individual space
ardboard
harm

athroom
living
hinge
relax
cket taste
water
concrete
vell-being
quiet
chisel
rable
decking
kids
kitchen
eautiful **do**
home-coming
hammer
it
raft
bedroom
dream
comfort
success
xtension cool
varm path
home-made tools
build
plans
drill plaster

build
glass-block wall
concrete
foundations
decking
plaster
roof tiles
electrical sockets
repair
floorboards
damp
tap washer
paint
renew
doors
kirting
tiling
wallpaper
coving
carpet
laminate flooring
shelving
patio
pond
living space
create
kitchen
bathroom
study

you can do it

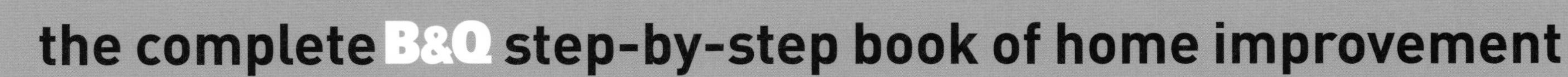

the complete **B&Q** step-by-step book of home improvement

with over 2200 colour illustrations

Thames & Hudson

Be safe

All home improvement activities involve a degree of risk. Skills of individual readers and site conditions vary widely. Although B&Q has made every effort to ensure that the instructions in this book are accurate, they are provided for general information only and you should always read and follow any manufacturer's instructions and, where appropriate, seek the advice of professionals.

In particular:

- All work on gas fittings and appliances must by law be carried out by a qualified professional.
- All electrical advice in this book assumes that you have an up-to-date system that complies fully with the latest IEE Wiring Regulations, or the Scottish Building Regulations in Scotland. If you are not sure whether your system is compliant you should get it checked by a qualified professional.
- Before working with electricity or water you should consult an appropriate professional. When working with electricity always turn the power off at the mains.
- Always read any relevant manuals or instructions for using tools and follow the safety instructions.
- The law concerning Building Regulations, planning, local byelaws and related matters can be complicated and you should take professional advice where appropriate. In connection with building work, B&Q cannot advise on planning permission or Building Regulations issues.

The techniques suggested in this book should not be used by anyone less than 18 years of age. To the extent permitted by law, B&Q accepts no liability for any loss, damage or injury arising as a consequence of the advice contained in this book. References to legislation and regulations are correct at the time of going to press.

FEEDBACK AND FURTHER ADVICE

B&Q welcomes your comments on this book and suggestions for improvements. Contact us by sending an e-mail to: thebook@b-and-q.co.uk

To find your local B&Q store, or for design and planning advice, indoors and out, visit **www.diy.com**

©

YOU CAN DO IT
The Complete B&Q Step-by-Step Book of Home Improveme

Commissioned by David Roth, Marketing Director, B&Q

Project Director and Writer Nicholas Barnard
Consulting Editor Ken Schept
Managing Editor Amanda Vinnicombe
Designer Aaron Hayden
Production Manager Philip Collyer
B&Q Project Manager Geoff Long
Photographer Lucy Pope
Illustrator Peter Bull Art Studios
Contributing Creative Director Bill Wallsgrove

First published in the United Kingdom by B&Q plc. This edition published in 2003 by Thames & Hudson Ltd, 181A High Holborn, London WC1V 7QX

www.thamesandhudson.com

Edited, designed and produced by Thames & Hudson Ltd, London, and B&Q plc

Reprinted 2004

British Library Cataloguing-in-Publication Data
A catalogue record for this book is available from the British Library
ISBN 0-500-51136-5

This book is printed on 130gsm Fineblade Extra, manufacture in the UK by Smurfit Townsend Hook in a plant with ISO 1400 environmental accreditation. The components of this paper a elemental chlorine-free (ECF) pulp plus filler and coating, all which are recyclable.

Printed and bound in the UK by Butler and Tanner

Introduction

Know your home

Inside the home

Outside the home

Home systems and services

The basics

Paul Mulready Astracast
Alan Fisher Trade B&Q
Angie Shawcroft Jeld-Wen
Geoffrey Evans Plumbing B&Q
Daryl Shaw Ceramic Prints
Mark Turner B&Q
Paul Town GE Lighting
Daz McDermid Decorating B&Q
Barry Batley Electrical B&Q
David Jennings Trade B&Q
Philip Taylor Flooring B&Q
George Siaperas G E T Electronics
Tony Rossi Frame 1 Windows
Keith Traynor Lighting B&Q
Bob Hesford Electrical B&Q
David Humphreys Tapis UK Ltd
Derek Spears Nexfor Ltd
Alison Morrisey Frame 1 Windows
James Eden Carpenter B&Q
Phil Duddridge B&Q
Nina Jones Interior designer B&Q
Sally Ockenden B&Q
Tony Royales Tools and hardware B&Q
Jim Chapman Plumbing B&Q
James Smith Ronseal Ltd
Alan Pearce Grange Sty
Ray Shaw Plumbing B&Q
Darren Kay Garden B&Q
Claire Cooper B&
Jackie Watson Twyford Bathrooms
Angela Lambert Q Lawns
Paul Tamlin B&Q
Geoff Long Project Manager B&Q
Jenny Woodyer Artex-Rawlplug Ltd
Sam Fowler Richard Burbidge
Arthur Weir B&Q
Martyn Underdown B&Q
Simon Bristow B&Q
Hugh Bracey B&Q
Robyn Barnes Earlex Ltd
David Westacott Clarksteel
Dan Bird B&Q
Paul Johnson B&Q
Ian Purkis Jeld-Wen
Murray Fraser Heissner
Neil Howarth B&Q
Debbie Berry Akzo Nobel
Claire Mitchell Sadolin Woodstains
Sally Gant Bradstone
Mark Lane Record Tools
Stuart Baker Yorkshire Building Supplie
Carol Bellwood Hanson Brick
Bernard Buckley B&Q
Barry Greening In Touch With Bricks Ltd
Mark Lopez Velux Windows
Geoff Menage Hanson Brick
David Boswell Halls Garden Products
Keith Dooley In Touch With Bricks Ltd
Gary Hatch Lingar Design Lt
Jerry Walker Kidde Safety Europe Ltd
Martin Cooper Henri Studios
Janine Dewar Graham & Brown Ltd
Derek Spears Nexfor
Peter Cox B&Q
Scott Trayhorn Lingar Design Ltd
Les Beech B&Q
Fiona Bashford Marley Exteriors
Steve Davis Premium Timber
Andy Ritchie In-Store Logistics
Adrian Clark Premium Timber
Stuart Watt B&
Brian Wiggins Screwfix Direct
Sharon Driscoll Halls Garden Products
Chris Smith Health and Safety B&Q

INTRODUCTION YOU CAN DO IT

You didn't know that B&Q was a publisher?

We're not. And that's why this book is so unique and important.

You Can Do It – The Complete B&Q Step-by-Step Book of Home Improvement puts in your hands knowledge we've gained from thirty-five years in the home improvement business. No publisher alone can make that claim.

Because we're not publishers, we took our own advice — go to experts you trust. Thames & Hudson is the world's leading publisher of illustrated books with a long list of titles that present complicated subjects with clarity and authority.

B&Q's customer advisers and in-store experts and Thames & Hudson's editors and designers collaborated on virtually every page. This extraordinary partnership has produced the United Kingdom's new and definitive home repair, maintenance, and decoration reference, unmatched by any book available today.

We started with an undeniable advantage. No company in the world understands home improvement and home trends better than B&Q. Our buyers search the globe every day for the newest products. Our stores operate in fifteen countries besides the United Kingdom.

But our greatest advantage is in the communities we serve at home – our customers. This book includes the features and qualities that you told us meet your needs, such as:

- An exhaustive, encyclopedic approach to basic and more advanced home maintenance and repair.
- Selected projects to improve your home's living space and enhance its value.
- Design options that inspire dreams and solutions that enable you to achieve them.
- Friendly, jargon-free language that imparts knowledge clearly and instils confidence.
- Colour photography and modern drawings that illustrate step-by-step instructions in logical, easy-to-follow fashion.
- Professional timesaving advice provided by our in-store experts. Look for the signature B&Q apron that marks these YOU CAN DO IT tips.

Whether your home was built during the reign of King George or the era of Boy George, *You Can Do It* is a book for how we live today. It addresses the distinct problems and untapped potential of homes both historic and modern. And it reflects the values we share as responsible citizens concerned with improving our properties while respecting the environment.

You can do it. We can help you – in our stores, on our website, www.diy.com, and now with our book. *You Can Do It – The Complete B&Q Step-by-Step Book of Home Improvement* is another part of our mission to keep home improvement affordable and to help you make your home better in every way.

Meanwhile, on behalf of everyone here, particularly those involved in bringing *You Can Do It* from idea to reality, thank you for shopping — and reading — with us.

David Roth Marketing Director, B&Q

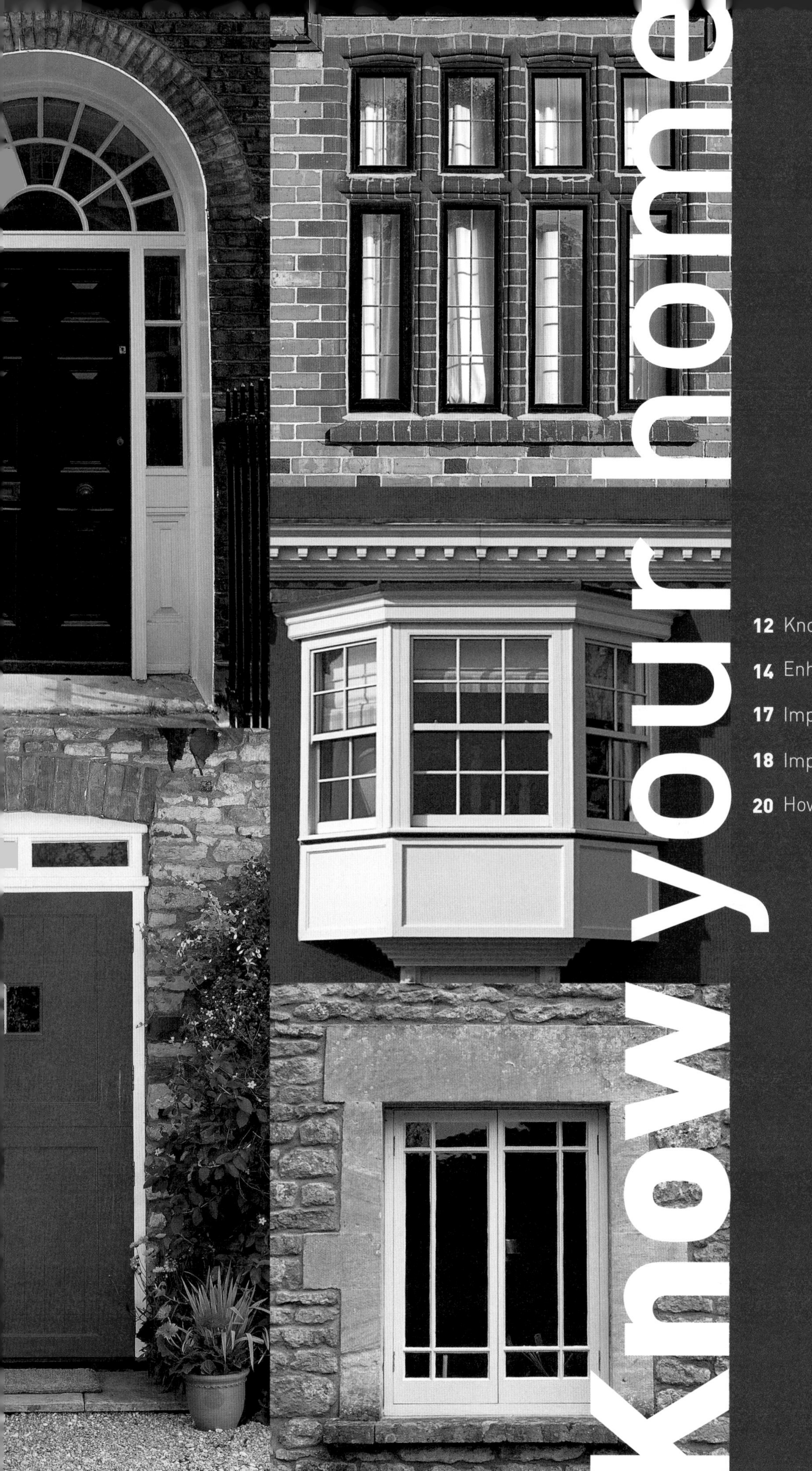

Know your home

KNOW YOUR HOUSE

Take a look at your house – at the architectural lines and details, brickwork, wall finishes or tiling. Get a feel for the character of your house as a house – not just as your home. Find out what period it belongs to, and get to know how it was built – how the roof, walls and floors were put together and what they are made of. This investigation can be fun. And it will help you assess what improvements can be made – and what improvements really should be made. It can reveal unforeseen problems, making it easier to plan and budget for maintenance work. Learning a little about your house before you start work on a project will make you a more knowledgeable homeowner, and could save you time and money too.

When was your home built?

Over half of us live in relatively modern suburban houses built in the past fifty or sixty years. Home improvement often is an opportunity to add a bit of character to dwellings designed for maximum efficiency. Those of us in period houses, however, sometimes face the opposite challenge of increasing efficiency without diminishing character. In general, improving living space while respecting architectural heritage will enhance both the quality and the market value of a property.

1714–1837 Late Georgian and Regency

A popular style of architecture with classical proportions. Original Georgian houses, whether terraced or detached, can be expensive to buy and costly to restore, but you can be fairly sure you'll get your money back. They will probably be listed, however, so you will have to take a conservative approach to home improvements. The kind of alterations you are allowed to make will be limited.

1837–1901 Victorian

Although Queen Victoria reigned from 1837, the term 'Victorian' is generally used to indicate the style of house popular from 1860 to the turn of the century, and in fact construction techniques for domestic buildings did not change significantly until the end of the First World War. Industrialisation led to a boom in house-building in towns and cities. The Health of Towns Act of 1848 initiated a series of housing acts that from 1875 prescribed minimum distances between dwellings, the inclusion of damp-proof courses in walls, and the provision of adequate natural lighting and ventilation. Doors, windows (sash rather than casement), and decorative details were mass-produced for the first time. One of the most popular styles of house was red brick with a plaster ground floor. Terraces, urban and suburban flats and detached villas flourished in this period. Their good, solid nature has ensured them lasting popularity.

1901–1939 Edwardian and Early Modern

After the Victorian era, the first significant changes in the materials and methods of domestic construction came with the large-scale private and public house-building after the First World War. The later Victorian development of back extensions, with porches and bay windows at the front, became universal in this period. The semi-detached house that still dominates suburbia first appeared in the 1920s, often in a mock-Tudor, half-timbered style.

Postwar to New Millennium

The level of home ownership in the United Kingdom grew following the Second World War, as new houses began to be more affordable. Less expensive materials were used and certain building modifications, such as thinner walls, also reduced costs. Semi-detached houses, compact easy-to-run flats, or bungalows, these properties usually offer plenty of scope for home improvement ideas. Modern flats, purpose-built and often budget-priced as part of an estate, are constructed of steel, concrete and glass in rectangular, geometric shapes.

In the 1960s and 1970s house design became more geared to informal, open-plan living, and at the end of the century natural materials and styles became fashionable again. New-build properties have state-of-the-art furnishings and fittings in more traditional-looking settings. Natural stone, brick and wood provide a warmer, softer-looking environment.

Retaining the character of an older house

Unless you are planning a total transformation, in which case you will want advice from a professional (see pages 370–73), aim to make improvements that are in keeping with the type of home that you have. Unsympathetic additions or changes can look ugly, and may cost you. If you change the windows in your Georgian terrace house to PVCu, for example, you will certainly bring the value of your property down, and probably flout conservation regulations. As far as possible, materials and finishes in older houses should be retained and cherished. Don't be tempted to add stone cladding or to paint brickwork, tile-hung bays and facades. Painting not only destroys the look of mellow brick and tile, but can also prevent these natural materials from breathing, and it is an unnecessary expense that will require continuous maintenance.

Creative salvage

Original features will enhance the aesthetics and value of your house. But if you decide to eliminate them don't throw them out – someone else is bound to want them. You can usually sell such items as iron fireplaces or old bathroom and kitchen fittings to a specialist company, which will probably come to remove them and give you some money for the privilege. Conversely, if you want to restore your property to its original condition, salvage yards can be a treasure-trove, and will no doubt fill you with inspiration for new projects.

ENHANCING VALUE

These days everyone's at it. You only have to turn on your television, or go into a newsagent or bookshop, to find people energetically working on their homes – or other people's. Home improvement, whether to sell, to let, or simply to enjoy, has become something of a national pastime.

From Mrs Beeton to Bob the Builder

We've come a long way since Mrs Beeton's *Book of Household Management* was first published over a century ago. Keeping an orderly home is not just a question of satisfaction or pride. For most of us buying a house is the biggest investment we will ever make, and it's much to our advantage to keep it in good shape. Thanks to the growth of home improvement stores as well as specialist outlets it's fairly easy to get the materials and equipment you need at an affordable price. Expert advice is also available from retailers as well as from books and magazines or online. As a result, we are tackling home and garden projects that a few years ago we would have left to the tradesman – or have left undone.

And there is much to tackle. Most houses were built in more traditional times. Life has changed. Today, individuals living alone comprise nearly a third of British households. And many of us work from home offices or joint bedroom/offices. Home improvement is the way we make space built for yesterday accommodate the way we live today.

Why move house?

You could be living in your dream home right now. It may be waiting to be discovered under frayed carpet and layers of paint. You can dramatically enhance the character of your home by restoring existing features or adding architectural mouldings and other details. A disused fireplace can be revamped and wooden floors made good by stripping and waxing, staining or painting. New lighting can transform the atmosphere and usefulness of a room. If you want a home office, a kitchen makeover, even another bathroom or bedroom, you can do it – and it will be a lot cheaper and easier than moving.

Express yourself

Gone are the days of wall-to-wall magnolia. Thanks to the influence of television, magazines and travel, we're better informed about design possibilities. A clean coat of paint will spruce up a room. But decorating can transform it. Combinations of colour, pattern, texture and light add interest and pleasure. They reflect your taste and point of view. Any four walls can be a shelter. Make yours a home.

Choose a green house

Products and materials that reduce environmental impact, such as low-solvent paints, timber from sustainable sources, and peat-free compost, are now widely available. And they are just the beginning of the changes you can introduce to make your home or garden more 'green'. Make the most of natural light, choose energy efficient appliances, recycle your waste and install effective insulation. Such improvements will conserve energy, help the environment, and in the long run can save you money too.

Cost-effective home improvements

Most home improvements will enhance the resale value of your home. But some are more profitable than others. Installing new windows, for example, or fitting a security alarm may not increase resale value. Loft conversions, surprisingly, also are not guaranteed to add value unless your house is in a fashionable area of a prosperous city. On the other hand, a kitchen or bath upgrade is likely to pay for itself in added market value. The same is true for investment in the garden.

But remember, the impact on resale value is only one consideration when contemplating a home improvement project. The first questions to ask are: is this what I want, will it make me happy, and can I afford it? If the answer to those questions is yes and you're ready to move ahead, then bear in mind the following dos and don'ts if you are eventually hoping to resell and recoup your costs.

Do

- Paint and decorate
- Replace outdated bathroom suites
- Choose a simple fitted kitchen
- Install central heating
- Fit or expose wooden floors
- Convert a cellar into living or storage space
- Add a garage
- Increase natural light
- Maximise views of a garden

Don't

- Rip out period features such as fireplaces
- Use textured plaster or woodchip to cover uneven walls
- Create windowless rooms
- Put in double glazing that doesn't open
- Split rooms to make more bedrooms, unless they are huge
- Economise by living with dated wallpaper or furnishings

IMPROVEMENT BY DESIGN

Sometimes we just need a change. Moving house is one option. But a redesign can be easier, cheaper and just as effective. It will renew your surroundings and can even revive your spirits. Be creative. Have fun. And don't hesitate to ask for advice – that's what the experts are there for.

Planning a new look

There's still a lot to be said for the quick-fix makeover, especially when you first move in to a place. Simple measures like hiding hideous wallpaper under white paint or screening out the neighbours with cheap fabric draped over curtain poles will rapidly create a neutral backdrop – just what you need as you get to know a new living space and plan exactly how you want it to look.

A good starting point when dreaming up a new decorative scheme are the two essential ingredients of colour and light.

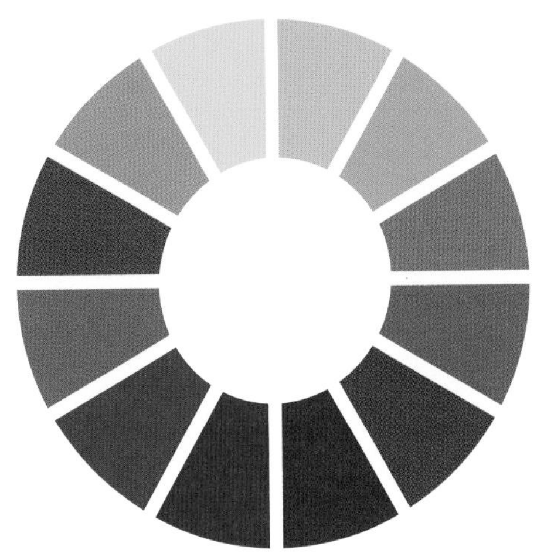

Colour

Look at the neighbouring colours on the colour wheel. They harmonise and produce a sense of tranquillity. Imagine placing opposite colours together. They clash and produce tension. It's easy to blend harmonising colours; more difficult to use the dramatic opposites, known as complimentary colours. If you're not sure about how to mix harmonising and complimentary colours, let nature be your guide. Think of a meadow dotted with vivid red poppies. Use small touches of a complimentary colour to spice up a scheme dominated by similar shades.

Colour gives shape to spaces. Need to make a small room feel larger? Ceilings lift and walls recede with pale, cool colours. Want something cosier? A warm-coloured finish will make a room feel snug. Colour also creates character. Use bold shades or daring contrasts for heightened drama; calm, harmonious, pale colours for understated elegance. The choice depends on the mood you want to create and the size, shape, lighting, and character of the interior.

Instant makeover

When it comes to redesigning your living space, there are no rules. You're really only bound by imagination and budget. But if such freedom strikes fear into your heart, you are not alone. Surveys suggest that more than half of us have had decorating disasters, which we often live with for years for want of the know-how, money or energy to put things right. Fortunately there are now more objective ways of testing out a new decorative vision than relying on your mind's eye. B&Q have developed easy-to-use digital software, available on CD-ROM, that enables you to see different combinations of pattern, colour and finish at the click of a mouse. You can either test out your ideas on a sample roomset (right) or use a digital photograph of the room you want to decorate. It's a confidence-inspiring way to get creative with your interior before so much as dipping a brush in a pot of paint.

Light

Light and colour are very closely related. Dark colours absorb nearly 90% of light, while pale shades reflect over 80%. On the other hand a silk paint finish will help reflect light, while matt absorbs it. Begin by thinking about natural light, and how to make the best of what's available to you. In a room used mainly at night, you can easily compensate for the effect of a dark colour scheme with extra artificial lighting. But during the day, a room decorated in dark shades will be very gloomy without natural light in abundance.

Like colour, light changes the atmosphere of a living space. There are three categories of indoor lighting, each serving a different purpose. Modern electric fixtures, such as recessed ceiling spotlights with flood bulbs, provide ambient, or general illumination. Task lighting is directed and functional — desk or bedside lamps are a good example. Accent lighting is directed but decorative – for example a narrow beam spotlight on a painting or sculpture. For best effect, mix the different types of electric light fittings. Don't forget candles either. A row of candles inside or outdoors on a summer evening will create a mellow mood. Finally, think of the environment too: though more expensive, energy-efficient lamps and bulbs last much longer and often use less electricity.

IMPROVEMENT IN ACTION

Ask yourself some questions about how you use – or underuse – your living space. Is the kitchen the hub of family life? Is the table piled with work clutter? Could you convert a spare room into a study? Is there a spot for proper storage cabinets? Do you retire with a bath, or wake up to a power shower? Might some decking, a table and chairs and an outdoor heater be as good as building a dining room extension, at least for half the year? Look at your home again and you will probably be amazed by how much unrealised potential it offers.

Kitchen

If, like so many of us, you live in the kitchen, then why not make it comfortable? Expand it to accommodate a table and chairs. Rearrange it to take advantage of a view. Whether from the sink or the cooking area, a view of the outside world, especially the garden, can be an uplifting distraction from the chores. Add windows or glazed doors to increase natural light. Tile the wall above your units to create an attractive waterproof splashback. Install good task lighting over the work surfaces. If an existing fitted kitchen is adequate but unattractive, consider giving it a decorative makeover by painting the units, or changing their doors and handles. These are only some of the possibilities for achieving your dream kitchen. But whatever you do, plan carefully, and take into account safety, convenience, and efficient use of space.

Living room

Arranging the sofa and chairs to form a comfortable cluster will instantly make a living room feel more relaxing. If you don't want the television to be a continual distraction, hide it away in a cabinet. Lighting a living room is another challenge. You may want to combine ambient lighting with table lamps to read by as well as spotlights to accentuate a special feature in the room. This is a good space to present a coordinated decorative look too, using textures, colours and patterns on the walls and furnishings.

Dining room

Enjoying food in company is one of life's great pleasures, so make the colours and lighting in a dining room match the desire for relaxation and calm. Lighting, as in a bedroom, should be versatile so that you can adjust the totally different levels of illumination required during daytime and evening with the flick of a switch.

Bathroom

We spend a surprising amount of our lives bathing and washing, and the bathroom can be a wonderful space for relaxation. It needs to be easy to clean and comfortable to use: consider tiles or mosaic finishes, moisture-proof downlighters, a heated towel rail and a well lit mirror. If you haven't room for a shower cubicle, look at installing a modern shower screen and power shower over the bath – taking a shower saves water and time. Don't forget to make room for storage too. And finally, if you are making significant changes to the bathroom, keep the plumbing as simple as possible by planning around the existing waste outlets.

Bedrooms

More storage space is number one on many people's bedroom wish list. Fitted cupboards offer the most efficient storage, and are now available with a variety of extremely useful accessories for stowing shoes and clothes. When lighting a bedroom, you will need to combine ambient lighting to illuminate the entire room with task lighting, such as bedside lamps. In this way you will be able to make best use of the room at any time of day or night. Finally, the bedroom is usually the one room where even those who prefer exposed wooden flooring find the warmth and comfort of carpeting or rugs irresistible.

Home office

Setting up an efficient home office requires planning, particularly in terms of services. You will be surprised how much storage and desk space an office needs, so prepare to install, and if necessary disguise, filing cabinets, computer equipment and a mess of cables. Make sure that you have an adequate electrical supply and good lighting for working. Think too about extra heating or cooling; sitting immobile at a desk can be chilly in winter and sweltering in summer – particularly if you have converted an attic or a shed.

Garden

Altering the landscape of your garden also takes careful planning and preparation. Look at photographs taken throughout the year and try to imagine how any improvements will be affected by the changing seasons. Draw an outline plan of the garden, make copies, and then experiment with sketching new ideas. There are any number of ways to increase the usefulness of your outdoor living space throughout the year: installing a deck, garden lighting, a dining area and outside heaters, a greenhouse, playhouse or shed. A new fence will increase your privacy, while a pond will add interest – and life.

HOW GREEN IS YOUR HOME?

Becoming more environmentally aware is not just about changing your habits – it's about changing your home as well. Adapting your home to make it a greener place to live in is one of the most important domestic improvement schemes you can undertake. It makes sense to conserve energy and recycle wherever possible. You'll not only be saving natural resources, but also a good deal of money.

Solar power

As oil prices continue to rise and experts estimate we have less than half a century of fossil fuels left, energy issues become ever more urgent. Increasingly mindful, too, of global warming and pollution, more and more people are now opting for free and cleaner solar power.

By installing a solar-powered electricity-generating system in a standard three- or four-bedroom house, you should be able to produce about half the electricity you need. During the 30-year lifetime of the panels you can expect to save around 50 tonnes in carbon dioxide emissions, the chief culprit of global warming.

Even if this is not practical for you, there are still ways you can reduce your energy usage with solar-powered products such as security and garden lighting, or garden water features.

Saving energy

By installing effective insulation you will conserve energy and reduce your heating bills by minimising heat loss. The average home can save over £250 per year by taking energy-efficiency measures:

- Loft insulation 270mm thick can cut 20% off your heating bills.
- Replacing an old, inefficient boiler could save 10–15% on bills.
- Lowering your thermostat by 1.25°C could cut 10% off your fuel bills.
- An energy-efficient fridge-freezer could save 50% on energy used.
- Energy-efficient light bulbs use 4 times less electricity and last 8 times longer, so continue to save you money month after month.
- Fitting a 75mm-thick insulating jacket to your hot-water cylinder can reduce heat loss by 75%.

Many appliances carry the European energy label which rates them from A to G according to their energy efficiency, with the most efficient being A grade.

Paints and finishes

The solvents and other chemicals released into the atmosphere by paints and varnishes are known as Volatile Organic Compounds. VOCs contribute to air pollution and climate change, and there are also reported links to complaints such as asthma, which could have an effect on us all. You can do your bit to minimise this harm by choosing products with low VOC levels. Labels now clearly state the level of VOCs contained in paint products. Be sure to choose from the wide range of decorative and speciality products with low VOCs that are kinder to you and to the environment. These include:

- Interior emulsions
- Quick-drying and low-odour trim paints and varnishes
- Masonry paint
- Textured wall finishes

Recycle your waste paint, or give it to someone else. Never pour it into drains or waterways, where it could cause land and water contamination.

Timber and other wood products

The destruction of the world's forests is probably one of the most high-profile global environmental issues. Do your bit to prevent it by choosing wood that has come from well-managed sources. Look for labels bearing the letters FSC (Forest Stewardship Council). These products have come from forests or woodland that are being managed according to an agreed set of ecological principles, and have been certified at every stage of the supply chain. FSC-approved products include:

- Exterior and interior doors
- Shelving
- Laminate flooring
- Fencing and garden sheds
- Garden and hand tools
- Garden decking
- Fire surrounds
- Lavatory seats
- MDF (Medium Density Fibreboard) sheets

Recycling and conservation

- Choose recycled products and packaging that bears the recyclable symbol.
- Segregate your waste and use recycling bins.
- Use water butts to collect rainwater for use in your garden.
- Reduce the water used when you flush the lavatory by placing a water-saving device in the cistern.
- Mend that dripping tap.
- Do without packaging whenever possible. When shopping, look for reusable crates or bag-for-life schemes. Try not to use too many plastic bags; reuse or recycle them where possible.
- Use household products that are phosphate-free, biodegradable and contain natural oils and plant extracts, which are non-polluting.

In the garden

Gardening without the use of artificial chemicals can reduce the build-up of potentially harmful substances in the environment. Organic products for gardeners are constantly being improved and expanded, giving everyone the opportunity to garden organically. To make sure you can trust the claims made for organic products, look out for those that have independent expert verification such as from HDRA.

Composting your own garden waste can create a great compost and save you money. Alternatively, choose a peat-free compost to avoid adding to the destruction of the natural environment that is caused by the harvesting of peat bogs.

ondary glazing
ble glazing
le glazing
Solar panels
Insulated storage tanks and lagged pipes in loft
Loft insulation
Thermostatic radiator valves
Room thermostats
Programmer for central heating
Brick or timber-framed external walls rather than concrete
Solar-powered lighting
Water-saving device in cistern
Shower rather than bath to reduce water consumption
Insulated hot-water cylinder
Rainwater butt for garden irrigation
CFC-free fridge-freezer
Energy-efficient appliances in kitchen
Condensing boiler
Recycling bins
ergy-efficient light bulbs
Compost bin
ity-wall insulation
mira

BRITISH MADE
2"
colourcraft

Inside the home

The ground floor of a house may be a solid floor sitting on a base of concrete and hardcore laid on the ground, or it may be a suspended floor built above the ground on joists. Floors on the first storey and above are always suspended.

Foundations

The floors of a house rest on the foundations, a solid base that supports the whole weight of the house. The loadbearing strength of the soil on which the house is built determines the type and depth of the foundations. Trench foundations are made by digging out trenches and filling them with concrete, then the external walls are built on top of them and a slab of concrete about 100mm–150mm thick is laid within the walls. Raft foundations consist of a reinforced-concrete slab laid on a layer of hardcore (coarse rubble), which covers the whole ground area and forms a base on which the walls are built.

Solid floors

A solid floor normally consists of several layers, although some old houses have flagstones or quarry tiles laid straight on top of the ground.

Screed

On top of the concrete there is a smooth screed of sand and cement. This is covered with the surface flooring, which may be wooden floorboards, man-made boards, tiles or carpet.

Insulation

Newly built houses must have a layer of thermal insulation beneath the ground floor. In a solid floor, this consists of rigid slabs of glass wool or polyfoam, laid either above or below the concrete. A strip of the same material is usually also run vertically at the edge to minimise heat loss at the bottom of the wall.

Damp-proof membrane

The damp-proof membrane (DPM) is a layer of moisture-resistant material that is usually laid on the layer of hardcore, although sometimes the concrete slab is laid first. The membrane may be either a thick sheet of polythene or a liquid coating of asphalt or bituminous material. The damp-proof membrane must be joined to the damp-proof course (DPC) in the walls. The damp-proof course is a layer of impervious material, such as polythene or bituminous felt, built into a joint between brick courses 150mm above the ground to prevent moisture rising from the ground into the walls.

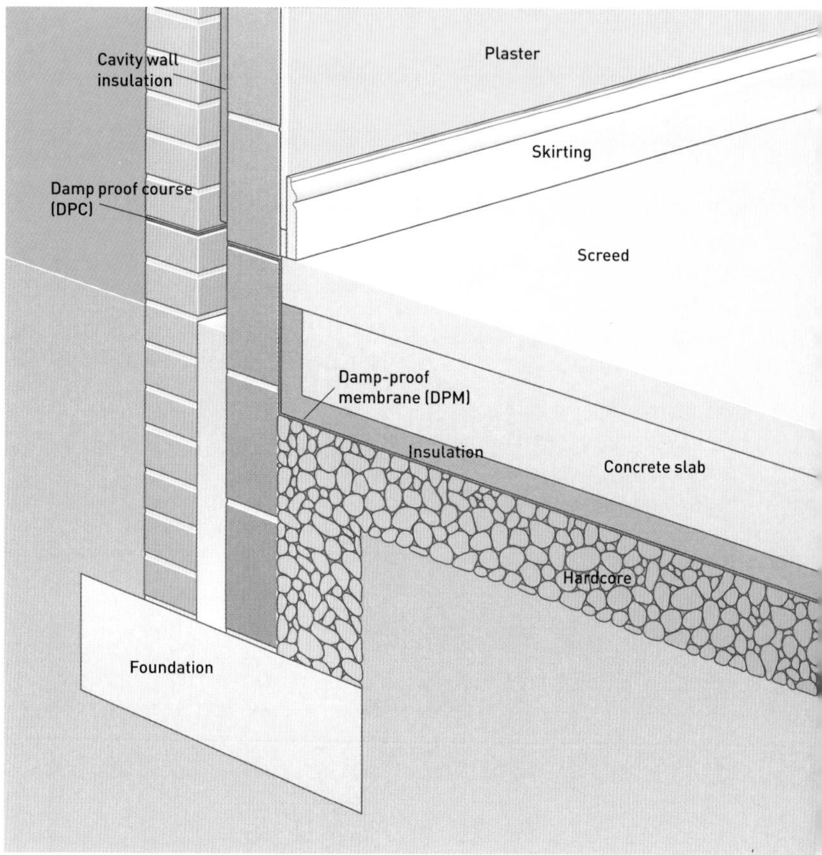

A solid floor on trench foundations

When the floor is built on trench foundations, it is constructed after the first few rows (courses) of bricks for the external walls have been laid above ground. The topsoil within the walls is removed, then hardcore is laid to level the ground. The rough surface of the hardcore is covered with a layer of sand before the damp-proof membrane, insulation, and concrete slab are laid.

Suspended floors

A suspended floor may be made of wooden floorboards or man-made boards set on timber beams called joists.

Ground floor

The joists supporting a ground floor sit on low sleeper walls inside the external walls. The bricks of the sleeper walls are laid in a honeycomb pattern to allow air to circulate freely. Alternatively, the ends of the joists slot into gaps or joist sockets in the outer walls, where they rest on timber beams called wall plates that are built into the wall. Often there will be sleeper walls in the middle of the floor space to give the joists extra support. Blocks of thermal insulation are positioned between the floor joists, supported by polypropylene netting. All the timbers are above the level of the damp-proof course to protect them from rising damp. Sleeper walls are also topped with a damp-proof course, then a timber wall plate to which the joists are secured.

Floorboards

Floorboards or chipboard are laid on top of the joists. Modern floorboards are most often tongue-and-groove design and slot together, while older ones are usually thicker and have straight edges that fit side by side. Flooring-grade chipboard may have either tongue-and-groove or straight edges.

Upper floors

Joists above the ground floor are fixed at each end but are unsupported in the middle. They may slot into sockets in the external walls or into metal joist hangers attached to the walls. Consequently upper floor joists need to be deeper than those on the ground floor to ensure they remain rigid without intermediate support; they also usually span shorter distances. For extra reinforcement, the joists may have wooden or metal supports called strutting nailed between them.

Suspended concrete floors

Timber is costly, and some houses have suspended concrete floors instead of wood. Rows of pre-cast concrete joists, which are shaped to hold concrete blocks, are placed on sleeper walls. Concrete blocks are set between the joists and covered with a concrete screed.

Flooring

A suspended floor made from soft- or hardwood boards can be sanded and sealed (see pages 34–35), or used as a sub-base for another flooring – carpet, laminate, vinyl or tiles. A concrete screed can serve as a sub-base (provided it is level and dry) or be covered first with flooring-grade plywood, chipboard or medium-density fibreboard (MDF).

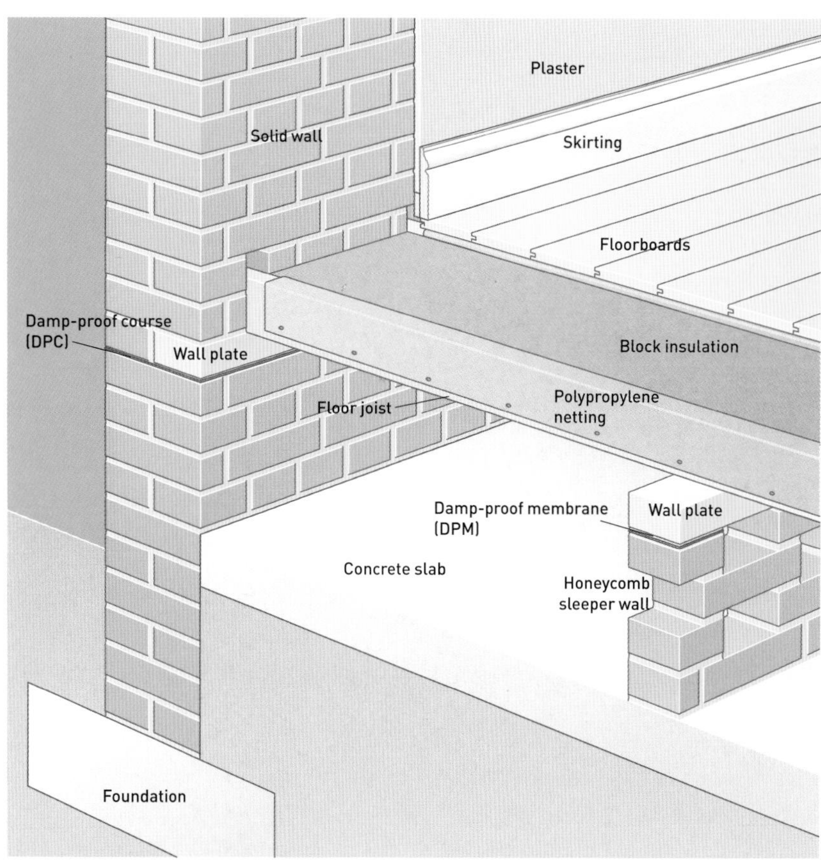

A suspended ground floor

CHOOSING FLOORING

Flooring	Advantages	Disadvantages
Laminate	Attractive, polished-wood look at less cost than new floorboards. Different finishes and wide range of colours.	May be damaged by heavy furniture. Not all types suitable for kitchens and bathrooms. Can be noisy.
Carpet	Large range of colours, designs and prices. Warm feel.	Good quality carpet is expensive. Spills can stain. May trap dust and allergens.
Sheet vinyl	Cheap and easy to clean. Cushioned vinyl is more comfortable to walk on, but more expensive.	Smooth vinyl feels cold underfoot and is slippery when wet.
Vinyl tiles	Large range of colours and designs. Easy to clean.	Can be slippery when wet.
Cork tiles	Warmer than vinyl. Easy to clean if varnished or sealed.	Does not wear well in areas of heavy use unless you choose the more expensive PVC-coated type.
Hard tiles	Hardwearing, resistant to stains and spills. Easy to clean.	Relatively expensive. Cold to bare feet.

Choosing flooring

Flooring is very much a matter of personal taste. But do give consideration to the practical pros and cons. If a family member is asthmatic, getting rid of carpets may make their life more comfortable; on the other hand, stripped wooden floors in a first-floor flat can be very noisy and may make you an unpopular neighbour.

FLOORS AND STAIRS STAIRCASES

A staircase can be anything from a simple straight flight of steps running from one floor to the next, to a grand feature with intricately carved balustrades. Even in an ordinary house it may curve or change direction, and there may be one or more intermediate landings between floors.

Parts of a staircase

The flat part of each stair (the part that you walk on) is called the tread. The vertical pieces that close off the treads are the risers. Treads and risers slot into long timbers on each side of the stairs called strings. Vertical balusters fit between the outer string and a handrail. Wider staircases are supported by a length of timber (the central bearer, or 'carriage piece') fixed underneath the stairs.

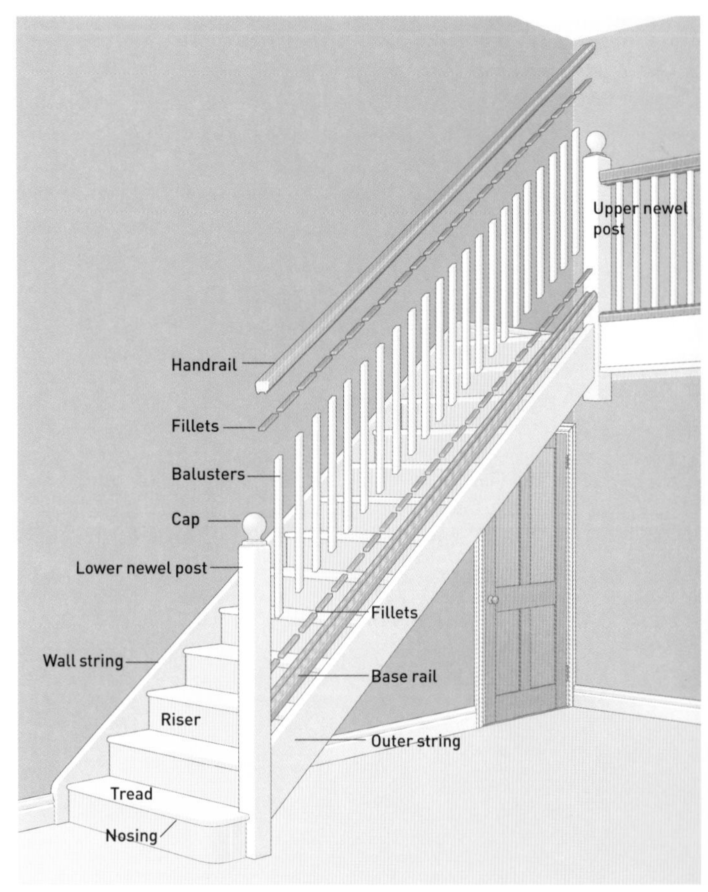

Treads and risers

The treads and risers in a staircase may have tongue-and-groove joints, or they may be nailed or glued together. The joints between them are often reinforced from beneath with triangular wedges of wood that are glued in place. The rounded front edges of the treads are known as the nosings. Some staircases have moulding the same shape as the nosings fixed to the cut end of the treads. The treads of a straight staircase are all the same shape; but if a staircase changes direction at some point, specially shaped treads called winders are needed as it turns the corner.

Open-tread stairs are built without risers. The treads are likely to be thicker than in a standard staircase, and horizontal rods or rails are fixed across the gap to ensure that no child can squeeze through.

Strings

The strings run the full length of a staircase from one floor to the next, on each side of the stairs. The wall string is screwed to the wall beneath the treads. The outer string may be 'closed' or 'cut' (see below).

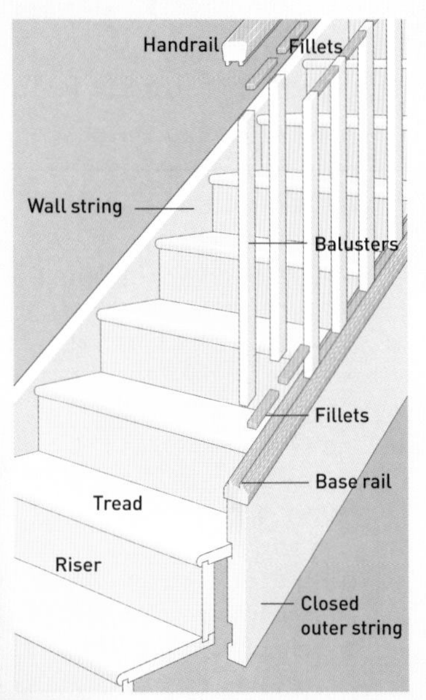

◂ Closed string construction

A closed string has parallel top and bottom edges. The treads and risers are fitted into narrow channels (housings) cut in the inner face of the string. They are secured with wedges of wood driven in from the underside and glued in place. The balusters shown here are fitted to the handrail and base rail between small lengths (fillets) of wood.

Cut string construction ▸

A cut string follows the shape of the steps. The treads are nailed on to the horizontal sections and the outer ends of the risers are cut to fit the vertical edges of the string. Here the balusters fit into housings cut in the treads and the cut ends of the treads are covered by lengths of moulding matching the nosings on the front.

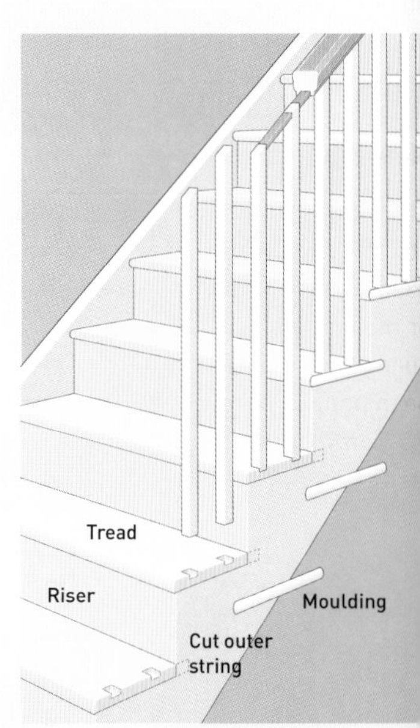

Balustrade

On the open side of the staircase vertical balusters are attached to the outer string at the bottom and a handrail at the top. They can be fitted in various ways (see below). Small wooden fillets may be fitted between the balusters to keep them evenly spaced. The handrail is held in place by newel posts. The balusters, handrail and string together make up the balustrade or banisters.

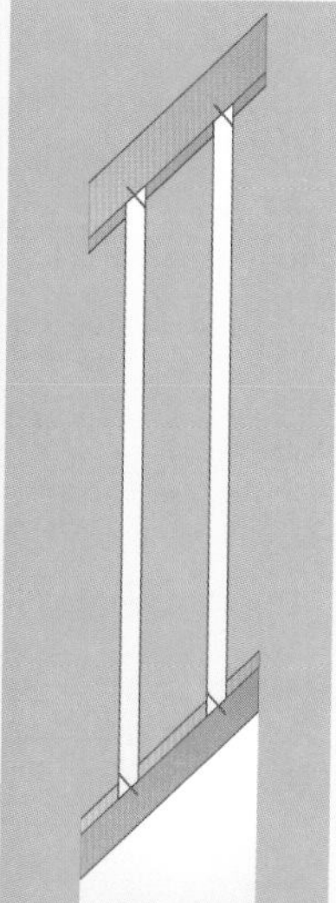

Butt-joint

Balusters may be simply butt-jointed and fixed to the handrail at the top and the string at the bottom by nails hammered through them at an angle.

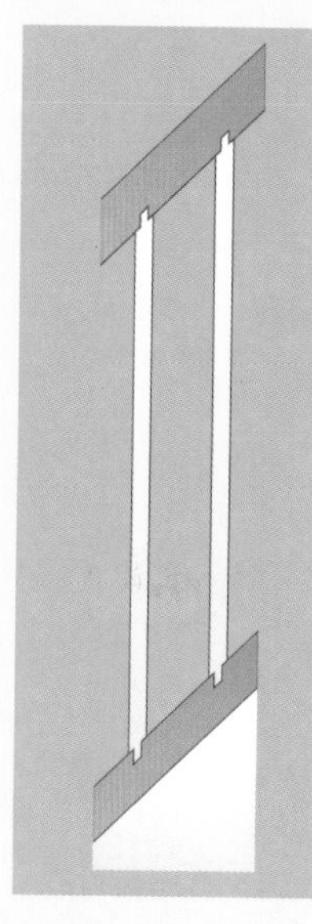

Projecting stub

Some balusters have a projecting stub on each end (known as a stub-tenon) that fits into a corresponding recess (mortise) cut in the underside of the handrail, and in the edge of a closed string or tread of a cut string staircase.

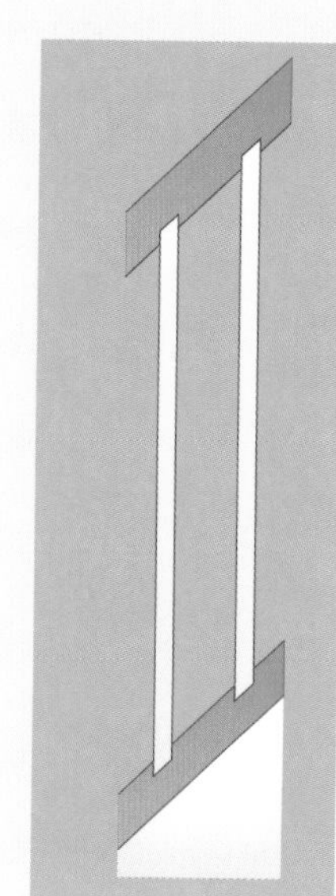

Housed balusters

Alternatively, balusters may be 'housed' or fitted into slots cut in the underside of the handrail and in the edge of a closed string or the treads of a cut string staircase. Some balusters are housed at the bottom, but nailed at the top.

Handrail

Staircases normally have at least one handrail; some have one on both sides. A handrail along the wall is attached with screws or brackets. The outer handrail is fixed to newel posts at the top and bottom of the stairs.

Newel posts

The newel posts hold the outer handrail in place and make the staircase stronger. The newel post at the bottom of the stairs is fixed to the floor and the top one may be fixed to the ground floor or the landing. The handrail is bolted to the newel posts with special angled metal handrail brackets. When the bolts have been tightened, cover caps are fitted to hide the nuts.

Newel posts often have a decorative cap on top, and grander staircases may feature beautifully carved newel posts.

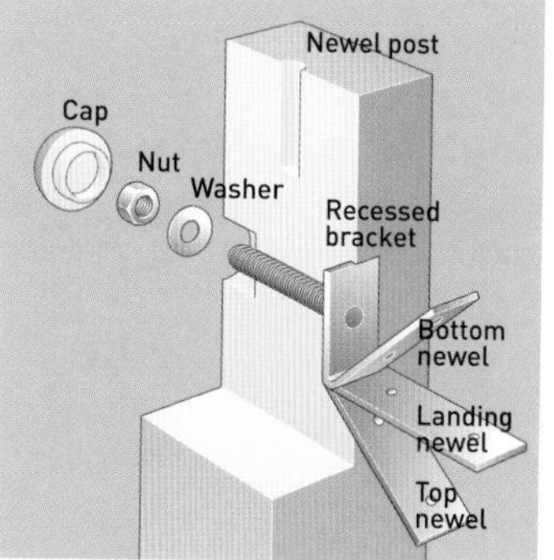

Newel post bracket

Under the stairs

The space below the staircase is known as the spandrel, and it is often enclosed to make a cupboard. If the underneath of the stairs is not plastered, you can gain access to them from inside the cupboard.

SAFETY FIRST

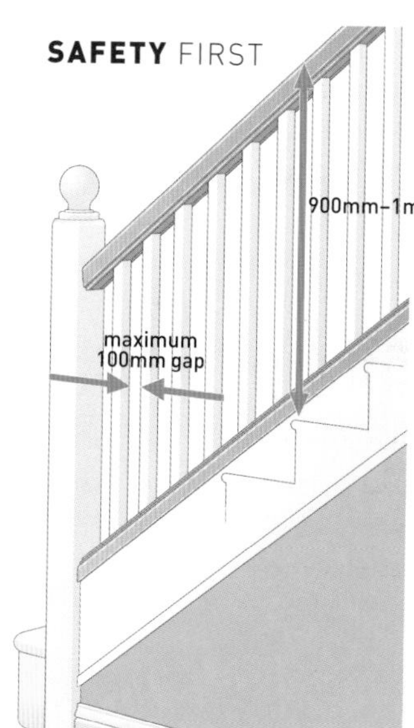

A stair balustrade should be no less than 900mm high and no more than 1m, with the measurement taken vertically from the pitch line – the line formed by the front of the treads. A balustrade edging a landing or upper floor must also be no less than 900mm high. The spaces between the balusters should not allow a 100mm-diameter sphere to pass between them, and the construction must not allow a child to climb over. The width of the treads, from back to front, must be at least 220mm.

FLOORS AND STAIRS CREAKING BOARD

Over the years, floorboards and stairs can work loose from their fittings, or dry out and shrink slightly, causing creaks and squeaks when you walk on them. If you take up a carpet in order to sand and seal a wooden floor, be sure to check for loose boards first – carpet and other floorcoverings can muffle a potentially infuriating problem.

Fixing creaking stairs

The way to fix a creaking stair depends on whether you can do the repair from underneath. If that would involve removing plaster from the underside of the stairs, it may be easier to work from above the stairs.

Fixes under stairs

Locate any loose steps by getting someone to walk up the stairs while you listen from underneath. Mark them with chalk. If the tread or riser has become loose in its string housing, the glued wedge securing the joint may have worked loose. Remove the wedge, clean it, apply PVA wood adhesive, then replace it.

Check the triangular blocks that fit in the angle between the treads and the risers. If they are not securely glued, remove them and scrape off the old adhesive. Prise open the tread/riser joint slightly and inject some adhesive. Apply adhesive to the block and press it in place, or screw it in place. If blocks were not fitted to the stairs, make some, each about 75mm long, and glue and screw them in place.

The joint between the back of a tread and the bottom of a riser can be strengthened by injecting PVA adhesive into the gap. Then drive three evenly spaced screws up through the tread and into the edge of the riser.

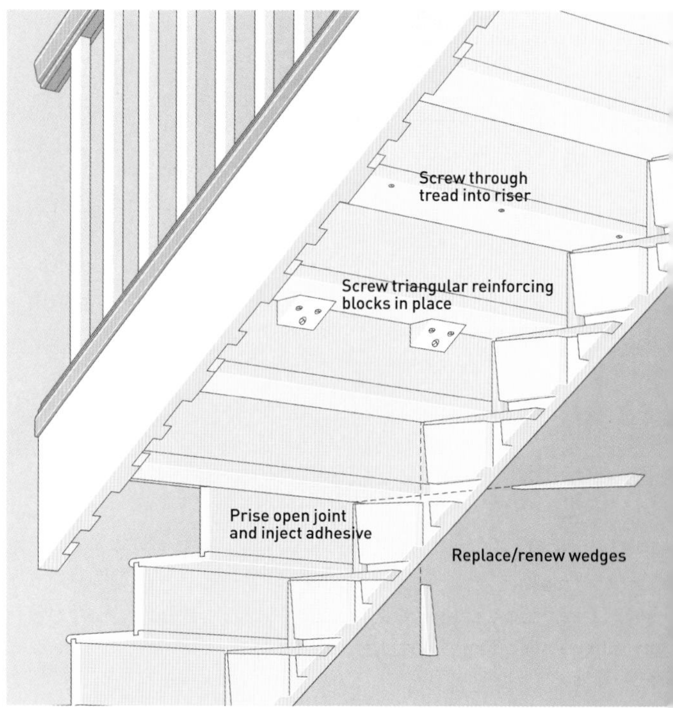
Screw through tread into riser
Screw triangular reinforcing blocks in place
Prise open joint and inject adhesive
Replace/renew wedges

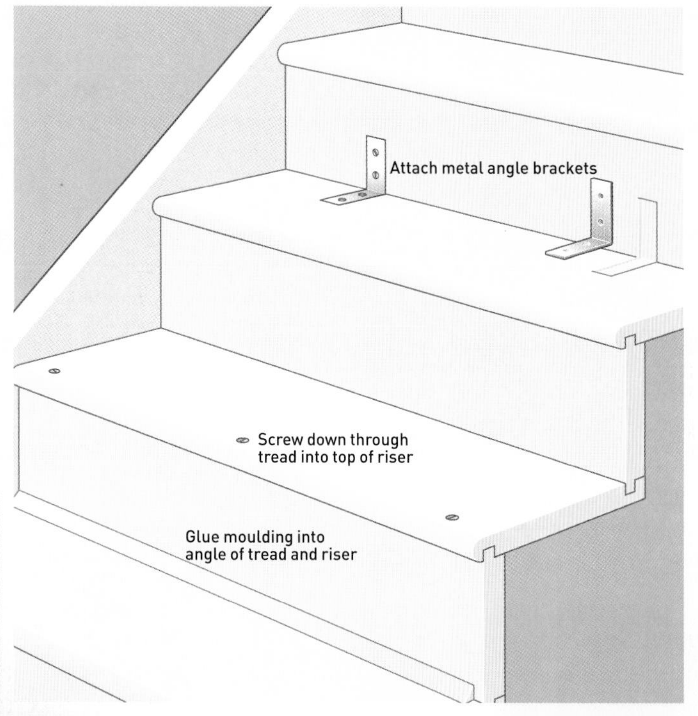
Attach metal angle brackets
Screw down through tread into top of riser
Glue moulding into angle of tread and riser

Fixes above stairs

Another way to cure creaking stairs is to screw down the front of the tread on to the riser. Drill clearance holes (for the thick part of the screws – the shank) through the tread and thinner pilot holes (for the point of the screws) into the top of the riser. Then drill the clearance holes with a countersink bit so that the screws will be just below the surface when they are screwed in place. Inject some PVA wood adhesive into the holes then screw the screws in tightly. Cover the heads with filler, using wood filler if the stairs are uncarpeted.

If the loose joint is at the back of the tread, you can strengthen it by gluing a length of triangular moulding, 12mm x 12mm, into the angle between the tread and the riser (as long as it does not make the tread narrower than the regulation 220mm). Alternatively, screw two thin metal brackets into the angle between the tread and the riser. For a completely flush surface, cut out a recess for the brackets using a sharp chisel and mallet.

Fixing creaking floorboards

A floorboard creaks when some of its fixing nails have worked themselves loose, so that it is no longer firmly attached to the joists. If the board is in good condition, you can prise out the nails and screw it down using the existing nail holes. In older houses, where floorboards may have been lifted many times before, the board may be badly damaged at the sides and corners so it is usually best to make new holes for the screws. Before drilling new holes in a floorboard, first lift the board to check for pipes and cables.

TOOLS MATERIALS

- **pincers**
- **pencil**
- **power drill with twist and countersink bits**
- **screwdriver**
- **knife**

- 50mm screws (4mm or 5mm gauge)
- talcum powder

Find the part of the floorboard t is loose by treading all over it d looking for movement. If the ard is damaged and cannot be nailed in the old holes, prise the nails with pincers, then the board to check for cables d pipes. Mark the top of the ard in pencil to show their sitions.

2 Drill a clearance hole in a sound part of the board, as near to the edge as you can. Insert the screw in the hole and screw it down firmly, seeing that it sits below the surface.

3 If the screw head projects above the surface, take it out, countersink the hole, and screw the board down again.

4 If you still have squeaks after re-fixing the boards, try sprinkling talcum powder along the joint and work it in with a knife. After a while, the squeaking should stop.

imber treatment

odworm and dry rot can do great harm to structural timbers such joists and roof timbers. Localised areas of woodworm infestation be treated using a chemical insecticide. Major infestations should treated by a specialist contractor, as should dry rot, which is far re serious.

Lift the floorboards. Wearing ves, pour some timber atment into a pot and brush n to the affected joists cording to the manufacturer's tructions.

2 Brush the underside of any floorboards showing signs of woodworm.

3 Turn the boards over and brush the top side with more of the insecticide.

YOU CAN DO IT

Spotting infestation
Woodworm holes are about 2mm in diameter. If dark in colour, they may have been treated before. Pale dust around the edge of a hole is a sign of recent activity and should be treated immediately. Wood that is infested with dry rot appears dry and spongy, with the fibres breaking down. Dry rot can do serious damage, and is best treated by a professional.

FLOORS LIFTING FLOORBOARDS

TOOLS MATERIALS

- **pipe and cable detector**
- **wide-bladed bolster chisel**
- **claw hammer**
- **wooden wedge or cold chisel**
- **try square**
- **pencil**
- **tenon saw**
- **ruler**
- **power drill with wood bits**
- **screwdriver**

- length of wood
- new floorboard
- 50mm cut floor brads or ring-shanked nails, or 50mm countersunk screws (4mm or 5mm gauge)

Over the years, floorboards may split, warp, shrink or break, and will need replacing. Or you may need to lift a board temporarily in order to access cables or pipes beneath. How you do this depends on whether your floor is made of tongue-and-groove boards, which are slotted together before being nailed to the joists, or square-edged boards, which are simply butted together.

Square-edged boards

Square-edged boards are easiest to take up. To remove a whole board that fits beneath the skirting at each end, however, you will have to saw through the board near the centre, or remove the skirtings (see page 70).

1 First locate any underfloor pipes and cables (see YOU CAN DO IT). Begin by driving a wide-bladed bolster chisel into the joint between the boards, close to one end. The blade will spread the load and keep damage to adjacent boards to a minimum.

2 Push down on the handle of the bolster chisel to prise the board up. Do the same on the other side until you can lift the end of the board high enough to insert a cold chisel or wooden wedge under it, to hold it clear of the joist.

3 Working on alternate sides of the board, insert the claw of your hammer under the edges and lever it higher. You can protect adjacent boards by placing a thin scrap of wood beneath the hammer head. Gradually work your way along the board.

4 When you have pulled most of the nails from the joists, you should be able to lift the free e of the board and lever up the remainder.

Replacing a section of board

If the damage affects only a small area of a floorboard, or if the board continues under the skirting, you may find it easier to cut out and replace a section rather than the whole board.

SAFETY FIRST

As soon as you lift a board, drive any projecting nails back through the wood, then prise them out with a claw hammer. This way you can't step on them. Any nails left in the joists should also be removed.

1 Prise the board up just enough to slide a length of wood beneath. Mark cutting lines with a try square and pencil, making sure they run along the centre-line of joists below.

2 Use a tenon saw to cut the section out, taking care not to damage adjacent boards and making sure that your cuts are square. Measure up for the replacement board. If the existing boards are not of a standard size, you may have to cut down a larger board to fit. If necessary, you can always notch the underside of a thicker board to fit over the joists.

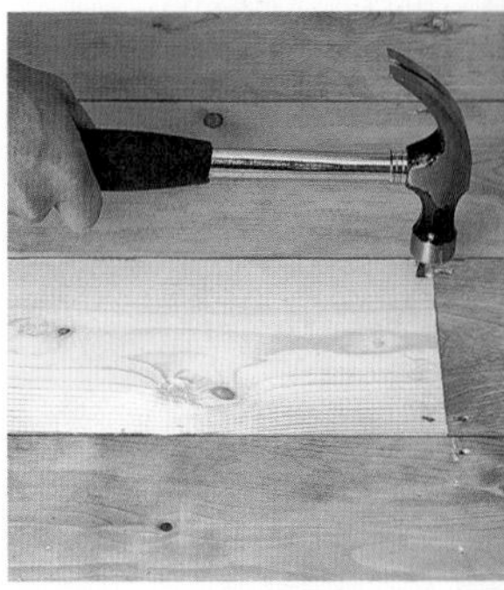

3 Position the new board anc secure with 50mm cut floor brads or ring-shanked nails, avoiding the existing holes in the joists. Drill pilot holes for the nails to prevent splitting. Alternatively, use 50mm countersunk screws (4mm or 5mm gauge).

Tongue-and-groove boards

A floor made from tongue-and-groove boards is more rigid and less likely to creak. However, to remove a board you will have to cut through the tongue. If replacing it, you will need a square-edged board.

TOOLS MATERIALS

- **pipe and cable detector**
- **wood chisel**
- **mallet**
- **floorboard saw**
- **padsaw**
- **narrow-bladed tool**
- **pencil**
- **try square**
- **ruler**
- **power drill with large wood bit**

- 50mm x 25mm softwood batten
- 50mm cut floor brads or ring-shanked nails, or 50mm (4mm or 5mm gauge) countersunk screws

IDEAL TOOL

Floorboard saw

This saw will make lifting tongue-and-groove boards easier. In addition to teeth along one long edge, the blade has a curved tip with more teeth. This allows a cut to be started directly down into the tongue. It also permits cuts to be made across boards without lifting them or damaging adjacent boards.

1 First locate any underfloor oipes and cables (see YOU CAN DO T). One way of freeing a board is :o use a sharp, wide-bladed (at east 25mm) wood chisel and nallet to cut down through the ongues on each side.

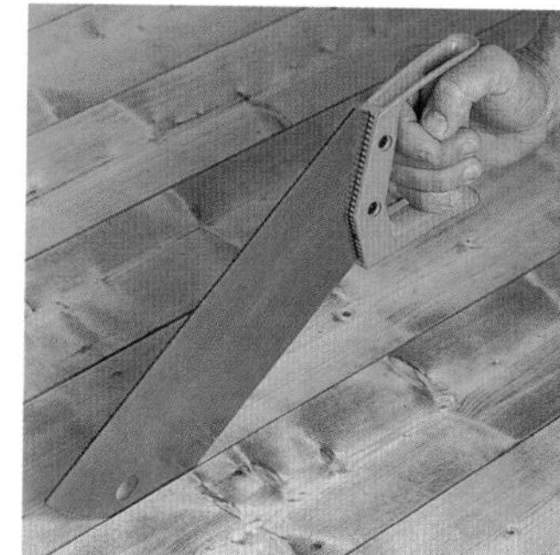

2 Alternatively, use a floorboard saw (see IDEAL TOOL). To begin, hold the saw upside-down and work the curved tip of the blade back and forth to cut into the tongue.

3 Once you have broken through the tongue, turn the saw over and continue cutting with the long edge of the blade. If the cut passes over a cable or pipe, use the curved edge of the blade again; work very slowly and apply minimal pressure so that you can control the blade as it breaks through the wood.

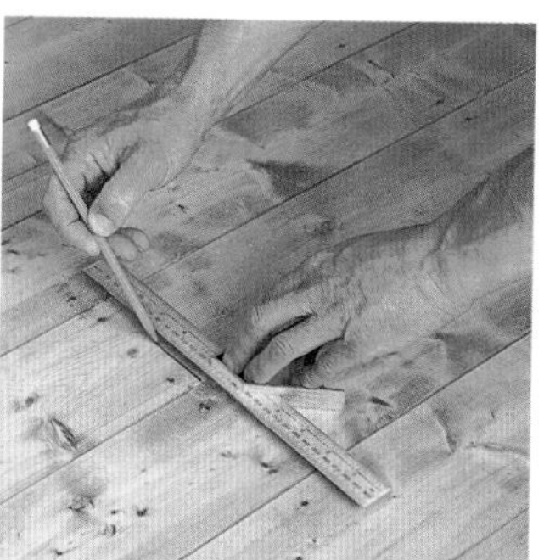

4 Once you have sawn through the tongues each side of the board, you should be able to see the joists below. If not, feel for them with a narrow-bladed tool. Using a pencil and try square, mark cutting lines across the board, in line with the edges of the joists.

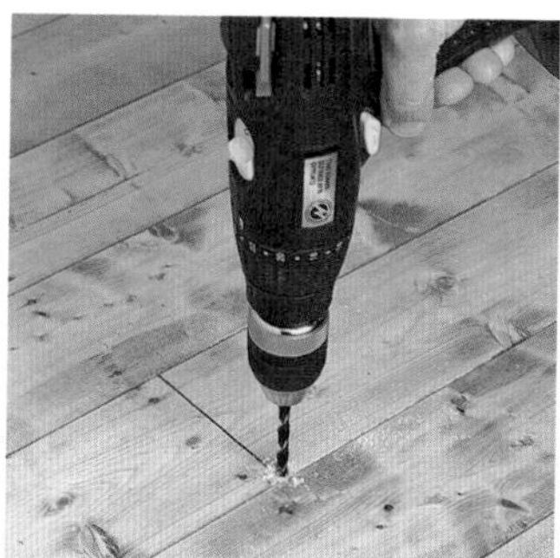

5 Using a large wood bit and electric drill, bore a hole near one edge of the board so that it just touches the cutting line across the board.

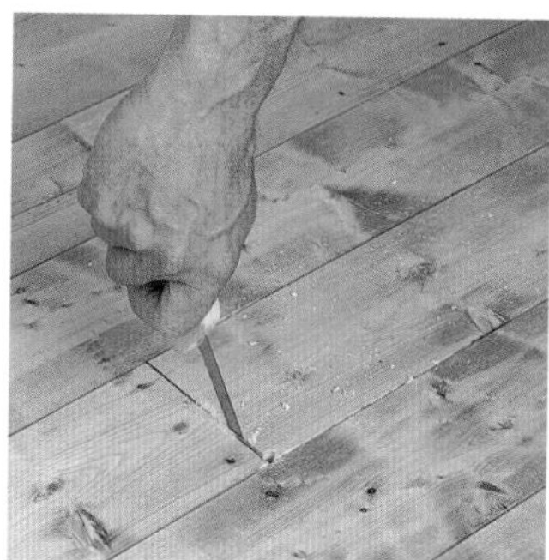

6 Insert the blade of a padsaw into the hole and cut along the line to free the end of the board from the joist. Do the same at the other end. Now the board can be levered up in the same manner as a square-edged board (see Steps 1–4, opposite).

7 Having cut the ends of the board flush with the joists there will be nothing to nail or screw the board back into. Get around this by nailing or screwing 50mm x 25mm battens to the sides of the joists, making sure they are tight against the undersides of the neighbouring boards.

YOU CAN DO IT

Locating underfloor pipes and cables

If you are lucky, you will find any pipes and cable runs already marked on the floorboards. Failing that, go over the area of floor you intend working on with an electronic pipe and cable detector. Look for signs that boards have been lifted before (damaged edges or multiple fixing holes). Mark the locations of any pipes or cables you find directly on the boards. Or if the boards are to be left exposed, draw up a paper plan and keep it somewhere safe.

SAFETY FIRST

Keep pets well out of the way whenever you lift floorboards. Before you nail the boards back down again double-check they haven't slipped underneath – getting trapped can be traumatic and dangerous for an animal.

FLOORS PREPARING FOR NEW FLOORIN

A change of floorcovering, be it vinyl, carpet or even ceramic tiles, can give a room a new lease of life. But before you start work, you must make sure that the underlying surface is sound and level. If it is not, the defects are likely to show through, spoiling the look of the new floor, and eventually resulting in uneven patterns of wear. Fortunately, there are simple ways of dealing with problem floors.

TOOLS MATERIALS

- **old paint brush or plant spray bottle**
- **claw hammer**
- **plane or sanding block**
- **long-nosed pliers**
- **nail spacing stick**
- **panel saw**

- 3mm-thick 600mm x 1220mm hardboard sheets
- 19mm ring-shanked nails

Levelling a wood floor

Hardboard sheets will not only level a boarded floor but will also reduce draughts from below. Buy 3mm-thick sheets, which you must first condition by brushing or spraying water over the textured side before stacking them on the floor of the room, back to back, for 48 hours. This expands them very slightly and means they will dry and tighten rather than expand and buckle once laid. Before laying them, drive all floorboard nails below the surface and plane or sand down any boards that are proud of the rest. Fix the sheets in place with 19mm ring-shanked nails, which are too short to penetrate right through the floorboards and damage any pipes and cables below.

IDEAL TOOL

Long-nosed pliers

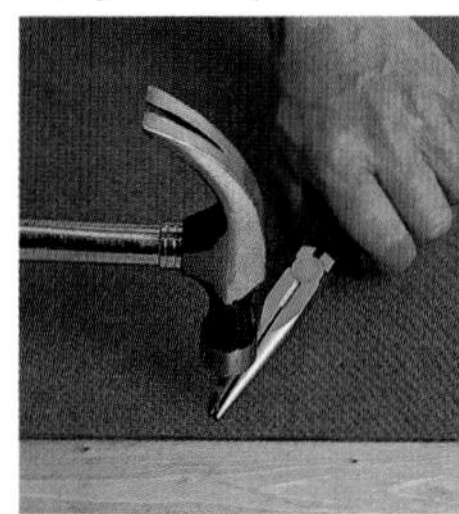

Use a pair of long-nosed pliers to hold a nail in position as you start it – not your fingers.

1 Lay the hardboard sheets textured side up (unless the instructions for the flooring that will cover them specify otherwise), as this will provide a key for the adhesive and accommodate the nail heads. Start in a corner of the room, setting the nails about 13mm in from the edges of the sheet in a pyramid pattern (see YOU CAN DO IT). Cut scraps of wood as nail spacing guides.

2 Butt the sheets tightly together, nailing along each meeting edge first, before continuing in pyramid fashion. When you reach the end of the first row of sheets, you will have to cut the last one to size.

3 Use the off-cut from the last sheet in the first row to start the second row. This will prevent wastage and ensure that the joins are staggered (see diagram, below). Continue in this way until you have finished the floor.

Staggered joints

By staggering the panel joins in adjacent rows, you will prevent the possibility of continuous undulations forming in the floor and showing through the floorcovering.

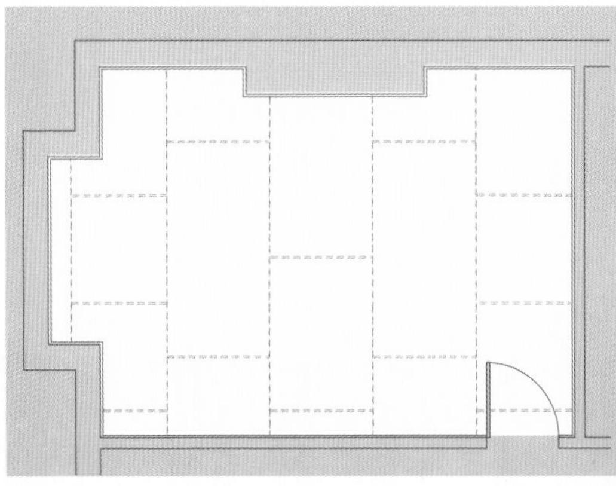

YOU CAN DO IT

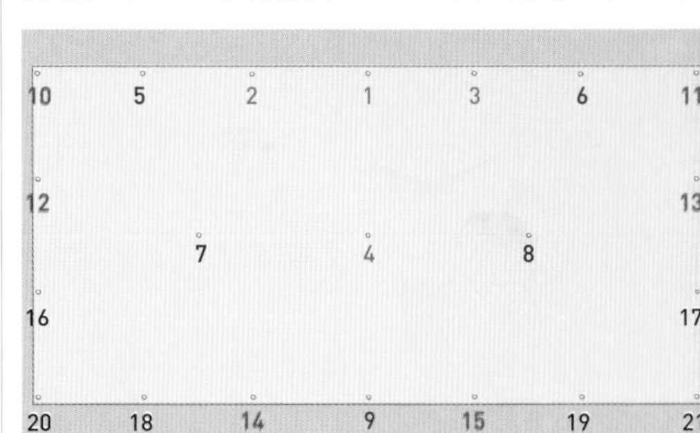

Pyramid nailing
To prevent hardboard sheets buckling as you nail them down, position nails in an expanding pyramid pattern, starting in the middle of one edge and gradually working across to the other side. Around the edge nails should be spaced at 150mm intervals, while in the centre they can be 225mm apart.

Replacing a wood floor

If a lot of floorboards are damaged, it will be cheaper and easier to pull them all up and fit tongue-and-groove chipboard flooring panels. These will provide a firm foundation for the final floorcovering.

TOOLS MATERIALS

- **claw hammer**
- **pencil**
- **try square**
- **panel saw or electric circular saw**
- **mallet**

- tongue-and-groove chipboard flooring panels
- 50mm ring-shanked nails
- PVA wood adhesive

1 Start in the corner of the room. Lay the first panel so that its long side spans the joists and its end rests on a joist – if you need to cut it down, do so on the skirting edge. Position the board about 9mm from the wall to allow for expansion. Nail along the joists, beginning about 18mm from the edge, using 50mm ring-shanked nails spaced at 300mm intervals. Remember to mark on the boards the location of any pipes or cables beneath.

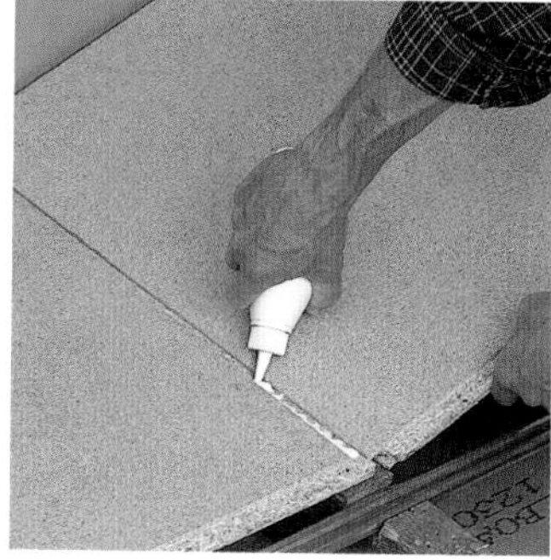

2 Check the fit of the next panel. If its tongued end does not meet a joist, cut it back as necessary. Then apply PVA wood adhesive to the end tongue of the first panel, slot the end groove of the second over the tongue, aligning the long edges, and nail down the second panel. Wipe off excess glue with a damp cloth.

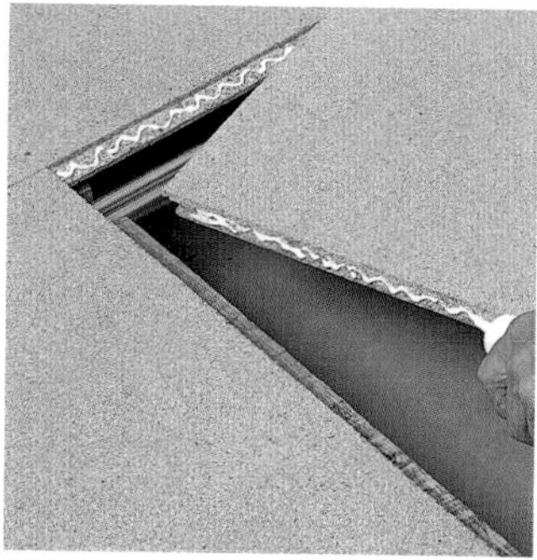

3 If you shortened the second panel to meet a joist, the grooved end of the next will also need cutting off so that you can butt and glue them together over the joist. Cut the last board in the row to size, remembering to leave a 9mm expansion gap at the wall. Lay the first panel of the second row against the last panel of the first so the joins are staggered.

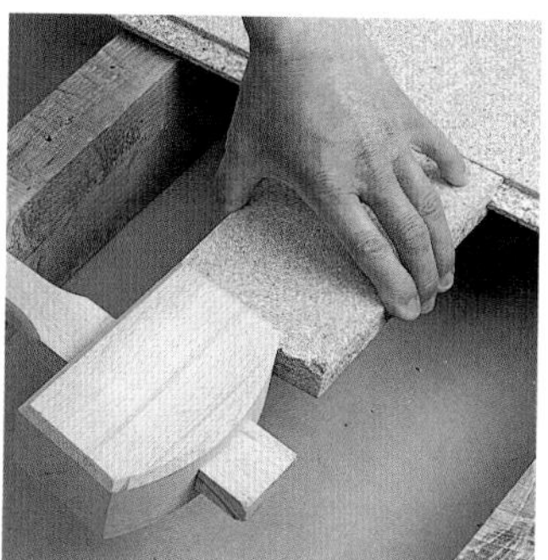

4 Make sure the panels fit tightly by driving each into place with a grooved panel off-cut. Continue until you reach the far side of the room, staggering the joins and allowing an expansion gap at the wall. Measure and cut the last row of boards to fit.

Levelling a concrete floor

Provided a solid concrete floor is basically sound, the simplest way of levelling it is with a self-levelling compound. This is poured on to the floor and trowelled fairly smooth. Any cracks or holes should be repaired first.

TOOLS MATERIALS

- **old paint brush**
- **small trowel**
- **bucket**
- **stirring stick**
- **plasterer's trowel**

- sand/cement mortar
- self-levelling flooring compound

YOU CAN DO IT

Smooth it over

If your trowel marks are still visible after a couple of minutes, sprinkle water on them and smooth the compound again.

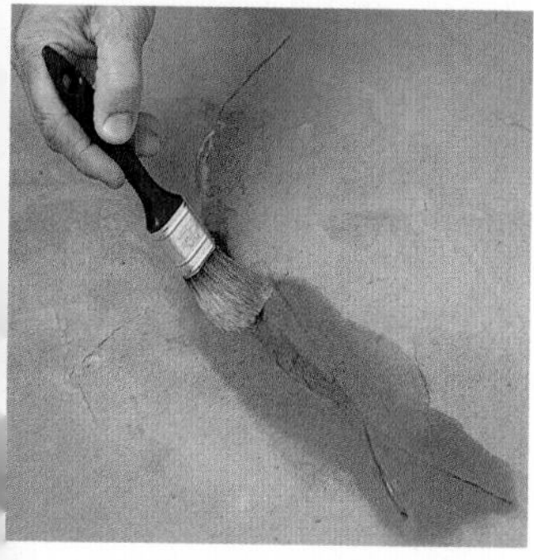

1 Dampen cracks or holes by brushing them with water. This will stop your filler from drying out too quickly and cracking.

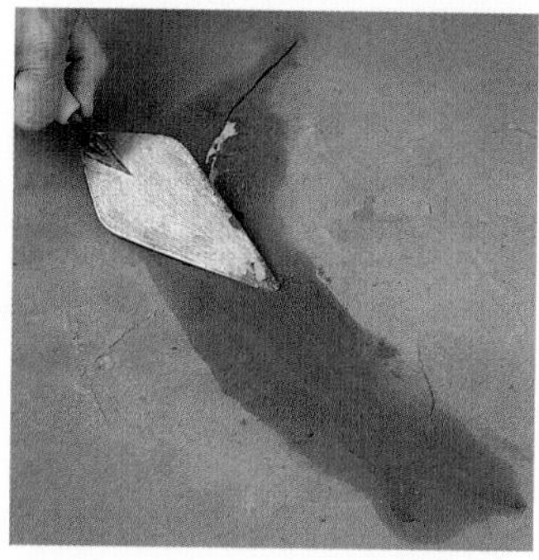

2 Fill large cracks or holes with a sand/cement mortar mix. Smaller ones can be treated with self-levelling compound. Trowel smooth and leave to harden. Once the floor has set, prepare it for the compound by pouring a little water on to the floor and brushing it out to dampen the surface. Do not flood it!

3 Mix the compound as instructed. Starting in the corner furthest from the door, pour it on to the floor and spread it to a thickness of about 3mm with a plasterer's trowel, using long, sweeping strokes. While you are doing this, get a helper to mix the next bucketful of compound.

4 Work quickly, but carefully; it will set in about 15 minutes, and you should be able to walk on the floor in a few hours.

FLOORS SANDING AND SEALING

You can greatly enhance the look of a room by stripping a boarded floor back to the bare wood and sealing it with a varnish, so that the beauty of the wood grain shows through. It is a dusty and noisy job, however, and as with so many home improvement projects the quality of the finish will largely depend on the effort you put into the preparation.

Preparing the floor

Before you begin sanding a floor, you must make sure that it is ready to be sanded, and that it will look good when finished. The boards must be in good condition, with no wide gaps or protruding nails.

1 Drive all the nails below the surface with a hammer and punch; protruding nails will tear a sanding sheet. Nail down loose boards and replace damaged ones, ideally using boards of similar age – you may be able to take these from other rooms in your home where the floorboards are not exposed.

2 Fill the gaps between the boards (see YOU CAN DO IT). If the gaps are very wide, you may be better off lifting and re-laying the boards more tightly, filling the final gap with an extra board. Otherwise, you can glue in narrow strips of wood, as illustrated.

3 Leave the filler strips slightly proud, and let the glue dry. Then plane or sand down the strips until they are flush with the surrounding boards. Sweep the floor clean.

TOOLS MATERIALS

- **hammer**
- **nail punch**
- **plane**
- **sanding block**
- **broom**
- **drum sander**
- **rotary edge sander**
- **electric hand sander**
- **vacuum cleaner**
- **lint-free cloth**
- **100mm brush**
- **fine wire wool**
- **dust mask**
- **safety goggles**

- thin wood strips
- PVA wood adhesive
- newspaper
- wallpaper adhesive
- water-based wood dye
- masking tape
- coarse-, medium- and fine-grade abrasive sheets
- white spirit
- varnish

YOU CAN DO IT

Mind the gaps

Papier mâché makes a good filler for gaps between floorboards. Mix a stiff paste with torn strips of newspaper (not coloured) and wallpaper adhesive. Colour this with a little water-based wood dye to match the sanded floor. Force the papier mâché into the gaps and smooth off flush with the boards. Allow to dry before sanding.

Sanding the boards

To sand floorboards effectively, you will need to hire a heavy-duty industrial drum sander and rotary edge sander; make sure you are shown how to change the abrasive sheets. Sanding produces a lot of dust, so seal doors to other parts of the house with masking tape, and sweep up after each sanding pass.

1 Fit a coarse abrasive sheet to the drum sander and work across the floor in overlapping diagonal strips. Sweep up the dust and repeat the process, working at right angles to the first sanding pass.

2 Each time you start or stop the machine, tilt the drum clear of the boards to stop it damaging them.

3 Having levelled the boards by
anding diagonally, fit medium-
rade paper to the drum and
and parallel to the boards, again
verlapping each pass. Then
nish off with fine-grade paper in
ne same manner. Do not work
cross the grain of the boards, as
nis will leave visible marks.

4 The drum sander will not sand right up to the skirting – for this you need the rotary edge sander. Use coarse, medium and fine grades of abrasive paper and keep it moving, otherwise it will score deep marks in the floor. Tilt the machine as you start and stop the disc.

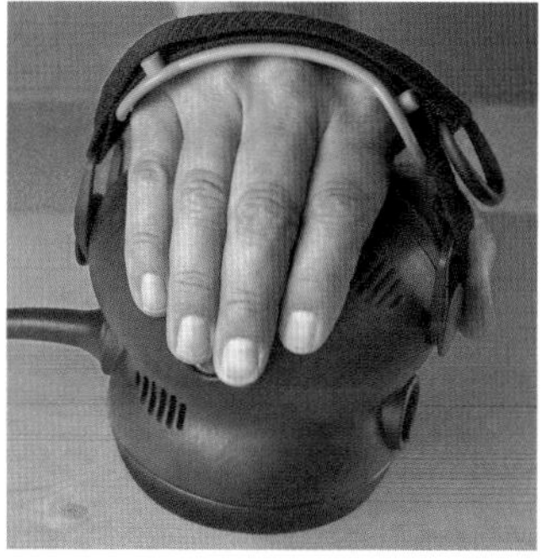

5 Finish the corners and inaccessible areas with abrasive paper wrapped around a sanding block or – much easier – a powered hand sander (see IDEAL TOOL).

IDEAL TOOL

Electric hand sander

A small hand sander will make light work of the bits that the drum and edge sanders cannot reach. It can be fitted with various grades of abrasive paper to ensure a fine finish.

SAFETY FIRST

Sanding a floor is a very dusty job, so you must wear a dust mask and close-fitting eye protection. Keep the flexes of sanders out of the way by draping them over your shoulder, and plug them into a residual current device (RCD) to protect you from shocks should the flexes become damaged (see page 290). Always unplug the sander before changing the abrasive sheet.

Sealing the boards

ou can use a clear or tinted varnish to seal the sanded
oorboards. Apply three coats for a really hardwearing finish.
ake sure the brush is completely clean before you start.

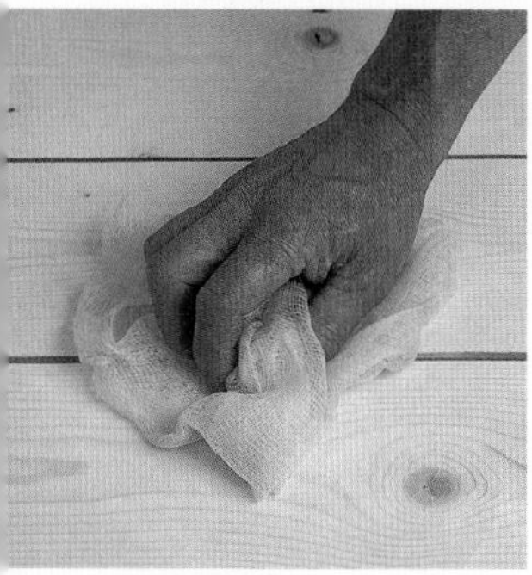

1 Sweep the sanded floor
noroughly, then vacuum it.
nally, go over it with a lint-free
oth dampened with white
pirit.

2 Thin the varnish for the first coat with 10% white spirit to make it more workable. The first coat seals the wood; working towards the door, brush out the varnish in the direction of the wood grain, making sure no pools form.

3 When the first coat has dried, remove any lumps or specks with fine abrasive paper and wipe clean with a lint-free cloth dampened with white spirit. Apply a second, unthinned coat and allow to dry. Then apply the final coat.

YOU CAN DO IT

Wire wool

Before applying the final coat of varnish, go over the dry floor lightly with wire wool for a really clean and polished finish.

FLOORS LAMINATE FLOORING

ECO WOODS 

Look for laminate flooring marked with the FSC symbol to show that a percentage of the wood fibre in the product comes from well-managed forests, independently certified in accordance with the rules of the Forest Stewardship Council.

Laminate flooring can transform a room, giving it an attractive, 'polished wood' look. It is made up of long, narrow lengths of high density fibre, coated with lacquer to make it scratch-, stain- and fade-resistant, and it can be laid on top of most surfaces. It is available in a range of colours and decorative effects, so you can create any style, from pale and contemporary to rich, dark and old-fashioned. Laminate flooring is laid 'floating', which simply means there are no fixings attaching it to the floor below. This allows it to expand and contract slightly without buckling. Visit www.diy.com for help planning and laying your laminate floor.

Preparing the existing floor

Laminate flooring can be laid on any smooth, flat surface as long as it is dry, firm and level.

Concrete floors

A newly concreted floor must be left to dry for one day per 1mm thickness of concrete before you can lay laminate flooring. If the old floor is uneven, level it with self-levelling compound (see page 33).

Wooden floors

Make sure all the floorboards are firmly screwed down and flatten all nails with a hammer. Wide gaps between floorboards can be filled with mastic or thin wedges of wood glued in place and planed flush with the boards when dry.

Which underlay?

All sub-floors need to be fitted with an underlay before laminate flooring can be laid. Concrete, asphalt, vinyl-, quarry- or similar tiled sub-floors should be covered first with a plastic-film moisture barrier (a damp-proof membrane), in addition to any damp-proof course that may be present in the sub-floor. Never use carpet underlay under laminate flooring.

If your door frame extends beyond the skirting, cut away a slot at its base before laying the underlay (see page 41).

Poly foam underlay

This is the thinnest of the underlays used beneath laminate flooring, and is suitable for any firm, dry and level sub-floor, such as a wooden floor. Prepare the floor and if necessary lay a damp-proof membrane. Lay the poly foam underlay over the entire floor area. Trim to fit with scissors or a knife, cutting a 10mm gap around pipes. Lay lengths side by side and secure them with masking tape.

Wood fibre

This is the thickest of the underlays used beneath laminate flooring, and you will need to use it if you have a slightly uneven sub-floor. Because they are more substantial, wood fibre boards also give good heat and sound insulation.

Prepare the floor and if necessary lay a damp-proof membrane. Allow the boards to acclimatise in the room for 24 hours. Stagger the joints and leave a 10mm expansion gap around the edge of the room and 5mm between the boards. They can be cut to fit easily with a knife.

Combined underlay and damp-proof membrane

The obvious advantage of combined underlay is that whatever your sub-floor, you only have to fit one layer rather than two. It is thicker than poly foam underlay so will absorb very slight irregularities in the floor, and it provides good sound insulation.

1 Prepare the floor. Lay the underlay over the entire floor area, placing the lengths side by side. Trim to fit with scissors or a knife, cutting a 10mm gap around pipes.

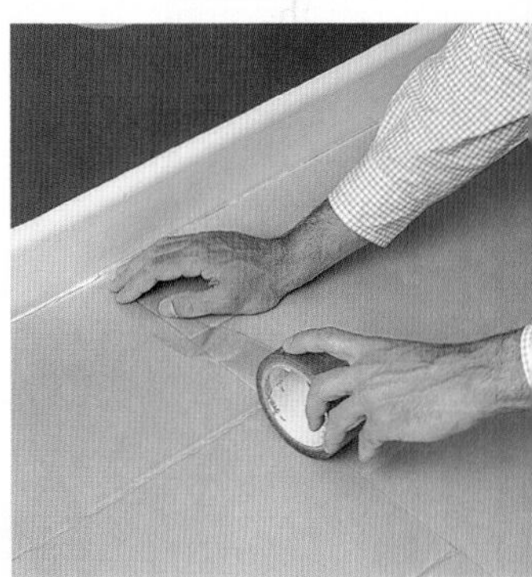

2 Tape the joins securely, making sure the lengths do not overlap.

Types of laminate flooring

Not all laminate flooring has a wood finish. There are new tile-effect laminates on the market – terracotta, slate or ceramic – that look absolutely convincing but are warmer and gentler underfoot than a true tile floor.

If you do opt for a wood-effect laminate, you don't have to just use one shade: mix different colours to complement your interior and subtly partition the space.

Locking and tongue-and-groove flooring

There are two main types of laminate flooring: locking and tongue-and-groove. Locking flooring planks have long and short tongues on their sides and ends which lock together to make tight joins with no glue required. It's easy to unlock the floor again if you want to move it or replace a damaged plank.

Tongue-and-groove flooring has a tongue on one side and a groove on the other. The tongue of one plank fits into the groove of the next. Planks are glued together at each join, so are not easy to take up again.

If you want laminate flooring in your kitchen or bathroom, buy one with a water-resistant core (though be aware that even this will not take a soaking).

What to buy

Laminate flooring is sold in packs to cover a given area. The number of planks in a pack varies, so be sure to read the specifications on the packaging. Calculate the area of your room by multiplying together the width and length measurements, and buy an extra 10%, just in case.

SAFETY FIRST

Protect your knees

Laying flooring is very hard on the knees, and can lead to painful injuries if you accidentally kneel on sharp objects. Let a pair of knee pads take some of the strain.

YOU CAN DO IT

Laying bathroom flooring

If you are refurbishing a bathroom and need to fit a new basin or lavatory, do so after the floor is laid. You'll avoid the problem of different floor levels, and you won't have to cut the flooring to fit around the pedestal.

Fitting kit

As well as the flooring, you need a fitting kit. This includes some essential items to help you lay the floor:

- Expansion spacers or wedges, to be inserted all the way around the edge of the floor (and removed when it is laid). These ensure that a 10mm gap is left for the floor to expand and contract without buckling.
- A tapping block which is used with a hammer to gently tap the ends of the planks together.
- A pulling bar, to pull the last plank in a row into place. One end hooks over the end of the plank adjacent to the skirting; the other is lightly tapped with a hammer.

Laminate flooring clamp

This is a very useful tool for tightening rows of tongue-and-groove planks. The clamp consists of a metal plate and a ratchet plate which are joined by a belt. First fit the metal plate and ratchet across three planks. Tighten gently, taking care not to overtighten and lift the planks off the floor. Leaving the metal plate in position, extend the ratchet plate another three rows and tighten again. Repeat across the floor. The clamp can extend up to 4.5m. If you want, you can use several clamps at a time on the floor.

SAFETY FIRST

Wear a dust mask while you saw the planks, and ensure the room is properly ventilated.

Laminate flooring that locks together with no need for glue or nails is the quickest type to fit. The boards must be conditioned before they are fitted, otherwise they could warp. Lay them horizontally in their packing in the room where they are to be used for at least 48 hours. Make sure the existing floor is properly prepared and underlay fitted (see page 36).

Fitting locking laminate

Laminate flooring expands and contracts naturally, so you need to leave a gap of 10mm between the planks and the skirting-board all around the room when you fit the floor. Expansion spacers or wedges are included in the fitting kit to allow for this.

TOOLS MATERIALS

- **try square**
- **pencil**
- **ruler**
- **dust mask**
- **hardpoint handsaw or jigsaw with a laminate blade**
- **hammer**
- **tapping block**

- locking laminate flooring
- fitting kit

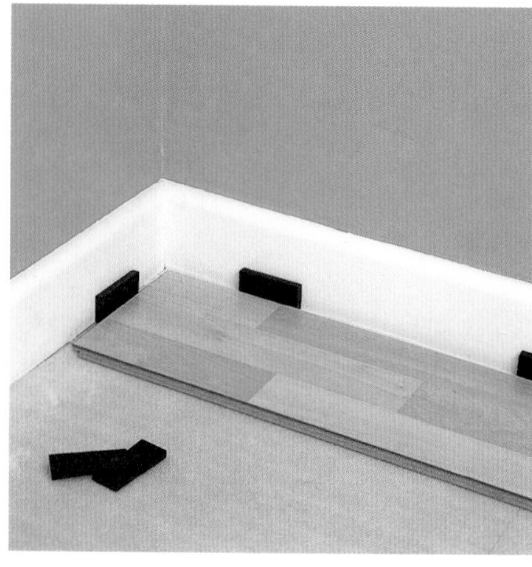

1 For the best effect, lay planks lengthways towards the light source. With the underlay in place, lay the first plank in a left-hand corner, the end with the short tongue against the wall. Place expansion spacers at intervals between the plank and the skirting, following the manufacturer's instructions, to ensure the correct gap is left for expansion. Check that the plank is aligned and square with the wall.

2 Lay the next plank end-on, placing the short tongue of the second board into the long tongue of the first board at a 30° angle. Lower the plank and lock it into place. Lay more planks in the same way until you reach the end of the row, where you will probably have to cut a plank to make it fit.

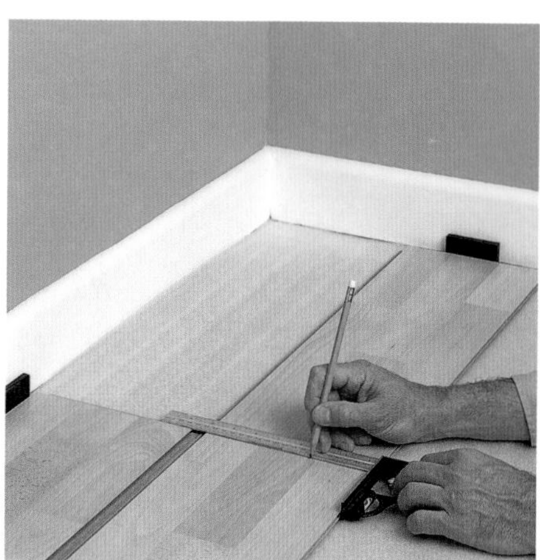

3 To measure the last plank, turn it 180° and lay it next to the previous one, with an expansion spacer directly against the skirting. Using a try square and pencil, draw a line across the last plank level with the end of the previous one. Cut to size and reposition it to complete the first row. The joins should be staggered: if the off-cut piece of plank is 300mm or more, it can be used to start the next row; otherwise cut a plank in half. Make sure the cut end is next to the expansion spacer, where it will be hidden by the floor trim.

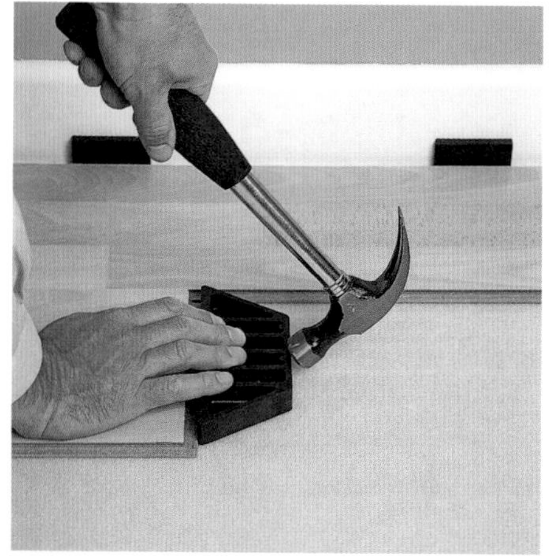

4 There are two ways of fitting rows of planks together. You can lock the planks on their long sides first, then tap each short end carefully to join it to the previous row, using a hammer and tapping block. Alternatively, clip a row of planks together on their short ends first, laying them next to the previous row. Then with a helper lift the new row to an angle of roughly 30° and push down to lock the long sides together.

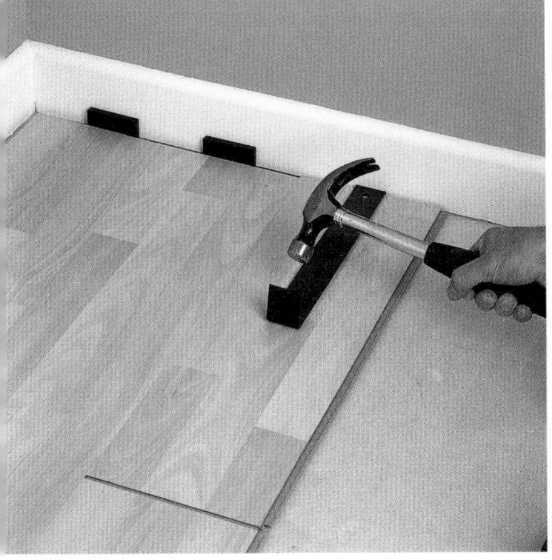

5 Measure and cut the last plank in each row as described in Step 3. Lock its long edge to that of the previous row. Fit the shorter end of a pulling bar between the last plank and the wall and tap the other end sideways with a hammer to lock the last plank into place.

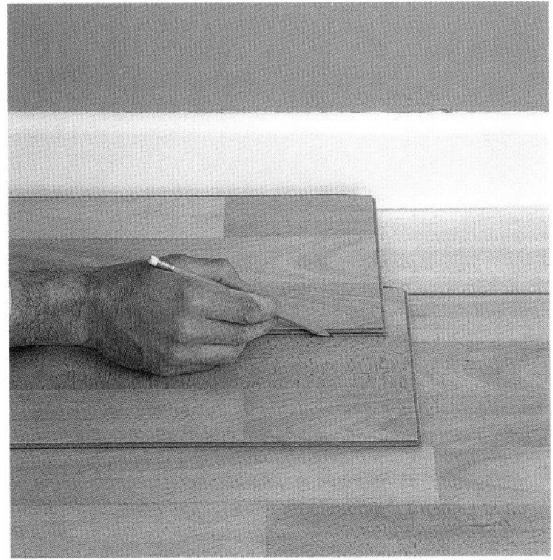

6 To cut planks to fit the last row, place a plank at a time directly over the previous row. Place a third plank on top so that its tongue touches the skirting. Use the edge of this plank to mark the cutting line with a pencil on the plank beneath. Cut the plank and ease it into position in the final row, using the pulling bar.

YOU CAN DO IT

Caring for laminate floors

- Clean regularly with a soft vacuum cleaner or brush.
- Wipe with a damp cloth to bring back the shine.
- Put felt pads and/or castor cups under chairs and heavy furniture to stop them denting the floor, and always move furniture carefully.
- Place a rug or mat inside the door and in front of a hand basin or sink to protect from marks or spills.

B&Q

Flooring trim

Once the flooring is laid, you can remove the expansion spacers and cover the gap around the room with a laminate flooring trim, chosen to match your floor. The trim should be fixed to the skirting – not the floor – with glue or nails. Tongue-and-groove laminate needs to settle for 12 hours first.

TOOLS MATERIALS

- **pencil**
- **ruler**
- **dust mask**
- **mitre saw or tenon saw and mitre block**

- laminate flooring trim
- adhesive

1 Measure and cut lengths of laminate flooring trim. For a really neat finish use a mitre saw, as here, or a tenon saw and mitre block to cut the corners to a 45° angle.

2 Apply a suitable grab adhesive (see page 369) to the back of a length of flooring trim (not the base) so that it will stick to the skirting-board rather than the floor.

3 Press the trim in place and if necessary hold it firm with a couple of bricks or heavy books while the adhesive dries.

This type of flooring is laid so that the tongue of one plank fits into the groove of the previous plank, with the joints glued. Remember to condition the flooring to stop it warping: lay it horizontally in its original packing in the room where it is to be used for at least 48 hours.

Fitting tongue-and-groove laminate

Apart from the need to glue the joints, fitting, cutting and laying tongue-and-groove laminate is in most respects the same as locking laminate. However, before gluing, you should measure up and dry-lay three rows of planks at a time to make sure they fit together correctly.

1 With the underlay in place, start in the left-hand corner of the room and lay the first plank with the groove on the side facing the wall. Insert expansion spacers from the fitting kit between the plank and the skirting at intervals, following the manufacturer's instructions, to maintain a 10mm gap. This allows the floor to expand.

2 Lay the next plank end-on, pushing the tongue of one into the groove of the other. Continue to the end of the row. To measure and cut a plank to fit, turn to Step 3 of Fitting locking laminate (page 38). If the off-cut from the last plank is 300mm or more, use it to start the next row. If it is less, cut a plank in half to start the row so the joints are staggered.

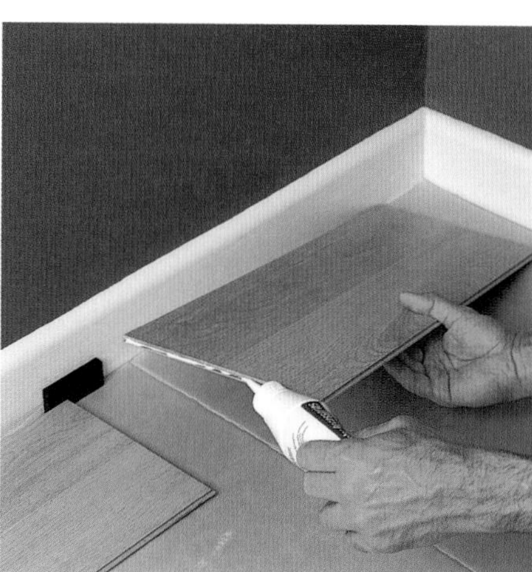

3 Once you have dry-laid three rows, take them apart and lay them again, this time applying laminate flooring adhesive to each joint. Gently push the planks together, if necessary using a hammer and tapping block from the fitting kit. Wipe away any excess adhesive immediately with a damp cloth.

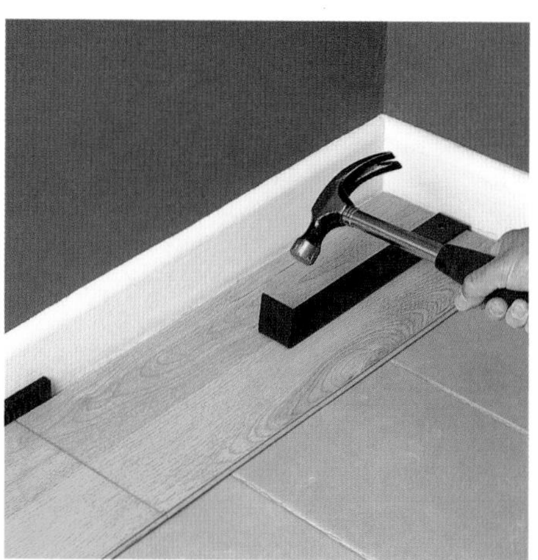

4 At the end of a row, fit the shorter end of the pulling bar between the last plank and the wall and tap the other end sideways with a hammer to pull the last tongue and groove together.

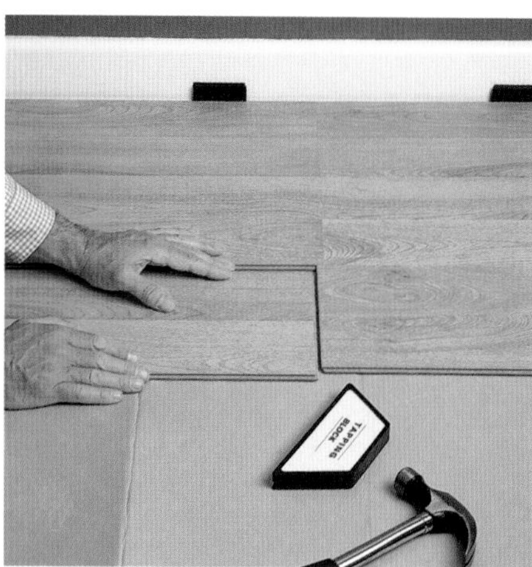

5 Once the first three rows are fitted and glued, continue working across the rest of the floor, three rows at a time. Use a flooring clamp to tighten the rows (see page 37). To cut the last row of planks to fit turn to Step 6 of Fitting locking laminate (see page 39).

TOOLS MATERIALS

- **try square**
- **pencil**
- **ruler**
- **handsaw or circular power saw**
- **hammer**
- **tapping block**
- **clean, damp cloth**
- **laminate flooring clamp**

- tongue-and-groove laminate flooring packs
- fitting kit
- laminate flooring adhesive
- flooring trim

Cutting around pipes

Obstacles such as radiator pipes are dealt with in exactly the same way whether the boards are locking or tongue-and-groove. Use a jigsaw to make curved cuts.

TOOLS MATERIALS

- **pencil**
- **tape measure**
- **try square**
- **dust mask**
- **jigsaw with laminate blade**
- **power drill with 20mm wood bit**

- laminate flooring
- expansion spacer
- radiator pipe cover
- laminate flooring adhesive

1 Lay the plank down so that the edge is touching the pipe, checking that it is in the correct position in relation to the end wall or the last plank fitted. Mark the position of the pipe, allowing some clearance for error and expansion. Place an expansion spacer from the fitting kit against the wall and measure from the front of the spacer to the front of the pipe. Mark this distance on the plank.

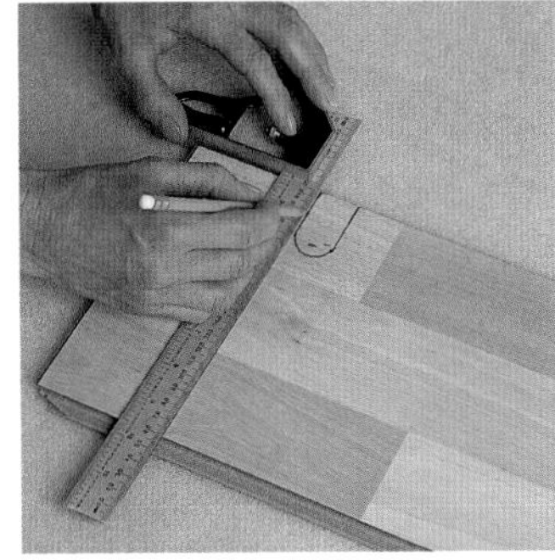

2 Join up the marks to outline the slot to be cut for the pipe.

3 Wearing a dust mask, cut the straight edges of the marked shape with a jigsaw, then release the piece by drilling through the board with a 20mm wood bit.

4 Position the plank, then glue down a radiator pipe cover (see YOU CAN DO IT), aligned with the grain of the wood.

Fitting around architraves and door frames

If the architrave extends beyond the skirting, don't try to cut the flooring to fit around it. You'll achieve a neater finish by cutting a slot into which the underlay and flooring will fit.

TOOLS MATERIALS

- **panel saw**
- **wood chisel**
- **tape measure**
- **pencil**
- **dust mask**
- **jigsaw with laminate blade**

- laminate underlay
- laminate flooring
- flooring trim
- PVA wood adhesive
- threshold bar

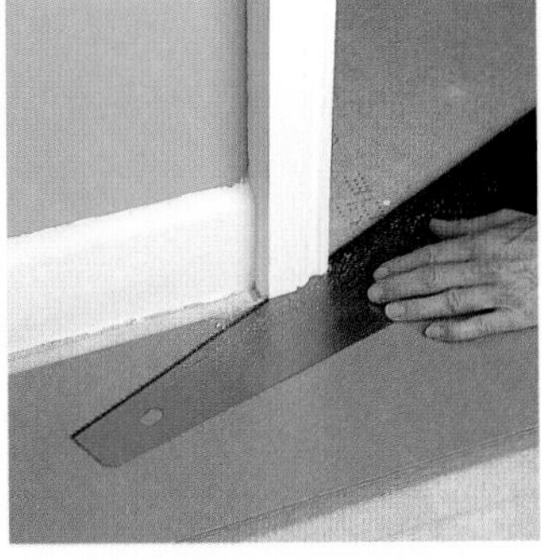

1 Lay a plank on a piece of underlay beside the door frame. Then place a panel saw flat on the plank and cut through the bottom of the architrave.

2 Use a wood chisel to remove the waste piece of wood, taking out an extra 10mm to allow the laminate flooring to expand.

3 To fit the flooring in the doorway measure the recesses in the door frame. The flooring should finish under the door when it is closed (but don't forget the 10mm expansion gap beneath the architrave). Transfer the measurements to the board with a pencil, cut it with a jigsaw and fit in position.

4 Cut a threshold bar to the width of the doorway and glue or screw it down (depending on the bar). When all the floor is laid, cover the gap between the laminate and the skirting with flooring trim (see page 39).

YOU CAN DO IT

Radiator pipe covers
These wood-effect discs will cover gaps or any untidiness around holes cut for radiator pipes. Align a disc with the grain of the flooring and glue it down.

Threshold bar
This is fitted in a doorway to make a neat join between the new floor and the flooring in the next room.

FLOORS LAYING SOFT TILES

Soft vinyl floor tiles are very versatile and make an excellent hardwearing floor in any room. The tiles can be stuck to the floor with tile adhesive or they may have a self-adhesive backing, so all you do is peel off the paper covering it. Tiles pre-coated with adhesive are quicker to lay, and there is no mess. They are light to work with and if you make a mistake, you only ruin one tile rather than a whole – and expensive – sheet of vinyl.

What to buy

When you are calculating the area of your room, remember to measure any alcove or bay separately and add it to the total. Also be aware that the size and number of tiles per pack do vary. Buy all your tiles at the same time. Check that the batch and item numbers are the same on each pack, since there may be slight colour differences between batches. When you get home, stack the tiles in the room where you are going to lay them for 24 hours, so they become acclimatised.

Preparing the existing floor

The old floor must be sound, dry and level. If you want to lay new tiles over old ones, these must be firmly stuck down – otherwise, remove them. If you have a timber floor, screw down any loose boards and then lay hardboard or plywood over it (do not lay tiles directly on floorboards – the boards may start to show through and cause premature wear). Lay hardboard smooth side up, and fix it with 25mm ring-shanked nails. Timber treated with wood preservative is not suitable as a sub-floor, even if overlaid; you must replace it (see page 33). Make sure there are no proud nail heads. Seal porous surfaces such as cement, plywood, hardboard or chipboard with a suitable primer.

Setting out

Don't be tempted to start laying tiles along one wall and then work your way round the room. The wall may not be straight and the room is unlikely to be square. It is better to find the centre point of the room and work from there towards the wall in each direction. You will then have a symmetrical design, with no unsightly narrow gaps at the skirting.

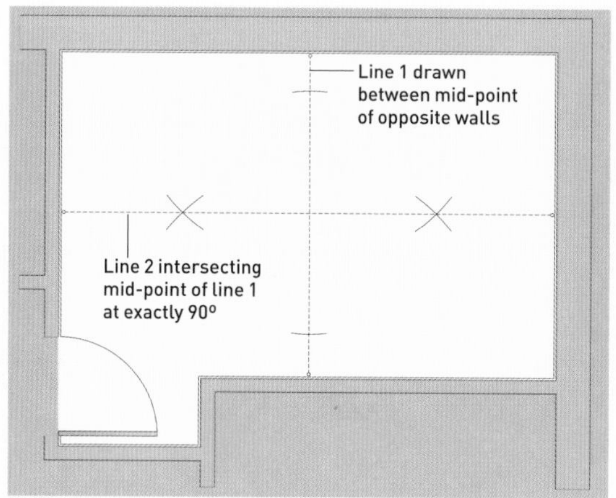

TOOLS MATERIALS

- **tape measure**
- **pencil**
- **chalk line**

- string

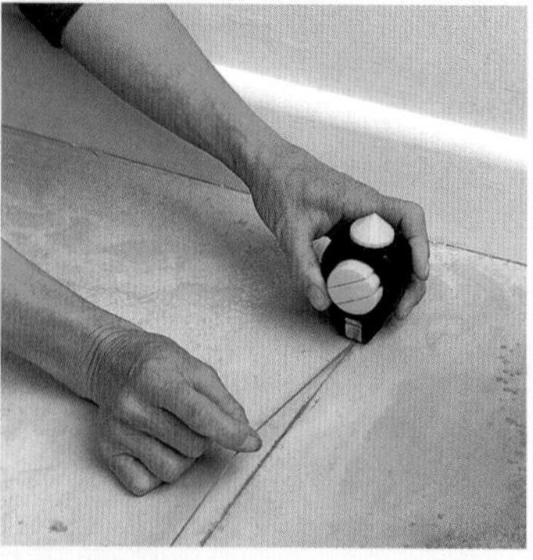

1 First measure one wall, calculate its mid-point and mark this on the floor. Repeat with the opposite wall. With a helper, stretch a chalk line between the two marks and snap a line across the floor. Calculate and mark the mid-point of this line. Tie about 1m of string to a pencil, and while your helper holds the end of the string firmly on the mid-point of the line, pull it taut and scribe an arc on the line either side.

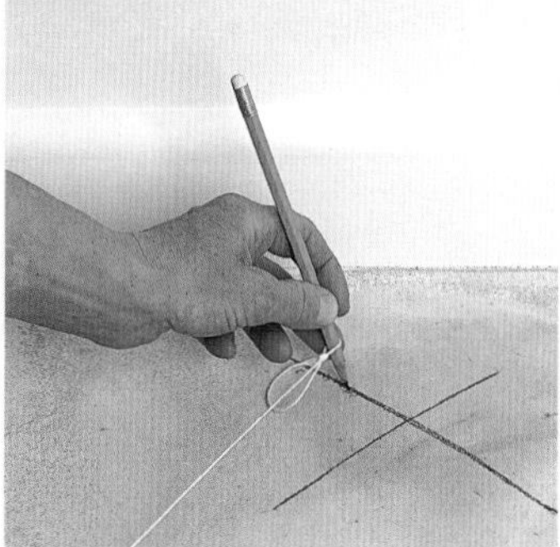

2 Now get your helper to hold the end of the string on the point that one arc intersects the line, and with the string pulled taut draw arcs at a roughly 45° angle either side of the centre line. When you repeat this from the other side, the arcs should intersect.

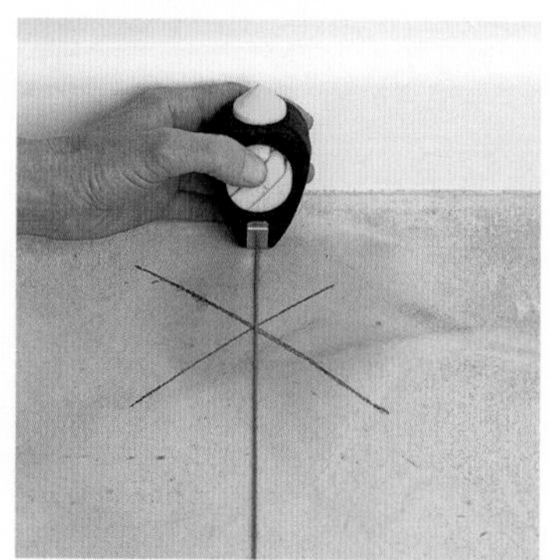

3 Stretch a chalk line between these intersecting arcs and snap a line across the floor. You now have two lines intersecting at a perfect right-angle in the centre of the room.

YOU CAN DO IT

Tiling awkwardly shaped rooms

If the dimensions of your room are irregular, the chalk lines will need to be snapped from a different place – the first line centred on a strong focal point such as a fireplace or patio doors, for instance. The room will still be divided into sections, but they will be different from one another.

Laying self-adhesive vinyl tiles

Once the intersecting lines have been marked, you need to decide the position of the first (key) tile, which will determine where the other tiles will go. To do this, dry-lay some of the tiles from the centre line to check how they fit at the skirting.

TOOLS MATERIALS

- **straightedge**
- **pencil**
- **chinagraph pencil**
- **craft knife**

- cushioned vinyl tiles

1 Starting at the centre line, dry-lay a row of tiles from the line to one of the walls.

2 When you reach the wall, check to see if you are left with a narrow gap (as above). This should be avoided – a thin strip of tile at the skirting will look ugly and may not stick well.

3 To avoid such a narrow gap, move the starting line back the width of half a tile. Repeat the dry-laying from the start line in the opposite direction and then towards the other two walls. Adjust the start line as necessary, until there is a reasonable gap of about half a tile all round the room.

4 Peel the backing paper off the first tile and press its edge against the start line. Lower the rest of the tile on to the floor and press down.

5 Lay the next tile on the other side of the chalk line, butting against the first tile. Form a square with two more tiles, and then lay tiles around the square to form a pyramid shape. Continue positioning the tiles until half the room is covered (except for the gaps at the skirting). Then tile the other half of the room. Position all the whole tiles before filling in the gaps at the edges and tackling the areas where there are fittings (see page 44).

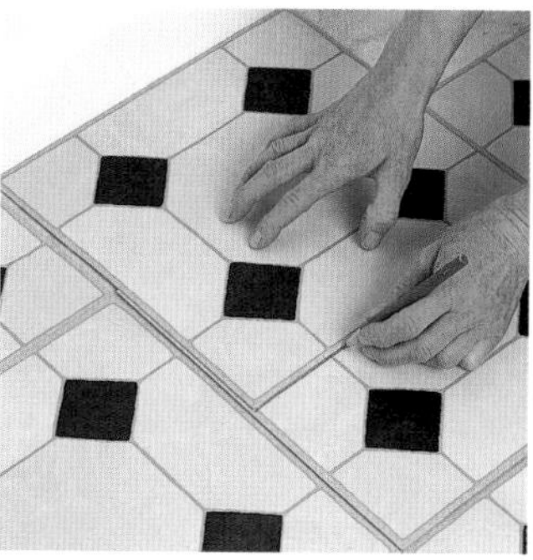

6 To cut the tiles for the gaps at the skirting, place the tile to be cut exactly on top of the last full tile. Place another tile on top, with its edge touching the wall. Using a chinagraph pencil, mark along the edge of the top tile on the face of the tile below.

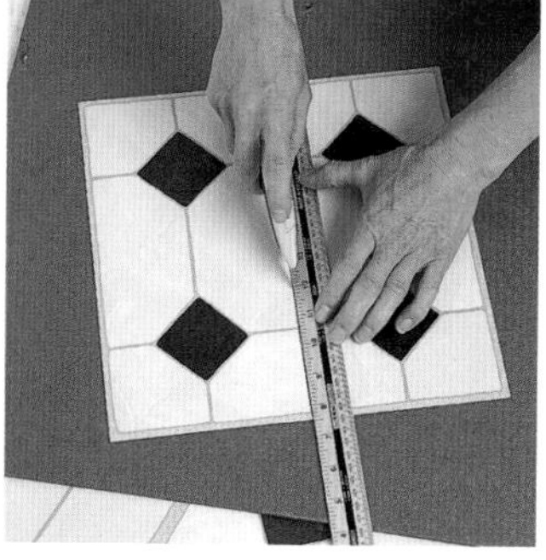

7 Put the marked tile on an old piece of board, place a straightedge along the marked line and cut part-way through the tile with a craft knife.

8 Break the tile by bending it at the cut line until it snaps.

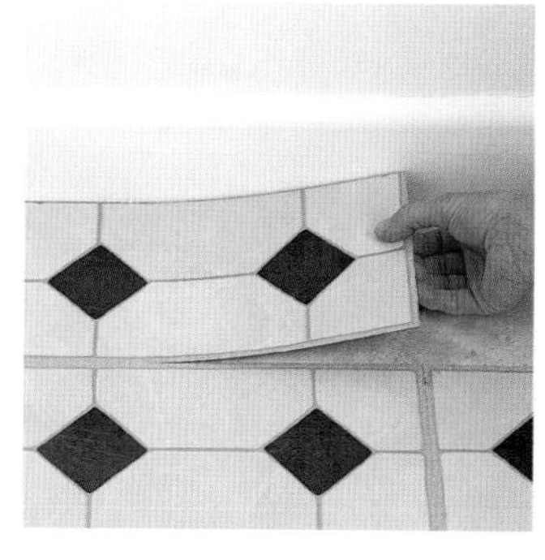

9 With the backing paper still on, check that the cut tile will fit into the gap without being forced, then remove the backing paper and stick it in place. Repeat the marking and cutting process all the way around the edge of the floor.

Once all the whole tiles are in place, you can deal with the awkward areas – round radiator pipes or lavatory and basin pedestals, for instance.

Tiling around basins and lavatories

To cut a tile to fit around a large awkward shape such as a basin pedestal, you need to make a template out of very thin card or paper to use as a cutting guide. Depending on your tiles, the object you are tiling around, and the layout of the room, you may require templates for more than one tile.

TOOLS MATERIALS

- **scissors**
- **blunt knife**
- **tape**
- **pencil**
- **craft knife**
- **round metalworking file**
- **off-cut of copper pipe**
- **hammer**

- vinyl floor tile
- thin card or paper
- block of wood

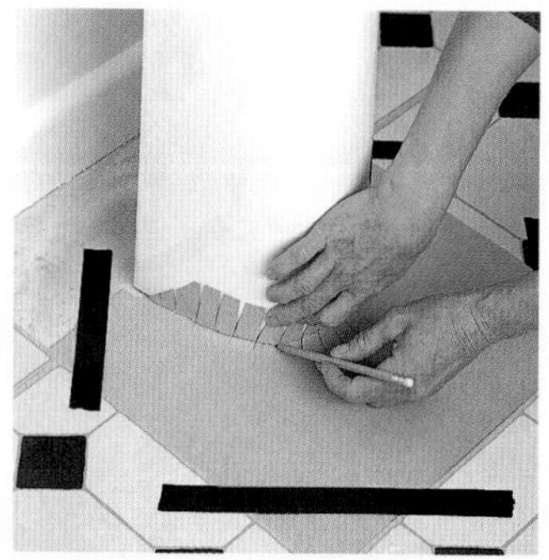

1 To make a template, cut a piece of thin card or paper the size of one of the tiles. Cut slits on the side where the pedestal will fit. Position the template against the pedestal with the flaps fringing it. Press the flaps against the pedestal with a blunt knife. Tape the paper to the floor and draw a pencil line where the pedestal and the floor meet.

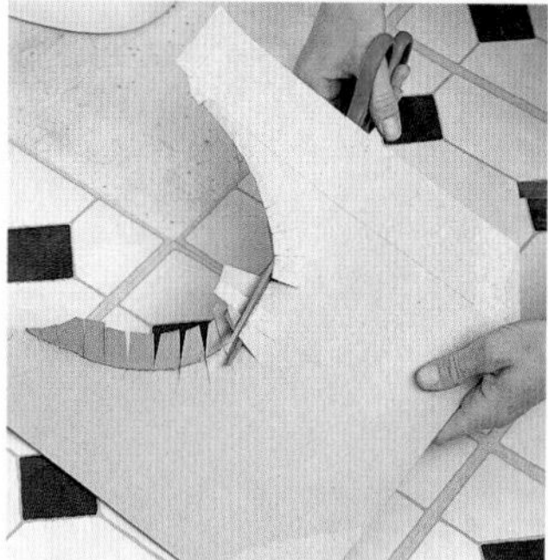

2 Remove the template and cut away the flaps, leaving the pencil guideline.

3 Place the template on a tile. If the tiles have a directional pattern, make sure the tile you are going to cut is the right way round. Draw the guideline on the tile and then cut it with a craft knife. Peel off the backing paper and fit the tile.

Cutting around pipes

The best way to cut a hole in a soft tile for a radiator pipe is to make a home-made punch from an off-cut of copper pipe the same diameter as the central heating pipe. You need a piece about 150mm long. Sharpen the inside of one end with a round metalworking file.

1 Hold the tile against the pipe and draw a line on it each side of the pipe to mark its width.

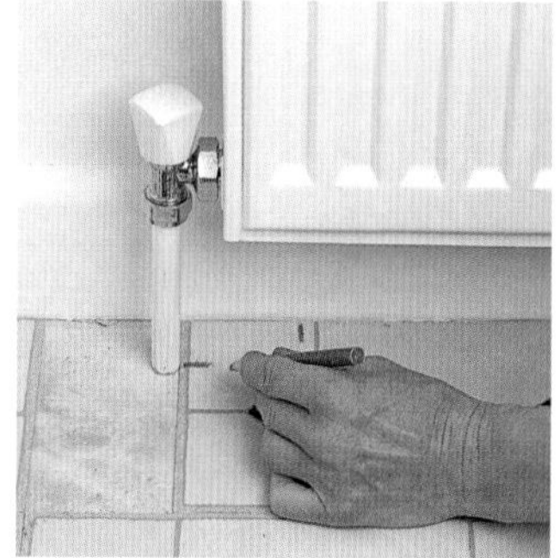

2 Move the tile so the marked edge touches the wall. Mark on the tile the distance to the front of the pipe.

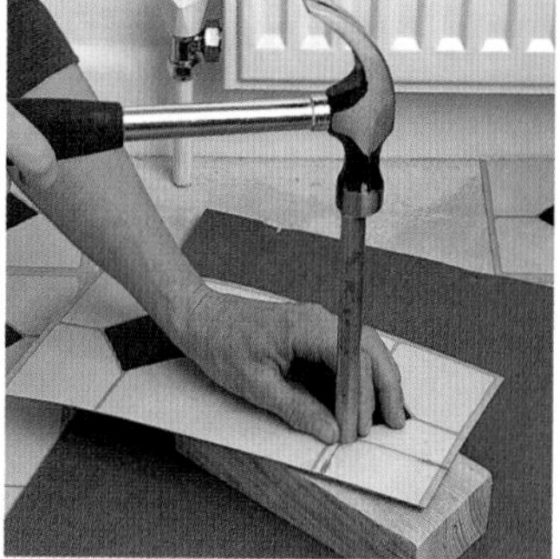

3 Rest the tile on a block of wood. Position the sharpened off-cut of copper pipe where the lines meet. Hit the other end of the pipe with a hammer to punch a neat hole through the tile.

4 Cut a straight slit between the hole and the edge of the tile. Dry-lay to check the fit, then stick the tile firmly in place.

Laying non-adhesive vinyl tiles

If you've chosen non-adhesive tiles, use the glue recommended by the manufacturer and apply it according to the instructions. The floor must be level and free from any sign of damp. Work out the start line in the same way as for self-adhesive tiles (see page 42).

TOOLS MATERIALS

- **paintbrush**
- **notched spreader**
- **small roller**
- **damp cloth or sponge**

- primer
- adhesive recommended by the tile manufacturer
- non-adhesive vinyl floor tiles
- white spirit

1 If you are laying the tiles on a porous surface such as concrete, apply primer with a paintbrush to seal it.

2 Working from the centre line, spread the tile adhesive evenly over the floor with a notched spreader. Check with the manufacturer's instructions, but for most adhesives you should cover an area big enough for about 15 minutes' work.

3 Carefully lay the tiles over the adhesive while it is still wet. Press the tiles into the adhesive, ensuring that every part of each tile is in contact with the sub-floor. Check that the tiles are level and butted tightly up against each other.

4 Roll a small roller over the tiles, particularly at the edges and corners, to make sure they are well stuck down.

5 If any adhesive comes through the joins, wipe it from the surface of the tiles immediately with a damp cloth or sponge. Adhesive that has started to set can be removed with white spirit. To measure up the edging tiles, turn to Step 6 page 43. Cut the tiles and stick them in place.

SAFETY FIRST

Take care when using adhesives for these tiles – the solvent- and spirit-based ones are highly flammable. Their fumes soak into clothing, so keep away from any fire and hang clothes outdoors when you have finished. If there is a pilot light in the room, turn it off while you lay the floor. Open all windows. Some manufacturers recommend wearing gloves when applying floor-tile adhesive: check the guidelines on the tin.

YOU CAN DO IT

Create your own floor pattern

Try combining different coloured tiles. Patterns can range from a simple chessboard of dark and light to more dramatic combinations of two or more colours. Draw a scale plan of your design before starting to lay a patterned tile floor.

B&Q

FLOORS LAYING HARD TILES

Hard ceramic and quarry tiles make an attractive floorcovering in kitchens, bathrooms, hallways or conservatories, and they are easy to care for and hardwearing. They can be expensive, however, so take care when laying them.

Preparing the existing floor

Hard tiles can be laid directly on a dry and level concrete floor, but a timber floor must be strengthened first with 13mm-thick exterior grade plywood fixed with countersunk 25mm screws (4mm gauge) or ring-shanked nails at 300mm intervals. Clean a concrete floor with detergent mixed with water; if it is uneven, level it (see page 33). If you intend to use a cement-based tile adhesive, first prime porous concrete surfaces and plywood with diluted PVA adhesive, so that the moisture is not drawn out of the adhesive before it has a chance to set. New tiles can be laid over old quarry or vinyl tiles as long as they are securely stuck down. Vinyl tiles should be coated with primer.

How many tiles to buy

Tiles are sold in packs and the size and number of tiles they contain will determine the area of floor they will cover. When you calculate the area of your floor, remember to include the dimensions of any alcove or bay. Round up the total to the nearest whole number to establish the number of packs of tiles you need.

TOOLS MATERIALS

- **rubber gloves, if required**
- **notched trowel or spreader**
- **chinagraph pencil**
- **tile cutter or diamond-wheel cutter**
- **rubber-edged grout spreader**
- **striking tool or wooden dowel**

- floor tile adhesive
- batten and nails (optional)
- hard floor tiles
- spacers
- damp sponge
- floor tile grout
- damp cloth
- dry cloth
- dark-coloured flexible sealant

Starting out

The first tile – the 'key' tile – determines the position of all the others, so it is very important that this tile is in the right place. Because rooms are seldom completely square, and the walls may not be straight, you cannot start by laying tiles right up against one wall and working your way out from there – you would end up with an untidy mess. The best way to ensure you have a symmetrical design is to start from the centre of the room and work out to the walls in each direction.

Positioning the key tile

First, find the centre of the room (see Setting out, on page 42). Starting at one of the centre lines, dry-lay a row of tiles from the line to the wall. When you reach the wall, make sure that you are not left with a narrow gap because a very thin strip of tile at the skirting will look very odd and may not stick very well. If necessary, move the line away from this wall the width of half a tile to create a larger gap. Repeat the dry-laying from this centre line in the opposite direction and then in both directions. perpendicular to it. Adjust the key tile position, as shown below, until there is an equal gap of about half a tile at all the edges of the room.

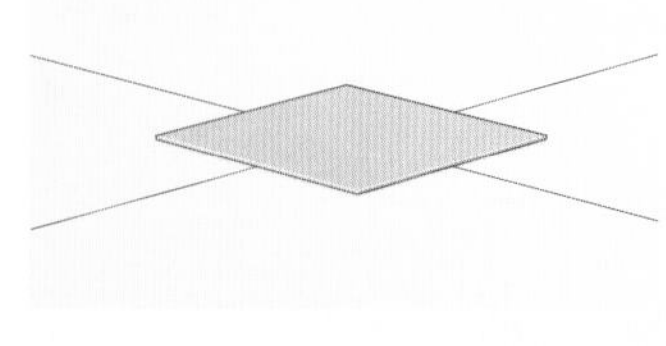

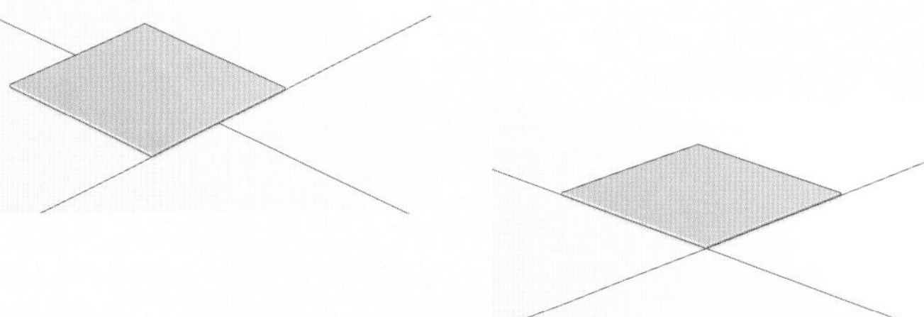

Laying the tiles

Start with the key tile, and work out towards one of the walls. Fix the tiles using a standard floor tile adhesive. When you have finished, you must let the adhesive set for 24 hours before you walk on the newly laid floor tiles. If you are laying them in a kitchen, tile half the room at a time so the whole kitchen is not out of action, and check you have left yourself an exit passage so you don't have to step on any tiles.

IDEAL TOOL

Notched trowel
Use the smooth side of this rectangular tool to spread the tile adhesive on the floor. Then draw its notched or serrated edge back through the adhesive to form ridges that leave the correct amount of adhesive needed to secure the tiles.

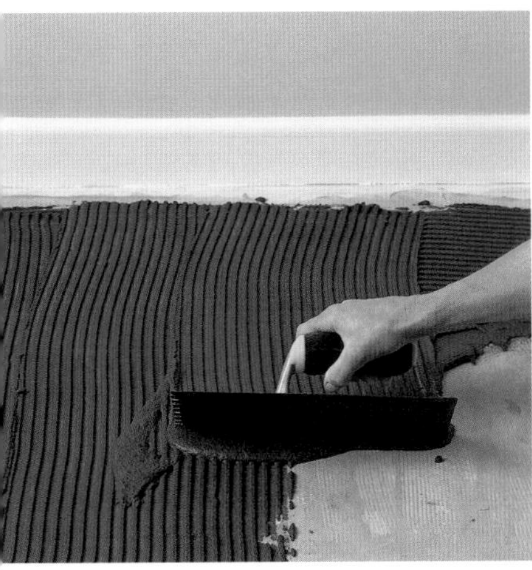

1 Starting in the centre of the room, pour out enough adhesive to cover about a square metre of floor. Spread the adhesive evenly using a notched trowel or spreader. The ribbed pattern leaves just the right amount of adhesive to make the tiles stick. Make sure you can still see enough of the chalk line to position the key tile. If you wish, nail a guide batten against one line to help align the first row of tiles.

2 Place the key tile in position, giving it a slight twist to bed it into the adhesive and to make sure that there is no air trapped underneath. Continue working out towards one of the walls to complete a row of whole tiles, fitting plastic spacers between them so they are evenly spaced. Check from time to time that the tiles are level using a spirit level. If you are laying thick handmade tiles, this may not be possible – you will need to rely on eye and judgment. Lay the next row of tiles out from the key tile, working at right angles to the first row. Continue working in rows in this quarter of the room.

3 When the first section of the room is complete, repeat the process until all but the cut tiles at the edges are laid. Wipe the tiles regularly with a damp sponge to remove any adhesive on the surface.

4 Using a trowel, clean out any adhesive remaining in the gaps around the walls before it sets. Leave the tiles for 24 hours before cutting and laying the edge tiles at the walls (see page 48).

YOU CAN DO IT

Tile spacers
Using tile spacers will give even grout lines between the tiles and a professional-looking finish to the floor. They come in different sizes, suitable for floor and wall tiles. Cross-shaped spacers are for use with standard square or rectangular tiles, while special Y-shaped spacers are for laying octagonal tiles. Press them well below the surface of the tile so that they do not protrude through the finished grout.

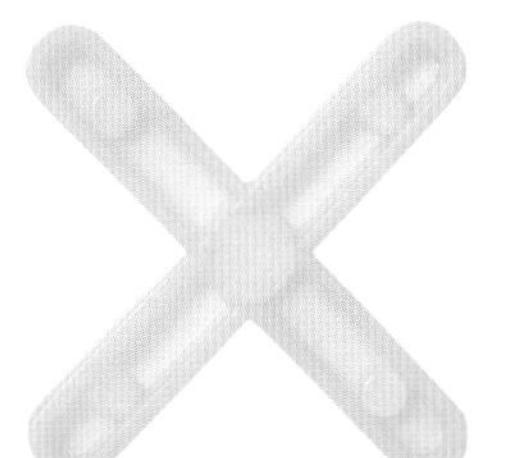

B&Q

Cutting and fitting edge tiles

Hard floor tiles are thicker than ceramic wall tiles, and to cut them you will need a heavy-duty tile cutter. Large tiles are easier to cut than smaller ones. A diamond-wheel cutter with water lubrication is expensive but will give perfect results every time. If you do use a hand-wheel type cutter, make a single score line in one pass and then snap the tile smartly. Hesitation will produce bad results.

1 To measure an edging tile, place it over the last full tile; align a third tile on top, with one edge touching the wall; use the inside edge as a guide to draw a line on the face of the tile below (see Step 6, page 43). Use a chinagraph pencil rather than an ordinary pencil, which may stain. Cut the tile just short of the marked line to allow space either side for the grout and sealant (see below).

2 Apply adhesive to the back of each cut border tile.

3 Place the border tiles in position and leave to set for 24 hours.

Grouting

The finished look of a tiled floor depends on careful grouting. Use floor tile grout and mix it thoroughly with water, making sure there are no lumps. Most grouts are best left to stand for a few minutes before use. Around the edge of the room use a similar-coloured flexible sealant instead of grout.

1 When the adhesive has set, mix the grout into a paste with water. If the surface of the tiles is glazed, you can pour the grout over them and spread it with a rubber-edged grout spreader, as here. If the surface of your tiles is absorbent, however, you should mix a very dry grout and press it into the joints one by one, taking care to keep the tiles as clean as possible to avoid staining.

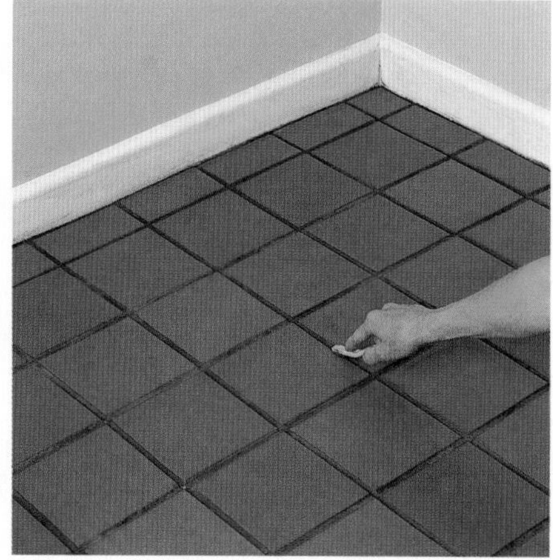

2 When the grout begins to set, press and smooth it into all the joints with a striking tool or a wooden dowel to compact it and make it water-resistant. Clean off the surplus grout with a damp sponge as you proceed.

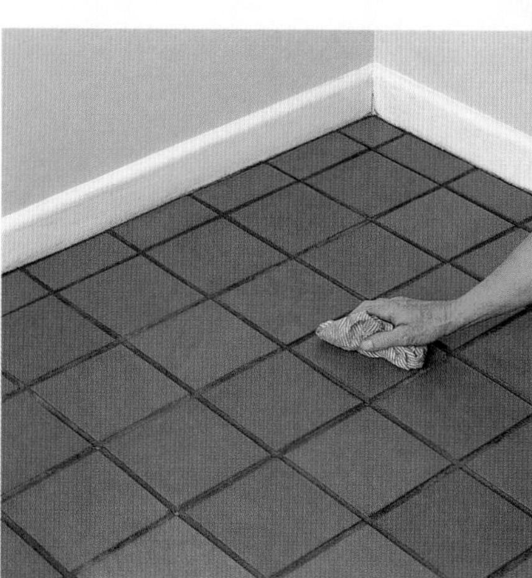

3 Leave the grout to harden for about an hour, wipe it again with a damp cloth and then polish the tiles with a dry cloth. Seal around the edge of the floor with a matching flexible sealant. Avoid giving the floor any heavy use for at least 48 hours after grouting.

Decorative border tiles

Count decorative border tiles as the last row of full tiles, and cut plain tiles to fit the gap around the edge of the room. Lay all the whole, plain tiles and allow the adhesive to set, then fit the decorative border tiles and the cut edging tiles the next day. Start by dry-laying all the border tiles. Measure a plain edging tile by first placing it exactly on top of the adjacent border tiles (aligned with their outer edge). Then position another plain tile on top, with one edge touching the wall. Use its inside edge as a guide to draw a line on the tile below with a chinagraph pencil (see Step 6, page 43). Cut the tile just short of the line to allow space for grout and sealant.

SAFETY FIRST

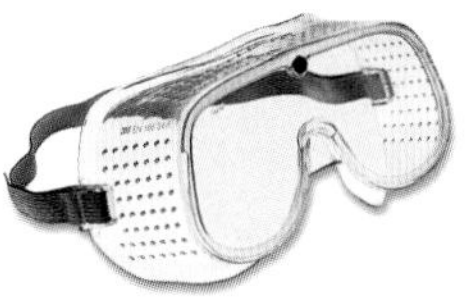

Always wear goggles and a dust mask when cutting ceramic floor tiles. Not only is it dusty work, but small fragments can fly up and cause injury.

1 Spread enough adhesive for a few border tiles and edging tiles at a time, using a notched trowel or spreader. Some manufacturers recommend wearing gloves when applying floor-tile adhesive: check the guidelines on the tin.

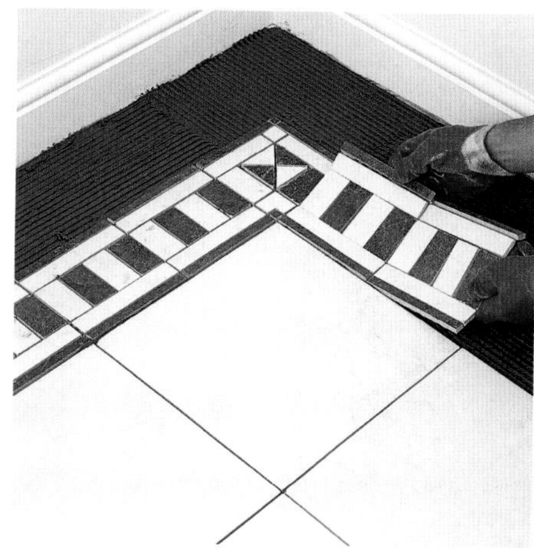

2 Carefully place the decorative tiles in position, making sure they align with the plain tiles. Insert spacers between them.

3 Position the plain, cut edging tiles, taking care that they align with the decorative tiles.

4 Leave the adhesive to set for 24 hours, then mix the grout and spread it over the border and edging tiles with a rubber-edged grout spreader.

5 Smooth and compress the grout into the joints with a striking tool or a wooden dowel when the grout begins to set. Clean off the surplus grout with a damp sponge as you proceed. When the grout has hardened for about an hour, wipe it with a damp cloth and then polish the tiles with a dry cloth.

6 Seal around the edge of the floor with a flexible sealant that matches the colour of the grout. Avoid giving the floor any heavy use for at least 48 hours after grouting.

FLOORS LAYING SHEET VINYL

Sheet vinyl is quicker to lay than tiles. Unless your room is very large, you can usually lay it in one seamless piece, which looks better than two or three strips, though it can be more difficult to fit. Calculate the area of the room and add 50mm–100mm to each edge. Don't forget to measure right into any alcoves and up to the halfway point in the doorway.

Sheet vinyl is available in different widths. If you do opt to lay it in strips, work out how many you need by measuring the wall that their narrow ends will meet. Measure the room in the other direction and multiply this by the number of strips to find the total length. Add 75mm to each end for trimming, and more if there is a pattern. In small rooms with lots of obstacles, you may be able to use the old flooring as a template. Just remember to leave 50mm–100mm all round the edge for final fitting.

TOOLS MATERIALS

- **scribing gauge**
- **craft knife**
- **scissors**
- **bolster chisel**
- **metal straightedge**

- cushioned sheet vinyl
- double-sided tape or adhesive (as recommended by the vinyl manufacturer)
- adhesive spreader
- threshold bar

Laying sheet vinyl flooring

Keep the roll of vinyl in the room where it will be laid for 48 hours to bring it up to room temperature. If the weather is cold, put the heating on to stop it becoming brittle. Skirting is rarely completely straight, and to cut the vinyl to fit the first wall – the longest clear wall – you will need to trace the skirting profile on to the vinyl using a home-made tool known as a scribing gauge.

1 Unroll the vinyl and start by fitting the longer side of the sheet parallel to the longest clear wall, about 25mm away from the skirting. To make a scribing gauge, take an off-cut of wood and hammer a nail into it about 30mm from one end until the point is just protruding from the other side. Carefully move the gauge along the skirting so the nail traces the outline of the skirting on to the vinyl. Cut the sheet along this line with a knife or scissors, then slide the vinyl against the skirting.

2 To get the vinyl to lie as flat as possible, cut a triangular notch at each internal corner with the scissors. The cut is made in the extra allowed along each wall.

3 Press the vinyl into the angle between the skirting and floor with a bolster chisel, to make a sharp crease.

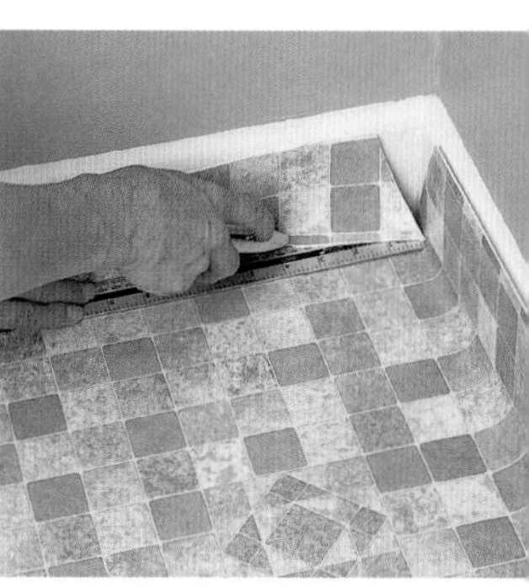

4 Holding a metal straightedge pressed against the crease, cut carefully along it with the knife held at a slight angle.

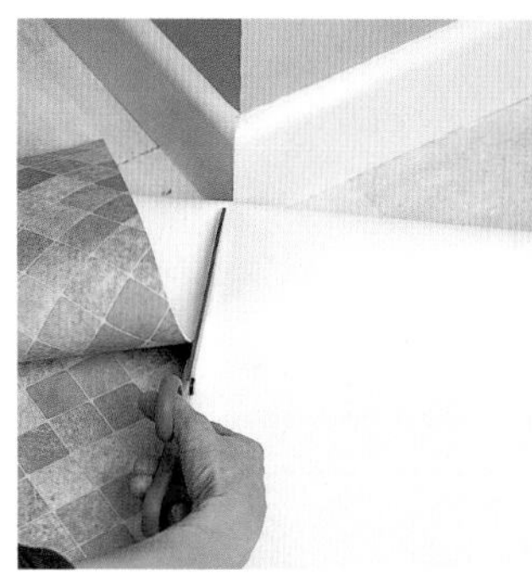

5 At external corners, make a straight cut from the edge of the vinyl down to the floor level. Cut away the excess vinyl, leaving 50mm–100mm turned up at the skirting.

6 Use a bolster chisel to press into the angle between the skirting and floor. Hold the straightedge against each crease and cut along it with the knife held at a slight angle to give a neat finish.

7 When the vinyl sheet has been fully laid, lift the edges and stick them to the sub-floor with double-sided tape or adhesive.

IDEAL TOOL

Bolster
A bolster chisel can apply a good deal of pressure in the junction between the skirting and the floor, creating a precise crease in the vinyl to act as a cutting guide. Hold the vinyl in place with a straightedge while you make the cut.

Fitting difficult areas

Most rooms have architraves and radiator pipes, and there will be lavatory and basin pedestals to deal with in the bathroom. It is a good idea to seal the edges of the bathroom floor with silicone sealant to create a waterproof barrier.

To fit the vinyl around a lavatory washbasin pedestal, lay it as - as the front of the pedestal, en fold it back on itself. Using issors, cut in from the edge in a aight line to the centre of the destal.

2 Make a series of cuts in the vinyl around the base of the pedestal until the sheet lies flat. Take care not to cut too far in, or to tear the vinyl.

3 Use the bolster chisel to make a sharp crease in the vinyl all the way round the base of the pedestal.

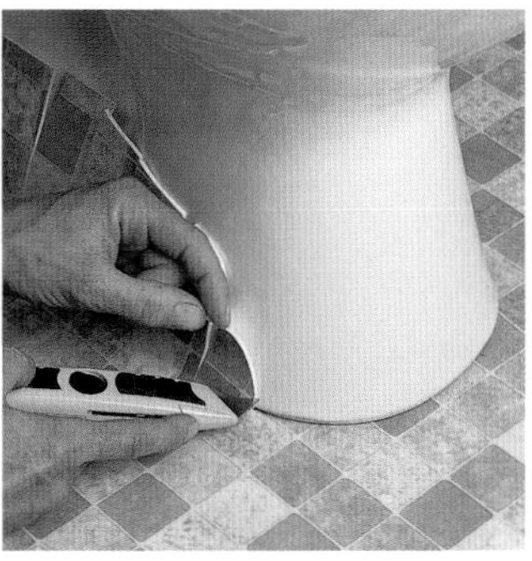

4 Cut around the crease, carefully trimming off each flap of vinyl until it fits. Then peel back the vinyl, apply adhesive to the floor around the pedestal, and press it back into place. You may wish to seal the edges with silicone sealant.

To fit the vinyl around a door ame, make a series of vertical ts to the point where the vinyl eets the floor. Cut off the cess, leaving 50mm–100mm rned up at floor level for more curate trimming.

6 Press the vinyl into the angle between the door frame and the floor and cut along the crease. Cut the vinyl straight across the line of the door so it ends halfway under the door. Fit a threshold bar to hold down and protect the edge of the vinyl.

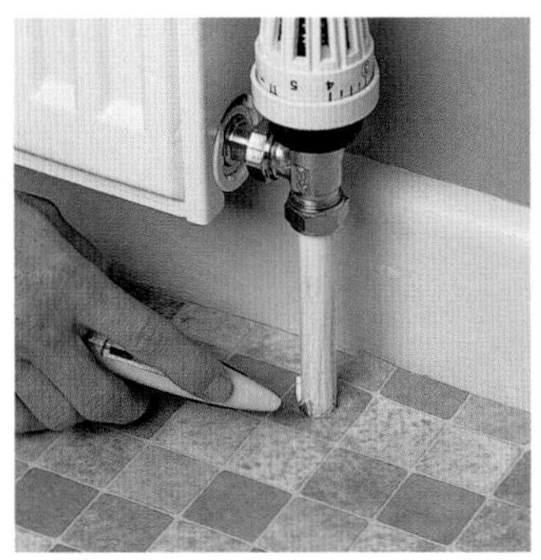

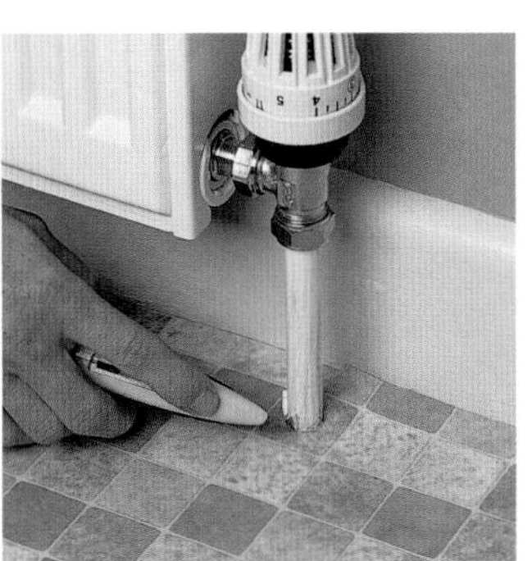

7 To fit vinyl around a pipe, make a straight cut in line with the pipe to the edge of the vinyl, then make a series of small cuts at the pipe end of the slit until the vinyl lies flat around the pipe. Trim off the slit pieces for a neat fit.

Joining vinyl

In a large room you may have to join two or more sheets to cover the whole floor. These should be from the same roll – different rolls may vary slightly in colour. Don't have a join in the doorway where it will get heavy wear.

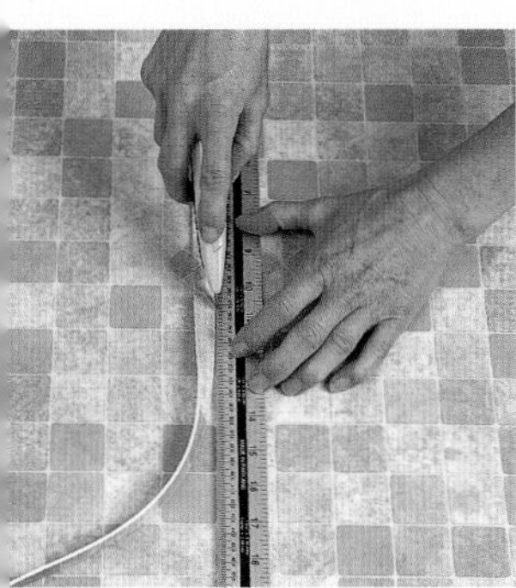

To join patterned sheets, slide e second sheet along until the ttern matches the first sheet. this will be difficult, overlap the eets until the pattern matches actly, then make a cut through th sheets using a straightedge d a knife.

2 Without moving the sheets, fold back the edges and use double-sided tape or adhesive to secure them to the floor. Press down well with both hands to glue the join.

YOU CAN DO IT

Gluing vinyl

Not all vinyl has to be glued to the floor. Heavy-duty 'stay flat' vinyl does not shrink or lift, so it can be laid without glue. Cushioned vinyl, however, should be glued around the edges and at joins. Thinner non-cushioned types need to be stuck down all over: once fitted, roll back half the vinyl and apply adhesive to the floor (use the adhesive supplied or recommended by the manufacturer). Fit the vinyl back in place and repeat for the other half of the room. When it is all back in place, press the vinyl flat with a soft broom.

B&Q

FLOORS CARPETING A SMALL ROOM

There is an enormous range of carpets available, with something to suit every room in the house and every budget. They all benefit from a cushioned underlay, which makes carpet more comfortable underfoot and last longer. A carpet with foam or rubber backing has a built-in underlay, so it is quite straightforward to fit, especially if you buy a carpet that can be laid in one piece. A hessian-backed carpet needs a separate underlay and must be stretched as it is laid, so the task of fitting may be better left to a professional.

Laying foam-backed carpet

If you are laying foam-backed carpet over floorboards rather than hardboard, put down a paper underlay to stop dust blowing up between the boards and making dirty marks on the carpet. But leave a gap of about 100mm around the perimeter of the room because you will need to attach the carpet to the floor with double-sided tape or carpet adhesive.

TOOLS MATERIALS

- **craft knife**
- **metal straightedge**
- **bolster**
- **bradawl**

- foam-backed carpet
- spray carpet adhesive
- threshold bar

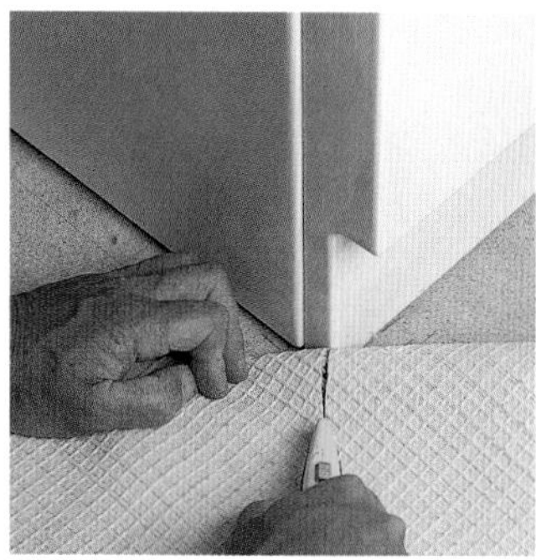

1 Starting with the longest clear wall, unroll the carpet and lay it loosely in place, allowing the excess to extend up the walls. Smooth it flat across the floor, then push it hard into the edges and trim it to leave an overlap of 25–50mm. At external corners use a craft knife to make a straight cut in the excess allowance; at internal corners cut a triangular notch.

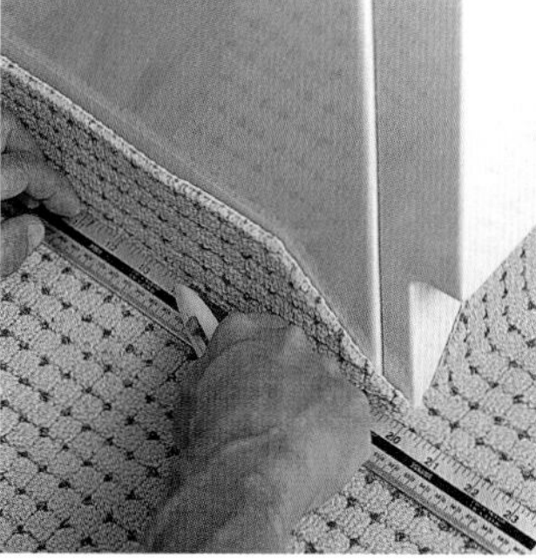

2 Use a metal straightedge to push the carpet firmly into the edges all around the room.

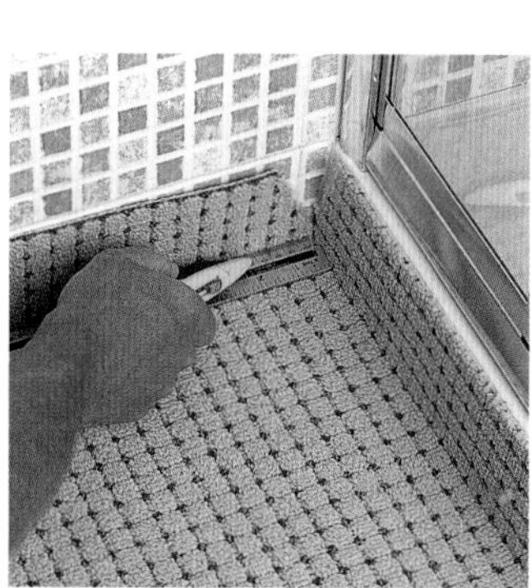

3 Cut around the edge with a craft knife held at a 45° angle. Push the carpet in place with the metal straightedge while you cut.

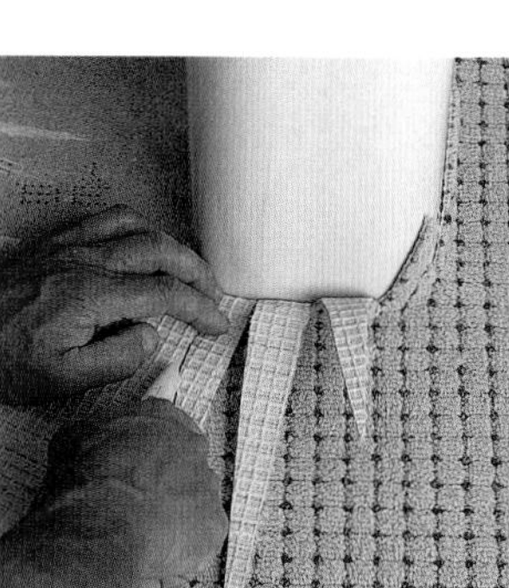

4 To fit the carpet around a lavatory or basin pedestal, lay it as far as the front of the pedestal, then fold it back on itself. Cut in from the edge of th carpet in a straight line to the centre of the pedestal. With a bolster press it hard into the junction between floor and pedestal on one side and cut it roughly, about 50mm above the floor. Then make a series of angled cuts to the curved edge of the pedestal so it will lie flat. Push it into the junction the oth side and cut it roughly in the same way.

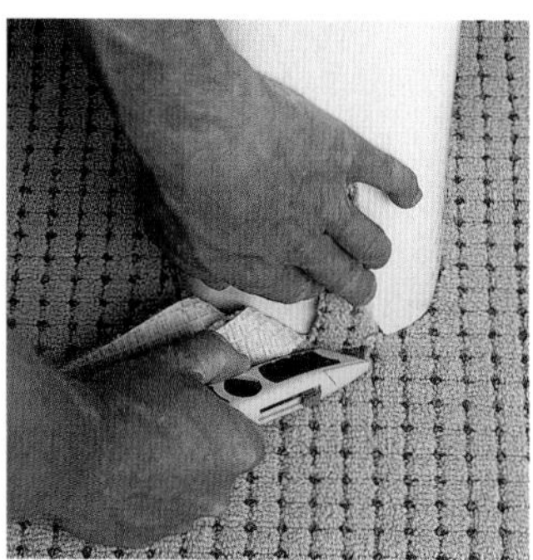

5 Trim around the base of the pedestal with the knife held at a 45° angle. When you have a neat join, peel back the carpet, apply adhesive to the floor, and press it firmly back in place.

6 To fit the carpet around a pipe, make a straight cut to the edge of the carpet in line with the centre of the pipe.

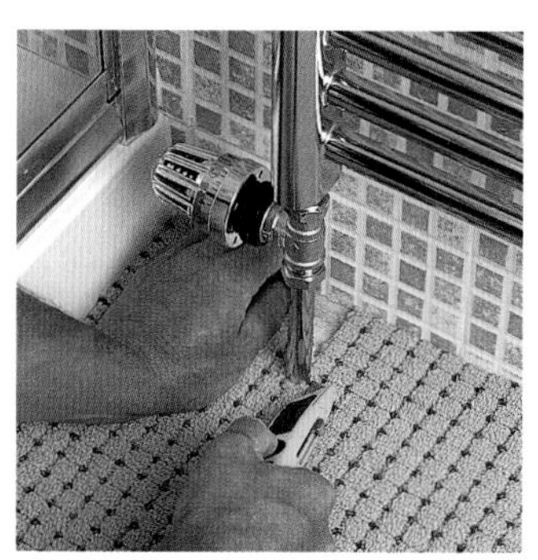

7 Press the carpet around the pipe, then trim it by running the knife around the base of the pipe at a 45° angle until the carpet lies flat.

Fitting the carpet across a doorway

A threshold bar fitted across the edge of the carpet in the doorway is essential to create a neat and safe transition from the flooring of one room to the next.

1 Make straight cuts at the external corners of the door frame so that the carpet will lie flat either side.

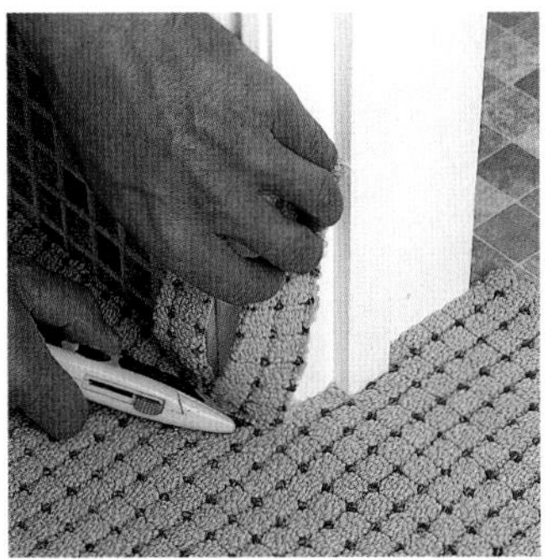

2 Press the carpet into the corners with a bolster and cut around the bottom of the frame with a craft knife held at a 45° angle.

3 Cut the carpet along the metal straightedge in line with the edge of the flooring in the next room.

4 Cut the threshold bar to length with a hacksaw. If you have a wood floor, make pilot holes for the screws with a bradawl and screw the strip to the floor. If you have a concrete floor, drill holes with a power drill and masonry bit, and insert wallplugs first.

5 Push the edge of the carpet under the threshold bar with a bolster.

ECO CARPETING

Minimise waste

The amount of wasted carpet is determined by the irregular shapes in a room, such as alcoves and bay windows. In some rooms, it may be more economical to lay one piece of carpet over most of the floor and then fit separate pieces in these awkward areas.

YOU CAN DO IT

Joining carpet

If you do need to join sections of carpet in a large room, try to join them along the factory-cut edges as these will be sharper. Stick double-sided tape to the floor, remove the backing tape and press both pieces of carpet on to the tape to make a neat join.

B&Q

Attaching the carpet to the floor

To fix the carpet to the floor you can use an aerosol carpet adhesive, as shown here, or special double-sided tape.

1 Pull back the edges of the carpet around the perimeter of the room, spray the floor with adhesive, then replace the carpet.

2 Press down firmly to make sure it adheres properly.

3 Retrim any untidy edges once the carpet is glued firmly in place.

WALLS INSIDE AND OUT

The majority of houses are built from a combination of bricks, concrete blocks and timber on a solid base known as the foundations. Older houses may be made of local natural stone. The construction of the walls depends on whether they are external or internal, and whether they are loadbearing or non-loadbearing.

The external walls of a house are all loadbearing – they support the weight of the roof, floors and internal walls. Internal walls divide the floor space into rooms and are generally made of less heavyweight materials. Many internal walls are not structural (ie they do not support the structure); these are known as non-loadbearing walls. Not all internal walls are non-loadbearing, however, some may partly support floor and ceiling joists while others add to the stability of the building. Never assume an internal wall is non-loadbearing – always seek professional advice before attempting major alterations.

Solid external walls

External walls can be either of solid or cavity (hollow) construction. Solid external walls, made of natural stone or brick, are mostly found in houses built before the 1920s. Traditional brick and stone walls vary in thickness depending on the age and size of the building, but they are usually at least 225mm thick (the length of a standard brick), and are often a brick and a half thick in places where houses are exposed to severe weather. These days when solid walls are required, concrete blocks will normally be used. Solid walls provide good sound insulation, but do not retain heat efficiently.

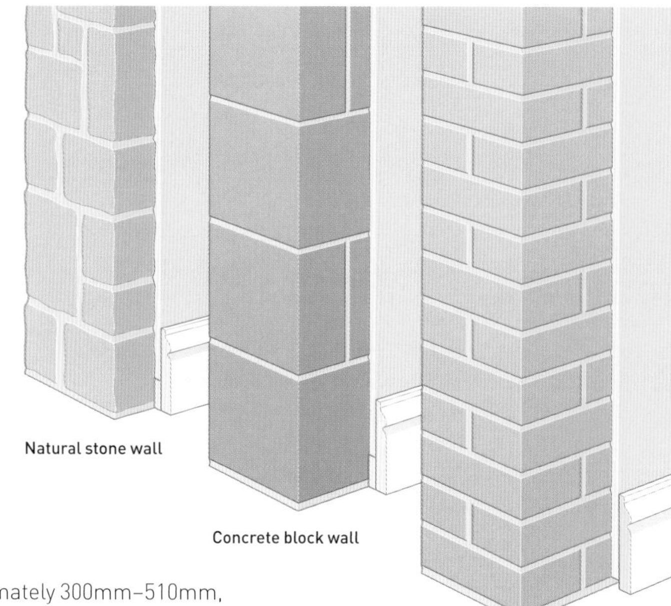

YOU CAN DO IT

Fitting a window
A window frame is not strong enough to support the weight of the structure above it in a loadbearing wall, so a rigid beam called a lintel must be installed. This spans the gap above the opening, transmitting the weight to the walls each side. A lintel may be wood, stone, brick, concrete or steel, depending on the span of the opening and the weight overhead; calculating this is a job for an architect or structural engineer. Wider openings need stronger support and for these rolled-steel joists (RSJs) are used.

Natural stone

In solid stone walls the entire depth, approximately 300mm–510mm, is made up of natural stone. In the days when houses were built this way, the best stone was used for the outer facing layer of the wall, which was left uncovered, and the inside of the wall was usually made from less attractive pieces of stone which were rendered (coated with a mix of builder's sand and cement) and plastered. Older houses may have lath and plaster on the inside, dating back to the days before plasterboard. Thin strips of wood (laths) were nailed horizontally to vertical timbers to act as a key for a covering of plaster. Many stone walls are rendered on the outside to improve their weatherproofing.

Concrete blocks

External walls made from concrete blocks usually have the external face of the wall covered with render, which is painted. The internal wall is rendered and plastered.

Bricks

With a solid brick wall the entire thickness of the wall is made from bricks, two or three bricks deep. The bricks are laid with mortar in overlapping bonding patterns. The outer wall is left as bare brick unless the brickwork has become shabby, in which case it may have been rendered and painted with masonry paint. The interior of the wall is normally covered with a coat of render, then plastered.

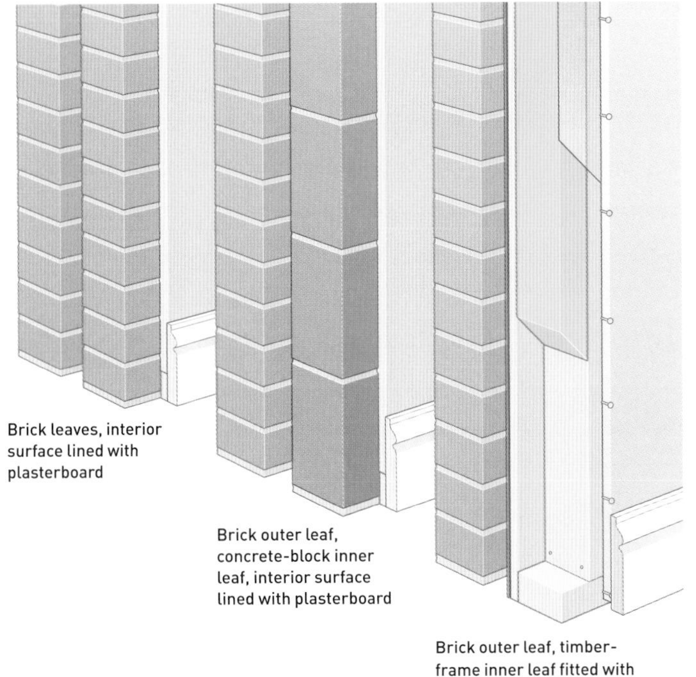

Brick leaves, interior surface lined with plasterboard

Brick outer leaf, concrete-block inner leaf, interior surface lined with plasterboard

Brick outer leaf, timber-frame inner leaf fitted with thermal insulation, the cavity side lined with plywood sheeting and the interior surface lined with plasterboard

Cavity external walls

Most modern houses have external walls that are constructed with a cavity in the middle. Typically the leaves (walls) are each about 100mm thick, separated by a gap of at least 50mm. The leaves are tied together with metal wall ties to make them stable. This type of wall is more effective in preventing moisture penetration and heat loss. For it to work as a moisture barrier, mortar must not drop on the ties during construction as this would bridge the gap. Cavity walls are built from bricks, concrete blocks or timber framing, or a combination of these.

Brick and block cavity walls

These walls have an outer leaf of brick and an inner leaf of either brick or concrete blocks. The inner wall may be rendered and plastered; alternatively, plasterboard may be attached directly to the wall or to a wooden batten framework.

Timber-framed cavity wall

With timber-framed walls the outer leaf is brick, or sometimes stone or wooden boarding, and the inner leaf is constructed of a timber framework with plywood sheeting on the cavity side and plasterboard attached to the inside. Thermal insulation may be fitted between the plywood and plasterboard.

Internal walls

There are two types of internal walls in a house: party walls and partition walls. Party walls are shared walls between neighbouring houses, detached or semi-detached. Partition walls divide up the floor space within a property into rooms and they are usually – though not always – non-loadbearing. Internal walls may be made from a variety of materials, including stone in older houses, brick and concrete blocks, and plasterboard or wallboard fixed to frames made from timber or metal. Lightweight internal walls can even be made from glass blocks.

Solid internal walls

In houses with stone external walls, the internal walls may be made from the same stone. Other solid internal walls may be constructed from bricks or lightweight concrete blocks, usually one brick or block thick. The grey blocks widely used for modern partition walls are made from cement and lightweight aggregate. They provide good sound and heat insulation and are fireproof. Their relatively large size (225mm x 450mm and anything from 75mm to 350mm thick) makes building a wall with blocks quick and simple. Solid internal walls may be plastered on both sides (in older stone-built houses, there may be a lath-and-plaster finish). Or plasterboard may be attached, either to timber battens or directly to the bricks or blocks.

Stud partition walls

Hollow partition walls called stud walls are a very common type of internal wall, and they may or may not be loadbearing. The cavity in the middle is ideal for running concealed water pipes and cables. In newer homes stud walls consist of plasterboard sheets fixed to each side of a timber frame. The vertical timbers in the frame are known as studs. In older houses, built before the days of plasterboard, thin strips of wood, called laths, were nailed to the studs. The laths provided a surface for the plaster to stick to. Some modern stud wall frames are made of metal rather than softwood.

Cellular-core wallboards

These wallboards are used to make a lightweight, non-loadbearing wall. They have plasterboard on each side and a centre of cardboard in a hollow grid pattern. They can be decorated as they are, or plastered first then decorated.

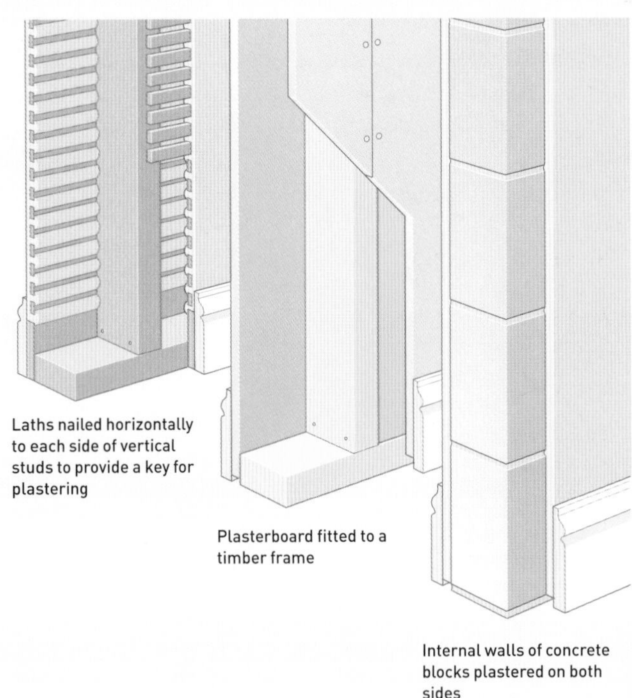

Laths nailed horizontally to each side of vertical studs to provide a key for plastering

Plasterboard fitted to a timber frame

Internal walls of concrete blocks plastered on both sides

WALLS REPAIRS

Wear and tear and slight movement in a building will often damage the plastering. Small cracks and holes can be repaired with filler. Where an area of plaster is seriously damaged or has come away from the wall ('blown'), it is better to repair it with plaster.

If the entire wall is in a bad condition it may need completely replastering – a job for the professionals. Put down dust sheets before you start any repair work.

Filling holes and cracks

You can choose from various fillers for minor repairs:

- Interior filler: a general-purpose cellulose filler available ready-mixed in tubs or as a powder for mixing to a stiff paste with water.
- Fine-surface filler: an ultra-smooth fine-particle filler for minor cracks and surface imperfections.
- Deep-repair filler: a ready-mixed lightweight filler for holes up to 20mm deep.
- Fast-setting filler: a filler that sets in 10–20 minutes.
- Flexible acrylic fillers: for gaps between plaster and woodwork.
- Foam or expanding filler: for large holes or gaps. Once dry, it needs trimming back with a craft knife.

For more extensive repairs there are two main types of plaster that can be used:

- Gypsum plasters: these are the ones used by professional plasterers. They are mixed with water and applied in two coats – an undercoat and a finishing coat. They are quick-setting and generally the most economical, but they are also the most difficult plasters to use.
- General plasters: these are available as two coats – an undercoat or 'repair' plaster, and a finishing coat – either ready-mixed or as powder to mix with water. If a wall is to be papered, plaster undercoat will give a good enough finish; if it is to be painted, you need a plaster finish (also known as plaster skim) as well. The finishing plaster is applied before the undercoat is completely dry. Application methods vary for finishing plasters, so check the manufacturer's instructions.

YOU CAN DO IT

Make it stick

If you are mixing your filler from a powder, add a squirt of PVA adhesive to make a smooth yet sticky paste.

Patching corners

The corners of walls are particularly vulnerable to wear and tear and often need patching. There are two ways to do this. You can repair the damage with undercoat plaster, using a nailed-on piece of board to help you achieve a neat edge. Or if a longer stretch is damaged, it is better to repair and reinforce the corner with metal or plastic corner beading. In either case, cut back the crumbling plaster to a firm surface with a cold chisel and hammer before you start.

Using plaster and a board

Hammer two nails into a piece of board slightly larger than the damaged area on one side of the corner, making sure that the nails will fit into firm plaster beyond the damaged area. Position the board's edge so that it is flush with the plaster surface on the adjacent wall. Nail the board to the wall. Dampen the broken edges on the uncovered wall with a large paintbrush and apply the plaster undercoat with a trowel. When the plaster has set, pull the board away from the wall. Once the plaster has completely hardened, nail the board to the repaired side and fill the other side of the corner in the same way. Leave the plaster to dry, remove the board then sand the corner to a smooth edge. Fill and sand the holes made by the nails.

TOOLS MATERIALS

- **hammer**
- **cold chisel**
- **large paintbrush**
- **plasterer's trowel**
- **sanding block**

- wooden board
- nails
- plaster undercoat
- medium-grade abrasive paper

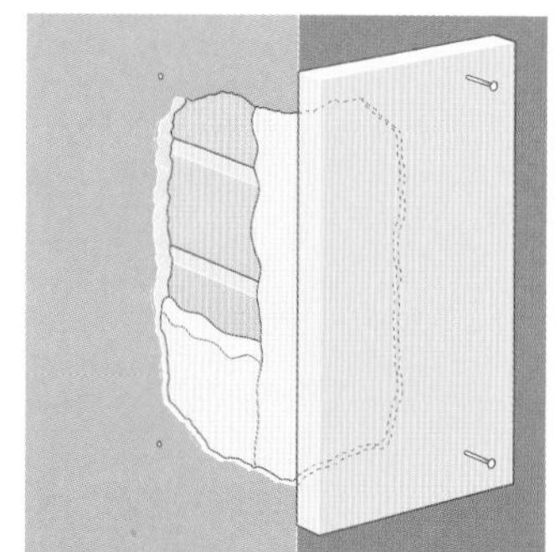

Using metal corner beading

Cut the expanded metal corner beading to the required length with a hacksaw. Paint the cut ends with metal primer to seal them. Wet the wall and apply patches of plaster undercoat each side of the corner, using a plasterer's trowel. Press the beading into position, allowing the plaster to squeeze through the mesh. Build up the undercoat plaster, then scrape it back to 2mm below the old finished level with the trowel. Apply a top coat of finishing plaster in a wide band and feather in the new plaster level with the existing surface. Take care not to damage the metal beading's coating or rust may come through later. To be on the safe side, brush metal primer over the corner before decorating.

TOOLS MATERIALS

- **hammer**
- **cold chisel**
- **hacksaw**
- **plasterer's trowel**
- **small paintbrush**
- **large paintbrush**

- metal corner beading
- metal primer
- plaster undercoat and finishing coat

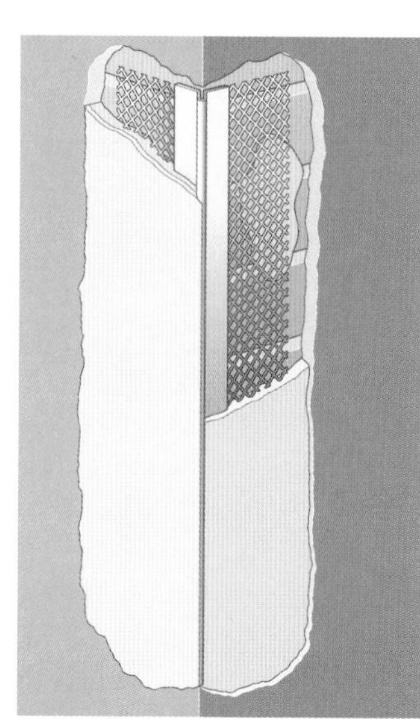

;racks and holes in plaster

deep crack can be filled with screwed-up newspaper to make a base ›r the filler. With larger holes you may need to build up several thin ›ats of filler rather than one thick one, letting each coat dry before ›dding the next.

TOOLS MATERIALS

- **filling knife or scraper**
- **small paintbrush**
- **sanding block**

- plaster filler
- medium-grade abrasive paper

1 Rake loose plaster from the :rack with the corner of a filling :nife or scraper. Using a small ›aintbrush, dampen the crack vith water to make the filler ›ry slowly – this helps to stop ‹ shrinking and falling out of he crack.

2 Load some filler onto a filling knife and draw it across the hole at right angles to the crack, firmly pressing it in until the filler is just proud of the surface. Leave to dry, then smooth with medium-grade abrasive paper wrapped around a sanding block.

Repairing holes in plasterboard

Small holes in plasterboard can be repaired in the same way as holes and cracks in plaster, but a hole bigger than about 125mm needs to have a plasterboard patch fitted into it otherwise the filler will simply fall into the cavity.

TOOLS MATERIALS

- **craft knife**
- **padsaw or hole saw**
- **power drill**
- **filling knife or scraper**

- off-cut of plasterboard
- string
- nail
- plaster filler
- pencils or timber off-cut

1 Neaten the edge of the damaged area with a craft knife. From an off-cut of plasterboard, cut a patch that will fit through the hole but is just larger than it. Drill through the centre and thread a piece of string through. Tie a nail to the end of the string at the back of the patch (the grey side). Make a loop in the string on the front side and apply filler around the front edge. Keeping hold of the string, push the patch through the hole.

2 Pull on the string to manoeuvre the patch into place, with the filler side facing you. Holding it taut, add more filler to the hole. To hold the patch in place while it sets, tie your string to a pencil or timber off-cut and 'wind' it taut against the wall. When the filler is set, cut the string flush with the wall and apply a finishing coat of filler.

Lath-and-plaster repairs

\As long as the laths are secure, you can fill small holes in a lath-and-plaster wall in the same way as ordinary plaster. Broken laths can often be the reason for plaster crumbling; if this is the case, they need to be reinforced with expanded metal mesh under the new plaster.

TOOLS MATERIALS

- **tinsnips**
- **small plasterer's trowel**

- expanded metal mesh
- plaster undercoat and finishing coat

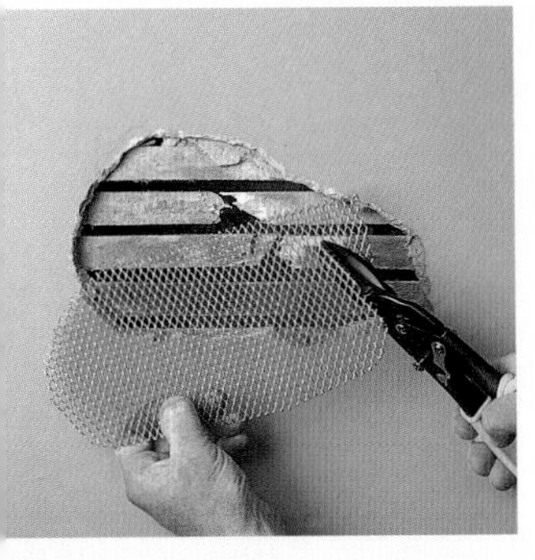

1 Remove any debris until you get back to an edge where the plaster is still firmly attached to the laths. Using tinsnips, cut a piece of mesh the size of the hole.

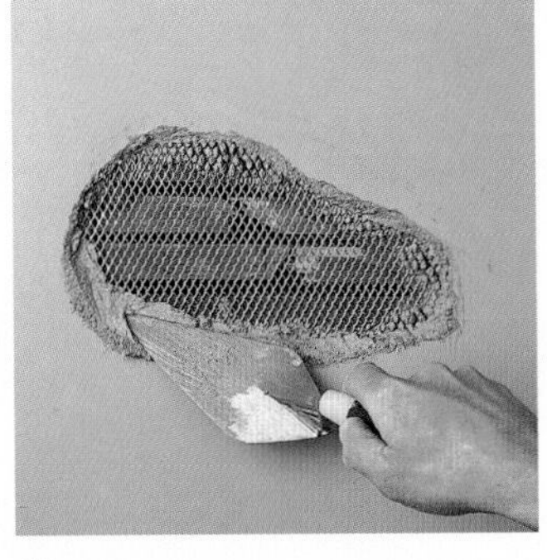

2 Position the mesh and secure it in place around the edges with plaster undercoat. (Nailing or stapling on to the laths may cause further damage to the surrounding plaster and lath.)

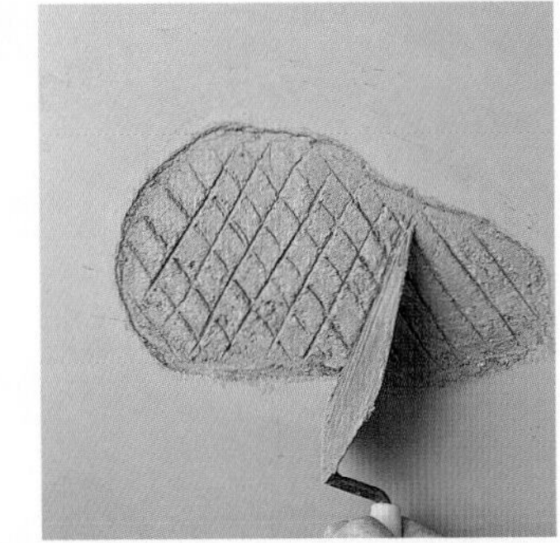

IDEAL TOOL

Tinsnips
Snips are made in different sizes and cut through sheet metals like scissors.

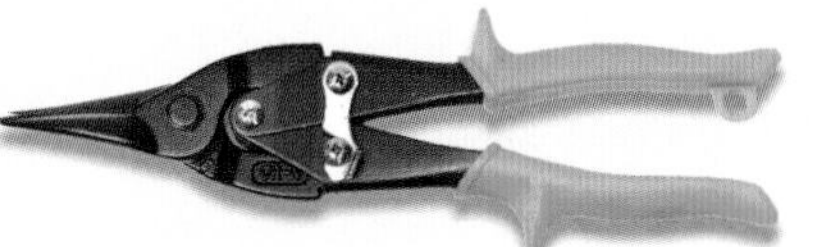

3 Dampen the laths and apply a plaster undercoat using a plasterer's trowel. Force the plaster between the laths to make sure it sticks well. Score the surface in a diamond pattern to create a key for the finishing coat. Allow it to set, then apply a finishing coat of plaster.

WALLS REPAIRS

The look of a tiled wall can be ruined by a broken tile or discoloured grout (the paste that fills the gaps between tiles).There is no need to retile the whole surface – both problems can be solved fairly easily.

TOOLS MATERIALS

- **grout raker**
- **power drill with tile and masonry bits**
- **dust mask**
- **heavy duty gloves**
- **safety goggles**
- **hammer**
- **cold chisel**
- **adhesive spreader**
- **wooden batten**
- **tile spacers**
- **small trowel or grout spreader**
- **sponge**
- **grout shaper or grouting tool**
- **soft cloth**

- new tile
- tile adhesive
- grout (ready-mixed or powder)

Replacing a damaged tile

The hardest part of replacing a damaged tile is removing the old one – very occasionally they lift out easily, but usually the adhesive holds the damaged pieces just as firmly as it held the whole tile.

1 Loosen the grout around all four edges of the damaged tile with a grout raker and rake it out. Drill some holes in the centre of the tile to weaken its surface, using an electric drill fitted with a ceramic tile bit. Wear a dust mask, gloves and safety goggles to protect your eyes. Change to a large masonry bit to increase the size of the hole, if necessary.

2 Use a hammer and cold chisel to cut through the tile between the holes and to chop out the central portion, taking care not to dig the chisel into the wall. Wear thick gloves to protect your hands.

3 Work towards the edges of the tile, gently breaking pieces away and being especially careful as you get close to neighbouring tiles. Once the tile is removed, scrape out as much adhesive as possible.

4 Make sure you have removed enough adhesive by inserting the new dry tile. It should not be proud of the surrounding tiles. Coat the back of the tile with tile adhesive, using an adhesive spreader, and position it in the hole.

5 Press the tile into place with a wooden batten to ensure that it is flush with the other tiles. Fit tile spacers perpendicular to the tile's surface to maintain the gap for grout and prevent the tile from slipping out of position before the adhesive is dry. When the adhesive has dried, remove the spacers and grout the tiles (see Steps 2–4 opposite).

YOU CAN DO IT

Leftover tiles

When you do any tiling, always save the leftover tiles – it can be tricky matching new tiles to the colours of older ones.

B&Q

Regrouting

Moisture from baths and showers, or food spills in kitchens can stain grout, leaving it looking shabby while the tiles themselves are fine. Simply replacing the grout can make the tiled surface look as good as new.

TOOLS MATERIALS

- **grout raker**
- **small trowel or grout spreader**
- **sponge**
- **grout shaper or grouting tool**
- **soft cloth**

- grout (ready-mixed or powder)

1 Use a grout raker to remove the old grout from around the tiles to at least half the thickness of the tiles, taking care not to scratch their edges. Do all the vertical joints first and then the horizontal ones, to make sure that you don't miss any.

2 If using powdered grout, mix it with water to a creamy consistency – a small amount goes a long way. Use a small trowel or grout spreader to press the grout firmly into the joints between the tiles. Move the trowel or spreader diagonally over the joints to prevent the grout being dragged out again.

3 Wipe the excess grout from the tiled surface with a damp sponge – don't press too hard or you may remove grout from the joints. Rinse the sponge frequently to keep it free from grout build-up.

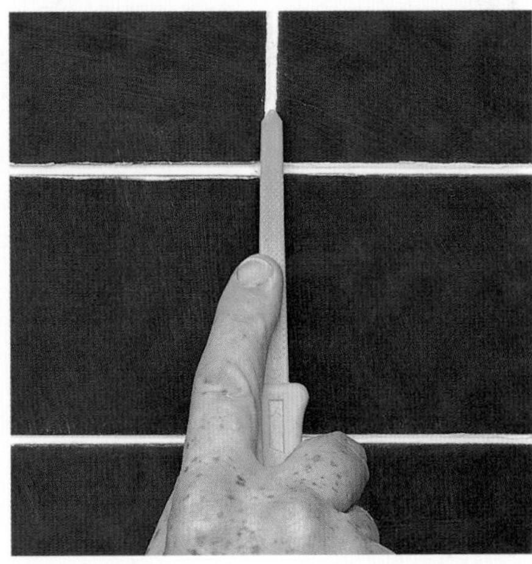

4 Run a grout shaper or grouting tool along the joints to give them a neat profile, and remove excess grout with the sponge. Leave to dry, then polish the tiles with a soft cloth.

IDEAL TOOL

Grout rakers

Grout is designed to provide a hard filling for the joints between the tiles, so it takes some effort to remove it. The only way this can be done is to scrape it out with a sharp point. While you may be able to improvise a tool for the job, you must take care not to damage the tiles themselves, and it is best to use a specially designed grout raker.

YOU CAN DO IT

Renovate, not replace

It's not always necessary to rake out dingy old grouting: minor staining and fungal growths can be removed with a specially formulated grout cleaner. This contains a variety of detergents and biological agents to clean the grout and discourage mould. Dilute with water and apply the cleaner, following the manufacturer's guidelines.

WALLS REPAIRS

Problems with painted and wallpapered surfaces are commonplace in many homes. They spoil the look of the surface and need attention. If you try a 'quick fix' by redecorating over damaged areas the finish will soon deteriorate again. It's much better to tackle the problem head on.

Curing paint problems

Problems on a painted surface are usually caused by poor preparation, incompatible paints on top of one another, and trapped moisture. Generally the only cure is to strip off the paint and redo it.

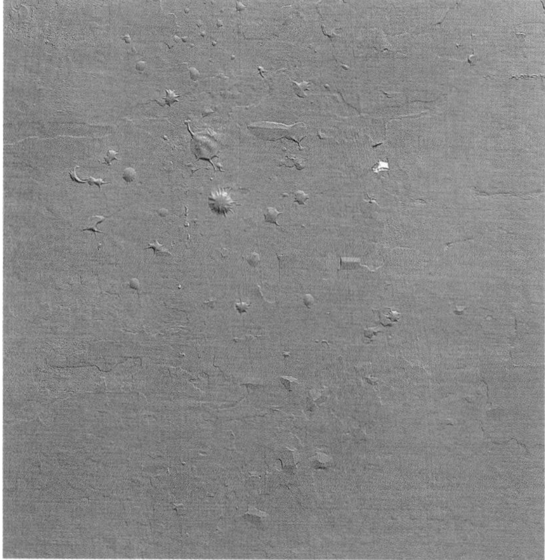

Paint blisters

Sometimes blisters will appear on painted woodwork. If pricking the blisters releases water then you know the surface is damp. Strip the paint with a hot-air gun, and when the wood is dry, prime and repaint.

Air can be trapped under the painted surface of open-grained wood. Strip the paint, and fill the grain with epoxy-based wood filler. This filler flexes with the natural expansion and contraction of the wood. Alternatively, repaint with microporous acrylic paint.

Paint flaking

Paint will flake off a surface that is already flaky, or is incompatible – emulsion over a gloss, for instance. The flaking paint must be stripped off with a wide stripping knife, sanded with medium-grade abrasive paper around a sanding block, then washed with sugar soap and water and repainted. Emulsion will also flake if painted over distemper – old-fashioned water-based paint containing glue. In this case you must treat the whole area with special stabilising solution before repainting.

Paint runs

Too much paint applied to the wall too quickly will result in runs. You can simply brush runs out of wet paint. Rub dry paint with fine abrasive paper until the surface is smooth. Then dust and wipe with a damp cloth, and carefully apply a new top coat.

YOU CAN DO IT

Tackling damp
Damp patches should be looked at by a professional, as there may be a problem that needs to be addressed. When you are ready to redecorate, apply a specially formulated damp sealant or oil-based undercoat over the stain first. You can also help to keep damp at bay with microporous acrylic paint, which is a water-based paint that allows the wall surface to breathe.

B&Q

SAFETY FIRST

Lead in paint
Paint with a high lead content can cause poisoning. Most paint you buy nowadays contains little or no lead, and any that does must bear a clear warning. But before stripping old paint, especially pre-1960s paint, you must use a lead-testing kit on it first. If the result is positive, you should use a specially formulated chemical stripper: don't dry-strip the paint either with a hot-air gun or a sander. Keep the windows open and children well out of the way.

Problems on wallpapered walls

Problems with wallpaper are often down to human error – rushing the job when hanging the paper, using too little paste, or not being careful enough with the paper. Take your time! ... but if it's too late, try these solutions.

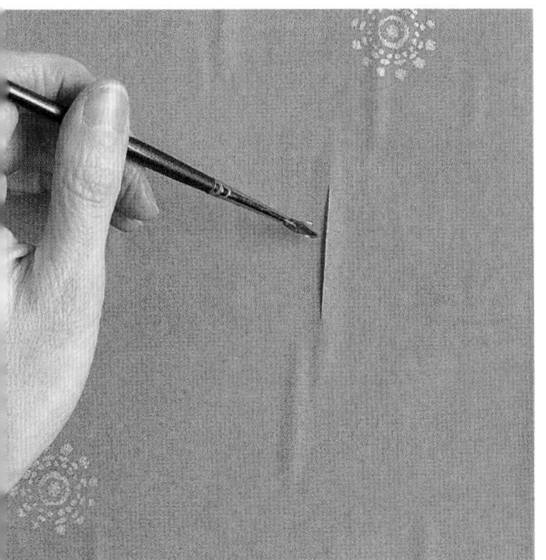

Bubbles under paper

Small bubbles should disappear as wallpaper dries. If the paper was not left to soak for long enough, however, it may expand on the wall and create air bubbles. Simply cut small bubbles with a razor blade and insert some wallpaper paste behind the flaps with a fine brush. Press the paper into place, then wipe off the excess paste with a damp rag.

Shiny patches

Shiny patches can appear on matt wallpaper if it was rubbed too hard when it was hung. Try gently rubbing the shiny areas with a ball of white bread to dull the shine. Bread can be used to remove dirty marks too. Next time you hang matt wallpaper, smooth it carefully with a clean dry sponge to avoid this problem.

Lifting seams

Seams can open up if too little paste has been applied at the edges, particularly with vinyl and relief papers. Lift the seam with a round-bladed knife and apply fresh paste with a fine brush. Run down the seam with a seam roller to press the edges together.

Damaged vinyl wallpaper

Since you can't tear vinyl paper, cut a square larger than the damaged area. Tape the square over the damage, then with a trimming knife cut within it (through both layers) a square large enough to take out all of the damaged area. Remove the old square of vinyl, apply paste to the patch, and fit it into the gap.

YOU CAN DO IT

Gaps at seams
Sometimes gaps appear at wallpaper seams, generally due to poor hanging, but occasionally because of shrinkage while the paper was drying. White gaps can be filled with felt-tip pen the same colour as the base colour of the paper. Some paper manufacturers sell special pens for this purpose.

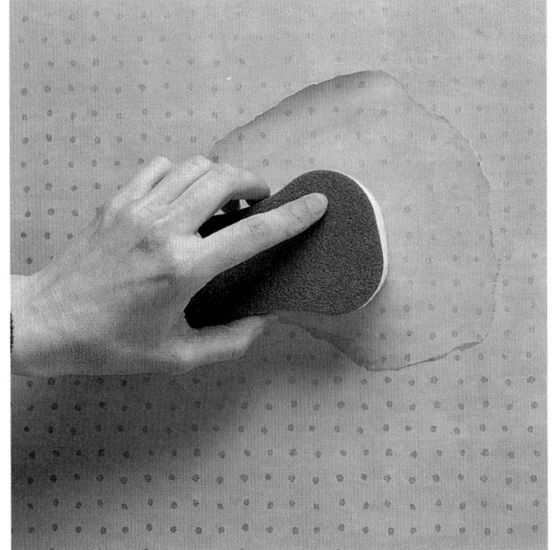

Torn patches

Remove all the damaged paper, leaving only paper that is firmly attached. Tear around the edges of a patch of fresh wallpaper – this will make a less noticeable repair than a square-cut patch – and paste it over the damaged area so that the pattern exactly matches. Smooth it down with a sponge.

Putting up a wall to create an extra bedroom, en-suite bathroom or shower is much easier – and cheaper – than moving house to get another room. A stud wall consists of a frame of timber studs secured to the floor, ceiling and walls, which is then covered with plasterboard; once decorated, it looks like an integral part of the house. While it is a fairly straightforward job, there are things that have to be considered before you start.

- Check with your local authority to make sure that the work involved conforms to the current building regulations relating to fire resistance, light and ventilation.
- Organise lighting, heating and, if necessary, plumbing for the new room.
- If the wall is going to have a doorway, buy a door and frame that matches the thickness of the timber and plasterboard you are using.

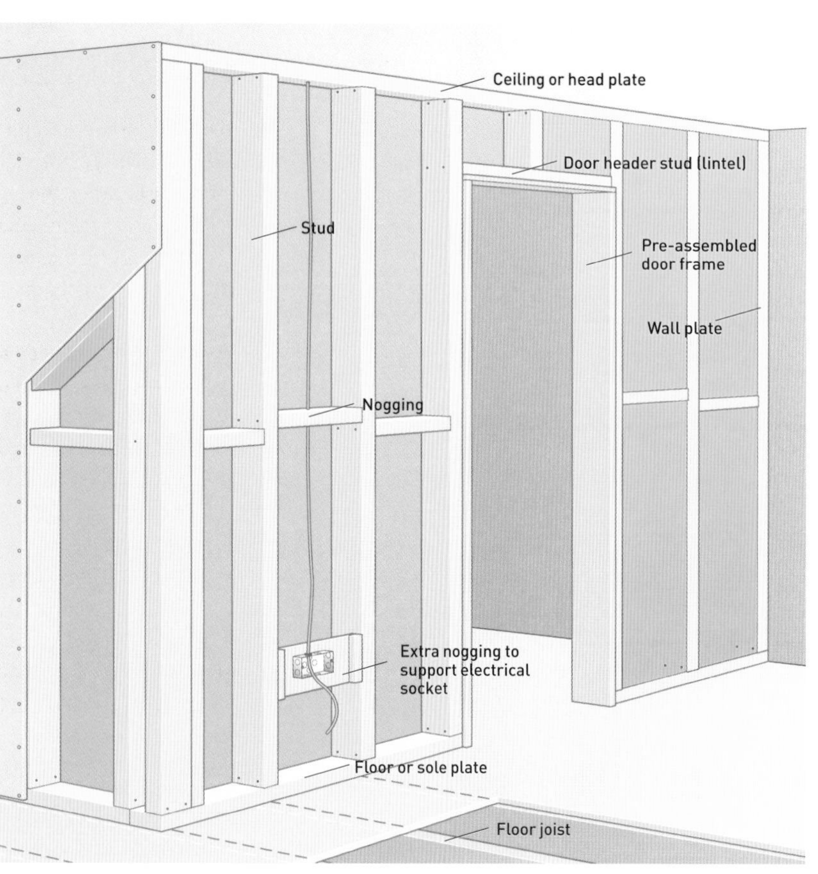

TOOLS MATERIALS

- **joist, pipe and cable detector**
- **pencil**
- **tape measure**
- **plumb line**
- **chalk line**
- **bradawl**
- **panel saw**
- **power drill and twist bits**
- **hammer**
- **tenon saw**
- **spirit level**

- off-cut of wood
- 75mm x 50mm or 100mm x 50mm sawn timber
- 100mm countersunk cross-head wood screws (5mm gauge)
- 100mm nails
- wallplugs

Making a frame

The stud wall frame can be made from 75mm x 50mm or 100mm x 50mm sawn timber. It consists of a ceiling or head plate, which is fixed to the ceiling joists; a matching length nailed to the floor, called the floor or sole plate; wall plates, at either end; studs that stand vertically between the plates, equally spaced and fixed with nails; and noggings, which are short, horizontal braces that give extra support and keep the frame rigid.

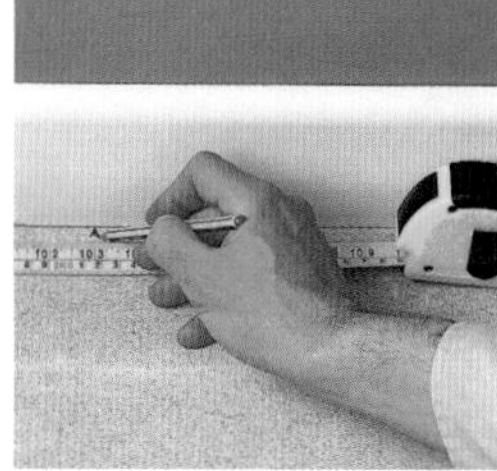

1 Decide where to position your wall, and use an electronic detector to trace joists, cables and pipes in the walls, ceiling and floor. If the new wall is to run at right angles to the floor and ceiling joists, it can be fixed at any point. If the wall is to run parallel with the joists, it must stand directly over one of them. (If the partition wall must be installed between joists, lift the floorboards below and above and secure 100mm x 50mm timbers at right angles between two joists at 1m intervals to support the new wall.) Measure from both ends of a wall in the room and mark the position for one edge of the stud wall on the floor or skirting-board.

2 Suspend a plumb line to the mark you have made and draw a line up the wall to the ceiling, following the plumb line.

3 Mark the ceiling line, using an off-cut of wood.

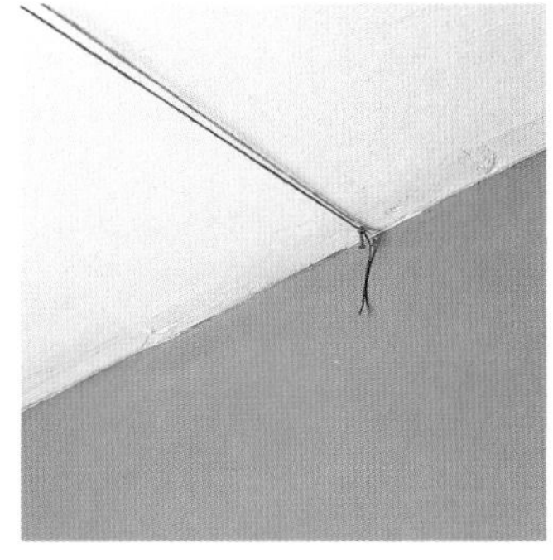

4 Knock a nail into the ceiling close to the wall junction at what will become the side edge of the ceiling plate. Measure and mark the opposite ceiling/wall junction. Make a guideline to show the ceiling plate position by snapping a chalk line between the two points. Use the detector to find the joists if they are at right angles to the new wall – you need to locate the joists so that the ceiling plate can be secured to them.

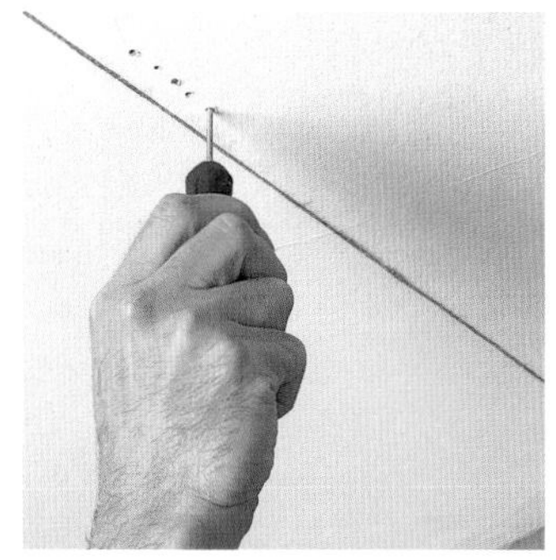

5 If the detector does not indicate the joist positions, use a bradawl to probe the ceiling along the length of the chalk line to find the joists. The holes you make will be hidden by the ceiling plate. Mark the positions for the fixing points on the ceiling adjacent to the chalk line.

6 Measure and cut the length of timber for the ceiling plate – it must fit exactly between the walls at the ceiling. Holding the plate in position, mark the fixing points along its length. If the wall runs directly underneath a parallel joist, these should be at 400mm intervals. Take it off the ceiling and drill clearance holes for the screws at the marked points. Fix the ceiling plate in position along the edge of the chalk line using 100mm countersunk cross-head wood screws (nails may crack the ceiling plaster). It's best to have some assistance, but failing that, use a wooden prop to help you to hold the ceiling plate in position.

7 Measure and cut the timber for the floor plate so that it fits exactly between the opposite walls (or skirting). If you're having a door, find the width of the opening you need by laying the pre-assembled door frame on the floor against the plate. Mark and cut the floor plate so that the frame will fit the gap exactly. Nail the floor plate to the floor at approximately 400mm intervals. If the joists run at right angles to the wall, follow the line of their fixings (or use the detector to find them) so that you can drive the nails into them (see diagram below). If the floor is solid, drill holes with a masonry bit and use plugs and screws.

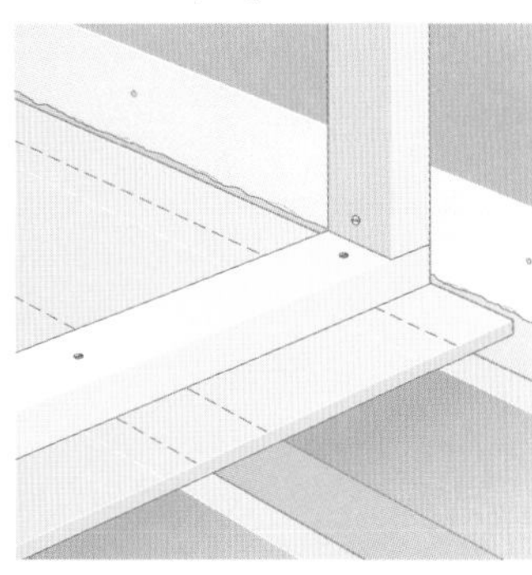

8 Measure the distance between the ceiling and floor plates at each end of the frame and cut two studs to length; these wall plates should be a tight fit. Place each one alongside the guideline you have drawn down the wall, and mark the clearance required for the skirting-board. Remove the wall plates, and use a tenon saw to shape a notch to fit around the skirting-board.

9 Drill clearance holes for the screws along the length of the wall plates, and mark the positions of the holes on the walls. The first fixings should be approximately 100mm up from the floor (just above the skirting-board) and 100mm down from the ceiling. The remaining fixings should be 410mm–450mm apart. Drill the marked points on the walls, fit wallplugs, and then reposition and screw home the two wall plates.

YOU CAN DO IT

Positioning a door

Stud walls are non-loadbearing, so you can make a doorway or opening exactly where you wish, in whatever shape you wish. Although it's a good idea to put a door hard up against a wall plate, as this braces the frame more securely, it really is up to you. Think about how you are going to use your new room, and where you want to put the furniture.

1 First, mark the floor plate at intervals to show the position of the vertical studs – this spacing of the studs is vital. If you are covering the frame with 9.5mm-thick plasterboard, the studs should be no more than 400mm apart (so that a standard 1200mm-wide plasterboard sheet is supported by four equidistant studs); if you use 12.5mm plasterboard, they can be 600mm apart. If you need a doorway, start measuring at the wall and work towards where you want the frame – the doorway will be better braced by an adjacent vertical stud. It is much easier to fix the vertical studs if you nail a supporting off-cut block of timber to one side of each vertical stud guideline.

Filling in the frame

Your frame is now ready to be filled in with timber studs and noggings.

2 Measure and cut your vertical studs. Hold them steady at the base, against the block supports. Fix them to the floor plate with 100mm nails skewed at an angle from both sides of the stud (see diagram, right). Fix to the ceiling plate in the same way, using a spirit level to make sure that each one is vertical.

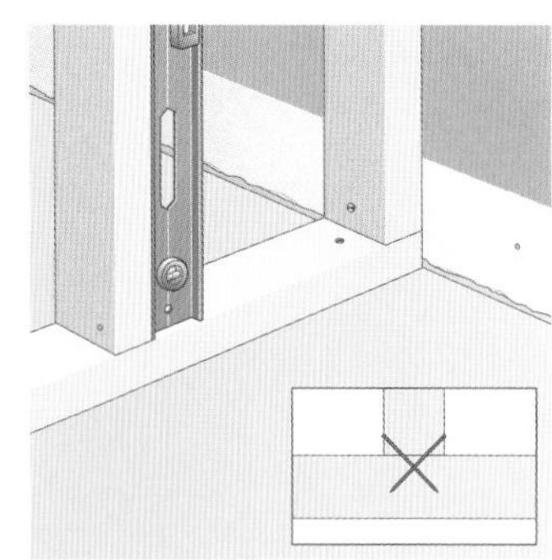

3 To reinforce the vertical studs, take a measurement at the ceiling plate and cut short lengths of timber (noggings) to fit horizontally between them. Fit the noggings about half-way between the floor and ceiling, staggering their positions so that nails can be driven straight through the studs into the ends of the noggings. If you are using a metal box to mount a socket outlet or switch, fit an extra nogging to support it, or else use a cavity socket box (see page 275). Noggings also need to be fitted if you intend to mount a heavy item such as a washbasin, WC cistern, radiator or kitchen cupboard on the wall.

4 Use the pre-assembled door frame to measure the width of the header stud that will run horizontally across the top of the door. Cut and nail in place the vertical stud to which the door frame will be fixed.

5 Tack (lightly nail) the door frame in place, checking it is vertical with a spirit level and packing out with off-cuts of wood or hardboard if necessary. Mark the position of the door frame header stud. Remove the frame and fit the header stud.

6 Strengthen the doorway by fixing a short vertical stud centrally between the door header stud and the ceiling plate, using skewed nails. Then nail the frame securely in place.

Working with plasterboard

Once the stud wall framework is in place, it needs to be covered with plasterboard. This comes in different widths and lengths, either 9.5mm or 12.5mm thick. Plasterboard sheets can be fixed horizontally or vertically (which is easier, as they are heavy and can be rested on the floor). Whichever way you choose, you should start at the doorway and work outwards at either side.

OOLS MATERIALS

tape measure
pencil
craft knife
straightedge
fine abrasive paper
bolster chisel
power drill with twist bits
tenon saw
chisel
mallet

2400mm x 1200mm sheets of plasterboard, 9.5mm or 12.5mm thick, or 220mm x 600mm sheets of plaster lath
off-cut of wood
32mm plasterboard nails

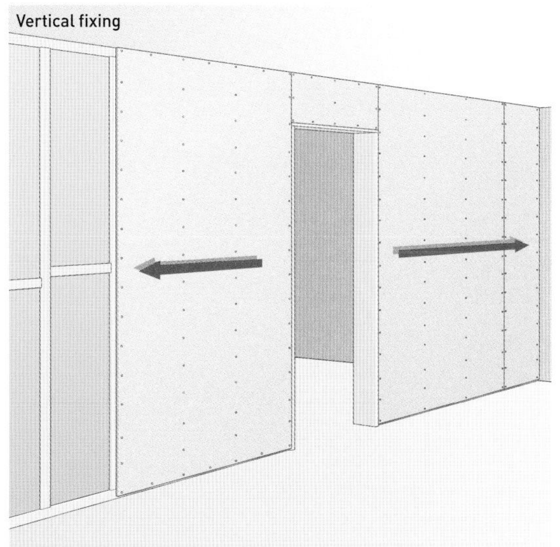

Vertical or horizontal?

If you are fixing your plasterboard sheets vertically, position each width so that the joins align at the centre of a stud. If you are fixing your sheets horizontally, start by nailing the bottom row of boards to the frame. Make sure the vertical joints are staggered.

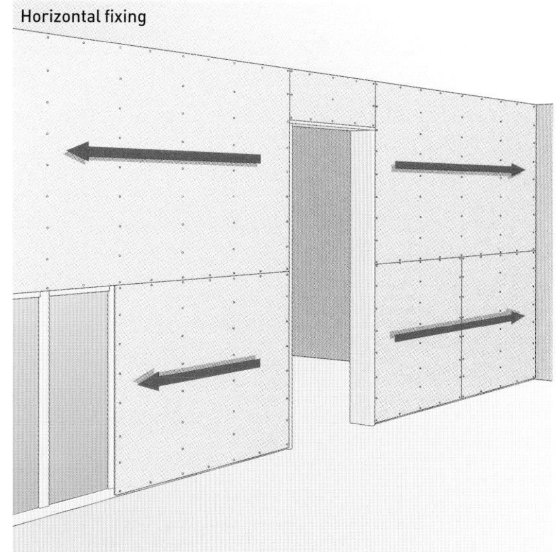

Using plaster lath sheets

If you're worried that you'll have trouble transporting or handling full-size plasterboard sheets, you can use 1220mm x 600mm plaster lath sheets instead. As these are smaller, they need many more fixings and therefore result in a patchwork finish. They are easier to manage, but securing them is very time-consuming. And think twice before you attempt to dry-line plaster lath sheets (see page 67), as it's difficult to achieve a smooth surface. You'll be better off getting in a good plasterer to complete the job with a full plaster coat.

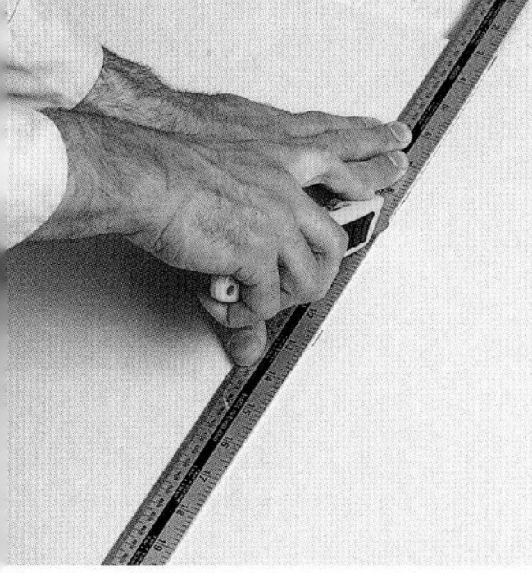

1 Measure the sheets to 12mm ›ss than the floor-to-ceiling ›eight. Mark the cutting line on the ›ory side of the plasterboard, then ›ut along it using a craft knife and ›traightedge.

Cutting plasterboard

Standard plasterboard has a grey side and an ivory side, which faces outwards. The sheets need to be cut to fit, especially where walls and ceilings are not completely straight. Be warned – your knife blade will become blunt very quickly, so a knife with a replaceable snap-off blade is a useful tool for this job.

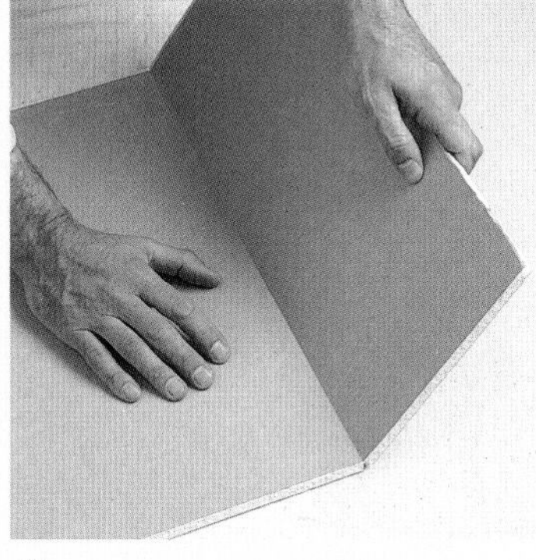

2 Turn the plasterboard over and fold the end along the cut to snap the board.

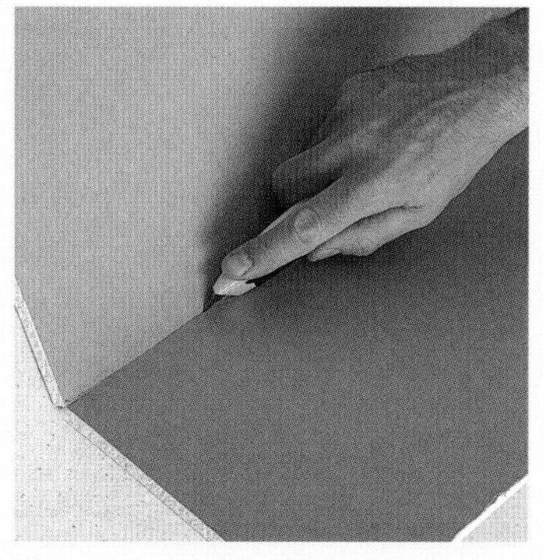

3 Cut through the paper backing with the knife.

Fixing plasterboard

Get someone to help you attach the plasterboard to the frame, if possible – it's much easier with two people, but you can do it by yourself if you use a wood off-cut as a 'floor lifter' to raise the board tight up against the ceiling. The plasterboard should be fitted with the ivory side outwards.

1 Starting at the door studs, carefully position a full-size board vertically, ivory side outwards, to cover half the width of the door stud and half of one other stud. Wedge a bolster chisel at the foot of the board, slide a wood off-cut underneath and use your foot to press down and force the board hard up against the ceiling.

2 Fix the board in place with 32mm plasterboard nails at approximately 150mm intervals, 15mm away from the edges. Continue to fit whole boards in the same way before cutting a board to fit above the doorway and before cutting boards to fit against the adjacent walls. If there is a skirting-board, notch the plasterboard to fit around it.

Cables and pipes

Once you've fixed plasterboard to one side of the frame, you must position all electric cables and plumbing pipes before covering the other side.

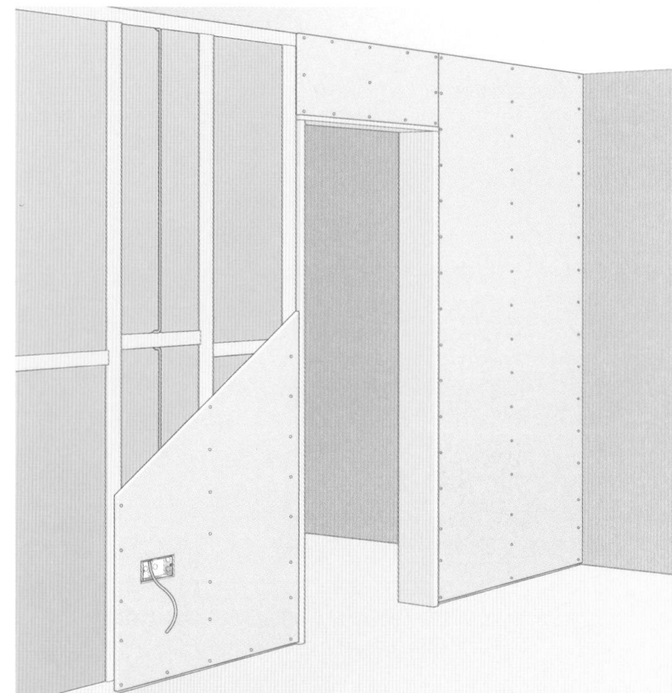

1 Drill holes for running cable through the middle of the studs, or through the noggings (see below). Either way, allow a generous air gap around the cable to prevent overheating.

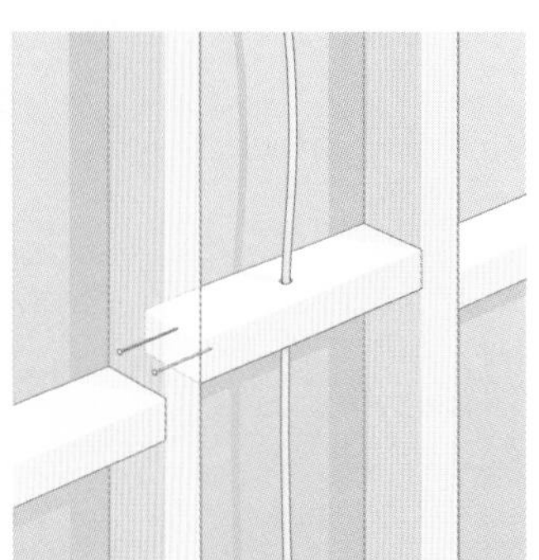

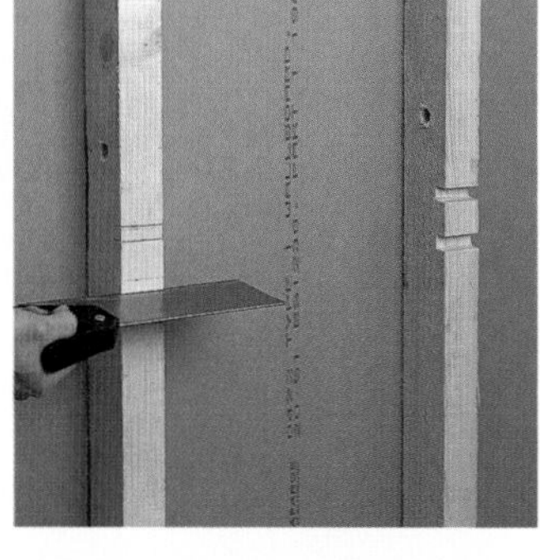

2 Plan the runs of plumbing pipes by marking the faces of the studs with a tenon saw. Carve out the pipe runs with the saw, or a chisel and mallet. Make the notches slope backwards very slightly, so they will hold the pipes while they are fitted. If you need a deep notch – for a waste pipe, for instance – reinforce the stud with a bridging piece.

3 Don't run electric cables and plumbing pipes through the same holes. As you plasterboard the second side of the frame, remember to mark the pipe and cable runs on the plasterboard.

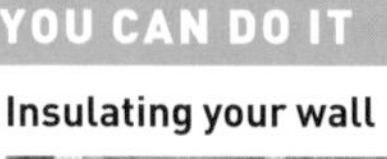

Insulating your wall

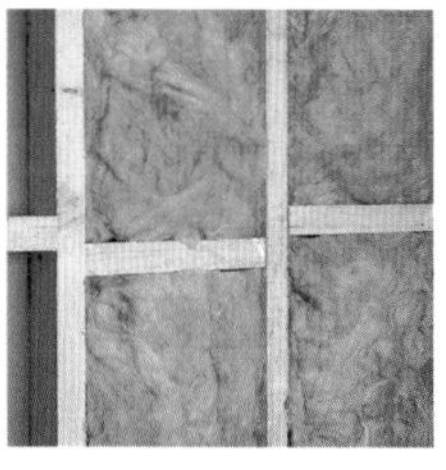

Improve sound and heat insulation by fitting 100mm-thick glass fibre insulation blanket between the studs before plasterboarding the second side. To stop electric cables from overheating, run them inside PVC conduit clipped to the studs or noggings, and passed through notches rather than holes.

Dry-lining

For the smoothest possible finish, plasterboard should be plastered – a skilled job best left to a professional. However, plasterboard joints can be finished with a dry-lining, which you can do yourself. Dry-lining is a way of joining sheets of plasterboard using jointing compound and jointing tape to give a smooth finish. When all the joints are dry, fill the join with the adjacent wall and any other gaps with filler, then all you need to do is apply a drywall primer to the surface and you're ready to decorate.

TOOLS MATERIALS

- **nail punch**
- **hammer**
- **bucket**
- **filling knife or scraper**
- **scissors**
- **coating knife**
- **clean sponge**
- **sanding block**

- jointing compound
- jointing tape
- fine-grade abrasive paper

1 Use a nail punch to make sure that the nail heads are just below the surface. Be careful – don't drive them in so far that they damage the board.

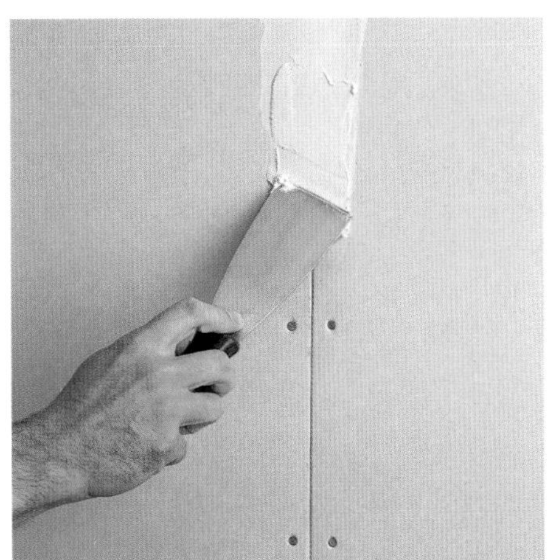

2 Mix the plasterboard jointing compound in a bucket. Smooth the compound down or along the joint with a filling knife or scraper.

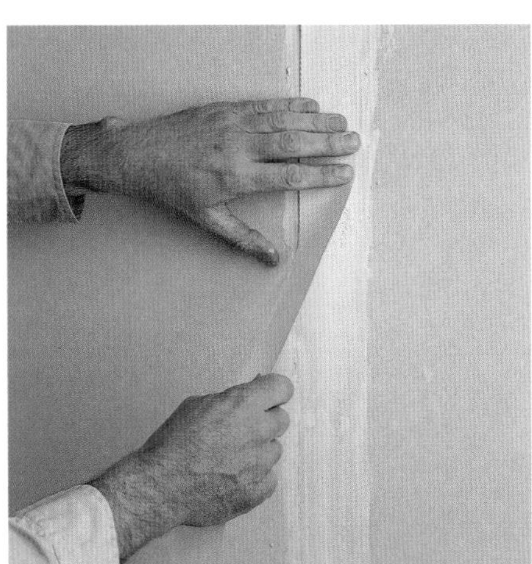

3 Cut a piece of jointing tape the length of the joint with scissors and press the tape in place.

4 Using the blade of a coating knife, press the jointing compound along the taped join so that the compound is flush with the surface of the tape.

5 Immediately smooth the surface with a clean damp sponge. Keep rinsing the sponge and wringing it thoroughly, as excess moisture will weaken the joint and cause cracking. Using the coating knife, apply a wide band of compound down the joint, then use the damp sponge to feather its edges. When all the joints have been done, cover the remaining nail heads with compound, sweeping it over them with a scraper – or better still, an old credit card – to give a smooth surface. Leave the compound to dry, then, if necessary, sand any bumps very lightly with a sanding block.

IDEAL TOOL

Compound coating knife
This has a metal blade wide enough to cover the jointing tape and a few centimetres either side of it. With this knife you can sweep over the compound and tape in one go, achieving a smooth finish. If you use a smaller blade, you have to go over the compound several times and this creates lumps and ridges.

ECO TIMBER

Do your bit to prevent deforestation and global warming: always buy timber that bears the stamp of the Forest Stewardship Council. That way you can be certain it has come from a well-managed source.

Tongue-and-groove panelling is both attractive and hardwearing. You can paint or stain it, or keep a natural wood finish. It is made from planks with a small tongue along one edge and a matching groove along the other. The tongue slots neatly into the groove of the neighbouring plank. The panelling can cover as much of the wall as you like – up to dado level is a popular height. It is usually easier to leave old skirting-boards in place and apply new skirting when you have finished panelling. Or, if the floor is uneven, it may be better to use a thin moulding and bend it to fit the contour of the floor as you fix it. The simplest way of covering the top edge of the panelling is to glue on L-shaped capping. Any switches and sockets will have to be moved forward and remounted.

Fixing the battens

The tongue-and-groove panels are nailed to horizontal battens which you should fit in place first. For panelling up to dado level, you will need to fit three battens, one at floor level, one level with the top of the panelling, and one half-way between the two. There should be approximately 400mm–500mm between them.

TOOLS MATERIALS

- **tape measure**
- **pencil**
- **tenon saw**
- **spirit level**
- **power drill with masonry bit**
- **bradawl**
- **pipe and cable detector**
- **screwdriver**
- **long-nosed pliers**
- **nail punch**
- **hammer**

- 50mm x 25mm softwood battens
- tongue-and-groove panelling
- 50mm screws (5mm gauge) and wallplugs
- abrasive paper
- panel pins
- L-shaped capping
- wood adhesive
- skirting

1 Cut battens to fit the length of the wall you wish to panel. Decide on the height of the panelling and cut each tongue-and-groove plank to length. Using one of the cut planks, mark the height on the wall with a pencil. Use a tape measure and pencil to measure and mark the other levels. If there is skirting on the wall, the lower batten should be fixed just above it. If there is no skirting, mark the lower batten position about 50mm from the floor to leave a gap for air to circulate.

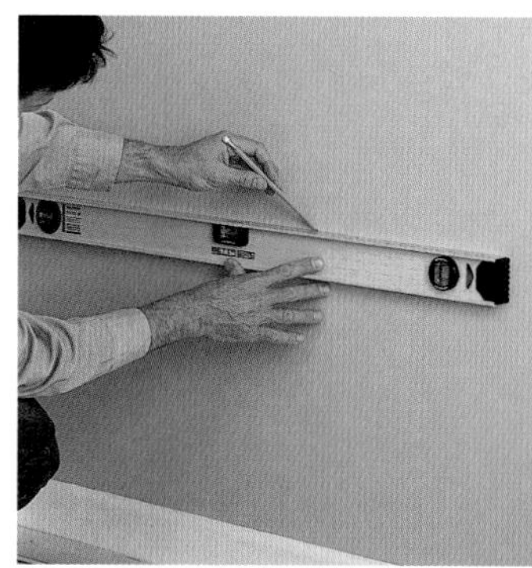

2 Using a spirit level, draw horizontal lines across the wall joining up the marks at the three batten levels. The top edge of the top batten should be exactly the same height as the top of the cut plank.

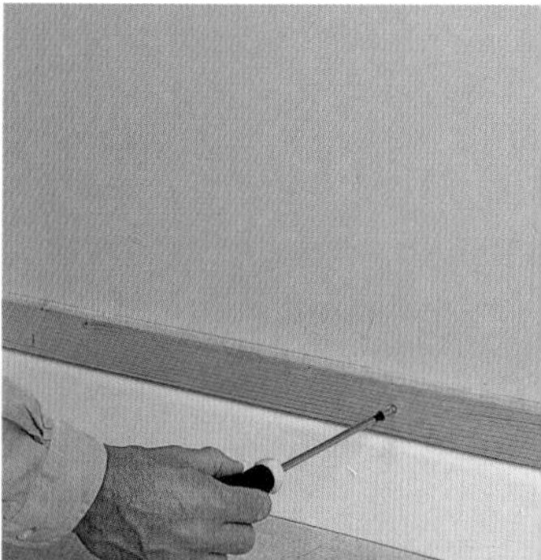

3 Drill the battens 50mm from each end and at about 400mm intervals in between. Hold each batten in position and mark the drill points on the wall with a bradawl. Remove the batten and check there are no hidden pipes or cables behind the fixing positions before you drill and plug the wall and screw the battens in place.

YOU CAN DO IT

Filling gaps

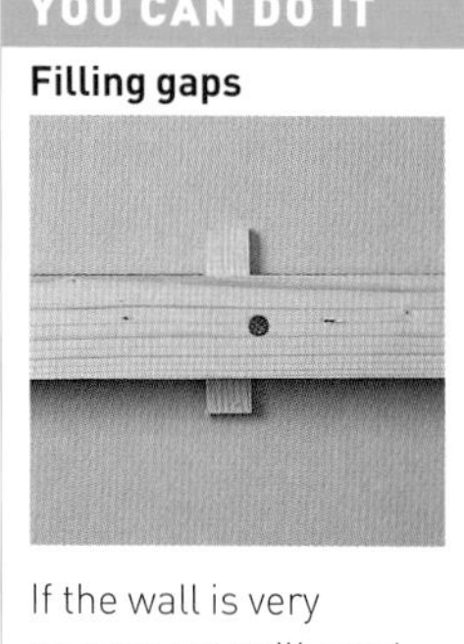

If the wall is very uneven, you will need some packing, such as cardboard or wood off-cuts, to fill any gaps behind the battens.

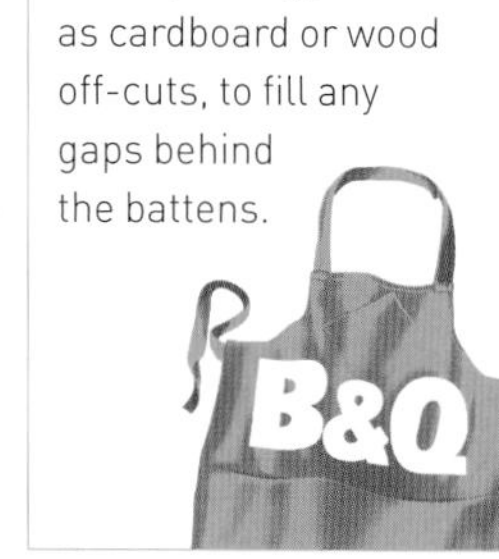

Attaching the panelling

The design of tongue-and-groove panelling allows for 'secret nailing' (see cross-section, right). Panel pins are nailed through the tongue of each plank and covered by the groove of the next plank as it is slotted in place.

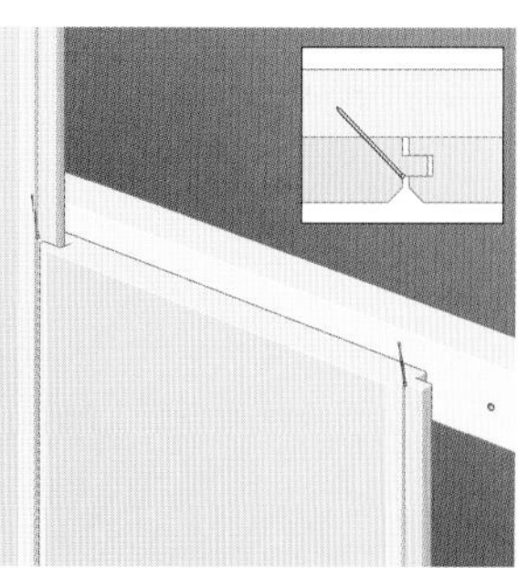

1 Sand any rough edges at each end of the planks. Starting on the left, hold the first plank in place (tongue side on the right), level with the top batten. Nail a panel pin through the top left-hand side of the plank face into the batten.

2 Use a spirit level to check the plank is vertical before fixing it to the remaining battens. Repeat this every 3 or 4 planks to make sure the panelling remains vertical.

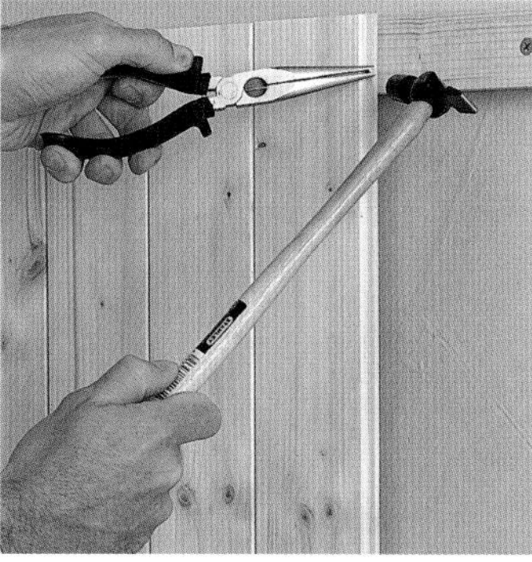

3 To 'secret nail' the planks, hold a pin with long-nosed pliers and hammer it at an angle through the corner of the tongue into the batten behind it. Repeat for each batten.

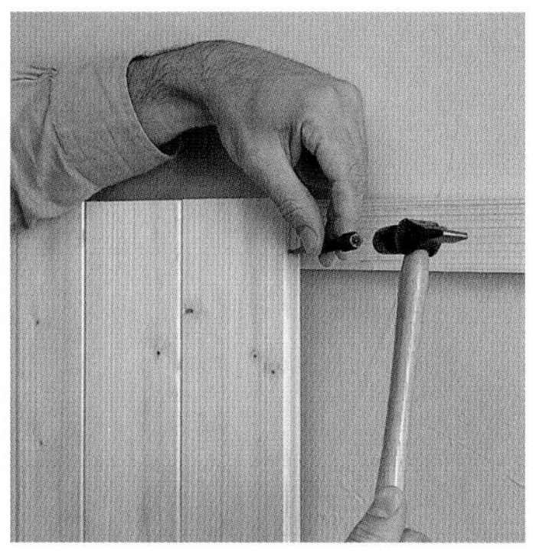

4 Sink the pin heads below the surface of the plank using a nail punch and hammer. Slot the next plank into place with its groove covering the tongue of the previous plank. Repeat for each plank until you reach the end of the wall. Cut the last plank to fit, and nail through the face into the battens. If you are panelling the next wall too, leave a 3mm gap between the last plank and the wall at the corner. Butt the grooved edge of the first plank on the adjoining wall against this last plank, and nail it though the face into the battens.

5 Cut the capping to fit the top edge of the panelling. Apply wood adhesive to the panelling, attach the capping, and leave to dry.

6 Cut a length of skirting to fit and nail it to the bottom of the panelling with panel pins.

YOU CAN DO IT

Panel pins

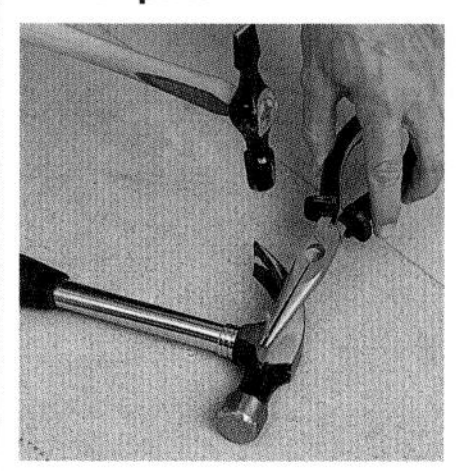

To prevent the panel pins from splitting the tongue on the panelling planks, you can blunt the point. Hold the head of the inverted pin with long-nosed pliers on a hammer. Tap the point of the pin with a second hammer just enough to blunt it.

Remounting a power socket

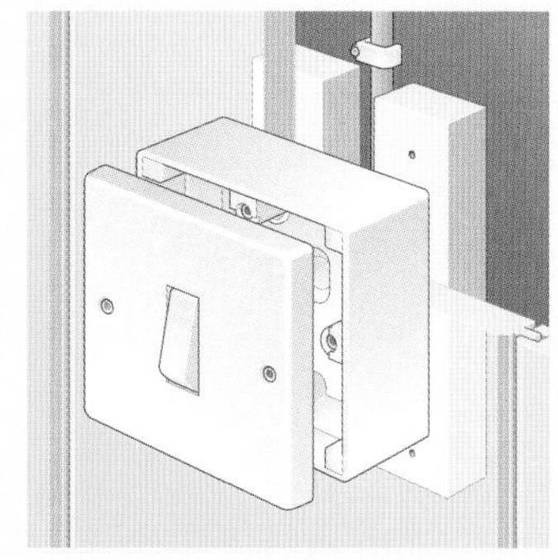

▲ Surface-mounted fitting

A surface-mounted switch or socket sits on the panelling, but remember to fit short battens to to the wall behind to support its fixing screws. Turn off the mains power. Drill a hole, disconnect the cable and pass it through the hole. Screw the box to the battens, reconnect the cable and replace the faceplate.

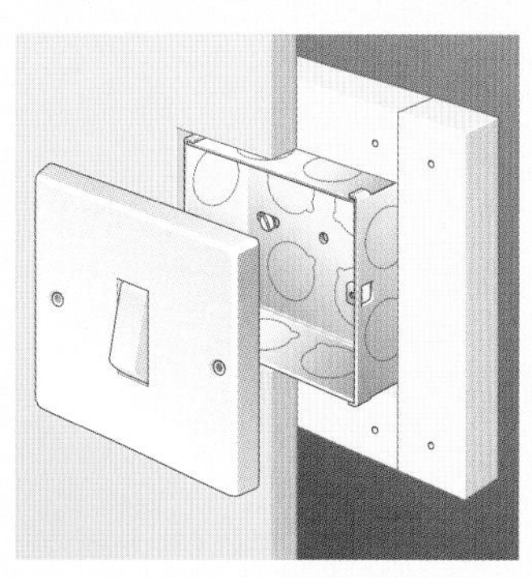

◂ Flush-mounted fitting

Cut a hole for the mounting box as you fit the panels at that point. With the power switched off at the mains, unscrew the faceplate. Move the mounting box forward and pack the recess behind it with short pieces of wood. Screw the box to the wall using wallplugs inserted into the masonry. The screws should penetrate about 25mm. Fit the planks, reconnect the cable and replace the faceplate.

SAFETY FIRST

Don't be tempted to move an electrical switch or socket by simply pulling the cable forward and refitting the cover on the panelling; you must also move the mounting box forward, otherwise the terminal connections are unprotected and a fire risk.

Skirting covers the joint between the wall and the floor. It makes a decorative border while hiding the gaps needed for the natural expansion and contraction that takes place in a house. It also suffers a lot of hard wear. Fortunately, replacing it is not complicated, and there is a range of profiles to choose from (see page 361). Or you may want to restore skirting to a property whose original mouldings have been stripped out, or fit it on a newly built stud partition wall.

YOU CAN DO IT

Removing old skirting

Take care when prising away old skirting not to damage adjacent plaster. Tap the blade of a bolster chisel between the wall and the skirting using a hammer. Lever the top edge away enough to insert the blade of a crowbar. Place a thin piece of wood behind the crowbar to protect the wall.

B&Q

IDEAL TOOL

Skirting-board mitre tool
This guiding tool is fixed in a vice or workbench, and the skirting is held steady in it by thumbscrews. It can be used for cutting left- or right-hand mitres, and for both internal and external corners.

Fitting new skirting

Coat the back of new skirting-board with wood preservative before fitting it. The type of fixing will depend on the construction of the wall and the previous fixings:

- masonry walls: use masonry nails or screws
- stud walls: use oval wire nails nailed into the studs (located with a stud detector, see page 62)
- grounds (timber blocks): if the old skirting was attached to these common fixing points, then use them again. Mark their position on your new skirting and fix onto them using lost-head nails.

You could just glue it in place with wood adhesive, and on damp-proofed walls you will have to in order to avoid penetrating the damp-proofing with nails or screws. It may be necessary to use a combination of methods. For long lengths, you will need a trestle on which to rest one end of the board.

TOOLS MATERIALS

- **tape measure**
- **pencil**
- **skirting-board mitre tool**
- **vice or workbench**
- **trestle**
- **panel saw**
- **pipe and cable detector**
- **power drill with 5mm gauge countersink bit**

- new skirting
- off-cuts of wood and hardboard
- wood preservative
- 60mm wallplugs and screws (5mm gauge)
- masonry, oval wire or lost-head nails, as necessary
- wood or PVA adhesive
- panel pins
- abrasive paper
- filler
- decorator's caulk
- primer
- undercoat and top coat paint

1 Start at the longest wall with internal corners. Measure the wall and mark the top edge of a length of skirting to show where it should be cut. Fit the skirting-board mitre tool (see IDEAL TOOL) in a vice or workbench. Put the left-hand end of the skirting in the mitre tool and rest the other end on the trestle, making sure the trestle is level with the base of the mitre tool. Protect the board face with a piece of hardboard placed under the thumbscrews, then tighten the screws. Cut the mitre for the left-hand corner with the saw, then move the skirting and cut the right-hand corner.

2 If fixing the skirting with masonry nails or screws, fit them to existing points where possible; otherwise, fix them approximately every 600mm at the highest flat point on the skirting, checking first that there are no pipes or cables behind the fixing positions. If there are timber grounds, fix the skirting to them with lost-head nails. If using screws, drill pilot holes and insert plugs then screws. For stud walls, locate the studs using a stud detector and nail oval wire nails into them.

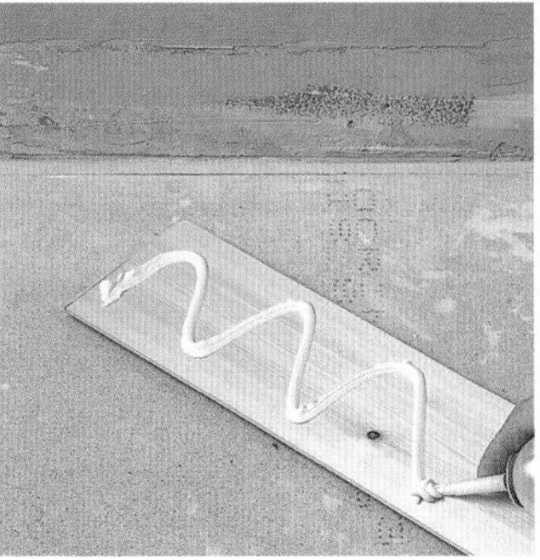

3 If gluing the skirting, apply adhesive evenly to the back. Press the piece in place and, if necessary, hold it in position with props made from off-cuts of wood until the adhesive has set.

4 Continue measuring, cutting and fixing skirting to one wall at a time. Turn the board the other way up in the skirting board mitre tool to cut mitres for external corners. To fix the skirting at external corners, use adhesive and then hammer two panel pins into the skirting each side of the corner for extra security.

5 When all the skirting is in place, sand the external corners and fill any gaps with filler. Sand them again when dry. Cover any nail or screw holes with filler.

6 Fill the gaps between the skirting and the wall with decorator's caulk. Leave to dry before applying primer, then undercoat and finally a top coat of paint. Or if you plan to varnish the new skirting, use an acrylic filler that matches the colour of your wood.

Cutting skirting profiles

Instead of cutting mitres for corners, you can fit boards at internal corners by profile cutting. The first board is fitted right into the corner, then the end of the second board is cut to fit around the profile of the first.

TOOLS MATERIALS

- **profile gauge**
- **pencil**
- **workbench**
- **coping saw**

- new skirting

1 Fit one skirting-board right into the corner, with the end butting up against the wall. Hold a profile gauge against this skirting to take a copy of its shape.

2 Measure and mark the next length of skirting to be fitted. Hold the profile gauge against the mark and draw round the shape with a pencil.

3 Alternatively, hold an off-cut of the skirting at 90° to the piece to be fitted and trace its profile with a pencil.

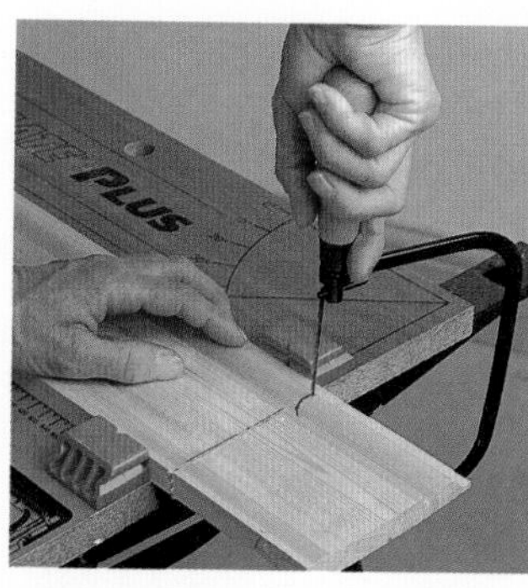

4 Cut along the pencil mark with a coping saw.

5 Check the fit – you may have to make small adjustments to get it absolutely right.

IDEAL TOOL

Profile gauge

A simple profile gauge will make numerous tasks easier – not just tracing skirting profiles, but laying tiles or flooring or anything that needs to be cut to fit an awkward shape.

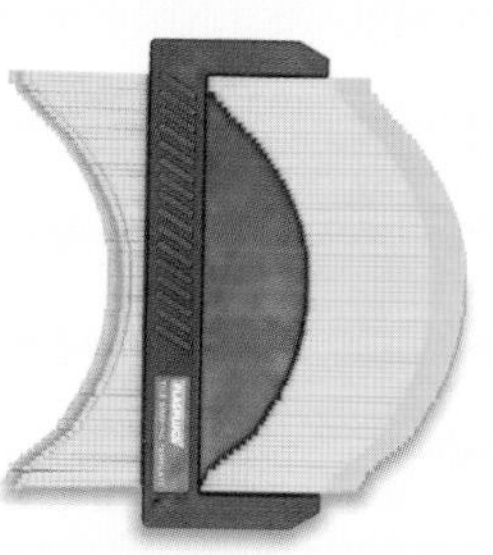

WALLS BUILDING A GLASS-BLOCK WALL

TOOLS MATERIALS

- **tape measure**
- **pencil**
- **panel saw**
- **pipe and cable detector**
- **power drill**
- **screwdriver**
- **hammer**
- **trowel**
- **spirit level**
- **craft knife**
- **damp sponge**
- **striking tool**
- **grout raker**
- **soft cloth**

- glass blocks and frame
- 38mm screws or 50mm screws and wallplugs (4mm or 5mm gauge); or hollow-wall fixings
- 20mm nails
- foam expansion-joint strip
- glass-block mortar
- plastic spacers
- panel anchors
- panel grout
- silicone sealant

Glass blocks make an interesting alternative to more traditional building materials. You can choose from a vast array of sizes, colours and designs. They are especially good in kitchens and bathrooms as they are resistant to grease and humidity, and they can even be used to build a curved wall.

While glass blocks are not suitable for a structural wall, they are a stylish way of dividing a room while making good use of the light. The blocks are simply laid within a wooden frame, which is fixed to the floor, ceiling and walls at either end. Special glass block frames are available, which you cut to size. Choose a frame to fit your blocks with the width the same as the thickness of the blocks. A flexible foam expansion-joint strip is fitted between the frame and the glass blocks to allow for slight movement. Panel anchors (hidden by mortar) are screwed to the sides of the frame to secure the blocks. Fit them every row or alternate row according to the manufacturer's instructions.

Building the wall

To work out the dimensions of the frame, lay a single row of blocks on the floor with plastic spacers between them, including one at each end. Measure the total length, then do the same for the vertical dimension. Cut the frame to fit.

Fit the frame into place, packing it with small off-cuts of wood to ensure it is level and square if necessary. Fix it to the walls, ceiling and floor: drill holes in the frame, mark the wall, and check for hidden pipes and cables. Then drill the fixing holes and insert either 50mm wallplugs and screws into masonry; 38mm screws into wood (ceiling joists or the studs of a stud wall); or hollow-wall fixings into plasterboard (see page 368).

SAFETY FIRST

A wall of glass blocks is heavy, so you must check that the weight can be supported by the floor below, especially if building on a suspended wooden floor. If in doubt, seek professional advice before starting the project.

1 Nail the expansion strip to the sides of the frame at intervals, stopping just short of the bottom of the frame to allow a spacer to be fitted against the frame. Mix the mortar to a smooth consistency and lay a bed of mortar on the bottom of the frame (the sill). Use enough mortar to give a 10mm joint when the blocks are in place.

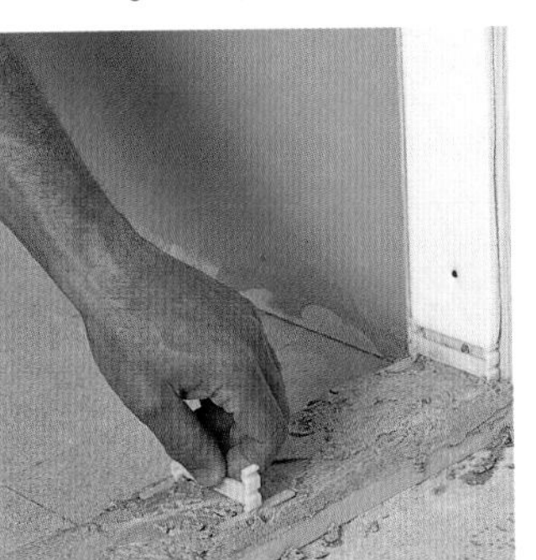

2 Starting at one corner, place an L-shaped spacer against the frame. Place a T-shaped spacer to support the other end of the block (use one of the blocks to mark out the right position).

3 Lay the first block in the corner and bed well down on spacers.

4 Position the next T-shaped spacer. Apply enough mortar to the side of the second block to fill the cavity between the blocks. Sit the second block on the spacers and push it against the first block, ensuring it is snug on the spacers.

Spacers

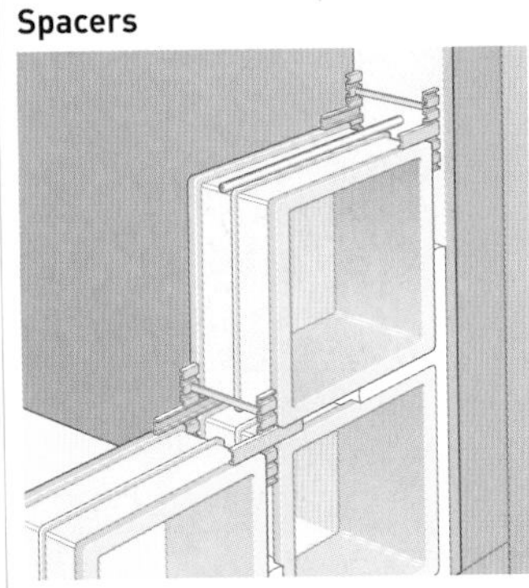

The cross-shaped plastic spacers sold with glass blocks are three spacers in one, as you can snap them off to make T-shaped and L-shaped spacers to fit around the frame. The tabs are twisted off once the mortar has set. To work out how many you need, allow 1.5 spacers per block plus 10%.

B&Q

5 Continue until the first row is complete, checking from time to time with a spirit level to make sure it is straight. Lay mortar on top of the first row and bed in full spacers between the blocks. Lay the second row.

6 Using a craft knife, cut the expansion strip level with the second row of blocks.

7 Lift the expansion strip and screw a panel anchor to the side of the frame at either end of the row. Drop the strip back over the vertical arm of the anchor. Its horizontal arm should fit over the block and the spacers; cover it with mortar and continue laying the blocks.

8 Clean the face of the blocks with a damp sponge from time to time.

YOU CAN DO IT

Reinforcing the wall

If the span of the wall is greater than 1.4m, steel reinforcing bars must be laid between each row of blocks. Lay the mortar on top of the blocks and press the reinforcing bar into it. If you need more than one bar for the length of the wall, overlap them by 150mm.

IDEAL TOOL

Striking tool

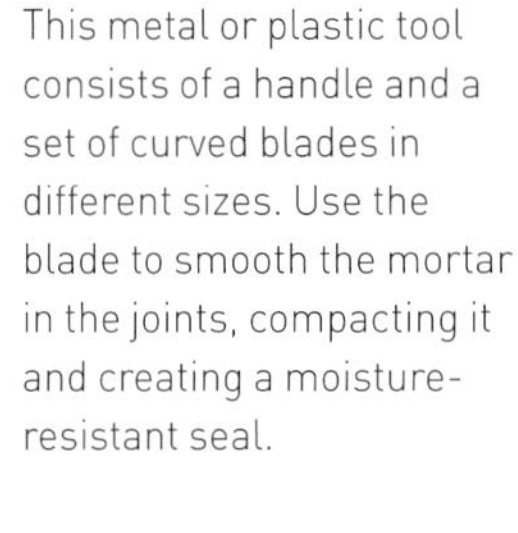

This metal or plastic tool consists of a handle and a set of curved blades in different sizes. Use the blade to smooth the mortar in the joints, compacting it and creating a moisture-resistant seal.

Finishing

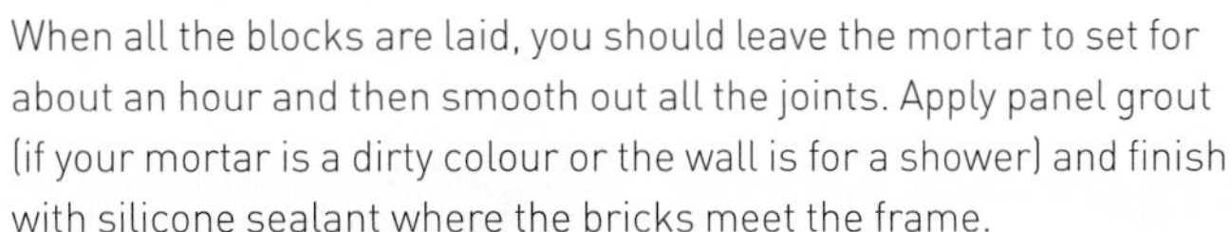

When all the blocks are laid, you should leave the mortar to set for about an hour and then smooth out all the joints. Apply panel grout (if your mortar is a dirty colour or the wall is for a shower) and finish with silicone sealant where the bricks meet the frame.

1 When the mortar has set, twist off the tabs on the spacers. Smooth the joints with a striking tool (see IDEAL TOOL). This compacts the mortar to create a moisture-resistant seal. After striking, all the joints should be full of mortar.

2 If the wall is being built for a shower, rake some of the mortar out of the joints with a small trowel so that a depth of 10mm remains, and leave for 24 hours. (You can also do this if your mortar is not white and you want a white finish.)

3 The next day, fill the joints with white panel grout, moulding and compacting them with a striking tool. Leave for 1–2 hours, then wipe the surface with a clean, soft cloth.

4 Apply silicone sealant in a continuous bead where the blocks join the frame, at the top, sides and bottom on both sides.

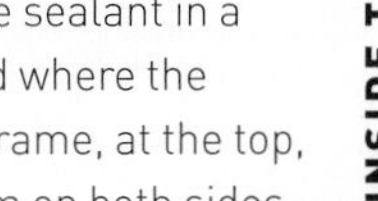

WALLS PREPARATION

Walls almost always need some surface preparation before you can apply paint. Even brand-new plaster needs priming. Cracks and holes must be filled (see page 56), and surfaces must be clean and dry (for problems such as damp, see page 60). Emulsion-painted surfaces in good condition can be painted over; peeling paint should be stripped back. Paint over wallpaper only if it is very firmly stuck to the wall.

Cleaning surfaces

Clear the room as much as possible. Move anything that has to stay into the centre and cover it with dust sheets. Use dust sheets to protect the floor too. Fill holes and cracks, then wash down walls, ceiling and woodwork with a sugar soap solution. Wear gloves and goggles as sugar soap can irritate the skin. Rinse with clean water and leave to dry. Depending on the wall, you may need to seal or prime it (see below).

PREPARING WALLS AND CEILINGS

Surface	Preparation
New plaster	Prime with a coat of plaster sealer.
Painted plaster	No need to prime a surface that has been painted previously unless tarnished by smoke stains, in which case coat with primer as for new plaster.
New plasterboard	Apply drywall primer, or seal with emulsion paint.
Old paint	Clean with sugar soap and water. Scrape off any peeling paint and sand the surface.
Distemper	Seal with special stabilising solution, or wash off completely.
Wallpaper	If the paper is firmly stuck down, clean with sugar soap and water; otherwise, strip it.
Stripped plaster	Seal with a plaster sealer.
Cork wall tiles	Prime absorbent cork with all-purpose primer.
Ceramic wall tiles	Paint with a special-purpose primer and compatible gloss paint.

TOOLS MATERIALS

- **dust sheets**
- **filling knife**
- **bucket**
- **large sponge**
- **protective gloves**
- **safety goggles**
- **orbital wallpaper scorer or wallpaper spiker**
- **wide stripping knife**
- **wallpaper steam stripper**
- **sponge**
- **hot-air gun, if removing cork tiles**

- filler, as necessary
- sugar soap
- liquid detergent
- wallpaper paste
- primer, as necessary (see chart)

Stripping wallpaper

Stripping wallpaper takes time, as it must be soaked with hot water before you scrape it off. If you make holes in the paper beforehand the water can get underneath, and this helps to lift it. You can perforate the paper by running an orbital scorer or a wallpaper spiker over it.

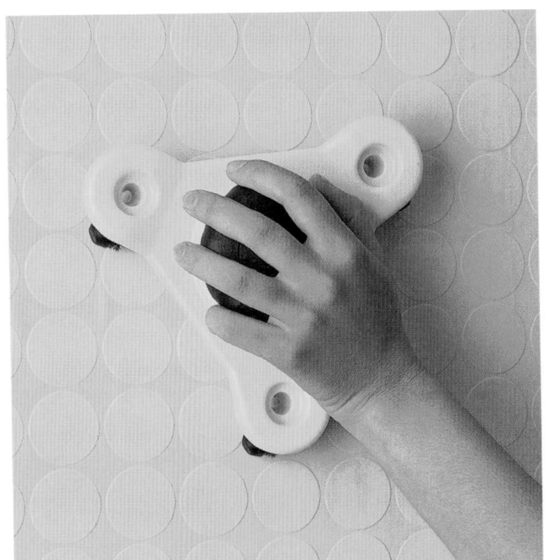

1 Run the orbital scorer over the paper, being very careful not to damage the plaster behind. Fill a bucket with hot water and add some liquid detergent and a handful of wallpaper paste to thicken the water, so that it doesn't run down the wall quite so fast.

2 Using a large sponge, wet the wall, covering a few square metres at a time. Leave it to soak for at least five minutes. Slide the edge of a wide stripping knife under the paper at a seam to see if it is ready to be stripped. Make sure the blade does not gouge holes the plaster. The paper should come away in a fairly big strip. If after lengthy soakings it still doesn't come away easily, you will need to use a steam stripper.

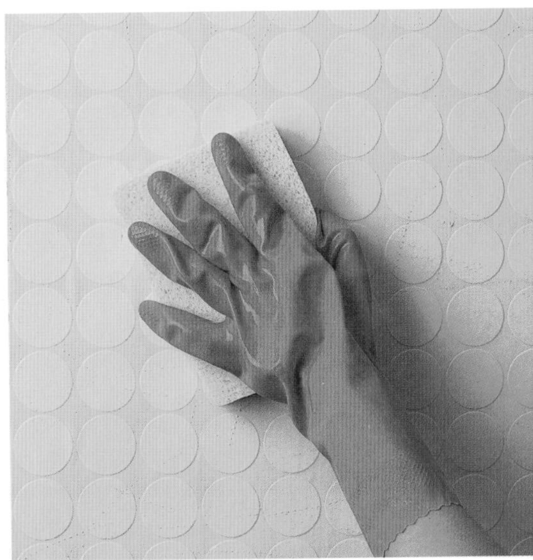

Jsing a steam stripper

steam wallpaper stripper speeds up the process considerably. Hold the stripper ɪd at the bottom of a wallpaper length for a minute or so, until the paper around appears damp. Pull away the damp paper, loosening any stubborn areas with a ripping knife. Hold the pad with the other hand over the next area to be stripped, orking up the wall. Start at the bottom of the wall to strip off the next length.

If you are stripping paper from plasterboard, take special care with the ripping knife – if you over-use it in one place, you risk damaging the board. And n't hold the stripper over one spot for too long, as this too can damage plaster.

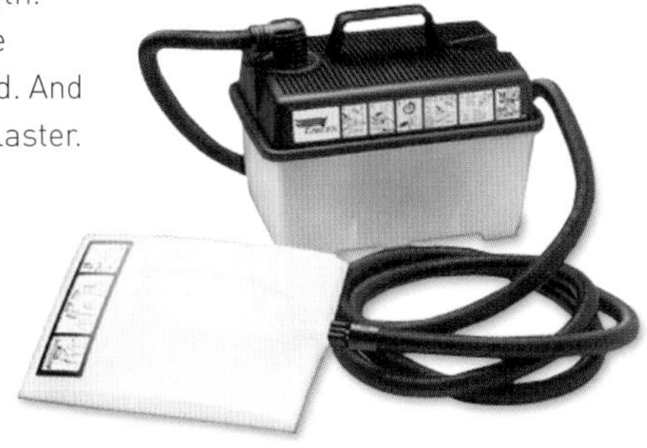

IDEAL TOOL

Steam stripper
An electric steam stripper consists of a tank and a pad, joined by a length of pipe. The tank is filled with water which is heated until it boils. Steam comes out of the pad, which is held against the wall to loosen the paper. Always turn the power off and leave to cool for two minutes before you refill the tank. Use warm water so that it comes to the boil faster.

Take care!

- Do not use around electrical switches and sockets.
- Wear heat-resistant gloves and goggles.
- Never leave a steam stripper unattended when it is turned on.
- Keep the boiler on a level surface.
- Never move it by pulling the pipe, and don't detach the pipe while it is switched on.
- Always read the instruction leaflet before you start.

Stripping cork tiles

emoving cork tiles is not difficult, but it is messy because they come away in ieces, leaving the adhesive still firmly attached to the wall. The best way to get e adhesive off is to soften it with an electric hot-air gun, also known as a hot-air ripper. For the non-professional, this is much safer than a blowtorch because ere is no naked flame – it simply blasts hot air.

1 Lever the tiles from the wall with a wide stripping knife. The tiles will break up, leaving the adhesive still on the wall.

2 Wearing safety goggles, soften the adhesive with a hot-air gun. Scrape the adhesive from the surface while it is still soft, using the stripping knife.

WALLS PAINTING

ECO DECORATING

The main environmental impact of paint is the release of VOCs (Volatile Organic Compounds), primarily solvents, into the atmosphere. These contribute to atmospheric pollution, smell unpleasant and can be harmful to people with respiratory problems.

B&Q has developed a VOC labelling scheme – now adopted across the UK paint industry – and has encouraged the development of water-based technology to provide alternatives to traditional products. All paint products, stains, varnishes and decorative sundries such as white spirit are now labelled to give information on VOC concentration, so low-VOC products are clearly identifiable.

YOU CAN DO IT

Recycle unused paint
Water-based paint is better for the environment than a solvent- or oil-based product, but whatever you use, never pour leftovers down the drain. Paint can pollute waterways. Contact your local authority to find out if there are any paint recycling schemes in your area.

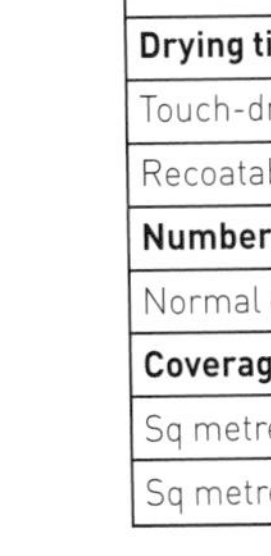

Once you have prepared the walls and cleared the room, you can start painting. This is one of the most pleasurable parts of decorating, but don't rush into it without thinking. Before you start, run through some final checks:

- Are you sure you have the right paint, and also enough of it (see below)?
- Do you have the right sort of cleaning fluid for your paint, and a good supply of it?
- Do you have the right tools for the job? Most paints can be applied with either a brush or a roller.
- Can you reach all the surfaces safely? You will certainly need a stepladder, and may have to hire or make a work platform (see page 347).
- Have you allowed yourself enough time? Take account not only of the drying time, but also the period between coats of paint (see the chart below).
- Are there children and pets around? Keep them away from wet paint!

Choosing your paints

Large areas like walls and ceilings should be painted with water-based paint. You can choose between traditional emulsion, acrylic emulsion, or the latest multi-surface formulas, suitable for wood, metal and even radiators. See below, and also the tables on page 364.

Emulsion

Emulsion is a water-based paint for walls and ceilings available in a large variety of colours, which usually need two coats. It can be applied directly on to walls that have been previously painted, or on to paintable wall coverings such as lining paper and textured wallpaper. Emulsion paint generally comes in two finishes – matt and silk. Matt has a flat, non-reflective appearance, which is useful for disguising uneven surfaces. Matt emulsion marks easily and is not washable, but new 'wipeable' matt paints are being introduced in many ranges. Silk emulsion has a shiny, reflective finish, and can be washed. It is useful for vulnerable areas such as halls, staircases and children's rooms. There is a third finish, often called soft sheen, satin or mid-sheen, which is basically half-way between matt and silk, with a wipeable surface.

One-coat emulsion

This special emulsion paint is thicker and has superior covering power. Just one coat will cover most surfaces. This paint usually comes in satin, mid-sheen and matt finishes.

Kitchen and bathroom emulsion

This is specifically formulated for areas of high humidity. It has moisture- and grease-resistant properties, and gives a tougher, scrubbable surface. This emulsion is available in a mid- or soft sheen.

Acrylics

These paints are similar to emulsion paints in that they are water-based, quick-drying and low-odour, but their advanced formula means they are tougher and washable, and many are suitable for other surfaces such as wood and metal (check the manufacturer's instructions). They are available in matt finish for a solid, flat colour, satin for a subtle sheen and gloss for a moderate gloss finish.

Multi-surface acrylics

These new generation paints can be applied to walls, ceilings, woodwork and radiators, meaning you only have to buy one paint for the whole job.

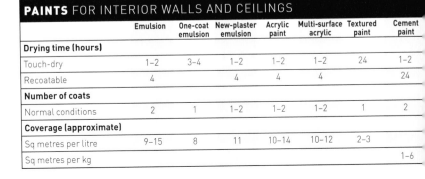

PAINTS FOR INTERIOR WALLS AND CEILINGS

	Emulsion	One-coat emulsion	New-plaster emulsion	Acrylic paint	Multi-surface acrylic	Textured paint	Cement paint
Drying time (hours)							
Touch-dry	1–2	3–4	1–2	1–2	1–2	24	1–2
Recoatable	4		4	4	4		24
Number of coats							
Normal conditions	2	1	1–2	1–2	1–2	1	2
Coverage (approximate)							
Sq metres per litre	9–15	8	11	10–14	10–12	2–3	
Sq metres per kg							1–6

Paint in sequence

Do you need to paint the ceiling? If so, paint it first, since you are bound to get some on the walls. Then paint the walls, and finally the woodwork. Start painting by the window or light source, and paint in bands away from and in parallel to it. Take a break when you reach the corner of a room, not in the middle of a wall. For a detailed guide to painting windows and doors, see pages 130–31.

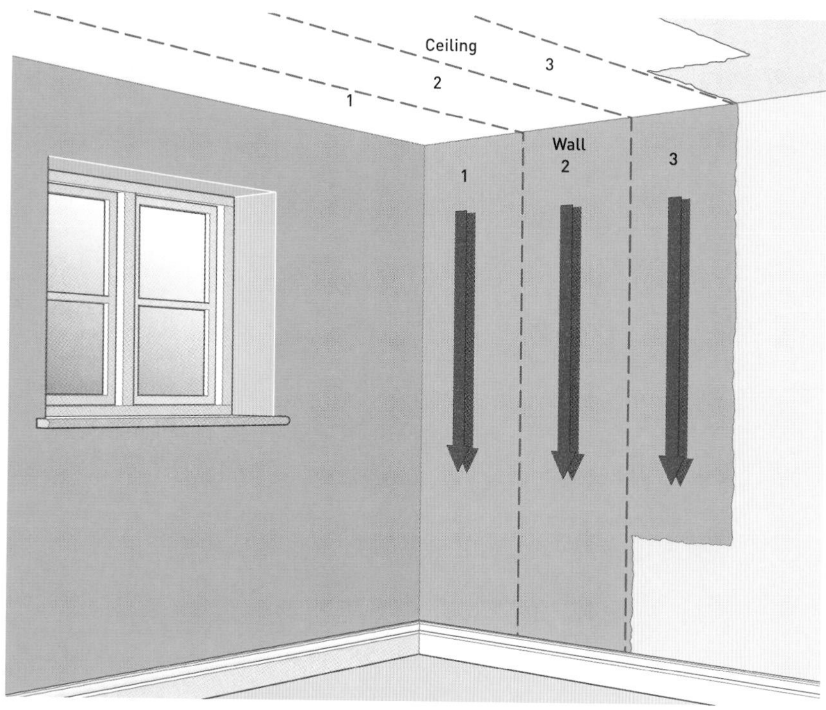

Tricks of the trade

Buying paint in quantity can save you money, but only if you know how to store and decant it effectively.

Storing paint

Paint will not keep indefinitely, as it deteriorates over time. Solvent-based paints have a longer storage life than water-based ones. You can store small quantities in an airtight jar. Choose a size that leaves as little air in the jar as possible, and always label the container with the code number, name and type of paint, and note the room it was used in.

When storing paint in the tin, reduce the risk of a skin forming by turning it upside-down for a few seconds (first making sure that it is tightly shut) to 'seal' the lid with paint, or cut a round of foil to the size of the lid and press it down on to the paint to eliminate air.

Using a paint kettle

A large tin of paint may be more economical, but it is cumbersome to work with. Professionals always decant paint into smaller containers known as 'kettles'. These are available in metal or plastic. It takes a lot of white spirit to clean oil-based paint from a container, so it is a good idea to use a throwaway lining of aluminium foil (right). Mould the foil into the kettle and if necessary use more than one layer to make sure it is fully leak-proof.

Paintbrushes

There is a vast range of paintbrushes to choose from, ranging from cheap ones that you use once then throw away to professional-quality brushes that will improve with use, careful cleaning and correct storage. You can also now buy high-quality synthetic brushes that minimise bristle-loss and have individually tapered fibres for a finer finish; some synthetic brushes are not compatible with all solvent cleaners, however, so do check the manufacturer's instructions when you buy them.

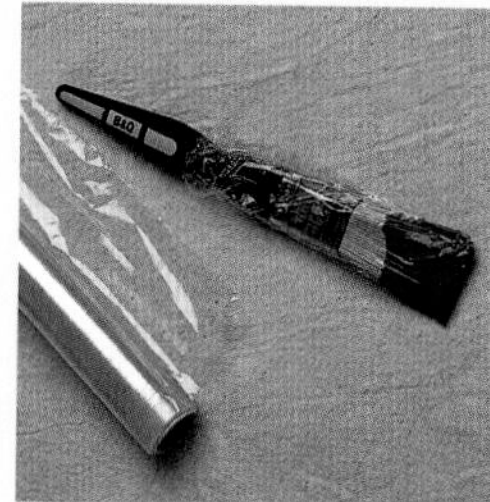

Taking a break?

Stop brushes or rollers drying out by wrapping them in cling film. If you make the wrap as airtight as possible, they will remain soft overnight.

Cleaning and storing

Brushes used with water-based paints are simply washed with water. Work a little soap into the bristles, rinse them clean and leave them to dry. Clean, dry brushes, rollers and pads can be stored wrapped in lint-free cloth, plastic bags, foil or brown paper. Brushes steeped in oil- or solvent-based paint can be stored immersed in an appropriate cleaner or solvent. However, resting the bristles on the bottom of a jar for any length of time is certain to ruin them, so suspend the brush, or use a specially designed cleaning tub.

Using a paintbrush cleaning tub

This is ideal for storing as well as cleaning brushes that have been used with oil- and solvent-based paints. With the lid on tight, store brushes with a small amount of cleaning fluid in the bottom. The vapours circulate, keeping the brush clean and fresh.

1 Snap the brushes into position.

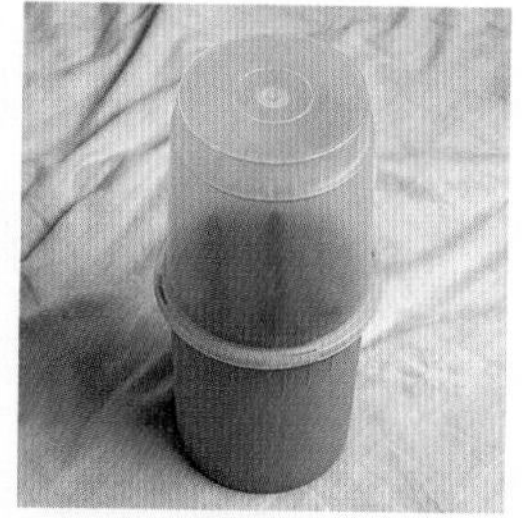

2 Add enough cleaning fluid to cover just the bristles, fasten the lid and rock the container backwards and forwards several times to clean the brush. Dispose of the fluid as instructed, and replace with fresh fluid up to the mark. Keep the lid on while the brush is in storage.

WALLS PAINTING TECHNIQUES

Walls and ceilings are usually painted with emulsion, acrylic or water-based eggshell. Non-drip emulsion is also available, in jelly or solid form, and this is particularly good for ceilings. Never stir non-drip paint, however lumpy it looks. You will cause the gel structure to break down and it will lose its non-drip quality.

Applying liquid emulsion with a brush

Stir the paint and pour it into a paint kettle so that it is about a third full. Dip a 100mm–125mm brush into the paint to cover about one-third of the bristle depth. Press the brush against the rim to get rid of the excess; don't scrape it on the edge – you'll take off too much paint and create a build-up on the inside of the kettle.

1 Start at the top of the wall and apply the paint with short, overlapping horizontal and vertical strokes. Work in panels about 1 sq m at a time, allowing each area to merge into the next one while the edge is still wet.

2 Work systematically across the wall. Try and finish a complete wall before you take a break or there may be a visible change of tone where you stopped.

Painting edges

Rollers and larger paint pads are very good for covering whole walls, but they cannot reach all the way to the edges; you will need to finish off these areas with a brush or small paint pad – a process often referred to as 'cutting in'. This can be done before or after the main painting, but you will get the most uniform finish if you do it before the main area is painted.

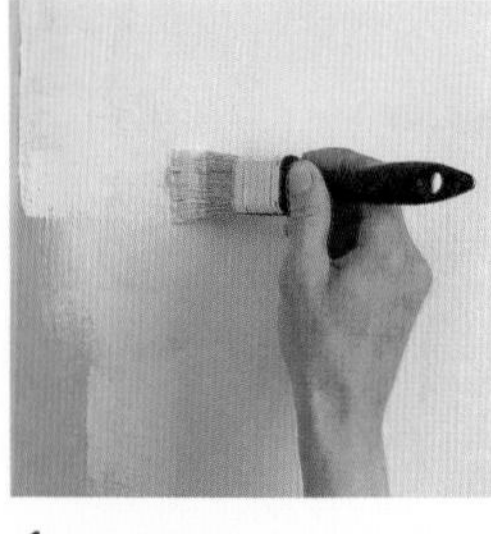

1 Paint four or five overlapping strokes at right angles to the edge to fill the gap between the edge and the new paint.

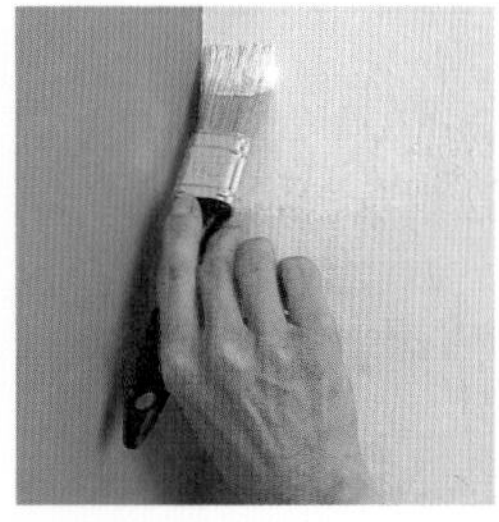

2 Painting parallel to the edge, go over the first brush strokes in a long sweeping motion. Repeat until the whole edge is painted.

Beading where colours meet

You can use masking tape to get a neat edge where different colours meet, such as at the junction of walls and ceiling, or where adjacent walls are a different colour. But professionals use a technique called beading, which is not difficult, provided you have a reasonably steady hand. The adjacent colour must be dry before you start.

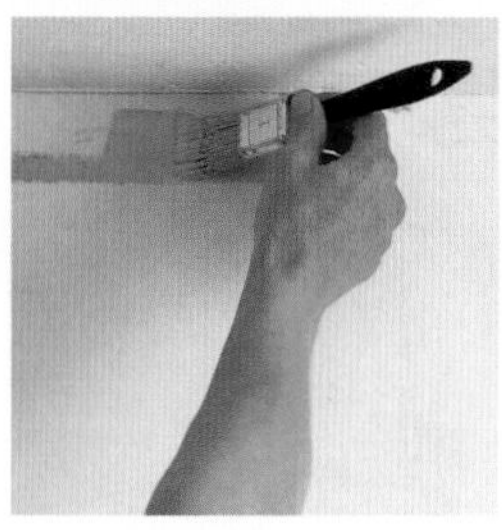

1 Load the brush with a little paint. Turn it edge-on and press it flat against the wall, a short way from the edge, so that the bristles are slightly splayed to create a bead of paint.

2 With a steady hand, draw the brush sideways or downwards along the surface, gradually working right to the edge to give a clearly defined line between the colours.

IDEAL TOOL

Paint shield

Known in the trade as a 'George', this is used to protect the skirting-board. Hold it at the bottom of the wall as you work your way along to stop the paint dripping down. When you are painting skirting-boards, you can use it to protect the floor and to ensure that no dirt or fluff sticks to the paintbrush.

YOU CAN DO IT

Protective clothing

Wear something like cotton overalls when you are painting – don't wear wool because fibres will stick to the paint. A mask will protect you from the paint fumes. Wear a cap or hat to stop your hair getting speckled when painting a ceiling.

B&Q

Painting with oil-based paint

Oil-based paint is slightly more difficult to apply and must be painted over an undercoat. Use a 75mm brush and work in 300mm-square areas. Clean brushes and any spillages with white spirit. It is not advisable to use oil-based paint on large areas like walls or ceilings (see SAFETY FIRST, below).

1 Paint three vertical, parallel strips, leaving a space slightly narrower than the brush between them.

2 Blend the strips together by painting horizontally, without reloading the brush with paint. With a nearly dry brush, make light vertical strokes over the painted area to give an even coating. Repeat the process on the area below, working the wet paint into the dry, so the sections marry into each other.

IDEAL TOOLS

Specialised rollers
Rollers designed specifically for awkward areas will make your life much easier.

- An extension pole fitted to your roller lets you paint the ceiling from the floor.
- A special corner roller is perfect for painting corners where both walls are going to be the same colour.

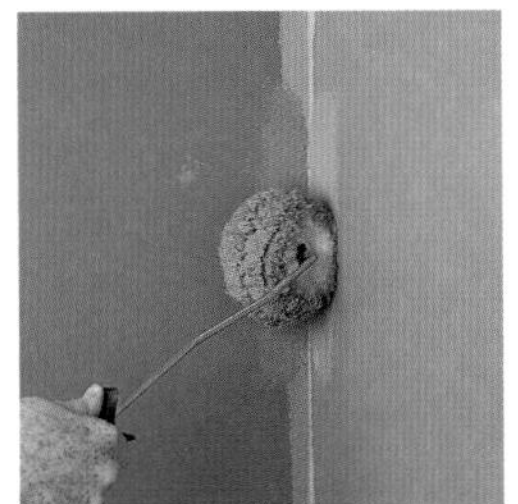

- A mini roller with an extra-long handle allows you to paint the difficult-to-reach bits behind the radiator.

Using a roller

Applying emulsion with a roller is the quickest way of covering a large surface area, although you may need more coats than when painting with a brush because the paint goes on quite thinly. Roller sleeves are available in a variety of sizes and textures. Choose a short-pile sleeve for a smooth wall surface, and a shaggy sheepskin-style sleeve for a more textured surface. The areas the roller cannot reach will need to be finished with a brush. Solid non-drip emulsion, which comes in a tray, is also applied with a roller. As you apply the roller, the paint liquefies and allows the roller to pick up the right amount of paint.

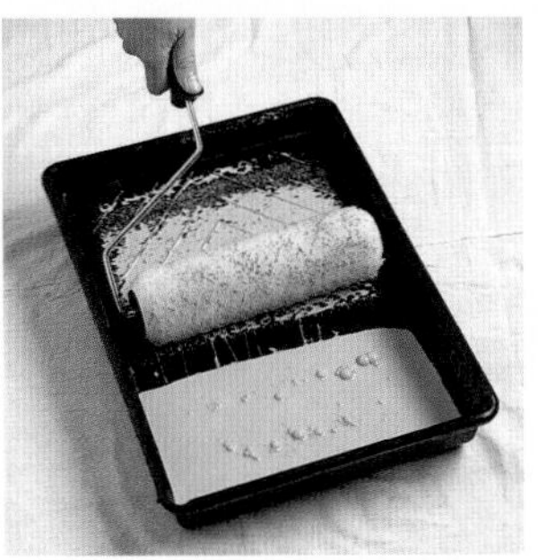

1 Pour the emulsion paint into the paint tray reservoir – it should be about a third full. Dip the roller sleeve into the paint and roll it firmly up and down the tray's ribbed incline to spread the paint evenly. Don't overload the sleeve or paint will splatter everywhere.

2 Move the roller over the wall surface, using random strokes applied with a light, even pressure. Try not to work too fast or you will create a fine mist of paint spray. Each time the roller is dipped in the paint, move it to an adjacent unpainted area and work your way back to the painted area in overlapping strokes to blend in the wet edges.

Using paint pads

Paint pads come in different sizes. They are flat and rectangular with closely packed, short fibres bonded to a foam backing strip, which makes the pad flexible. Pads are good for painting large areas with liquid paint – the bigger the pad, the faster you cover the surface. They make less spray and mess than rollers, but they do need reloading more often. Use a paint pad tray with a built-in ribbed roller on which excess paint can be removed.

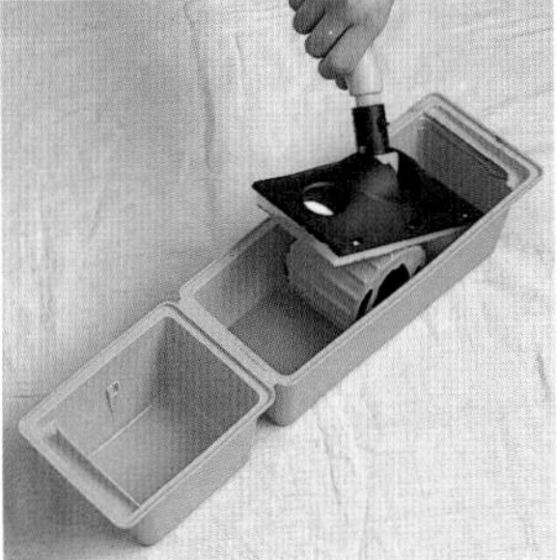

1 Pour the paint into the paint pad tray, then draw the pad over the built-in roller to distribute the paint evenly and remove any excess – a paint pad will give a patchy finish if it is loaded unevenly, and will drip if there is too much paint.

2 Start painting near a corner and work in strips about four times the width of your pad. Keeping the pad flat on the wall, move it up and down the surface with a gentle scrubbing action.

SAFETY FIRST

Oil- and solvent-based paints give off fumes that are harmful to your health and to the environment. Always make sure there is very good ventilation while applying them, and while they dry. Avoid using them on large areas like walls and ceilings.

WALLS SIMPLE PAINT EFFECTS

YOU CAN DO IT

Shielding ceilings and walls When working close to the ceiling or into corners, shield them off with a piece of stiff thin card.

Sponging, colourwashing and ragging on are simple but stunningly effective decorative techniques that create a finish of hazy, broken colour on walls. They use a mix of dilute emulsion applied over a base coat of matt emulsion that has been allowed to dry. Dilute emulsion has a short drying time, which can cause problems, so make sure the room you plan to decorate is not too hot or dry. It's also a good idea to experiment on a piece of card or an out-of-the-way patch of wall before you start.

Mixing your colours

Matt emulsion is mixed with warm water to make the colours for these effects.

- For **colourwashing**, the colour can be diluted from 1:4 to 1:10
- For **sponging**, it can be as much as a 1:30
- For **ragging on**, anything from 1:5 for bold colour to 1:25 for a soft colour

Not all emulsion paints can be diluted without loss of performance, however, so always check the manufacturer's instructions first. The alternative is to use effects paints, which are widely available. These are specially formulated to have extended drying times and can be used straight from the container.

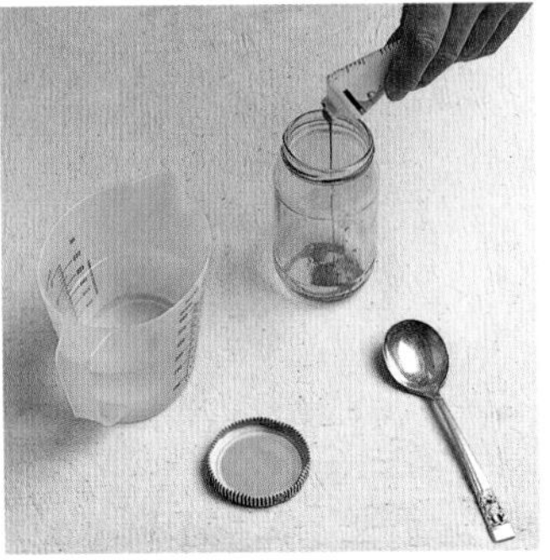

1 Pour a measured amount of emulsion into a mixing jar and add the right amount of warm water.

2 Secure the lid, cover with an old towel – just in case – and shake well.

Sponging

Sponging is the fastest way to add interest to a dull wall or hide imperfections on its surface. If you make a mistake, simply sponge on some of the base colour to cover it. You need a natural sea sponge, an old plate or paint tray, a cloth and colour mix in two or three colours.

1 Pour a little of the first colour mix on to the paint tray or plate and dip the sponge into it. Test the colour on a piece of paper and experiment to achieve the desired effect before you start on the wall.

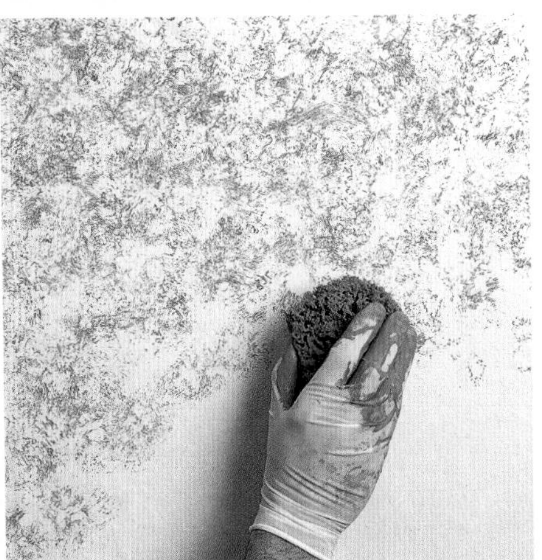

2 Gently pat the sponge on the wall, constantly changing the angle and position of your hand and the sponge so you get an even but random build-up of colour. Step back from time to time to look at your work. One 'loaded' sponge should cover about 8 sq m, producing a light colour effect.

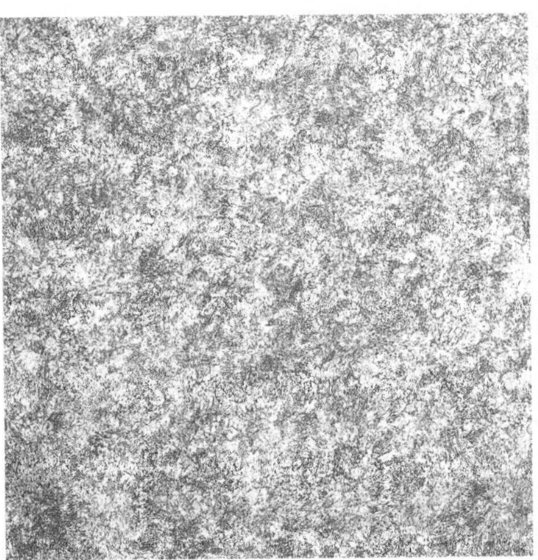

3 For a dense effect, go over the wall several times, gradually building up the colour. If using a second and third colour, add the next one immediately, washing and drying the sponge between colours.

YOU CAN DO IT

Throwaway gloves

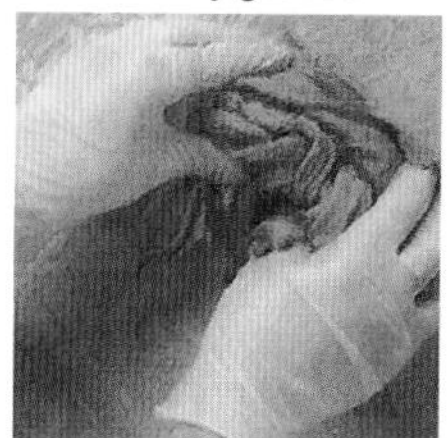

Applying paint effects is a messy business. These paints are water-soluble, so do wash off easily, but it's still a good idea to wear throwaway decorator's gloves, made from thin rubber or plastic.

Colourwashing

Colourwashing is probably the simplest paint effect. Using a decorator's sponge, and an old plate or paint tray containing the colour mix of your choice, you can cover a large wall very quickly with a wash of textured colour. For a deeper hue, apply two or more coats of the same or different tones.

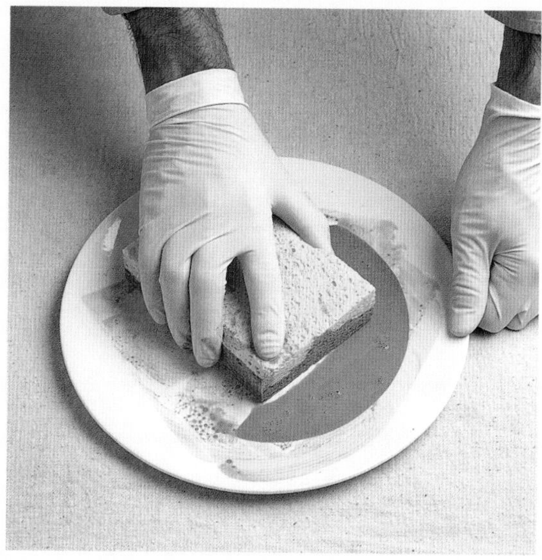

1 Pour your colour mix on to an old plate or paint tray and work it into the sponge.

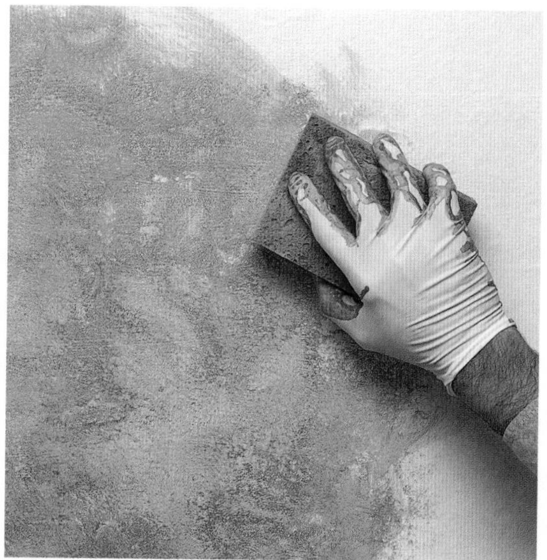

2 Apply it to the wall with either circular shapes, random patterns or regular horizontal or vertical movements. Work quickly in areas of about 1 sq m at a time, and try to maintain a wet edge. If you're adding more colours, allow the paint to dry between coats.

Ragging on

This paint effect is quite literally dabbed on the wall with a rag, and can range from a soft, subtly textured look to a bold, eye-catching vibrant finish. You need pieces of clean cotton or cotton and polyester rag, about 300mm square and with no seams or hems, a plastic tub and colour mix in two or more colours.

1 Transfer your first colour mix to a plastic tub. Immerse the rag in the mix, then squeeze out.

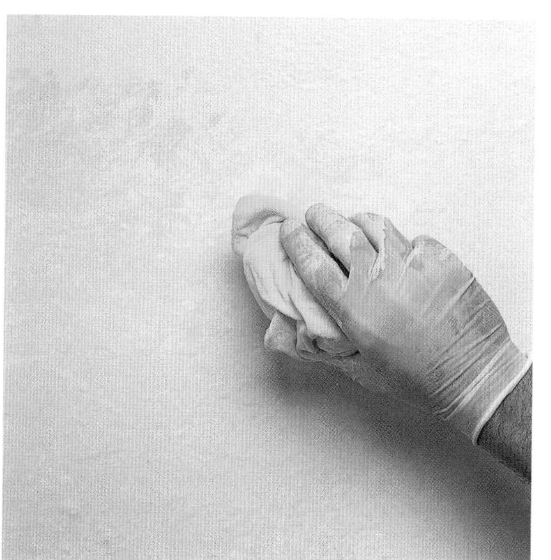

2 Scrunch the rag into a ball. Don't fold it or your patterns will be too regular. Gently pat the colour onto the wall, layering and building up the colour as you like. When the rag starts to dry out – after about 1 sq m – immerse it in the colour mix as before. Leave the colour to dry before adding a second or third colour in the same way.

IDEAL TOOL

Ragging roller

Even easier than a rag is a special ragging roller, which looks like a roller with a rag wrapped around it.

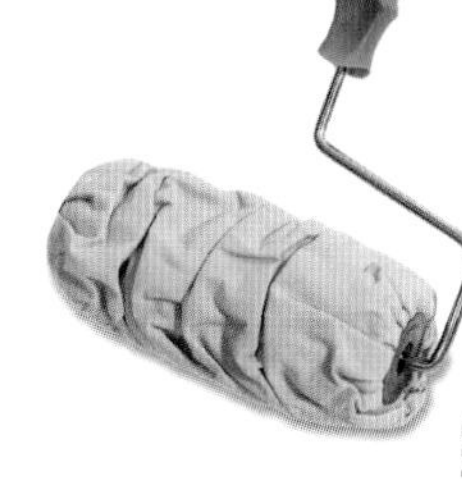

WALLS ADVANCED PAINT EFFECTS

To create elaborate paint effects, you need more time to work on the designs before the paint dries. Water-based acrylic glaze, also known as scumble glaze, doesn't dry quite as fast as dilute emulsion. It gives you enough time to work on textured designs, using techniques such as dragging, stippling and bagging. Buy a ready-mixed coloured glaze or make your own by mixing uncoloured acrylic glaze with water, then tinting it. The glaze is applied over a base coat of vinyl silk emulsion or eggshell paint.

Mixing your own glaze

Mix uncoloured acrylic glaze and water in a jam jar to roughly a 4:1 ratio, then tint it to the colour you want with acrylic paint. Secure the lid and shake well. If using a specially formulated clear base with emulsion, mix it with the emulsion paint of your choice to a ratio of two parts base to one part emulsion. Test the colour and also the 'workability' of the glaze to make sure it is not too thick.

Dragging

Dragging is a decorative technique that gives a softly striped effect on walls that have been painted with silk emulsion or eggshell paint. The glaze is applied with a decorator's paintbrush or a short-haired roller and then dragged with a mixed bristle dragging brush or a large flogging brush. You will need an old plate or a paint tray and an old towel. Dragging is equally effective on doors and wooden panelling.

1 Pour the mixed glaze on to an old plate or a paint tray and apply it to the wall with a decorator's paintbrush or a short-haired roller. Don't paint the whole wall at once – cover an area about 600mm wide at a time.

2 Slightly dampen a dragging or flogging brush with glaze. Starting from a top corner, drag the brush down through the glaze, at an angle of about 30° from the wall. Continue down the wall as far as possible in a single stroke to avoid making joins.

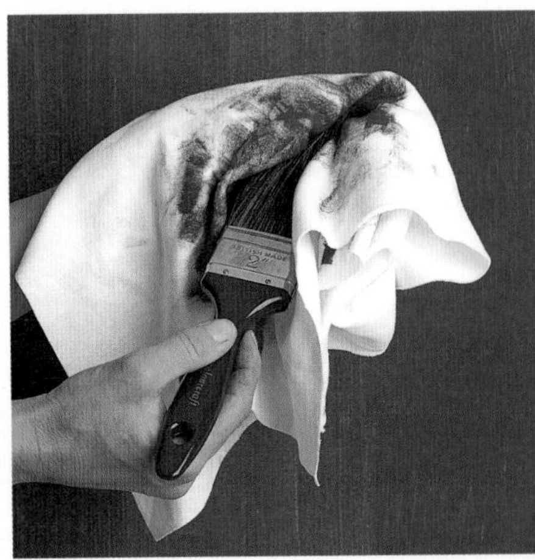

3 Wipe the brush from time to time on an old towel to keep the bristles dry.

4 The brush only leaves a mark when it first touches the surface. If you have several join marks down the wall, drag up from the floor to cover them over. In this way the only marks visible will be at the bottom of the wall.

Stippling

Stippling creates soft, shaded colour – glaze and base coat merge with no obvious brushstrokes or texture. You'll get the best effect if you stipple a strong glaze colour over a pale base coat of eggshell. You will need a paint tray, decorator's brush or a short-haired roller, a stippling brush and an old towel.

1 Apply the glaze randomly to the wall, using either a decorator's paintbrush or a short-haired roller. Dip the bristle tips of the stippling brush into a little of the glaze in the paint tray.

2 Keeping the bristles at right angles to the wall, pound the surface to make imprints in the glaze. Control the depth of colour as you stipple the pattern by wiping the build-up of glaze from the brush with a towel.

YOU CAN DO IT

Testing colours
You can choose from a range of acrylic paint colours, but you may need to mix several in order to achieve the shade you want. Add some of your mixed colour to a small quantity of glaze on an old saucer and test it on an out-of-the-way part of the wall – you don't want to end up with a large quantity of glaze that is not the right colour. You need very little colour for these special paint effects, so you can use the tiny paint colour testing tubes, tins or pots as your colour source.

Bagging

Every household has plenty of them: plastic bags. Scrunched up, they are just what you need for this dappled paint effect. Alternatively, you can get the same effect by using a special bagging roller, which looks like a roller with a plastic bag wrapped around it. You will also need a decorator's paintbrush or a short-haired roller.

IDEAL TOOL

Plastic bag
Use your B&Q plastic bag as a decorating tool! But do remember to turn it inside out as the glaze may dissolve the print and ruin your work.

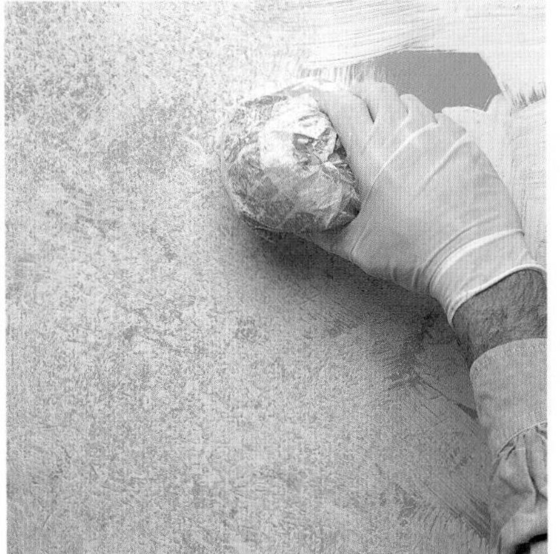

1 Apply the glaze randomly with a decorator's paintbrush or short-haired roller. Turn your plastic bag inside out, then scrunch it up so that it's comfortable to hold. Gently pat the surface with the bag, which removes some of the glaze to leave an attractive grainy pattern. Reform the bag from time to time to create new and original patterns.

2 For a softer effect, clean the glaze off the bag from time to time with a towel or rag.

WALLS WALLPAPERING BASICS

Wallpapering is usually the final stage of decorating, as the ceiling, doors, windows and skirting-board should be painted first. Wallpaper allows you to change the colour, pattern and texture of your walls with immediate effect, and you can choose from an extensive range. Standard patterned wallpaper is ideal for most wall surfaces. It's available as traditional paste-the-back paper, or ready-pasted, or the newer paste-the-wall types. Textured wallpaper has a built-in relief pattern, making it suitable for rough wall surfaces. Vinyl paper can be wiped with a damp cloth, so it is good for kitchens and bathrooms.

TOOLS MATERIALS

- **dust sheets**
- **step-ladder**
- **bucket**
- **paper-hanging brush**
- **pasting brush**
- **pasting table**
- **tape measure**
- **plumb line**
- **pencil**
- **wallpaper scissors**
- **sponge**

- sugar soap
- size
- wallpaper paste
- wallpaper

Planning

Expect to make a mess! Move furniture and soft furnishings out of the room, and cover carpets and anything that can't be moved with dust sheets. Most wallpaper can be papered over provided it is in good condition (but remove relief or washable paper). If it's in a poor state, strip it off and line the walls. You can paper directly over painted surfaces, but be sure to wash them thoroughly with sugar soap first. Your walls must be clean, dry and smooth before you can begin.

- Use the chart below to estimate the amount of wallpaper you are going to need – a standard roll of wallpaper is approximately 10.05m long and 530mm wide. When you measure around the room include the windows and doors – this allows for wastage when the paper is trimmed.
- Allow for extra when using a paper with a large repeat pattern – the size of the pattern is usually stated on the roll label.
- Make sure all the rolls you buy have the same batch number, to be certain the colours will match.
- Coat the wall surfaces with size, a special sealer that prevents them soaking up the wallpaper paste. Use a size recommended by the paste manufacturer. Or you can seal the walls with dilute wallpaper paste painted on with a large decorating or pasting brush.

Lining the walls

Lining paper helps to cover imperfections, giving you a smoother surface for the wallpaper. Lining paper is pasted and hung in the same way as wallpaper. Leave the lining paper to dry (this can take up to 12 hours) before applying the wallpaper. When hanging lining paper, always use a size and paste that are compatible with the manufacturer's recommended adhesive for the wallpaper.

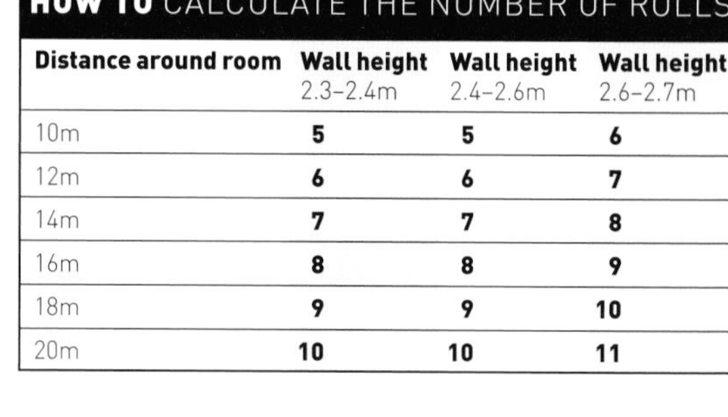

HOW TO CALCULATE THE NUMBER OF ROLLS

Distance around room	Wall height 2.3–2.4m	Wall height 2.4–2.6m	Wall height 2.6–2.7m
10m	**5**	**5**	**6**
12m	**6**	**6**	**7**
14m	**7**	**7**	**8**
16m	**8**	**8**	**9**
18m	**9**	**9**	**10**
20m	**10**	**10**	**11**

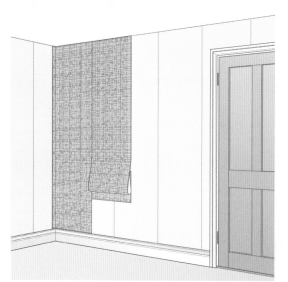

Hanging lining paper horizontally

Wallpaper is usually hung vertically, so it's quite a good idea to apply the lining paper horizontally – that way the two lots of seams will not fall in the same place.

Hanging lining paper vertically

If you do want to hang the lining paper vertically, start from the place where you are going to hang the first length of wallpaper and hang a half-width of lining paper. Continue with full widths across the rest of the wall.

Cutting the paper

Wallpaper is expensive, so don't waste it by cutting the lengths too long or too short. Measure the wall at your starting point, from the ceiling to the top of the skirting board. If you are going to cut several lengths of paper before you start hanging it, check that the height of the wall is the same all the way around the room.

1 Measure the height of the 'all in several places around ne room with a steel tape neasure. Add 100mm to the ongest measurement, to allow r trimming at the top and ottom. Check which way round ne wallpaper pattern goes and here any pattern should be in elation to the top of the wall. nroll the paper on the pasting able, pattern-side down, and raw a straight line across the vidth at the measured point. sing wallpaper scissors, cut ne first length.

2 Turn the cut length over. Unroll the next length, place it edge-to-edge with the first length, and match the pattern. Use the cut length as a guide to cut the second length. Continue cutting several lengths, numbering them at the top corner on the wrong side so that you know the hanging order. Mark the hanging direction, too.

Pasting the paper

The most common type of wallpaper is the traditional kind that you paste yourself. Use the paste recommended by the paper manufacturer and mix it according to the guidelines. You can lay several lengths of paper on top of each other on the pasting table and paste and hang them one after the other.

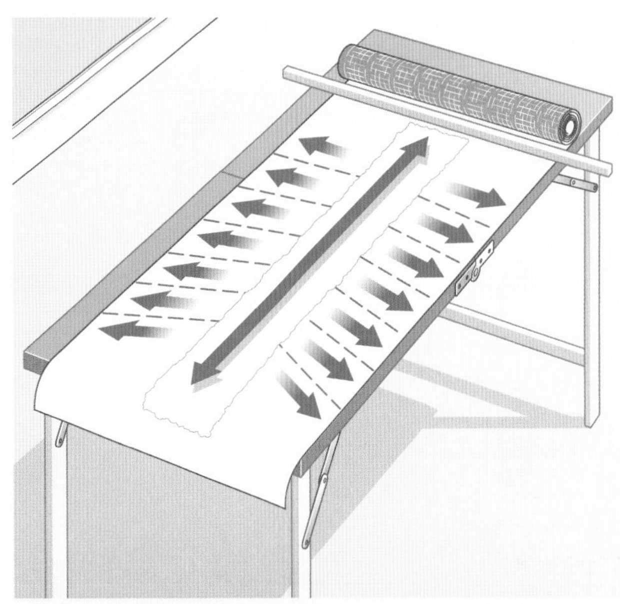

Lay the cut length on the pasting table (pattern-side down), so that the paper hangs over the end of the table. If you are pasting a shorter length, use a weight to stop it rolling up. Load the pasting brush and wipe off excess paste. Paste along the centre of the paper, working the paste from the middle to the edges in a herringbone pattern (see diagram above). It is easier to spot areas you have missed if you use coloured paste (which dries clear). Between lengths, wipe any paste spills off the table with a clean, damp sponge.

YOU CAN DO IT

Paste brush rest

Most new pasting brushes have a lug at the handle end which you can rest on the rim of the bucket when you want to take a break, so that the brush hangs down inside it. If you have older brushes, tie a length of string taut across the rim, from one handle end to the other, and rest your brush on the string.

Folding the pasted paper

Most lengths of wallpaper are longer than the pasting table. When the ength on the table has been pasted, it needs to be loosely folded over n to itself in a concertina shape. You can then carry on pasting the est of the length without paste getting on to the patterned side.

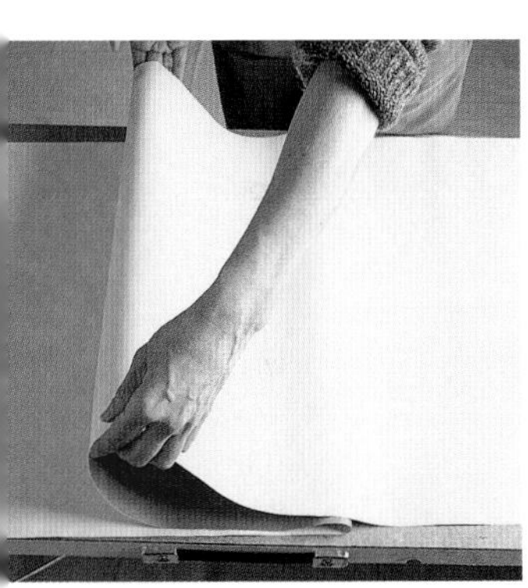

1 When the paper covering the able has been pasted, fold it over on itself, taking care not to crease t, and start a concertina. Move the concertina to one end of the table, using a weight such as a large brush to stop the unpasted end rolling up.

2 Paste the entire length, folding the paper as you go. Lift up the completed concertina of paper and set it aside to allow the paste to soak into the paper for as long as the manufacturer recommends. The paper needs time to expand before it is hung. Soaking prevents bubbles appearing as the paper continues to expand on the wall. In the meantime, paste more lengths.

WALLS HANGING WALLPAPER

Walls and corners are rarely straight, so don't rely on them as a guide when you are hanging paper. Instead, mark a vertical guideline on the wall, using a plumb line or a spirit level, before you hang the first length. Always read the instructions to see if there are any specific requirements for your paper. Check the markings you have made on the back when cutting the paper, to make sure that you hang the lengths in the correct order and the right way up.

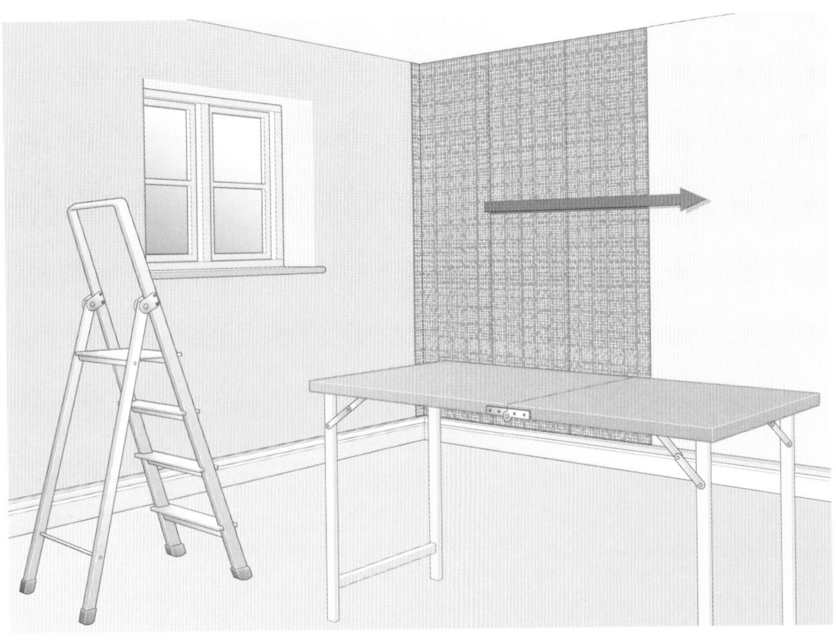

Where to start

- Try to hang the first length of wallpaper on a wall that has neither door nor window, so you can hang a full length from the ceiling to the top of the skirting-board.
- Choose a wall to the right of the window if you are right-handed, to the left if you are left-handed.
- Work away from the window, so that the paper edges will not cast a shadow if they overlap slightly.
- If your wallpaper has a large pattern, you should hang the first length over a fireplace or other focal point and then work away from it in both directions, so that the design is central and symmetrical. Complete this area before papering the rest of the room.

TOOLS MATERIALS

- **step-ladder**
- **tape measure**
- **plumb line or spirit level**
- **pencil**
- **pasting table**
- **paper-hanging brush**
- **wallpaper scissors**
- **seam roller**

- lengths of pasted wallpaper

Hanging the first length

You should always take your time hanging paper, but be particularly careful with the first length – it's very important to get that one straight.

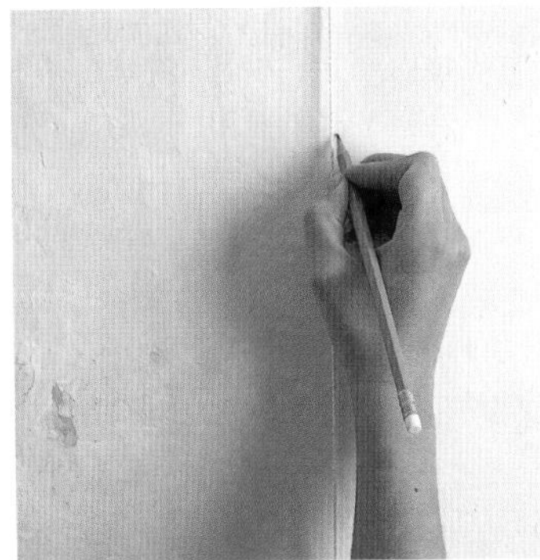

1 To position the first length of wallpaper, draw a line from ceiling to skirting-board 480mm out from the corner, using a plumb line (see IDEAL TOOLS) or a spirit level. This allows a 50mm overlap on to the window wall.

2 Position the first pasted length at the top of the wall with its right-hand edge running down the vertical line. This is easier if you can keep the left-hand edge of the paper off the wall. Make sure about 50mm of excess paper is left above the top of the wall for trimming. Hold the paper at both sides and don't let the lower paper drop suddenly, as it may tear or stretch.

3 Once the right-hand edge is positioned, smooth the paper down with a paper-hanging brush. Work from the centre of the paper to the edges, making sure that there are no bubbles. Check the edge stays on the pencil mark.

Plumb line
A plumb line will give you a true vertical guideline. Most plumb lines are a length of builder's string with a pointed weight (a 'bob') attached to the end. Hammer a small nail into the wall near the ceiling, and hang the plumb line. Use a pencil to mark the wall down the length of the line, then join up the marks with a ruler.

Seam roller
This small, narrow roller is just the right size for running down the wallpaper seams to make sure they are flat and sticking to the wall.

Cutting guide
Instead of creasing the paper at the skirting-board and trimming it with scissors, you can use an L-shaped piece of metal called a cutting guide. Hold the guide against the skirting-board (or picture rail or coving), tucking the paper into the crease of the guide, then trim the paper with a sharp knife.

4 With the first length in place, crease the top and bottom of the paper against the ceiling and skirting-board junctions. Gently pull the paper away from the wall and cut along the creases with wallpaper scissors. Brush the trimmed edges back into place.

5 Butt the next length against the previous one, matching the pattern at eye level. When two or three pieces are in place, run the seam roller lightly down the joins. Don't press down on heavily textured paper or you'll flatten the pattern.

YOU CAN DO IT

Keeping scissors clean

Occasionally dip your wallpaper scissors into a jar of clean, warm water to loosen the build-up of paste.

Hanging paste-the-wall paper

There is one type of wallpaper – known as 'paste-the-wall' or 'dry-hanging' paper – that is hung 'dry' because the wall is pasted rather than the paper. The paper features a special backing that does not expand when wet, which means you can hang it straight from the roll on to the pre-pasted wall. Don't paste the entire wall before starting to hang the paper. Just paste one section at a time.

This type of paper peels off easily, so there's no need for steaming or soaking when you want to redecorate. Simply lift a corner at the bottom of the wall and pull steadily upwards.

1 This paper can come in a variety of widths, so measure your roll, allowing a 50mm overlap on to the next wall. Use a plumb line or spirit level to draw a vertical line marking this width from the ceiling to the skirting-board. Using a pasting brush or a roller, apply a generous, even layer of strong wallpaper paste to the wall where the first length of paper will hang. Make sure that the pasted area is slightly wider than the width of the roll.

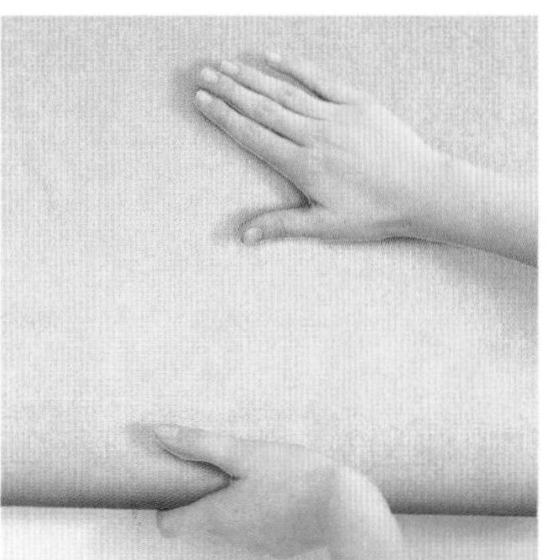

2 Apply the wallpaper directly from the roll (or, if you prefer, measure and cut lengths as for other wallpapers). Slide the paper into position, aligning the right-hand edge with the vertical marked line. The left edge will wrap around the corner.

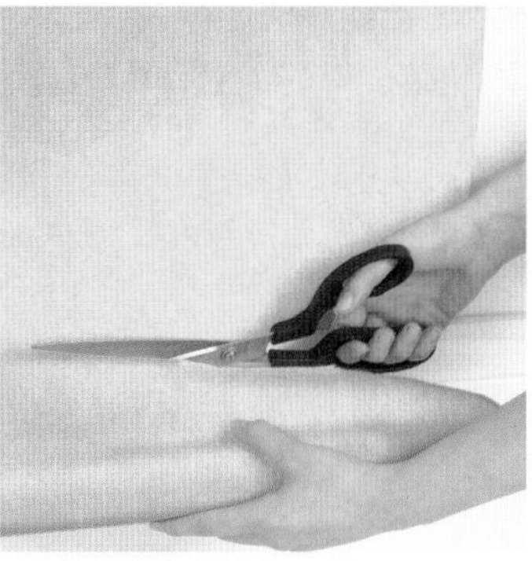

3 Smooth the paper with a brush or damp sponge, pushing any bubbles to the edges. Do not attempt to remove small blisters – they will disappear when the paper has fully dried out. Trim the top and bottom with sharp scissors or a metal rule and craft knife. Repeat the process for each length, ensuring that the edges exactly meet and the pattern is matched.

WALLS PAPERING CORNERS AND DETAILS

You will probably have started hanging your wallpaper on a straight wall without obstacles, but there's no way of papering all the way around a room without tackling corners and fittings such as light switches and sockets. If you know the right technique, however, you can paper neatly from one wall to the next in a smooth operation.

Internal corners

When you reach a corner, it's much easier to hang a length of paper that has been cut into two vertical strips than to fold the paper into the corner – especially when you are papering a wall that is slightly crooked and your corner is not completely square. Measure and cut the paper so that it reaches slightly beyond the corner, then paste the off-cut over the overlap.

1 Measure the distance between the edge of the last hung length and the corner, at the top, bottom and middle of the wall. Using the widest measurement, allow an extra 25mm for turning on to the next wall. Cut a length of paper to this width, reserving the off-cut for papering the first length of the adjoining wall. Paste and hang the length, butting the paper to the edge of the previous strip. Align the pattern at eye level and allow the extra 25mm to stick lightly to the next wall. Use a paper-hanging brush to smooth the paper into the internal corner.

2 Make sure that the paper is firmly pressed against the wall by running the seam roller along its edge. Wipe excess paste from the roller before it dries. If any creases have formed, tear the paper and overlap the pieces so they lie flat – a tear will show less than if you cut the paper (although it is better to cut vinyl paper).

3 Measure the width of the reserved off-cut and hang the plumb line that distance from the corner to find a vertical line. Make pencil marks behind the vertical line at intervals down the wall. This will give you a completely vertical edge for starting the next wall.

4 Hang the off-cut with its right-hand edge aligned with the pencil marks, overlapping the paper turned from the previous wall. If the paper is patterned, make sure that you match the two pieces as closely as possible.

External corners

Some rooms have external corners – round a chimney breast, for instance – as well as internal ones. They are treated in a similar way: the paper is hung slightly beyond the corner, then an off-cut is pasted next to or over the overlap. Measure at the top, bottom and middle of the wall, as before, in case the wall is not completely straight.

1 Continue papering the wall until there is less than the width of a length of paper before you reach the corner. Measure from the edge of the last full width to the corner, then allow an extra 25mm for the turn on to the next wall. Cut a length of paper to this width, reserving the off-cut. Hang the length as far as the corner and bend the excess paper around the corner on to the next wall. Smooth away any bubbles with the paper-hanging brush.

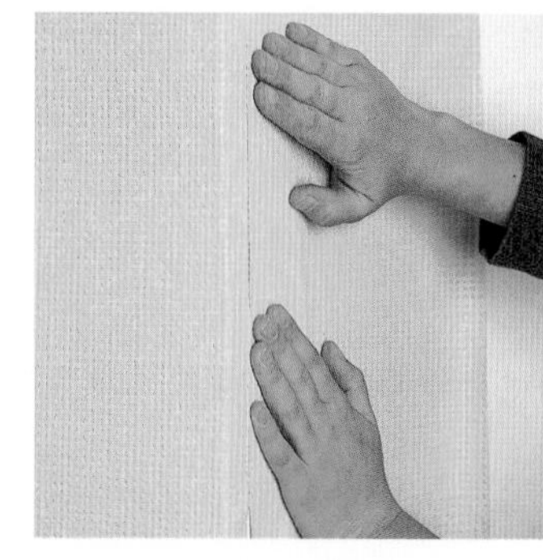

2 Run a seam roller up and down the edge of the overhang to make sure that it is firmly stuck to the wall. Hang the reserved off-cut next to the overlap, matching the pattern and butting the joins. If the walls are not straight, it may be easier to overlap rather than butt the joins – make sure that the pattern matches up exactly. Smooth along the overlap with the seam roller. Continue to hang lengths until you reach the internal corner. Before you paper the next wall, use the plumb line or spirit level to get a vertical start.

Papering around light switches or sockets

Every room has light switches and sockets – there's no avoiding them, so it's worth knowing how to deal with them. If you don't do it properly, you'll notice every time you turn on the light. Always switch off the electricity at the mains before you start work.

Make sure the electricity is off. ang the wallpaper from the top of e wall straight over the switch or cket. Brush gently over the fitting th a dry paper-hanging brush to ake a slight impression on the per, but take care not to tear it. olding the paper over the fitting, ake a small pencil mark from ch corner into the centre of the ceplate. Pierce a hole in the paper the centre point with a small pair scissors. Cut the paper to the rners and pull back the flaps.

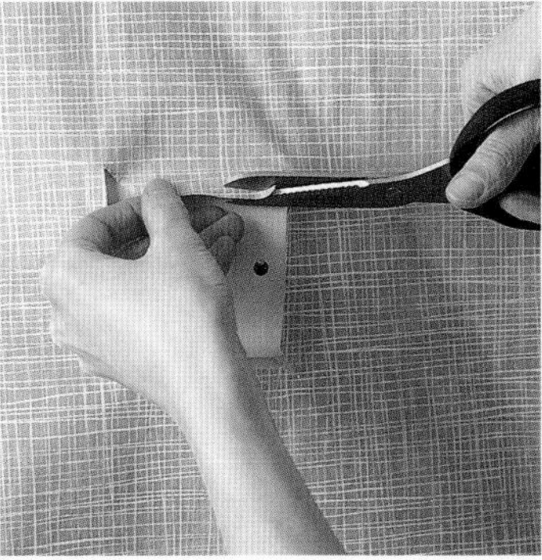

2 Trim the flaps just inside the outer edge of the switch or socket so there is an overlap of about 6mm covering the fitting. Partially unscrew the faceplate and pull it about 6mm away from the wall.

3 Carefully ease the faceplate through the hole in the paper. Use the brush to push the trimmed edges gently behind the faceplate and smooth away any air bubbles. Put the faceplate back in place and secure the screws. Let the paste dry before turning on the power.

YOU CAN DO IT

Wallplug markers

Unscrew all wall fixings before papering, leaving the wallplugs in place. Mark the position of each one by pushing a matchstick (with the head broken off) into the plug, leaving it slightly proud. As you hang the paper, bring it over the marked position and press the paper on to the matchstick, so it pierces the paper. Smooth the paper with a paper-hanging brush. When the paper is quite dry, remove the matchstick and replace the fitting.

3orders

any wallpaper manufacturers produce borders and friezes to mplement their wallpaper. These can be applied to a painted or papered ırface (but not a heavily embossed one) for a decorative border or frame, create a dado or picture rail effect, or simply to disguise a less-than-erfect line at the ceiling by making a patterned cornice.

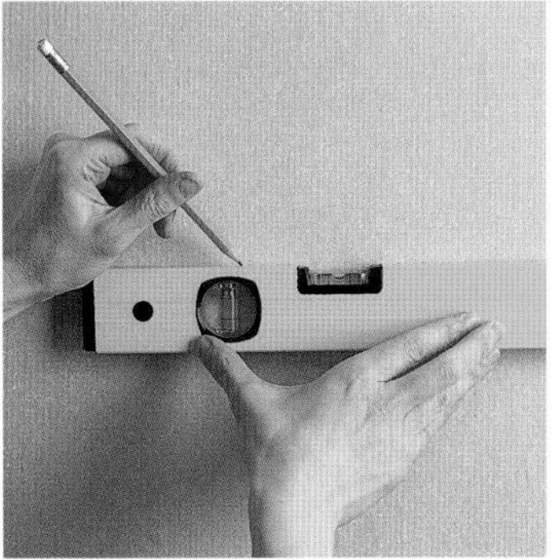

1 Use a spirit level and pencil to mark a horizontal line around the room at the place where you want the border. Measure the width of the first wall and add 50mm to each end. Cut a piece of border this length. Border adhesive dries quickly, so do one wall at a time, rather than trying to go right around the room in one go.

2 Apply border adhesive to the back, brushing it over the edge and folding the border like a concertina. Take care not to crease the folds. Leave it to soak in for the required time. Starting at a corner, apply the border to the wall, carefully releasing the folds and lining up the top edge of the border with the horizontal pencil line. Smooth it into place with the paper-hanging brush.

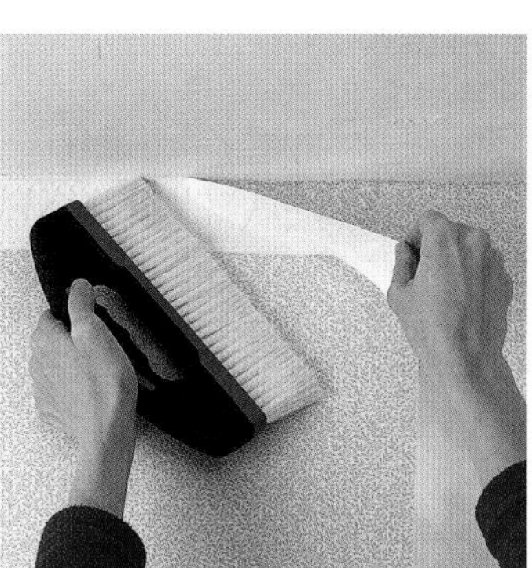

3 For a cornice, apply the border along the line between the wall and ceiling, releasing the folds of the pasted concertina as you work along the wall. Smooth it into place with the paper-hanging brush. Wipe any excess paste from the wall or ceiling with a damp cloth.

WALLS PAPERING DIFFICULT AREAS

Wallpapering around obstacles such as windows and doors is a job that needs special care. It is best to cut lengths of wallpaper roughly to size before you apply the paste so that the amount of pasted paper is manageable.

Windows and door frames

When you are trying to trim around a frame, allow for at least 30mm overhang of paper. It is better to make small cuts and to try to fit the paper several times than cut away too much in one go. It helps if you apply size to the wall because this will make it easier to peel back and reposition the paper. The paper will be soft and tear easily when pasted – small scissors are the best tool for cutting around fiddly corners and mouldings.

1 Cut lengths of wallpaper roughly the right size to go around the frame. Paste and hang the paper in the ordinary way as far as the frame. Push the paper into the frame surround with the paper-hanging brush.

2 Smooth the paper on to the frame with your fingers so that the outline of the moulding shows through.

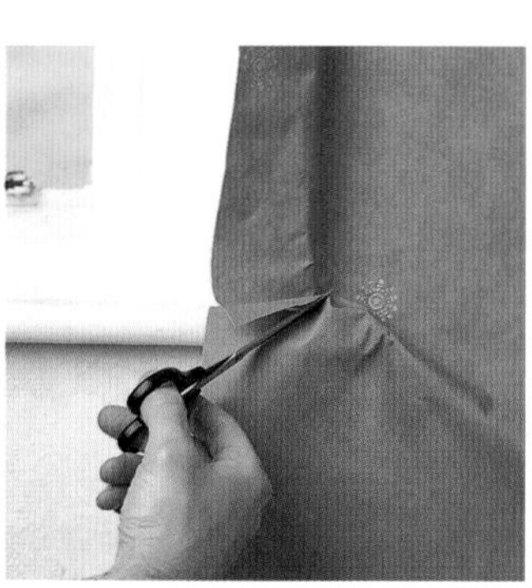

3 Use small scissors to cut diagonally towards the corner edge of the frame. Peel back the paper and cut in with short v-shaped cuts, peeling and repositioning as necessary. Repeat this process until the paper fits around the corner.

4 Smooth the paper with the paper-hanging brush, using the bristles to press the paper into the corner. Make diagonal cuts in towards the next part of the moulding.

5 Continue snipping around the corner of the frame. If necessary, press in with your fingers to mould the outline in the paper. Pull the paper away and cut along the outline.

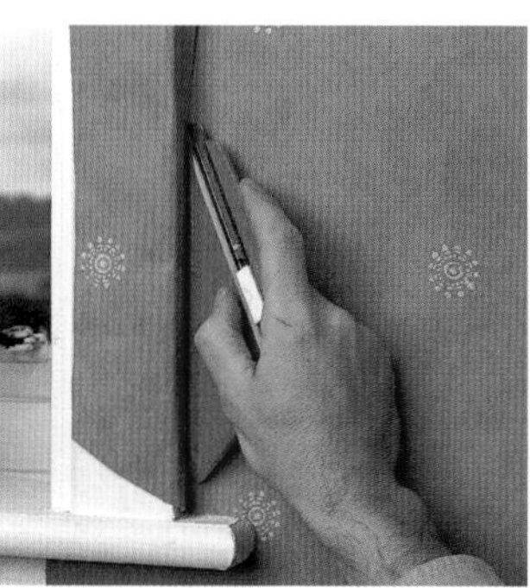

6 Use a smoothing/cutting tool (see IDEAL TOOL) to cut the paper to fit right up against the frame. If the paste on the paper starts to dry before you have finished trimming, apply extra paste to the wall rather than the paper.

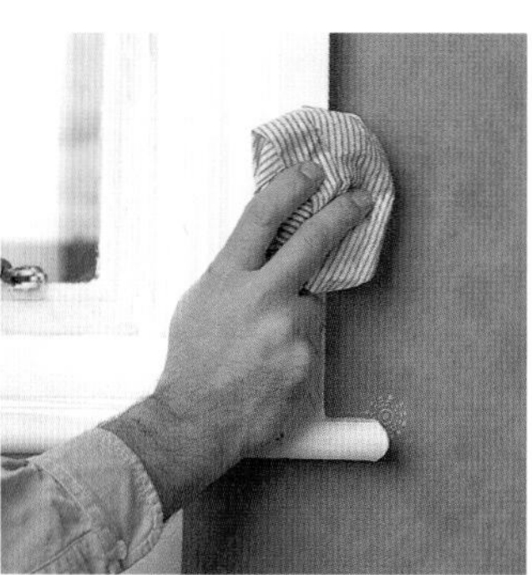

7 Wipe the paste off the woodwork before it can dry and become much harder to remove.

IDEAL TOOL

Smoothing/cutting tool
A combination wallpaper smoothing/cutting tool will help you cut paper close to a frame for a good fit. It works best along straight edges rather than around curves. Smooth the paper into a recess or corner so that it's easier to push the cutting knife along the crease to cut the paper. Peel away the unwanted paper.

INSIDE THE HOME

Radiators

Ideally, you should drain a radiator and take it off the wall so that you can paper behind it. If that is not possible, turn off the heat and wait for the radiator to cool.

Hang the length of paper on the wall, letting it cover the radiator. Mark the position of the fixing brackets on the paper, then cut from the bottom up to the pencil marks. Cut out a rectangular shape to accommodate the bracket. Push the paper into place each side of the supporting bracket using a narrow radiator paint roller. Trim the paper at the skirting.

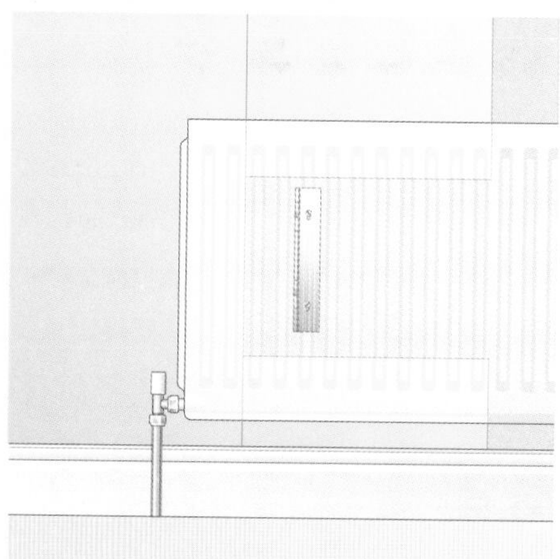

Alternatively, cut the paper so that it covers approximately 150mm of wall behind the top of the radiator. Cut another length to fit the gap at the bottom of the radiator.

YOU CAN DO IT

Roll it

Smoothing the paper behind the radiator is a fiddly job. First of all hoover out the inevitable cobwebs and dust, and then use a clean and dry radiator paint roller to push, guide and smooth the wallpaper into place.

Papering stairwells

Choose a good quality wallpaper with a non-matching pattern, as hanging long lengths can be difficult – they tear easily and tend to stretch. You are working with heavy lengths of pasted paper: if possible, get someone to stand on the stairs and hold the bulk of the paper while you hang the top part.

Making a platform

You need to be able to reach both the head wall and the well wall from a safe working platform (see diagram). Place a pair of steps on the top landing, lean a ladder against the head wall, with the ladder feet resting against a riser halfway down the stairs, and lay a scaffold board between them. Wrap the end of the ladder in a cloth to protect the wall. Tie the board to the ladders with rope to stop them slipping. Use one board on top of another if the gap between the steps and the ladder is more than 1.5m.

Hanging the paper

Paper the longest drop first. Cut the required length, remembering that the skirting will be at an angle. Begin attaching the paper at the top of the wall, allowing the folded length to hang. Unfold it as you work down the wall. If you have someone helping you, they can fix the lower half in place. If the stairwell is deep, you'll need to remove the ladder and place one end of the scaffold board on a stair tread and the other on steps at the bottom of the stairs so you can reach the lower half of the wall.

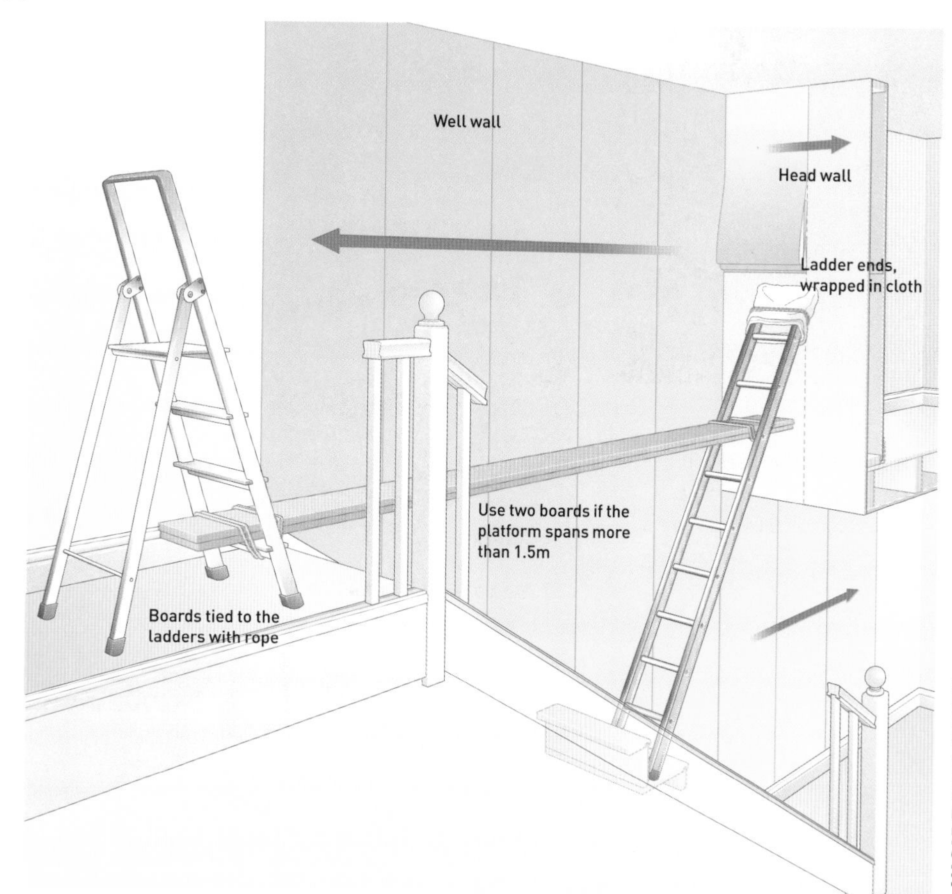

Tiling is a skilled job, but with care there is no reason why you should not produce good results. The surface to be tiled must be clean, dry and flat. Strip wallpaper back to the plaster, remove any crumbling plaster and fill any holes. Allow new plaster to dry out completely – this will take at least two months. Prime porous surfaces with a PVA-based adhesive.

YOU CAN DO IT

Making a tiling gauge rod

A gauge rod is essential for any tiling job, allowing you to work out the positioning of the rows and determine the size of any cut tiles that may be needed at the ends of the rows. A 50mm x 25mm wooden batten is ideal, but any convenient size will do. Make it 1.8m long when tiling a wall, but shorter for a smaller area.

Lay out a line of tiles, inserting tile spacers between them. Place the batten alongside, lining up the end with the edge of the first tile.

Mark the positions of the tiles and gaps on the rod with a pencil. By numbering the tile positions, you will have a quick means of working out how many tiles you will need in each row.

B&Q

Calculating quantities

Most modern ceramic tiles are supplied in packs that will cover 1 sq m. So to work out how many packs you need, simply measure the height and width of the area to be tiled and multiply the figures to obtain the area in square metres. Allow 5–10% extra for cutting and breakages. If your wall has doors, windows or fixed cupboards, calculate their area and subtract this from the total area to be tiled. It may help to draw a rough sketch of the wall and mark all the dimensions on it.

Setting out

Because of the obvious grid pattern formed by the joints between tiles, finding the best starting point for the first row of tiles is crucial. It is no good simply starting in one corner and working across the wall – the corner may not be truly vertical and you may end up with tiny slivers of tile to cut at the far corner. It is much better to centre the grid on the wall, producing cut tiles of equal size at the ends of the rows and an overall symmetrical appearance.

Vertical rows

The first job is to establish the position of the vertical rows. This will allow you to find the starting point, which should be near the centre of the area to be tiled. Measure the width of the area and mark its mid-point with a pencil.

TOOLS MATERIALS

- **tape measure**
- **pencil**
- **gauge rod**
- **spirit level**
- **pipe and cable detector**
- **claw hammer**

- three 50mm x 25mm softwood battens
- tiles
- tile spacers
- 50mm masonry nails

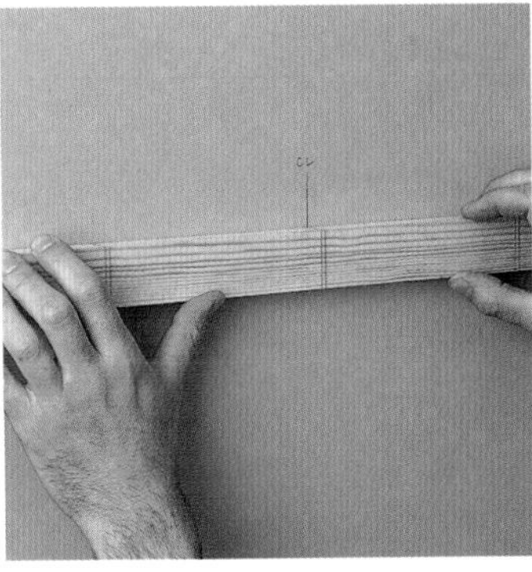

1 Hold your gauge rod (see YOU CAN DO IT, left) so that one of its marks aligns with the centre-point on the wall. Step off the tile positions across the wall.

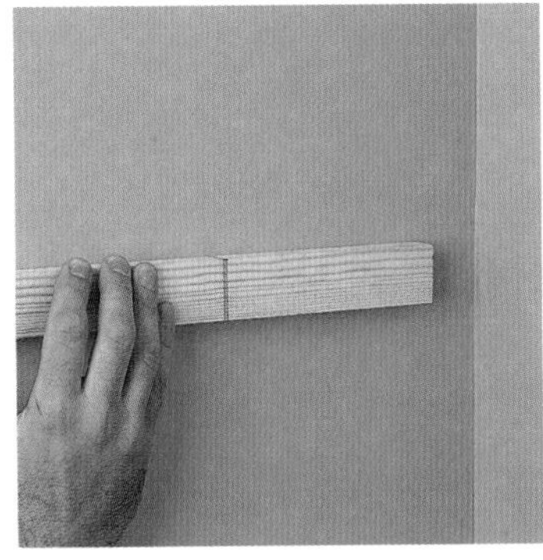

2 When you reach a corner, you will see if you need to cut the last tile in the row to fit. If this will be less than half a tile wide, it is best to reposition the starting point.

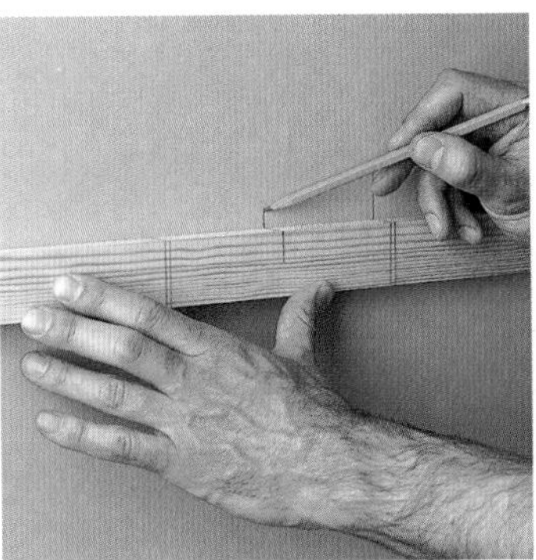

3 Reposition by aligning the rod with the centre-point as before, then pencil a new mark on the wall so that it falls halfway between two tile marks on the rod. This will be the actual starting position for tiling and will ensure that the cut tiles at each end are more than half a tile wide, and that the centre-line of the wall passes through the centre of a tile.

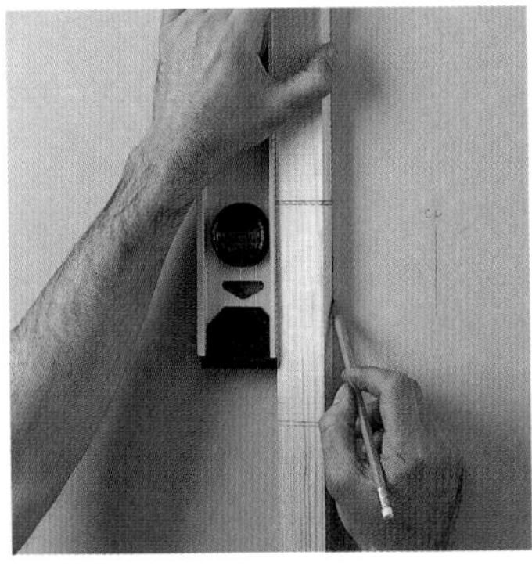

4 Hold the gauge rod against the new wall mark, using a spirit level to ensure that it is truly vertical, and draw a line from top to bottom.

Horizontal rows

Having established the positions of the vertical rows, you can check where the horizontal rows will fall and determine where the first row should be. Use wooden battens nailed to the walls as guides for positioning the tiles and to support them while the adhesive sets, so that they don't slide down the wall.

1 Position the gauge rod against the vertical pencil line on the wall, with its end touching the floor (or skirting). Put a pencil mark on the wall in line with the top tile mark on the rod. Now move the rod up the wall, still following the vertical pencil line, until it touches the ceiling. If you are very lucky, the pencil mark on the wall will align with one of the marks on the rod, indicating that you will not have to cut any tiles for the top and bottom rows. If there is no alignment, however, look at the mark on the rod below the wall mark; halving the distance between them will give you an idea of the size of the cut tiles required. As with the vertical rows, it is best if these are at least half a tile deep. If they will be narrower than this, make a mark on the wall in line with the next mark down on the rod.

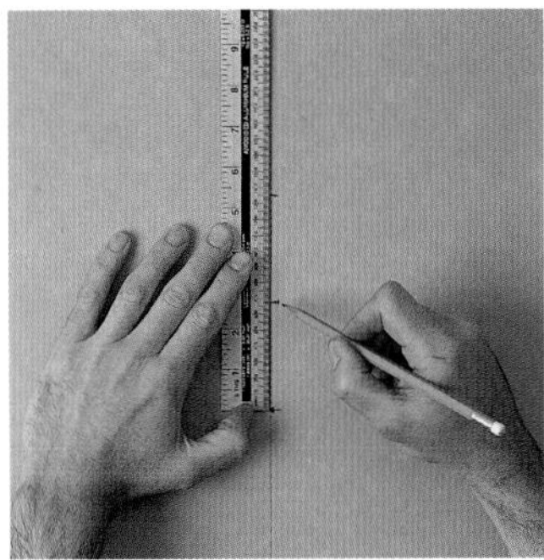

2 Measure the distance between the two marks on the wall and make a third mark exactly halfway between them.

3 Hold your gauge rod so that the end is just clear of the skirting or floor, moving it until one of its marks aligns with the mark you have just made. Make another mark on the wall, level with the foot of the rod. This will be the starting point for the first horizontal row of whole tiles. Use a long straightedge and spirit level to draw a perfectly level line across the wall at this point.

Tiling over tiles
Rather than remove old ceramic tiles, you can simply tile over them. Check that they are all firmly fixed in place, and reglue any that are loose. Make sure that the joint lines of the new tiles do not lie directly over those of the old.

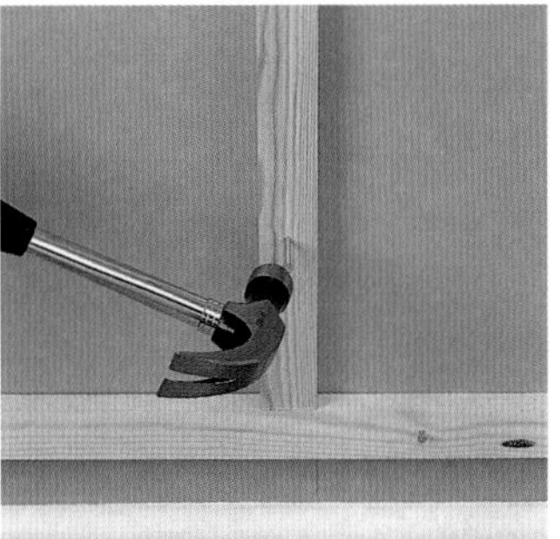

4 Check there are no hidden pipes or cables behind the wall, then nail a 50mm x 25mm batten with its top edge aligned with the horizontal pencil line. Double-check with a spirit level that it is straight. If necessary, use more than one batten to span the wall. Then nail on another, this one aligned to the vertical line. Again, check for pipes or cables first, and ensure it is upright with a spirit level. Leave the nail heads slightly proud so the battens are easy to remove later.

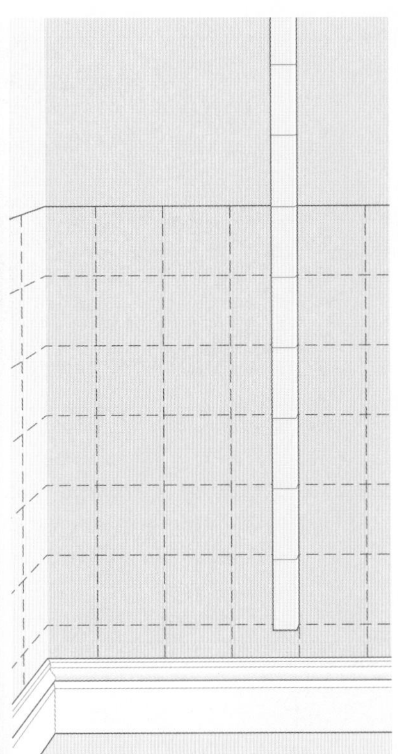

Part-tiled walls

When part-tiling a wall, set out the horizontal tile rows so that the top row consists of whole tiles; this will look much better. Mark the position of the top row on the wall and use the gauge rod to determine the position of the lowest horizontal row. Fill the gap between this and the skirting with cut tiles. Move the top row up or down so that you don't have to cut narrow slivers of tile. You may even be able to avoid cutting tiles altogether, although if the skirting is uneven, some trimming will be necessary. In this case, you will need to start from the lowest point of the skirting. Find this by holding a long straight batten along it, levelled with the aid of a spirit level.

WALLS APPLYING TILES

When you have a large area to tile, it is best to begin in the centre and work outwards, applying all the whole tiles – known as field tiles – first. Then you can fill in around the edges with cut tiles. Work on small areas at a time and pay particular attention to spacing and bedding the tiles properly. Your aim should be to achieve a perfectly flat tiled surface with a grid of uniform-thickness grouted joints.

Applying whole tiles

When applying the field tiles, it is essential to bed them so that their faces are level; any unevenness will spoil the overall effect. Lift any that are high or low, adding or scraping away adhesive as necessary.

TOOLS MATERIALS

- **trowel**
- **notched spreader**
- **sponge**
- **claw hammer**
- **scraper**
- **felt-tip pen**
- **tile cutter**
- **tile file**
- **hacksaw**

- tile adhesive
- tiles
- tile spacers
- corner trim

1 Beginning in the corner formed by the two wall battens, scoop up a quantity of adhesive with a trowel and press it on to the wall. Then spread it out with a notched spreader, working away from the vertical batten with horizontal strokes and holding the blade at an angle of about 45°. The ridges produced will ensure that there is an equal quantity of adhesive behind each tile, making it easier to set them all level. Work on no more than 1 sq m at a time, or the adhesive may begin to harden before all the tiles are in place.

2 Set the first tile into the corner between the two battens, pressing its edges against them and the whole tile firmly against the wall. Add the tile above it and the one next to it, spacing them initially by eye and pushing them firmly into the adhesive.

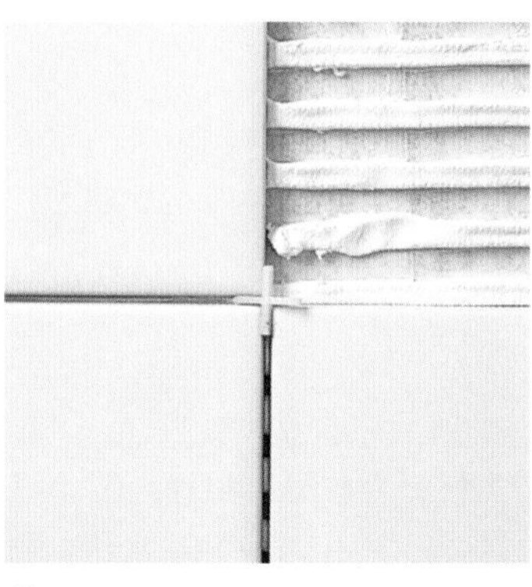

3 Insert a tile spacer into the angles between the tiles and adjust the tile positions as necessary. Plastic tile spacers make it easy to obtain uniform joints. Push them in well so that they can be grouted over. (Alternatively, simply insert one leg of the spacer between two tiles and pull it out once the adhesive has set.)

4 Continue in this way, until you have tiled the area of adhesive. Apply more adhesive and tiles to the wall until you reach the point where you need to finish off with cut tiles. As you work, wipe off splashes of adhesive with a damp sponge. If you allow it to dry, it will be very difficult to remove.

5 Take off the vertical batten by prising out its nails. You may find that you need to remove hardened adhesive that has spread from under the tiles. Do this with the edge of a scraper. Continue adding field tiles to the rest of the wall. After that, you can finish off with cut tiles.

YOU CAN DO IT

Glazed-edge tiles
If you buy tiles with bevelled or rounded glazed edges, you should be able to finish an external corner without using corner trim. Simply tile the first wall as normal, taking the tiles right up to the corner. Then tile the return wall, working away from the corner and allowing the tiles to overlap the edges of the tiles on the first wall. Make sure you provide a gap for grouting by inserting spacers between these tiles and the tiles on the first wall.

Internal corners

Corners between walls are rarely truly vertical, so resist the temptation to cut all the edge tiles to the same size – you will probably find that some do not fit. Instead, measure up for each tile separately. For a summary of tile-cutting techniques, see overleaf.

One way of marking a tile for utting is to hold the tile exactly ver the last whole tile in the row, hen butt another against the all, marking where it overlaps he one below with a felt-tip pen. lternatively, take separate easurements at the top and ottom of the space to be filled.

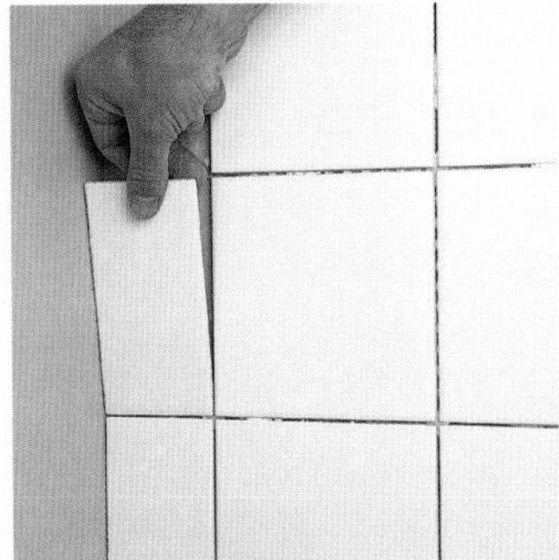

2 After cutting, check the fit of the tile; you can make small adjustments with a tile file. If the adjoining wall is to be tiled, total accuracy is not crucial, since the edges will be hidden by the tiles on the adjoining wall; if only one wall will be tiled, make sure you allow room for a grouted joint at the corner.

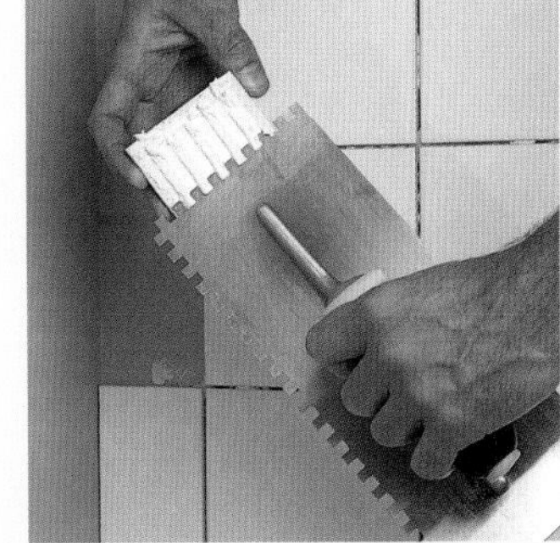

3 Use the narrow end of the notched spreader to apply adhesive to the back of the cut tile, then press it into place so that it is level with the adjacent tile. Insert joint spacers as necessary.

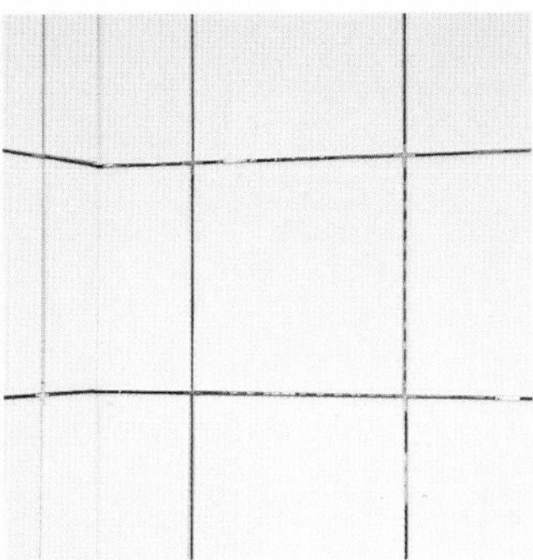

4 When you have completed one wall, you can tile the next. Care is needed when cutting these edge tiles, to ensure a uniform grouted joint where they meet the tiles on the facing wall.

External corners

t an external corner, you can achieve a neat finish by using plastic orner trim. This comes in various sizes and colours, and normally as a quadrant shape. It has the added advantage of protecting the dges of the tiles from knocks, which could cause chipping.

1 Complete one wall. Use a acksaw to cut the corner trim o length, apply a narrow strip of ile adhesive to the return wall and press the trim into it. Align he trim with the tiles of the first wall, using spacers to ensure here is a gap for grouting. Carefully apply more adhesive to he return wall with the notched spreader. Make sure that you apply it vertically, so that you are ess likely to catch the teeth of he spreader in the corner trim's lange and dislodge it.

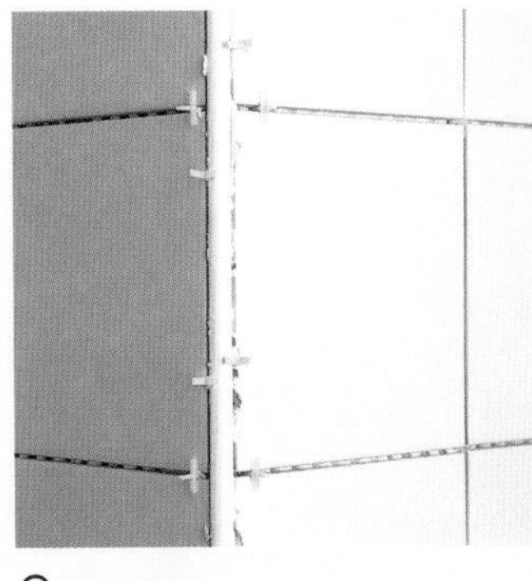

2 Begin tiling the return wall, working away from the corner trim. As you set the tiles in place, remember to allow a narrow grouting gap between them and the trim, inserting spacers and adjusting the tiles as necessary so that the gap is uniform. Make a final check to see that the trim has not moved.

Obstructions

The best way to deal with obstructions such as doors and windows is to work from the vertical centre of the most obvious feature. For example, with a single window or door, begin setting out from its centre-line; if there are two windows, use the centre of the space between them; if a window or door is near one end of the wall, work from the centre of the space between its frame and the far corner. Use the gauge rod to check for cutting problems around the feature, moving the starting point as required. The same applies for the horizontal rows.

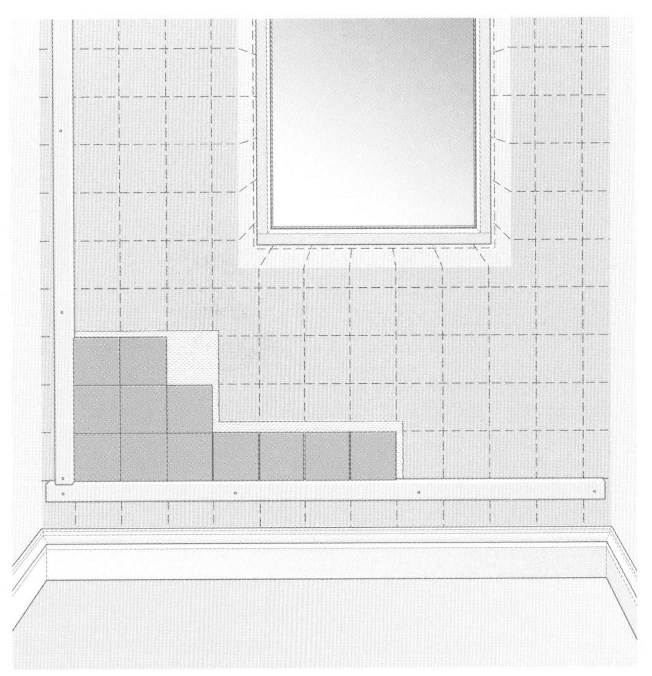

WALLS CUTTING TILES

Unless you are tiling a small area, such as a splashback (see page 100), which you can restrict to whole tiles only, you will be faced with cutting tiles to fit. You can choose from a variety of hand and power tools to do this, and some will be easier to use than others. What you go for will depend on the size of the job and your budget.

YOU CAN DO IT

File your tiles

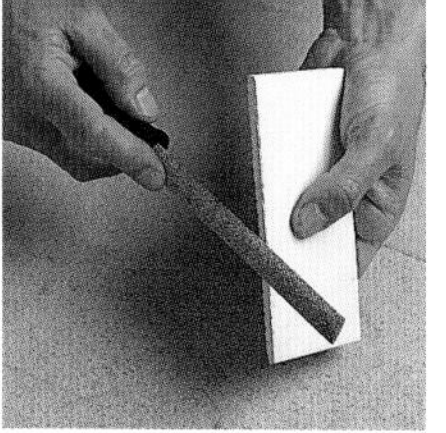

Any rough edges should be removed from a cut tile with a tile file. Hold it square on to the edge.

Tile spike

The simplest and cheapest tool for making straight cuts through tiles is the tile spike, which has a specially hardened tip.

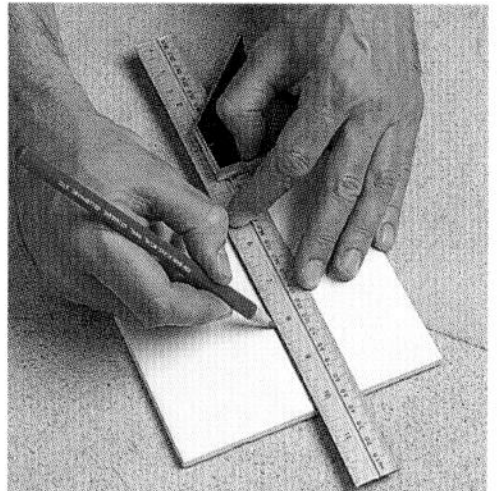

1 Having measured the gap to be filled, transfer the measurements to the tile, then use a steel rule and chinagraph pencil or felt-tip pen to mark a cutting line across the tile. Make sure that the rule does not slip as you make the mark.

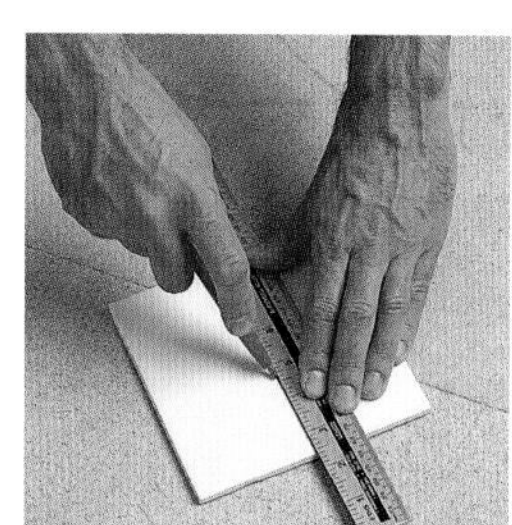

2 Holding the rule firmly, score along the line with the tile spike in one stroke, applying enough pressure to cut through the glaze. Place a pencil beneath the scored line and press down each side. The tile should snap cleanly in two.

Combined scorer/snappe

Snapping the tiles is not always easy with a tile spike; a combined tile scorer/snapper is very effective and requires only a little pressure to operate successfully.

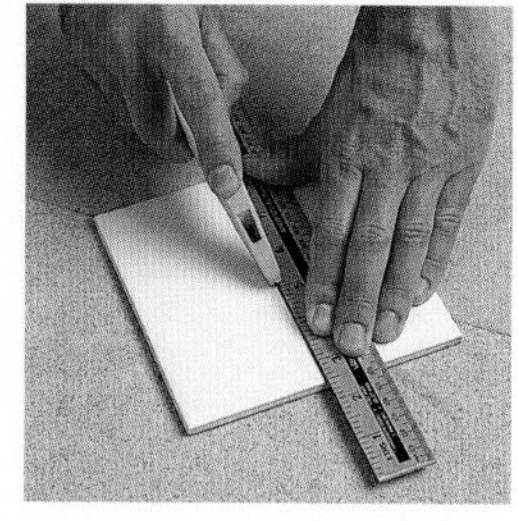

1 Mark the tile for cutting in the normal manner. Then, using the steel rule as a guide, run the cutting wheel of the tool along the line, pressing down firmly to score the glaze.

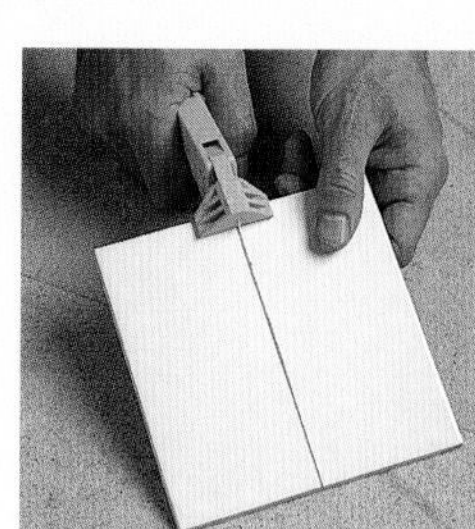

2 Insert the tile between the jaws of the tool, aligning the scored line with the centre mark. Squeeze the handles and the tile will snap in two.

Cutting curves

There are various methods of making curved cuts in tiles; one of the simplest is to use a tile saw, which has a round blade, allowing you to change direction easily.

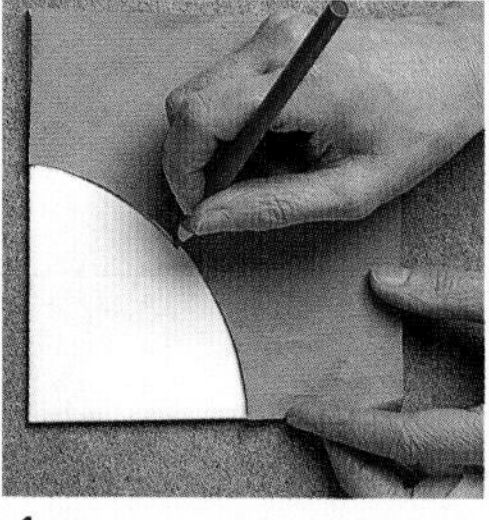

1 Take a piece of paper or card of the same size as the tile and cut it to the required shape. Lay it over the tile and mark the shape on the face.

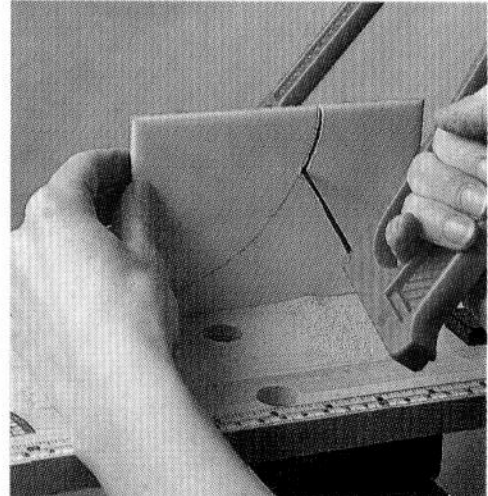

2 Clamp the tile securely and cut along the line with a tile saw. Check the fit of the tile, making any necessary adjustments with a tile file.

Tile-cutting machine

This robust device combines a scorer and snapper with a sturdy bed to support the tile. Some incorporate a removable gauge for measuring the tiles and will even make an allowance for a grout gap and tapered cut. They are relatively inexpensive and the easiest of all these tile-cutting tools to use.

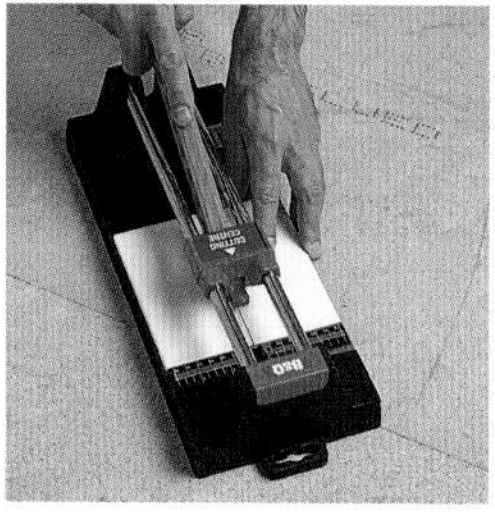

1 Mark the tile for cutting and insert it into the machine, lining up the mark with the tool's guide. Lower the handle to bring the scorer into contact with the tile, press down and push the handle forward to score the tile.

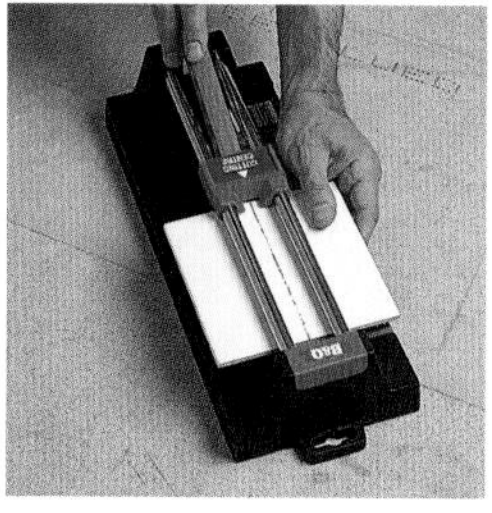

2 Fit the tile into the slide of the handle, carefully aligning the scored mark with the guide. Lower the handle until you feel the snapper touch the tile's underside.

3 Apply firm pressure to the handle to snap the tile along the cutting line

Cutting around pipes

If you are lucky, a projecting pipe may fall on the joint line between two tiles. If not, you will have to split a tile on the pipe's centre-line, then make cut-outs in each piece.

1 Tile the wall to one side of the pipe and just below it. Then, using another tile as a guide to ensure square lines, make pencil marks on the wall, level with the top, bottom and both sides of the pipe.

2 Now transfer the marks to the tile for cutting, using a felt-tip pen or chinagraph pencil. Support the tile on tile spacers while you do this, otherwise the marks will be in the wrong place.

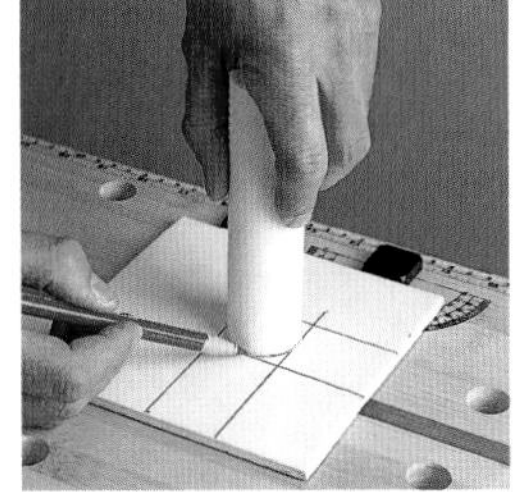

3 Using a try square, or even another tile, join up the lines across the tile. Where they cross, they will form a square. Stand an off-cut of pipe (the same size as the wall pipe) in the square and draw around it. Then cut the tile in two, so that the cut passes through the centre of the circle.

4 To remove waste from the two pieces of tile, you could use a tile saw, a jigsaw fitted with a tile-cutting blade or a rotary cutter. With the last two, choose a slow speed, hold the tool still and rotate the tile around the blade. Keep inside the marked line, using a tile file to make final adjustments. Or you can simply break away small pieces with a pair of tile nippers until the cut-outs are of the correct size.

IDEAL TOOL

Rotary cutter

This has a narrow, round saw blade that rotates as it cuts. It can be used to make very tight circular cuts.

5 Check the fit of the two pieces of tile around the pipe. If all is well, apply adhesive to the back of each piece and stick to the wall. You should find that the joint between the two pieces is virtually invisible, while any gap around the pipe can be filled at the grouting stage.

Window recesses

Window recesses, being narrow, will need tiles cut to fit all round. Treat them in a similar manner to external corners. After tiling the face of the wall, tile the head of the recess, then the sides and lastly the bottom.

Glazed-edge tiles

If you are using glazed-edge tiles, you don't need corner trim. Tile the face of the wall up to the recess, then tile the recess, placing the tiles so that they cover the edges of those on the face of the wall. Work back towards the window frame.

Using corner trim

Tile the face of the wall, making sure that the edges of the tiles are flush with the window recess. Fit lengths of corner trim around the recess so that they are flush with the tile faces; mitre the ends for neatness. Then tile the recess, working back from the trim.

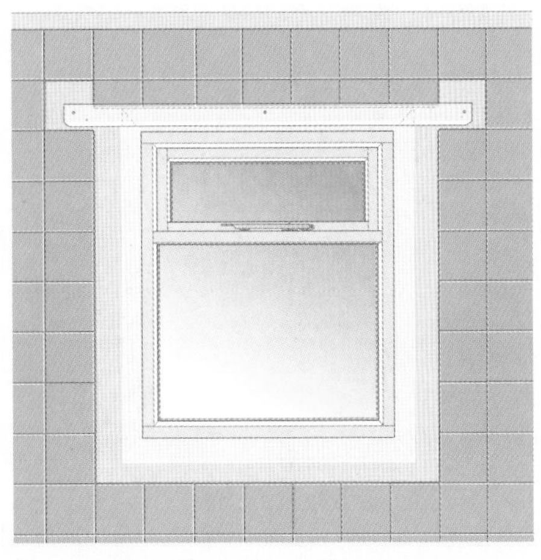

Supporting tiles above the recess

When tiling the wall face, you must provide support for the tiles above the recess. Do this by nailing a temporary batten to the wall so that its top edge is flush with the top of the recess.

Supporting tiles in the recess

When tiling a window recess, you must support the tiles at the head of the recess while the adhesive sets. The simplest way to do this is with a length of wood wedged in place by two more pieces.

WALLS GROUTING AND FINISHING TILES

Once you have applied all the tiles to the wall, they should be left for the adhesive to dry. How long depends on the product – check with the maker's instructions. Then you can finish off all the joints with grout, a special hard filler. To complete your tiling, you may also need to add a waterproof seal along the bottom of a splashback and possibly mount some fixtures.

Grouting

You can buy grout in powder form for mixing with water, or pre-mixed and ready to apply. Whichever you choose, check that you have enough for the job, and remember to use waterproof grout anywhere the tiles are likely to be splashed. You can also buy coloured grout to match or complement your tiles.

TOOLS MATERIALS

- **trowel**
- **grout spreader**
- **sponge**
- **bucket**
- **grout shaper**
- **soft cloth**
- **sealant shaper (optional)**
- **chinagraph pencil**
- **pipe and cable detector**
- **power drill**
- **ceramic tile drill bit or masonry bit**
- **tile scorer**

- grout
- silicone sealant
- masking tape

1 Press a small amount of grout on to the face of the tiles with a trowel. Use a grout spreader to spread it, making long, upward diagonal strokes and working it into the joints between tiles. Continue until you have grouted all the joints. Do this as quickly as possible, since the grout will soon begin to harden.

2 Immediately you finish applying the grout, go over the tiles with a damp sponge to remove any excess. It will be very difficult to shift once hard. Take care not to drag any grout from the joints.

3 After leaving the grout to harden slightly, use a grout shaper to finish off the joints and give them a neat appearance. Pull the shaper along the joints in one continuous movement. If any gaps appear in the joints, press in some more grout with the tip of your finger. Sponge off any excess grout.

4 Leave the grout to dry; as it does, you will notice a powdery film appear on the tiles from all the sponging. Simply polish this off with a soft, clean cloth to leave your tiles sparkling.

IDEAL TOOL

Grout shaper
Giving grouted joints a neat, uniform appearance is easy with a grout shaper. This simple plastic tool usually comes with interchangeable heads, offering a choice of profiles. Simply draw it along each joint so that it touches the tiles on each side, then wipe any grout from the faces of the tiles.

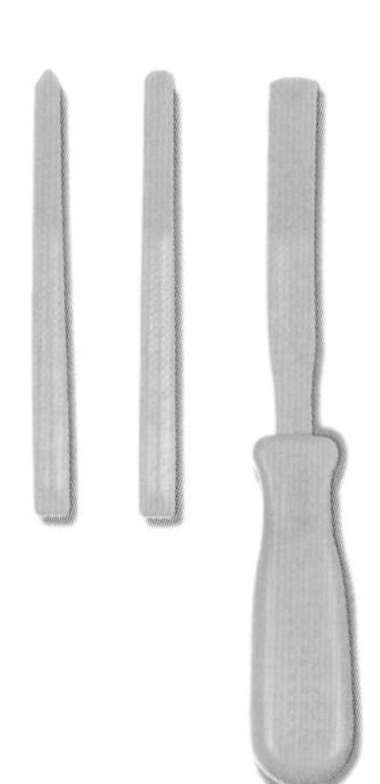

YOU CAN DO IT

Sealing around a bath
To be sure of a waterproof seal around a bath, fill it with water, then apply the silicone sealant. Leave it for 24 hours before emptying. That way, you will have allowed for any movement caused by the weight of the full bath.

Waterproof seals

Although there are waterproof varieties of grout, the joint between a basin or bath and a splashback should be protected with a flexible silicone sealant. This will accommodate any movement in the fitting, which could cause the grout to crack and allow water through.

1 Working from one end of the splashback to the other, apply a continuous bead of sealant. Maintain a steady pressure and speed.

2 Any irregularity in the shape of the bead can be smoothed with a special sealant shaper, or even a soapy wet finger, but take care not to pull the sealant from the surface.

Mounting fixtures

The idea of drilling holes in brittle ceramic tiles to mount something like a toilet roll holder can seem daunting, but actually it is not difficult. If you don't have a proper tile bit, you can use a normal masonry bit.

IDEAL TOOL

Ceramic tile bit
If you have to drill holes in tiles to mount fittings, a ceramic tile bit is the best tool for the job. It is shaped to break through the glaze immediately, reducing the likelihood of skidding, and it makes short work of boring through the tile, with no risk of cracking. You can choose from a range of sizes.

1 Hold the fitting in place on the tiles and mark through one of its fixing holes with a chinagraph pencil. If you drill this hole first, you can fit a plastic wallplug and screw to support the item while you level it and mark the remaining hole. Before drilling, check there are no hidden pipes or cables behind the wall surface.

2 Although ceramic tile bits are designed to cut into the glaze instantly, for peace of mind – or if you are using a masonry bit – you can break the glaze at the drilling point with a tile scorer, twisting the tip to create a starter hole.

3 A piece of masking tape over the hole position will also help to stop a bit skidding across the surface. Mark the position of the hole on the tape, then begin drilling, using a slow speed at first to establish the hole.

WALLS SPLASHBACK AND MOSAIC TILES

A panel of tiles above a sink or basin will protect a non-waterproof wall covering from water damage. As well as being practical and easy to clean, a tiled splashback can add a dash of colour to an otherwise plain bathroom.

Mosaic tiles are not as fiddly as they look, since they are usually supplied in sheets with either a mesh or paper backing, or a facing paper that is removed once they are laid. Use them on their own, or as a decorative detail within a large area of standard tiles.

Tiling a splashback

If the top edge of your basin is straight or only slightly curved, then measure the depth of the splashback in multiples of whole tiles. If its curve is pronounced, however, you will have to cut tiles to fit. In that case, allow for a row of half tiles along the line of the basin.

TOOLS MATERIALS

- **tape measure**
- **pencil**
- **spirit level**
- **notched spreader**
- **cloth**
- **chinagraph pencil**
- **tile spike or cutting machine**
- **tile file**

- tiles
- tile spacers
- wooden batten
- 2 x 50mm masonry nails
- tile adhesive
- grout
- edging trim
- silicone sealant

1 Measure the width of the basin and mark the centre-point on the wall. The width of the splashback should be measured in whole tiles plus edging strip.

2 Lay out a full row of tiles with spacers between and edging strip at either end. Cut a piece of wooden batten to the same length and mark on it the position of the tiles and joins. This is your gauge rod (see page 92) and will also act as a lower batten if you are cutting half-tiles for the bottom row.

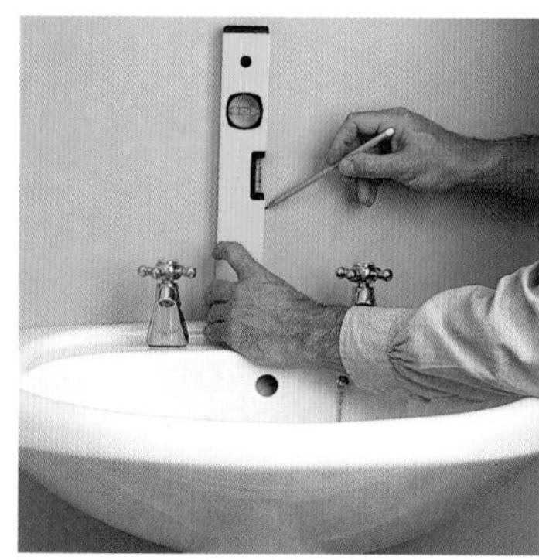

3 Use a spirit level to draw a line vertically from the centre-point of the splashback up the wall to its upper limit.

4 If you are cutting the bottom row of tiles, then fix the batten to the wall using two 50mm masonry nails. Centre it on the vertical line. Its upper edge should be about half a tile width from the top of the basin. Check it is level with a spirit level.

5 Use a notched spreader to apply tile adhesive evenly across the area of the splashback.

6 Apply the first tile, starting in the middle of the row and aligning it with the guide marks on the gauge rod/batten. Complete the row and then build above it, fitting tile spacers between the tiles as you work.

YOU CAN DO IT

Tiling without a batten
If the upper edge of the basin is straight or only slightly curved, you can lay the first whole row of tiles along it. That will save you cutting tiles – but it is more tricky to ensure the tiles are exactly level. Use paper or cardboard spacers beneath the tiles to hold them level while the adhesive dries. When you have finished, remove the spacers and fill in the join between the splashback and basin with silicone sealant.

7 Wipe off any stray adhesive as you work – it is much easier to clean off when wet than dry.

8 Finish the upper and side edges of the splashback with matching glazed trim. Mark and cut the trim to match the length of your tiles so that the joins align neatly. Cut the corners at a 45° angle to create a neat mitre; use a tile file to shave off small amounts to refine the fit.

9 Remove the batten and measure the gap below. Cut the lowest row of tiles to fit, remembering to allow for a bead of silicone sealant between sink and tiles. When the adhesive is dry, grout the tiles and seal the gap at the bottom (see pages 98–99).

IDEAL TOOL

Tile file

If a cut tile is too big and doesn't quite fit, don't waste it – file it to size with a tile file. Cheap, durable and easy to use, this is an essential tiler's accessory.

Mosaic tiles

Setting out for mosaic tiles is much the same as for regular tiles (see pages 92–93) – just treat a panel of tiles as you would a whole tile. It isn't so important to centre the panels on the wall, since the individual tiles are so much smaller. But you should still establish horizontal and vertical starting lines, and work from the centre outwards for the neatest results. Once you have finished and the adhesive is dry, grout the tiles in the usual way (see page 98).

Applying mosaic tiles

Handling sheets of mosaic tiles takes a little practice, but the results are more than worth it.

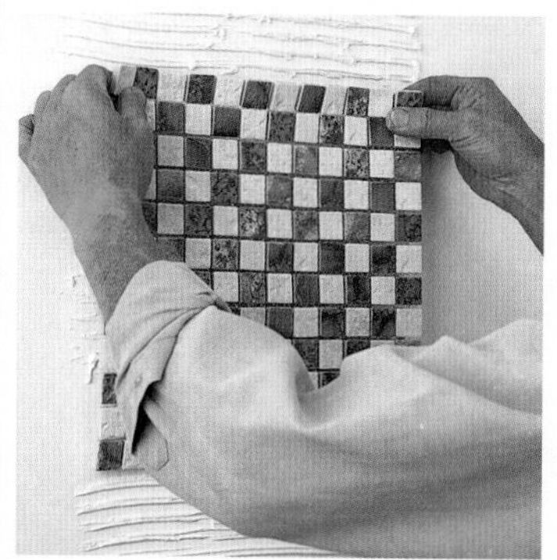

1 Spread tile adhesive on the wall with a notched spreader, then place a panel of tiles onto it. Press evenly across the surface with spread fingers. You need to work accurately: once the backing paper or mesh is moistened by the adhesive it disintegrates, making the panel very difficult to adjust.

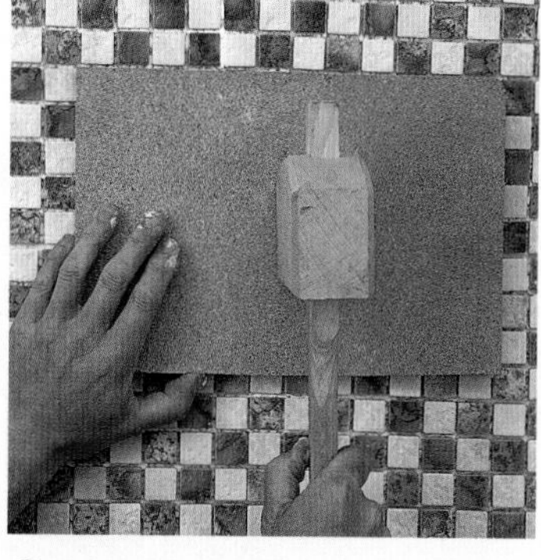

2 Hold a piece of scrap board over the tiles while the adhesive is wet and tap lightly with a wooden mallet. This will give the tiles a flat, even finish.

3 If you need to reduce the size of a panel, either use a craft knife to cut between two rows of tiles, or use tile nibblers to cut the tiles. There's no need to score them first.

TOOLS MATERIALS

- **notched spreader**
- **wooden mallet**
- **craft knife or tile nibblers**

- tile adhesive
- mosaic tiles
- scrap board

CEILINGS AND LOFTS ROOF SPACE

ECO INSULATE

Because heat rises, much of the heat in your house goes straight through the roof. When you insulate a loft space, you reduce the rate at which heat is lost. Since less heat is then needed to keep rooms warm, you will conserve energy and your heating bills will be reduced.

The construction of the ceilings and roof space in your house depends on its age. Older houses built with traditional pitched roofs have open space below the rafters. Some have a attic room or rooms built into this space as part of the original structure; others have been converted, as below, to create extra living space. Modern roofs usually have roof trusses – prefabricated timber frames incorporating rafters and ceiling joists – which are easier to erect but leave less open space under the roof.

Using roof space

In many houses there is scope to create a good storage area under the roof as long as there is easy access and a safe, solid flooring (see pages 112–15). If the available space and the roof construction allow for it, the loft can be converted into extra living space, but the joists must be strengthened, or new joists must be inserted. A living space also requires a fixed staircase, ventilation and a window, all of which are subject to building regulations, and this scale of loft conversion is better left to the experts.

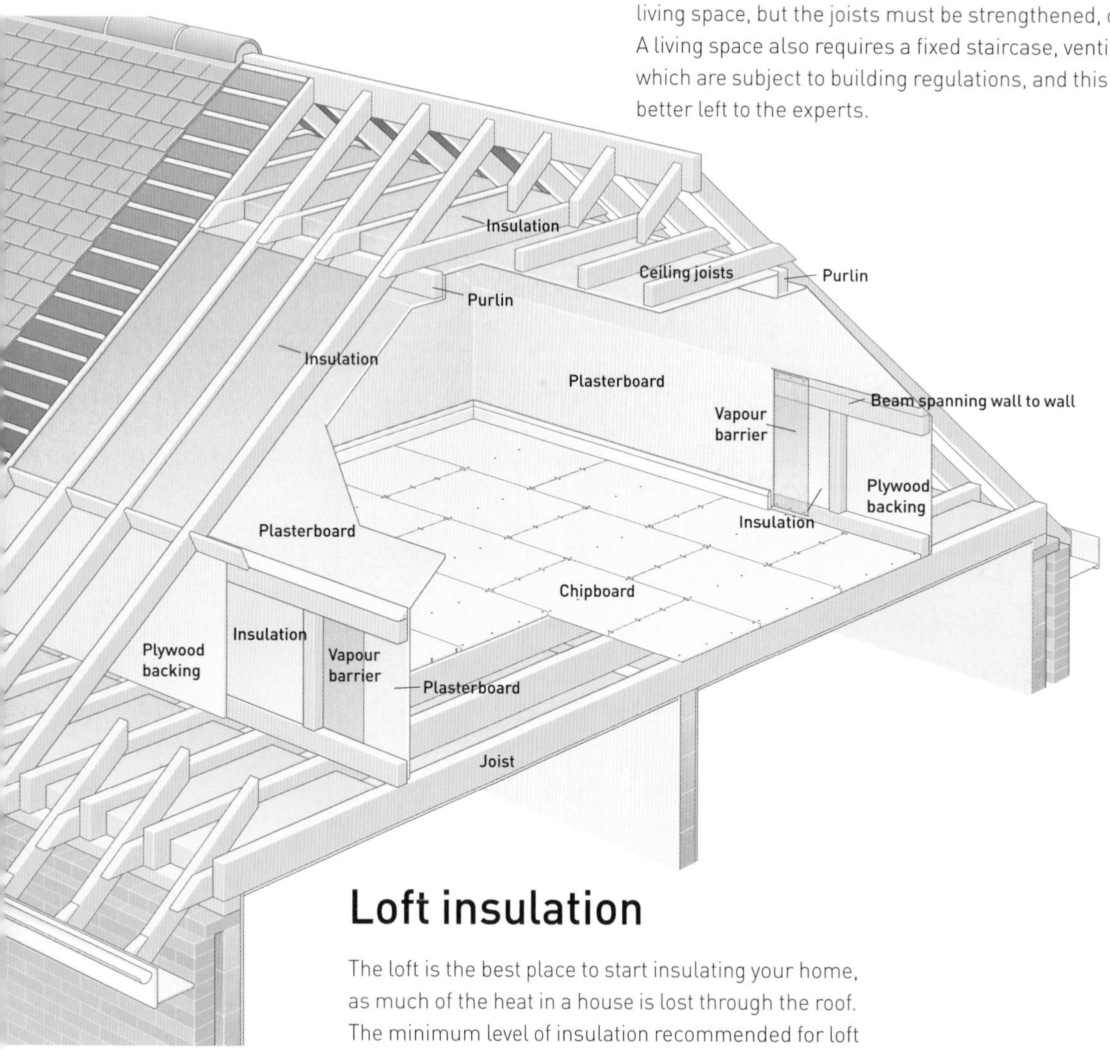

SAFETY FIRST

When working in a dusty loft space, wear protective overalls, gloves, eye protectors and a face mask. If the loft is unboarded, lay planks across the joists to make a safe walkway.

YOU CAN DO IT

Bats in your roof?

All bats and their roosts are protected by law and must not be harmed. But this does not necessarily mean that you can't work in your loft. Contact the Bat Conservation Trust (details on page 371) for help and advice.

Loft insulation

The loft is the best place to start insulating your home, as much of the heat in a house is lost through the roof. The minimum level of insulation recommended for loft floors is 270mm, but it is common to find as little as 25mm, particularly in older houses. Existing insulation can be topped up quite easily using blanket insulation or loose-lay material. If you are planning to lay boards on the joists in the loft, the depth of the insulation will be limited by the depth of the joists, unless you build up the joists with strips of wood. Blanket insulation is available in different thickness and widths. Use rolls that are the same width as the gap between the joists and simply lay it between them. Loose-lay insulation comes in bags and can be tipped between the joists and levelled using a straightedge. It is ideal for topping up existing insulation.

Insulating loft rooms

When the loft space is going to be used as a room rather than storage space, the sloping roof needs to be insulated to keep the heat in. Insulation laid under the roof felt must have a ventilation gap of 50mm behind it. Roof insulation has the effect of making the uninsulated parts of the roof colder than before, so increasing the risk of condensation. This can be reduced by a vapour barrier, usually foil-backed plasterboard, on the inner side of the insulation.

Types of ceiling

In old houses the ceilings may well be constructed from lath and plaster, while in modern houses they are likely to be of plasterboard. Both kinds of ceiling will be fixed to the joists supporting the floor above. The depth of the joists varies according to the age of the building (older ones are often deeper than modern ones) and their length. The ceiling between the top floor of the house and the loft space should have a layer of insulation between the joists to prevent heat loss.

Lath and plaster ◢

This was a time-consuming method of building walls and ceilings, as individual laths (thin strips of wood) had to be nailed to the joists and then covered with layers of plaster. The plaster was squeezed between the laths so that 'nibs' formed – ridges of plaster that squeezed through the laths and set hard, holding the ceiling plaster in place. The room above would traditionally have had floorboards.

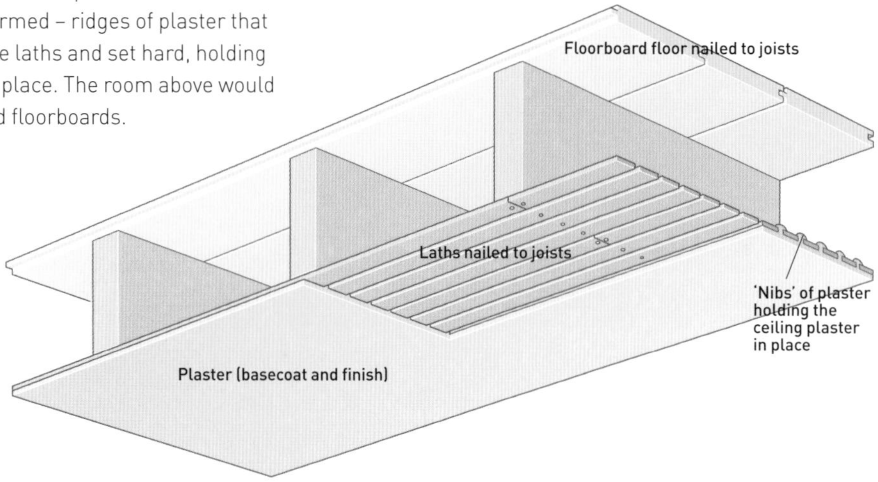

Floorboard floor nailed to joists

Laths nailed to joists

'Nibs' of plaster holding the ceiling plaster in place

Plaster (basecoat and finish)

YOU CAN DO IT

Repairing plaster around a ceiling rose
First switch off the power at the mains and put the circuit fuse in your pocket, or leave a sign at the consumer unit indicating that you are working on the circuit (see page 264). Unscrew the cover of the light fitting, and then the screws supporting the rose, so that the fitting drops away from the ceiling. Scrape away loose plaster and then apply new plaster with a trowel. Smooth it off and leave to dry for an hour before replacing the rose and then restoring the power.

B&Q

Plasterboard ◢

Most modern ceilings are constructed from plasterboard which is either plastered or dry-lined. Sheets of plasterboard are nailed to the joists and the joints are taped with scrim – a very open-weave, self-adhesive tape – before plaster is applied. Dry-lined ceilings are finished with jointing tape and jointing compound, which seals the joints and creates a surface ready for decorating without any need for plastering (see page 67). The floor of the room above a plasterboard ceiling may be laid with floorboards or chipboard.

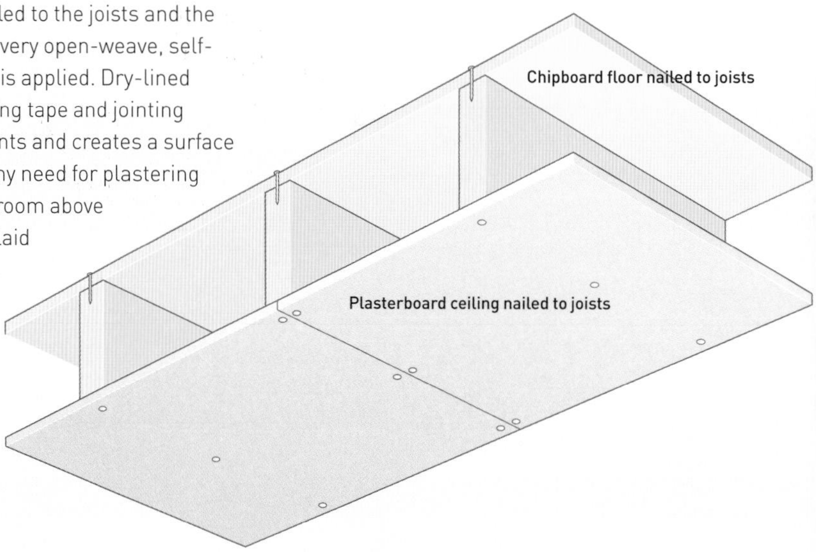

Chipboard floor nailed to joists

Plasterboard ceiling nailed to joists

Suspended ceilings

Very high ceilings are sometimes lowered by fitting a suspended ceiling. Panels or tiles are fitted to a lightweight framework consisting of an outer frame – called the angle section – which is fixed to the walls, a main bearer section spanning the width of the room, and a cross-bearer section which fits between the main bearers. Wires fixed to angle brackets attached to the original ceiling hold the framework in place. Panels may be decorative and translucent or may have sound-proofing and/or thermal properties.

Ceiling repairs

Small areas of damage on a ceiling can be repaired in a number of different ways. Crumbling areas in a lath-and-plaster ceiling can be patched with conventional plaster (below) or a plasterboard patch (overleaf). Slight bulges can be repaired from the floor above. If a ceiling is damaged all the way through – for instance, if someone slips off a joist and puts a foot through it when walking in an unboarded loft – you can repair the hole with a plasterboard patch supported by noggings nailed between the joists.

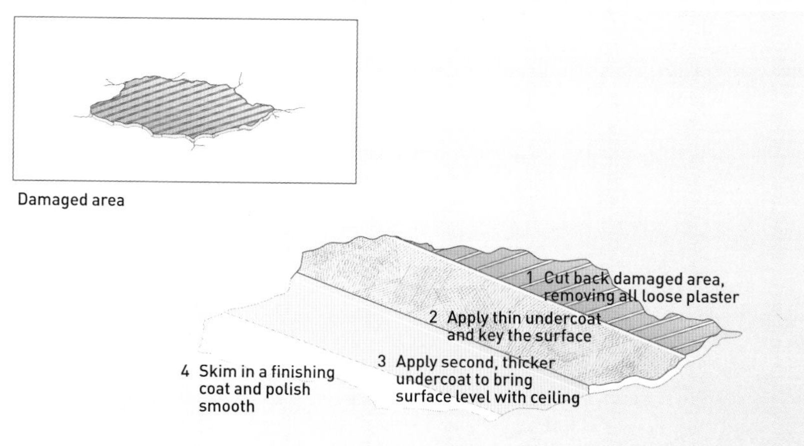
Damaged area
1 Cut back damaged area, removing all loose plaster
2 Apply thin undercoat and key the surface
3 Apply second, thicker undercoat to bring surface level with ceiling
4 Skim in a finishing coat and polish smooth

Replastering a damaged section on a lath-and-plaster ceiling

Where the laths are still intact, damaged plaster can be repaired with new plaster. Carefully cut back the damaged area, removing all loose material, until you reach sound plaster. Dampen the laths and apply a thin coat of bonding undercoat plaster. Score the surface of the plaster in a diamond pattern with the side of the trowel to create a key for the next coat. Allow it to set, then apply a second coat of undercoat plaster. Scrape it back 2mm below the surface and lightly score it. When it has set, apply a finishing coat of plaster to bring it down level with the rest of the ceiling.

Repairing a lath-and-plaster bulge from above

An area of plaster that is sagging away from the laths can be repaired from above if you have good access to the upstairs floor. Prop up the sagging plaster using a flat piece of chipboard or plywood nailed to a length of 38mm-square timber that reaches from floor to ceiling (this is known as a 'deadman'). Lift the floorboards in the room above and vacuum between the joists over the bulge to collect up the loose plaster. Mix fairly runny bonding undercoat plaster and pour it over the damaged area to replace the broken plaster. Leave the supporting prop in place until the plaster has dried and bonded to the laths.

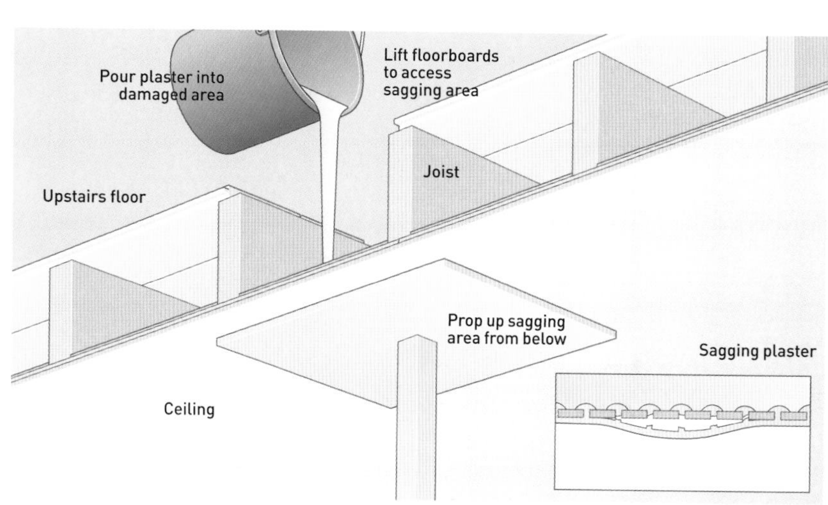
Pour plaster into damaged area
Lift floorboards to access sagging area
Joist
Upstairs floor
Prop up sagging area from below
Sagging plaster
Ceiling

Joist
Upstairs floor
Nail noggings between joists to support new plasterboard patch
Cut back damaged area to joists
Ceiling
New plasterboard patch

Repairing a hole

Locate the joists each side of the hole with a stud detector. Draw a line along each joist, half-way across its width, with a straightedge and pencil, and then join them up to mark a square or rectangle around the damaged area. Cut away the laths and plaster or plasterboard inside the marked area with a padsaw. Remove any protruding nails in the joists with a claw hammer. Cut two noggings from 100mm x 50mm sawn softwood to fit between the joists and form the other two sides of the opening. Half the thickness of the noggings should project into the exposed area. Drive nails into the noggings at an angle to secure them to the joists. Using plasterboard that is slightly thinner than the ceiling depth, cut a piece the same size as the hole. Fix it in place with plasterboard nails along the joists and noggings. Fill the join with bonding undercoat plaster. When it is dry, apply multi-finish plaster to the patch to bring it level with the rest of the ceiling. If necessary, apply two thin coats rather than one thick coat.

CEILINGS PATCHING A CEILING

The lath-and-plaster ceilings in older houses often crack with age and the plaster may bulge where it begins to break away from the laths. If only a small area of a ceiling is affected, a simple repair can be made with a plasterboard patch using dry-lining techniques that do not require plastering skills.

1 Areas of loose, bulging plaster should be dealt with promptly, as they are not only unsightly but also dangerous. Put on a dust mask, protective goggles and, preferably, a hard hat before you start. Open up one of the cracks with a filling knife or similar bladed tool until you can insert your fingers in it.

Making the patch

Remove the old plaster before you buy the plasterboard to make the repair patch, so that you can choose the thickness closest to the depth of plaster.

2 Pull away the loose sections of plaster to expose the wooden laths, continuing until you have reached sound plaster and have exposed the joists to which the repair patch can be nailed.

3 Undercut the edges of the plaster slightly with a filling knife. Then tape a sheet of newspaper over the hole, stretching it as taut as possible, and trace around the edge of the plaster with a crayon or felt-tip pen.

TOOLS MATERIALS

- **dust mask**
- **safety goggles**
- **hard hat**
- **filling knife**
- **crayon or felt-tip pen**
- **scissors**
- **pencil**
- **padsaw, jigsaw or plasterboard saw**
- **wooden props**
- **straightedge**
- **tape measure**
- **hammer**

- newspaper
- masking tape
- plasterboard
- abrasive paper
- packing pieces

4 Remove the newspaper and cut around the outline of the hole. Then lay it on a sheet of plasterboard and draw round it to obtain the shape of the patch.

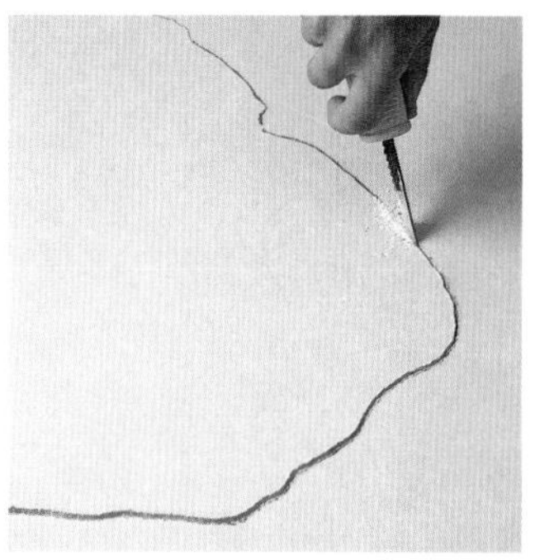

5 Lay the plasterboard on a firm surface, such as a portable workbench, and cut out the patch. You can use a padsaw, a powered jigsaw or, as here, a plasterboard padsaw. Gently rub down any ragged paper edges with abrasive paper.

6 Check the fit of the patch; if necessary, scrape away more of the ceiling plaster to leave a gap of about 3mm. Prop the patch in place, or have someone support it, hold a straightedge across the ceiling and measure the vertical gap between it and the patch. This will show the thickness of packing needed to set the patch flush with the ceiling's surface.

7 The packing can be made from stiff card (make sure it cannot be compressed), hardboard, plywood or even plasterboard. Nail it to the joists.

IDEAL TOOL

Plasterboard padsaw
This saw is designed for cutting holes in plasterboard sheets (for electrical fittings, etc). Its pointed, tapering blade is inserted initially into a drilled hole, much like a padsaw, but its narrow blade also makes it ideal for cutting out an irregularly shaped patch. The coarse teeth will cut through the plasterboard quickly.

Fixing the patch

The edges of the repair can be disguised and reinforced by using plasterboard jointing tape (in the same manner as dry-lining; see page 67).

TOOLS MATERIALS

- **hammer**
- **pencil**
- **small brush**
- **coating knife**
- **sponge**
- **sanding block**

- plasterboard nails
- PVA adhesive
- ready-mixed filler
- abrasive paper
- plasterboard jointing compound
- jointing tape

1 Hold the patch in position and check that it is flush with the ceiling; adjust the packing if necessary. Then nail the patch to the joists with plasterboard nails. It may help to mark the positions of the joists with pencil on the surrounding plaster.

2 Brush a PVA solution on to the edges of the patch and surrounding plaster and allow it to dry. Then fill the gap around the patch with a ready-mixed filler, pressing it in well; the undercut edges of the plaster will help retain it. When dry, sand the filler lightly.

3 Spread a layer of plasterboard jointing compound over the joint and press jointing tape into it, applying another wide layer of compound with a coating knife.

4 Smooth the compound with a damp sponge, feathering the edges. When it has dried, sand it smooth before decorating.

YOU CAN DO IT

Containing the mess

Removing the old damaged plaster will be a very messy job, with a lot of dirt and dust flying about. To reduce the amount of clearing up to do afterwards, cut two holes in a rubbish sack and pass your arms through them. That way, the sack will catch most of the debris as you take it out.

B&Q

Redecorating

It is best to paint a patched ceiling with a textured paint. Because it is thicker than ordinary paint, textured paint will disguise an uneven wall or ceiling that is dry-lined or plastered (but not papered). Various attractive textured paints or coatings are available; some have a matt or silk finish, others can be covered with emulsion. Some are applied with a brush, others with a coarse foam roller for a rough texture or a synthetic fibre roller for a finer texture.

TOOLS MATERIALS

- **roller**
- **25mm paintbrush**

- textured paint

1 Apply the textured paint over the patch and then over the rest of the ceiling, using a roller.

2 Finish off around the edge of the ceiling with a 25mm brush, drawing it through the wet coating to create a neat junction between the wall and the ceiling. If you are finishing with an emulsion paint, leave the textured paint to dry before adding any more coats.

CEILINGS DECORATING A CEILING

You must have a solid platform from which to work when decorating a ceiling – scaffold board resting on trestles will do. If possible, construct a platform that allows you to paper or paint the length of the room without having to move it along. A ceiling surface should be prepared for papering or painting in the same way as walls (see page 74).

TOOLS MATERIALS

- **step-ladder**
- **tape measure**
- **pencil**
- **hammer**
- **chalk line**
- **pasting table**
- **wallpaper scissors**
- **bucket**
- **pasting brush**
- **paper-hanging brush**
- **seam roller**

- small nails
- lining paper, if necessary
- wallpaper paste
- wallpaper

Papering a ceiling

As with walls, it is particularly important to get the first length of paper absolutely straight. Ceiling/wall junctions are not usually true enough to use as a guide. It is better to mark a chalk line and then position the first length along it. Don't worry about a guideline for lining paper – just align the paper with the wall where you start and butt-join the edges (taking care not to overlap them).

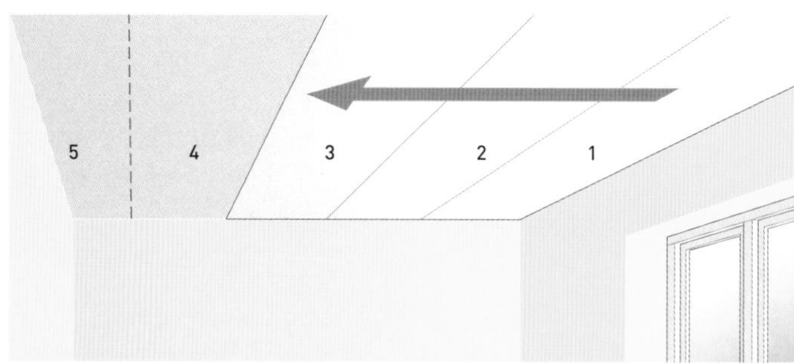

Papering away from a window

Start next to the window wall, so that if the joins overlap slightly they will not cast shadows. If the room has windows on two walls, you may not be able to avoid some shadows, so hang the paper across the narrowest part of the ceiling, as this will be easiest.

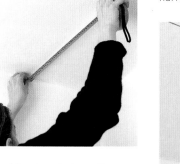

1 Decide where to hang the first length, and at either end of the ceiling measure out from the side wall a distance exactly 25mm less than the width of the paper. Hammer a small nail a little way into the ceiling at each point. If your ceiling is obviously uneven, measure its width at each end of the room, calculate the difference, and at the narrower end move the nail towards the wall junction by half of that amount. This will avoid the final strip of wallpaper appearing skewed.

2 Attach a chalk line between the two nails. From the centre of the trestle platform, pull and release the line to snap on to the ceiling. Remove the line and nails. Measure, cut and paste the paper (see pages 84–87).

3 Position the edge of the first length of paper against the chalk line and smooth the other edge into the ceiling/wall junction to give a 25mm overlap on to the wall. If the junction is not straight, the overlap will be uneven rather than the paper on the ceiling.

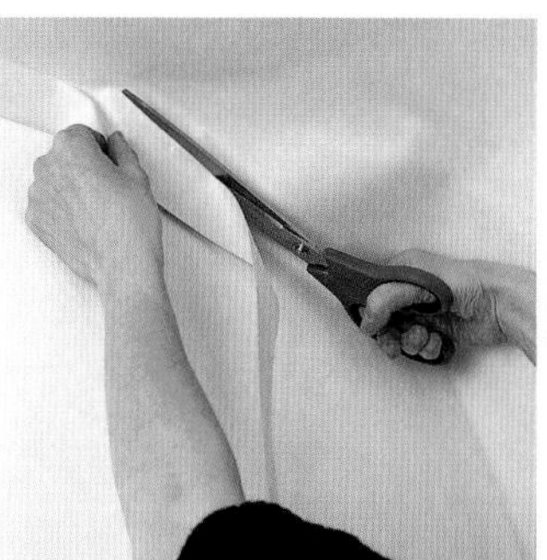

4 Brush out the bubbles with a paper-hanging brush, and then run wallpaper scissors along the ceiling/wall junction to make a sharp crease. Gently pull back the paper and cut along the crease. Brush the trimmed edge back into place, applying extra paste at the edges if needed. Butt the next length of paper against the first. Run a seam roller lightly along the joins.

YOU CAN DO IT

Papering around a light fitting

When you reach a pendant light, turn off the power at the mains (switching off at the wall is not enough). Unscrew the cover and paper up to and over the base. With scissors, puncture the paper at the centre of the fitting and make a series of snips outwards, being careful not to cut beyond the fitting. Then trim away the flaps of paper, cutting just inside the rim of the base. Wipe away any paste. When the paper is completely dry, replace the cover and then turn the power back on.

Painting the ceiling

Paint a ceiling with a roller or a broad emulsion brush. To avoid having to stretch up continually, either construct a platform so that you can walk along the length of the room, or buy an extension pole to fit on to the end of your roller handle – some can extend to over 3m. If you are redecorating a room, you should paint the ceiling first. For general painting techniques, see pages 78–79.

IDEAL TOOL

Roller with extension handle
This is an integrated roller and small telescopic extension handle tool – useful for both ceilings and walls.

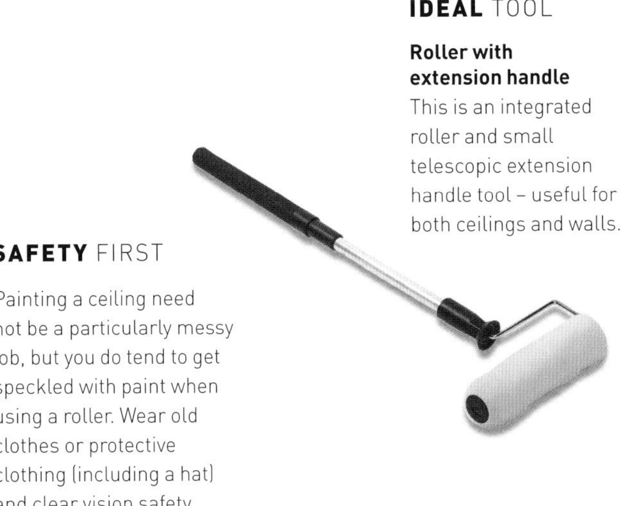

SAFETY FIRST

Painting a ceiling need not be a particularly messy job, but you do tend to get speckled with paint when using a roller. Wear old clothes or protective clothing (including a hat) and clear vision safety glasses or goggles to keep the paint out of your eyes.

Painting the edges

Either before or after you paint the bulk of the ceiling with the roller, you will need to paint into the edges of the room with a brush. If you are going to paint the walls after the ceiling, use a 25mm–50mm brush to carry a strip of paint on to the walls which you can later paint over. If you are not going on to paint the walls, bead the edges or use a 'George' (see page 78).

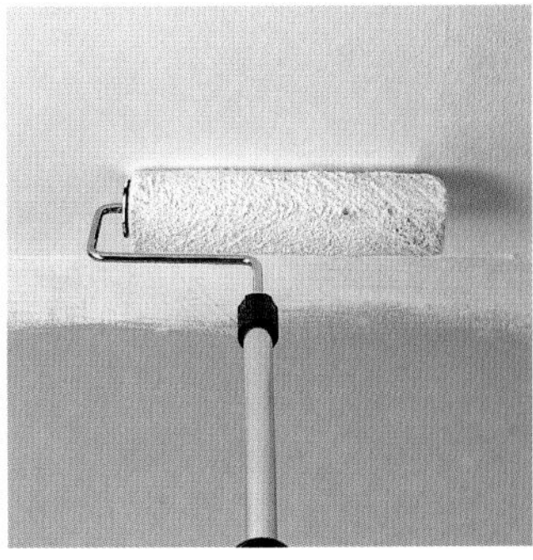

Painting with the roller

Dip the roller sleeve into the paint and roll it firmly up and down the tray's ribbed incline to spread the paint evenly, then apply it to the ceiling at an angle of about 45°. Experiment with the amount of paint on the roller. Too much and you will spray paint everywhere; too little and you will take forever! Move the roller over the wall surface, using random strokes applied with a light, even pressure. Each time you dip the roller in the paint, move it to an adjacent unpainted area and work back to the painted area in overlapping strokes to blend in the wet edges.

Fixing a plaster ceiling rose

When you have painted your ceiling, you can create an interesting focal point by adding a plaster ceiling rose. Lightweight ceiling roses can be secured with adhesive alone. If you want to fit a large one, you may need to use screws driven into the joists as well as adhesive. In that case, drill pilot holes for the screws through the rose into the joists above, then screw in place with brass screws.

TOOLS MATERIALS

- **drill**
- **screwdriver**

- plaster ceiling rose
- adhesive
- damp sponge
- screws

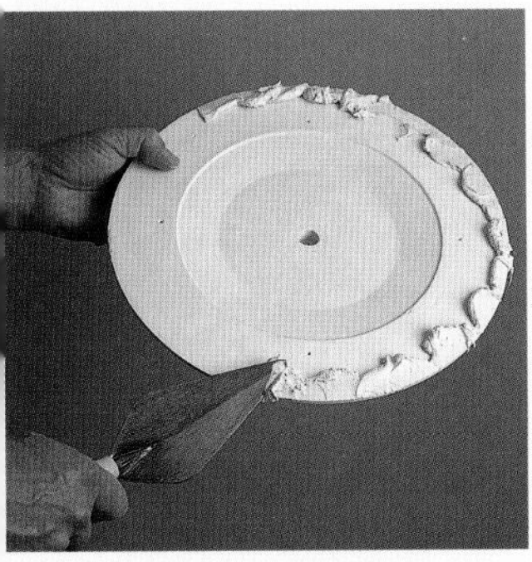

1 Turn off the electricity at the mains (see page 264). Then disconnect and remove the light fitting. Drill a hole for the cable in the decorative rose (don't press down hard or you may crack it). Apply adhesive all round the edge on the back of the decorative rose.

2 Pass the lighting cable through the drilled centre hole. Position the rose on the ceiling and press it in place until the adhesive secures it.

3 Wipe off the excess adhesive with a damp sponge. When it has set completely, refit the light fitting using screws long enough to pass right through the rose and into the joist above. Drill pilot holes first. Reconnect the wires and then turn the power back on.

YOU CAN DO IT

Painting with a brush
If you are using a brush instead of a roller, pour the paint into a paint kettle, so that it is about one-third full. Dip the brush into the paint to cover about one-third of the bristle depth. Apply the paint with short, overlapping strokes in different directions. Then, with a fairly dry brush, lightly draw the bristles across the painted surface, again in a criss-cross pattern, to remove any visible brush marks and achieve an even surface.

CEILINGS FITTING COVING

Coving is a prefabricated decorative moulding fitted at the junction of the wall and ceiling all the way around a room. It is excellent for hiding any unsightly cracks that can open up between walls and ceiling. Traditional types of coving are made from fibrous plaster, but coving made from expanded polystyrene or lightweight paper-wrapped material is also available. There's a selection of sizes; generally, the smaller the room, the narrower the coving. Many old properties have had their original mouldings stripped out. Fitting traditional style ceiling coving will instantly restore period character.

Before you start

Coving should be applied before you decorate a room. To mark out the area that it will cover, go around the room holding a piece of the coving in position, pencilling its upper and lower edge on the wall and ceiling. Coving can only be fixed to a sound, dry, clean surface, so remove all traces of distemper, loose plaster, wallpaper or flaking paint from this area. Strip off wall or ceiling paper by cutting through the paper 2mm inside the pencil guidelines with a sharp knife to give neat edges, and removing the paper between the marks with a scraper. Key the area between the guidelines by scoring the plaster with a series of criss-cross lines to give the coving adhesive a better grip. Brush away any loose particles.

TOOLS MATERIALS

- **tape measure**
- **pencil**
- **mitre block**
- **fine-toothed panel saw**
- **scraper or trowel**
- **filling knife**
- **pipe and cable detector**
- **hammer**
- **sponge**

- coving
- fine-grade abrasive paper
- coving adhesive
- nails
- coving primer

Cutting corners

Check you have the coving the right way up before starting to cut or fix it. The edges are generally clearly marked on the reverse side.

Measure the length of the first wall and mark the coving where you need to cut mitres for the corners. Lay the coving on the mitre block with the wall edge of the coving upright against the side and the ceiling edge flat against the base. Use a panel saw to cut the mitres for the corners. Lightly sand the cut edges.

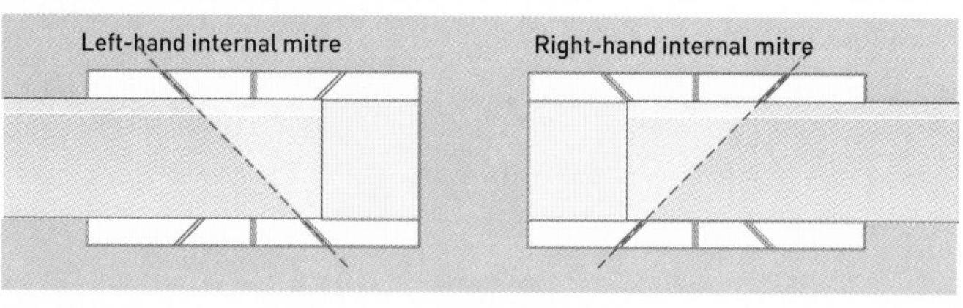

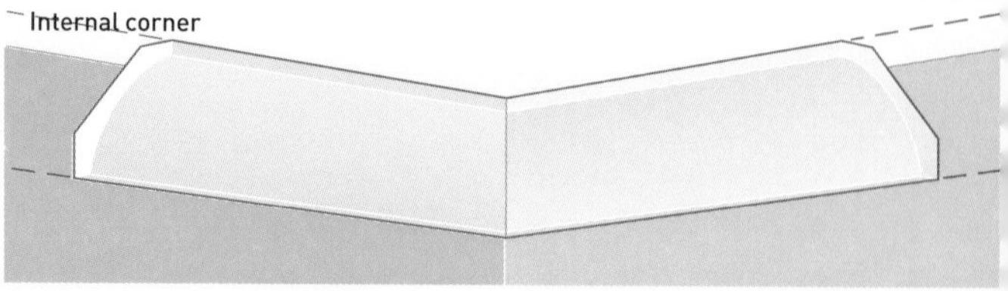

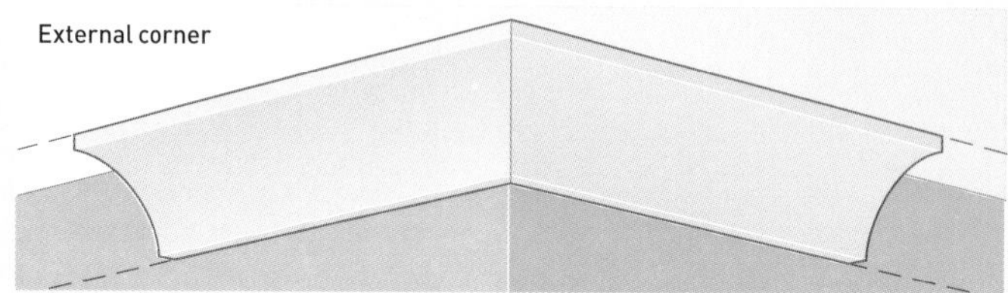

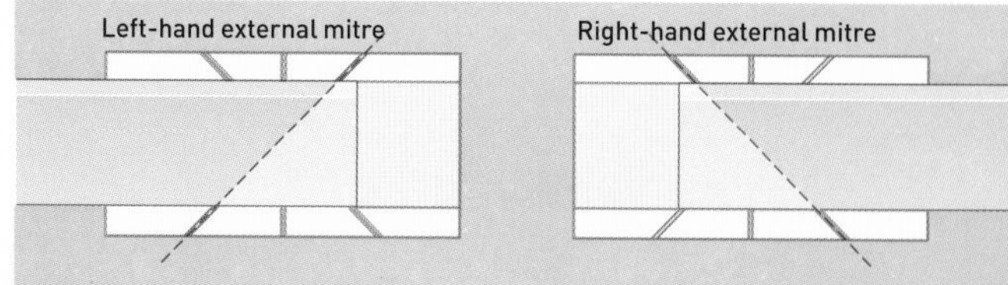

Fixing coving

Always read the manufacturer's fixing instructions carefully before starting work – they may vary slightly, depending in the type of coving.

1 Use a scraper or trowel to apply coving adhesive all the way along the back edges of your length of coving. You don't need to apply it to the central area as this does not come into contact with the wall or ceiling.

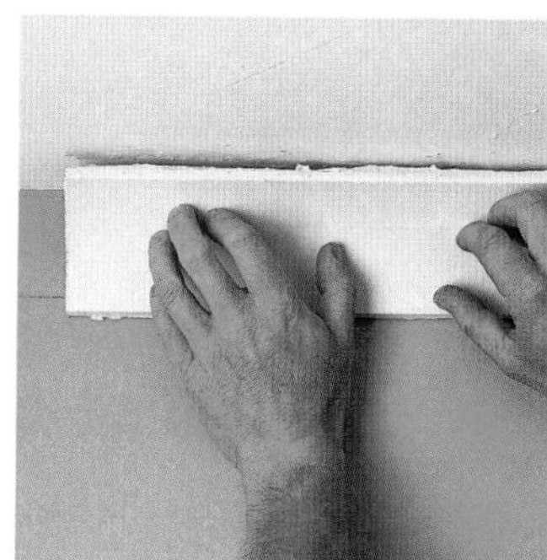

2 Press the coving into place along the pencil guideline. Allow excess adhesive to squeeze out, making sure there is firm contact along the entire length. Remove the excess with a filling knife or your finger and use it to fill in any gaps in the mitred corners and the joints between lengths. If any adhesive splashes on to the coving, wall or ceiling, wipe it away with a damp sponge.

3 Check there are no hidden pipes or cables then tap in nails just below the bottom edge of the coving to support it as the adhesive dries. You can remove the nails later, but if you are fixing plaster coving to a very uneven surface, you may have to reinforce the adhesive with galvanised nails or countersunk screws driven into wallplugs set in the wall. Continue to add lengths, butt-joining and gluing to the previous length.

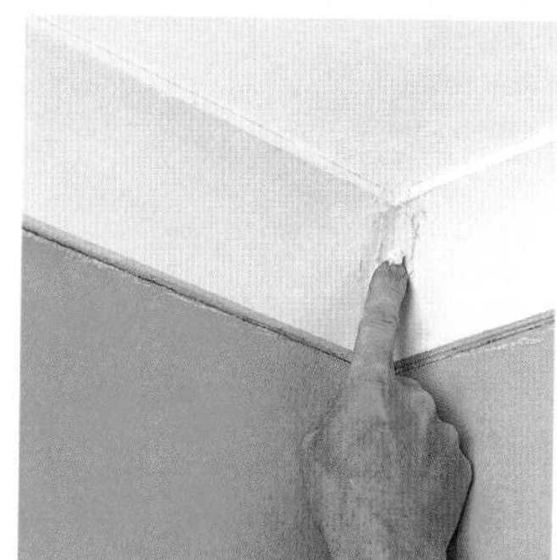

4 When the room is complete, fill any gaps and joints with adhesive, then wipe with a damp sponge. Allow the adhesive to dry, then lightly sand the joints and corners with fine-grade abrasive paper.

YOU CAN DO IT

Mixing adhesive

Coving adhesive can come ready-mixed, or in powder form to be mixed with water. It sets very quickly, so if you are mixing it up yourself, check its setting time and only mix the amount you can use in that time.

Adding cornerpieces

Some manufacturers make coving cornerpieces, differently shaped to fit internal and external corners. They will give an elegant finish to your coving, and hide any less-than-perfect mitre joints. Simply apply adhesive to the back, hold the cornerpiece in place until it is secure, then wipe away any excess adhesive.

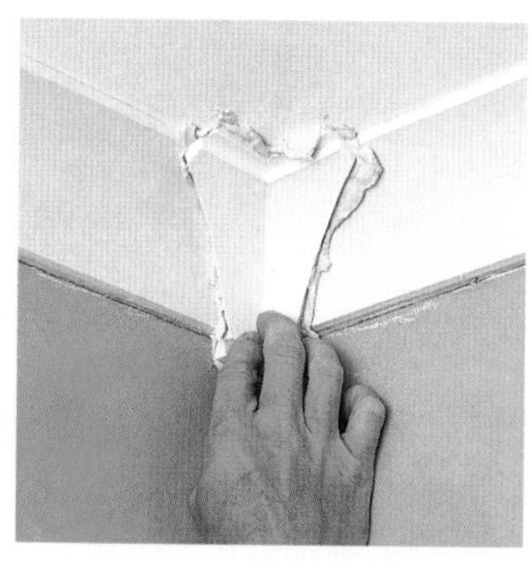

Decorating with coving

Coving can offer more than period elegance. By adding a lighter band at the highest point in a room, it can be a great way of making a ceiling seem higher, especially if you want to decorate the walls and ceiling in strong or dark colours. Modern designs are available that will give a bold lift to any design scheme. Before you paint coving, seal its porous surface with coving primer.

LOFTS CREATING SAFE ACCESS

The loft is a very handy storage place, but to make use of it you need to be able to access it easily. The best way to do this is via a fitted, extendable loft ladder, which folds back and is stored out of the way in the loft space. To install it, however, you may need to enlarge your existing hatch or create a completely new opening in a better position. It may also be necessary to board the loft to provide a safe surface on which to walk and store items.

TOOLS MATERIALS

- **dust sheets**
- **ladder**
- **electronic joist detector**
- **hammer**
- **bradawl**
- **straightedge**
- **pencil**
- **trailing light**
- **padsaw**
- **panel saw**
- **mitre saw**

- tongue-and-groove chipboard boards
- length of timber the same size as the joists
- 100mm round wire nails
- 30mm plasterboard nails
- 25mm thick planed timber, deep enough to form the hatch lining
- 50mm lost-head nails
- filler
- door architrave

Choosing a ladder

Loft ladders are made of wood or aluminium, and come in either fold-and-slide or concertina designs. They are made in different lengths (to suit heights of 2.3m, 2.5m and 2.9m–3m, measured from the floor of the landing to the top of the loft joists). All are hinged to the hatch; some have a handrail and some can be operated from inside the loft. The manufacturer will specify the size of hatch opening required and the pivoting height needed inside the loft (usually 1.1m above the loft floor). Make sure you have enough space.

A sliding ladder is simple to install and operate: it is lowered by means of a pole hooked over the bottom rail. It has two or three sections, with spring-locking catches to hold it in the fully extended or closed position. Some are fitted with a sprung power pivot arm to prevent the ladder from dropping down under its own weight. This also makes it easy to raise the ladder into the roof.

SAFETY FIRST

If you intend to store heavy items in your loft, be sure to keep them at the sides rather than in the middle of your loft space.

Cutting a joist

If you need to enlarge your present hatch, you will probably have to cut away part of a joist – that is, part of the roof structure. You should cut no more than one joist. In some post-war houses, you may not need to cut any joists as they may be spaced as much as 600mm apart. In modern houses, lightweight timbers are used for the joists and the roof is designed in such a way that each joist plays a vital role – any alteration may weaken the structure, so check with your Building Control Officer before proceeding.

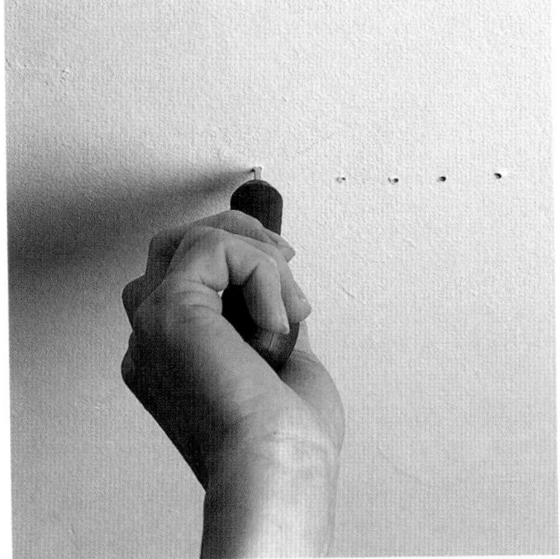

1 Locate three ceiling joists where you want the hatch to be. Use an electronic joist detector, or tap lightly on the ceiling with a hammer until you hear the sound change. This will mean you are under a joist, and you can then find the edges of the joists and the direction in which they lie by probing the ceiling with a bradawl. The outer joists will form parallel sides of the new hatch, while a section of the central joist will have to be removed.

Making a new opening

Put down dust sheets before you start. You will need good lighting when working in the loft. An inspection lamp hung from a rafter will do while you are installing the hatch and ladder, but consider finishing the job by adding a permanent light within easy reach of the new opening (see pages 284–87).

2 Draw the outline of the hatch on the ceiling using a straightedge and a pencil. The ladder manufacturer's instructions will give you the minimum opening size.

3 With a hammer knock an inspection hole in the ceiling within the marked area. Make it large enough for your head and the trailing light so that you can inspect the area for hazards and assess the space available.

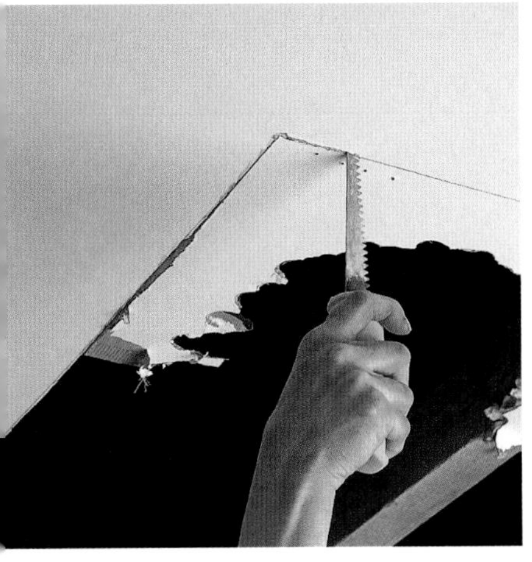

4 Provided all is safe and clear, use a padsaw to cut out the marked area.

5 Climb up between the joists and lay a board across them to support yourself. Saw through the central joist, cutting it back 50mm from the edges of the new opening. Remove the cut piece. Place more boards in the loft around the opening to prevent accidental damage to the ceiling below.

SAFETY FIRST

- Lay planks over the loft joists so that you don't put your foot through the ceiling of the room below
- Lofts can be full of fine dust, so wear a dust mask if you are cleaning up debris or removing old insulation
- If you don't have the necessary skills, get an electrician to fit a loft light

6 Cut two lengths of timber ('trimmers') to fit between the joists and form the other two sides of the hatch. Fix the trimmers in place with 100mm round wire nails.

7 Nail the ceiling to the underside of the trimmers with 30mm plasterboard nails.

IDEAL TOOL

Mitre saw
This saw is designed to lock in place and cut at an angle of 45°. You can use it to cut mitred corners in mouldings such as the door architrave to go round the hatch or to cut skirting-boards.

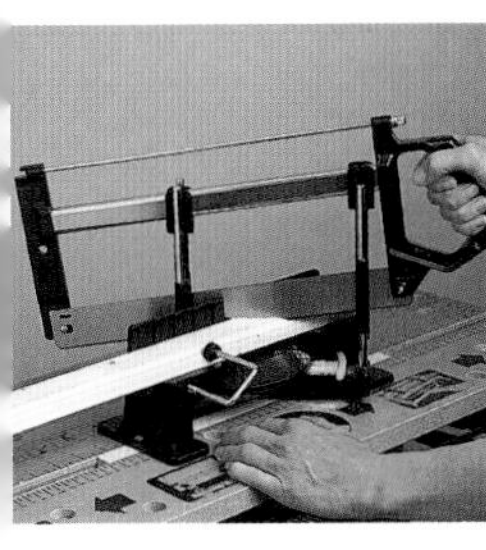

8 Cut the planed timber to make facing boards. These cover the joists and the edges of the ceiling plaster to form the hatch lining. They should be about 25mm thick and sufficiently deep to fit level with the ceiling on one side and the finished loft flooring on the other. Nail them in place with 50mm lost-head nails. If the ceiling plaster is damaged round the edges, repair it with filler.

9 Cover the joint between the ceiling and the hatch lining with door architrave. Cut the corners of the architrave to fit using a mitre saw, then nail the architrave in place.

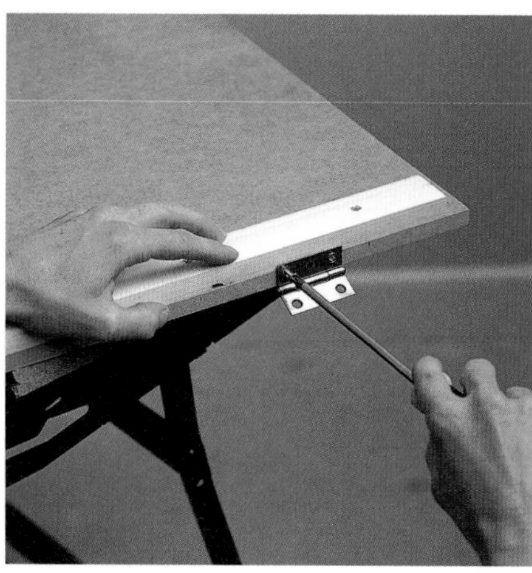

1 Measure the hatch opening and cut a door from your blockboard, MDF or plywood. If the 12mm board is too thin to take the hinges, nail a strip of 50mm x 25mm batten to the hinge end of the board. Screw the hinges on to the door.

Making a hatch door

Some ladders come with a hatch door, but if yours does not, or if your old hatch door is not strong enough, you can make a new one. You can choose from 12mm or 19mm blockboard, MDF or plywood. The thicker board is very heavy to work with, but the thinner board may need a batten added to take the hinges.

2 The door should open downwards, so fix the other side of the hinges the same side as the ladder will go, screwing through the hatch lining into the joist or trimmer.

TOOLS MATERIALS

- **tape measure**
- **pencil**
- **tenon saw**
- **screwdriver**
- **adjustable spanner, if necessary**

- 12mm or 19mm blockboard, MDF or plywood
- 50mm x 25mm batten if required
- two 65mm or 75mm hinges and screws

3 Most ladders come with a push or turn lock/release catch which has to be fixed to the other side of the door. Follow the manufacturer's instructions for fitting it.

SAFETY FIRST

- Re-route any electric cables lying on top of the joists before boarding the loft, running them between the joists. Don't cut channels for them in the ceiling joists as it will weaken the joists. If the cables need to cross over the top of the joists, they can do this at the eaves.
- Check that no wires or pipes will be damaged when drilling or screwing the boards.
- Wear a mask to cut the boards, and don't do it in the loft, as ventilation up there is probably very limited.

Boarding the loft

If the floor of your loft consists of exposed joists, you will need to lay down a safe, firm flooring before you can use the space for storage. Tongue-and-groove chipboard 1220mm long and 18mm thick is designed specially for loft boarding. The boards are easy to pass up through a hatch, and they are long enough to cover three joists.

Start beside the hatch hinges, and fit the ladder once the first couple of boards are down. If boarding all the way to the rafters, leave a gap of at least 10mm around the edge of the loft to allow the boards to expand in wet weather.

TOOLS MATERIALS

- **circular saw or jigsaw**
- **power drill with 4mm gauge countersink bit**
- **screwdriver**

- tongue-and-groove chipboard boards
- PVA wood adhesive
- 40mm screws (4mm gauge

Laying the boards

The boards should be laid with their long sides at right angles to the joists, with joins staggered wherever possible. Fit tongues into grooves and glue the joins. Where necessary, cut the boards so that they meet at the centre-line of a joist and are properly supported. Screw them down along the length of the joists. Drill pilot holes with a 4mm countersink bit, and drive in the screws so the heads are flush with the boards or slightly recessed. For future reference, mark on the boards the position of any cables or pipes lying beneath.

Fitting the loft ladder

you are boarding the loft, fit the ladder as soon as the first ouple of boards are down – it will much easier and safer to nish the job of boarding with a fixed ladder in place. Ladders ill differ, so always follow the manufacturer's instructions.

TOOLS MATERIALS

- **power drill with twist bits**
- **screwdriver**
- **bradawl**
- **adjustable spanner, if required**

- loft ladder and fittings

1 Lower the ladder to the floor. Fit the top tops on the ladder, according to the nstructions. Drill pilot holes then screw the adder hinge screws through the board into he joist or trimmer below and on to the front ace. Fit the loft ladder guide assembly to the rame. You can fit the handrail now or, if you ave a power pivot system, you may find it asier to fit it after this is installed.

2 If the ladder has a power pivot system, use the template supplied to mark the position for the pivot arm on the floor of the loft. Mark the position of the screws with a bradawl. The pivot system can usually be fitted to either side of the ladder.

3 Position the power pivot arm according to the manufacturer's instructions and screw it to the loft floor. With the ladder in fully stowed position in the loft, attach the pivot arm to one side of it.

4 Follow the manufacturer's instructions for lowering and storing the ladder. This usually involves putting the hook on the end of the ladder's pole into the catch on the underside of the door and rotating the catch to lower the door. Then place the pole hook into the socket in the centre of the bottom rung on the middle section of the ladder and lower it until the stops are reached. Release the locking catches and lower all sections of the ladder.

5 To store the ladder, release the catches, move the ladder into a closed position and engage the catches. Slide the ladder upwards until it is able to swing through the loft opening and ease it into the loft space with the pole. Hook the end of the pole into the catch on the door, raise the door and twist the catch to close it.

YOU CAN DO IT

Loft insulation
Before boarding the loft, check you have adequate insulation. The minimum recommended depth is 270mm, but many houses – old and new – will have less. If so, take the opportunity to top it up using blanket or loose-lay insulation (see page 102). This will make your heating system more efficient, and may bring the bills down significantly.

B&Q

As glass-making developed over the centuries, windows progressed from open slits in walls to the great variety of styles available today. Windows can have a dramatic effect on the appearance of a house, both from the outside and the inside. Choices range from old-fashioned windows in stained wooden frames to large single panes of glass that allow lots of natural light to flood indoors, with countless variations in between.

Choosing windows

The part of the window that opens is called the sash, and it consists of a fitted frame that either slides vertically or is hinged from one edge. Vertically sliding windows are usually known as sash windows, while hinged windows are called casements, and, although there are lots of styles to choose from, most windows are variations of these two main types.

When fitting new windows always choose ones that suit the style of your house and the neighbourhood.

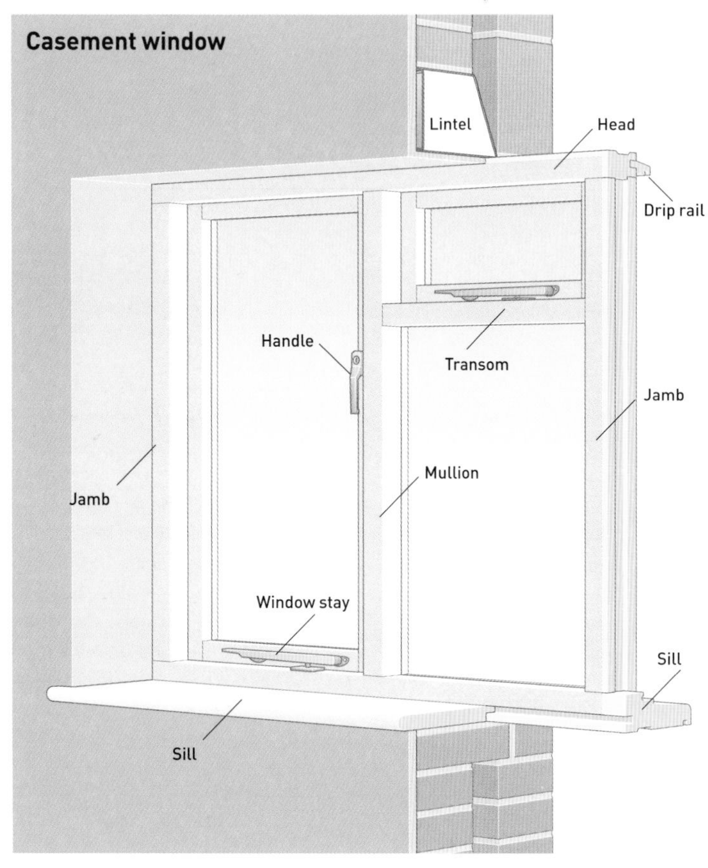

Casement windows

Casements are the most common windows. They are often a mixture of fixed panes of glass and opening casements, which may be hinged either at the side or the top. Side-hinged casements are usually larger than the top-hinged ones. Wooden casement window frames have a vertical piece, called a jamb, at each side of the frame; there is a piece called a head at the top and a sill at the bottom, all joined by mortise-and-tenon joints. The frame may be divided vertically by a piece called a mullion or horizontally by a transom. The glazed areas of some windows are divided into smaller panes by moulded strips of wood called glazing bars.

Larger windows are conventionally fastened with a handle and mortise plate at roughly the mid-point and a window stay and locking peg at the bottom of the window; top-hinged windows may have just a window stay and locking peg.

Modern window frames are sometimes fitted with ventilators to give a constant supply of fresh air without having to open the window.

Pivot windows

Pivot windows are made like casement windows but they have a hinge mechanism on each side so the sash can pivot at its mid-poin allowing both sides of the glass to be cleaned from inside the house Special weatherproof pivot windows, double-glazed and with ventilation in the frame, are made for installation in pitched roofs. These are often used in loft conversions.

Tilt-and-turn windows, which are usually made to measure, open inwards at the top or may open at the side.

Louvre windows

This type of window is usually found in a kitchen or bathroom. Horizontal strips of glass are attached to a frame with metal clips, and these enable the strips to pivot simultaneously to control the flow of air. With some windows the strips can be lifted out of the clips, which poses a security problem, but locking ones are available. Louvre windows are often fitted above or beside a fixed pane of glass.

Bay windows

A bay window is built into the external wall of the house, so the roor extends into the bay. The window frames are built to fit the shape of the wall, and the sides of each frame may be set at an angle of 90° or less to the flat front of the house. They can be fitted with casement or sash windows. To make a curved bay, frames of equal size are set at a slight angle to each other.

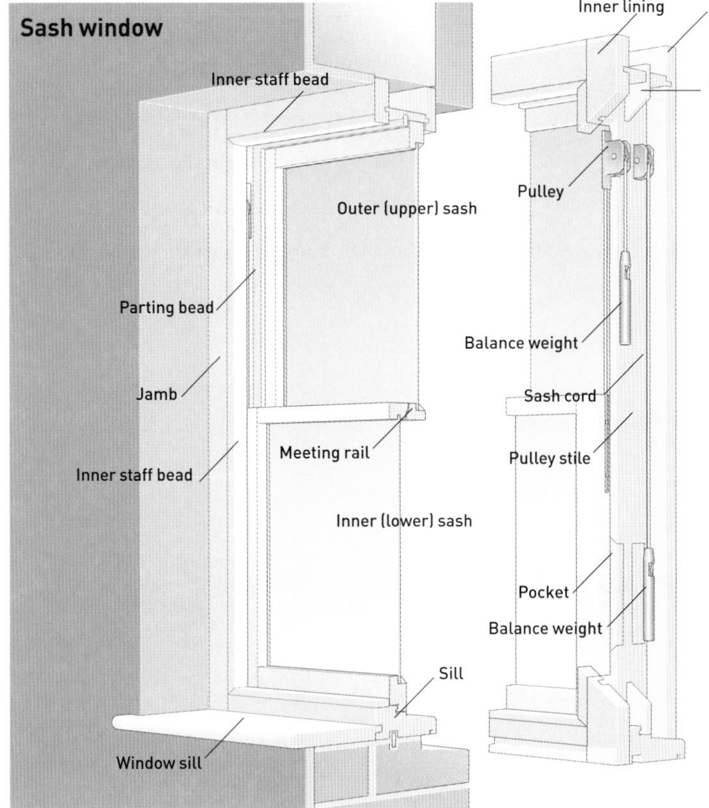

Sash windows

Traditional sash windows slide up and down, whereas some modern ones, especially those with metal frames, slide from side to side.

Traditional sash windows are operated by sash cords attached to cast-iron or lead weights. The cords and weights are concealed in a box-like compartment inside the vertical jambs at each side of the frame. These compartments consist of inner and outer linings and a pulley stile. The cords move over pulleys set in the pulley stiles. Access to the weights is through panels of wood, known as pockets, in the lower part of the stiles.

When both the top and the bottom sashes open, the window is known as a double-hung sash window. The sashes are held in runners formed by the outer lining of the jambs, parting beads – which keep the sashes apart – and inner staff beads. The beads can be removed if you need to carry out work on the sash mechanism. The upper sash moves up and down in the outer runner, and the lower sash in the inner runner. They overlap at horizontal meeting rails, and they are secured by fasteners which are screwed to the two meeting rails.

Modern sash windows have spring-action spiral balances which are not boxed in. Instead they are set into the frame and move up and down in grooves cut in the side of the sashes.

Bow windows

The frames for bow windows are ready-made from a series of casements set at an angle, so they form a curve. They may be fitted into a flat wall or a slightly bow-shaped one, but unlike bay windows the curve is too shallow to actually extend the size of the room.

French windows

These are really doors, hinged on the side, with the bottom of the frame level with the floor.

Window materials

Windows may be made of wood, plastic, steel or aluminium. These materials all require different amounts of maintenance.

SAFETY FIRST

Safety glass

Glazed doors must be fitted with safety glass, which is reinforced or strengthened by a toughening process. Windows close to the ground and other vulnerable glazed areas, such as shower screens or large panes of glass, should also be fitted with safety glass.

Wood

Wooden windows look good but they do need regular maintenance. Cheaper softwood windows must be painted; hardwood and some better-quality softwood ones can be stained or painted. Modern wooden windows are often double-glazed. When buying new wooden windows, always check that they have been treated with preservative.

Plastic

Plastic, or PVCu, windows are very practical and hardwearing. They do not warp, rot or rust, and aside from cleaning the glass they are virtually maintenance free.

Steel

Steel windows have slim welded frames which make them strong and durable. Newer ones are galvanised before they are painted or given a polyester coating; in older ones, the galvanised coating can deteriorate, leaving them prone to rust.

Aluminium

Aluminium windows are often used in new houses and they are usually double-glazed. They require no maintenance unless they are fitted in a wooden frame, which will need regular painting or varnishing.

WINDOWS AND DOORS TYPES OF DOOR

There are plenty of styles and materials to choose from when you buy a new door. Most fall into one of two main categories: panel doors or flush doors. Houses built before the 1940s (and most built in the past decade or so) are likely to have panel doors; flush doors were popular in the post-war period.

Choosing a door

When buying a new door, choose one that matches the other doors in the house. Internal doors may be made from softwood or hardwood, and they may be painted or stained and varnished for a natural-wood look. Glazed doors are generally used for front and rear entrances, but are increasingly used for internal doors. The door frame may be made from timber, or aluminium if it's a PVCu plastic door.

Doors are sold in standard sizes of varying thicknesses to fit modern houses. Interior doors are thinner and less strong than exterior doors, which have to be weatherproof (see page 173). Older houses often have non-standard size doors so, if you have to replace one, you may need to have it made to measure. Alternatively, you may be able to buy a larger door and trim it to fit (see page 124), but check when you buy it how much can be safely removed without weakening the structure.

SAFETY FIRST

Fire safety

Fire-resistant doors can delay the spread of fire. They are primarily installed in multiple-storey buildings to prevent fire blocking the escape routes, but the door to a garage attached to a house must also meet fire-resistance requirements. Fire doors are usually the wooden flush type with a core of solid board material. Any window opening must be glazed with fire-resistant glass. Fire-resistant door frames have a recess containing a special strip that swells when hot and seals the gap around the door. If you are replacing an old fire door, make sure the new door is at least the same fire rating. Follow the instructions carefully and make sure the seals and special fittings are all properly installed. If you are considering fitting a new fire door, you should consult your local Fire Prevention Officer.

Panel doors

Panel doors consist of a wooden frame with panels of wood, plywood or glass in the centre. At one time there might have been as many as eight or ten panels in a door; doors manufactured today are more likely to have four or six.

The frame has a vertical piece called a stile on either side – the hinges fit on one stile (the hanging stile) and the lock is attached to the other stile (the shutting stile); three cross rails running horizontally at the top, centre and bottom of the door are jointed into the stiles; and the final piece of the framework is a vertical piece in the centre, called a muntin, which is joined to the cross rails. The panels fit into grooves in the frame and may have decorative moulded borders.

Plain moulding

The panel is slotted into a groove in the stiles and left without any moulding.

Planted moulding

The inside edge of the frame is fitted with a planted moulding. This type can shrink away from the frame and cause cracks in the paint if the door is painted.

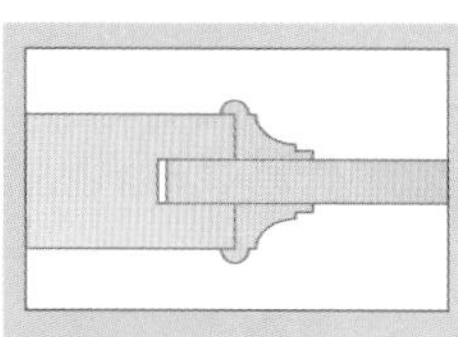

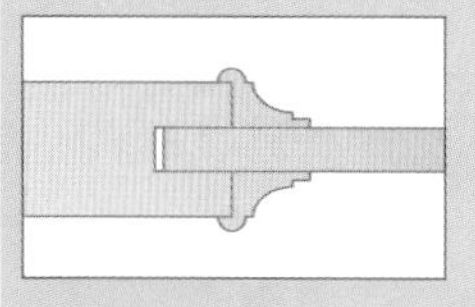

Bolection moulding

A bolection moulding is shaped so that it overlaps the door frame, making it less likely to shrink away from the frame.

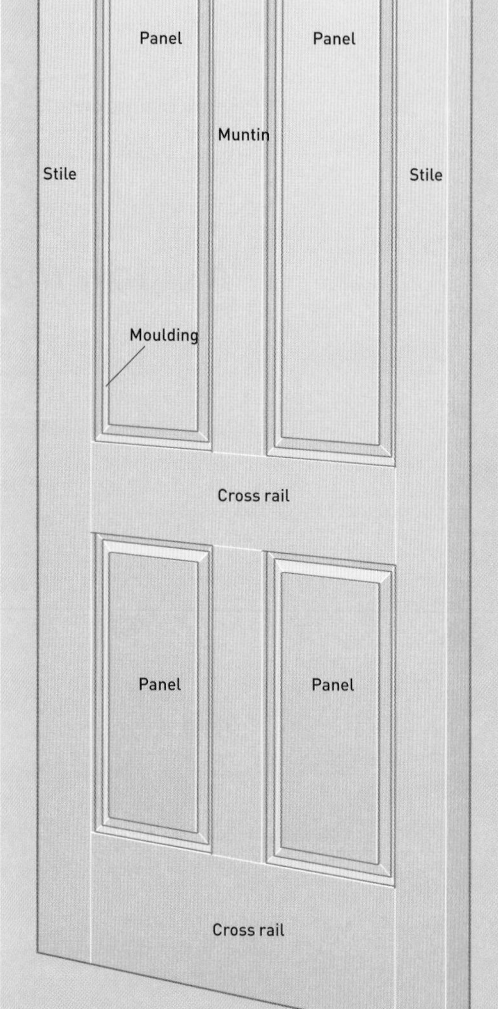

Panel door

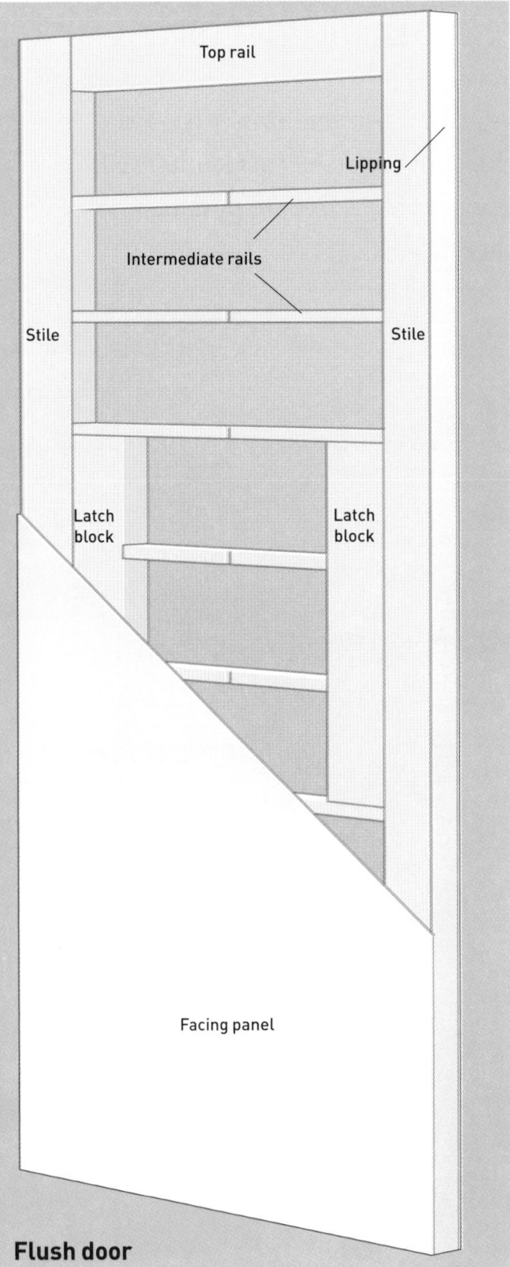

Flush door

Flush doors

Flush doors usually have completely flat facings of man-made board attached to a softwood frame. The frame consists of a stile on either side, and a top and bottom rail jointed into the stiles. A vertical block is glued to the inner side of each stile to take the door latch.

The frame is covered on both sides with sheets of plywood or hardboard, which may be painted or covered with a wood veneer. Some facings are embossed to look like a panelled door; others have mouldings fixed to them to look like panels. The edges of the door are covered with lipping.

Between these facing sheets, the core of the door can vary. The framework of a lightweight door may be filled with a honeycombed paper or cardboard material. Heavier alternatives include sheets of chipboard, laminated vertical strips of timber or horizontal timber rails, known as intermediate rails, attached to the stiles all the way down the door.

Door frames

n internal door is hung on a wooden frame screwed ıto the walls on both sides. If the door is in a ıasonry wall, a rigid beam called a lintel is set in ıe wall over the door to support the structure bove the opening. Special brackets fix the frame ɔ the walls. A door frame in a stud partition wall (see age 55) is attached to the timber studs supporting ıe plasterboard walls and extra studs are fitted over ıe doorway to strengthen it.

The top of the door frame is called the soffit asing and the sides are jamb casings. The door ɜ attached to the frame with two hinges set in ecesses cut out with a chisel. The line where ıe casings and the wall meet is covered with a ecorative moulding called an architrave. The oor closes against a doorstop, which is usually separate piece of wood fitted to the frame.

Architrave
Soffit casing
Lintel
Recess for hinges
Doorstop
Jamb casing
Jamb casing
Securing bracket attaching frame to masonry wall
Recess for hinges
Threshold

Door frame casing

YOU CAN DO IT

Interior doors

Panel door
A traditional panelled door, whether painted or stained and varnished, gives privacy and elegance.

Glazed pine door
Partially glazed doors are great for diffusing natural light through an interior.

Glazed french doors
Double doors with lots of glass look good leading to a conservatory or extension.

WINDOWS REPLACING SASH CORDS

TOOLS MATERIALS

- **wood chisel**
- **wooden mallet**
- **table or workbench**
- **craft knife**
- **pincers**
- **old screwdriver or chisel**
- **plane or sander**

- string
- new sash cord
- 50mm nail or screw
- 25mm or 32mm galvanised clout nails
- parting beads, if old ones are damaged
- 25mm oval nails
- wood filler

The most common repairs to sash windows are replacing broken sash cords and repairing damaged or loose beads. When a cord breaks you have to take the sash right out of the frame to replace it, so it's a good idea to replace both at the same time. You can be sure that if one breaks, the other will soon go too.

Sash cord

Sash cord is made from various materials, including waxed and unwaxed hemp and synthetic fibres, and is available in different diameters. Make sure your new cord is the same diameter as the old one – take a piece to the shop, if necessary. Most sash cord is sold in a pack containing enough for all types of window. Alternatively, measure from the top of the window to the sill and add about two-thirds as much again for each length of cord. Each sash – upper and lower – requires two lengths of cord. Don't cut it to length in advance.

Pulley
Sash cord
Upper sash
Parting be
Staff bea
Lower sash

Gaining access to the broken cord

If you remove both the sashes, label the weights so that you know which ones are from the upper (outer) sash and which from the lower (inner) one. Although they look the same, they may be slightly different and if you put them back the wrong way round, it could affect the smooth running of the sashes.

1 To replace a lower sash cord, you must take out the lower sash window; to replace an upper sash cord, you will need to take out both the lower and then the upper sash.

2 Prise off the left- and right-hand staff beads from the inside of the frame. Start in the centre of each bead to avoid damaging the corners and tap a chisel into the joint using a mallet.

3 Once a staff bead has lifted in the middle, the rest of it should pull away from the frame and spring out from the mitred corners.

4 If either cord was unbroken, tie some string around it near the pulley; this will be used to pull the new cord into place. Cut through the old cord below the string and gently lower the weight to the bottom of its compartment, running the strin over the pulley. Lift out the lowe sash and support it on a table or workbench. Remove the piece o cord from each side of the sash, pulling out any securing nails with pincers.

5 Prise the narrow parting beads out of their grooves. They should be wedged in place, but may be nailed or screwed. Lift the upper sash into the room if you are replacing all the cords (otherwise it can stay in place). Cut and remove the cords in the same way as for the lower sash.

6 Use a chisel to prise off the pocket cover from each side of the frame. The covers should be just pushed in place but some may have been secured with screws or nails that you will need to take out.

7 Lift out the weights in the pockets and remove the old cords. If you have attached string to a cord, leave it in place over the pulley with one end in the pocket.

Replacing the cords

If you have removed both sashes, replace the cords on the upper sash first and fit it back in the frame, then do the same for the lower sash.

1 Where the cord was broken, tie a 50mm nail or screw to a piece of string and push it into the hole above the pulley. Feed the string through the hole so that it drops down into the weight compartment and you can retrieve it from the pocket.

2 Tie lengths of new cord – each at least one and a half times the depth of the window frame – to the ends of the strings hanging from the pulleys. Pull each cord over the pulley, down into the weight compartment and out through the pocket.

3 Remove the string from each cord, thread the cord through the hole in the top of the weight and tie it with a stop knot (see YOU CAN DO IT). Tuck the end into the cavity at the top of the weight. Put the weights back in the pockets and replace the pocket covers.

YOU CAN DO IT

Stop knot
A figure-of-eight knot in the sash cord will stop the weight slipping off the end. Make a loop in the cord about 75mm from the end. Take the end round the back of the cord to form a figure-of-eight. Bring it back to the front and pass it through the first loop.

Reassembling the window

Before you can replace the lower sash in the frame, you will need to refit the parting beads – unless you have taken out the upper sash, in which case put that back in first.

1 Tap the parting beads back into their slots with a mallet. If necessary, use an old screwdriver or chisel to clean out any debris first. If the parting beads were nailed rather than pushed in, they are likely to have split when you removed them and you will need to replace them. Measure the window and cut new parting beads to the correct length. Plane or sand them if they are too thick, then tap them into place.

2 Rest the lower sash on the sill and get a helper to pull the cords and raise the weights to their highest position. Tie a knot in each cord level with the knot holes in the sides of the sash, then cut off the surplus cord. If the knot holes are damaged, as here, you will need to secure the cord with 3 or 4 galvanised clout nails. Then replace the sash in the frame.

3 Refit the staff beads on each side of the frame: tap them into place with the mallet, then nail with 25mm oval nails, but don't drive the nails all the way in. Check first that the sashes move up and down without sticking, and adjust the beads in or out accordingly.

4 When you are satisfied with the operation of the window, drive the nails fully home. Use wood filler to repair any damage before touching up or repainting the whole window (see page 131).

DOORS FIXING FAULTS

Doors can develop a variety of faults, any of which may prevent them opening and closing smoothly. Faults may be due to heavy wear and tear, age, previous damp or a build-up of paint layers over the years. Fortunately, they are quite easy to cure.

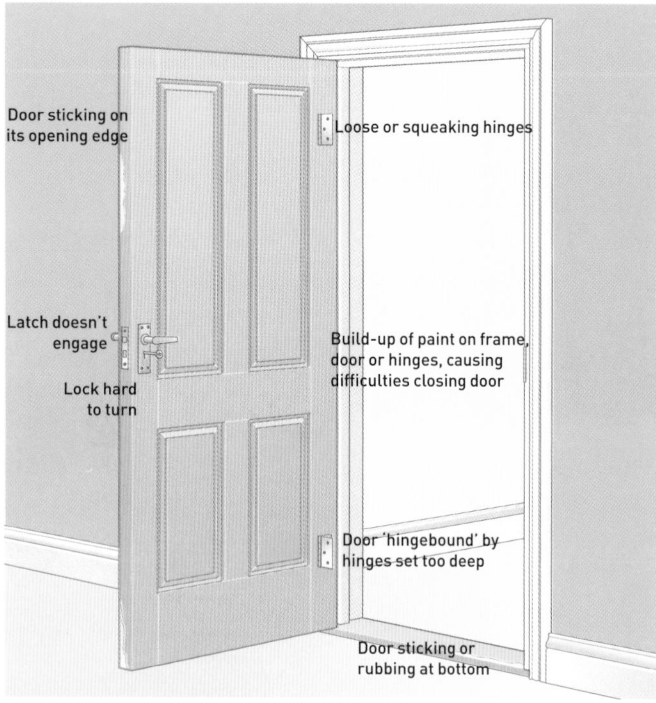

Squeaks and stiffness

Squeaking hinges and a lock that is hard to turn can both usually be solved by a squirt of aerosol lubricant, either into the latch mechanism or on to the hinge pins. When you have sprayed the hinges, open and close the door a few times to allow the oil to flow through them, then wipe away any excess before it runs down to the floor.

Fixing a dropped door

A door may drop because its hinges have worn loose. Check all the hinge screws to make sure they are tight. If a screw will not tighten properly, you may need to replace it with a larger size or plug the existing hole with matchsticks.

TOOLS MATERIALS

- **screwdriver**
- **wood chisel**
- **wooden mallet**

- wood adhesive
- matchsticks

1 Remove the screw. Apply wood adhesive to one end of some matchsticks and tap two or three into the screw hole.

2 When the adhesive has set, cut off the matchsticks level with the hinge flap, using a chisel and wooden mallet, then replace the screw.

Sticking door

A build-up of paint on the edge of the door and the frame can make the door stick or bind, either at the top, bottom or the side. You may be able to sand any high spots away, using coarse abrasive paper around a sanding block, but if it is sticking badly you will need to plane off the excess material.

TOOLS MATERIALS

- **plane**
- **workbench, if necessary**

- abrasive paper
- sanding block
- wood primer
- paint

1 Marks on the paintwork will indicate where the door is sticking – in this case, the edge of the door. When a door is sticking along the top or upper side edge, you may be able to plane it without taking it off its hinges. If it is sticking near the floor, however, you will need to remove the door and secure it in a workbench in order to plane it.

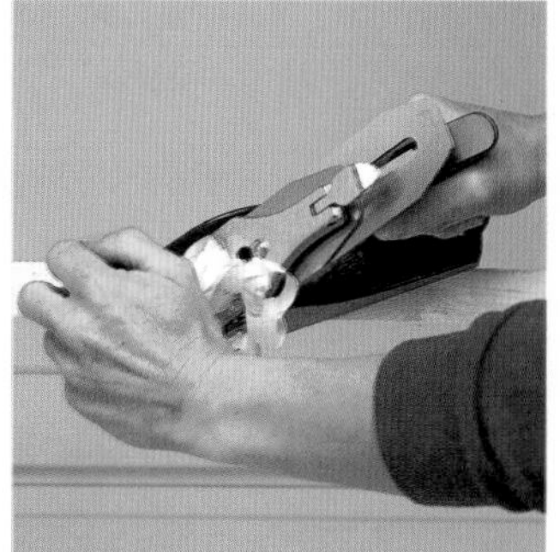

2 Plane the edge, allowing sufficient clearance for repainting. Remove the lock first if you need to plane near it.

3 Sand the planed edge of the door and the top and bottom corners, using a sanding block. Prime the wood before repainting it.

1 If there is no clearance on the hinge side, remove the screws from one hinge at a time. Prise the hinge out of the recess – it helps to have an assistant holding the door steady while you do this. Cut some cardboard to fit the recess and pack it into the space.

YOU CAN DO IT

Jamming at the bottom

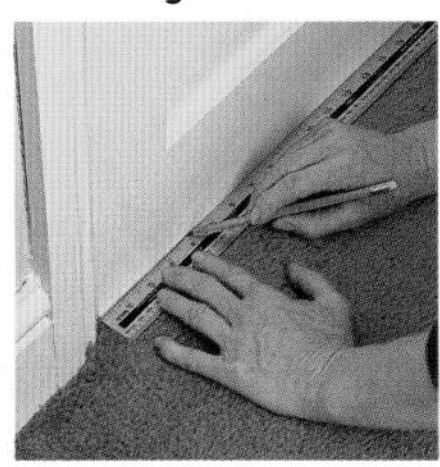

If the door is jamming at the bottom or there is insufficient clearance over the carpet, position the door where it is sticking the most. Rest a piece of thick card or a steel rule on the flooring against the door and mark a pencil line at that height along the bottom of the door. Take the door off its hinges and saw or plane off the excess material. Smooth the edges with abrasive paper and refit the door.

Springing door

If a door springs open all the time, this usually means the hinges are set too deep in the door or frame and the door is straining against them. Alternatively, the door may not be closing properly against the doorstop, the thin strip of wood nailed on to the frame. Examine the paintwork around the door to locate the problem.

TOOLS MATERIALS

- **screwdriver**
- **wood chisel**

- cardboard
- 30mm nails

2 Screw back the hinge and repeat the process for the other hinge. The packed-out recesses will give the required clearance, but they may cause sticking on the lock side. If this happens, you will need to plane the edge of the door (see opposite).

3 If the door will not stay closed against the doorstop, tap a wood chisel into the joint between doorstop and door frame and lever the doorstop off.

4 Close the door, then reposition the doorstop to give the door enough clearance to close without catching. Nail it in place with 30mm nails roughly 300mm apart.

Misaligned lock

If the door latch is out of line with the striker plate, it will not engage. It may be possible to fix a very small misalignment without removing the plate by enlarging the cut-out area in the striker plate with a metal file. However, the plate may have to be taken off and repositioned.

TOOLS MATERIALS

- **screwdriver**
- **pencil**
- **crayon (optional)**
- **wood chisel**
- **power drill with twist bit**

- small round wooden pegs

1 Unscrew and remove the striker plate. Rub a pencil or crayon on the tip of the latch, then close the door and operate the handle several times. Open the door and you will see marks on the frame at the position of the latch. Mark over these with a pencil to show the new position for the striker plate.

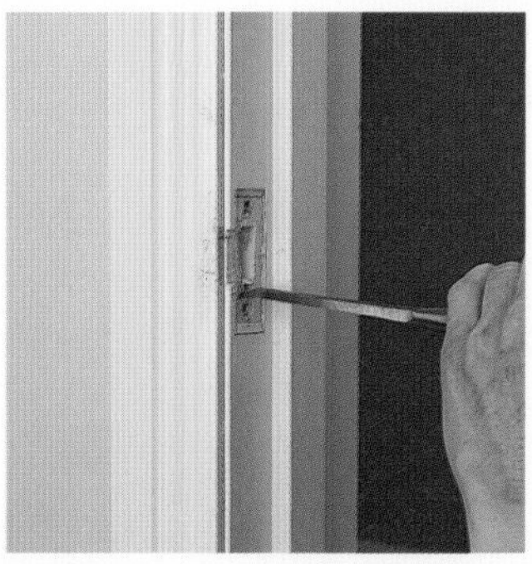

2 Use a wood chisel to enlarge the cut-out area in the frame as far as the pencil marks.

3 Reposition the striker plate in the new position, making sure that its cut-out area fits over the cut-out area on the frame. If the plate has moved only a small distance, plug the old screw holes with small wooden pegs before drilling new pilot holes for the screws.

Whether you are hanging a new door in a new frame or a new door in an existing frame, you must make sure that the door fits into it before fitting the hinges. Allow a clearance gap of about 2mm at the top and sides, and 6mm–12mm at the bottom, depending on the thickness of the flooring.

Fitting a new door in a new frame

YOU CAN DO IT

Plane talking

When trimming the top or bottom of a door, plane from both ends towards the centre to avoid splitting the end grain.

B&Q

New doors may have extensions to the stiles, known as horns, which prevent the corners being damaged. These should be sawn off before trimming the door.

TOOLS MATERIALS

- **tape measure**
- **pencil**
- **plane**
- **panel saw**
- **marking gauge (optional)**
- **wide-bladed wood chisel**
- **wooden mallet**
- **power drill with twist and wood bits**
- **screwdriver**
- **try square**
- **narrow chisel**
- **craft knife**
- **vice**
- **hacksaw**
- **mitre saw or mitre block**
- **long-nosed pliers**
- **nail punch**

- new door
- abrasive paper
- two 100mm butt hinges and screws
- wooden wedges
- cardboard
- masking tape
- door latch and handles
- 30mm nails
- panel pins
- thin strip of wood for doorstop

1 Measure the door frame, allowing for the necessary clearance, and transfer the measurements to the door. Plane equal amounts from the two side edges of the door to a maximum of 5mm.

2 If you need to trim more than 6mm excess wood from the bottom edge of the door, use a saw, then finish with the plane. Sand the cut edges with abrasive paper until smooth.

Fitting the door hinges

Two hinges are generally enough to support a standard internal door, though in the humid environment of a bathroom or kitchen fit three to help prevent bowing. Hinges fit into recesses of an equal depth in the door frame and the stile. You need a very sharp wood chisel with a wide blade for making them.

1 Mark the position of the upper hinge on the stile, 175mm from the top edge of the door. The lower hinge should be 250mm from the bottom edge of the door. Stand the door on its side edge with the hinge edge uppermost. Hold each hinge on its marked position with the knuckle protruding from the door. Draw round the hinge flap with a sharp pencil.

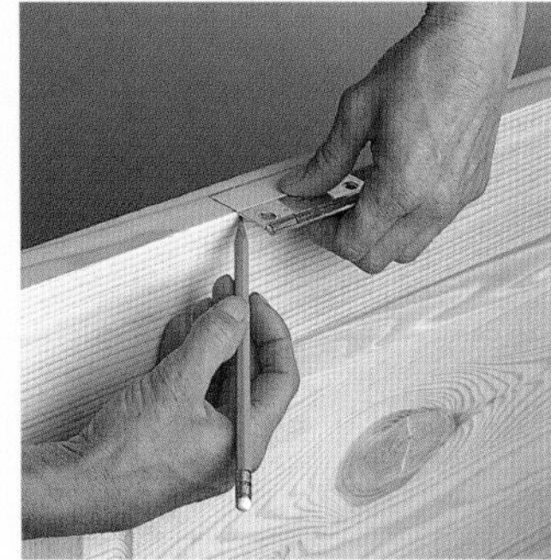

2 To mark the depth for the hinge recess, use a marking gauge or hold a hinge flap level with the edge of the door and mark the depth with a pencil.

3 Cut out the hinge recess using a sharp wide-bladed wood chisel and a wooden mallet. First cut the ends and then make a series of cuts along the length of the hinge to approximately the correct depth.

4 Use the chisel to pare away the surplus wood and trim the recess until it is level.

YOU CAN DO IT

Testing the fit

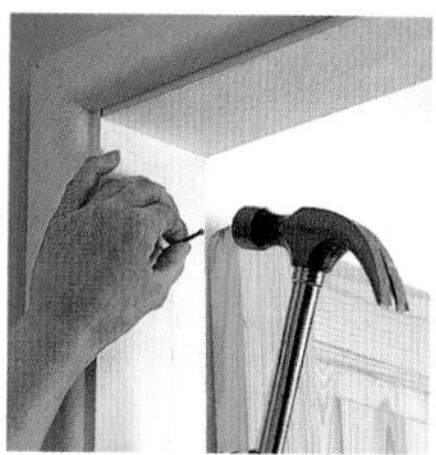

Before test-fitting the door, partially hammer four nails into the frame at the depth of the door to prevent it from falling through.

IDEAL TOOL

Door/board lifter
Use this specially designed tool to lever the door into position with your foot, leaving your hands free to mark the hinge positions.

5 Test-fit the hinge in the recess and trim it again as necessary. Repeat the process for the other hinge. Position each hinge flap in its recess and drill pilot holes in the screw positions. Screw in the screws with a screwdriver to secure the hinges to the door.

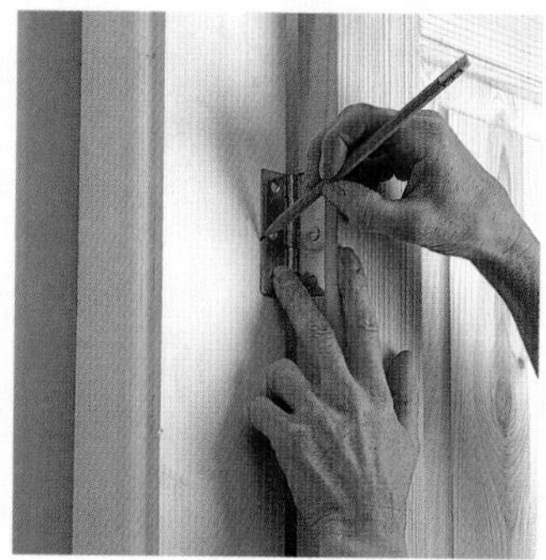

6 Get a helper to hold the door in the open position in the frame with the hinge flaps against the frame. Tap two screwdrivers or wooden wedges under the door to raise it to the required height to clear the flooring. Make sure the hinge knuckles are parallel with the frame, then mark the frame with a pencil. Remove the door. Chisel out the hinge recesses in the door frame in the same way as those in the door.

7 Wedge the door in the open position and check that the hinges fit into the recesses. Adjust them, if necessary. Drill pilot holes and screw the hinges to the frame using just one screw per hinge, then check to make sure the door closes smoothly. If it is straining against the hinges (hingebound), undo the screws and pack out the flaps with cardboard. If it rubs on the latch side of frame, make the hinge recesses slightly deeper. Screw in the remaining hinge screws.

Fitting the latch

Door latches, locks, knobs and handles are available in a vast range of shapes and sizes, including reproductions of many traditional styles and designs. Here a brass door knob is fitted to a panelled door (Steps 1–12).

1 Measure and mark the middle point of the centre rail on the side of the door, using a pencil and a try square.

2 Centre the latch on this line. Holding it in place, draw round the latch. Use the try square to transfer the dimensions to the edge of the door.

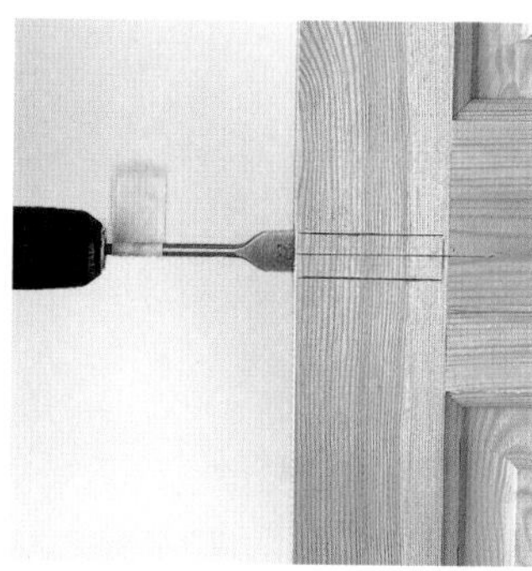

3 Measure the depth of the latch then mark this measurement with a piece of tape on a wood cutting bit the same diameter as the latch (in this case 22mm). Drill a hole to the correct depth (as far as the tape) in the edge of the door, keeping the drill horizontal and in line with the door. Prise out the debris with a narrow chisel or suck it out with the nozzle of a vacuum cleaner.

4 Hold the latch in the correct position on the side of the door and, using a bradawl, mark the position of the handle spindle. Do the same on the other side of the door.

5 Using a drill with a wood bit, drill a hole at the marked position large enough to give the handle spindle plenty of clearance. Drill from both sides into the latch hole already drilled.

DOORS HANGING AN INTERNAL DOOR

6 Slide the latch into the hole on the edge of the door and mark the position of the rectangular edge plate with a pencil.

7 Score around the edge of the plate with a craft knife. Do use a knife for this – it is very easy to accidentally split the wood with a chisel.

8 Remove the latch and cut out a slight recess for the rectangular latch plate, using a chisel and mallet.

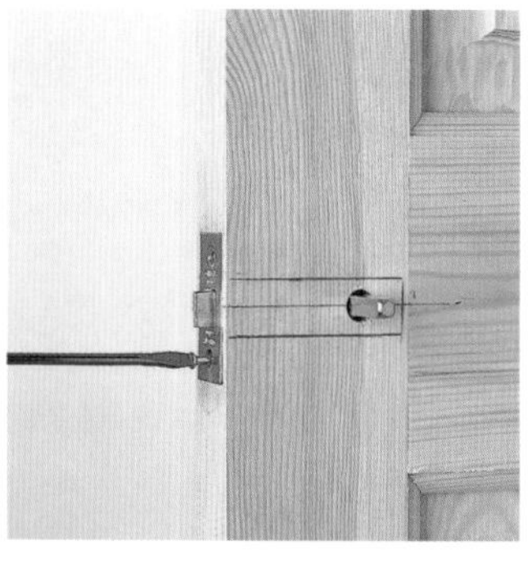

9 Refit the latch. Fit the handle spindle and make sure that it will turn freely. Adjust the hole, if necessary. Screw the latch plate in position. Sand off the pencil marks.

10 To fix the handle plates to each side of door, start the screw holes with a bradawl, then screw in the screws. If the spindle is too long for the thickness of the door, secure it in a vice and saw to the correct length with a hacksaw.

11 Close the door so that the latch is touching the frame and mark its position on the frame with a pencil.

12 Hold the striker plate in position and mark the shape on the frame, including the central cut-out area. Use a narrow chisel to cut a recess for the latch and a wider one to cut around the outer shape and pare away the wood to the depth of the striker plate.

YOU CAN DO IT

Door details

Door furniture isn't just about function – choose from a huge range to complement the style and materials of your interior.

Fitting the doorstop

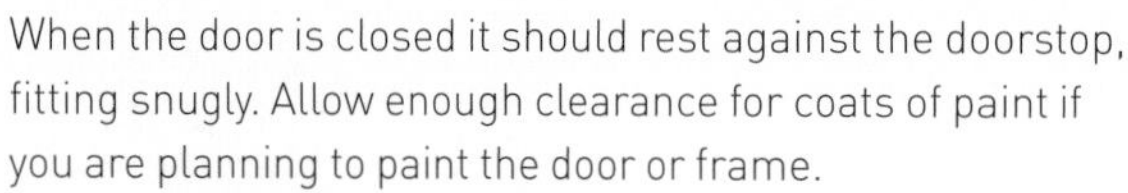

When the door is closed it should rest against the doorstop, fitting snugly. Allow enough clearance for coats of paint if you are planning to paint the door or frame.

1 Measure and cut the doorstop for across the top of the door. With the door shut, position the strip and partially knock in some 30mm nails to hold it.

2 Open the door and finish knocking in the nails. They should be roughly 300mm apart. Repeat the process for the strips at either side of the door.

Fitting the architrave

The architrave – the timber moulding that hides the joint between the door frame and the wall – is made from three lengths of moulding, a top and two sides, joined with mitred corners.

1 Hold a length of architrave beside the door frame and mark the internal height of the door frame plus 3mm. This is the position of the internal edge of the mitred corner. Cut the mitre at the marked point on the architrave, using a mitre saw or a mitre block and panel saw.

2 Nail the architrave in place with panel pins. Measure and fit the other two lengths of architrave in the same way.

3 Secure the mitred corners by nailing across them with a panel pin. To avoid hitting your fingers, hold pins with long-nosed pliers as you begin to drive them.

4 Tap the pin heads below the surface with a nail punch.

Fitting a new door to an existing frame

The doors in many older houses are not a standard size so you may need to trim a replacement door to fit, or even have one specially made. You should not cut more than 10mm off each side edge of a flush door, or 5mm off a panel door, or you will weaken the structure. Be aware that the old door frame may not be straight. Buy new hinges the same size as the existing ones or reuse the old hinges if they are in good condition.

1 Remove the old door. If it was a good fit, use it as a guide to measure and mark the new door; otherwise, hold the new door against the frame and mark where it needs to be trimmed. Shorten it, if necessary, before adjusting the width. Cut from both top and bottom if a large amount has to be removed so that you retain the symmetry of the panels. When the door is the correct height, position the hinge side in the door frame and insert two wedges or screwdrivers underneath to keep it in place.

2 It is much easier if two people mark the door width, one each side of the door. Run a pencil down the door against the frame on the lock side to mark the trimming line. Remove the excess equally from each side using a plane. Smooth the sharp edges with abrasive paper. Test-fit the door in the frame and trim again if necessary.

3 Measure the hinge positions on the door frame and transfer them to the new door. Hold each hinge in position and mark with a sharp pencil. Cut out the hinge recesses and fit the hinges to the door following Steps 2–5 on pages 124–25.

4 Use the existing striker plate if it will work with the new latch (otherwise fit a new one). Close the door and mark on it the latch position with a pencil. Fit a latch following Steps 1–12 on pages 125–26. Remove and reposition the doorstops if necessary.

DOORS STRIPPING AND FINISHING

If an old door has been painted and repainted many times, or if its paintwork is blistered or flaking, adding another layer will only exacerbate the problem. But stripping off the old paint can make a shabby door look like new. You could then repaint it or, if the wood is good quality, bring out its natural warmth by varnishing, or staining and varnishing.

Stripping with chemical stripper

Read the instructions, and take all the precautions recommended for the product you are using. If you can, take the door off its hinges and work in a garage or workshop, especially if you have small children or pets.

TOOLS MATERIALS

- **protective gloves**
- **safety goggles**
- **old paintbrush**
- **flat-bladed scraper**
- **shave hook**
- **cloth or brush**

- chemical paint stripper
- white spirit

1 Apply paint stripper using an old paintbrush; remember to wear protective gloves and goggles. Stipple it into the mouldings and corners and brush liberally over the flat areas. Leave for the recommended length of time. The chemical will begin to react with the paint, and the surface will rupture and bubble.

2 Use a flat-bladed scraper to try scraping back the paint on a test patch. If the paint is several layers thick you may need to stipple in some more paint stripper and leave it a little longer. Once the stripper has done its job you can scrape back the paint to reveal bare wood.

3 Use a shave hook to scrape paint from mouldings. Draw the hook back towards you, removing paint from the crevices. Continue until all the paint has been removed.

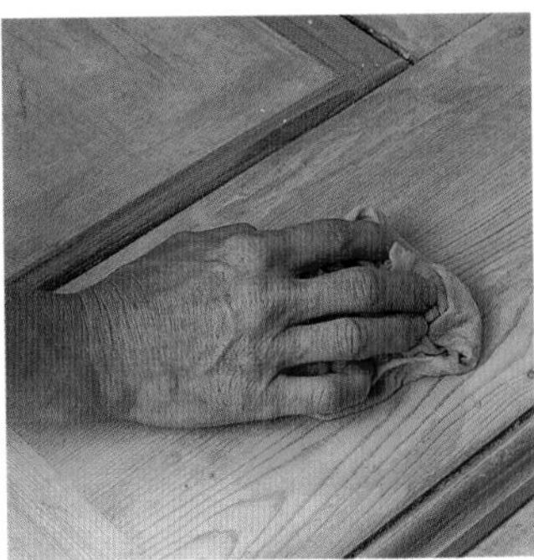

4 Neutralise the surface using either white spirit or water (depending on the product – check the instructions on the tin). Work it into the surface with a cloth or brush to remove all traces of the stripping solution before sanding and finishing.

Stripping with a hot-air gun

Hot-air guns usually come with a selection of nozzle attachments. Use the one that spreads the heat over a wide area, or use the gun with no attachment fitted. A conical nozzle is more likely to scorch the wood and should only be used when you are working next to an area that you don't want to damage.

TOOLS MATERIALS

- **protective gloves**
- **safety goggles**
- **hot-air gun**
- **flat-bladed scraper**
- **shave hook**

1 Strip paint from the flat areas first. Wearing protective gloves and goggles, direct the heat over a small area of paint, moving the gun slowly back and forth. Use a flat-bladed scraper to lift the paint as it softens.

2 Use a shave hook to strip paint from the mouldings. Keep the hot-air gun moving, or you will scorch the wood. Pull the shave hook towards you, working methodically on each section in turn.

SAFETY FIRST

Always wear protective gloves and goggles when using a hot-air gun or when handling paint-stripping chemicals. Never check that a hot-air gun is working by placing your hand in front of the nozzle.

ECO LEAD TESTING

Before stripping old paint, especially pre-1960s, it is important to check that it doesn't contain lead pigments. You can buy a lead testing kit, which is quick and simple to use. If the result is positive, you must use a special chemical stripper, and take all the precautions advised by the manufacturer.

1 Wearing a dust mask, sand the flat panels with a medium-grade abrasive paper. Wrap the paper around a piece of wood or use a sanding block and work in the direction of the grain. Take care not to round off any sharp corners on mouldings. Or you could use a small hand-held electric sander (see page 35), but again take great care not to damage the mouldings. Go over the area a second time using a fine-grade abrasive paper.

Sanding and filling

A newly stripped door will usually reveal imperfections. Previously hidden cracks in the wood and blemishes may become apparent. Use wood filler to hide them. If you intend to stain or varnish the door, choose a filler to match the colour of the finished effect, since wood filler does not absorb stain or varnish in the same way as natural wood.

2 Fold the abrasive paper into a suitable shape and work on the mouldings. You could wrap the paper around a piece of dowel. Take care when working on corners and edges not to damage the mouldings. Fine-grade wire wool can be used instead of abrasive paper (except on natural oak, which it will mark).

3 To sand into corners and crevices in mouldings, fold the abrasive paper and use the fold edge to reach into the joint.

TOOLS MATERIALS

- **wood filler**
- **dust mask**
- **sanding block**
- **hand-held electric sander (optional)**
- **fine-grade wire wool (optional)**
- **tack cloth**
- **25mm and 50mm paintbrushes**
- **lint-free cloth**
- **medium- and fine-grade abrasive paper**
- **piece of dowel**

- wood stain
- varnish

Staining and varnishing

Wood stains and varnishes are available in a wide range of colours, though bear in mind that the final colour may differ from that shown on the tin, since it will look different on different woods. Wood stain can be mixed or diluted to achieve a particular shade. Test it on a piece of timber similar to the door before you begin.

1 Brush down the door and use a tack cloth to remove all traces of dust. Apply the stain with a paintbrush. Start with the panels, staining the mouldings first, then work around one half of the door and then the other. Follow the grain and pick up wet edges before they dry. Work quickly and apply the stain evenly, without overlap. While still damp, rub the door with a lint-free cloth to even out the stain and take off any excess.

2 Use a good quality clean brush to apply the varnish, and be sure to read the application instructions on the tin. Follow the sequence for painting a door (see page 130). Dip the brush to one third of the bristle length and touch the excess off on the inside of the container. Allow the first coat to dry thoroughly then go over the surface lightly with a fine-grade abrasive paper. Wipe the door using a tack cloth. Apply a second coat and, for a really tough finish, a third.

IDEAL TOOL

Tack cloths

These specially impregnated cloths are sticky to the touch – perfect for removing fine dust prior to painting or varnishing. They are cheap, reusable and endlessly useful.

WINDOWS AND DOORS PAINTING

Doors and windows are constructed using lengths of wood with grain patterns that inevitably run in different directions. To achieve an even, professional-looking finish, free from brush marks, you need to paint them in a sequence that takes account of the grain. Think ahead when painting windows using oil-based paints, as they may take longer to dry than you expect. Or use water-based paint, which dries more quickly and releases much less odour and fumes.

TOOLS MATERIALS

- **knotting solution, if required**
- **soft brush**
- **tack cloth**
- **25mm and 50mm paintbrushes**
- **cutting-in brush**

- combined primer/undercoat
- top coat

Painting doors

If you are painting a new wooden door you will need to apply knotting solution to any knots in the wood to prevent resin seeping through the new paint. If you are painting a stripped door this is not necessary as the surface will already be sealed. However, the door will need to be primed and undercoated.

Before starting, take off the door handles and wedge the door open. Keep the handle in your pocket in case the door is accidentally closed. Remove any dust using a soft brush and wipe the surface with a tack cloth.

Painting technique

Take care when painting corners and mouldings as paint can collect in crevices and create runs. Make your last brush strokes in the same direction as the grain, and pick up wet edges before they begin to dry.

Panel door

Start with the panels (1) and the mouldings that surround them. Next paint the muntin or centre vertical (2). Then paint the cross rails (3), starting with the top rail and working down. Paint the stiles or outer verticals (4) and finish by painting the three exposed door edges (5). If you are painting the door a different colour on each side, the hinged edge should be the colour of the closing face, and the outer edge that of the opening face.

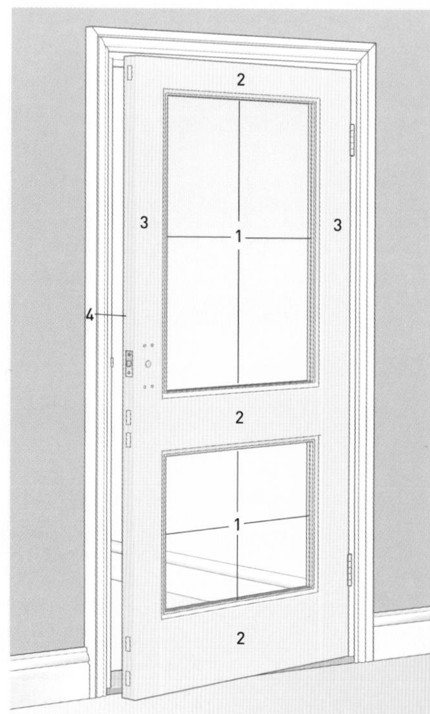

Glass door

Use masking tape or a paint shield to protect the glass in a glazed door. First paint the mouldings around the glass (1) with a cutting-in brush. Next paint the cross rails, starting with the top rail and working down (2). Then paint the stiles (3) and finally all three exposed door edges (4).

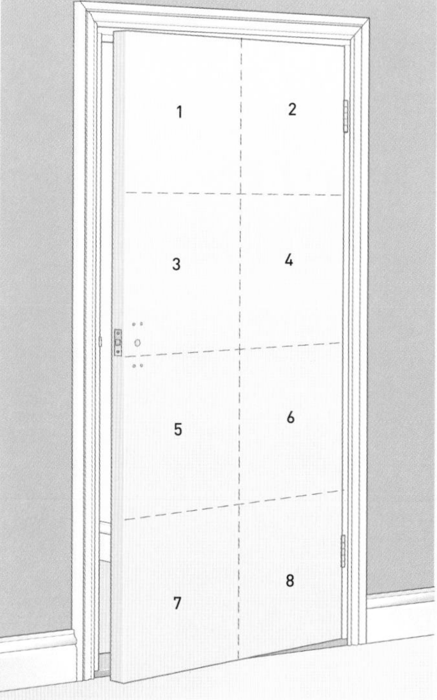

Flush door

Divide the door into eight imaginary sections, as shown. Start at the top left (1) and work down from left to right. Blend each area into the next while the paint is wet, finishing with vertical strokes in line with the grain. Paint the door edges last.

TOOLS MATERIALS

- **abrasive paper**
- **soft cloth**
- **masking tape or paint shield**
- **25mm and 50mm paintbrushes**
- **cutting-in brush**

- filler
- window cleaner
- white spirit
- combined primer/undercoat
- top coat

Painting windows

Prepare the frame by filling and sanding as necessary, and clean the glass before starting. Overlap the paint onto the glass by about 2mm to seal out water. It will make the job easier if you use a cutting-in brush for the glazing bars.

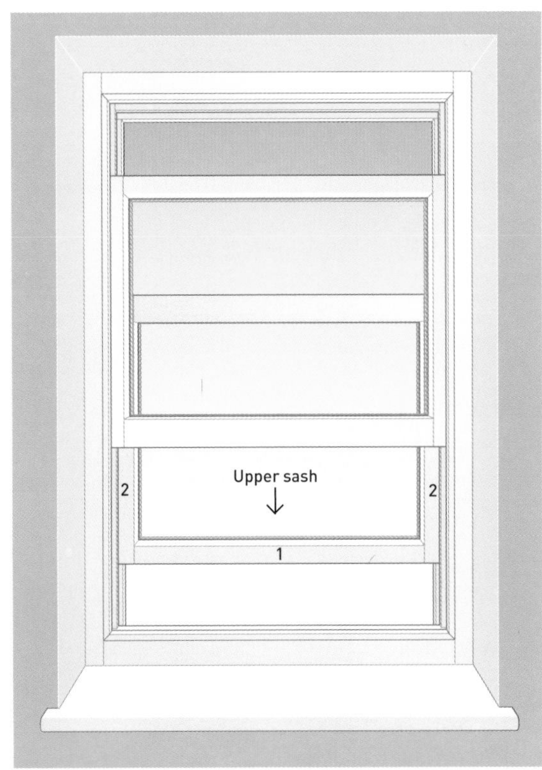

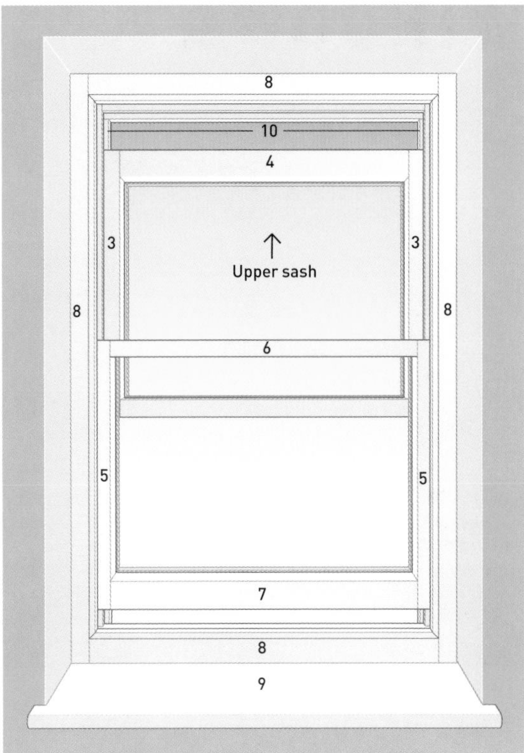

Painting a sash window

Start by painting the bottom meeting rail of the upper sash (1). To expose it, raise the bottom sash and lower the upper one. Also paint the vertical bars (2) of the upper sash as far as you can. When it is touch-dry, raise the upper sash again, and lower the bottom, leaving a small opening top and bottom. Finish painting the upper sash (3,4). Now paint the bottom sash (5,6,7), including the underside of the cross rail (7), followed by the frame (8) and window sill (9). Wait until the paint is dry before you start painting the runners (10). Apply a thin coat to the inner runners and the upper section of the outer runners. Try not to get paint on the cords; pull them out of the way as you paint. Carefully check that the sashes are running before the paint has dried.

IDEAL TOOL

Cutting-in brush
This has specially angled bristles that make it much easier to paint the rebates around a window pane and get a clean line along the glass.

YOU CAN DO IT

Painting windows
If you are not confident that you can keep a straight line, use a paint shield (see page 78) or masking tape to protect the glass. Set tape back 2mm from the edge of the glass and remove it before the paint is dry, or the paint may lift off at the same time. Or you can use a masking pen, which leaves a layer of wax on the glass. This can be removed (along with any drips of paint) with a window scraper once the paint is dry.

B&Q

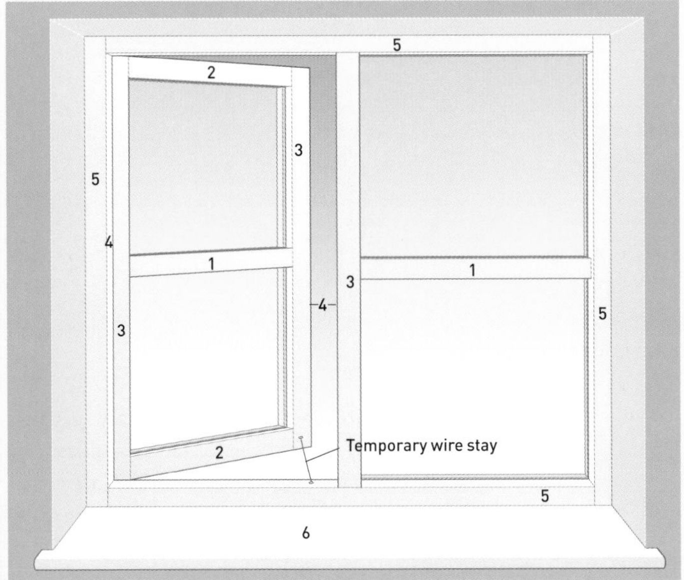

Painting a casement window

Remove the window furniture and fit a temporary wire stay to hold the window open (see page 132). First paint the transoms (1), using a cutting-in brush against the glass. Next, paint the top and bottom cross rails (2) followed by the vertical mullions and jambs (3). Paint the edges (4) and then the frame (5) and lastly the window sill (6).

If the window must be closed before the paint is quite dry, rub a little talcum powder along the frame to prevent it sticking.

WINDOWS FINISHING

Give a new lease of life to old window frames by painting them in a fresh colour and fitting new window furniture. Anyone can achieve a professional-looking finish by following the painting sequences described on page 131 and the step-by-step instructions below.

Painting a casement window

Prepare the frame carefully before you begin to paint, stripping back old paint if necessary and filling any holes in the wood. You'll need an undercoat and a top coat for a hardwearing finish.

TOOLS MATERIALS

- **screwdriver**
- **hammer**
- **soft brush**
- **paint shield or masking tape**
- **25mm paintbrush or paint pad**
- **cutting-in paintbrush**

- wood filler
- medium-grade abrasive paper
- stiff wire
- small nails
- combined primer/undercoat
- top coat paint

1 Remove catches and stays from the window frame before you begin. If you intend to fit new window furniture once the frame is repainted, fill the old fixing holes with wood filler and sand smooth.

2 Make a temporary stay to hold the window open while you are painting it (see YOU CAN DO IT).

3 Prepare the surface by lightly sanding over the old paintwork using medium-grade abrasive paper.

4 Brush away dust and debris, paying particular attention to the corners.

5 If you don't have a steady hand, use a paint shield (see page 131) or cut some masking tape to fit around each pane of glass. Set the tape 2mm in from the frame so that paint will just overlap on to the glass.

6 Use a combined primer/undercoat and paint the frame in the painting sequence described on page 131.

YOU CAN DO IT

Temporary wire stay

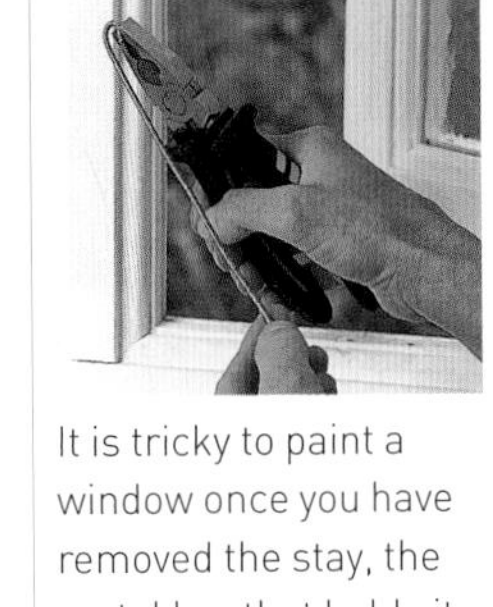

It is tricky to paint a window once you have removed the stay, the metal bar that holds it open. Make a temporary window stay using stiff wire; an old coat hanger will do the job. Cut to length and bend the ends into a small loop just large enough to drive a nail through. Fix one end to the sill and the other end to the frame, using small nails.

7 When the first coat is dry, apply the top coat in the same sequence.

8 Keep checking that there are no runs, particularly on edges and in corners.

9 Paint the sill last. Remove the masking tape when the paint is just touch dry. Once it is completely dry, remove the temporary wire stays.

IDEAL TOOL

Paint pad

You could use a paint pad instead of a brush. Its small square foam pad is designed to fit easily around mouldings and into corners. Pour some paint into a shallow bowl and dip the pad into the paint. It will produce a smooth painted surface with no visible brush strokes.

Replacing window furniture

A change of window furniture can make a big difference to the appearance of your windows. Try to choose fittings that will complement the style of the window frame and are in keeping with the age of the house.

TOOLS MATERIALS

- **bradawl**
- **power drill with twist bits**
- **screwdriver**
- **narrow chisel**

- window furniture and fixings

1 Decide on the best position for the stay. Read the instructions, since different designs are fitted in different ways. Mark the position of the fixing screws with a bradawl.

2 Drill pilot holes where you have marked the fixing positions, and fit the stay using the screws supplied.

3 Find the correct position for the locking pegs. Check that the stay will fit over them and mark the position of the fixing screws. Drill pilot holes, and screw the locking pegs to the frame.

4 Fit the handle by marking the screw positions and drilling pilot holes, then screwing it into place. Hold the mortise plate in position and draw around the mortise slot with a pencil. Chisel out the slot using a narrow chisel. The precise depth will depend on the position of the handle; use trial and error and keep checking. Cut out just enough to allow the latch to enter fully.

5 Drill pilot holes for the fixing screws and screw the mortise plate into position.

SAFETY FIRST

Before drilling into a wall always check first for pipes and cables with an electronic detector. Never drill directly above or below a light fitting or power socket.

Whether you decide to put up a curtain track or a pole, make sure you either buy the correct length or get one longer than you need and cut it to fit. To look good and let in plenty of light, curtains should draw back clear of the glass. To achieve that you wi probably need to fit the track or pole to the wall or ceiling above the window recess. However, they can also be fitted within the recess. To hang curtains over a bay window you will need to use flexible curtain track that will bend around the corners c the recess.

Putting up a curtain track

The screws supplied with your curtain track may not be long enough to achieve a secure fixing, particularly if your plaster is old and and slightly crumbly. In that case use longer screws and wallplugs, or screw into sound ceiling timber. The window top or ceiling may not be quite level, so mount the track parallel to whichever is the most horizontal.

TOOLS MATERIALS

- **fine-tooth hacksaw**
- **craft knife or file**
- **pencil**
- **ruler**
- **pipe and cable detector**
- **power drill with masonry bits**
- **screwdriver**

- curtain track and fixings
- wallplugs

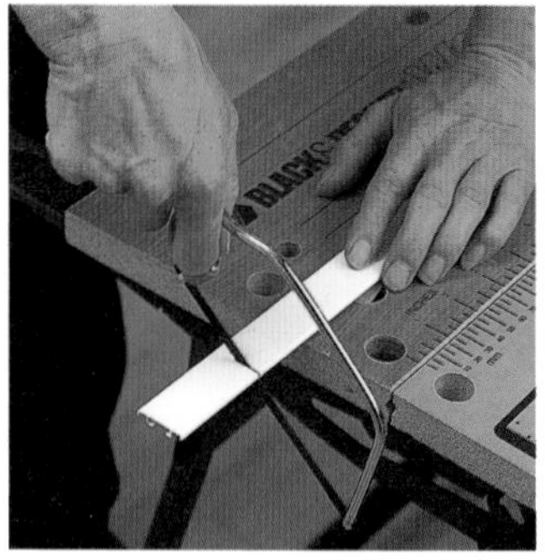

1 Decide on the correct length of track to accommodate your curtains and cut it to length using a fine-tooth hacksaw. Remove any burrs from the cut ends with a file or craft knife. If the window is wide and the curtains thick then the track will need to extend further than if the material is lightweight.

2 Calculate how much the track will reach beyond the recess. Use a ruler to extend the top line of the recess by this amount with a pencil either side. You can rub the line out later.

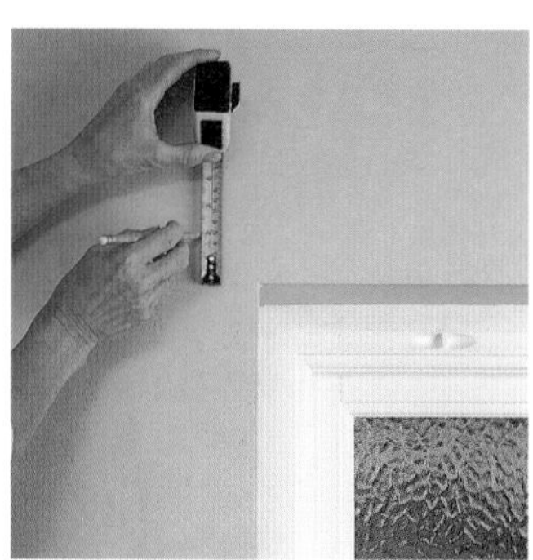

3 Measure 25mm in from the end of the line and 50mm up; this is the fixing position for the end bracket. Repeat to find the position of the other end bracket.

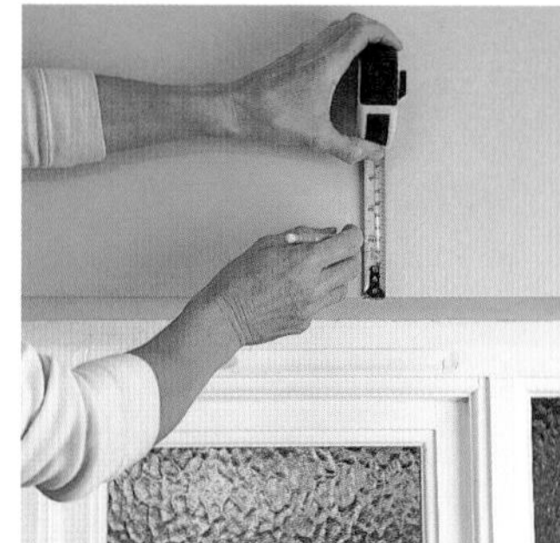

4 Mark the remaining fixing positions at equal intervals between the two end brackets, measuring 50mm up from the top of the window recess each time.

5 Check at each fixing position that there are no hidden pipes or cables. If all is clear, drill the fixing holes and insert wallplugs of the correct size for your screws.

6 Screw the mounting clips into position, following the manufacturer's instructions. The bracket latches that the track fits into need to be facing forward.

7 To fit the end stops, slip one over each end of the track and tighten the retaining screws.

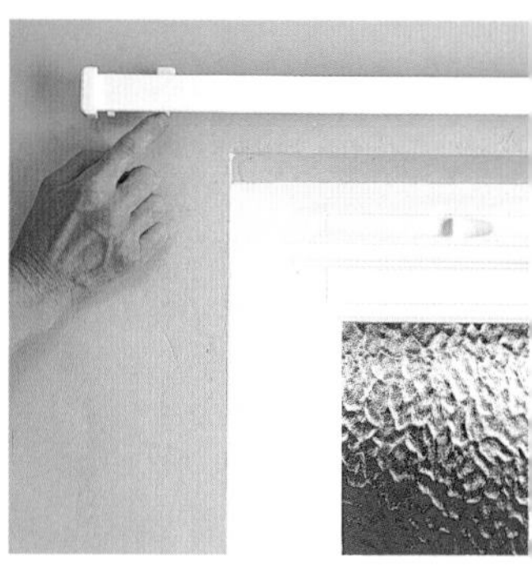

8 Place the track into the slot in one of the end brackets. Push the bracket latch until you hear a click. Clip the remaining track into place in the same way.

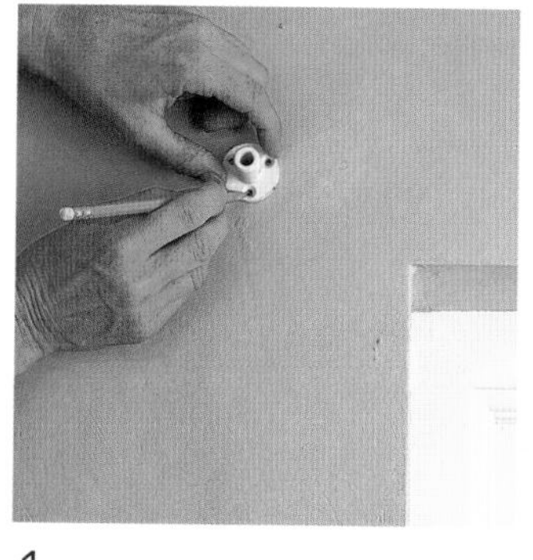

1 Find the positions for the two end brackets (see Steps 2 and 3 opposite). For a curtain pole, however, the brackets should be at least 50mm from either end. The decorative brackets often fit over fixing bosses. Hold a fixing boss over the mark and use a pencil to mark the screw positions.

Putting up a curtain pole

Curtain poles were used in Victorian homes, and have become popular again. They are available in metal, wood or plastic. The curtains hang from large matching rings or loops of fabric. The length of some curtain poles is adjustable; others you can cut it to fit using a fine-tooth hacksaw. You may need to use longer screws than those supplied with the pack if you intend to hang particularly heavy curtains.

2 Check there are no hidden pipes or cables then drill at the marked positions with a masonry bit. Insert wallplugs and screw the bosses into place.

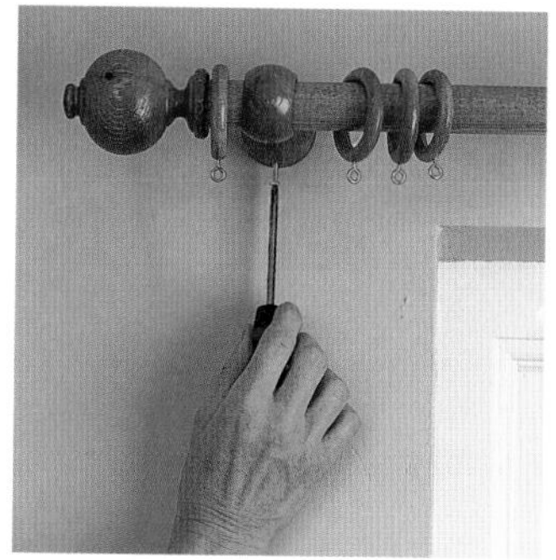

3 Fit the wooden wall brackets over the boss and secure with a screw. Assemble the pole and slide it through the two brackets. Leave one curtain ring on the outside of each bracket, with the remaining rings between them. Tighten the retaining screw on each fixing boss and push on the finials.

TOOLS MATERIALS

- **ruler**
- **pencil**
- **pipe and cable detector**
- **power drill with masonry bits**
- **fine-tooth hacksaw**
- **screwdriver**

- curtain pole pack
- wallplugs

YOU CAN DO IT

Create the look

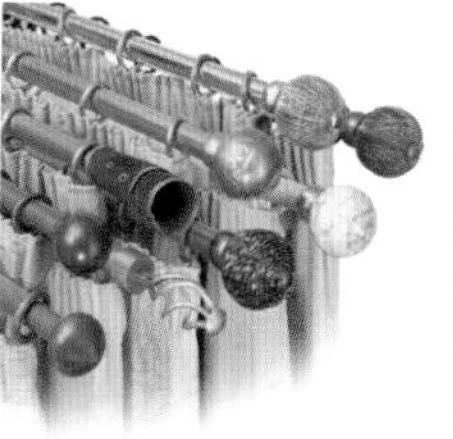

Gold, silver, pewter, iron and wood are just some of the finishes available in curtain poles. Decorative end-stop finials can bring an element of fun or elegance to your window; mix and match poles, brackets and finials to create your own unique style.

Fitting a roller blind

Roller blinds come in a vast array of colours, designs and sizes. As with curtains, you need to decide if you want the blind to fit inside or across the top of the window recess. For a blind inside the recess (shown below), remember that you will need a little clearance space either side for it to operate smoothly – check the instructions when you buy the blind.

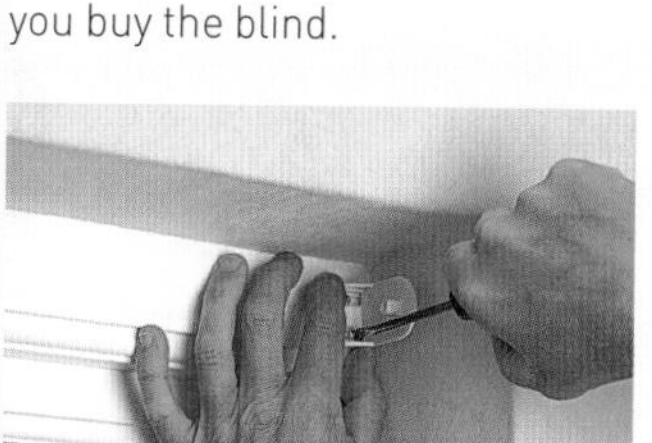

1 Measure the width required. Some blinds can be cut to fit (check the manufacturer's instructions). Mark the positions for the brackets in the corners of the window. Fit the bracket for the blind control on the side from which you want to operate the blind. Use a bradawl to make starting holes, then drill and plug the wall and screw the brackets into place, checking they are level.

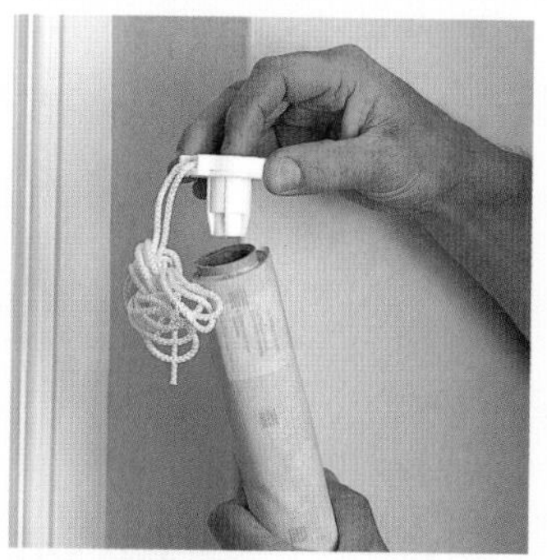

2 Fit the side control into the end of the blind, then fit the dummy pin into the other end. Push it into place by pressing against a hard surface or by tapping gently with a hammer.

3 Slot the blind into the fixing brackets. Ensure the cords are hanging downwards.

TOOLS MATERIALS

- **tape measure**
- **scissors**
- **pencil**
- **bradawl**
- **power drill with masonry bits**
- **screwdriver**

- roller blind and fixings

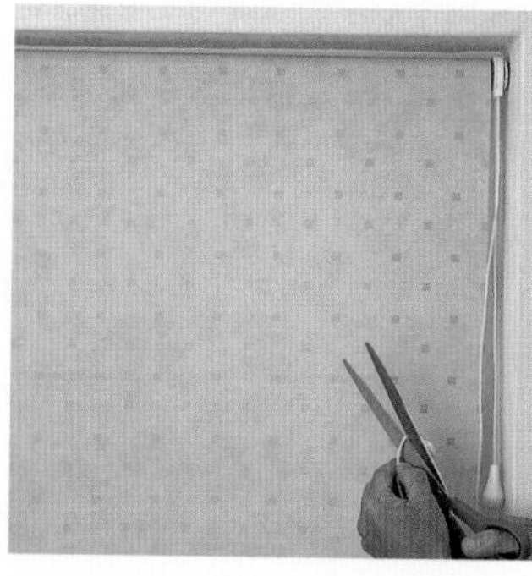

4 Operate the blind to ascertain the correct length for each pull cord. Cut the cords, and fit a cord pull to each one.

FIREPLACES AND FIRES

Fireplaces can provide an attractive focal point in a room, especially with a glowing fire in them. Open fires can be a lot of work to maintain and some urban areas have restrictions on burning wood and coal, but there are many alternatives. Controlled-draught slow-burning fires and enclosed stoves are easy to clean, they burn all day without attention and if you add a back boiler, they can be used to heat water and central heating. Even easier, and no less cosy, is a flame-effect gas or electric fire. There is a huge range of models that will work with your existing fireplace and decor: see www.diy.com.

SAFETY FIRST

Carbon monoxide

This poisonous gas has no smell, taste or colour. It is produced by the incomplete combustion of fossil fuels – gas, oil, coal or wood. Damaged or badly installed appliances, combined with poor ventilation, can cause it to accumulate in the home. Protect yourself and your family by fitting an approved CO detector – and testing it regularly.

Types of gas fire

Gas fires need an outlet for the fumes produced during combustion. If your fireplace has a chimney, then a gas fire can easily be installed. If not, you must choose a flueless model with a catalytic converter to clean waste gases, or a balanced flue model, which expels gases via an outside wall. Either way, a CORGI-registered gas fitter must do the installation. Some fires come with surround and hearth included.

Wood-effect fire

The natural gas flame of this fire is energy-efficient, as most of the heat is radiated or convected into the room. Before selecting a model to be set in an existing flue, make sure you check the depth of recess.

Radiant gas fire

This retro-styled gas fire can be hung on a wall or stood on a hearth. It does require a chimney.

Coal-effect gas fire

It's possible to buy a fire separately and then add your own choice of hearth, surround and mantelpiece to create an original effect.

YOU CAN DO IT

Decorative fireplaces

Got a redundant fireplace? Don't brick it up – a fireplace doesn't have to be functional. Instead, fit a fire surround that complements your interior and place candles, dried flowers or a sculpture in it to create a decorative focal point. To keep out debris and draughts, close off the flue with a piece of hardboard nailed to wooden battens screwed into the sides of the chimney opening, just out of sight. Cut some ventilation holes in the board to prevent damp.

B&Q

Types of electric fire

Electric fires are made in a wide range of designs and can be freestanding or fitted into a surround. The advantage of electric is versatility: you can reposition a freestanding fire as you like, and you don't need a chimney. Choose between radiant, convector or fan heaters, with or without a thermostat to regulate the temperature.

Freestanding stove

This freestanding cast-iron stove, with flickering flame effect, can be sited anywhere there is a convenient power point.

Coal-effect fire and surround

Electric heaters can be installed in existing fireplaces, with or without a chimney. Make sure you take all the measurements carefully before selecting a model.

FIREPLACES AND FIRES

Coal and wood fires produce a mixture of gas and solid waste products which are carried up the chimney. Some of these deposits settle in the chimney as soot. Too much soot will narrow the chimney and reduce the flow. If the build-up becomes too great, most likely at a bend in the chimney, a severe blockage may occur. This could cause a chimney fire or divert poisonous gases back into the room. Chimneys over an open fire should be swept annually and it is a good idea to sweep old chimneys and install a flue liner.

The working fireplace

To work efficiently, a fireplace needs a supply of oxygen and a means of removing smoke and fumes. Most fires have a barred grate where ash can fall through into a removable tray. The burning fuel produces gases which are lighter than air and so they rise up the chimney. This creates a draw, pulling fresh oxygen into the grate to feed the fire.

Occasionally a fire will smoke. This may be because the chimney needs cleaning; any partial blockage can prevent smoke being drawn up the flue. Double-glazing or draught-proofing can also prevent a fire from burning properly, as a constant supply of fresh oxygen is essential. Provide ventilation by inserting an airbrick into an outside wall or by fitting a window vent.

If the chimney is old and much used, it may have become damaged inside. The easiest way to prevent damp patches on walls or smoke seeping into the room is to put in a flexible flue liner. A flue liner may also be needed if you are installing a new gas fire into the fireplace. You will need a liner to suit the type of appliance you are fitting, so do consult a professional installer.

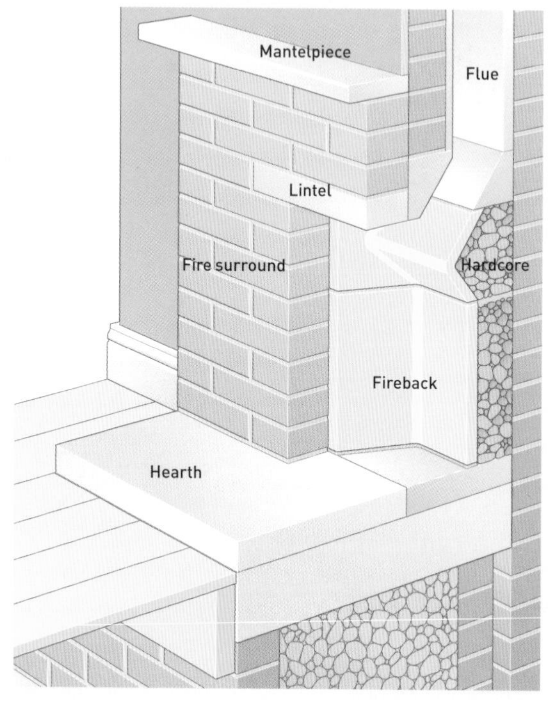

YOU CAN DO IT

Changing fireplaces

Fitting a new fire surround and hearth can make a terrific difference to the overall look of a room. Most surrounds are fitted to the wall with screws hidden by the plaster on the chimney breast. Surrounds are usually very heavy, so get help when removing an old and fitting a new one.

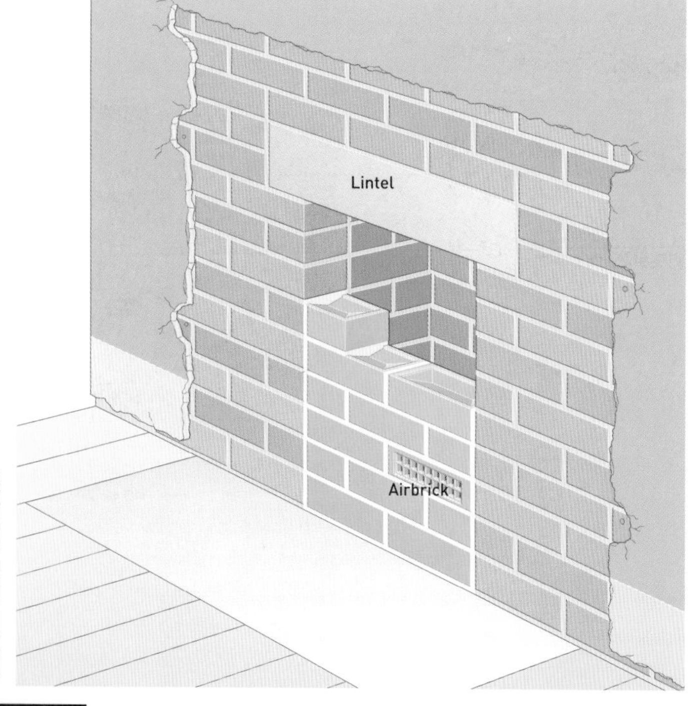

Removing a fireplace

Removing a fireplace from a room is a messy job that creates lots of dirt and dust. First you must remove the fire surround, hearth and adjacent skirting, then level the surrounding floor. If you suspect that you might want to use the chimney again in future, you can simply panel over the opening with a piece of plasterboard cut to the appropriate size and nailed to a wooden frame set within the fire opening. If you don't want to use the chimney again, you can brick it up then plaster over the top.

Whichever method you choose for enclosing your fireplace, it is crucial that you fit a ventilator in the opening, so that there is still a flow of air through the chimney. Otherwise, condensation could form in the chimney, which would eventually seep through and stain the wall. In the case of plasterboard, cut an opening just above skirting level and fit a ventilator into it. If you are bricking up the fireplace, fit an airbrick in the lowest course of bricks above the skirting.

Sweeping a chimney

Sweeping a chimney does not have to be excessively messy if you prepare the area carefully. Wear safety goggles and a dust mask to protect your eyes and lungs.

TOOLS MATERIALS

- **dust sheets**
- **chimney sweeping brush and canes**
- **shovel**
- **safety goggles**
- **dust mask**

- plastic refuse sack

1 Roll back any carpet, remove nearby objects and cover everything in the vicinity with a dust sheet. Drape another dust sheet over the fire surround and use heavy objects to weight it down on the mantelpiece. Put a heavy object like a brick on each side of the opening against the fire surround to seal the chimney space. Screw the brush head to the first cane.

2 Lift the sheet and push the brush inside the flue above the fireplace.

3 Screw on another cane and push the brush up the flue. Continue adding canes and pushing the brush upwards. If the brush gets stuck, pull back a little and push up again, working to and fro. Don't use a screwing action or the canes might unscrew at a joint. You will be able to feel when the brush comes out at the top. If there is a cowl on the chimneypot, be careful not to push it off.

4 Pull the brush back down, unscrewing the canes as you go. Shovel the soot and debris from the grate and into a plastic refuse sack.

Repairing a cracked fireback

The extreme heat generated by a fire can easily damage a fireback over time. Fine cracks can be repaired quite simply, following the steps below. If the damage is severe, however, it may be better to replace the fireback.

TOOLS MATERIALS

- **dust sheet**
- **wire brush**
- **small trowel**
- **paintbrush**

- fire cement

1 Let the fireback cool for 48 hours. Spread a dust sheet around the fireplace and use a wire brush to clean away soot deposits and expose the damaged areas. Use the point of a trowel to clean out the cracks.

2 Brush dust out of the cracks with a wire brush and then brush water over the area using a paintbrush. This will help the fire cement to bond.

3 Use a small trowel to work fire cement into the cracks.

4 Trowel away any surplus fire cement then brush the surface with a wet paintbrush to get a smooth finish. Leave the cement to harden for a few days, or light a small fire to warm the area and dry it more quickly (follow the instructions on the cement tin).

STORAGE SHELVING

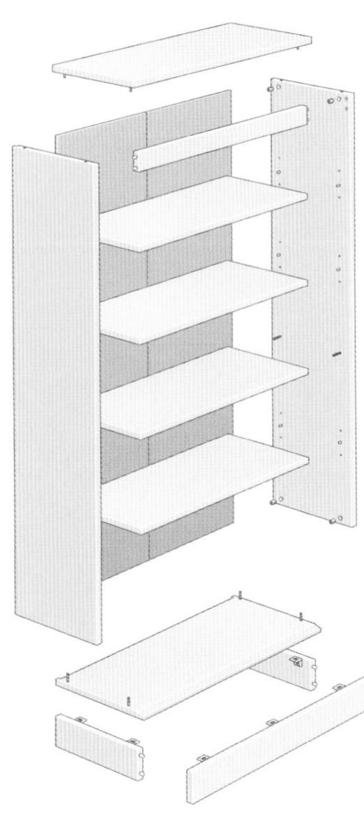

Most of us wage a never-ending war with household clutter. One easy way to gain extra storage space without having to embark on major building work is to put up a shelf or stack of shelves. You can put them just about everywhere – on the wall, under the stairs, in an alcove – and they will take a surprising amount of overspill from other areas of the house. You can choose from a vast range of shelving and brackets, adjustable shelf systems, or flatpack sets of shelves with pre-drilled holes for easy assembling (left).

Shelving materials

Shelves can be made from a variety of materials, ranging from cheap chipboard to extremely expensive hardwoods like oak and beech.

Chipboard

Chipboard, which consists of small pieces of wood glued together, is the cheapest material for shelves and is easy to cut and fit to brackets. It is available with a wipe-clean melamine coating, or a wood veneer which needs to be sealed with varnish or wax.

MDF

Medium-density fibreboard, or MDF, is made from wood fibres very firmly stuck together under pressure. It has a smooth surface – including the edges – and can be painted, stained or varnished.

Blockboard

Blockboard is cheaper than solid wood but very strong. It is made from strips of softwood running parallel between two outer layers of veneer. If cut edges split, they can be covered with veneer or wooden lipping.

Plywood

Plywood consists of thin wooden sheets glued together, with the direction of the grain alternating at right angles in each layer. The two outer sheets have the grain running in the same direction. Edges are smooth enough to leave plain or they can be covered as for blockboard.

Wood

Solid wood is the most traditional shelving material and it makes very attractive, but relatively expensive, shelves. The wood needs to be sealed with wax or varnish to protect it from dirt.

Acrylic sheet

Acrylic sheet, such as perspex, can be used for shelves displaying light- to medium-weight objects as long as it is a thickness of 12mm. The cut edges can smoothed with a fine file and then with progressively finer abrasive paper.

Glass

Glass makes an attractive shelf, but it must be toughened and a minimum of 6mm thick. Also, glass is heavy, so you will need to use medium- or heavyweight brackets.

Brackets

Brackets may be fixed or be part of an adjustable shelf system (see pages 143–45). Both types are available in light-, medium- or heavyweight versions. It is vital that you make sure your shelves and brackets can support the weight they will have to bear. Use this table as a guide, but always read the shelving manufacturer's instructions as well.

Fixed brackets

Fixed brackets may be made from aluminium, pressed steel, pressed and welded steel with an epoxy-coated finish, pressed steel with a snap-on coloured plastic cover, wrought iron or solid brass.

Adjustable shelving brackets

Adjustable shelving systems consist of metal or wooden tracks that are fitted to the wall. Removable flanged brackets slot into place to support the shelves. The cheaper, lightweight systems are often made of aluminium; medium-weight and heavyweight systems are made of steel or wood.

SPACING BRACKETS

Material	Thickness	Space between brackets (load)
Chipboard (coated)	16mm	610mm (medium)
	18mm	510mm (heavy); 700mm (medium)
Chipboard (veneered)	32mm	915mm (heavy)
MDF	18mm	510mm (heavy); 700mm (medium)
	25mm	700mm (heavy); 915mm (medium)
Blockboard	18mm	700mm (heavy); 750mm (medium); 800mm (light)
Plywood	18mm	700mm (heavy); 915mm (medium)
	25mm	915mm (heavy)
Softwood	16mm	400mm (heavy); 610mm (medium)
	18mm	510mm (heavy); 700mm (medium)
	25mm	700mm (heavy); 915mm (medium)
	32mm	915mm (heavy)
Hardwood	18mm	510mm (heavy); 700mm (medium)
	22mm	700mm (heavy); 915mm (medium)
	25mm	915mm (heavy)
Acrylic sheet	12mm	400mm (light-medium)
Toughened glass	6mm	400mm (light)

SAFETY FIRST

Estimating the load

Unless you intend taking your shelf systems with you when you eventually move house, it is best to assume that at some point your shelving will have to bear a fairly heavy load. If your chosen shelving is really only appropriate for light, decorative objects, be sure to inform the new owners when you leave.

The simplest shelf supports are non-adjustable brackets, which are ideal for putting up a single shelf. Space the brackets according to the shelf material, its thickness and the load the shelf will be supporting (see page 140), or you may end up with a sagging shelf.

Fixing sagging shelves

If you have a shelf on the wall that is sagging under the weight of its load, you can either reinforce the edges to keep it straight or you can reposition the brackets to redistribute the weight.

Reinforcing shelves

A shelf can be reinforced quite easily by fixing a wooden batten, lipping or metal strip to its front or underside. Metal reinforcements, which come in various designs, are slimmer and less noticeable than wooden ones. The reinforcement should run the full length of the shelf. Fix wooden battens and lipping with wood glue and screws, and metal strips with screws.

When putting up shelves that will bear a heavy load, reinforce them before fitting them. You could make the reinforcements a design feature – or even use them to hide strip lights, if you wanted.

YOU CAN DO IT

Will it sag?

You can test to see whether a new shelf might sag by resting it on bricks or books, spaced as you plan to space the brackets. Put your items on the shelf and then place a straightedge along it. If the shelf sags, bring the bricks closer together until it is straight. If the brackets can't be fixed that close, you will need to use a thicker material for the shelf.

Type of reinforcement

1. Wooden batten
2. Rebated wooden strip
3. Rebated wooden batten, with a rectangular recess cut out to fit around the shelf edge
4. Semi-circular wooden lipping – its shape gives the shelf a rounded front edge as well as extra support
5. Metal screwed angle
6. Metal grooved T-section
7. Metal grooved angle
8. Metal screwed T-section

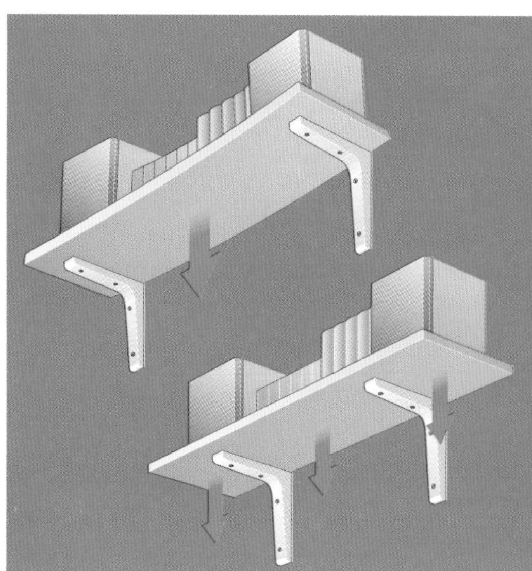

Repositioning brackets

Instead of reinforcing your shelves, you can move the brackets further in so that the load at each end balances the central load. Unscrew the shelf from the bracket, take the brackets off the wall and reposition them following the steps opposite. Fill and sand the old holes and touch up with paint.

Getting a strong fixing

On masonry walls, you will need a hammer action drill with a masonry bit and at least 50mm screws and wallplugs, to go through the plaster and into the wall behind. For stud partition walls, the screws need to go directly into the timber noggings or studs (find them by tapping and listening, or by using an electronic stud detector). Use 38mm screws, or 50mm screws for heavy loads (there is no need for a wallplug). The screws should be the heaviest gauge that the holes in the bracket will take – generally 4mm gauge on small ones and 5mm or 5.5mm on larger ones.

SAFETY FIRST

Safe drilling
Always check for pipes and cables with an electronic detector before drilling into a wall. Never drill directly above or below a light fitting or power socket, as that is where its supply cables are most likely to be.

Putting up a fixed shelf

Brackets are fitted with the longer arm against the wall and the shorter one under the shelf, so the length of the longer arm will determine how closely shelves can be fitted one above the other.

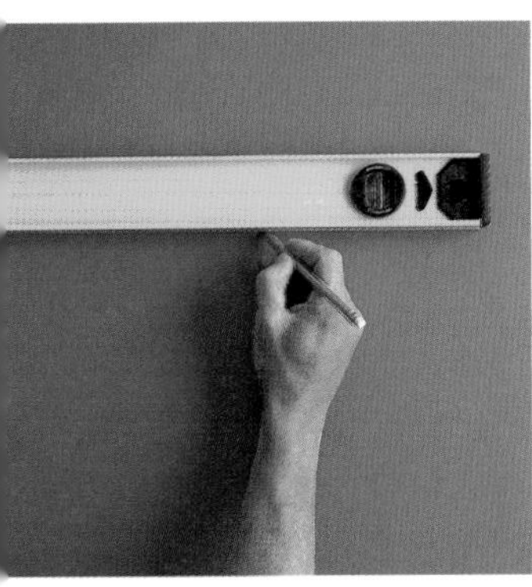

1 Check that the area is free from hidden pipes or cables (see SAFETY FIRST). Hold the shelf against the wall and mark where you want the bottom to go. Then mark where the first bracket should be, as well as the distance to the next bracket (see page 140). Check the marks are level with a spirit level.

2 Hold the first bracket up to the mark, checking it is vertical, and mark the wall through the fixing holes. Repeat with the second. If there are more than two brackets, fit them between the outer brackets, equal distances apart.

3 Drill into the wall, insert wallplugs if you have a masonry wall, and screw the brackets in place. Lay the shelf across, and make a mark through the holes in the brackets for the fixing screws underneath it. Take the shelf down and drill pilot holes for the short screws, but be sure not to go right through the shelf. Replace the shelf and screw home the fixing screws.

TOOLS MATERIALS

- **pipe and cable detector**
- **pencil**
- **straightedge**
- **spirit level**
- **safety goggles**
- **power drill with masonry or twist bits**
- **screwdriver**

- shelf
- brackets
- 50mm or 38mm screws and wallplugs (4mm, 5mm or 5.5mm gauge)
- small screws for fixing the shelf to the brackets

Hidden fixture shelving

This is a storage system with no visible means of support. It comes as a kit with a ready-prepared shelf, available in different lengths. The shelf is supported by a metal strip you fix to the wall, from which project two or more bars that support the pre-drilled shelf. Some of these systems also have pre-drilled holes for small locating screws that go through the underside of the shelf into the bar to make the shelf more secure.

These systems look great, but they do have drawbacks: if your wall is not perfectly flat, the metal strip will not fit against it properly; the shelf itself looks overly thick, since it has to accommodate the bars; and it is really only strong enough for light objects.

TOOLS MATERIALS

- **tape measure**
- **pencil**
- **spirit level**
- **power drill with masonry or twist bit**
- **screwdriver**

- hidden fixture shelf kit
- 50mm or 38mm screws and wallplugs (4mm, 5mm or 5.5mm gauge)
- small screws for fixing the shelf to the bars

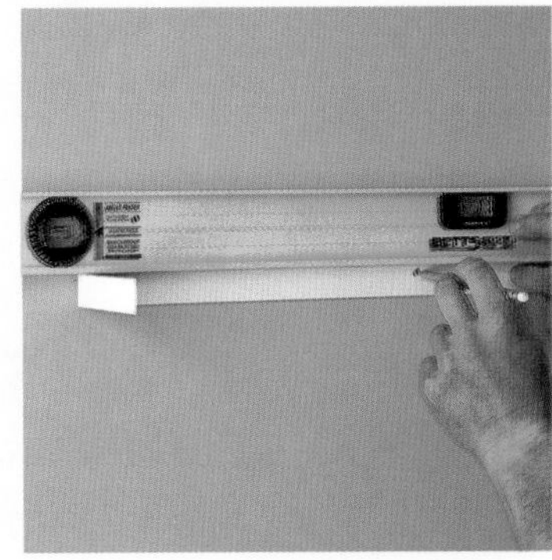

1 Check there are no hidden pipes or cables (see SAFETY FIRST). Hold the metal strip on the wall, level it with a spirit level, and mark the fixing hole positions. Drill the holes, insert wall plugs and screw the strip in place.

2 Slide the shelf on to the bars. If your kit has pre-drilled holes in the underside of the shelf, fit small screws through them into the holes in the bar.

YOU CAN DO IT

Shelves in alcoves
One of the most popular places for shelves is in an alcove, and here you need fixings on the side walls. Cut 50mm x 25mm wooden battens the width of the shelf and screw them horizontally to the side walls of the alcoves. If the shelf is long, a batten can be fixed to the back wall as well. For extra security, the shelf can be screwed to the battens by means of a metal plate positioned between batten and shelf.

STORAGE STACKS OF SHELVES

If you need a stack of shelves, you can choose fixed shelves or an adjustable track system. Fixed shelving is usually cheaper, but a track system lets you adjust the height of the shelves.

1 Lay the battens side by side and mark and cut them to length (measure from the top of the top bracket to the bottom of the bottom bracket, plus about 30mm to prevent splitting when the screws are fitted). Mark the position of each bracket's top fixing hole on each batten, then mark the position for the wall fixings – these should go where they will be hidden by the brackets. Drill the fixing holes. Use three fixings per batten, or four if there are more than three shelves. Sand, paint or varnish the battens. Check for hidden pipes or cables (see SAFETY FIRST, page 143) before fixing the battens to the wall.

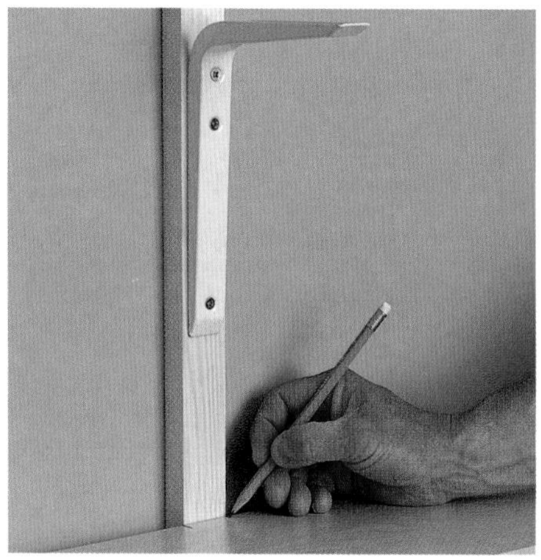

4 If you want the backs of the shelves to sit flush against the wall, you will need to cut slots in them to fit around the battens. Position each shelf in turn on its brackets, and mark where the sides of each batten are.

Fitting a stack of fixed shelves

Stacks of fixed shelves are supported by brackets attached to wooden battens fixed vertically to the wall. If you want the backs of the shelves to touch the wall, the shelves must be cut to fit around each batten. The shelving material will determine the number of battens you need (see the table on page 140), and the length of the battens will depend on the number of shelves and the distance between them.

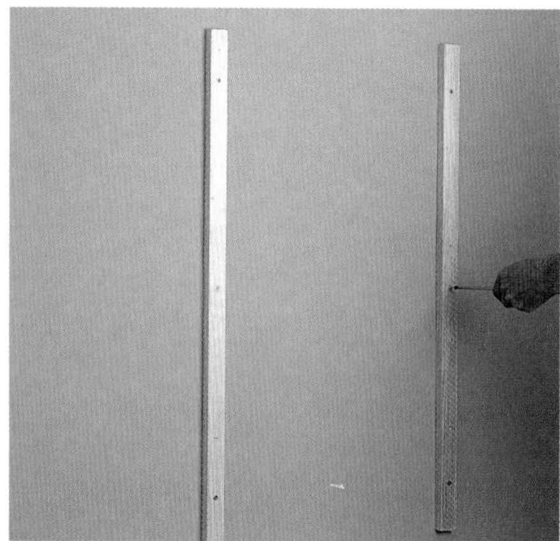

2 Hold the left batten in position and mark the place for the top fixing hole with a bradawl. Drill the hole and screw the batten loosely in place. Check it is vertical with a spirit level, and mark the other fixing holes. Swing the batten to one side to drill the holes, then screw it firmly in place. Measure the distance to the right batten and mark the wall. Position the right batten, using a spirit level to check it is level with the top of the left batten, and fix it as before.

5 Remove the shelf. Use an off-cut of batten to mark the piece to be cut out. Make two saw cuts into the shelf and chop out the piece with a wood chisel and mallet. Repeat for all shelves except the top one (see YOU CAN DO IT).

TOOLS MATERIALS

- **tape measure**
- **pencil**
- **ruler**
- **panel saw**
- **abrasive paper**
- **paint brush**
- **pipe and cable detector**
- **bradawl**
- **power drill with twist or masonry bit**
- **spirit level**
- **screwdriver**
- **straightedge**
- **wood chisel**
- **wooden mallet**

- 50mm x 25mm battens
- paint or varnish for the battens
- 50mm or 38mm screws and wallplugs (4mm, 5mm or 5.5mm gauge)
- small screws for fixing the shelf to the brackets
- brackets
- shelves

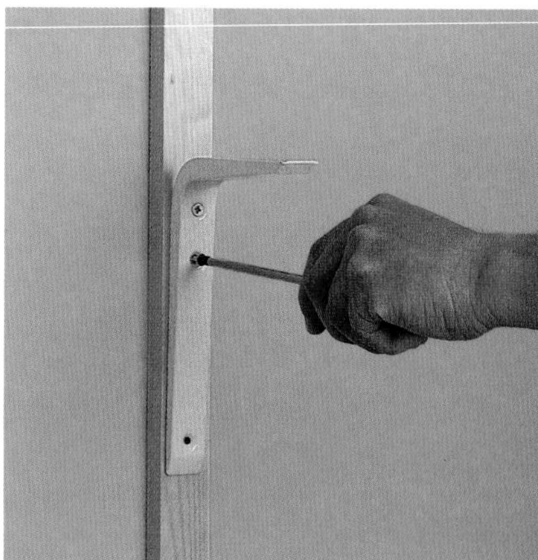

3 Fix a third batten, if required, exactly mid-way between them, checking that all three are exactly level. Fix the brackets to the battens, starting at the top hole.

YOU CAN DO IT

Top notch?

If you sit the top shelf on top of the battens, it will sit flush against the wall without needing slots cutting. Simply position the top of the top bracket level with the top of the batten.

6 Fit the shelves in place around the battens. Mark the positions for the fixing screws through the holes in the brackets on to the underside of the shelves.

7 Drill pilot holes for the screws, taking care not to go right through the shelf. If necessary, remove the shelf to drill it. Drive home the fixing screws.

Fitting adjustable shelves

Ready-made adjustable shelving sits on brackets slotted into metal tracks screwed into a wall. The track and brackets create a small gap behind the shelves, which can be useful for running electric cable for a lamp. If you prefer the shelves flush with the wall, you must cut notches in them (see Steps 4 and 5 opposite).

TOOLS MATERIALS

- **pipe and cable detector**
- **spirit level**
- **pencil**
- **tape measure**
- **bradawl**
- **power drill with twist or masonry bit**
- **screwdriver**

- adjustable track and bracket shelving system
- 50mm or 38mm screws and wallplugs (4mm, 5mm or 5.5mm gauge)
- small screws for fixing the shelf to the bars

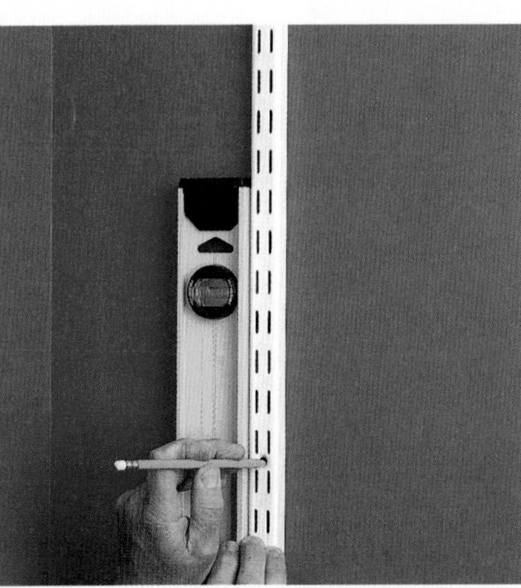

1 Check there are no hidden pipes or cables (see SAFETY FIRST, page 143). Using a spirit level, draw a vertical line down the wall the length of the track. Position the next track (manufacturer's guidelines will specify the distance between them), and draw another vertical line. Hold the left track on the wall and mark the top fixing hole. Drill the hole and screw the track loosely in place. Holding a spirit level to the side of the track to check it is vertical, mark the other fixing holes.

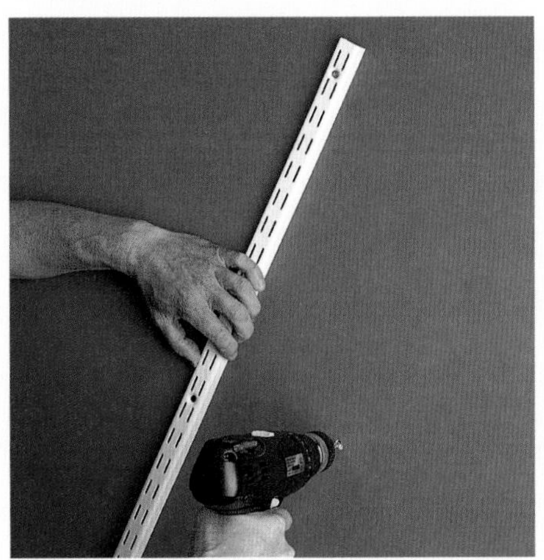

2 Swing the track to one side, drill the holes and fit wallplugs, then screw it in place. Slot in a bracket near the top of the track, and insert another in the same position in the second track. Hold the second track at the next marked vertical line. Lay a shelf across the two brackets and use a spirit level to get it exactly horizontal. Mark the top fixing hole for the second track, remove the shelf, and fix it in place at the top fixing hole.

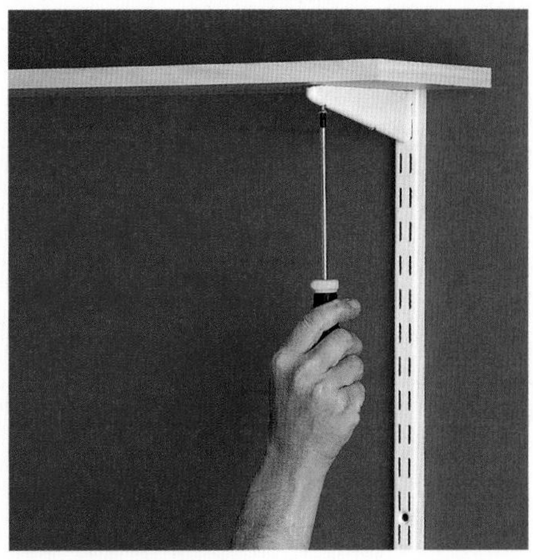

3 Position the top shelf centrally on the brackets and use a bradawl to mark the drilling points for the small securing screws through the underside of the shelf. Drill pilot holes, removing the shelf if necessary, and screw home the shelf fixings to the brackets.

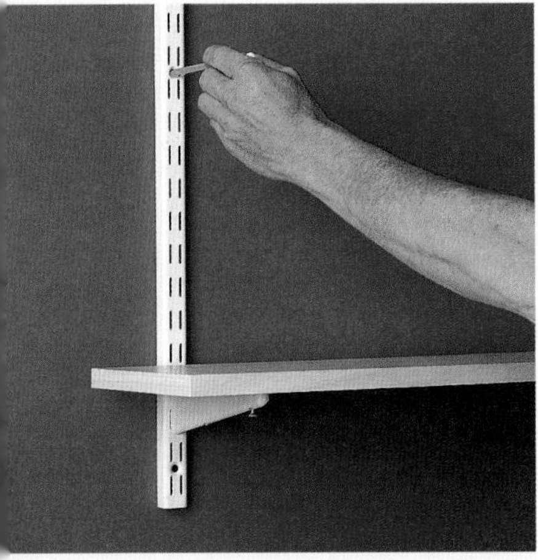

4 Remove this shelf with its brackets and refit it at the bottom of the tracks. Mark the lower fixing holes of the second track and secure it to the wall. This way the tracks will be perfectly parallel and the shelves all interchangeable. Slot the remaining brackets into the tracks and screw the shelves to them.

STORAGE ASSEMBLING FLATPACKS

Flatpacks have been available for many years but they just keep getting better. The choice is almost endless. Whether you need a fully fitted kitchen or just an extra set of shelves, you will find a flatpack to suit you.

Convenient

Flatpacks have become so popular because they are readily available and easy to transport. Most are packed so that they will fit into a normal family car.

Versatile

Flatpacks are a convenient way of creating attractive storage space, and many ranges are so versatile that with a little imagination you can create almost any design to suit the style of your home. They are made in a wide range of wood, coloured or glass finishes.

Flexible

B&Q flatpacks allow you to choose your own accessories. When you make your purchase, check what has been included in the pack. You may need to buy handles, drawer fronts or legs separately; this is a good opportunity to add your own design touches. You can even buy conversion kits to transform a simple cabinet into a filing cabinet, or a set of drawers. You can mix and match finishes, or replace the doors or drawer fronts to match a new colour scheme.

There is no need to feel limited by the size of unit available. Measure the space you wish to fill and then work out if a combination of units will fit the area. The units are designed to fit together horizontally, vertically, or both. Once they are secured to the wall, they will be perfectly stable and look just like fitted units.

Logical

All B&Q flatpacks follow the same basic principles. The steps are logical and each part will be numbered clearly on the accompanying instructions. The most important thing is to read them carefully first, check nothing is missing before you begin, and allow plenty of uninterrupted time for assembly.

Assembling a small cabinet

This compact cabinet is a typical building block in a flexible, modular storage system. You can fit drawers, or a shelf and door to make it into a cupboard. Buy several to make a unit that is purpose-built for your storage needs. Always read the manufacturer's assembly instructions too, since individual products may differ.

TOOLS MATERIALS

- **cross-head screwdriver**
- **small hammer**
- **trimming knife**
- **power drill with 3mm twist bit**
- **ruler**
- **pencil**
- **bradawl**

- small cabinet flatpack
- shelf pack
- door pack
- handle pack

1 Lay panels out on the floor so that you can easily see each part. Use the packaging to protect the panels from scratches, if necessary. Keep screws and fixings inside their packaging until you need to use them.

2 Push the legs into the pre-drilled holes underneath the base panel. If you are using decorative legs that have been purchased separately, refer to the fixing instructions supplied with them.

3 Turn the base panel over so that it is standing on the legs. Using a screwdriver, screw four cam studs into the pre-drilled holes closest to each corner.

4 Apply a little of the PVA wood adhesive supplied to one end of four wooden dowels and insert them into the pre-drilled holes either side of the base panel.

5 Tap the dowels into place with a small hammer. They should fit snugly. Take care not to damage the end of the dowels; a light tap should be sufficient.

6 Insert a locking cam (see below) into each of the larger holes at the bottom of the side panels. The arrows embossed on the cams must point towards the end of the panel. Use a trimming knife to remove any excess edging at both ends of the grooves running along the length of the side panels. This is where the back panel will be fitted.

7 Apply a little PVA wood adhesive to the protruding end of each dowel.

8 Fit the first side panel to the base. It should slide neatly on to the already glued dowels. Keep the panel at right angles to the base, or you risk damaging the dowels. The grooves in the base and side panels should line up.

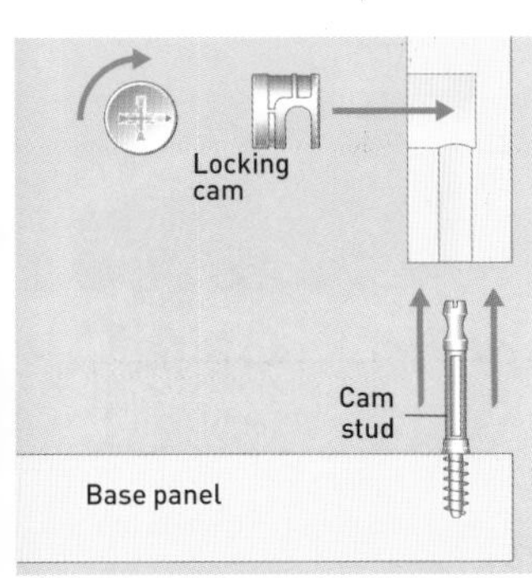

9 Secure the first side panel by tightening the two locking cams. Use a screwdriver, and turn them clockwise.

10 You are now ready to fit the back panel. Run a bead of glue along the grooves in the side and base panel you have already assembled. Slide the back panel into place.

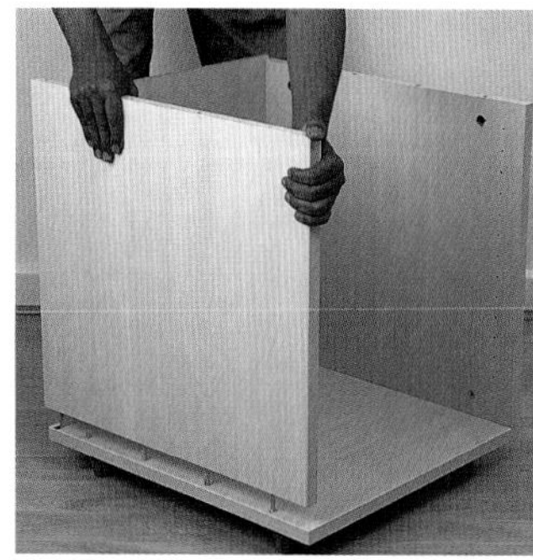

11 Slide the second side panel into position. Tighten the two locking cams.

12 Insert four locking cams into the holes on the top of the side panels, with their arrows pointing towards the end of the panel. Glue four wooden dowels and fit them into the top panel. Insert four cam studs into the pre-drilled holes and run a bead of glue into the groove. The top panel can now be fitted. Tighten the locking cams and fit cam covers to all of the exposed locking cams.

Fitting a shelf

This cabinet is supplied with a shelf, but you can fit shelves into any flatpack cabinet. Buy a shelf pack to match the cabinet and all the fixings you need will be included.

IDEAL TOOL

Gofer
This ultra-compact rechargeable screwdriver is perfect for assembling a flatpack, or any job that involves a lot of screwing. Just press it onto the screw head and it will work automatically.

1 Decide on the height of the shelf. Use a screwdriver to fit two shelf support screws into each side panel. Make sure all four screws are at the same height. Avoid using any of the pre-drilled holes that you will need to fit door hinges to the cabinet.

2 Place the four shelf support inserts into the pre-formed holes in the shelf. You may need to use a small hammer to tap them into place.

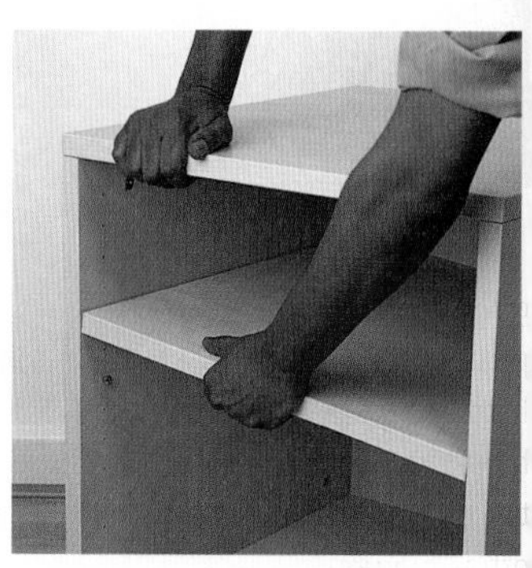

3 Simply slide the shelf in and clip into place by pressing down. The shelf will rest on the exposed screw heads on the side panels.

Fitting door handles

If handles have not been supplied with the unit, you will need to buy them separately. Always drill at a 90° angle to the door, and select a drill bit that allows half a millimetre clearance around the screw.

IDEAL TOOL

Bradawl
Bradawls are mainly used to start holes in a piece of wood in which you want to insert screws. They help to prevent the wood splitting or the drill bit slipping.

1 Decide where you want the handle. It can be in the centre of the door or towards the upper corner if that's more convenient. Mark the position on the front of the door with a pencil (you can easily rub the marks out later if they are visible after the handle is attached).

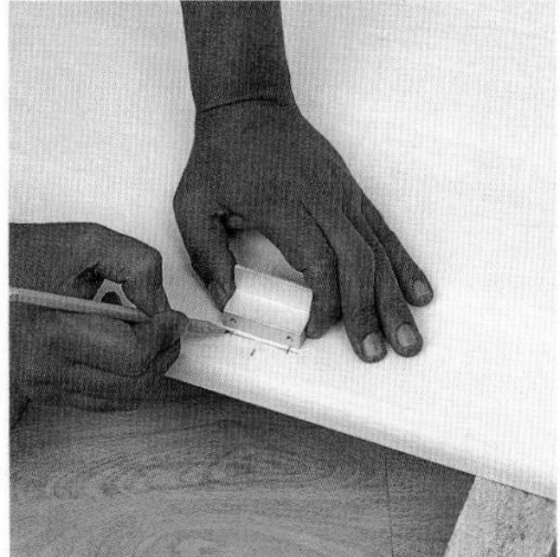

2 Place the handle on the pencil marks. Tip the handle back a little and mark the position of the fixing holes.

3 Using the recommended drill bit (normally 3mm), drill the holes ready to attach the handle.

4 Place the handle on the front of the door. Line up the holes and insert screws from the back of the door to secure it.

5 Stick one door buffer to the front edge of the base panel and another to the front edge of the top panel. Position them both 15mm–20mm in from the side panel.

Fitting door hinges

Hinges are usually supplied with all the necessary fixings, and doors and cabinets have cut-outs and guide holes for easy fitting.

1 Use a bradawl to make guide holes in the pre-marked positions on the cabinet door. Insert the circular part of the hinge into the large hole in the door. Repeat with any other hinges.

2 Fix the hinges to the door using the screws provided. Make sure they are fitted squarely. Once all the hinges are in position on the door, fix them into the guide holes on the side panel of the cabinet. Do not overtighten the screws.

Adjusting door hinges

You may find that the doors need some adjustment after you have completed assembly of a new unit. On most modern cabinets, badly fitting doors can be adjusted in the same way.

1 If a door is hanging either too high or too low, use a screwdriver to loosen the top and bottom screws on the hinge mounting plates. Slide the door up or down until it is level with the top. Re-tighten the screws. To adjust the door to the left or right, turn the front screw on the arm of the hinge.

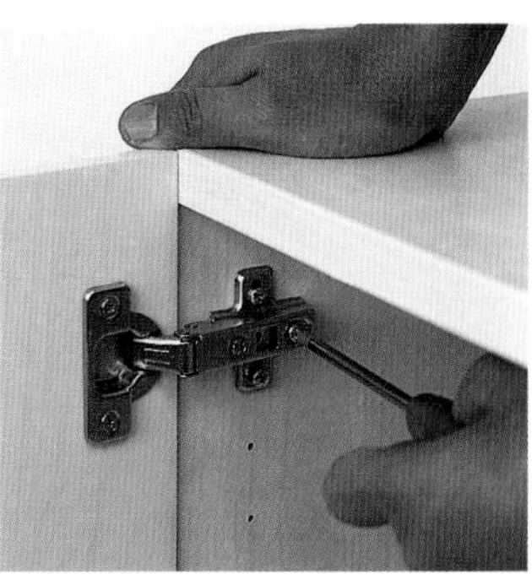

2 If a door does not fit flush against the cupboard front, loosen the screws at the back of all hinges. Reposition the door and re-tighten the screws. Adjust the screws at the front of the hinge if the door is not square with the cabinet. Re-tighten once you have a good fit.

STORAGE MIX AND MATCH FLATPACKS

YOU CAN DO IT

Lay it out

When assembling any flatpack, it's a good idea to begin by laying out all the parts so that you can clearly see how they will fit together.

Once you have grasped the basics, there's no end to what you can create by mixing and matching flatpack units, whether for bedroom, study, bathroom or kitchen.

Drawer unit

Most flatpack systems give you the option of fitting drawers instead of a shelf and cupboard door to a small cabinet (see pages 147–48). You could of course create a combined drawer and cupboard unit by joining the two together either vertically or horizontally (see opposite); or use them as components of an entire built-in storage system, carefully designed to meet your own individual needs.

As always, do read the manufacturer's instructions as well, since different products are often assembled in slightly different ways.

TOOLS MATERIALS

- **bradawl**
- **power drill with 3mm gauge twist bit**
- **screwdriver**

- small cabinet flatpack
- drawer pack
- drawer front pack

1 Push the drawer sides on to the drawer back to form a frame. The sides will be marked left and right. Make sure you fit them the right way around.

2 The drawer base has two different sides. Decide which you want to be visible, then slide it into the groove that runs around the lower part of the frame.

3 With the drawer upside down, make guide holes with a bradawl for the four screws that will hold the base in place. These holes are pre-drilled on some units. Screw the base panel into place.

4 Each drawer front will be marked top, bottom or middle, indicating the drawer's position i the finished cabinet. Take note o this order. Fix two retaining clips into the pre-drilled holes in the back of the drawer front. Each cl requires two screws. Swivel the clip round to cover the screws.

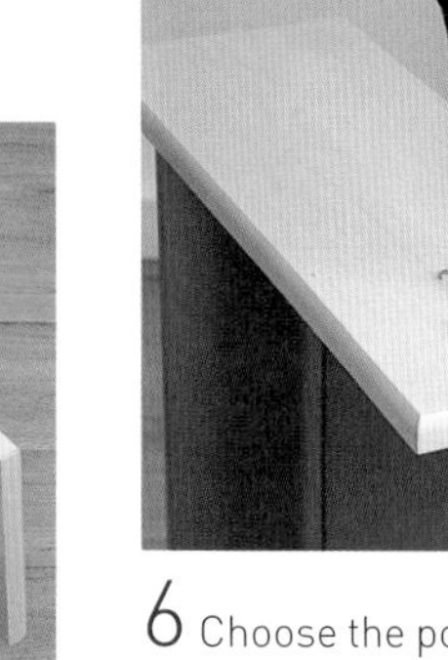

5 Push the drawer front into the drawer sides. Repeat Steps 2 to 5 for each drawer to complete the set.

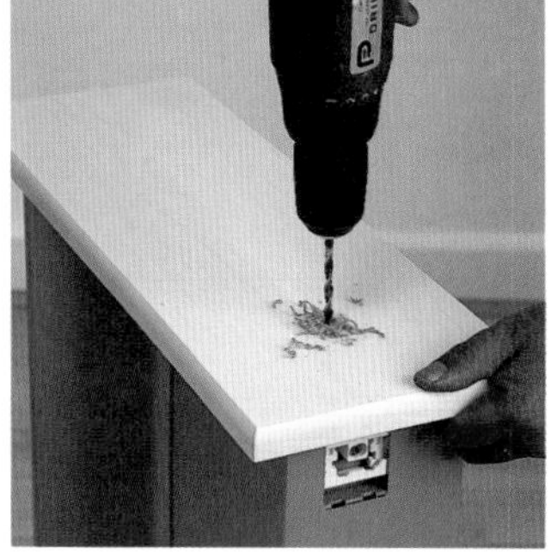

6 Choose the position for the drawer handles. Measure accurately, so that the handles are neatly parallel. Use a bradawl to mark hole positions and then drill clearance holes for fixing. Insert screws from the back of the drawer and fix the handles in place.

7 There will be pre-drilled holes in the side panels of the cabinet to which the drawer runners will fit. Use two screws to fix each runner on to the side panels, making sure that you fit left- and right-hand runners on the correct sides. Make sure that opposite pairs of runners are at the same height.

8 Engage your assembled drawers on to the running mechanisms, making sure that the top, middle and bottom drawers are in the correct order. Check that the drawer fronts are aligned. If they need adjustment to left or right, turn the screws nearest to the drawer front. Do this at both sides, or you may create uneven pressure. To adjus up or down, turn the rear screws Once you have completed all adjustments, fix the two locking plates into position.

Joining Units

You can join units vertically or horizontally using the same method. Three or more units joined vertically need to be secured to the wall with steel angle brackets for stability.

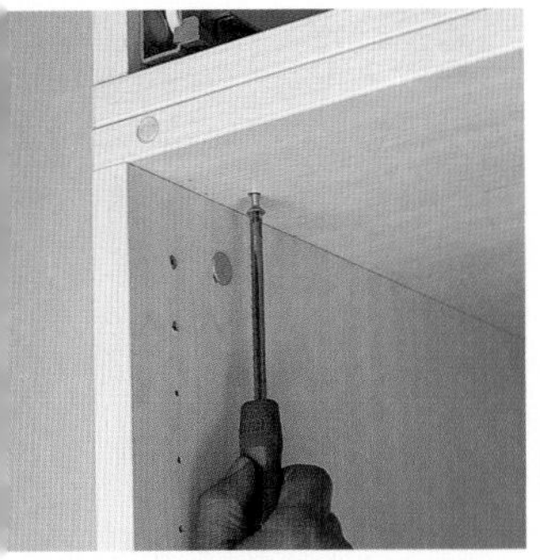

1 To join units vertically, locate the four joining points marked on the inside of the top panel. Wrap masking tape 30mm from the end of a 3mm bit and drill through the top of one unit into the base of the next, stopping when you reach the tape. Screw in 30mm screws and cover the heads with screw caps.

2 Position steel angle brackets on top of the uppermost unit close to its outer edges. Mark the screw positions then drill pilot holes with a 3mm drill bit. Don't drill right through the top panel. Screw the brackets to the units. Then put the units in position and mark the screw holes on the wall. Fix to the wall (see right).

TOOLS MATERIALS

- **power drill with twist and masonry bits**
- **pipe and cable detector**
- **screwdriver**
- **bradawl**

- masking tape
- 30mm screws (3mm gauge) and screw caps
- steel angle brackets
- hollow-wall fixings or wallplugs

SAFETY FIRST

Safe drilling

Never drill directly above or below a light fitting or power socket. Always check for pipes and cables with an electronic detector before drilling into a wall.

Safe fixing

How you fix the units to the wall depends on what your wall is made from:

- Plasterboard: push a bradawl through at the fixing position. If you hit a stud, drill a pilot hole and fix with a 30mm screw; if not, use a special hollow-wall fixing (see page 368).
- Solid plaster: drill with a masonry bit, insert a wall plug and fix with a 30mm screw. If the plaster is old or crumbly, use longer screws and plugs.

Kitchen unit

You could adapt this kitchen unit to take a sink base, if you like, but the back would have to be altered to accommodate all the pipework. For more advice see Kitchens, pages 156–59.

TOOLS MATERIALS

- **cross-head screwdriver**
- **small hammer**
- **power drill with 3mm gauge twist bit**

- kitchen unit flatpack
- plinth

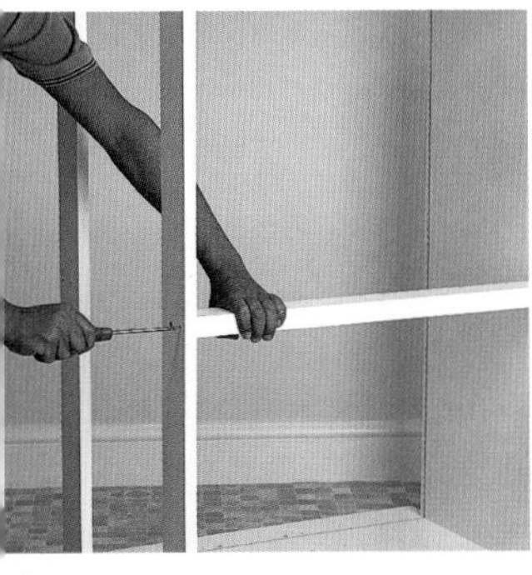

1 Assemble the base unit as you would a small cabinet (see pages 147–48). Fit the central support and secure with four screws.

2 Position the leg brackets into the pre-drilled holes on the underside of the base panel. Ensure that the screw holes will not lie over panel joins.

3 Using a small hammer, tap in the central plastic lug.

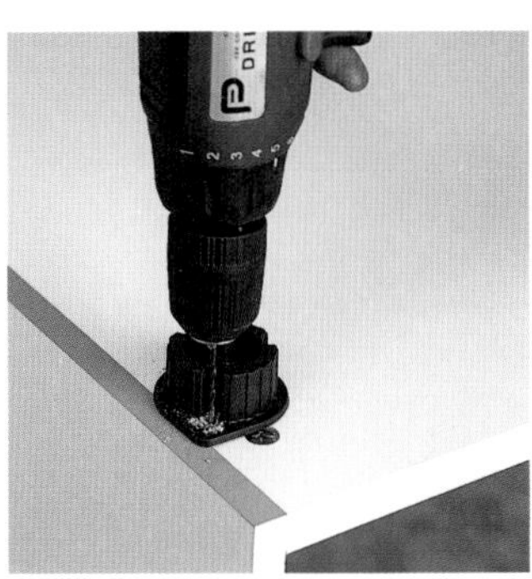

4 Using a 3mm bit, drill pilot holes through the screw holes in the leg bracket and into the base panel. Then secure each bracket with three screws.

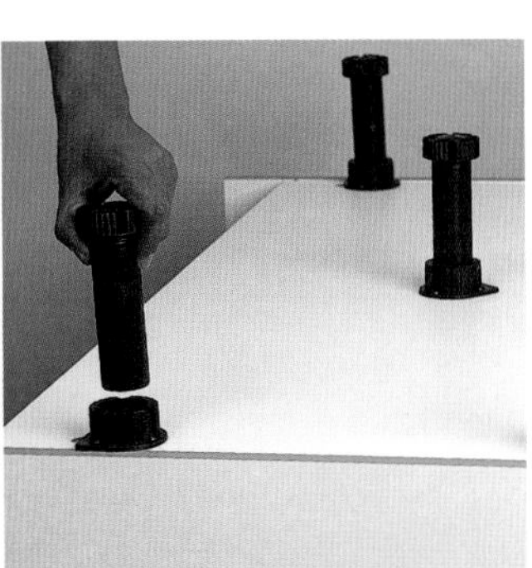

5 Fit the plastic legs into the brackets. Place the unit in position and adjust the legs until the unit is level at the correct height.

6 Push shelf supports into the pre-drilled holes at the required height. Turn the shelf on its side to feed it through the opening then rest it on the supports. To fit the doors, see page 149.

KITCHENS PLANNING

Modular kitchen systems are designed to be flexible and simple to install. Before planning the layout, consider your lifestyle and the way you and your family use the room. Do you gather and entertain in there – or is it simply a room to cook and do the chores? If you prefer not to do the planning yourself, B&Q have a design service to do the work for you.

Before you start

It is tempting when planning a new kitchen to keep the arrangement of appliances much the same as they already are. But there may be a better way. Start from scratch and think about what can be improved.

Refurbishing a kitchen is a great opportunity to upgrade the electrics and lighting. Plan for plenty of sockets on the walls behind the worktops – you won't regret it. Also think carefully about lighting. You will need directed task lighting over the work surfaces as well as overall illumination. There are so many options these days – from adjustable spotlights recessed into the ceiling or on tracks to lights installed under, on or inside cupboards, shielded by pelmets or cornices. Think about mood too – bright white light creates a brisk, efficient atmosphere; pools of subdued illumination are more relaxing. Why not allow for both, especially if you have a dining table in the kitchen?

If the kitchen does double up as a dining area or faces a dining room, make sure that there is a clear path to the table – this will make it easier to serve food, as well as bringing together the diners with those hard at work preparing the meal.

Finally, don't forget the flooring. This needs to be easy to clean and hardwearing. Water-resistant laminate or ceramic tiles are practical, popular choices.

Convenience and safety

- It is possible to move fixed elements, such as water pipes, power points, windows and doors, but it will be a lot easier and cheaper to work around them.
- Make sure there is easy access to cupboard doors and drawers, particularly in corners, or they won't get used effectively.
- Measure the height of window ledges and double-check that any units will fit underneath them.
- If you can, position the sink under a window to let in light and give you a view.
- Choose energy-efficient appliances to help reduce energy consumption.
- For safety, avoid placing the cooker or hob near to an inward-opening door or under a window. Allow at least 100mm of workspace either side of the hob so that pans sit safely on it.
- Don't put a fridge beside hot appliances, or it will have to work harder to keep food cold.
- Make sure there is enough space in corners for doors and drawers to open properly. Don't put an appliance like a washing machine in a corner where its door will obstruct access to other units.
- If possible, keep washing machines and dishwashers close to a sink to keep the plumbing simple.
- Do not position cooker and sink any less than 600mm apart.
- Any fitting or moving of gas appliances must be carried out by a CORGI-registered professional. Any modifications to plumbing or electrics must be in accordance with the Wiring and Building Regulations; if in doubt, consult a professional.

Drawing up a plan

Start by making a rough sketch of the room showing fixtures, doors, windows, plumbing and electrical sockets, and gas outlet. Then take accurate measurements of every dimension and transfer them to the drawing. The walls and floor of your kitchen may not be regular. To measure the length and width, take three measurements at different wall heights and work with the smallest. Finally draw a plan of the kitchen to scale, either on ordinary graph paper or on a special kitchen planning grid that you can download from www.diy.com.

- If you are using a kitchen planner it will have ready-made shapes of kitchen units and appliances. Simply put the ones you want on the plan and move them around to create different designs. If you are using graph paper, cut out your own shapes.
- Most work in a normal kitchen revolves around the 'work triangle' of sink, fridge and cooker, so start with these and position your units around them. Try them in different arrangements and draw lines between them to form a triangle. For maximum efficiency a work triangle should be neither too cramped nor too spread out: the combined distance of its three sides should be no less than 3.6m but no more than 7m.
- Mark where you would like to install new sockets and light fittings.
- Allow for adequate ventilation – an extractor fan is a must.
- Is your boiler in the kitchen? If it is in the way, could it be moved?

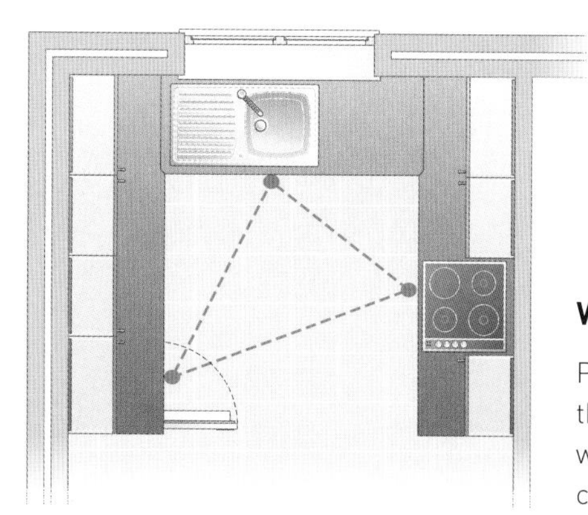

Work triangle

Plan your kitchen around the three hardest-working elements: sink, cooker and fridge.

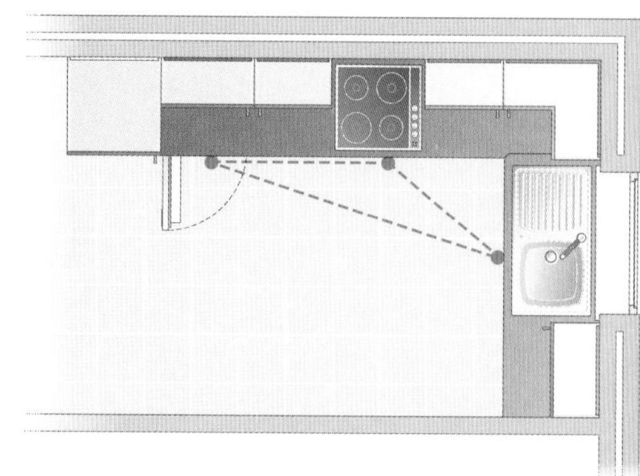

KITCHEN MAKEOVER

Bored with your kitchen? Want to change the style, but don't want the expense of a complete refit? There is no need to despair. You can completely alter the feel of your kitchen by changing the colour scheme and taking a critical look at all the accessories; with the choices available you can quickly make an older kitchen look like new.

Changing doors and worktops

The beauty of modular kitchen systems is that everything is made to mix and match. You may want to break up a solid run of cupboard doors by adding glass panelled ones for a softer look. Or convert cupboards to drawers or vice versa to make the most of the space. Base and wall units come in standard sizes, so doors, drawer fronts and worktops are interchangeable – though do check all measurements carefully before you buy.

Gloss white

For a clean, bright, modern kitchen, cool in summer and full of light in winter, a gloss white finish is hard to beat, and it won't go out of style.

Solid pine

Warm, cosy and welcoming; solid pine recreates the feel of a country kitchen. Natural wood is also a good choice if you want to coordinate your kitchen and dining room decor.

Birch effect

Modern style in a natural wood effect; the pale, soft, smooth finish of birch will give a contemporary kitchen a real touch of sophistication.

Cherry effect

Rich, warm and elegant: the red finish is a strong statement, so use contrasting colours and textures to bring out the stunning colour.

Stainless steel

For the ultimate in modern design and simplicity, stainless steel is stylish and practical.

YOU CAN DO IT

Focus on detail

Give your door fronts a facelift by changing the handles. You'll be surprised what a difference it can make.

Traditional ceramic

The large capacity of this timeless design makes it ideal for the busy family and it looks great in a traditional style of kitchen.

Update your sink

As the mainstay of the kitchen, your kitchen sink should be good-looking as well as functional. See pages 159 and 310 for instructions on how to fit a sink.

Round bowl and drainer

This modern stainless steel sink has a separate matching drainer. It's easy to keep clean and compact, giving you useful extra worktop space.

Bowl and half-bowl

Impact-, stain- and scratch-resistant, this practical sink is ideal for food preparation, as the smaller half bowl can be used independently.

Stainless steel bowl and half-bowl

Tough, hygienic and functional. Stainless steel looks good in any kitchen.

Painting doors and drawers

Your melamine kitchen units may not be compatible with readily available replacement doors. Don't worry: painting cupboard doors and drawer fronts is a perfectly good option. Either buy a special paint designed for use on melamine, or apply a melamine base paint and then a topcoat of your choice. Provided you prepare all the surfaces carefully, a good result is easy to achieve.

TOOLS MATERIALS

- **power drill with twist bit**
- **medium-grade abrasive paper**
- **screwdriver**
- **50mm paintbrush**
- **measuring tape**
- **pencil**

- timber off-cuts
- melamine paint, or melamine basecoat and topcoat of your choice
- handles, if required
- wood filler

1 Remove all the handles and hinges, and rub down surfaces using a medium-grade abrasive paper. Carefully work into recesses and mouldings.

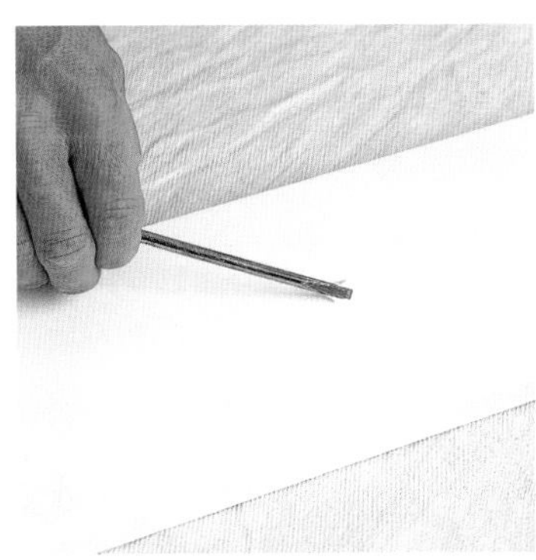

2 If you intend to change the handles, fill the fixing holes with wood filler; use an old screwdriver to work it well into the hole. When the filler is dry, sand the area smooth.

3 Apply the paint with a 50mm brush. Blend in wet edges and make your final brushstrokes in a consistent direction.

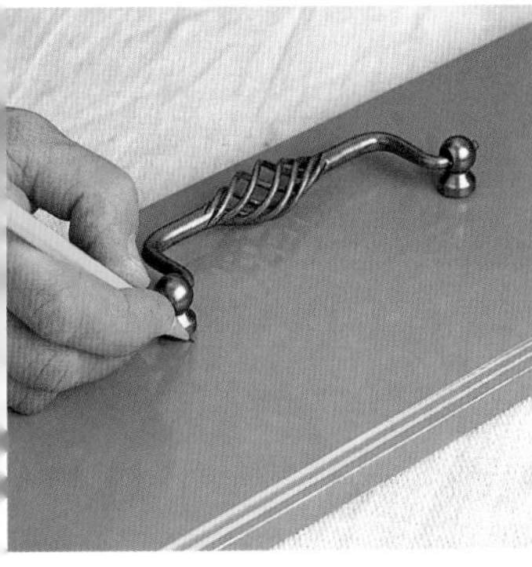

4 Once the paint is thoroughly dry you can replace the drawer handles. Measure the width and depth of a drawer front and mark the centre point very lightly in pencil. Centre the handle on your mark, ensuring it is level. Mark the fixing points. You can rub the guidelines out later.

5 Support the drawer front on two pieces of wood and drill clearance holes right through it for the handle screws. Make sure the drill is at exactly 90° to the surface or the handles won't fit properly.

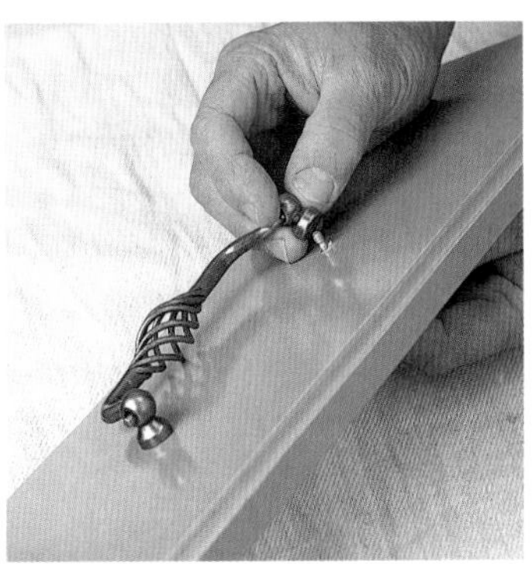

6 Push the screws supplied through the holes from the back, and screw them into the handle.

7 Fit handles on all the cabinets and drawers. You will have to decide on the most convenient position for cupboard handles. On wall units, they are usually more practical at the bottom.

YOU CAN DO IT

Change your plinths

You can buy plinths, cornices, end panels and mouldings to match your kitchen units...but you don't have to. Take a look at other finishes and use a contrasting colour for a more unusual effect.

You could even do away with plinths and show a bit of leg!

KITCHEN UNITS

Creating a new look for your kitchen is a great opportunity to stamp your personality onto the busiest room in the house. Base and wall units come in standard sizes and form the basis of a kitchen. Draw a detailed plan on graph paper or use a purpose-designed kitche planner (downloadable from www.diy.com), and double-check all measurements before you begin. Products may differ, so do read the manufacturer's installation instructions toc

Fitting the base units

Remove the old units, disconnect power and water supplies and do any preparatory work necessary on walls and ceiling. It is a good idea to apply the first coat of paint to walls and ceiling before fitting the units. The top coat can be completed after they are in place. See page 151 for guidance on assembling kitchen units.

TOOLS MATERIALS

- **tape measure**
- **pencil**
- **spirit level**
- **cross-head screwdriver**
- **power drill with 3mm twist bit**
- **masonry drill**
- **clamp**

- base cabinets
- base corner cabinet
- base corner post
- wall cabinet
- wall corner cabinet
- wallplugs or plasterboard fixings
- screws, 25mm and 30mm
- masking tape

1 Using a spirit level as a straightedge, mark a horizontal guideline on the walls level with where the top of the units will be. Align them with any existing appliances. Remember to allow for the legs when working out the height of the units.

2 Assemble the base units (see page 151) and move them into position, starting with a corner cabinet. Rotate the legs of each unit to adjust the height until it aligns with the pencil guideline on the wall. Use a spirit level to check that the run of cabinets is level.

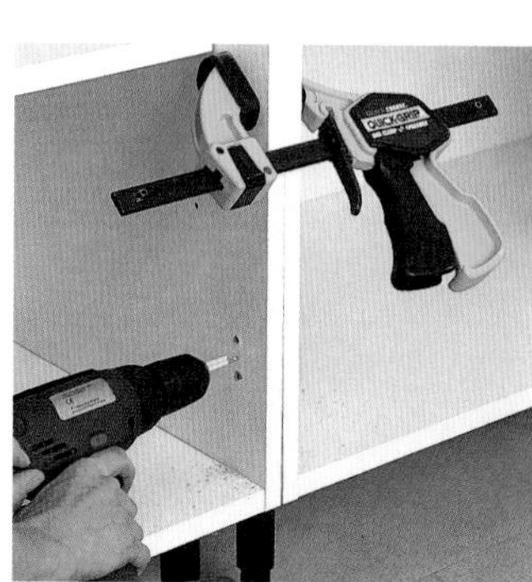

3 Clamp adjoining cabinets together to hold them securely. Wrap masking tape 20mm from the end of a 3mm gauge bit as a depth guide. Drill between the two hinge holes, through one cabinet and 4mm into the next, stopping when you reach the tape. Do this at both hinge positions. Screw the units together using the 25mm screws supplied.

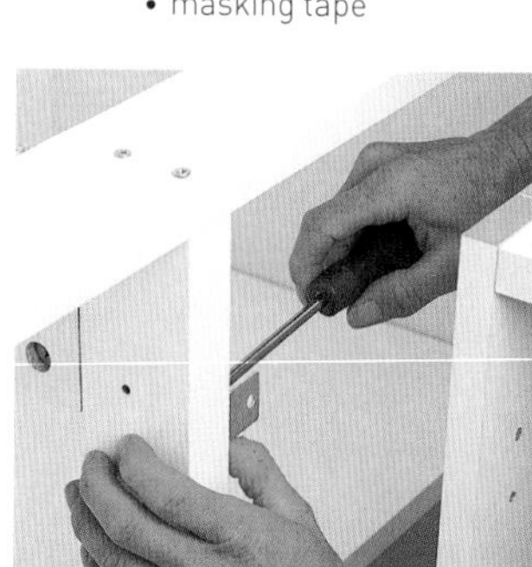

4 To turn a corner with a run of cabinets, you need to fit a corner post or there will be an ugly gap. Screw two brackets at top and bottom of the inside face of the central post of the cabinet that extends into the corner.

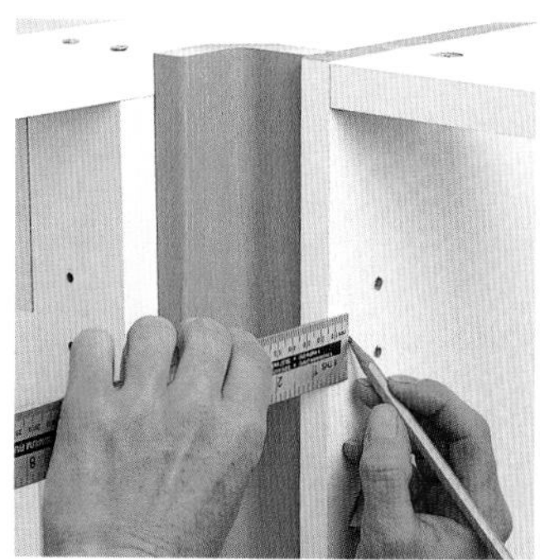

5 Screw two 30mm screws from behind through each bracket into the corner post. Drill two pilot holes through the side panel of the next unit, 13mm in from the outer edge. Keep clear of the hinge positions. Screw 30mm screws through the holes and into the corner post.

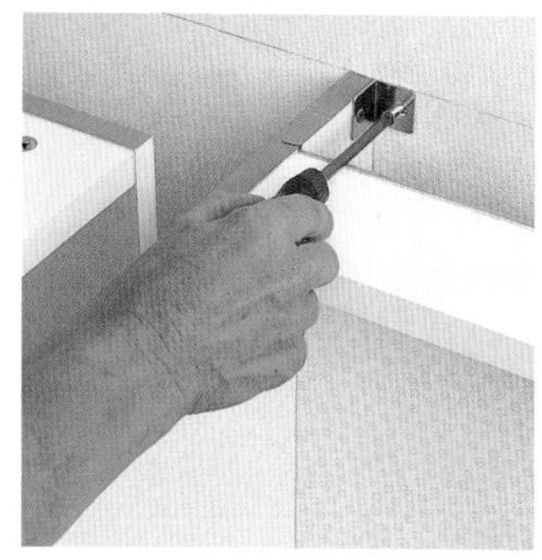

6 Each base is secured to the wall with two brackets. Mark the drilling positions in pencil on the wall and cabinet. Check for pipes and cables before drilling into the wall. On solid masonry use a drill with hammer action and a masonry bit, and fit a wallplug. On plasterboard use plasterboard fixings. Drill a pilot hole into the cabinet and secure the bracket with a 15mm screw.

IDEAL TOOL

Pipe and cable detector

Whenever you need to drill into walls, you must make a thorough check for pipes or cables hidden behind the plaster. The simplest and most effective way of doing this is to use a battery-operated detector. Run it over the surface of the wall where you intend to drill a hole and it will indicate where any hazards lie.

Planning the vertical layout

The distance between the top of the base units and bottom edge of wall units is up to you. However, wall units must not be directly above a hob, and you should check the hob manufacturer's instructions for the necessary clearance either side. Position all the wall units at the same height if possible and take into account the heights of the people who are likely to be using them. If you intend to tile between the base and wall units, calculate the gap in terms of whole tiles (plus grout and sealant) to make your life easier and the finish neater.

Fitting the wall units

The wall units hook onto brackets that must be very securely fixed to the wall.

1 Measure up from the top of the base unit and mark the bottom edge of the wall unit, allowing for the thickness of the worktop. Then use a spirit level to mark a horizontal guideline on the wall, stretching as far round as your wall units will go. Draw another line marking the top of the wall units. Then consult the kitchen plan and draw vertical lines where the cabinets will meet.

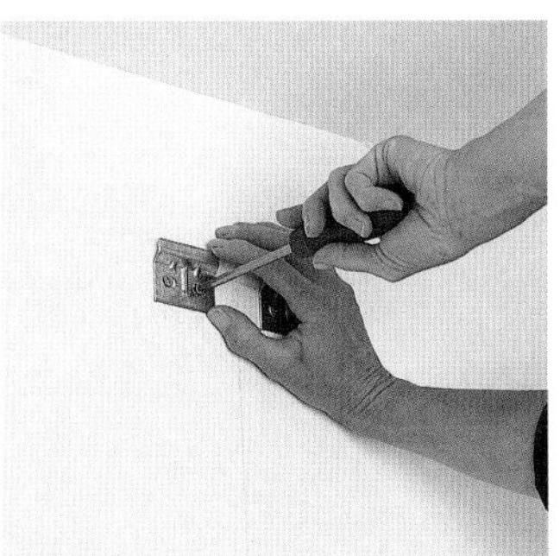

2 Check the manufacturer's instructions to find the correct position for the wall fitting brackets. Each unit will require two brackets, one in each top corner. Hold a bracket in place and mark the position of the fixing holes. How you fix the brackets to the wall depends on what kind of wall you have – see below.

3 Hook the wall cabinets onto the brackets. Use the adjustment block in the top internal corner to position them accurately. Lie a spirit level across the top of the cabinet and turn one screw to level it horizontally, then place the spirit level against the front face and adjust the other screw until it is vertical. Also check that the units are level with each other.

4 Join adjacent wall cabinets in the same way as base cabinets (see Step 3, opposite). Finally, decide on the best position for the shelves and push the shelf supports into the pre-drilled holes. Tilt the shelves and slide them into place.

Fixing units to different types of wall

Always check for pipes and cables before drilling into any wall. If you have solid plaster walls, then use a power drill with hammer action and insert wallplugs and then screws. If you have slightly crumbling plaster, use longer plugs and screws.

If you have plasterboard walls, use hollow-wall fixings to secure the brackets (see pages 368–69). But for safety you must add extra fixings to the wall units. Hang the cabinet on the brackets and adjust it as described above. Then unhook the cabinet. Use a stud detector to locate a stud or nogging behind the wall. Pack out the cavity at the back of the cabinet with a length of timber, rehang it on the brackets, and drill right through the back of the cabinet and packing to screw it firmly into the stud or nogging. Use two additional screws per cabinet.

KITCHEN WORKTOP, SINK AND PLINTH

TOOLS MATERIALS

- **panel saw**
- **power drill with 4mm and 2mm gauge twist bits and 12mm flat bit**
- **cross-head screwdriver**
- **hacksaw**
- **craft knife**
- **fine file**
- **pencil**
- **ruler**
- **power jigsaw with wood blade**
- **try square**
- **bradawl**

- worktop
- profiled joining strip
- kitchen sink
- plinth with fixings
- masking tape
- 16mm (3.5mm gauge) and 38mm (5mm gauge) wood screws
- contact adhesive
- silicone sealant

It's the finishing touches – sinks, worktops and plinths – that will make your kitchen units look professionally designed and, most important of all, make them easy to work on and keep clean.

Fitting the worktop

Kitchen worktops can be made from a variety of materials, including wood, real or synthetic slate or marble, or laminated chipboard. Laminate worktop is the simplest to fit, and is available in a wide range of colours and textures. It also comes in different thicknesses; the worktop fitted here is 45mm thick. Use a panel saw to cut laminate board to the right length before you begin fitting. Factory-cut edges will inevitably be more accurate than those you cut yourself, so position factory cuts where the edge will show and hide your own cuts against wall junctions or under a joining strip.

1 Choose where to make the fixing positions for the worktop: three screws at the back and front of each unit will usually be about right. Using a 4mm gauge bit, drill clearance holes through the support panels on each unit.

2 Put the laminate worktop in position, checking it fits tightly against the wall, and that edges butt up snugly.

3 Where the run of units turns a corner, there has to be a join in the worktop. The front edge of a worktop is profiled, so to create a neat join you have to insert a specially profiled aluminium joining strip. Use a hacksaw to cut the strip to exactly the width of the worktop. Apply silicone sealant along the cut edge of the worktop, and then screw the strip in place using 16mm (3.5mm gauge) wood screws. Apply more sealant to the profiled edge of the adjoining worktop and slide the two sections together.

4 Now fix the worktop to the units. Wrap masking tape 38mm from the end of a 2mm gauge drill bit as a depth guide. Working from beneath the worktop and inside the cabinets, drill through each of the clearance holes you have already made, and into the worktop. Stop when you reach the masking tape so that the drill doesn't break through. Screw a 38mm (5mm gauge) wood screw through each fixing position.

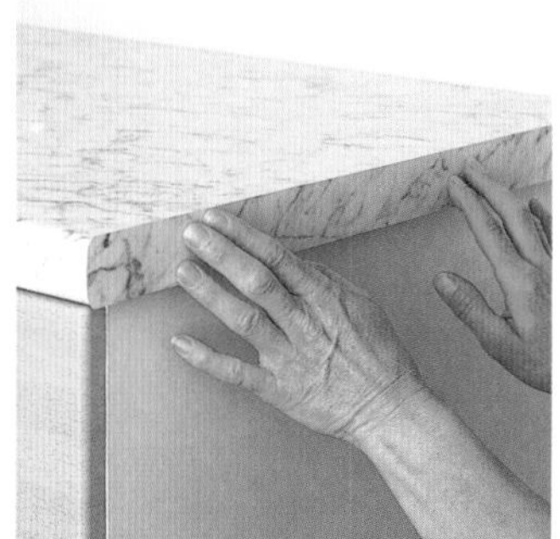

5 Apply matching laminate strip to exposed worktop edges; this will be supplied with the worktop. Cut the strip to the right length. Apply contact adhesive to both the back of the edging strip and the worktop edge. Leave for the recommended time and then stick into place.

6 Once the glue has dried completely, trim the edge with a craft knife and file off rough edges with a fine file.

YOU CAN DO IT

Splashbacks

A splashback doesn't have to be tiled. Specially designed splashbacks are available in various finishes, including toughened glass and stainless steel. They are waterproof and easy to clean, and much quicker to fit than tiles.

Fitting a sink into a laminate worktop

Although kitchen sinks come in a variety of designs, the basic technique for fitting them into a worktop remains the same. Check the instructions supplied with the sink for any variation.

1 Use the template supplied, or turn the sink upside down on the worktop (with the bowls in the right position – the sink may not be exactly rectangular). Make sure it is an equal distance from the front and back edges, and will fit into the base unit underneath. Trace its outline directly onto the work surface in pencil or – if pencil won't mark the laminate – stick masking tape on the surface beneath the sink edges and trace their outline onto it.

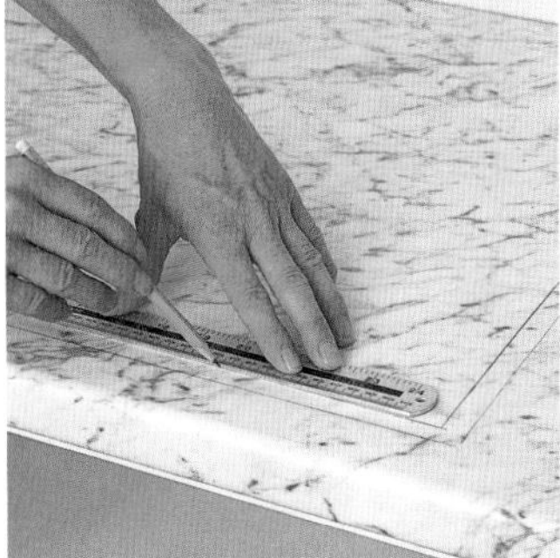

2 Take the sink away and measure the overlap required for the sink edge to rest on the worktop. The manufacturer's instructions should give you this measurement. Use a ruler to draw another line at this distance inside the first.

3 Using a 12mm gauge flat bit, drill a hole through the worktop at each corner of the inner line to enable you to insert the blade of a jigsaw. Be extremely careful that you don't stray over the line.

4 Cut along the inner line with a power jigsaw using a wood blade suitable for laminated chipboard. Stick masking tape on the jigsaw plate to avoid scratching the surface. Support the piece you are cutting out as you get to the end, to prevent the worktop splitting. To plumb in a sink, see page 310.

Fitting the plinth

A plinth running round the bottom of your units will give a neat finish and make cleaning easier. It is held in place by special brackets that clip to the units' legs.

1 Measure the distance of the run of units corner to corner, and cut the plinth to fit. Lie the plinth on the floor adjacent to the front edge of the units and, using a try square, draw lines level with either side of each leg.

2 Hold a fixing bracket between two lines and use a bradawl to make a starting hole. Screw the bracket in place using the screws supplied. Fit the other brackets in line with each leg along the entire run of units.

3 Clip the plinth into place by simply pushing each bracket onto the legs of the unit.

YOU CAN DO IT

Seal the joints

Kitchen surfaces endure a lot of cleaning and are often left wet. It's a good idea to seal all joints, particularly along the back of a worktop and around the sink. Sanitary silicone sealant is easy to apply, forms a flexible waterproof seal, and will prevent any water from penetrating.

B&Q

outside the home

GUTTERING AND DRAINAGE

For a house to remain in a good condition it must be weatherproof. Rain that falls on the roof or is blown against the external walls must drain away efficiently, or it will penetrate the structure of the house and cause damp problems – or even leaks.

Walls

The external walls of a house are built with weather-resistant materials on the outside, normally stone, brick or concrete blocks. Stone is usually left in its natural state; concrete is most often covered with render – a weather-resistant finish of cement or cement and lime mortar; and brick may or may not be rendered, depending to a large extent on its condition. Some houses have a finish of timber boarding (also known as weatherboard cladding) or plastic cladding. Timber cladding must be protected by wood preservative or exterior paint.

The walls are shielded from rainwater that falls on the roof by the guttering, but all parts of the external walls, including doors and windows, must be maintained in good order so that any water that blows against them can run off the surfaces and drain away. Water will always find any cracks or gaps in render and mortar, and they must be repaired as soon as possible.

Roof

Guttering is the roof's drainage system. The size and layout of guttering is designed to enable it to cope with all the water that falls on a roof. It may be made of cast-iron, aluminium or – most often these days – plastic, and can have different shapes in cross-section (see below). If you need to replace a gutter, make sure the new one is the same size or even slightly larger than the old one and check that it can be joined to the old system – it's not always easy to join one manufacturer's guttering to another's and you may need a plastic adaptor.

Gutters must be kept clear of leaves and other debris or water will flow over the top rather than down the downpipe. Cast-iron downpipes can crack if damp material gets stuck inside and freezes.

Types of guttering

There are three different types of guttering: eaves, parapet and valley gutters.

Eaves gutters

These are the gutters found at the bottom edge of a sloping roof. They are usually attached to the fascia boards with brackets. They are available in different shapes and styles (see right), in plastic or metal. Old guttering is often cast-iron, whereas modern guttering is usually plastic, but aluminium is also used.

Parapet gutters

A parapet gutter drains a flat roof between parapet walls (which are walls that continue above the roof level by one or more courses of bricks). One of the parapet walls contains a gap or channel, and the roof slopes slightly towards it. This allows water to drain into a hopper fitted at the top of a downpipe.

Valley gutters

The junction between different sloping roofs – such as between a gable and hipped-end roof (see page 181) – is called a valley. Metal flashing runs the length of a valley and forms a watertight gutter that channels water into eaves or parapet guttering.

Guttering shapes

Gutters are available in several different shapes or profiles, both plain and decorative.

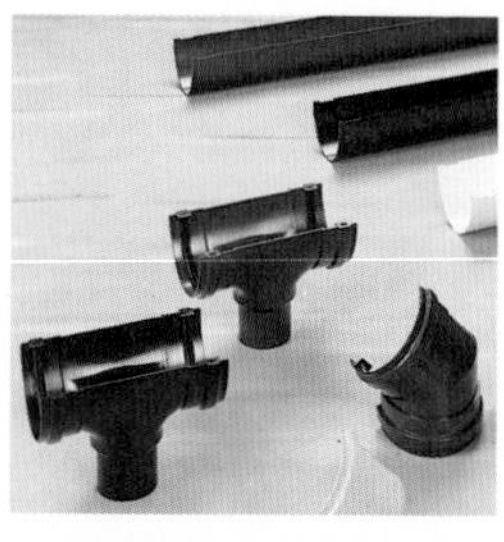

Half-round gutters

Standard 112mm half-round gutters are used with a 68mm circular downpipe for houses and large detached garages.

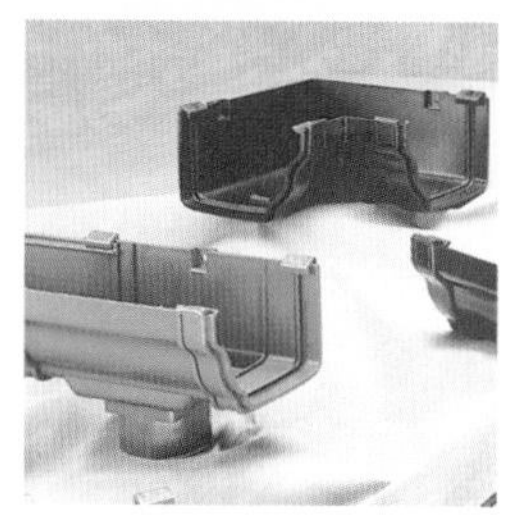

Ogee gutters

These have a straight back edge and a fluted front edge, which makes them wider at the top than at the bottom. The fluted shape can be plain or elaborately moulded. They can be used with square or round downpipes.

Square gutters

If you live in a large house or in an area of high rainfall, you may need a gutter with a greater capacity, such as 116mm x 60mm 'square' guttering which has a straight back, front and base.

Guttering system

Lengths of guttering either have a socket at one end into which the plain end (the spigot end) of the next piece fits, or they are plain at both ends and two lengths are joined by a union piece.

Gutter brackets

Gutter brackets are screwed to the fascia board or the rafters and the guttering then fits onto the brackets.

Downpipe

The downpipe is the pipe running from the guttering to the drain at ground level. You can buy wire or plastic covers to prevent debris entering the downpipe at the guttering outlet. Special offset bends are added to the downpipe if it has to fit round overhanging eaves.

Pipe clips

Plastic downpipes are attached to the wall of the house with clips that are screwed into mortar joints or bricks. Cast-iron pipes are secured with integral lugs fixed with large nails to wooden plugs in the mortar joints.

Angle fittings

Angled pieces, either 90° or 45°, are used when the guttering turns a corner.

Outlets

A stop-end outlet is an end piece with an outlet to attach to a downpipe. A running outlet is attached to a downpipe positioned mid-way along a length of guttering. Two lengths of plastic guttering can be connected with a union piece, which contains gaskets to make the connections watertight.

Hopper head

Some downpipes incorporate a hopper head to take a wastepipe or pipes from another source.

Stop-end

This plain piece stops the flow of water off the end of a length of guttering.

Shoe

This angled piece of downpipe is fitted to the bottom of the pipe to direct the water away from the wall and into the drain.

YOU CAN DO IT

Gutter size

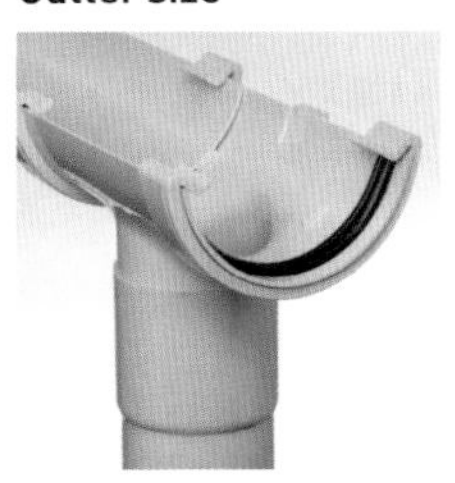

When fitting guttering on a shed, greenhouse or small detached garage, use 75mm half-round gutters and 50mm circular downpipe. This is smaller than the guttering on a house, which usually has 112mm half-round gutters and a 68mm downpipe.

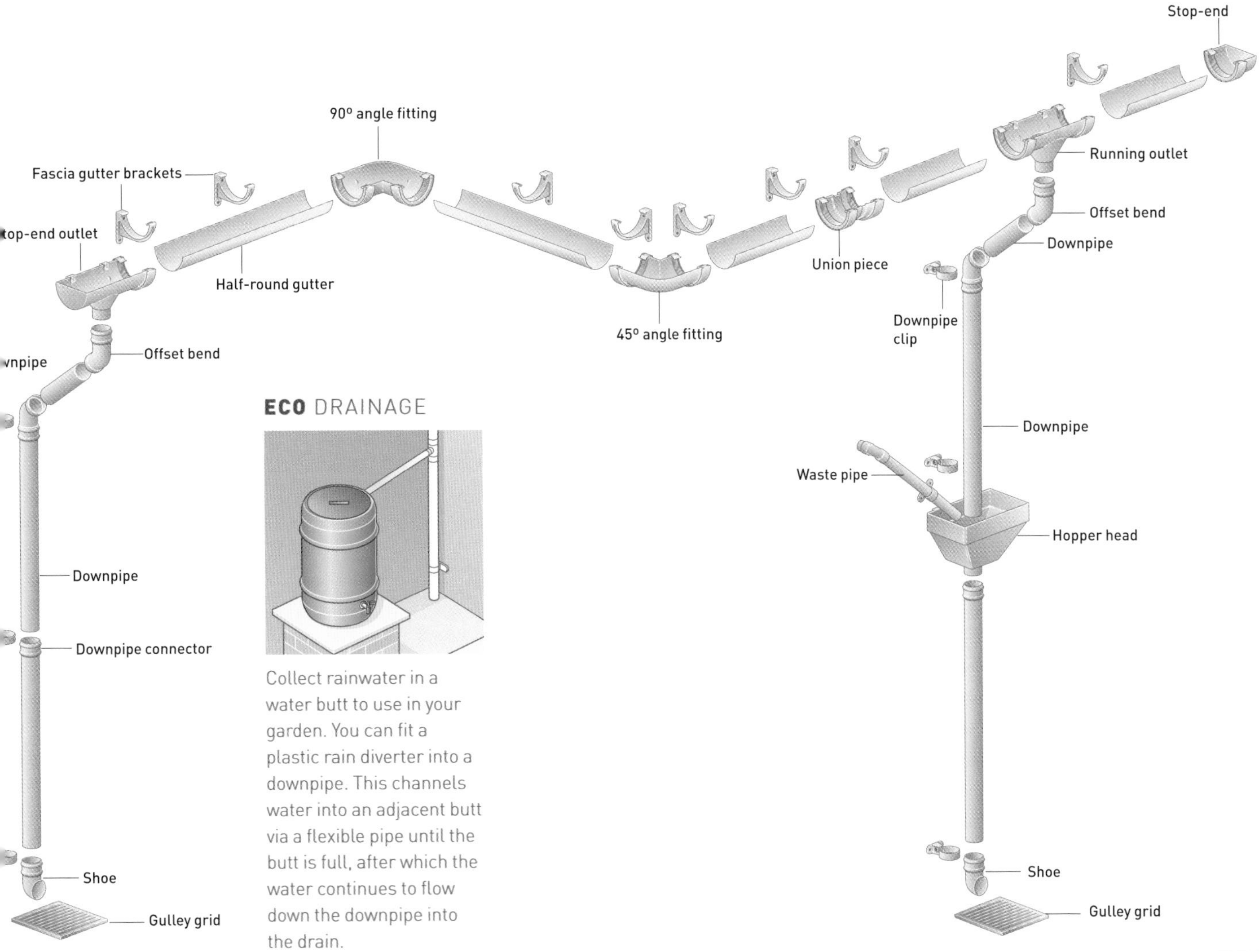

Stop-end
90° angle fitting
Fascia gutter brackets
Running outlet
Stop-end outlet
Offset bend
Downpipe
Half-round gutter
Union piece
Downpipe clip
45° angle fitting
Offset bend
Downpipe
Downpipe
Waste pipe
Hopper head
Downpipe
Downpipe connector
Shoe
Gulley grid
Shoe
Gulley grid

ECO DRAINAGE

Collect rainwater in a water butt to use in your garden. You can fit a plastic rain diverter into a downpipe. This channels water into an adjacent butt via a flexible pipe until the butt is full, after which the water continues to flow down the downpipe into the drain.

GUTTERING PROBLEMS

SAFETY FIRST

Working at heights
Take time to make sure that your ladder is secure before you start work, and never rest it against guttering. Use a ladder stand-off instead (see page 349). A scaffold tower is not as easy to manoeuvre as a ladder but it provides a safe working platform and plenty of room for tools. Assemble the components carefully and check that the platform boards are secure. Construct a guard rail around the platform. On soft or uneven ground, stand the feet of the tower on level scaffold boards.

The exterior of the house takes a constant battering from the elements, especially wind and rain. This can take its toll on the masonry and guttering systems, and can sometimes overwhelm them.

Wall drainage problems

Masonry in good condition is waterproof; but if allowed to deteriorate, render, stone and bricks can let water through to the inside of the wall, and must be repaired.

Porous bricks or stones soaking up water

If the affected area is small, cut out the damaged bricks or stones and replace them (see page 171). This is impractical for a large area; in this case repoint the joints and coat the bricks or stones with silicone water-repellent fluid, which prevents water getting into the bricks but allows them to breathe so that the moisture that has already penetrated can evaporate.

Water seeping into cracks in the render

Fill cracks with exterior filler. If there is extensive damage, hack off the render in the damaged area and patch it with new render, then paint the wall with exterior paint.

Crumbling mortar joints

Rake out the mortar with a raking-out tool, or a cold chisel or plugging chisel and a club hammer, to a depth of 13mm. Clean out any dust and brush water into the joints before repointing them. Mix some mortar (see page 215); pick up a small amount on the back of a trowel and push it into the joints. Leave until semi-dry, then shape the joints to match existing brickwork (see page 219).

Water penetrating window or door frames

Wooden door and window frames tend to shrink and sometimes the mortar around the edges falls out, allowing rainwater into the gaps. Frames should be repaired, if necessary (see page 177), then cracks up to 10mm can be sealed with frame sealant; cracks more than 10mm wide should be filled with mortar.

Guttering problems

If the guttering does not work efficiently, water will overflow and saturate the wall below. Any problems with gutters should be remedied as soon as possible.

Rusted cast-iron gutter

Patches of rust can be smoothed off with an emery cloth but take care not to rub so hard that you make a hole. If there are large areas of rust, brush them off with a wire handbrush or use a round wire cup brush fitted in an electric drill. Then paint the affected area with a rust-inhibiting metal primer, then with black bitumen or gloss paint. If there are any small holes in the gutter fill them first with roof-and-gutter sealant. A bigger hole can be filled with glass-fibre filler, but if the guttering is in poor condition with a lot of holes you should replace it altogether (see pages 168–69).

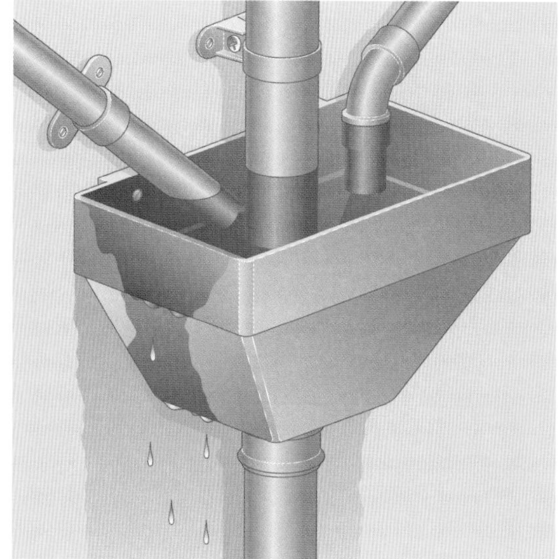

Overflowing hopper head

Water overflowing from a hopper head indicates leaves or other debris in the hopper head itself or a blockage in the downpipe below the hopper head. Scoop out any leaves in the hopper head. If the downpipe is blocked, try unblocking it from ground level. Cover the drain, turn on the water in a garden hose and push it up the pipe to dislodge the debris; if that doesn't work, use drain rods to unblock it from the top.

IDEAL TOOL

Wire brush drill attachment
A wire cup brush attached to a drill will quickly clean off rust on old cast-iron guttering. It's also useful for cleaning paint off stone or concrete surfaces. Be sure to wear a dust mask and protective goggles while you work.

Leaking gutter joints

For a metal gutter, scrape any dirt out of the joint and dry it. Inject roof and gutter sealant into the joint with an applicator gun. If it is plastic guttering joined with a union piece, one of the gaskets (seals) may be damaged. Squeeze the gutter to release the union piece, peel the gasket away and replace it with a new one.

It may be that a loose or wongly positioned bracket has caused the guttering to sag, so that the water forms a pool rather than flows away. If the screw had worked loose, you should be able simply to insert a wallplug and rescrew the bracket; if the bracket was wrongly positioned, fill the hole and refix it. If the guttering still sags, fit extra brackets to support it.

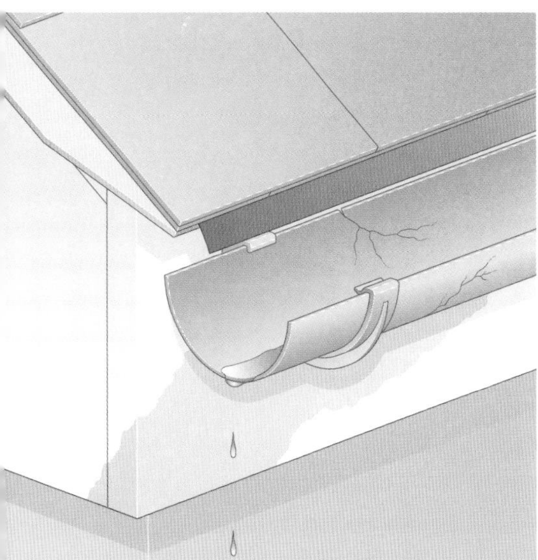

Leaking from the end of a length of guttering

Water will run off the end of a length of guttering if the stop-end has come away, or one was never fitted. Check the dimensions and profile of your guttering, and buy one to fit.

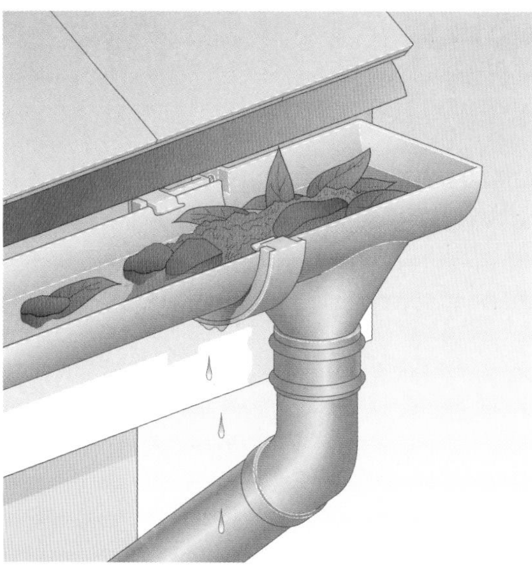

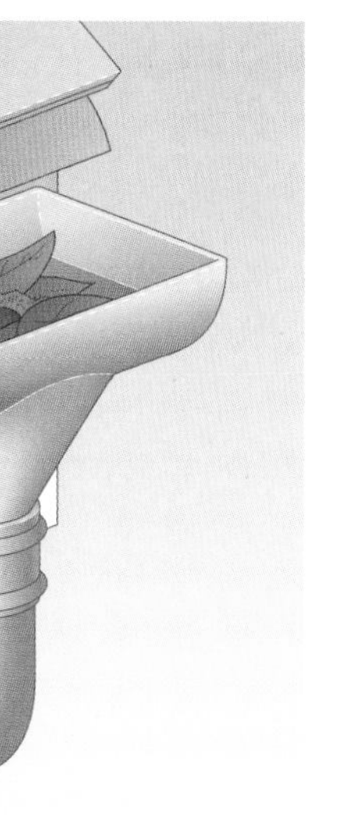

Blocked outlet

Block the bottom of the downpipe with a rag to stop debris getting into the drain, then scoop out leaves and silt from the gutter with a small trowel. Remove the rag and rinse out the gutter and downpipe with water. To prevent the problem recurring, fit a leafguard cover over the outlet, and gutter guard (right) over the guttering. Gutter guard is simply cut to size and clipped in place.

YOU CAN DO IT

Scoop it out

A plastic milk bottle with the base cut off makes a perfect scoop for clearing old leaves and debris from your gutters.

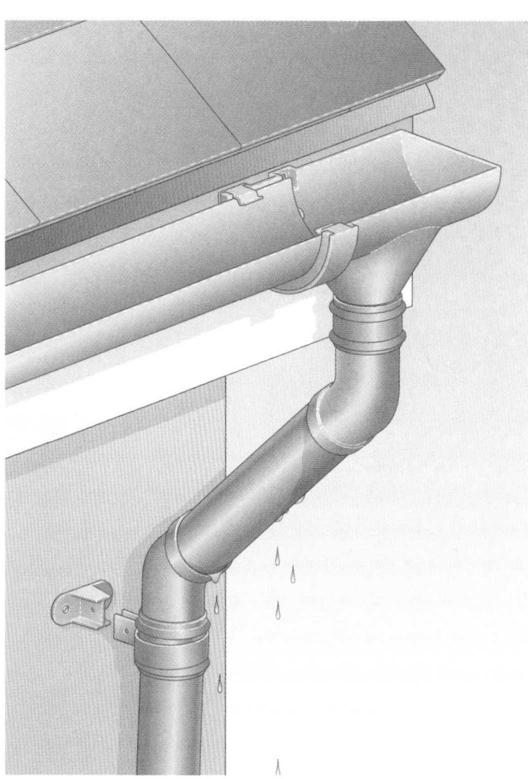

Loose downpipes

If a plastic downpipe is loose, check to see if one of the clips has lost a connecting screw, as here. Replace it with a galvanised screw of the same size. Or the wallplugs may have worked loose: replace them and refix the screws or fit new 6.5mm gauge galvanised screws. If a cast-iron downpipe is loose, take out the fixing nails or screws and insert wallplugs. Then drive the nails back in or fit galvanised screws. If wooden plugs are loose, remove and replace them.

GUTTERING REPAIRS

TOOLS MATERIALS

- **ladder, if required**
- **heavy-duty gloves**
- **wire brush**
- **scissors**

- joint repair tape

Plastic guttering is lightweight and easy to replace if part of it goes wrong. But it is also quite straightforward to carry out minor repairs to old cast-iron guttering. Take care, though, because cast-iron guttering is very heavy. If it is in very poor condition, you would be better to replace it altogether (see pages 168–69).

Repairing a leak with tape

You can use joint repair tape to fix minor leaks or cracks in a joint in cast-iron guttering or downpipes.

1 Clean around the area to be repaired with a wire brush to remove loose paint or rust. Cut off a length of repair tape a few centimetres longer than the diameter of the downpipe and remove the paper backing.

2 Wrap the repair tape around the joint and overlap the ends.

3 Press the tape firmly with your hand to mould it around the shape of the joint.

YOU CAN DO IT

Leaking downpipes
If a downpipe leaks during heavy rain, it may be a sign that the section of pipe below the leak is blocked by leaves or some other obstruction. You may be able to dislodge it with a garden hose: cover the drain, turn on the water, and direct it up the downpipe. If that doesn't work and the blockage is near the top of the pipe, use a length of wire to clear it. If it is near the bottom, you may need to use a drain rod or take a section of the pipe apart to clear it.

Repairing a leak with sealant

Roof and gutter sealant should be used to repair bigger leaks in metal guttering or a damaged union piece in plastic guttering. Protect your hands with heavy-duty gloves, especially while applying the sealant.

TOOLS MATERIALS

- **ladder, if required**
- **heavy-duty gloves**
- **wire brush**
- **old screwdriver**

- roof and gutter sealant

1 Clean around the area to be repaired with a wire brush to remove loose paint or rust.

2 Use an old screwdriver to dig out old jointing material.

3 Insert the nozzle of a sealant gun into the joint and run a bead of roof and gutter sealant around the pipe, making sure the cavity is filled.

4 Smooth the sealant with your finger to leave a neat filling.

Repairing a leak in cast-iron guttering

Lengths of old cast-iron guttering may be joined together with bolts. If these have rusted in place, you will need to saw them off with a hacksaw.

TOOLS MATERIALS

- **ladder**
- **spanner**
- **hacksaw**
- **nail punch**
- **hammer**
- **heavy-duty gloves**
- **wire brush**
- **screwdriver**

- roof and gutter sealant
- galvanised gutter bolt

1 Try to undo the old securing bolt with a spanner. If you can't, use a hacksaw to cut through the bolt then tap its shank upwards through the gutter with a nail punch and hammer.

2 Wearing heavy-duty gloves, separate the gutter joint – you will probably need to tap it to loosen the old putty or mastic. Clean the joint with a wire brush.

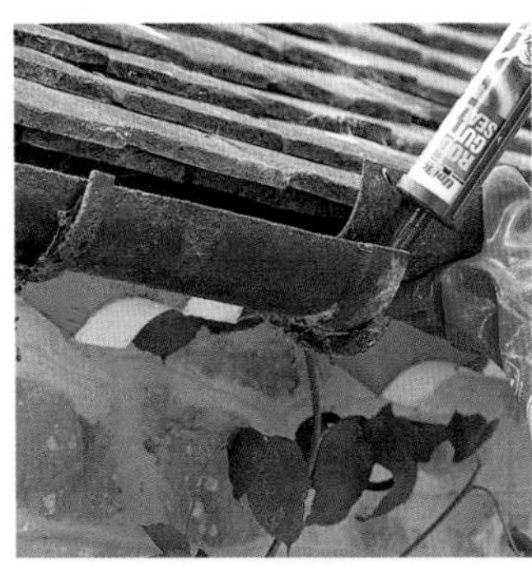

3 Run a bead of sealant into the joint.

4 Press the guttering into the sealant and fit a new galvanised gutter bolt. With gloves on, smooth the excess sealant with your finger.

Unblocking a drain

You will need special drain-cleaning rods to clear a blocked drain and some disinfectant to clean them afterwards.

TOOLS MATERIALS

- **heavy-duty waterproof gloves**
- **rubber plunger**
- **drain rods**
- **hose-pipe**
- **watering can**

- disinfectant

1 Lift the inspection cover of the blocked drain. Fit a rubber plunger to the end of two drain rods and insert them into the bottom of the inspection chamber. Slide the rods into the drain outlet pipe – if the inspection chamber is full you will have to probe with the plunger to find it. Push the rods into the drain, adding more rods as required. Use a push and pull action as this will help to dislodge the blockage. Or turn them in a clockwise direction – but not anti-clockwise, or they may unscrew in the drain and add to the blockage.

2 Remove the rods from the drain and see if the waste water drains away. If not, repeat the process, adding more rods. When the drain is clear, dismantle the rods and stand them in the inspection chamber. Using a hose-pipe, wash the rods and flush the drain with clean water, then drench the rods and the gloves in diluted disinfectant, pouring it from a watering can.

Clearing a valley gutter

Valley gutters can be difficult to reach, but a long-handled garden hoe will help you clear any trapped debris.

TOOLS MATERIALS

- **heavy-duty waterproof gloves**
- **garden hoe**
- **bucket**

1 Use a garden hoe to pull the debris towards you until you can reach it with your hand.

2 Hold a bucket beneath the end of the gutter and slide the debris into the bucket.

REPLACING GUTTERING

TOOLS MATERIALS

- **2 ladders**
- **hammer**
- **hacksaw**
- **nail punch**
- **pincers or crowbar**
- **scraper**
- **paintbrush**
- **screwdriver**
- **builder's line or string**
- **plumb line**
- **pencil**
- **spirit level**
- **hammer action drill with masonry bits**

- large nails
- rope
- filler
- paint or stain
- plastic guttering system
- wallplugs and screws (in sizes recommended by guttering manufacturer)
- solvent glue

If you need to replace your guttering and plan to do the work yourself, new plastic guttering is the easiest type to fit. Measure all the way round the house to calculate the length of gutter you will need. Check the manufacturer's guidelines to determine the number of fittings you will need.

Removing the old guttering

Old plastic guttering is easy to remove but cast-iron guttering is extremely heavy and the edges can be sharp, so it takes two people to remove it.

1 Drive large nails into the fascia board beneath a section of guttering at either end to hold it and prevent it falling.

2 Cut through the bolts joining two sections of gutter with a hacksaw then tap them out with a nail punch and hammer.

3 Tie a rope around each end of the section of guttering to be removed. Break apart the gutter joint and unscrew the brackets holding the section to the fascia.

4 Use the ropes to carefully lower the gutter section to the ground. Repeat the process to remove all the sections, then remove the downpipes. Use pincers to remove the pipe nails or, if they are rusted in, use a crowbar to lever them out of the wall. Remove downpipes one section at a time, starting from the top. Finally, repair the fascia board: fill in screw holes, strip off flaking finishes and repaint or restain.

Fitting new guttering

Start by fitting the section of guttering with the outlet since this will be joined to the downpipe which must be positioned directly over the ground-level drain. It may be a stop-end outlet at the end of a run of gutter or a running outlet in the middle of the gutter.

YOU CAN DO IT

Heat and cold
Plastic guttering expands in hot weather and contracts in cold. To allow for that, gutter fittings all have a depth mark. When you join sections of gutter, or fit a section into a bracket, carefully line the pieces up to this mark, and don't go past it.

1 Fit a gutter bracket near the top of the fascia board at one end of the run of guttering (the opposite end to the stop-end outlet, if you have one). Tie a builder's line or piece of string around the base of the bracket.

2 To position the gutter outlet accurately, hold a plumb line against the fascia directly over the drain. Mark the position on the fascia with a pencil. Fit the gutter outlet no more than 50mm below the level of the roof tiles, following the manufacturer's advice about the size and number of screws.

3 Stretch the string or builder's line from the bracket along the fascia board and tie it to the outlet. Using a spirit level, check that the string slopes towards the outlet to allow water to drain; it should ideally fall 10mm every 6m of gutter.

4 Mark the position of the other rackets, spacing them no more han 1m apart and no more than 50mm from any joint or fitting. f the outlet is in the middle of the utter, repeat the process with a racket at the other end of the uttering run so that it too slopes owards the outlet.

5 Fit the rest of the brackets.

6 Fit a stop-end to the first length of gutter and clip the gutter into position on the brackets. The easiest way to do this is to tilt the gutter to fit under the back clip and then straighten it under the front clip. Line up the gutter end with the insertion depth mark on the bracket (see YOU CAN DO IT, opposite).

7 Fit a union piece at the other end of the first length and screw it into the fascia, then fit the next length of gutter into it. Continue joining lengths. Cut the last section to fit using a hacksaw and fit a stop-end. Make sure all joints line up with the insertion depth marks on the fittings.

itting a downpipe

lere, the downpipe is fitted directly into the outlet. If your eaves verhang, however, you will need to bridge the distance between the utter and the house wall with two downpipe fittings called offset ends, with an off-cut of downpipe fitted between them (see page 163).

1 Using a spirit level or plumb ine, mark a vertical line on the vall from the outlet to the drain.

2 Hold a downpipe clip centrally over the line and mark its fixing holes on the wall with a pencil. Repeat down the wall with clips no more than 1.8m apart.

3 Drill the fixing holes with the size of drill bit recommended by the guttering manufacturer. Insert wallplugs into the holes.

4 Fit the first length of downpipe with its socket uppermost. Allow a 10mm gap between the end of the outlet and the bottom of the socket to allow for expansion in hot weather.

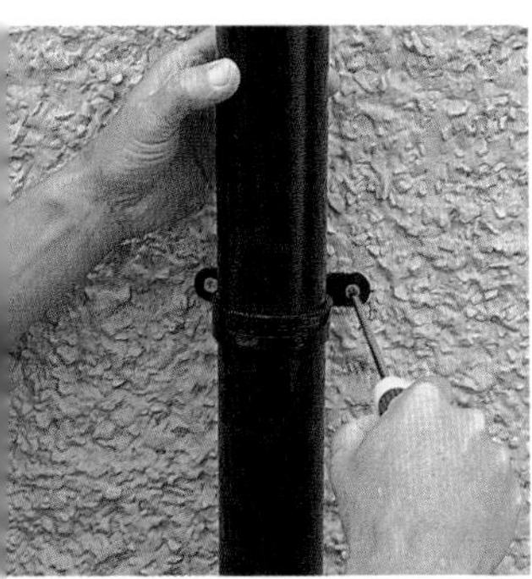

5 Fit the clips to the pipe and screw them into the wallplugs. Continue fitting the pipe until you each the bottom of the wall.

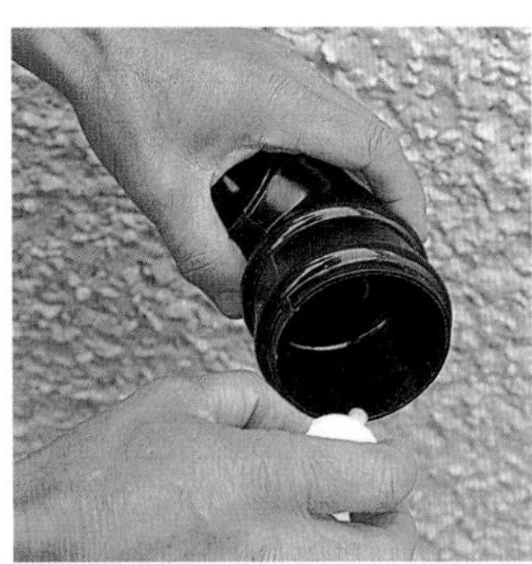

6 Use a hacksaw to cut the pipe to the correct length above the drain. Apply solvent glue to the socket of the downpipe shoe.

7 Fit the shoe to the bottom of the pipe so that it directs water into the drain.

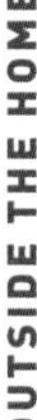

WALLS PAINTING AND REPAIRING

ECO PAINT

Water-based masonry paint dries faster than solvent-based paint. It is less harmful to the environment, produces less odour, and you can wash your brushes in water.

Maintaining the exterior of your house in good condition helps to keep it weatherproof. There should be no need to paint brickwork. If the walls are porous, protect them with a clear waterproofer. If one brick becomes porous or damaged, it should be replaced to avoid damp problems developing. Render and pebbledash need regular painting with masonry paint, which is available in two basic versions – smooth and textured. Smooth masonry paint goes a lot further than textured, but textured paint is better for covering minor blemishes and hairline cracks.

Preparation

Good preparation before you start painting will make the finished surface much more durable.

- If necessary, trim back creepers and shrubs, or cover plants with plastic or dust sheets.
- Use a pressure washer to clean off dirt and mould from the walls.
- Scrape away any thick growths of mould with a spatula, then treat the masonry with fungicidal solution. Leave it on for 24 hours before washing the wall thoroughly with clean water.
- Fill cracks and holes in a rendered wall with fresh cement containing a little PVA adhesive to help it stick to the masonry.
- Fix gutters if they are loose or leaking. If you are painting the gutters as well, do this before you start on the walls.
- Paint powdery or chalky surfaces with a stabilising primer to bind the loose material to the wall.
- Cover extension roofs and porches, and wrap newspaper around drainpipes to protect them from paint splatters.

YOU CAN DO IT

Stipple action

When painting heavily textured walls, hold the brush at 90° and dab the bristles into the surface with a stippling action.

TOOLS MATERIALS

- **ladder or scaffold tower**
- **100mm or 150mm paintbrush or a long-pile roller**
- **paint kettle or roller tray**

- newspaper
- adhesive tape
- masonry paint

1 Wrap newspaper around the downpipes and secure it with tape. Start painting at the top of the house and work downwards so the newly painted surface does not get splashed. Push the brush carefully right behind downpipes.

Calculating the amount of paint

As a rough guide, smooth water-based masonry paint will cover 10–12 sq m of flat wall per litre, but may cover only 4 sq m of a very rough surface. Unpainted render will probably need more paint than render that has been painted before. To work out the area of your wall, multiply the length by the height. To calculate the height, climb a ladder, hold the end of a ball of string against the top of the wall and drop the ball to the ground (a helper is a good idea), then measure the length of the string. If you are not painting the whole house, work out the area of each section to be painted and deduct the combined area of the doors and windows. Some manufacturers recommend that the first coat of paint is thinned, so always read the instructions on the can.

Painting exterior walls

Pour the paint into a paint kettle (see page 77) – this will be lighter and easier to handle than a can of paint, and safer at the top of a ladder. A long-pile roller on an extension pole is faster than a paintbrush, but it can be difficult to work with a roller tray up a tall ladder. Only paint when the weather is fine and dry. Painting in direct sunlight can be difficult, especially if you are using white paint, so try and follow the shade. Divide each wall into manageable sections that you can finish in a single session – use features like windows and drainpipes as your boundaries.

2 Use short horizontal or vertical strokes, applying a loaded brush to an unpainted area and working back to a painted area.

3 Paint in the opposite direction to make sure that the surface is completely covered. On rough surfaces, it is better to rotate the brush in all directions to ensure even coverage. If using a roller, vary the angle of the strokes. Cut into corners and obstructions in the same way as you would when painting interior walls (see page 78).

Replacing a damaged brick

Keep an eye on your brickwork – the outer face of an old brick can break down and become porous, allowing rainwater to soak through to its inner face. Eventually a damp patch will appear on the plaster indoors. The same will happen when a brick gets cracked. Much better to fix the problem before the damage is done.

TOOLS MATERIALS

- **hammer-action drill with 10mm gauge masonry bit**
- **heavy-duty gloves**
- **cold chisel or bolster chisel**
- **club hammer**
- **trowel**
- **raking tool**
- **old paintbrush**
- **soft brush**

- ready-mix mortar
- replacement brick

1 Drill a series of 10mm holes into the mortar joints around the damaged brick.

2 Use a cold chisel or a bolster chisel and a club hammer to cut into joints until the brick becomes loose.

3 Tap and wriggle the brick until you can remove it.

4 Scrape out the old mortar in the cavity with a trowel or bolster chisel. Brush away the dust.

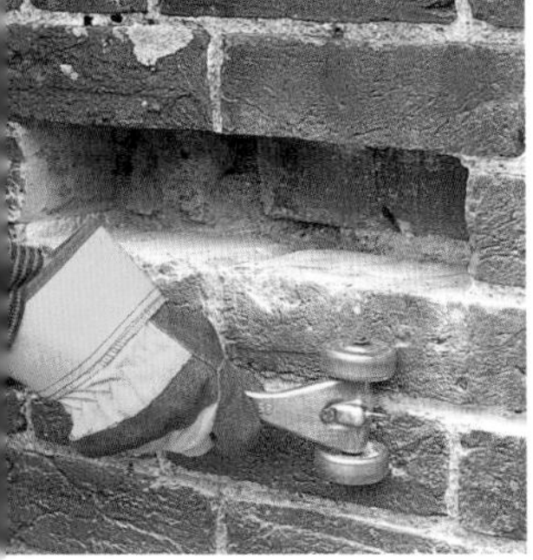

5 Use a jointing tool to rake out any loose or flaking mortar from the surrounding joints (see IDEAL TOOL, page 219).

6 Wet the surfaces of the cavity with an old paintbrush.

7 Spread mortar on the base and ends of the cavity with a trowel.

8 Wet the surface of the replacement brick and spread mortar on all sides.

9 Insert the brick into the cavity and tap it with the trowel handle until it aligns with the other bricks. Repoint the surrounding brickwork (see page 219).

10 When the mortar starts to harden, brush the surface of the bricks with a soft brush.

WINDOWS AND DOORS EXTERIOR

Windows and doors have a big impact on the external appearance of your home. Their most important job is to keep heat in and moisture out, but it's also desirable that they are in keeping with the style of the house and you might decide to replace them as part of a general 'exterior facelift'. The way they are fitted depends on whether the exterior of the house is constructed with solid or cavity walls (see pages 54–55).

Windows in solid walls

In houses built with solid external walls of stone or brick, a wooden window frame often fits snugly in a slight recess (reveal) on the inner side of the opening in the wall. The window will either be flush with the inner wall surface or set back from it, depending on the thickness of the wall. The frame is held in place with nails or screws. Windows in old houses usually have a stone or concrete subsill which sits below the window frame and any wooden sill on the outside of the house.

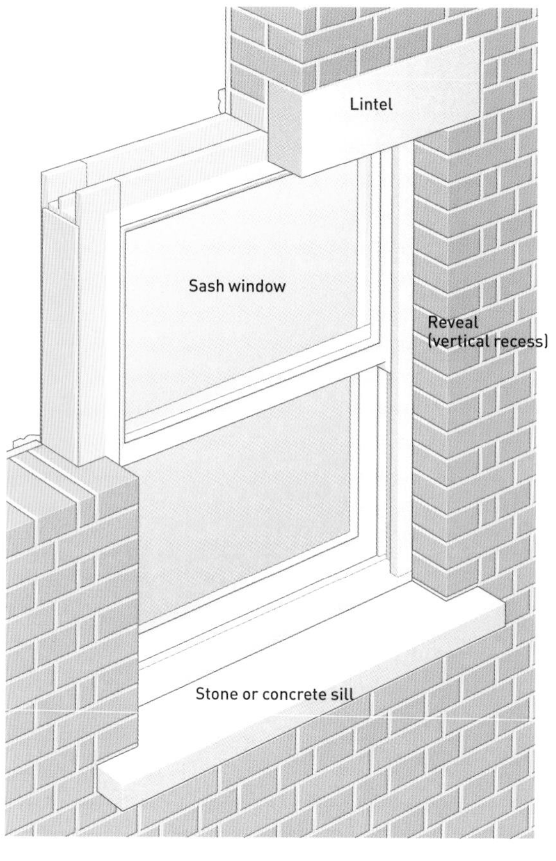

YOU CAN DO IT

Preventing wet rot

The best way to protect wooden window frames against wet rot is to apply wood preservative, paint or varnish regularly. Always ensure that any new timber used for repairs or replacement is treated with wood preservative. You should also seal any gaps around the outside of window frames with frame sealant if it is a small gap, and mortar if the gap is more than about 10mm wide.

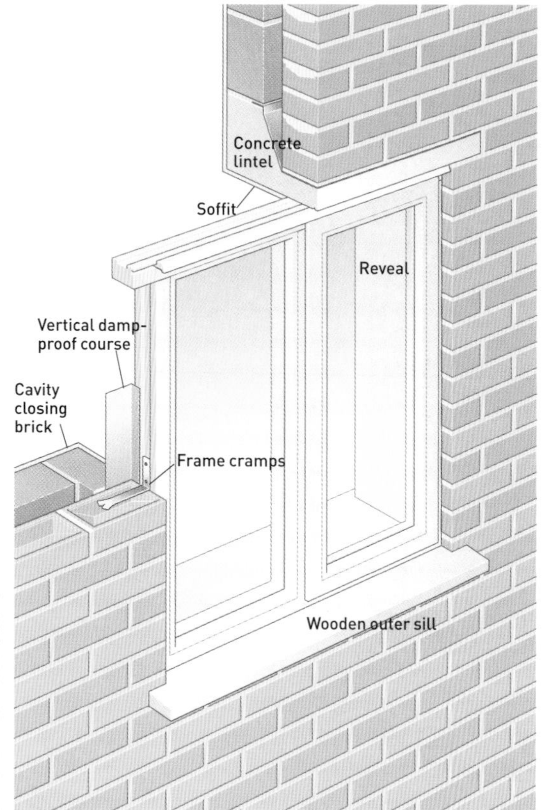

Windows in cavity walls

These days most houses are built with cavity walls and window frames are attached to metal brackets, known as frame cramps, fitted into the walls as they are built. Special bricks are fitted between the window frames and the cavity to close the gap and prevent heat escaping. There also has to be a damp-proof course in line with the frame to prevent moisture transferring from the outer to the inner wall. On the inside wall, the sides and top of the window opening (the reveals and the soffit) are plastered once the window frame is in place to give a neat finish. The window frame's wooden sill sits on a wooden window board that is screwed or nailed directly to the masonry.

ECO GLAZING

Make sure your windows are all draughtproofed to help retain warmth and conserve energy (see page 331). New outside doors and windows must be made with low-emissivity glass, which reduces heat loss and so makes your home more energy efficient. Look for products labelled 'Part L compliant.'

Door frames

Doors are usually fitted into a wooden frame consisting of a head at the top, a sill at the bottom and two side posts. The head has projections called horns supporting the frame joints and these are built into the masonry to secure the frame. The sides of the frame are fixed to the wall by wooden plates called pallets, or by metal brackets. Some aluminium and PVCu doors are supplied with their own frames.

Lintels

Where doors and windows are fitted in a loadbearing wall, a rigid horizontal beam called a lintel is installed over the window or door opening to support the masonry above. In an old house the lintels are often stone or wood, which cannot support a wide span. Some brick walls may have a decorative arch of bricks instead of, or as well as, a flat lintel. Each brick in the arch is narrower at the bottom than at the top so that they form a neat curve.

Nowadays, lintels are made from reinforced concrete or steel and they can support a much greater weight and span of masonry. The invention of plate glass coupled with stronger lintels means that single large panes of glass can be fitted safely into loadbearing walls.

Types of exterior doors

Besides a front door, a house may have many other kinds of door leading to the outside, including french doors, aluminium-frame glass doors, and up-and-over or sectional overhead garage doors.

Panelled and flush doors

Main front and back doors are generally panelled or flush wooden doors. Panelled doors may be made from expensive hardwoods or softwood, which may be solid, laminated or veneered.

Flush doors are cheaper than panelled doors. They are usually faced with plywood which needs to be painted to make it weatherproof. Some doors are fitted with panes of glass or leaded lights – small panes of plain or coloured glass held together with lead strips.

Doors often have a moulding called a weatherboard fitted at the bottom to encourage water to flow away from the doorway. Some frames have a weather bar – a metal or plastic strip fitted in the sill to stop rainwater leaking under the door. The door or weatherboard will have a rebate (recess) cut in the bottom in order to clear the bar.

Glazing

Window glass is secured in a bed of putty or glazing mastic in the frame. Small headless nails called glazing sprigs are tapped into the frame to hold the glass while the putty dries. Spring clips hold the glass in metal frames. More putty is smoothed over the top to make a neat finish.

Sometimes glass is secured with thin strips (beads) of hardwood instead of putty. The beads are cut and mitred individually, stuck in place with putty or glazing sealant, then secured with nails or brass screws.

Aluminium-frame glass doors

These doors are made from special double-glazed glass, which is sometimes opaque. The glass is fitted into an aluminium frame and may be one large single pane; if it is a front door, it will have a central aluminium rail fitted with a letter-box. At the back of the house, french doors often lead on to the garden or patio. One panel is fixed and the other slides horizontally on rollers. The panels are usually double-glazed for heat- and sound-insulation.

Garage doors

There are various types of garage doors. In the past, they were usually hinged, but modern garage doors are much more likely to be the up-and-over kind, which is lifted upwards and backwards to clear the opening. These operate either on vertical tracks to the sides of the door, or on horizontal tracks fixed to the garage ceiling. Most types of garage can be fitted with an automatic door-opening system that is operated by remote control from inside the car.

WINDOWS REPAIRS

TOOLS MATERIALS

- **protective gloves**
- **safety goggles**
- **tape measure**
- **craft knife**
- **hammer**
- **pincers**
- **old chisel or hacking knife**
- **putty knife**
- **paintbrush**

- thin hardboard or plywood
- panel pins
- wood primer paint
- putty

Cracked or broken glass in windows or doors can be very dangerous, especially if you have small children or pets. Security could be compromised and the glass will no longer be weatherproof. If you can't do a full repair straight away, you should at least make a temporary repair and ensure the area is safe. If you have to replace glass in an upstairs window, work from a scaffold tower rather than ladder and avoid working on a windy day. Carry panes on edge to prevent bending and always wear protective gloves. It will take two people to handle large pieces of glass safely.

Making a secure temporary repair

If security is not a problem, polythene sheeting will make a window opening temporarily weatherproof. Remove the broken glass, spread the polythene across the gap and secure it with thin wooden battens nailed to the edges of the frame. If the glass is cracked rather than broken, seal it with waterproof glazing tape. But on an accessible exterior window you will need a more secure repair.

1 Wearing protective gloves, remove any loose pieces of glass.

2 Measure the space and cut a piece of thin hardboard or plywood to fit.

3 Fit the cut board into the frame and tap panel pins into the surrounding wood.

Taking out a broken pane

Spread newspaper on the floor around the window to make it easier to clear up afterwards, and be sure to wear sturdy footwear. If the pane is only cracked, score it with a glass cutter about 25mm from the edge all the way round. Stick strips of adhesive tape across the cracks and scored lines and then tap each piece of glass free with a small hammer. The tape will hold the pieces safely together.

1 If the pane is smashed, remove jagged pieces still stuck in the putty by gripping each one in turn and working it loose. Wear protective gloves and goggles. Working from the top down, knock out the remaining glass by tapping it gently with a hammer.

2 Use a chisel or glazier's hacking knife and hammer to remove the old putty. Take out panel pins as you go using a pair of pincers.

3 Brush away any dust, then seal the wood with primer paint.

YOU CAN DO IT

Weatherproof repair

If weather conditions are bad and a full repair cannot be done straight away, use silicone sealant to make a temporary repair weatherproof.

Leave the broken glass in place and apply silicone sealant around the edge of the pane. Cut a piece of board to fit, and press into the silicone. Run another bead of silicone around the gap between board and frame.

Buying replacement glass

A glazier will cut glass for you and advise on the best type of glass for the window to be replaced. If you are replacing glass in a large picture window, or within 800mm of the floor, use safety glass (see page 362).

Measuring pane size and thickness

It will help to ensure you buy the correct thickness if you take a piece of the broken glass with you, wrapped carefully in newspaper. If that isn't possible, measure the thickness of the pane to the nearest millimetre. You may not be able to find an exact match if the glass is old. If so, buy glass slightly thicker, as this will be safer. As a rough guide, use 3mm glass for very small panes, 4mm for windows up to 1 sq m, and 6mm for larger areas.

Measure the height and width of the area, measuring into the frame rebate on each side. Have the new glass cut to 3mm less than both the length and width measurements. Check that the window is square by measuring the diagonals. If they differ by more than a couple of millimetres, make a cardboard template of the window pane and take it to the glazier to use as a guide.

SAFETY FIRST

Broken glass must be disposed of safely. Wrap it in old newspaper, tape it up securely and label clearly 'Danger broken glass'.

Types of putty

You will need about 500g of linseed oil putty to fill a rebate about 4m in length. Use linseed oil, all-purpose or acrylic putty when glazing painted wooden frames. Brown putty is available for use in stained and varnished wooden frames. For metal frames use all-purpose, acrylic or butyl rubber-based putty.

Installing a pane of glass

Working from outside, clean any debris from the rebate in the frame with a brush or old screwdriver. Rest the pane on a pad of newspaper away from where you are working. Don't stand it on a hard surface such as concrete or it may well crack. Linseed oil putty can be messy to work with. Wet your hands to prevent excessive sticking, and if necessary roll the putty on newspaper or card to remove some of the oil.

1 Knead the putty until it is soft and pliable. Take a palm-sized ball and squeeze a continuous band into the rebate, using your thumb to press it into place. It should be about 3mm thick all around the window.

2 Wearing gloves, sit the new pane of glass into the bottom edge and then gently push it into place. Exert gentle pressure around the edges of the glass – not in the middle, especially when working with a large pane, or it may break. Allow the glass to squeeze the putty until you have about a 2mm bed of putty behind the glass.

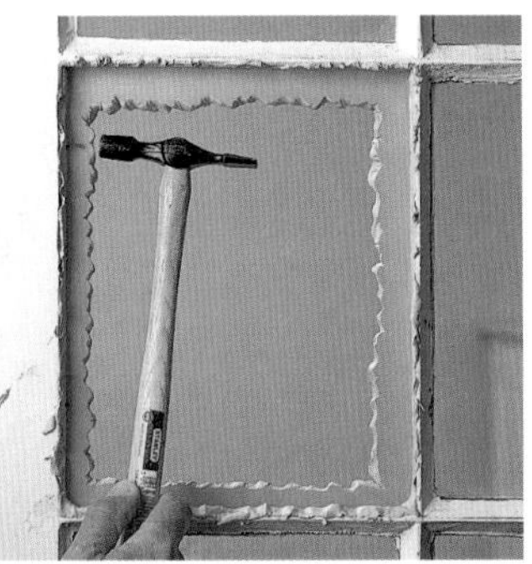

3 Secure the glass in place by tapping in glazing panel pins at 200mm intervals with a small hammer. They should lie flat against the surface of the glass and protrude 5mm from the frame. Remove surplus putty from the other side of the glass with a putty knife.

4 Run more putty into the rebate around the window, using your thumb to push the putty well into the edge. Use a putty knife to smooth the putty into a neat fillet running at an angle of 45°, covering the heads of the panel pins and lining up with the putty on the inside of the window. Wet the putty knife to get a really smooth finish and a clean angle at the corners. Allow the putty to harden for about two weeks before painting. When painting the frame, overlap paint from the new putty onto the glass by about 3mm to prevent water from penetrating.

IDEAL TOOL

Putty knife

Use a putty knife to create a neat moulding or fillet around the pane. The blade is shaped on one side to help you get a smooth finish.

Replacing a pane in a beaded casement

To repair a broken pane in a beaded casement window you will need to take out and replace the wooden beads – a slightly more complicated procedure, but not difficult.

1 Working from inside the room, prise off the beads. Using a large old screwdriver or chisel, start from the middle of the bead and work out, being careful not to damage the mitre joints at the corners.

2 As you remove the beads, lay them out carefully so that you can replace them in the same positions.

3 Remove the broken glass as described on page 174. Do remember to wear protective gloves and goggles.

TOOLS MATERIALS

- **protective gloves**
- **safety goggles**
- **large screwdriver or chisel**
- **hacking knife**
- **paintbrush**
- **tape measure**
- **hammer**
- **putty knife**

- primer or primer/undercoat paint
- putty
- panel pins

4 Once all the glass is safely cleared, scrape out the old putty from the rebates with a hacking knife or old chisel. Brush away any dust and paint the rebate with wood primer or primer/undercoat. Allow it to dry thoroughly.

5 Measure up for the new pane. Take the horizontal and vertical dimensions to the inside of the rebates and reduce the measurements by 3mm to allow some tolerance when fitting.

6 Knead a palm-sized ball of putty until it is soft and pliable then press it into the rebate with your thumb. It should be about 3mm thick all round. Insert the new pane, slotting it into the bottom rebate first. Press the glass gently around the edges (not in the middle) until you have a 2mm bed of putty behind it.

7 Run another band of softened putty around the pane, pressing it well into the edges.

8 Press the casement beads into the putty in the same positions as before. Fit the top bead first, followed by the bottom, then the sides. Tap panel pins through the existing holes.

9 Clean away the excess putty on both sides of the glass with a putty knife. Repaint the woodwork in the sequence described on page 131.

Repairing a rotten window sill

There are many wood repair compounds on the market that will make an effective repair to a rotten window sill. However, if the sill is stained or varnished rather than painted, the repair will remain visible unless the filler is the same colour as the wood.

TOOLS MATERIALS

- **old chisel**
- **narrow bladed scraper**
- **protective gloves**
- **paintbrushes**

- exterior wood repair compound
- waterproof frame sealant
- paint or varnish

1 Remove all rotten wood using an old chisel or narrow-bladed scraper. Dig into the frame until you reach firm, sound wood.

2 Knead the repair compound until thoroughly mixed. Follow the manufacturer's instructions and wear protective gloves.

3 Press the compound into the damaged area with a narrow bladed scraper and smooth the surface to follow the sill profile.

4 If there are gaps between window frame and wall, seal them using a waterproof frame sealant. Then repaint or varnish the window and frame (see page 131).

Repairing a rusted window frame

Galvanised metal window frames will eventually succumb to rust. Most paints will slow down the rate of corrosion but cannot stop it altogether. When repainting the frame, use a good-quality primer and be sure to reach into any crevices and awkward areas. Pay particular attention to outer corners and edges.

TOOLS MATERIALS

- **scraper**
- **wire brush**
- **paintbrushes**

- medium-grade abrasive paper
- rust remover
- metal primer
- undercoat paint
- top coat paint

1 Use a scraper to remove loose and flaking paint.

2 Go over the metalwork with a wire brush until you have removed all loose paint or rust.

3 Smooth the entire surface with medium-grade abrasive paper, paying particular attention to rough edges. Brush off the dust.

4 Paint the frame with a rust remover and allow it to dry thoroughly for the period advised on the tin. Next paint the frame using a zinc-based metal primer.

5 Repaint the frame. Apply an undercoat first then a top coat. Follow the sequence on page 131.

DOORS LETTERPLATE AND CAT FLAP

The procedure for fitting a letterplate or cat flap is similar. Both are simple jobs but always follow the instructions carefully and double-check all measurements before making the first cut.

Measuring up for a letterplate

Letterplates are available in a range of designs and materials. Some have a handle incorporated that doubles as a door-knocker. You can also fit an internal flap cover on the inside of the door, which will reduce draughts and look neater. If using solid brass screws, which are relatively soft, drill full-length pilot holes and don't use a power screwdriver or the screw slot may be damaged.

TOOLS MATERIALS

- **long ruler**
- **pencil**
- **power drill with 6mm and 8mm gauge twist bits**
- **padsaw or jigsaw**
- **narrow chisel**
- **mallet**
- **small adjustable spanner**
- **hacksaw**

- letterplate with fixings
- adhesive tape
- medium-grade abrasive paper

1 Working from the outside of the door, measure the depth of the cross rail and make a pencil mark at the mid-point in two places, about 35mm apart.

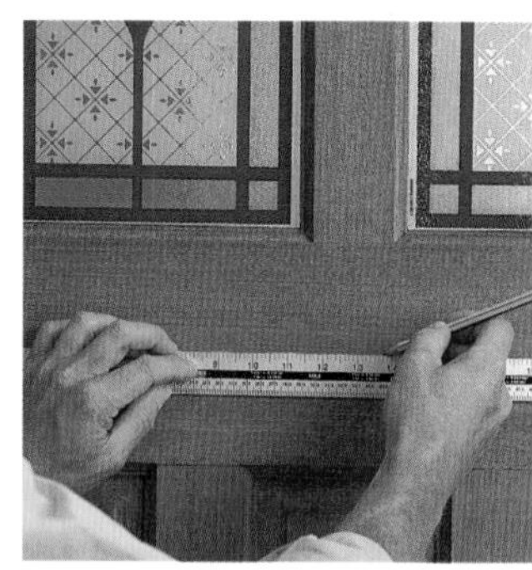

2 Draw a horizontal line between the two marks.

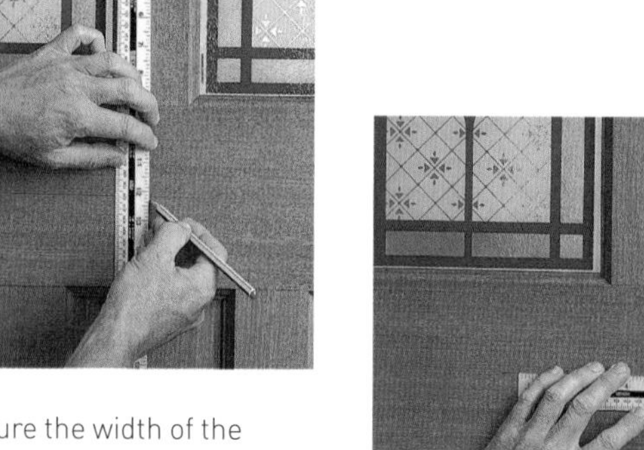

3 Measure the width of the cross rail and find the centre point. Draw a short vertical line across the horizontal one you have already made.

4 Centre the letterplate over the intersection of the lines and mark the position of the fixing bolts on either side.

Fitting the letterplate

This job will be far quicker and easier if you use a power jigsaw to cut the opening (see IDEAL TOOL, opposite).

1 Drill clearance holes for the fixing bolts. Make the holes slightly larger than the diameter of the bolt shank – normally about 6mm.

2 With a pencil, mark where the opening will be cut. It should be a fraction larger than the hinged part of the letterplate.

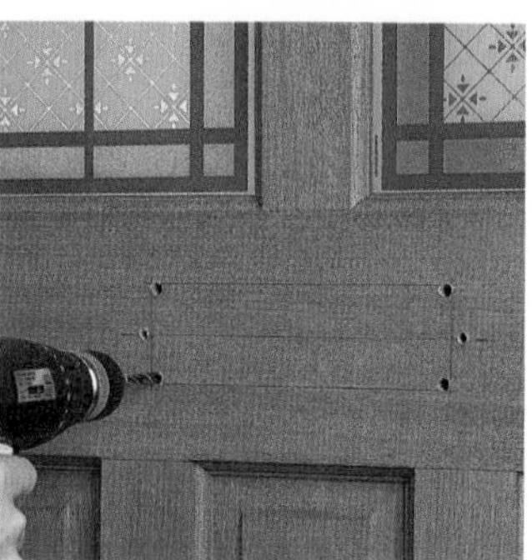

3 Drill a hole at each corner of the slot. Select a drill bit large enough to create a hole into which you will be able to insert the blade of a padsaw or power jigsaw – normally about 8mm.

4 Insert the blade of a padsaw or power jigsaw into one of the corner holes and carefully cut around the rectangle all the way through the door.

5 After cutting the opening, use a narrow chisel and mallet to cut recesses for the hinge-pin. Clean out the corners of the opening and smooth the edges with abrasive paper.

6 Fit the letterplate into position using the nuts supplied. If the bolts are longer than the thickness of your door, shorten them with a hacksaw.

IDEAL TOOL

Power jigsaw

A power jigsaw will make light work of cutting out difficult holes in wood. It is ideally suited for working in a restricted space. Blades are available with different numbers of teeth. Before use, check that the blade is fitted securely and that the roller guide is lubricated.

Fitting a cat flap

There are many types of pet door on the market. The majority have a simple locking mechanism but more sophisticated versions have a remote-controlled door operated by a collar worn by the resident pet. Whichever type you choose, it will come with a full set of fixing instructions, which you should read carefully before starting work.

TOOLS MATERIALS

- **power drill with 8mm gauge twist bit**
- **long ruler**
- **pencil**
- **padsaw or power jigsaw**
- **screwdriver**

- cat flap with fixings
- adhesive tape
- medium-grade abrasive paper

1 Decide where to position the cat flap, taking into account ease of installation and ease of use. Stick the template supplied to the door with adhesive tape. Check it is level and drill through the four points indicated on the template. The holes need to be big enough to insert the blade of a padsaw or jigsaw to begin cutting – normally about 8mm.

2 Remove the template and, using a ruler, draw lines between the four holes. These mark the outline of the opening.

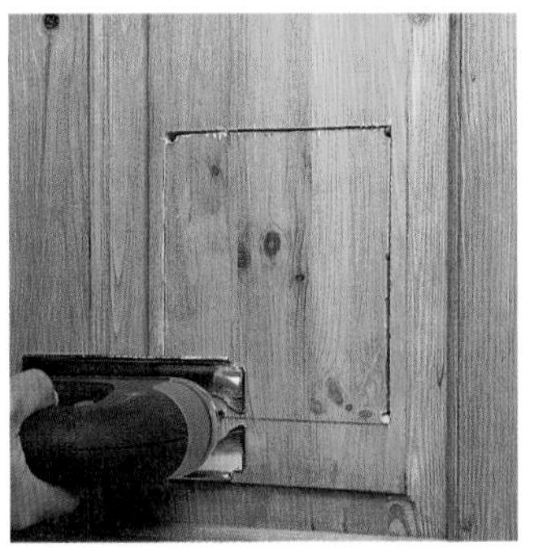

3 Use a padsaw or power jigsaw to cut through the door along the line. Push out the piece and smooth rough edges with medium-grade abrasive paper.

4 Hold the cat flap in position, aligned with the hole. Check it is level and drill clearance holes for the screw fixing positions.

5 Hold both sides in place through the open flap and screw them together, fixing each screw through the clearance holes. Check that the flap is swinging freely.

ROOFS CONSTRUCTION

Most houses have a pitched or sloping roof, made from a triangular-shaped wooden frame which is covered with tiles or slates. The weight of the tiles is supported by pairs of sloping rafters, whose heads meet at a central ridge board and whose lower ends are fixed to timber wall plates on the external walls of the house. Tiles are made from baked clay or concrete, and may be flat or moulded into various profiles. Slates are smooth flat pieces, either cut from rock (natural slate) or man-made.

Pitched roofs can be constructed in several different ways, depending on the size and design of the house.

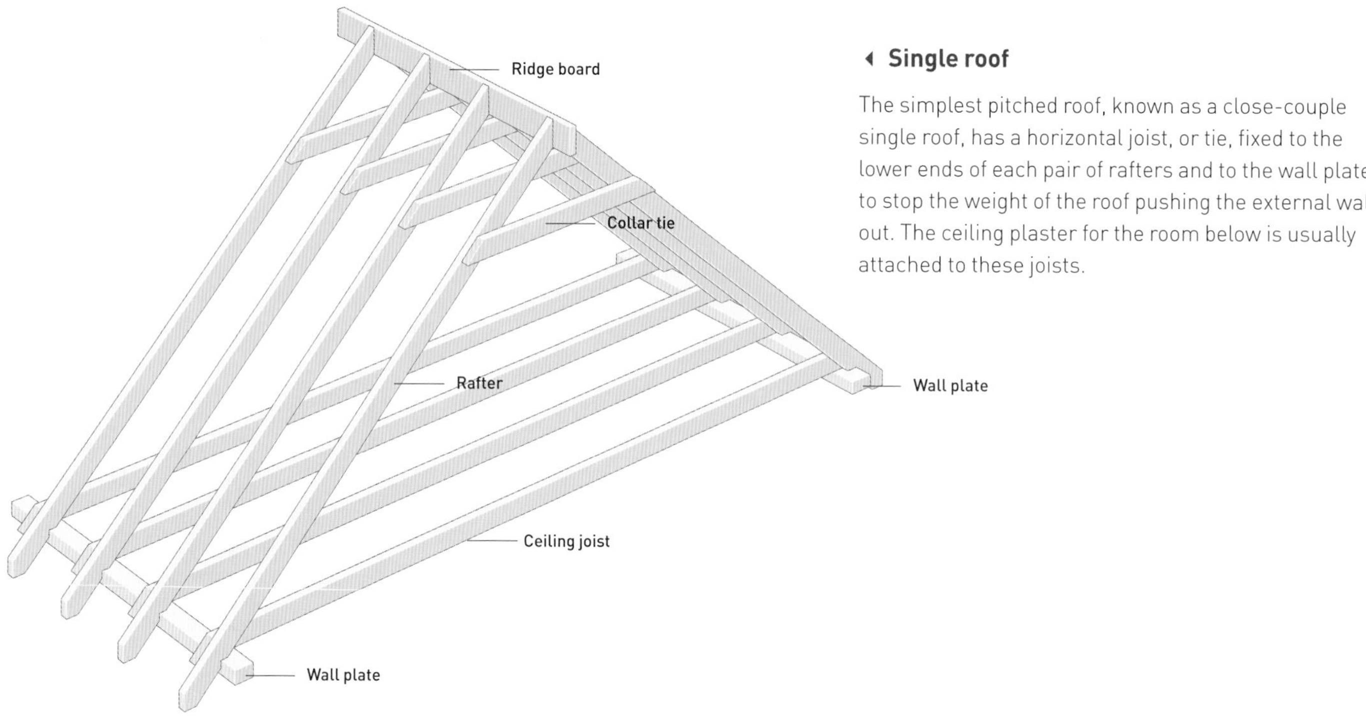

◂ Single roof

The simplest pitched roof, known as a close-couple single roof, has a horizontal joist, or tie, fixed to the lower ends of each pair of rafters and to the wall plates to stop the weight of the roof pushing the external walls out. The ceiling plaster for the room below is usually attached to these joists.

Double roof ▸

A roof spanning a large area may have horizontal beams called purlins fixed halfway down the rafters, in addition to the joists or ties across their lower ends. This type of roof is know as a double or purlin roof. A very large roof may have several purlins fitted at intervals down the rafters. Diagonal struts give extra support to the purlins. They are fixed at one end to the purlin and at the other end to the wall plate of a central, loadbearing partition wall. Horizontal timbers called binders and vertical ones called hangers may also be fitted to support the joists.

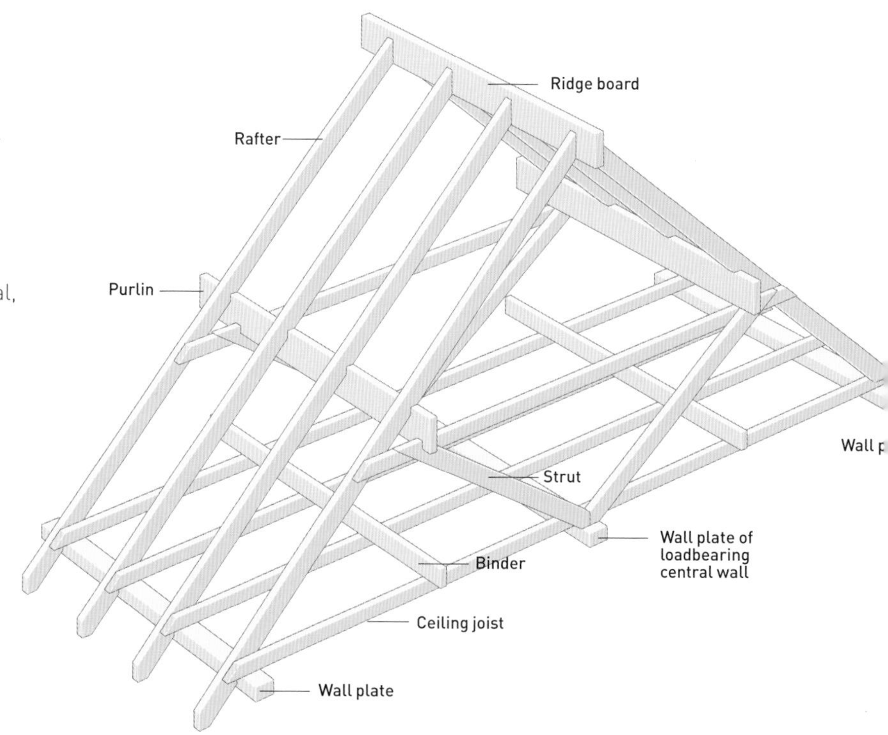

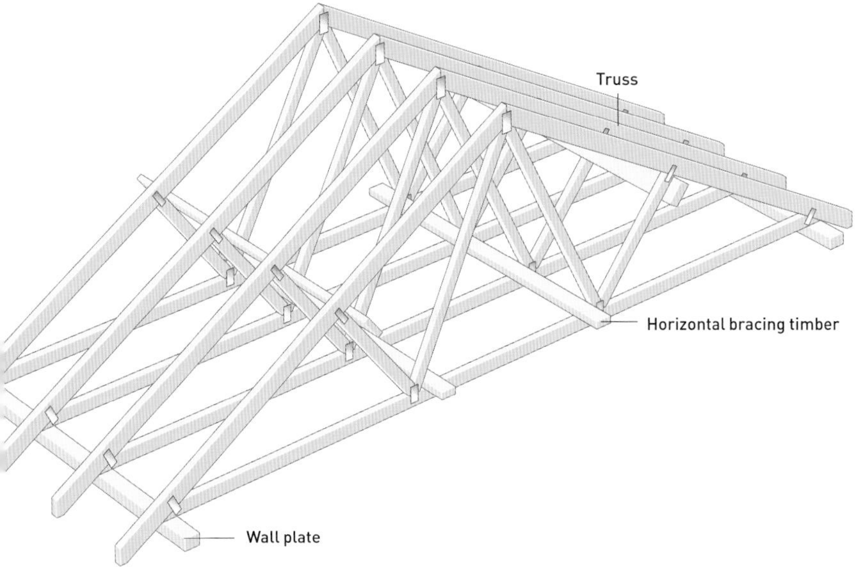

◂ Trussed roof

This type of roof is constructed from individual prefabricated trusses. Each truss is a triangle made from a pair of rafters and a joist braced with struts. These trusses are linked to each other by horizontal and diagonal bracing timbers, which means that very few trussed roofs can be converted into living space, and you must not cut into one without seeking professional advice. The trusses are usually fixed to the walls with metal straps. Trussed rafters are relatively light, they allow for a fairly wide span, and there is no need for a ridge board or a loadbearing partition wall. Older houses with this type of roof may have purlins adding support to the rafters.

Covering a pitched roof ▸

Before the tiles or slates are fixed in place, a roof is lined with sarking, which may be bituminous roofing felt or polythene. To make sure it is waterproof, the sarking is laid horizontally in strips with each new section overlapping the one below it, working from the bottom of the slope up to the ridge. Sawn softwood battens are then nailed to the rafters, over the sarking.

Tiles and slates are laid across the roof in rows or courses, with the bottom of each course overlapping the one below. As with sarking, they are laid starting at the eaves and working up the slope to the ridge. Tiles have a nib that hooks over the battens and holds them in place, though some are fixed with nails or clips as well. Slates are held in place with nails alone or nails and copper rivets. The size and type of tiles and slates and the pitch of the roof all determine the fixings that are used.

Curved tiles are used for capping the ridge (or the hips of a hipped-end roof, see below), to keep the junction of the two slopes weatherproof. Where a tile or slate meets a wall or chimney, a strip of lead, zinc or mortar, known as flashing, covers the join to make it weatherproof. Flashing, or specially formed valley tiles, are fitted along the valley where two roofs meet.

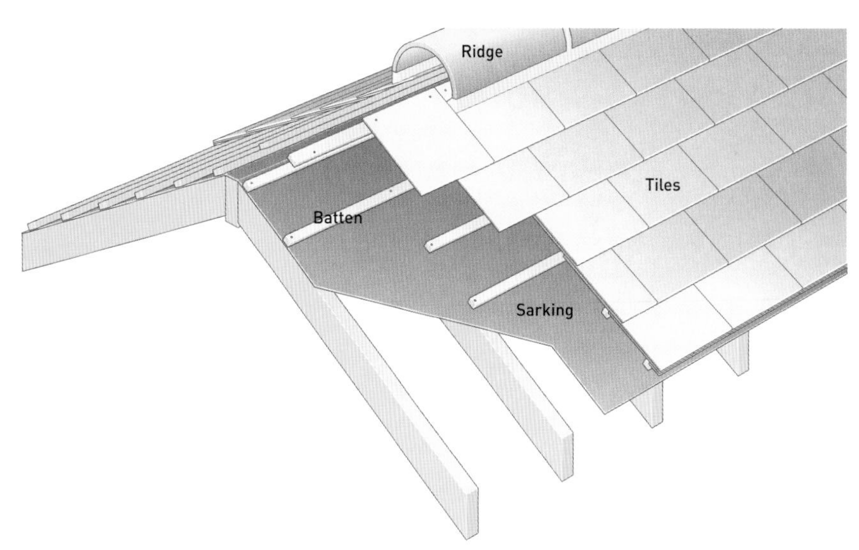

Gable roof

Hipped-end roof

◂ Roof shape

Gable and hipped-end roofs are the two most common pitched roof shapes. With a gable roof, the end walls of the house are built right up to the ridge, following the pitch of the roof and forming a triangular gable end. Hipped-end roofs slope down at the end as well as the sides, making them a more elaborate construction. They require additional timbers known as hip rafters, jack rafters, crown rafters and cripple rafters. A large house may well have both types of roof, and the junctions where they meet form 'valleys'.

ROOFS CONSTRUCTION AND REPAIRS

There are different types of eaves and verges protecting the edges of roofs where they meet the house walls. This is where guttering is attached, to drain water that falls on the roof (see pages 162–63). Flat roofs are usually covered in bituminous-based asphalt or roofing felt. Flat roofs tend to have a shorter life than pitched roofs and most problems should be left to the professionals, but you can buy a special sealant for making your own repairs to splits or blisters in the roofing felt.

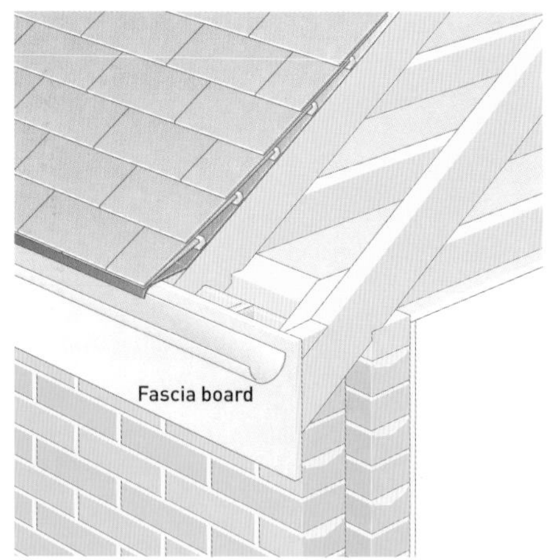

Flush eaves

Eaves

The eaves are the bottom edges of the roof where the lower ends of the rafters join the external walls of the house. The ends of the rafters may be cut level with the walls, in which case they are called flush eaves. Fascia boards are nailed across the ends of the rafters to protect them from the elements and the guttering is fixed to the fascia boards. Alternatively, the ends of the rafters may project beyond the walls and the guttering is fixed to them. These are known as open eaves. Projecting rafters are sometimes boxed in by a fascia board and a soffit board, in which case they are called closed eaves.

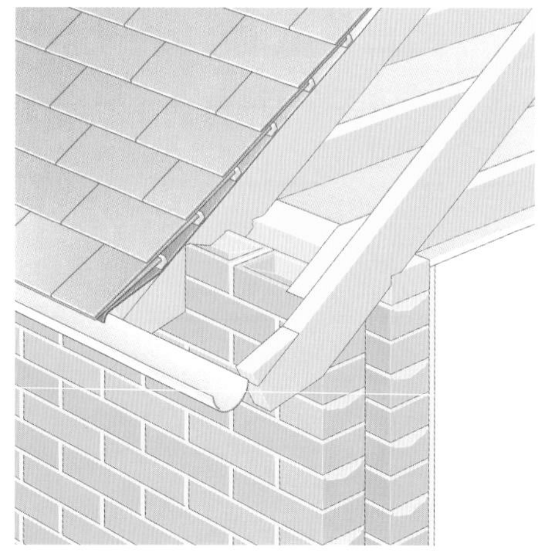
Open eaves

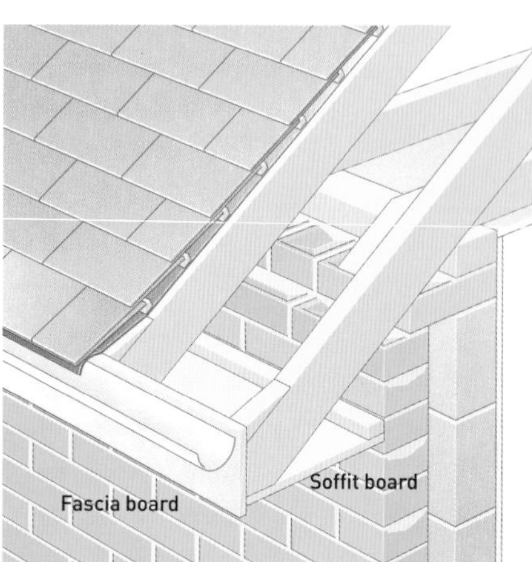

Closed eaves

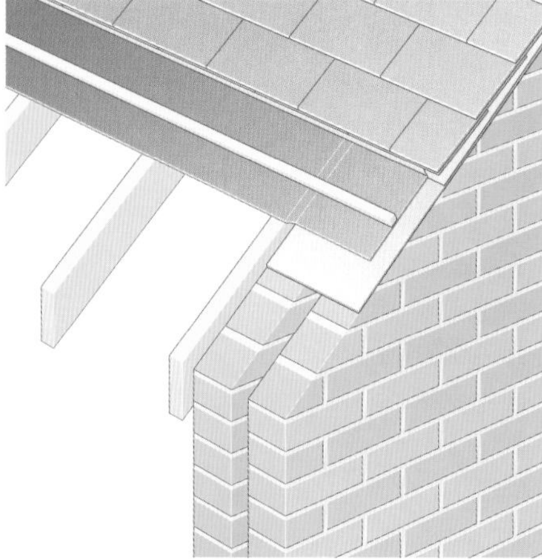
Flush verge

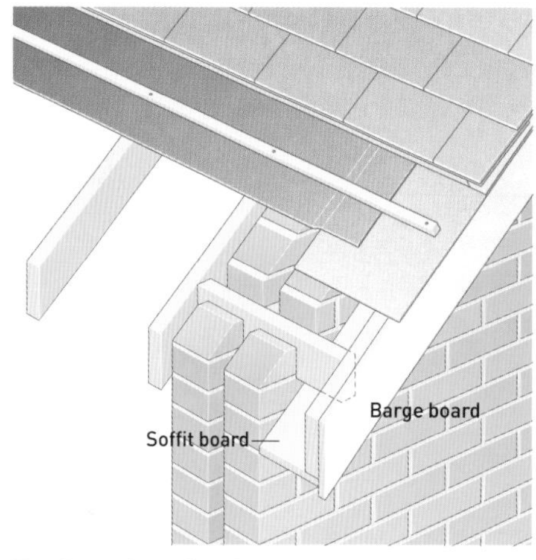

Enclosed projecting verge

Ventilation

It's essential that air can circulate through a roof space so that condensation cannot build up and cause the timbers to rot. There may be vents at the eaves and ridge, in addition to breathable roofing felt and ventilation tiles at the upper edge of the roof slope.

Verges

The sloping edges of a gable roof are called the verges and, as with the eaves, they may be level with the exterior walls or extend beyond them. If the verges are level with the walls, the last rafters are on the inside of the walls and the gap between the roof covering and the brickwork is sealed with mortar. Where the verges extend beyond the walls an outer rafter is fitted beyond each wall to cover the ends of the battens and wall plate. Long timbers called barge boards are fitted to the ends of these rafters, and the underside may be enclosed with soffit boards.

Flat roofs

Rear extensions and outbuildings often have a timber-framed flat roof covered with roofing felt. In fact no roof can be totally flat, or rainwater would just settle and cause it to collapse. Timbers in the roof frame called firring strips taper slightly so that the roof can drain. Roofing boards are laid on the firring strips, and three layers of roofing felt, bonded together with bitumen, are laid on top of the boards. The joint between a flat roof and an adjacent wall is sealed with metal flashing.

Vents at the eaves are essential so that air can circulate and moisture escape; there may also be vents through the roof alongside the junction with the house wall. Insulation is vital over a living space, either blocks of insulating material between the firrings, or sheet insulation laid on the ceiling.

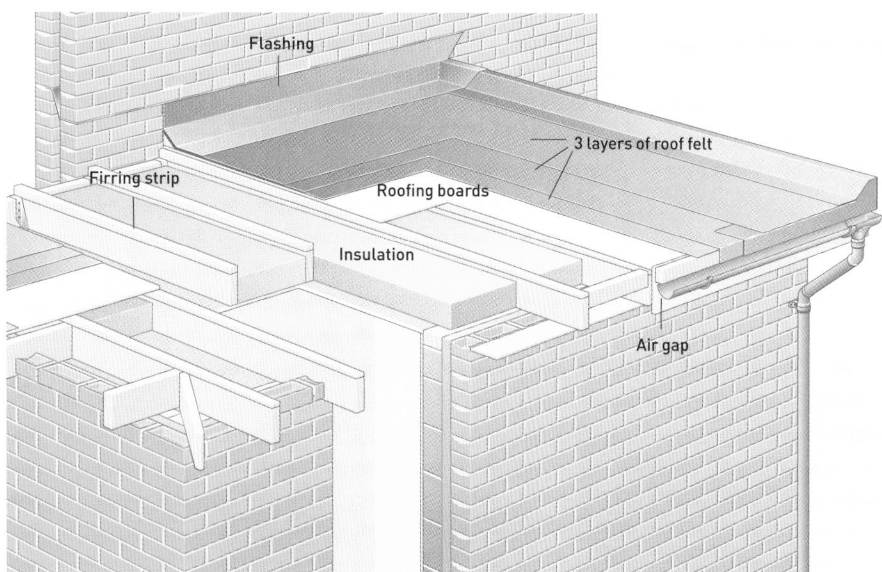

TOOLS MATERIALS

- **protective gloves**
- **stiff brush**
- **craft knife**

- card
- fungicide, if required
- roof and gutter sealant
- repair felt to match

Repairing roof felt

Flat roofs are not particularly durable, and it will pay you to keep a close eye on one. Besides weathering, the felt is prone to damage by careless feet and ladders. A prompt repair will stop rainwater seeping through and causing more serious structural damage.

If the edge of a strip of roofing felt is lifting from the surface, you can stick it down with specially formulated roof and gutter sealant. Wear protective gloves while you work to avoid getting the spray on your skin. If there is moss and lichen on the roof surface, treat the area with a fungicide before starting. Try to work on a warm day and avoid damp conditions.

Use a stiff brush to clean away loose chippings and dirt. Align a piece of card against the raised edge to protect the adjacent area from any stray sealant. Lift the flap of felt and spray the roof underneath with roof and gutter sealant. Leave to dry for the specified time then press the felt down firmly.

Patching a tear

Fix tears in roofing felt by inserting a patch of new felt underneath. Check the instructions and make sure you leave enough time for the sealant to dry before you stick the new patch down.

1 Lift the torn edge of felt and spray roof and gutter sealant underneath it and on the area adjacent to it. Allow to dry for the time specified by the manufacturer.

2 Cut a patch of matching felt, large enough to fit under the torn portion and cover the area around it. Slide the patch into place underneath the tear, and stick it down firmly.

3 Lift the torn section and spray sealant onto the upper surface of the new patch underneath it, and again leave it to dry.

4 Press the felt down and spray sealant liberally along all the joints.

ROOFS TILES AND SLATES

Check your roof regularly for broken tiles or slates. If you wait for it to spring a leak, you will find that much unnecessary damage has already been done. Provided you are comfortable working at heights, and you have proper, safe access equipment (see pages 347–49), there's no reason why you shouldn't make repairs yourself. When buying replacement tiles or slates, it will help if you can take one with you to get the best match.

Temporary repair of a roof tile

If you can't replace a cracked tile straight away, do a temporary repair to stop the leak.

1 Thoroughly clean the area around the crack using a wire brush and wipe away the dust and debris. Apply a coat of flashing strip primer to the crack and the area around it.

2 Cut off a piece of flashing strip to fit the length of the tile.

3 Peel off the backing from the flashing strip, lift the lower edge of the tile above the broken one and stick the flashing strip over the crack, making sure it is completely covered.

4 Press the flashing strip securely into place

TOOLS MATERIALS

- **wire brush**
- **scissors**
- **ladder with stand-off bracket**
- **roof ladder**
- **bucket on rope**
- **slater's ripper, if required**

- flashing strip primer
- self-adhesive flashing strip
- replacement tiles

Replacing broken tiles

Tiles are usually simply hooked in place on nibs that fit over wooden battens. But occasionally alternate courses will be nailed or clipped to the battens: it depends on the type of roof you have and the weather conditions in your area. If so you may need to cut the tiles free with a special tool called a slater's ripper, which you can hire.

1 Take out the highest broken tile first. Slide the adjoining ones up, and tilt the broken one sideways to separate it. The tiles below that can simply be lifted off. Carry the tiles to the ground one at a time, or lower them in a bucket to a waiting helper. Replace the lowest course first, working from right to left. Carefully lift the adjacent tile and hook the nibs over the batten as you slide each one into place.

2 When you get to the last tile of the course, lift the tiles on either side and wiggle the new tile until it hooks over the batten and sits correctly.

3 Move to the next course up. When you get to the last tile you must raise the lower edge of the tile above and slide the new tile under the tiles on either side. This can be a bit awkward, but shift the tile from left to right and it should slot into place.

SAFETY FIRST

Ladders and scaffolds

To make even minor roof repairs, you must have an ordinary ladder *and* a roof ladder (see page 347). The ladder to the roof should have a stand-off bracket, so that it rests against the wall not the guttering. A roof ladder has rubber wheels and hooks at one end. The wheels allow it to be pushed up the roof without dislodging loose tiles. When the top is level with the ridge, you turn the ladder over and hook it on the ridge. It must reach from the ridge all the way to the gutter so that you can step onto it easily from the ordinary ladder. For more extensive roof repairs you must have proper scaffolding – it's the law.

'emporary repair of a slate roof

nlike roof tiles, slates are all nailed to battens below. If a slate has racked and you are having difficulty finding a replacement, make a mporary repair to prevent water from seeping through. Wear protective loves to avoid cutting yourself on sharp edges.

TOOLS MATERIALS

- **ladder with stand-off bracket**
- **roof ladder**
- **heavy-duty gloves**
- **wire brush**
- **scissors**
- **bolster chisel**

- flashing strip primer
- self-adhesive flashing strip

1 Clean the crack and the area round it with a wire brush and pply flashing strip primer.

2 Cut a piece of self-adhesive flashing strip long enough to run the entire length of the slate.

3 Gently raise the lower edge of the slate above and insert a bolster chisel to hold it up. Peel off the backing and insert the strip.

4 Press the flashing strip firmly into place.

Replacing a slate

Vhen you replace a single slate – or the last in a group of slates – you on't be able to nail it to the batten, so you will need to secure it with a netal strip. Removing broken slates can be tricky. If the nails are old and usty, they may just pull out or break, but you might need to cut through nem with a slater's ripper, which you can hire.

TOOLS MATERIALS

- **ladder with stand-off bracket**
- **roof ladder**
- **heavy-duty gloves**
- **slater's ripper, if required**
- **bucket and rope**
- **hammer**
- **tinsnips**

- 25mm-wide strip of aluminium or copper
- 100mm large-head galvanised clout nails
- replacement slates

1 Remove the first broken slate arefully, wiggling it from side to ide to dislodge it. Take it to the round, or lower it in a bucket to helper. Slates have sharp edges o don't risk letting any fall from he roof, which could be langerous. Use tinsnips to cut he metal strip to the length of he slate plus about 100mm.

2 You should just be able to see the wooden batten between the two slates above the one you are replacing. Hammer a galvanised clout nail through the metal strip, about 25mm from the end, and fix it into the batten between the slates.

3 Slide the new slate under the two slates in the course above, with the bevelled edge facing outwards. Align the lower edge with the adjoining slates. Bend the end of the metal strip up and over the bottom edge of the new slate and press it down flat.

FENCES GATES AND STRUCTURES

Whether you are looking for privacy from the neighbours, protection from wind or sun, to enhance the look of your property or to make your home more secure, there is a fence, gate or garden structure for you. Before investing, consider the location and period of you property. Choose something in keeping with the style of your home and environment.

Fencing

Fencing is the most popular way of marking a boundary. It is fairly easy to erect and cheaper than building a wall, though don't overlook the cost and effort of maintenance over the years – you will have to treat the timber regularly to protect it from insects and weathering. Privacy is likely to be your primary concern, and there are a number of options offering good screening. However, if the site of your fence is exposed to prevailing winds, take care not to choose one that offers so much resistance that it falls down. A fence with an open structure, such as a picket fence, would be a better option.

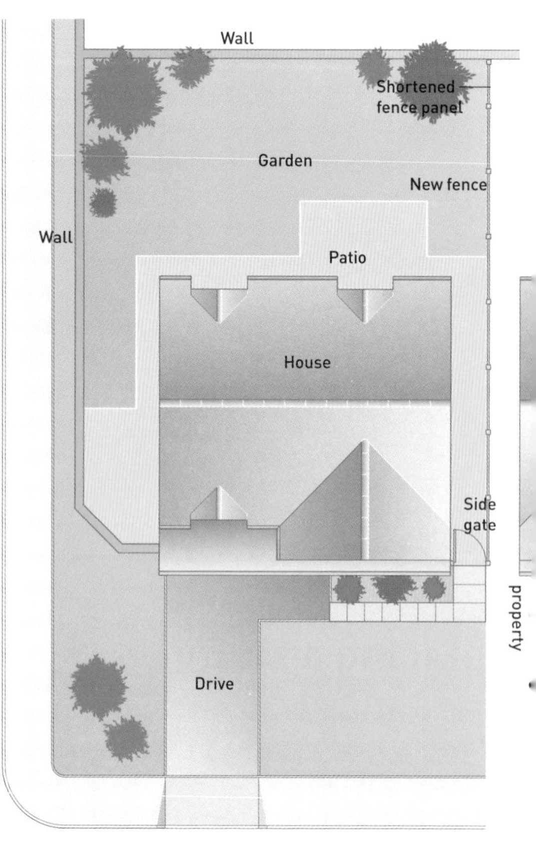

Planning your fence

Before putting up a fence discuss the plans with your neighbours. You need to check the exact line of the boundary and make sure the posts are positioned on your side. Before you take down an old fence first make sure it's yours. If it belongs to a neighbour and they won't allow you to take it down, you can erect another alongside provided it is on your side of the boundary. There is an unwritten rule that a good neighbour puts up a fence with the post and rails facing their own property, but this is not a legal obligation. Unless the boundary line meets a highway, you generally do not need planning permission for a fence less than 2m high.

Lap panel

Easy to put up, offering good screening and value for money, a lap panel fence is a popular choice. Ready-made panels are fitted between posts cemented into the ground. The panels usually come in standard 1.83m widths but can be cut down. They are available in heights of 0.6m–1.83m. Like all timber fences, a lap panel fence will need periodic treatment with wood preservative.

Combination trellis and lap panel

Add a trellis to the top of your panel fence to give increased height where you need it. The trellis is ideal for training climbing plants, creating a less stark effect than a solid fence, and offering more natural shade and privacy.

Closeboard

A closeboard fence consists of vertical featheredge boards (tapered on one side) which are nailed onto horizontal arris rails secured to the posts. It offers excellent screening and security – the vertical boards make a sturdy fence, good for keeping out intruders.

Picket

A picket fence is formed of a row of vertical pales with rounded or pointed tops. Available in panels usually no more than 1.2m high, this kind of fence is often used at the front of a house, where a boundary mark rather than screening is needed.

Willow or hazel pane

Panels of interwoven willow or hazel are ideal in a cottage garden, giving an informal, rustic feel. They are just one of a range of more unusual fencing options that can dramatically enhance your outdoor space.

Trellis

Trellis comes in a variety of forms and materials, including softwood, wood-effect synthetics and recycled material. It can be nailed between fence posts or fixed to the top of an existing fence or wall to give added height. It is perfect for supporting climbing plants, which will create their own natural leafy screen.

Trellis panels

Rigid panels of trellis made from softwood can be secured between fence posts to create a substantial and attractive freestanding screen. Or choose curved-profile trellis to create a striking garden feature.

Gates

Gates come in many different designs and may be made from wood or metal. They can be hung from timber posts, attached to a wall or hung on brick or concrete piers. Before you buy a gate, consider carefully your needs: how wide should it be and how will you hang it? You also need to establish which way the gate should open – both right- and left-handed gates are available. You may need one of each if you are putting up a pair of gates.

Entrance gate

An entrance gate needs to be sturdy enough to withstand continuous use. For additional strength, a wooden gate can be braced with a diagonal strut running from the latch to the opposite corner.

Metal gate

An ornate metal gate is an elegant feature that will complement brick or stonework equally well. They are often supplied with built-in hinge and latch fittings.

Boarded gate

Creating perfect privacy in a rustic-style garden, a boarded gate is also designed to form an unobtrusive entrance within a panel fence.

Picket gate

A picket gate will sit attractively alongside picket fencing, a wall or hedge. The pale tops can be square, rounded or pointed, and the wooden pales can be painted or stained.

Driveway gate

Choose a single gate or a pair that meet in the middle. Check you have space across the drive for it to swing fully open.

Structures

A pergola or an arbour can add a whole new dimension to even the smallest garden. Carefully situated, such a feature will draw the eye and entice visitors to explore. Climbing plants such as wisteria or honeysuckle can be trained to grow around the structure to create natural shade and a leafy retreat.

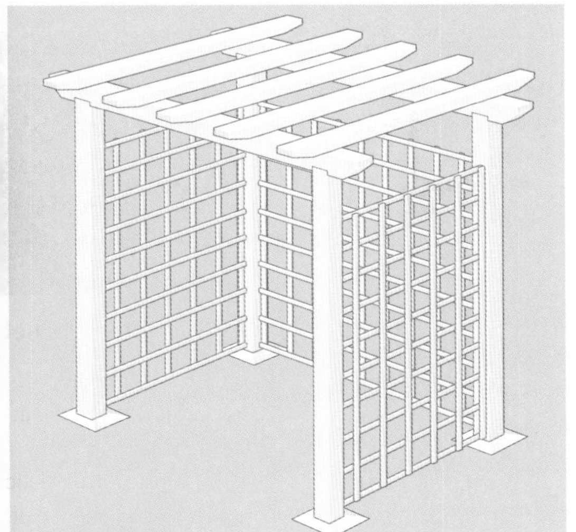

Timber arbour

An arbour provides a secluded spot and outlook from which to admire the garden.

Timber pergola

A pergola, when supporting climbing plants, creates a natural 'roof' over a patio or walkway.

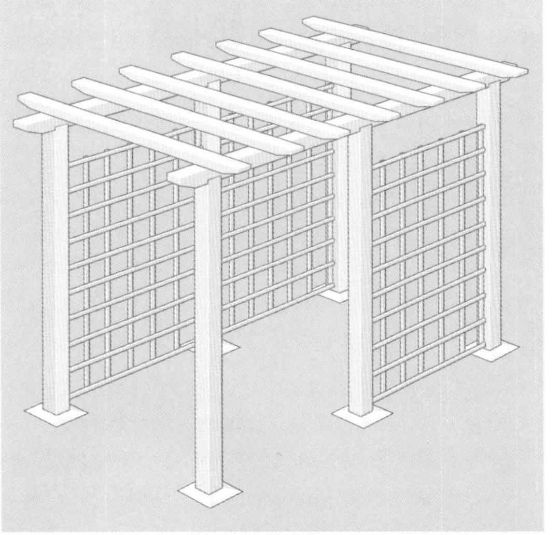

FENCES AND GATES REPAIRS

Wooden gates and fences are prone to rot or attack by insects. To prolong their life, treat them regularly with wood preservative. You should also avoid piling earth up against a fence and where possible install gravel boards at its base.

Repairing an arris rail

A broken arris rail can be fixed with an arris rail bracket, a length of galvanised steel specially shaped to fit the rail and ready drilled with holes through which you secure it with galvanised screws or nails. If the arris rail is cracked near the post use a flanged bracket and fasten the flanges to the post.

Reinforcing a rotten fence post

The part of a wooden fence post most likely to rot is the section buried underground. If not reinforced in time, it will eventually collapse and pull down the fence.

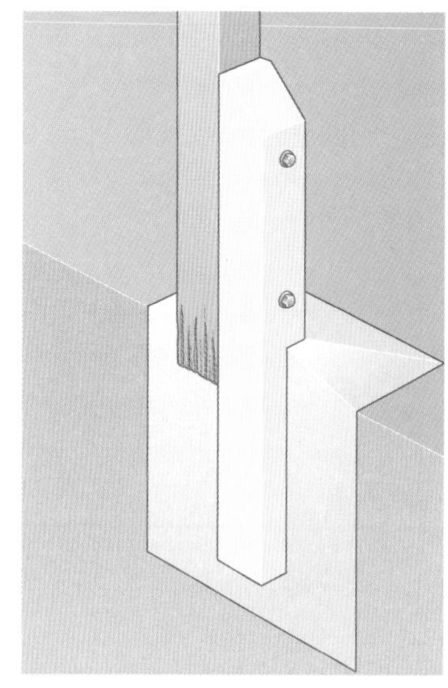

Support the fence with lengths of timber on either side. Dig a hole around the base of the post, cut the rotten part away and remove any concrete. Coat sound wood with preservative. Place a concrete spur in the hole against the remains of the post. Insert coach bolts through the holes in the spur and tap them with a hammer to mark the post. Then drill holes through the post at the marked spots. Push the bolts through the post and spur so the tails appear on the spur side. Put on the nuts and tighten with a spanner. Brace the post with lengths of timber, checking it is vertical with a spirit level. Fill the hole with concrete, leaving the timber supports in place for 48 hours while it sets.

Replacing a panel or post

If a post or panel is rotten it may need replacing altogether. Panels come in a standard size so finding a new one to fit shouldn't be difficult.

TOOLS MATERIALS

- **nail bar**
- **hacksaw**
- **hammer**
- **pincers**
- **power drill with twist bit**
- **spirit level**
- **long bar**
- **shovel**

- fence panel or post
- 75mm galvanised nails
- timber props
- cement and aggregate or post cement

1 Lever back the side frame of the panel with a nail bar to expose the nails joining it to the post.

2 Saw through the old nails with a hacksaw. Hammer in protruding nails or pull them out with pincers. If removing a panel, repeat at the opposite end. If the new panel isn't an exact fit, plane it a little each side, or close any gap with a thin fillet of wood. Drill six evenly spaced pilot holes horizontally through the framing batten at each end of the new panel, front and back, and fix it to the post with 75mm galvanised nails.

3 To remove a post, detach the panels on either side and pull them away from it. Dig out the base of the post and remove any concrete. If this proves difficult, cut a notch in the old post and lever it out with a long bar. Ensure the replacement post is the same size as the original and place it in the hole. Support the fence with timber props while you renail the panels either side (see Step 2). Check the post is vertical with a spirit level and concrete it in place, sloping the surface of the concrete away from the post to drain off rainwater. Leave the props in place for 48 hours while it sets.

YOU CAN DO IT

Wood preservative

A coat of preservative will drastically extend the life of a fence or gate. Most treatments will keep fungi and insects at bay for several years. The wood needs to be completely dry, so the best time to apply it is in late summer after a dry period and when no rain is expected for a day or so. Paint it on with a block paintbrush or use a garden pressure spray; wear protective gloves and, if spraying, safety goggles and a mask.

B&Q

Repairing a small area of rot

Small patches of rot on a wooden gate area easily treated without having to replace the whole gate.

1 With a small wooden mallet and a chisel, chip away the rot back to sound wood. Coat the area in preservative and allow to dry.

TOOLS MATERIALS

- **wooden mallet**
- **chisel**
- **sanding block**

- wood preservative
- outdoor wood filler
- abrasive paper

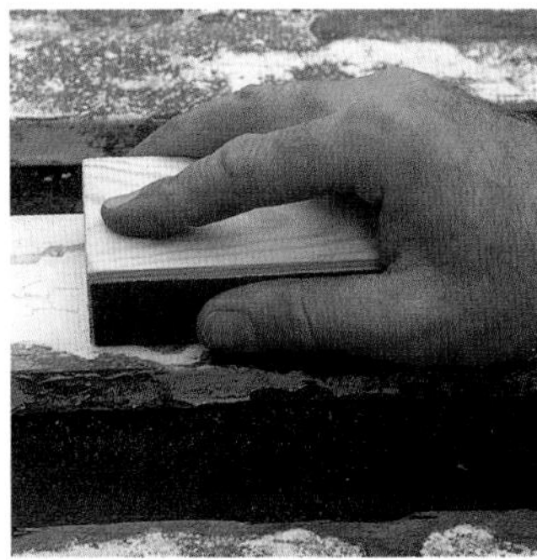

2 Fill the cavity with wood filler, which sets in about 15 minutes. Then sand it flush with the timber.

ECO PRESERVATIVE

Old-fashioned wood preservatives made from tar oil were foul-smelling and could be harmful to plants. Modern preservers are much more pleasant to work with. They are usually solvent- or water-based. The odourless, water-based preservers are the least environmentally harmful. They are also available in a wide variety of stylish colours.

Strengthening a gate corner

If your gate sags, first check whether the hinges are loose. If not, the problem may be caused by the timber joints having worked loose at the corner of the gate.

1 Force waterproof adhesive into the loose joint and press it together with a sash clamp.

TOOLS MATERIALS

- **sash clamp**
- **screwdriver**

- waterproof adhesive
- metal bracket
- galvanised screws

2 When the glue is dry, leave the sash clamp in place while you screw a metal bracket to the front of the gate to hold the joint.

Adding a brace to a sagging gate

A gate may sag if it has no diagonal brace or if an existing brace is not strong enough. Lift and wedge the gate into its proper position before measuring a new brace. The brace should fit snugly between the cross-rails on the back with the top pointing towards the latch. Cut it from a length of wood the same thickness as the cross-rails. Take the gate off its hinges, drill pilot holes, and fix the new brace to the pales with countersunk galvanised screws.

Treating a rusting gate

Old metal gates and railings will quickly deteriorate once rust gets in, but you can give them a new lease of life with special rust-inhibiting metal paint.

One coat should be enough over a previously painted surface, but always read and follow the guidelines on the tin.

TOOLS MATERIALS

- **wire brush**
- **safety goggles**
- **cloth**
- **paintbrush**

- medium-grade abrasive paper
- white spirit
- metal paint with rust inhibitor

1 Remove loose rust and paint with a wire brush or abrasive paper. Wear safety goggles, especially on a windy day.

2 Wipe down the surface with a cloth soaked in white spirit.

3 Apply one coat of rust-inhibiting metal paint.

If you are building a new fence with a gated opening, erect the gate and posts first and build the fence from them. If replacing an old gate, be sure to measure up precisely. Gates are sold in metric and imperial sizes and conversions are not always accurate, so note down the exact size you need and take a tape measure with you. Consider also which way you want it to open. Most gates open into a property rather than out.

Installing a picket gate

For a light gate the gateposts should be about 100mm square and 610mm longer than the gate height. For heavier gates – over 1.2m high or wide – posts should be thicker and at least 760mm longer than the gate height; check the manufacturer's specifications. Wooden gateposts should be treated with preservative before installing. They must be set in concrete since post spikes do not give enough support. Choose fittings that have been japanned (lacquered) or galvanised to deter rust.

TOOLS MATERIALS

- **panel saw**
- **sliding bevel**
- **pencil**
- **power drill with twist bits**
- **screwdriver**
- **trowel**
- **spade or post-hole borer**
- **spirit level**

- 2 gateposts
- wood preservative
- gate
- 5 lengths of timber (braces and supports)
- 2 hinges
- gate latch
- galvanised screws
- cement and aggregate or post cement

1 If your gate posts have not been 'weathered' – cut the top to a slant so that rainwater will run off – you will need to do this first. Use a sliding bevel to mark a 20° angle from the top of the post.

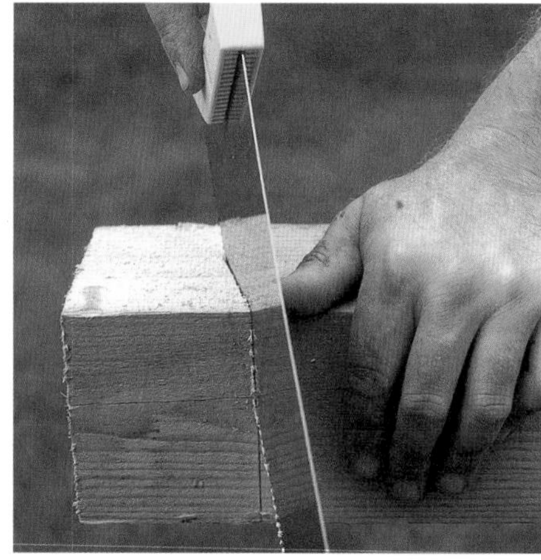

2 Continue the line square down the face of the post and saw neatly along it. Paint the cut edge with wood preservative; if the wood is untreated, paint the whole post.

3 When you have decided which way you want the gate to open, lay it face down on level ground. Position the posts either side with their tops 50mm higher than the top of the gate and a 5mm gap either side of the gate to allow it to open and close freely. Use two timber lengths to raise the gate slightly so that it sits flush with the gateposts. Adjust as necessary with timber off-cuts or wedges.

4 Place the hinges in position on the back of the gate. Mark the screw positions and drill one pilot hole. Test it by driving in a screw to check that the drill bit is not too large. Drill the remaining pilot holes.

5 Screw the hinges in place using galvanised screws. If you find it tricky to position them accurately on the post (see YOU CAN DO IT), wait to fit them and the latch until the gate is hung.

Drill pilot holes for the latch screws, then rew the latch in place. Don't forget to allow 5mm gap between gate and post.

7 Brace the gate and posts with three lengths of timber to make sure the construction is solid. Use the braced gate to mark the position of the post holes.

8 Use a spade or post-hole borer to dig post holes roughly a spade and a half wide, and deep enough to leave a 50mm clearance gap beneath the gate so it can open freely. Check this is sufficient by laying a spirit level on the ground that the gate will open over. If necessary, level the ground. In soft ground, you should dig a trench between the post holes about 300mm wide and 200mm deep and fill it with concrete. This will help prevent the posts being pulled inwards by the weight of the gate. Lower the gateposts into the holes and check they are level with a spirit level.

Use timber props to hold the gate and osts in position. Mix the concrete (see page 36) then concrete the posts into the ground, oping the surface downwards to direct inwater away from the wood.

10 Allow the concrete to set for 48 hours before removing the props and brace.

YOU CAN DO IT

Adjusting the hinges

With some hinges, you may find there is movement or 'play' when you try to screw them to the gate, making them difficult to position accurately. If so you will need to adjust their position once the posts are set. This will be easier if you fit only two holding screws per hinge into the post while it is still lying flat. Likewise, wait to fit the latch until the gate is hung.

Fixing a gatepost to a wall

If you need to attach a gate to a wall, fix the first post using expanding masonry bolts. These have an expanding section that fits into a drilled hole in the masonry. The post is then fitted over the stud and the nut tightened, causing the expanding section to open out and grip the sides of the hole.

Use three fittings for a post 1.2m or higher; two for anything less. First use a flat wood bit to drill recesses in the post just deep enough for the nuts and wide enough to allow access for a socket spanner. Then change bits and drill clearance holes for the studs right through the timber. Take a long masonry bit of the same diameter and, holding the post against the wall, drill pilot holes into the masonry. Accuracy is crucial, or the bolts will not function! Remove the post and enlarge the holes in the wall using a masonry bit the same size as the expanding section. Insert the expanding section into the wall, hang the post on the studs, place the washers and nuts on the ends and tighten with a socket spanner, taking care not to overtighten.

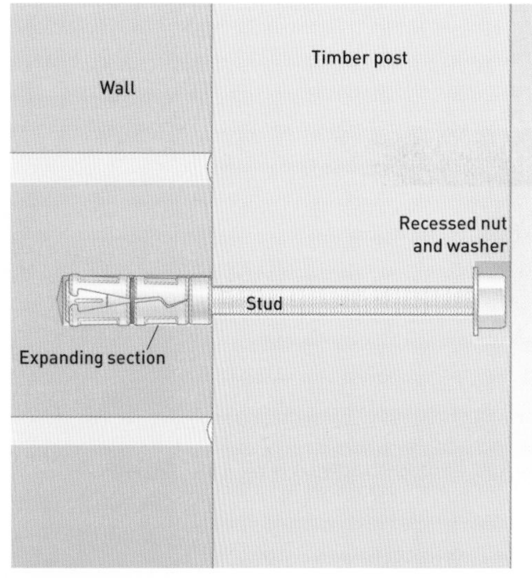

Expanding masonry bolt

FENCES ERECTING A PANEL FENCE

SAFETY FIRST

Wear strong gloves to protect your hands from splinters. Take particular care when applying wood preservative, and wear safety goggles if recommended by the manufacturer.

The secret to a successful panel fence is in the preparation. Bear in mind that this project is hard work and you'll find it a lot easier if you have at least one helper. Clear away vegetation and pot any shrubs or plants that you will want to replant once the fence is up. To give your plants time to recover, the best time to erect a fence is early spring and late autumn. Prefabricated fence panels come in a standard 1.83m width and are generally available in four heights (900mm, 1.2m, 1.52m and 1.83m).

Marking out and digging post holes

First decide whether you want to set your posts in concrete or in post supports. The former produces a sturdier fence but is harder work and the posts need to be at least 600mm taller than the fence panels. Metal post supports (see YOU CAN DO IT) are a quicker and easier alternative, but the resulting fence will not be as solid. Fencing timbers come ready-treated, but it's still a good idea to soak the feet of your posts overnight in a bucket of wood preservative.

TOOLS MATERIALS

- **protective gloves**
- **long tape measure**
- **spade or post-hole borer**
- **club hammer**
- **spirit level**
- **2 builder's lines**
- **panel saw**
- **power drill with twist bits**
- **trowel**
- **hammer**

- canes
- fence posts and panels
- timber props
- bricks
- 75mm galvanised nails
- cement and aggregate or post cement
- post caps
- silicone sealant

1 Stretch a long tape measure taut from end to end along the line of the fence. Measure out the position for each post and mark it by pushing a cane into what will be the centre of each post hole. If you are using 1.83m-wide panels and your posts are 100mm wide, the centres of the posts will be 1.93m apart.

2 Dig all the post holes. If there are a lot, consider hiring a post-hole borer. A standard depth of 450mm is usually enough, though in soft ground you should dig deeper holes and use longer posts to compensate.

3 With a club hammer, drive in temporary wooden props to hold the first post in place, using a spirit level to make sure it is vertical.

4 Erect the last post the same way, checking it is vertical and supporting it with props. Run two builder's lines between the top and bottom of these posts, along the line of the fence. Rest the other posts loosely in their holes.

Cutting fence panels

Your fence run is unlikely to divide into an exact number of panels, so you will need to know how to cut one down to fit.

1 Carefully remove the framing battens from one end of a panel and move them in to the required width. Sandwich them either side of the panel and nail them in place.

2 Saw the panel flush with the outer edge of the repositioned framing battens.

YOU CAN DO IT

Using post supports

Metal post spikes are an alternative to setting fence posts in concrete, provided the ground is firm. Buy supports that match the size of your fence posts. Fit the driving tool or dolly (left) into the cup of the spike and hammer it into the earth with slow firm strokes. If you hit a rock, dig it out and start again or the finished post will not be true. Keep checking the spike is vertical with a spirit level. Continue driving into the earth until the top of the cup is level with the ground. Use a sledge-hammer to hammer the fence post into the cup.

B&Q

Building the fence

Posts and panels should be erected alternately as you work down the line of the fence. Remember to keep checking that the panels are level and straight using a spirit level.

1 Drill six evenly spaced pilot ıoles into the batten framing ›f the panel on both sides and ›t each end. Raise the panel ›0mm–75mm above the ground ›y temporarily supporting it on ›ricks. This gap will help prevent › rotting from the bottom up.

4 Make sure each post is ·ouching both builder's lines, ›nd check that it is vertical using › spirit level. Mix the concrete ›see page 236) and fill the post ›ole to just above ground level. Smooth the surface downwards so that rainwater will drain away ·rom the wood.

2 Lay a spirit level on the panel to check it is level, then nail it to the post with galvanised nails. The top of the panel should be a consistent distance (at least 25mm) below the top of the post.

5 Soak the post caps in a bucket of water – this will help prevent splitting as you nail them on. Apply a silicone-based sealant to the underside to reduce the chance of water seeping beneath and rotting the top of the post.

3 Attach the second panel to the post, using temporary props to keep the fence vertical. Continue working this way until all the panels are in place.

6 Nail a post cap to the top of each post.

YOU CAN DO IT

Fence clips

As an alternative to nailing panels directly to the fence posts you can use fence clips. First attach the fence clips to the post, then slide the panel between the jaws of the clips and nail or screw the panel to the clips. If at a later date you want to remove a panel, fence clips will make this a little easier. However, fence clips are very visible on a finished fence.

B&Q

Fencing on a slope

To erect a panel fence on a slope, you still need to fix the posts vertically and the panels horizontally, as you would on flat ground, but you should step the fence panels to match the gradient. Remember when ordering materials that longer posts will be required to compensate for the stepped panels. If you can, try and keep the steps even, if necessary digging out or building up the ground beneath to ensure the triangular gap below each section is roughly equal. Fill this gap with a length of gravel board, which is easily cut to fit

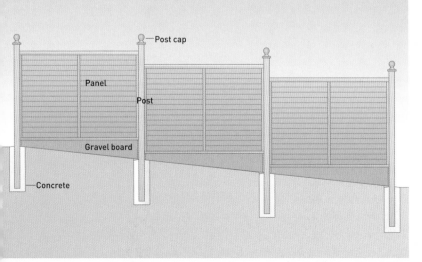

Post cap
Panel
Post
Gravel board
Concrete

Gravel board

Gravel boards are specially treated timbers that are fitted horizontally at the base of a fence. They protect the fence panels from rot by raising them off the ground. A rotten gravel board is much easier to replace than an entire fence panel. To fit gravel boards as you build a panel fence, leave a 150mm gap below the panels. Measure and cut 25mm-thick boards to fit between the posts. Fix them with galvanised screws or nails inserted at an angle into the posts. Countersink screws, or drill pilot holes for nails.

A closeboard fence is a popular alternative to panel fencing. Featheredge boards, tapered on one edge, are nailed to horizontal arris rails which are secured to the fence posts. This kind of fence is very good for privacy and security but can be quite expensive.

1 Put the first three posts in their holes and prop each one up with temporary supports. Insert one end of the upper arris rail into the notch of the first post and the other end into the third post. Check the arris rail is level and mark and saw off any excess: the end of the rail should reach exactly half-way across the third post. Nail it in place using 75mm galvanised nails and fit the lower arris rail in the same way. Keep checking both are level.

Erecting the posts and arris rails

Some fence posts come with ready-made slots (housings) for the triangular arris rails; others will need to be notched prior to installation. Use three arris rails for a fence over 1.2m high; two for anything lower. Make sure each post is the right way round: the back of the fence is the side where the arris rail is visible. The distance between posts should be half the length of your arris rail sections, less 50mm (cut this off each rail). Mark out the line of your fence, dig the holes and run two builder's lines between the first and last posts as in Steps 1–4, page 192. Remember to position the posts on your side of the boundary.

2 The joins in the arris rail sections need to be staggered for added strength. Therefore measure and cut the central arris rail to the distance from the outer edge of the first post to the mid-point of the second.

3 Nail the central arris rail into position using galvanised nails. The next section of the central arris rail should be a standard two-post width.

TOOLS MATERIALS

- **spirit level**
- **panel saw**
- **hammer**
- **power drill with twist and wood bits**

- fence posts
- timber props
- arris rails (3 x length of fen
- 50mm and 75mm galvanis nails
- cement and aggregate or post cement
- gravel boards
- featheredge boards
- capping strip

4 As well as making sure each post touches your builder's lines, keep using a spirit level to check the fence is vertical and level.

5 Continue fitting posts and rails to create your skeleton fence, supporting it with timber props as you go. Mix the concrete (see page 236). Checking again that each post is vertical, concrete them into the ground and leave to set for 48 hours. Slope the concrete away from the post to drain off rainwater.

6 Fit gravel boards horizontally to the front of the posts across the base of the fence. Drill pilot holes for the nails before attaching the board to prevent the wood from splitting.

YOU CAN DO IT

Post cement

Instead of aggregate and cement, consider using special rapid-setting post cement to secure your posts. It sets in about ten minutes and one 25kg bag should suffice for each post.

Attaching the boards

he first featheredge board is fitted with its thicker edge aligned to the outer edge f the first post and the bottom standing on the gravel board. Cut all the boards to e correct length before you begin and treat the end grains with wood preservative. he boards should stand 25mm taller than the fence posts.

1 Using 50mm galvanised nails, ail the centre of the first board o the upper arris rail. Check the oard is vertical before nailing it o the bottom rail and finally the entral rail. Make a spacer by utting an off-cut of timber to 0mm less than the width of a eatheredge board. Align this to he thicker edge of the first board. Butt the second board up against it nd fix it in the same way.

2 Continue fitting boards, using the spacer to maintain an identical overlap between them and checking that each is vertical with a spirit level. When you are six boards from the last post, measure how much space you have left and increase or decrease the overlap of the last few boards so that you meet the outer edge of the post neatly.

3 Run the capping strip across the top of the featheredge boards. Nail it in place using galvanised nails. If you find the wood is splitting, drill pilot holes before nailing.

Closeboard fencing on a slope

f you need to erect a closeboard fence on a slope, keep the posts and eatheredge boards vertical, but slope the arris rails evenly parallel to the round. When the boards are all in place, saw them across top and bottom n a line parallel to the arris rails. Finish the top of the fence with capping.

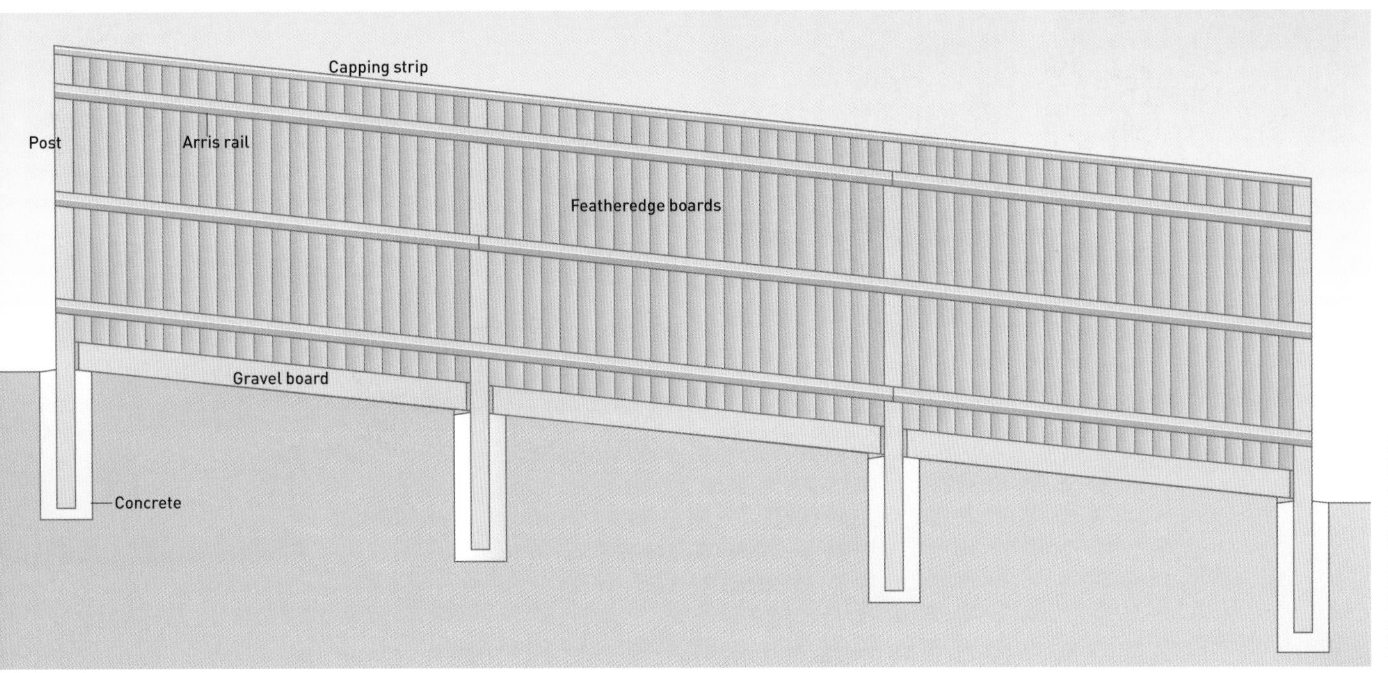

YOU CAN DO IT

Galvanised brackets

Another method of building a closeboard fence is to fix the arris rails in place using specially made galvanised brackets. These allow you to use standard fence posts without needing to cut

mortises to hold the arris rails. The brackets come ready-drilled with holes for nailing them in place. End brackets have additional flanges through which they are nailed to posts. These brackets are also ideal for reinforcing a broken arris rail.

B&Q

STRUCTURES BUILDING A PERGOLA

A pergola is basically an open roof set on posts or columns. Netting or trellis can be fixed to its timbers to encourage trailing plants such as wisteria or honeysuckle to spread up and over it and provide welcome shade in a sunny patch. Position it at the entrance to a garden, over a pathway or against a wall to shade a seating area or frame an ornament. If you want to pave the area beneath, it's best to do so after the structure is erected.

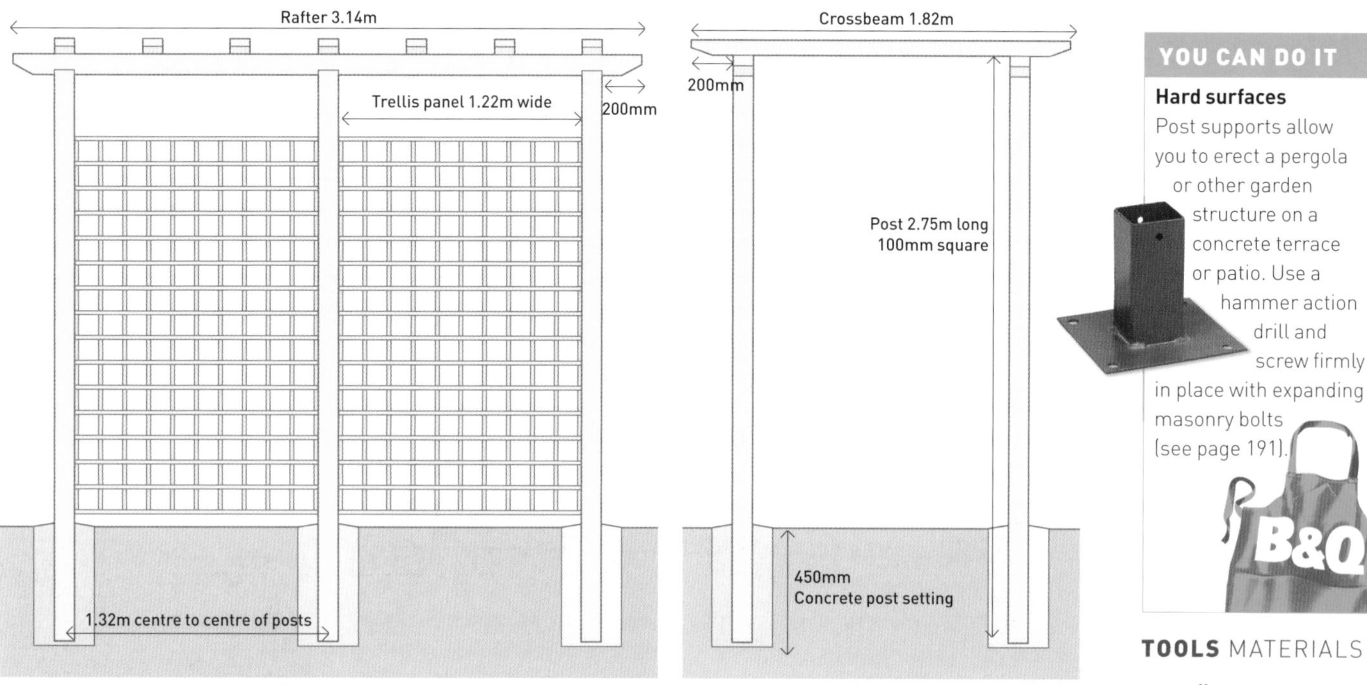

Side view

Front view

YOU CAN DO IT

Hard surfaces

Post supports allow you to erect a pergola or other garden structure on a concrete terrace or patio. Use a hammer action drill and screw firmly in place with expanding masonry bolts (see page 191).

TOOLS MATERIALS

- **pencil**
- **panel saw**
- **wood chisel**
- **mallet**
- **power drill with twist bits**
- **hammer**
- **try square**
- **spirit level**

- 6 posts 2.75m x 100mm x 100mm
- 2 rafters 3.14m x 100mm x 100mm
- 7 crossbeams 1.82m x 100mm x 75mm
- 4 trellis panels 1.83m x 1.22m
- cement and aggregate or post cement
- 65mm and 125mm galvanised nails
- timber props

Building a pergola

Pergolas can be bought in kit form but are also relatively easy to construct from scratch using treated softwood. Be sure to paint the cut ends of the timbers and the feet of the posts with wood preservative before you start.

1 Lay the three upright posts for one side of the pergola on the ground. Cut two lengths of timber to 1.22m and use them to mark the correct distance between the uprights, top and bottom.

2 Lay a rafter in position, jutting 200mm from the edges of the outer posts. Mark the outline of the post tops on the rafter. Since the timbers may not be identical, number each upright and the rafter in pencil so you can match them up again. Repeat this process with the other side of the pergola.

3 Mark up the rafter for a 25mm deep slot or housing for the top of each post. Saw down the side of the housing.

4 Cut out the housing with a wood chisel and mallet. It should be a neat, tight fit.

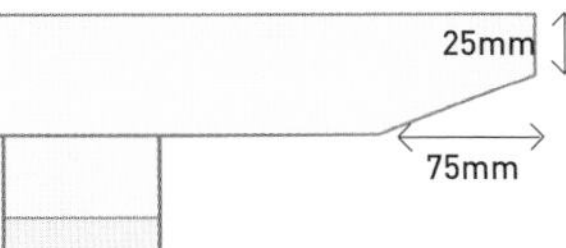

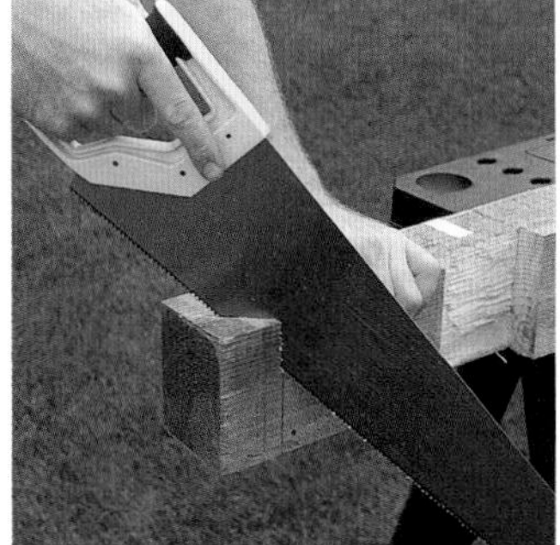

5 Profile the ends of the rafters and crossbeams. Measure 25mm down from the top and 75mm in from the outer edge. Draw a line between the points with a pencil and extend it square down the adjacent faces of the timber. Saw off the marked wedge. Or design a decorative profile of your own.

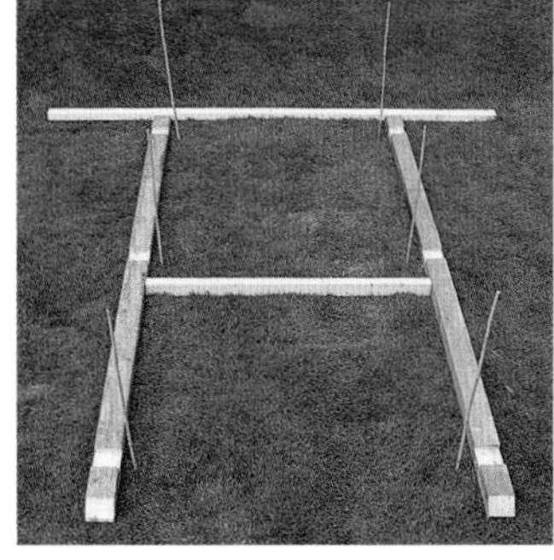

6 Use the rafters as a guide to mark out the post holes. Square their ends with a length of timber and line them up exactly parallel using a 1.32m measure. This will give you the precise position for the centre of each post hole. Mark with canes, remove the timbers, and dig the holes to a depth of 450mm.

7 Fit the posts into the housings in the rafters. Drill pilot holes and then secure with two 125mm galvanised nails.

YOU CAN DO IT

A tight fit

The posts should fit tightly into the housing in the rafters and you will need to tap them in with a wooden mallet. To avoid bruising the wood, hold an off-cut of timber between the mallet and rafter.

8 Use the 1.22m length of wood to space the uprights accurately and a try square to check they are square to the rafter. Then brace the structure with three lengths of timber.

9 Raise one side of the pergola into the post holes and prop it up with temporary supports. Double check that the posts are vertical, in line with each other and the rafter is level.

10 Raise the other side of the pergola and use a spirit level to make sure both rafters are at the same height. You may have to adjust the depth of the holes. Concrete the posts in and leave to set for 48 hours.

Fitting cross bars and trellis

Trellis is optional on a pergola, but it will help plants to climb.

1 Rest three crossbeams across the rafters at the post positions and nail into position. Then nail the remaining four crossbeams in place, evenly spaced between the first three.

2 Drill pilot holes and nail the first trellis panel into position using 65mm galvanised nails, remembering to leave a gap between the bottom of the trellis and the soil to avoid rot.

3 Complete by nailing the final three trellis panels in place.

DECKING THE BASICS

A deck is essentially an open-air extension of your living space. Freestanding or built against a wall, it can be a place for barbecues or outdoor entertaining, a surround for a pool or sandpit, a play area for children or simply a place to relax outdoors. It can also create an ideal surface for an urban roof garden. A deck may also be a solution to a garden problem – occupying a shady area where the grass won't grow, for example, or levelling a slope and so removing the need for expensive landscaping.

Are decks easy to build?

Yes! You really don't need to be a carpenter to build a deck – only basic skills are required. Just make sure you plan very carefully and check and re-check all measurements both at the planning stage and as you build. A second pair of hands will often be useful. Decking timbers are pressure-treated softwood carrying a fifteen-year guarantee against rot or insect attack, but do remember to treat any cut timber ends with end-grain preserver.

Designing your deck

Start by drawing up a simple plan of the house and garden and mark where you intend to build the deck. The south-facing side of the house will give you maximum sunshine, but if that isn't an option, build it where it will be of most use. Take into account the view from the deck, privacy (your own and your neighbours'), access to the garden and proximity to the house.

If your deck adjoins the house make sure the exit door opens over it easily. Check for any amenities your deck will obscure such as a drain cover and if necessary install a hinged trap door to allow future access. You can always build around a tree – just remember to give it enough room to grow and to move with the wind. If necessary install temporary deck boards around the trunk that can be removed as it thickens.

An oversize deck can overwhelm a house. Planning permission may be required. If in doubt, always discuss your plans with the local Building Control office, since local restrictions can vary. And it may be a good idea to let your neighbours know too.

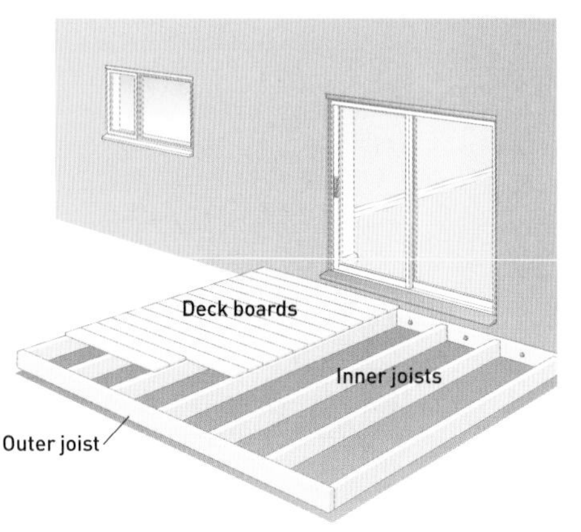

Simple ground-level deck

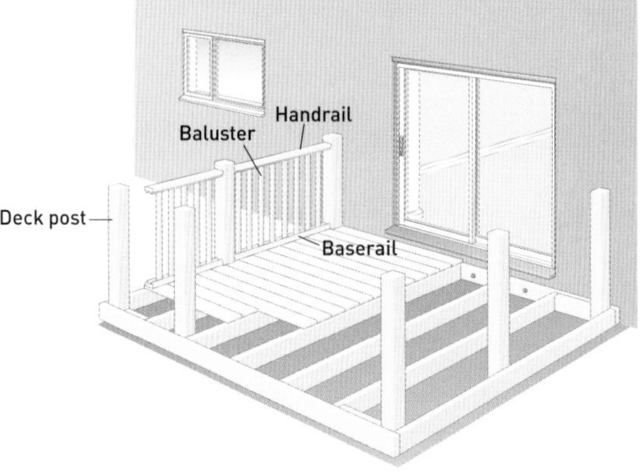

Ground-level deck with balustrade

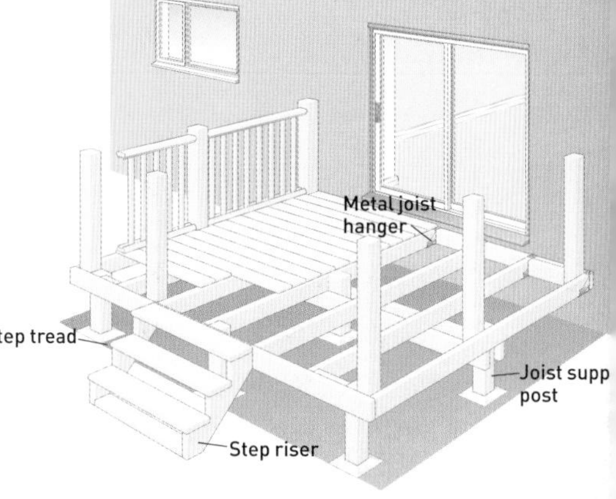

Elevated deck with balustrade and steps

Balustrade, steps and skirting

To make a deck safer and give it some style you can add posts and a balustrade. For peace of mind, fit a gate to stop children or pets straying.

Pre-cut treads and risers make easy work of adding steps to an elevated deck. A handrail will help prevent falls, and is essential if you have more than five steps, or they rise more than 600mm from the ground. Finally, if you don't need to use the space under an elevated deck for garden storage, you can finish it off with attractive latticed panels. Fit fine wire mesh behind them to prevent leaves and garden debris collecting beneath the deck.

DECKING A GROUND-LEVEL DECK

TOOLS MATERIALS

- **tape measure**
- **builder's line**
- **wooden pegs**
- **hammer**
- **spade**
- **straightedge**
- **spirit level**
- **pencil**
- **protective gloves**
- **safety goggles**
- **panel saw or circular saw**
- **dust mask**
- **power drill with twist and countersink bits**
- **jigsaw, if required**
- **screwdriver**
- **socket set for coach screws and bolts**
- **paintbrush**

- building membrane
- gravel
- quick-drying concrete, if required
- damp-proof course, if required
- deck joists
- coach screws
- coach bolts
- 50mm or 63mm deck or galvanised screws (depending on thickness of deck boards)
- abrasive paper
- deck boards
- end-grain preserver

A simple deck at ground level is a straightforward project – a perfect starting point if you are not completely confident of your carpentry skills. You can always add on features like posts and balustrade later. A walkway made from patio tiles looks great, and will prevent turf being worn away if your deck is accessed from a lawn.

Deck boards

Deck boards are laid with a 3mm gap between to allow rainwater to run through. Reversible deck boards can be laid smooth or ridged side uppermost, or you can combine the two finishes for decorative effect. The easiest way to arrange them is at right angles to the supporting joists – but you don't have to. Decide on the pattern before you start, as the choice will affect the spacing and number of joists.

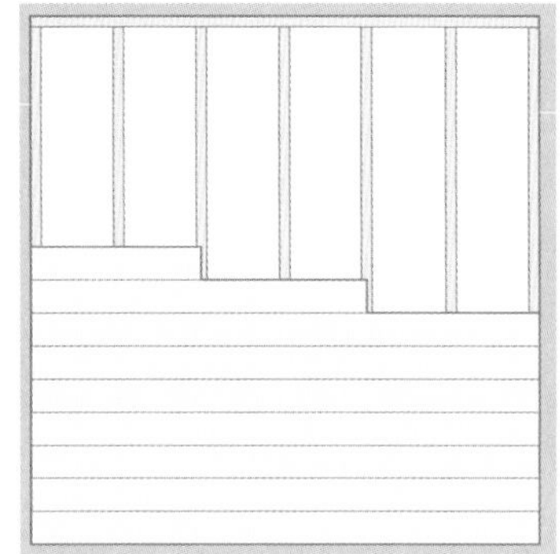

Horizontal
For standard right-angled decking, measure 400mm between the centre of one supporting joist and the next.

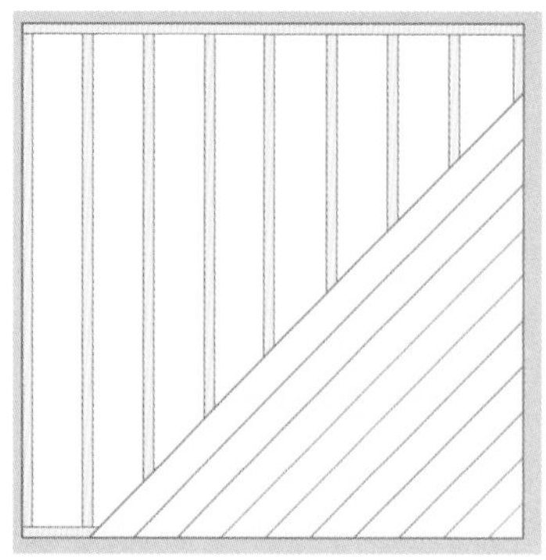

Diagonal
Boards laid diagonally need joists spaced 300mm centre-to-centre for the structure to be secure.

Chevron
For a chevron pattern, joists should measure 300mm centre-to-centre and you must lay a double joist where the boards meet in order to have space to fix them securely.

Preparing the site

A ground-level deck must be laid on even, level ground. Once you have decided on the size and location of your deck, mark out the area with pegs and builder's lines.

1 Clear away any turf, plants or weeds, taking care not to disturb any drains or underground cabling. Use a straightedge and spirit level to check that the whole area is level, and level out any slight unevenness in the ground.

2 To stop weeds growing back, cover the area in a layer of black building membrane and then 40mm–50mm of gravel.

Decking on damp ground

If drainage is a problem in your garden, you must raise your deck off the ground on concrete pads topped with a layer of damp-proof course. Dig holes roughly 150mm square and 150mm deep at intervals of 1.2m around the deck. Fill the holes with quick-drying concrete to just above ground level. Use a spirit level and straightedge to level the pads top-to-top while the concrete is still semi-dry. When it is dry, cover the whole area with black building membrane (making cut-outs for the concrete pads) and a layer of gravel. Finally, cut squares of damp-proof course to sit between the concrete and the decking timbers.

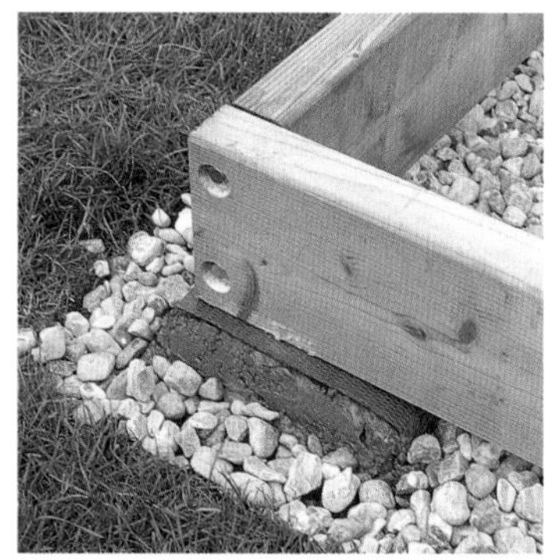

Assembling the deck

Even a small deck will be very heavy, so do build it on site. A ground-level deck is basically an elevated deck without the deck support posts. Begin by assembling the sub-frame – the outer and inner joists – and then screw down the deck boards. Remember when measuring and cutting the outer joists that the timbers will overlap at the corners.

1 Drill holes and assemble the sub-frame with two countersunk coach screws at each corner and two through the outer frame into each end of all the inner joists. If you want to join the deck frame to a building (see page 202) or add balustrade, do so before laying the deck boards.

2 Use two deck screws or galvanised screws to fix the deck boards to every joist along the sub-frame. If you are using deck screws, you don't need to drill pilot holes; if galvanised screws, you do. Deck boards must be spaced 3mm apart to allow for drainage and expansion. A 3mm gauge deck screw makes an ideal spacer.

3 Position joins between deck boards exactly halfway across a joist, so that both boards can be screwed into it. Stagger the joins for greater strength, and arrange them in a regular pattern for an attractive finish.

4 Remember to coat all the cut ends with end-grain preserver.

SAFETY FIRST

Wear gloves and safety goggles when sawing timbers. Make sure the work area is well ventilated and wear a mask to avoid breathing sawdust. Always unplug power tools when not in use. Do not burn off-cuts of treated wood – the smoke and ash are toxic; dispose of them as ordinary household waste.

YOU CAN DO IT

Joining joists

If you are extending your deck further than the length of a joist, you will need to join lengths. Clamp the joist sections end-to-end in a work-bench. Place a joist off-cut about 600mm long across the join and clamp it temporarily to the joists. Secure it with eight coach bolts sunk from the outside of the frame. When joining lengths of internal joist, which will be hidden by the deck boards, use two 600mm sections of joist off-cut, sandwiched either side of the join.

A walkway of patio tiles

A series of patio tiles is a quick and easy way to construct an attractive walkway. The frame comes in a kit form, is simple to assemble and available in a variety of sizes. The corresponding patio tiles slot into place. You could lay it over a bed of gravel and builder's membrane to deter weeds.

TOOLS MATERIALS

- **power drill with twist bits**

- deck frame
- 50mm deck or galvanised screws
- patio tiles

1 Fit the frame together with deck screws or galvanised screws.

2 Add the cross-bars to the frame. The wooden struts are rebated to hold the tiles.

3 Drop the patio tiles in each of the square frames, creating an alternate or continuous pattern with the patio tiles as you wish. The frame will hold the tiles in place, but for a more secure structure and to prevent the tiles warping screw each one down using four deck screws per tile.

DECKING BUILDING AN ELEVATED DECK

An elevated deck is a great way to take advantage of sloping or uneven land, and it will make an attractive and highly versatile addition to your house. Add balustrade, skirting, and steps for even greater usefulness and effect.

ECO TIMBER

Before buying timbers always check for the FSC symbol. That way you can be sure that they come from a sustainable source certified by the Forest Stewardship Council.

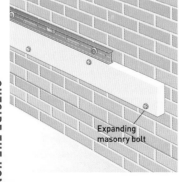

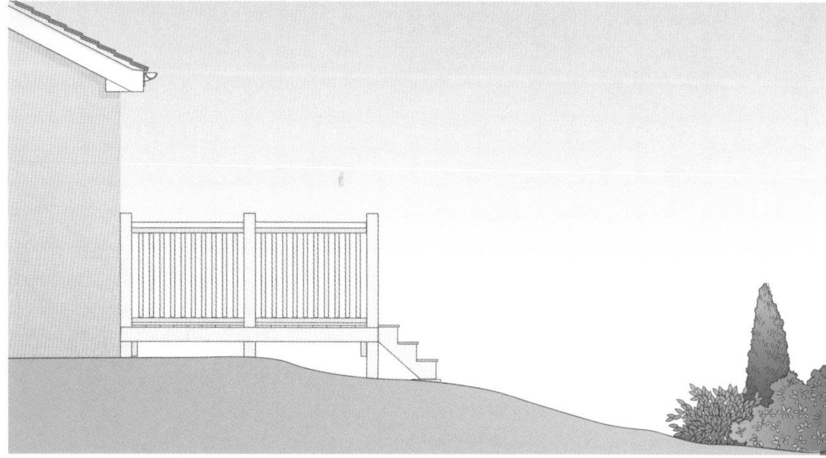

TOOLS MATERIALS

- **tape measure**
- **mallet**
- **builder's line**
- **spade**
- **protective gloves**
- **safety goggles**
- **dust mask**
- **panel saw or circular saw**
- **socket set for coach screws and bolts**
- **hammer**
- **line level**
- **spirit level**
- **builder's square**
- **pencil**
- **power drill with twist and wood bits**
- **workbench**
- **screwdriver**
- **quick-release clamps**
- **jigsaw**

- wooden pegs
- deck joists
- expansion bolts, if required
- 25mm x 100mm lengths of timber for profiles
- joist support posts
- quick-drying concrete
- building membrane
- gravel
- end-grain preserver
- metal joist hangers and 50mm galvanised nails
- coach screws
- deck posts
- handrail and baserail
- balusters
- 50mm or 63mm deck screws or galvanised screws (depending on thickness of deck boards)
- masking tape
- 12mm wooden dowels, 75mm long
- exterior wood adhesive
- deck boards

YOU CAN DO IT

Elevated decking on concrete

If part of your elevated deck extends over concrete, you don't have to take the concrete up. Instead position the posts in metal post supports, screwed down with expanding masonry bolts (see page 191). When marking out the site use chalk instead of pegs, and when squaring it drive in the wooden profiles beyond the concrete (even if this is some distance from the site).

Preparing the site

Begin by clearing away all vegetation, rocks and any trees not featuring in your deck design, taking care not to disturb any drains or underground cabling. If the site is lawned, take up the turf and make sure there is adequate drainage (see page 233).

According to your deck plan, measure out the site and hammer in four wooden pegs at each of the corners. Run a builder's line from each of the four pegs. This will help you visualise the site. Use a spade to lift the turf in manageable strips. Save some turf for making good around the site later. Level off the earth where necessary if the site is not quite flat.

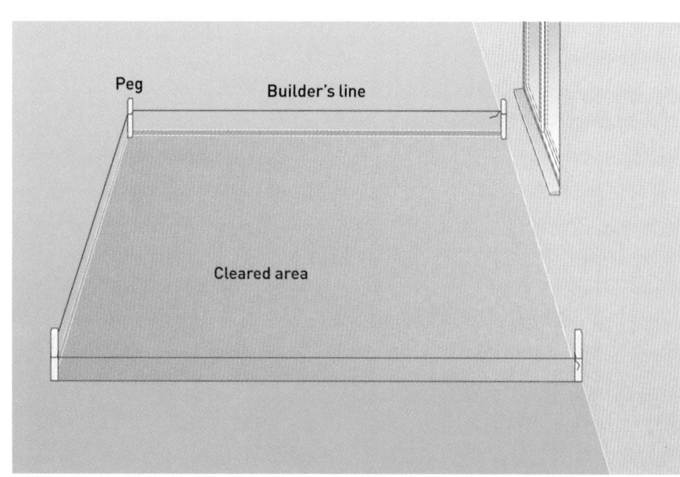

Attaching a deck to a building

If you decide to adjoin your deck to the house, be careful not to block off any air bricks or interfere with the damp-proof course. You need to fix one joist directly to the masonry and then set out the rest of the sub-frame in alignment with it. Drill holes at 400mm intervals along the length of this joist. Arrange the holes alternately at the top and bottom so as not to weaken the joist, and make sure they do not coincide with the eventual positions of the joist hangers (see page 204). Check the joist is level and make a mark on the wall through each hole. Remove the board and drill through the masonry at the marked points. Place the board back in position and insert expanding masonry bolts (see page 191) into each of the holes, remembering to include the washers, and tighten with a spanner.

Expanding masonry bolt

IDEAL TOOL

Line level

This is a quick and easy method of checking that a line is level. Stretch the line taut and hang the level from a central position to take a reading.

1 Make timber profiles to help you set out the deck sub-frame accurately. Cut three 600mm lengths of 25mm x 100mm timber for each profile. Two of them will form stakes that are driven into the ground; the third is a crosspiece. Cut the stakes to a point at one end and nail the crosspiece 50mm from the top of the stakes.

Squaring the site

Time spent on careful measuring at this stage is well worth it in the long run. Use the 3–4–5 triangle method (see below) to ensure that the corners are accurate and the finished deck looks professional.

2 Take up the pegs and lines and hammer two profiles into the ground at each corner, about 450mm beyond the cleared area. Run a builder's line from each profile to its opposite and tie it taut. Place a line level in the middle and hammer the profiles in until you get a level reading. Use a spirit level to ensure each crossbeam is level.

3 To check that the lines are crossing directly at the corners, first lay a joist along the edge of the cleared area to represent the edge of the sub-frame. Then stand a spirit level vertically against it at the corner. Adjust the position of the lines on the profiles until they cross directly above the corner of the cleared deck area.

YOU CAN DO IT

Corner to corner
As a final check, measure the diagonal distances from corner to corner. If they are the same, then each corner will be a right angle.

4 Use the 3–4–5 triangle method to square the corners, making any adjustments by sliding the string along the profiles. When the lines are perfectly level and square, mark the position of the string on each crosspiece with a pencil. Move it to one side and make a saw cut or hammer in a nail at the pencil mark. Then tie the line firmly in position.

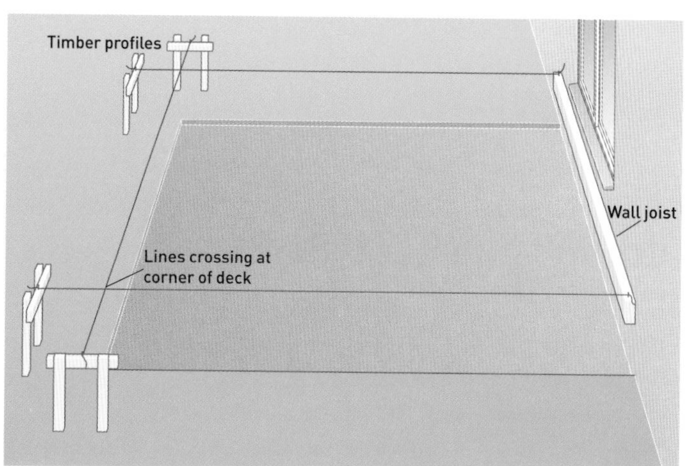

3–4–5 triangle

It is vital at this stage of the project that the sides of the deck are square to each other. The easiest way to achieve this is by the 3-4-5 triangle method, which uses simple geometry to create perfect right angles at the corners. In a triangle with sides exactly 3, 4 and 5 metres long, a right angle will form at the corner where the shorter sides meet. Any multiples of 3, 4 and 5 will follow the same pattern.

First ensure that the lines between the profiles cross directly above the four corners of the site – use a spirit level or run a plumb line down to check that they do. Then either use a wooden builder's square (see page 217) or measure and stick masking tape 900mm from the corner on one line and 1200mm from the corner on the other. When the diagonal distance between these two marks measures exactly 1500mm, the corner is a true right angle. Make any necessary adjustments by sliding the string along the profiles.

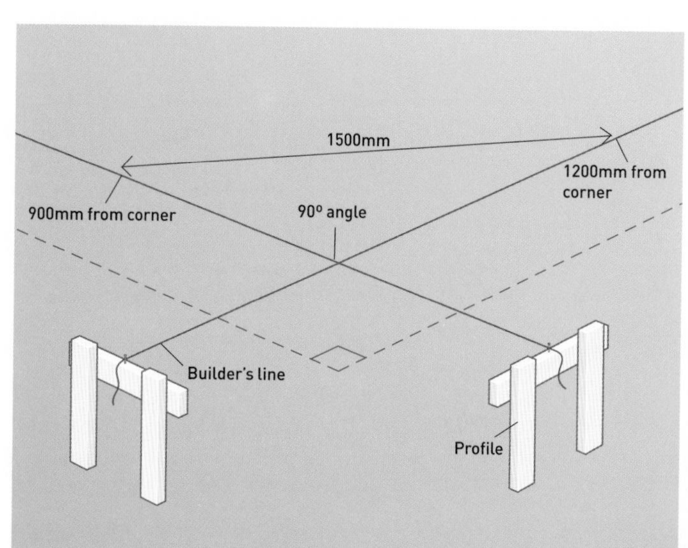

Fixing the joist support posts

An elevated deck is raised on joist support posts. The corner posts don't sit right in the corners of the sub-frame but are offset by the width of a post to allow deck posts to be slotted in later. A lot of the work at this stage requires two pairs of hands.

1 Dig out 600mm deep holes for each of the joist support posts. Ideally the holes need to be about 300mm in diameter at the top and 400mm at the bottom. The gap between the centre of one post and the centre of the next must be a maximum of 1.2m. The corner posts should not be right in the corners but offset to one side (it doesn't matter which) by the width of a post.

2 Place the post in the hole and check it is vertical using a spirit level. Hold the post in position with temporary supports and pour quick-drying concrete into the hole.

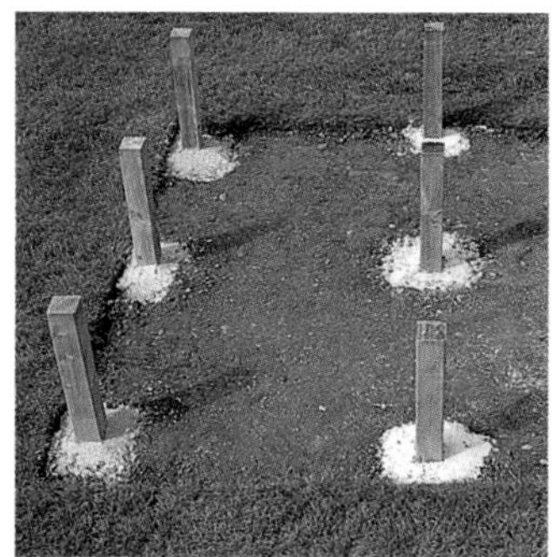

3 When all the posts are in place and the concrete is firm, remove the lines and profiles.

4 Fit a sheet of black building membrane around the posts and cover it with gravel to stop weeds growing through and allow water to drain away. Then allow the concrete to set for 48 hours before building the sub-frame.

Building the joist sub-frame

The sub-frame forms the deck's outer skeleton. Remember that joists run in the opposite direction to the deck boards, so decide now which way you would like the deck boards to run.

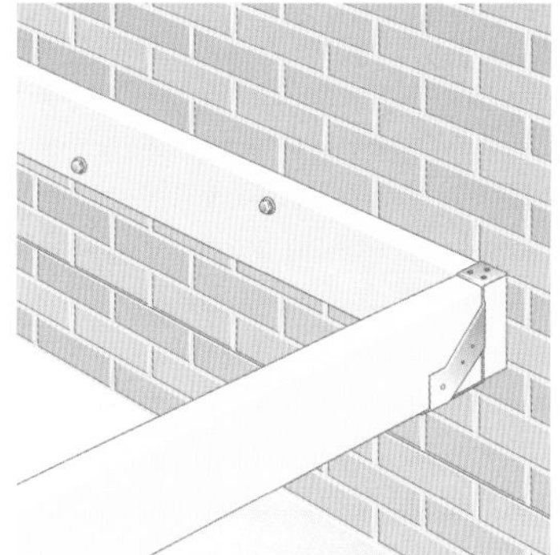

1 Cut the outer joists of the sub-frame to length, remembering to allow for overlapping corner joints. Paint the cut ends with end-grain preserver. Attach the sub-frame joists to the wall joist with metal joist hangers and 50mm galvanised nails.

2 Fix the side joists to the off-set corner posts, first checking that they are level. They need to protrude by the width of a deck post. Drill holes through the joist into the post and attach with two countersunk coach screws. Drive in two more coach screws at the corner to join the outer joists together.

3 Continue round the deck fixing the joists to each post with two countersunk coach screws.

4 To give extra strength to the sub-rame, screw two support beams onto every second post along the ength of the deck. Position them mmediately beneath the joists of the sub-frame.

5 Cut the inner joists to length and attach to the joist sub-frame with two countersunk coach screws at either end, or to the wall joist using joist hangers. If you plan to lay the deck boards in a horizontal pattern, the distance between the centre of one joist and the next should be 400mm; for diagonally laid boards, measure 300mm.

YOU CAN DO IT

Bowed joists

If you find that any of your joists bow, fix them with the bow projecting upwards. Even if you don't notice an obvious bowing, check the joists are level with the sub-frame using a straightedge and if necessary plane any excess to ensure the deck boards will lie flat.

B&Q

Fitting a balustrade

Attach railings to a deck after you have built the sub-frame but before you lay the deck boards. Work out how high you would like the railings to be and cut the balusters down to size if necessary, bearing in mind that for safety the handrail must be between 900mm and 1m above the finished deck and the base rail a maximum of 75mm. Don't forget to allow space beneath the baserail for the deck boards.

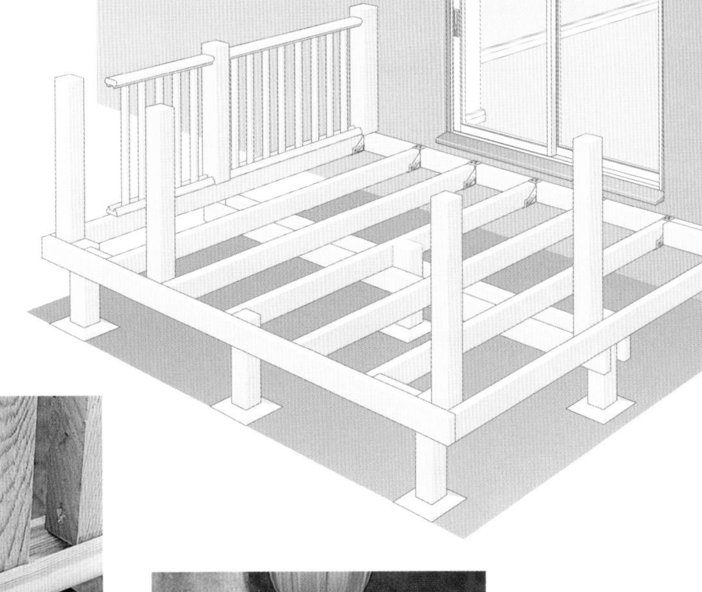

1 Decide how to space the deck posts (remembering they should be a maximum of 1.2m apart) and cut the base- and handrails exactly to length. Clamp a length of baserail in a workbench and drill pilot holes 100mm apart (or less if you decide you want your balusters more closely spaced) all the way through the rail.

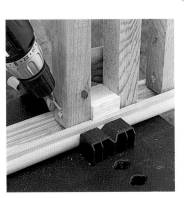

2 Slot the balusters into the underside of the handrail and secure them by screwing diagonally through the baluster into the rail. For accuracy measure the intervals using a spacer made from a wood off-cut, as shown. Remember the slotted sides of both the rails are fitted facing downwards so that rainwater cannot collect in them.

3 Fit the baserail onto the balusters and screw 50mm deck screws or galvanised screws through the pilot holes into the bottom of each. Use the wooden spacer again to align the balusters precisely.

4 Slot a deck post in the gap between the joist support post and the corner of the sub-frame and hold it in place with a quick-release clamp. Fix the post to the sub-frame with two countersunk coach screws.

5 To make the corner post more secure, fit a piece of joist off-cut between it and the first inner joist, screwed to the sub-frame with deck screws. Then position the next deck post and fix it with just one coach screw for now, so that you can push it to one side while you fix the railings.

IDEAL TOOL

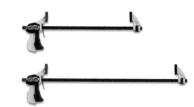

Quick-release clamps
These easy-to-use clamps hold timbers accurately in position while you drill and screw, allowing you to do much of the job without a second pair of hands.

6 Mark a 12mm drill bit with masking tape at 38mm from the tip and drill two holes to that depth on either end of both the hand- and baserails. Fit 12mm wooden dowels into the holes and mark the corresponding positions on the adjoining posts at top and bottom. Then drill 38mm holes in each post at the four marked points.

7 Glue the wooden dowels into the holes and slot the railing assembly into place. Use quick-release clamps to hold the posts and railings together while the glue dries. Then add another coach screw to the base of the second post to secure it.

Laying deck boards

With the railings in place, you are now ready to lay the deck boards. Remember that they must run in the opposite direction to the joists.

1 Begin laying boards at the outer edge of the sub-frame and move inwards. You will have to cut notches in the first board to fit around the deck posts. Cut the board to length and clamp it in position in front of the deck posts, overhanging the sub-frame. Measure and mark the outline of the deck posts accurately on the deck board.

2 Remove the deck board and clamp it firmly to a workbench. Cut out the shape of the deck posts using a jigsaw.

3 Slot the cut deck board into position. If necessary plane or saw down its outer length to ensure that the inner edge is flush with the inside edge of the deck post – this will give you a straight edge from which to lay the rest of your deck boards. Screw the board down into each joist using 50mm or 63mm deck screws or galvanised screws (depending on the thickness of your deck boards).

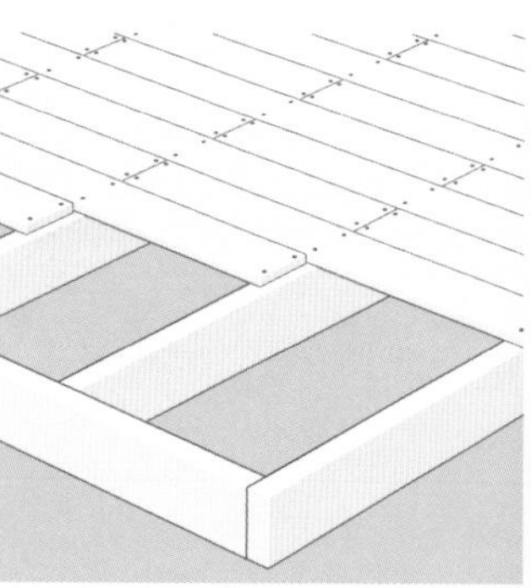

4 Fix each deck board with two screws into every joist before moving on to the next, remembering to leave a 3mm gap between boards. Position joins exactly halfway across a joist – that way both boards can be screwed down into it. Stagger the joins, and for a professional effect arrange them in a regular pattern across the surface of the deck.

Working around existing features

Don't cut down a tree: build your deck around it. All you need do is include a bit more sub-structure to frame the trunk. Simply block off the area around the tree by positioning joist off-cuts between the inner joists, secured either end with two coach screws. Remember to leave enough space for the tree trunk to thicken and for it to sway in the wind. Cut and fix the deck boards to fit around the tree.

Adding a gate

If you have small children or pets, a gate will make your deck a safer place. It's best to use a lightweight gate that can hang from a deck post. If you opt for a ready-made gate this needs to be sourced and measured before you draw up your plans so that you can position the deck posts and steps to fit it. Alternatively you can make a gate yourself or have one made to fit the gap. If you choose a metal gate, these usually come complete with a hinge assembly and automatic latch. For how to fit hinges and a latch to a wooden gate, see pages 190–91.

Fitting skirting panels

On a raised deck, lattice panels can be cut to fit beneath the sub-frame, creating an attractive skirting. Attaching a wire mesh behind the lattice will stop bits of garden debris and small animals from getting under the deck.

TOOLS MATERIALS

- **tape measure**
- **jigsaw**
- **hammer**
- **screwdriver**
- **wire cutters**
- **power drill with twist bits**

- lattice panels
- 30mm galvanised screws
- 75mm deck or galvanised screws
- fine wire mesh
- 20mm wood staples

YOU CAN DO IT

Deck protection
Coat a finished deck or walkway with colourless deck seal, which locks out moisture but still lets the timbers breathe. You can also revive older decking with specially formulated deck cleaner, which removes mildew and dirt and visibly refreshes greying timbers.

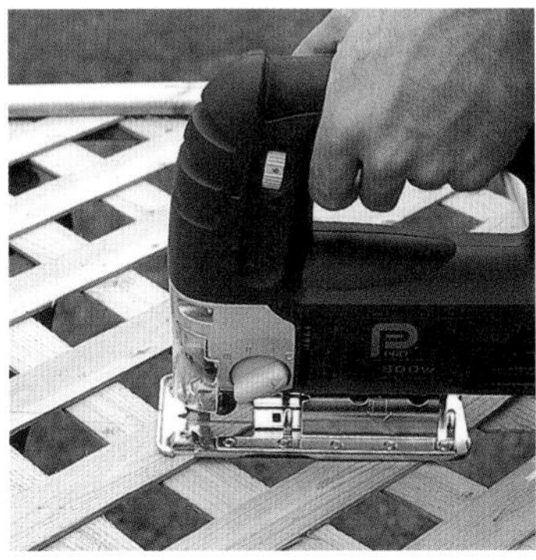

1 Measure from the bottom of your sub-frame to the ground. With a jigsaw, cut the latticed panel to fit these measurements. Remove the frame batten from the discarded section by gently knocking it away from the lattice with a hammer. Then use 30mm galvanised screws to fix it back into place on the lattice that you intend to fit.

2 Measure the lattice panel (within the frame) and cut a section of fine wire mesh with wire cutters to fit. Attach the wire mesh to the batten frame with wood staples and a hammer.

3 Drill pilot holes and screw the upper frame of the panel into the deck sub-frame.

DECKING EXTENDING A DECK

TOOLS MATERIALS

- **screwdriver**
- **goggles**
- **gloves**
- **try square**
- **spirit level**
- **tape measure**
- **pencil**
- **hammer**
- **circular saw or handsaw**
- **mitre block**
- **power drill with twist and countersink bits**
- **2 quick-release clamps**

- joist support posts
- deck joists
- deck boards
- 50mm or 63mm deck screws or galvanised screws (depending on thickness of deck boards)
- metal joist hangers and 50mm galvanised nails
- end-grain preserver
- coach screws
- coach bolts
- deck boards

The flexibility of decking is one of its great joys. As your needs change, you might find your initial deck too small and feel it could benefit from an extension. This is simply a matter of adding on another sub-frame. If your extension runs over a downward slope, you can accommodate the change of level by adjusting the length of the joist support posts and, if you wish, by installing a set of steps to lead down to the garden (see pages 210–11). To extend up a slope, step the deck up by starting the new sub-frame on top of the last.

Extending on the same level

The most straightforward way to enlarge the area of your deck is by extending the sub-frame and boards at the same level. You may need to remove a section of balustrade first.

1 Unscrew the outermost boards along the edge you want to extend to expose two joists. To enlarge the sub-frame, you will need to erect additional joist support posts and fix to them three sub-frame joists defining the extended area. Follow the method detailed on pages 202–5.

2 Fix new deck boards across the exposed joists, staggering the joins between boards. Remember to position the joins halfway across a joist and screw both boards into it. When you reach the edge of the extension, saw off the excess deck boards flush with the sub-frame.

Extending in a new direction

If your extension changes direction or is a walkway to another section of the deck, you may need or want to change the direction of the boards.

1 Attach a new joist to the sub-frame with coach screws. Mark out the area of the extension and erect joist support posts and the remaining sub-frame joists. Nail internal joists to the connecting joist using metal joist hangers. If the deck boards are to lie diagonal to the joists, the joists must be spaced 300mm centre-to-centre; if horizontal, then 400mm centres will suffice.

2 Screw each deck board down with two screws into every joist. If they lie diagonally, clamp each onto a workbench, use a builder's square to mark the ends at a 45° angle, and cut neatly with a circular saw or handsaw. When they are all screwed down, saw the edges in line with the sub-frame.

1 Centre the first joist of the new sub-frame along the edge of the deck – this will provide the step. The joist must be the length of the deck less 150mm (the thickness of two joists and two deck boards). Clamp a joist off-cut across the sub-frame and new joist and secure it with four countersunk coach screws.

Extending with a change in level

If you are building a deck over rising land you may need to step up part of it to accommodate the change in level. Or you might choose to add a new level as a design feature or to access a door. The higher level is achieved by building a new sub-frame on top of the existing one.

2 Build the rest of the new sub-frame as described on pages 202–5. This time the new joist support posts will be higher to accommodate the stepped deck.

3 Attach internal joists to the new sub-frame spaced 400mm centre-to-centre using two countersunk coach screws at either end of each joist. Remember that the deck boards must run in the opposite direction to the joists; here the direction has been reversed for decorative effect.

4 Cut three lengths of deck board to make a fascia that will give a neat finish to the face of the step. Mitre the corner joints for a really professional finish.

5 Cut the deck boards to length and position the first board flush with the face of the step. Secure the boards with two screws into each joist along their full length.

Decking an angled corner

If you want to make your deck really stand out, an angled corner is a striking and easy-to-achieve feature. Both the outer and inner joists of the sub-frame are cut to the required angle, and the deck boards then fitted and cut to match.

1 Using a straightedge or a long spirit level, mark the angle across the outer and inner joists with a pencil. Cut the joists along the line.

2 Measure a length of joist and cut its ends flush with the adjacent joists of the sub-frame. Then screw it to each inner and outer joist with two countersunk coach screws.

3 Lay the deck boards overhanging the angled outer joist and screw them down. Clamp a spare board to the deck to mark the line of the angled corner. Use a circular saw or handsaw to cut the ends of the overhanging boards flush with the sub-frame. Remember to coat all the sawn ends with end-grain preserver.

IDEAL TOOL

Circular saw

A circular saw is extremely useful for cutting through timber. The cordless variety is particularly convenient. You can control the depth of the cut of a circular saw – in this instance, set the blade to cut the depth of a deck board to avoid damaging the edge of the sub-frame.

DECKING STEPS AND RAILS

Unless the deck is at ground level, you will need steps to give easy access to the garden or link different levels within the deck. A handrail and balusters will not only help prevent slips and falls, they will turn a functional stairway into an attractive feature. And if, as you use or extend your deck, you decide you want a balustrade after all, this is easily added on.

TOOLS MATERIALS

- **tape measure**
- **handsaw or jigsaw**
- **power drill with twist bits**
- **hammer**
- **screwdriver**
- **pencil**
- **spanner**

- concrete slabs
- step treads
- 2 step risers
- 75mm coach screws
- joist off-cuts
- 50mm deck or galvanised screws

Steps

The easiest way to build steps is to buy pre-formed components. You will need a set of two risers and as many separate step treads as you require. A basic open stair is all that's necessary but you can build a more solid construction if you prefer.

To prevent steps sinking into soft ground, you need to sit them on a durable surface. Concrete paving slabs are ideal, but any material suitable for a path or terrace will work well – block paving or a bed of gravel on building membrane, for example. Remember to calculate the height of the step riser from the surface of the step support pad.

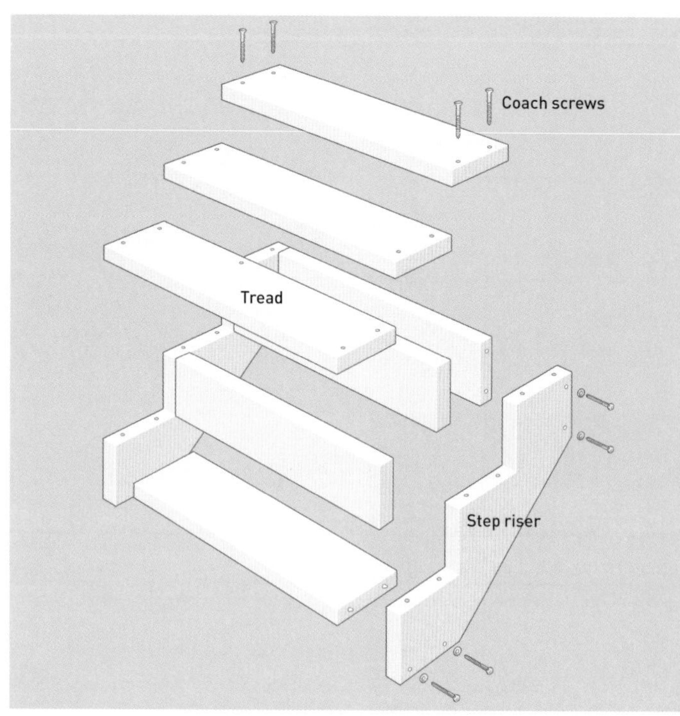

Measuring up

A comfortable width for an average stair is 900mm, but it should not be less than 760mm. If your stair is wider than 900mm you will need a central step riser to support the steps and prevent them buckling. If you do build your own riser, make sure the steps are a comfortable depth – ie not so deep that they are an effort to climb but not so shallow that you trip on them; 150mm–180mm is an ideal height.

1 Cut two sections of joist off-cut to the same width as the step treads. Attach them to the step risers at the top and bottom using two countersunk coach screws on each side.

2 Position the solid step assembly against the sub-frame of the deck and in the centre of the step support pad. Drill pilot holes through the step assembly and the sub-frame joist. Screw the step assembly securely to the sub-frame with four more countersunk coach screws.

3 Screw the treads into the riser supports at either end with two 50mm deck screws or galvanised screws to make a sturdy step.

4 If you would prefer a solid stairway to an open stair, you can fill the gaps with joist off-cuts or deck boards. Simply measure the height and depth of the gap and screw the timber into the step riser with two screws at either end.

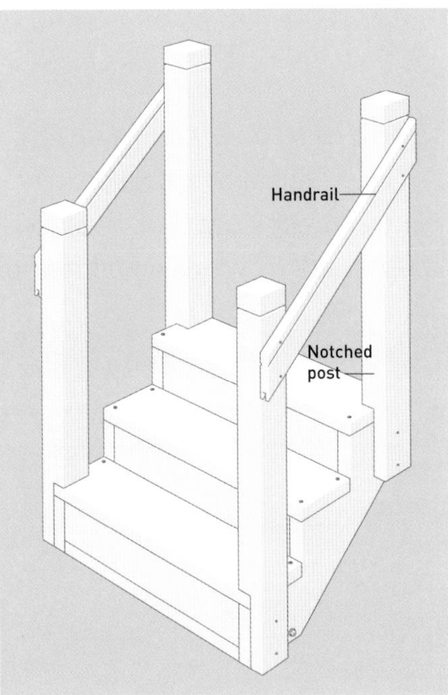

Fitting a handrail to steps

In order to fit handrails to your steps, you first need to fix notched deck posts at the top and bottom. Drive two coach bolts through each into the step riser. Position a length of handrail on the outside face of the posts parallel with the angle of the steps and with a pencil mark the line of the outer edges of the posts. Then cut along this line with a jigsaw. When the handrail is bolted to the posts the edges should be neatly flush.

Balusters

To attach balusters, you will need to fit a baserail in the same way as the handrail. Then cut the balusters to length and screw them in place.

Fitting balustrade to an existing deck

A simple run of hand- and baserails with upright balusters will prevent falls and instantly transform a basic deck into a more elegant feature. Notched posts are specially profiled at the bottom so that they can be attached to a completed deck.

TOOLS MATERIALS

- **tape measure**
- **pencil**
- **jigsaw or handsaw**
- **spanner**
- **quick-release clamp**
- **spirit level**
- **power drill with twist bits**

- notched deck posts
- coach screws
- deck joists
- hand- and baserails
- 50mm or 63 mm deck or galvanised screws (depending on thickness of deck boards)
- timber off-cut

1 Decide how to space the deck posts (no more than 1.2m apart) and fix the first notched post to the sub-frame with coach screws. Measure lengths of joist to sit on the outer face of the sub-frame between deck posts. Attach these with deck screws as you fix the posts. When you reach a corner, measure and cut the length of joist to the outer edge of the sub-frame. Position the corner post on the adjacent side of the sub-frame, overlapping this joist. This will keep the posts in alignment.

2 Measure and cut lengths of handrail, mitring the corners for a neat finish. Clamp a length of handrail into position with its grooved edge facing down. Check it is level with a spirit level, then drill countersunk pilot holes and screw it into the deck posts.

3 Use a baluster, aligned with the groove in the handrail, to determine the position of the baserail. Ensure any gap between the baserail and the decking boards does not exceed 75mm. Clamp the baserail in place and fix to the deck posts with countersunk screws.

4 Position the first baluster, checking it is vertical with a spirit level, and fix it to the hand and baserail with countersunk screws. Use a wood off-cut or, as here, a length of base rail as a spacer to maintain an even distance between balusters. Remember that the maximum gap by law between railings is 100mm. Ensure the spacing of the balusters and deck posts achieves a uniform design.

GARDEN WALLS BRICK AND STONE

A well-built garden wall in brick or stone is more expensive than a fence, but it will weather attractively and last a lifetime. Planning permission is needed for any wall over 1m high on the edge of a public highway and for any freestanding wall over 2m in height. Large retaining walls may need a structural engineer's specification, and in any case shouldn't be attempted without some experience on less ambitious building projects.

The techniques for building a wall are straightforward, but if it is to be strong and stable it is essential that it be properly planned and designed. The design will depend to a large extent on what it is for.

What is the function of your wall?

Garden walls may serve a variety of purposes.

- To retain earth so you can create a terraced area or to stop a steeply sloping bank from collapsing.
- To create a solid barrier adjacent to a highway or footpath, to reduce noise or for privacy.
- To divide a garden into different areas, or provide extra seating around a feature like a terrace or pond.
- To provide a low, solid base on which to erect fencing or build piers to support an overhead structure such as a pergola.

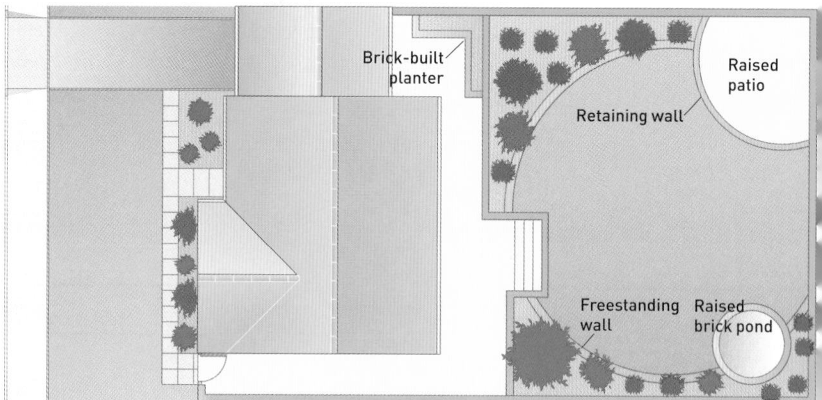

Decorative garden walls

Garden walls can be built from bricks, natural stone or reconstituted stone. There is a large range of reconstituted stone on the market, made from concrete blocks that are finished and coloured to look like stone.

Brick wall

Bricks are the cheapest material and they come in a range of colours, depending on the type of clay they are made from and the manufacturing process. They may also be multi-coloured or mottled and have a rough or smooth texture. Second-hand bricks often have a weathered look that blends with old house walls, but they are not cheap and there is usually no way of knowing whether they are frost-resistant.

Natural stone wall

Natural stone can be bought from quarries or reclamation yards, but it is very expensive. Stone bought in its natural state is classed as random rubble or undressed stone. Semi-dressed stone is cut into fairly uniform blocks with uneven surfaces. Fully dressed stone with machine-cut faces is called Ashlar. The wall pictured above is built with semi-dressed stone.

Semi-dry stone wall

A genuine dry-stone wall is built from stones that are carefully chosen so that they are perfectly stable without needing mortar to bind them together. This wall is a semi-dry stone wall. It looks like a true dry-stone wall but it has hidden mortar joints (see page 222).

Dry-stone effect

This wall is made from reconstituted stone blocks that allow you to create the look of a dry-stone wall at a fraction of the cost or labour of the real thing.

Types of brick

Bricks come in different shapes, sizes and levels of durability. The standard size brick is 215mm x 102.5mm x 65mm, but this can vary by a few millimetres. Most bricks are solid and they may have flat surfaces or a depression, called a 'frog', on one face. Some bricks have holes through them – these are known as perforated or cored bricks.

Facing bricks

These bricks are available in a wide variety of different colours and textures. They are the type of brick most likely to be used for a garden wall.

Common bricks

There are lots of different kinds of common brick, but all are generally cheaper and less attractive than facing bricks. They are usually used where they won't be visible, though they can't be laid below ground.

Engineering bricks

These dense, strong bricks are usually used underground, particularly for foundations or manhole construction. Many facing bricks also have engineering qualities.

TALKING ABOUT BRICKS

Face	Any flat surface of a brick
Bedding faces	The top and bottom faces
Stretcher face	The long side
Header face	The short end
Frog	The indent in one of the bedding faces, used to key the brick to the mortar
Course	A row of bricks
Stretcher course	A row of bricks with stretcher faces outwards
Stretcher	A brick from a stretcher course
Header course	A row of bricks with header faces outwards
Header	A brick from a header course
Single-skin wall	Wall the thickness of a stretcher brick
Double-skin wall	Wall the thickness of two parallel stretchers or one header brick
Coping	The top course of a wall with overhang
Capping	The top course of a wall without overhang
Bond	Interlocking arrangement of bricks in a wall
Bat	A brick cut widthways
Queen closer	A brick cut lengthways

Wall ties

These galvanised metal or stainless steel strips (often butterfly-shaped) are used to bind sections of masonry together. They are laid in the mortar as the wall is built.

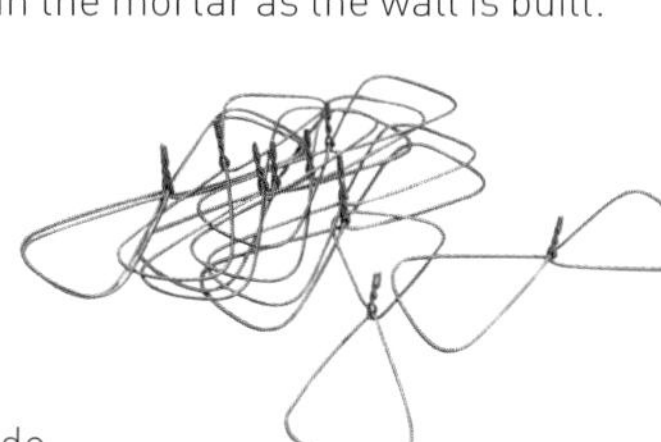

BRICK GRADING AND DURABILITY

F2 category	Completely frost-resistant
F1 category	Moderately frost-resistant
F0 category	Not frost-resistant; for internal use only
S2 category	Low salt content; suitable for most applications
S1 category	Unsuitable for foundations or retaining walls

Specials

Different shaped bricks – known as specials – are made for decorative brickwork, for fitting into corners and angles and for coping, the top course of a wall. Whether of brick or stone, the coping is there not only for decorative reasons but also to ensure that water runs off the wall rather than soaking into it (where it could freeze in winter and cause serious damage). Coping bricks are available in different shapes and widths, some with attractive patterns, to suit walls of all different thickness.They usually project 25mm on each side of the wall and may slope in one or both directions. All coping bricks should be fully frost resistant.

Reconstituted stone

Reconstituted bricks and blocks are available in all kinds of colours and finishes. Buy them either as single blocks or as composite blocks that resemble a number of laid stones.

Keybricks

Keybrick is an innovative system that allows you to create exactly what you want by simply locking the bricks together. No mortar is required. Keybricks can be used to build a low wall, a planter (see page 223) or even a garden bench.

Pitched walling

These reconstituted stones have a rugged, protruding face typical of quarry-dressed stone. You can buy them in a range of natural shades.

Composite dry-stone walling

These slate-effect blocks interlock, making them very straightforward to lay.

Composite block walling

The false joints in these easy-to-lay blocks do not need pointing.

GARDEN WALLS MATERIALS

Choosing the type of material for your garden wall is the start of the process. If you are building a brick wall, you must also decide on the pattern, or bond, for your wall. And whatever material you choose, you will need to make sure you have a suitable mortar.

Choosing walling materials

Your choice of materials for building a garden wall will depend on a number of factors.

- The material your house is built from, and other houses and walls in the immediate vicinity.
- Your budget. Natural stone is by far the most expensive option and prices will vary from region to region. The amount of dressing the stone has received is also reflected in the price – perfectly cut Ashlar stone is more expensive than undressed stone. In order to calculate the cost, a rule of thumb calculation is to allow 1 tonne of stone for about 3.3 sq m of finished stonework. But this is very approximate, as stone varies in size and weight.
- Bricks demand a degree of accuracy when building a wall and are less forgiving than natural stone. Once the basic techniques are mastered, however, brick-building is much quicker than laying stone.
- Reconstituted stone is easy to lay and relatively inexpensive. The stones come in varying sizes, so estimate the number you need by dividing the area of walling by the dimensions of the blocks you plan to use.

Cutting bricks

To build any kind of brick wall you will need to get the hang of cutting bricks. It's not quite as easy as a professional bricklayer can make it look – but it's also not too hard to master. Measure the brick with a ruler and mark the cutting line on all four sides with a pencil. Tap a bolster gently with a club hammer to score along the cutting line all the way around the brick. Then lay it, frog down, on grass or sand and hit the bolster firmly to cut right through it. Always wear safety goggles when cutting bricks or blocks.

Types of bond used in brickwork

A brick wall is constructed of layers of bricks, known as courses, cemented together with mortar. The pattern in which the bricks are built up is known as the bond. The idea of a bond is to stagger the vertical mortar joints so that they are not in the same place in two or more consecutive courses. The wall load is then transmitted along its length, making it stronger and more stable. The three types of bond most often used for garden walls are stretcher bond, English bond and Flemish bond. When estimating the number of bricks for a particular bond, add an extra 5% to allow for cutting bricks and breakages.

Stretcher bond

This is used for a single-skin wall, the thickness of a single brick, and for double-skin walls when they are joined with wall ties. All the bricks are laid lengthways with the long face exposed. Half-bricks (half-bats) complete the end of every other course on a straight wall, so that each vertical joint centres on the bricks above and below. A corner is made by alternating headers and stretchers. You will need approximately 60 bricks per sq m.

English bond

This pattern is formed by laying alternate courses of stretchers and headers. Queen closers inserted before the last header are used to maintain staggered joints at the ends of the wall, and at right-angled corners. You will need approximately 120 bricks per sq m.

Flemish bond

Headers and pairs of parallel stretchers alternate on each course to make a double-skin wall. Queen closers are used on alternate courses to stagger the joints. You will need approximately 120 bricks per sq m.

Mortar

Mortar is what sticks the bricks or stones together in a wall. General-purpose mortars are a mixture of soft sand, lime, cement and water, or soft sand, cement, plasticiser and water. Some masonry cements have plasticiser already mixed with them.

- Plasticisers and frost-proofers create small air pockets in the mix, making it smoother. They are used as a substitute for lime in colder conditions. Frost-proofer gives some protection against freezing but only in the case of slight frosts. Don't build your garden wall in freezing conditions.
- Bags of mortar ready-mixed to the correct proportions are more expensive, but are convenient for smaller jobs.
- Hydrated lime is added to mortar to slow down the drying process, thus preventing cracking. It also makes the mortar much easier to use.
- Always follow the manufacturer's instructions when adding plasticisers to the mix – too much will result in a weak mortar.

SAFETY FIRST

Wear safety goggles, gloves and a face mask when mixing mortar or concrete. Never put your hands or the shovel into a mixer while it is running.

Storing materials

It is important to keep bricks, cement and the materials for mixing mortar dry until you are ready to use them. Bricks, sand and aggregate should all be covered with a plastic sheet. Bags of cement should be raised off the ground and covered with a plastic sheet, or stored indoors.

Mixing mortar

Mortar can be mixed by hand or with a cement mixer; there is no advantage in mixing it by hand unless you only need a small quantity. Mortar should be used within two hours of being made, less in hot weather, so mix as much as you think you can use in that time – as a very rough guide, allow about two minutes to lay each brick. Mix mortar on a level surface, such as a sheet of plywood. If using a mixer, position it on flat ground.

By hand

Thoroughly mix the dry mortar ingredients together. Using a shovel, make a hole in the centre of the pile and pour clean water into it (mixed with plasticiser, if you are using it). Carefully push the dry mix into the water, letting it absorb. Mix it thoroughly, adding more water as necessary. The consistency of the mortar is important – it mustn't be too dry or too runny. To test it, make a depression in the mix with a shovel – if this is easy to do and the mortar holds its shape, the consistency is correct.

In a mixer

Put about a quarter of a bucket of water into the mixer. Add half the sand, then the cement and lime if you are using it. Run the mixer, then add the rest of the sand and more water if necessary. Mix it thoroughly until you have a good consistency.

YOU CAN DO IT

Keep it clean

Don't allow mortar or concrete to dry on your tools. Clean them with a stiff brush from time to time.

Mortar mixes

One 25kg bag sand, with the other ingredients mixed in the proportions shown below, is enough to lay approximately 55 bricks.

MORTAR MIXES

General-purpose mortar (moderate conditions)	1 part cement 1 part lime 6 parts soft sand
Strong mortar (severe conditions)	1 part cement 6 parts soft sand plasticiser
Very strong mortar (exposed to snow, heavy wind and rain)	1 part cement 4 parts soft sand plasticiser

Gauging mortar

For most purposes, mortar ingredients can be measured out with a shovel. But on some types of wall, such as faced brick or pointed stonework, it will spoil the finish if the mortar varies in colour. To prevent this, the mortar is gauged – the proportions of the mix are measured more precisely, using a bucket rather than just a shovel. Draw a line on the inside of a bucket with a felt-tip marker indicating one unit of the mix. Shovel the ingredients in turn into the bucket, making sure each measure is level with the line.

GARDEN WALLS FOOTINGS

TOOLS MATERIALS

- **hammer**
- **builder's line and line pins**
- **saw**
- **spirit level**
- **tape measure**
- **spade**
- **mattock, if required**
- **heavy-duty gloves**
- **club hammer**
- **shovel**
- **wheelbarrow**

- 25mm x 50mm lengths of timber for profiles
- large and small nails
- spray paint (optional)
- cement
- aggregate
- 50mm x 50mm lengths of timber
- plywood shuttering board, if required

Garden walls must always be built on a solid foundation, consisting of a trench filled with concrete. This is known as the footing. The importance of footings can't be overstated – the life expectancy and even the ease with which the wall is built will depend on substantial and accurate footings. When mixing concrete for the footing, don't skimp on materials by adding large stones or blocks – this will weaken it.

Setting out the footing

Before you start marking out the position of the trench, check that the ground is firm and well drained with no obstacles such as pipes or tree roots. The position of the edges of the wall and the edges of the footing are marked with builder's lines.

1 You must use timber profiles to get the footing absolutely straight. Each one is made from three lengths of 25mm x 50mm timber: two are sharpened to a point at one end, and the third is nailed to them as a crosspiece. Hammer a profile into the ground at either end of the site, about 450mm beyond the area to be excavated. Make sure each crosspiece is level and the profiles are at the same height.

2 Gently tap two small nails into the top of the crosspiece of each profile to indicate the width of the wall (in this case, 215mm), and another two beyond these to indicate the width of the footing (in this case, 120mm beyond the wall on each side).

3 Attach builder's lines to the outer nails on the profile – the ones which mark the edge of the footings – and secure the line with pins in the ground. If the footings incorporate a right-angled corner, set two more profiles at right angles to your existing ones. Check that the lines cross at a true right-angle using a builder's square (see opposite).

4 Hold a spirit level vertically against the lines to mark the edge of the footing on the ground. Mark this edge with builder's line nailed into the ground or use spray paint or a line of nails. Remove the above-ground builder's lines so they don't get in the way while you are digging out the trench.

Digging the footing trench

The depth of the footing will depend on the nature of the ground. The chart below is a rough guide in average soil. 'Made up' ground (on a new site, with recently dug-up and put-back soil or filled holes), loose sandy soils and soft clay soils need deeper footings. Particularly soft soils may even need a layer of compacted hardcore on top of geotextile permeable fabric in the bottom of the trench. Allow an additional depth of two bricks above the concrete for replacing the top soil, or to give room to pave against the wall.

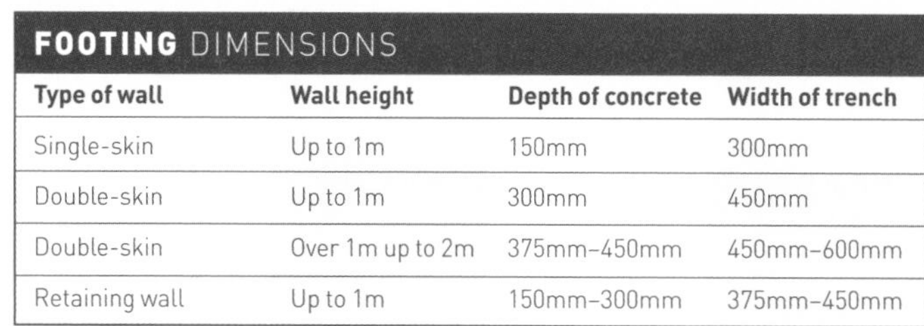

FOOTING DIMENSIONS

Type of wall	Wall height	Depth of concrete	Width of trench
Single-skin	Up to 1m	150mm	300mm
Double-skin	Up to 1m	300mm	450mm
Double-skin	Over 1m up to 2m	375mm–450mm	450mm–600mm
Retaining wall	Up to 1m	150mm–300mm	375mm–450mm

Keep it level and vertical

Use a spirit level to make sure the sides of the footing are vertical. To check the bottom is level, place a long straight piece of wood in the trench and lay a spirit level on top of it.

IDEAL TOOL

Mattock

When you are digging a trench for the footing, the wide blade of a mattock makes short work of breaking up heavy soil, and it is ideal for grubbing out stones or chopping through old tree roots.

Filling the trench

The footing trench is filled with concrete made with five parts mixed aggregate to one part cement. Levelling pegs are driven into the bottom of the trench as a guide to make sure that the trench is filled to the correct level.

IDEAL TOOL

Builder's wheelbarrow
For building tasks such as moving the earth you dig out of the trench or carrying concrete you will need a heavy-duty wheelbarrow. An ordinary garden wheelbarrow is unlikely to be strong enough.

1 Cut pegs from 50mm x 50mm lengths of timber and sharpen them to a point at one end. They should measure the depth of the footing plus enough to ensure the pointed end is solidly held in the bottom of the trench. Hammer in a peg at one end of the trench until it is level with the finished concrete height. Use a spirit level to set further pegs at the same height about 1m apart along the rest of the trench.

2 Pour the concrete and aggregate mix into the trench until it is level with the tops of the pegs. Leave it to set for 48 hours before starting to build the wall.

Stepped footings

When building a wall on a slope, the footing should be stepped, but the concrete must always be level. The step size depends on the slope and the material being used to build the wall; calculate it in multiples of the depth of a course. Make each step by placing a length of plywood shuttering board across the trench; secure it with a length of wood attached to pegs on either side and pour concrete behind it to make the higher step.

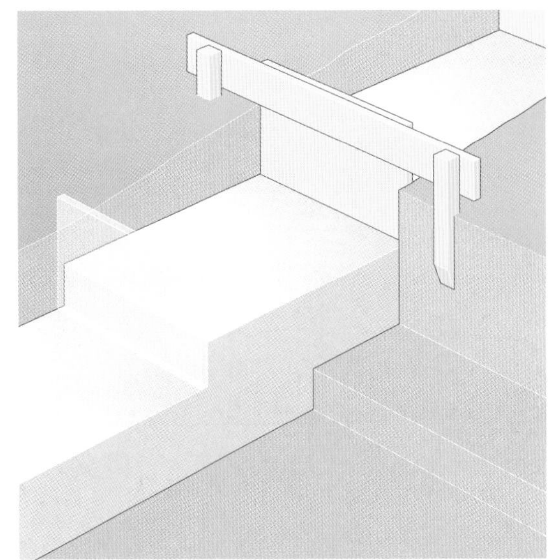

Make your own bricklaying guides

Gauge rod

A gauge rod is used for checking that each course of bricks is the correct height. Make one from a length of timber batten and mark it every 75mm (65mm for the depth of the brick plus 10mm for the mortar between each course).

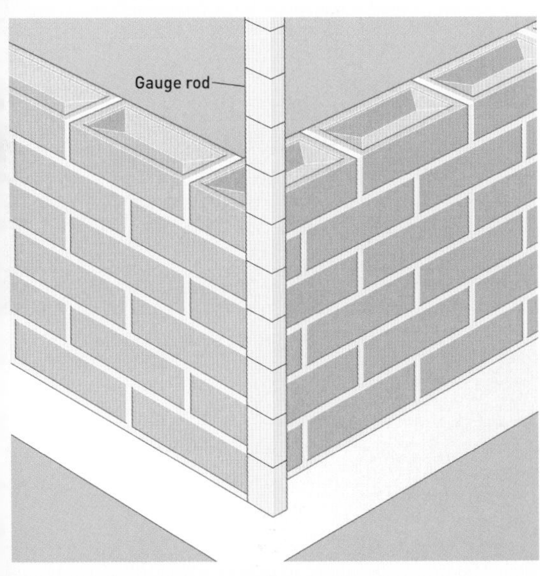

Builder's square

A builder's square is a large set square used for making sure right-angled corners in brick or stone walls are completely accurate. It is based on the simple geometry of the 3-4-5 triangle (see page 203). You need three lengths of wood about 50mm wide and 20mm thick. Mark one piece 450mm from one end, the second 600mm and the third 750mm. Nail the first two pieces at right angles, then align the third piece between the marks. Nail it in place and saw off the excess wood, then reinforce the right-angled corner with a piece of hardboard.

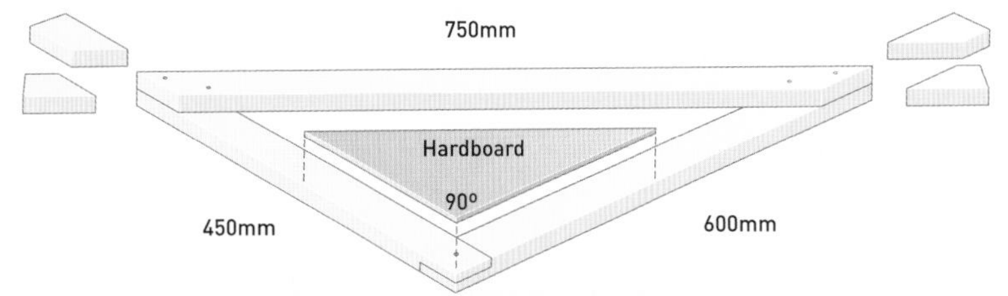

Setting out the first course

The wall built here is a double-skin brick wall using stretcher bond. The two skins are tied together with wall or butterfly ties. Use engineering bricks for the first two courses, below ground level, and frost-resistant F category bricks above ground. Mix up the mortar (see page 215) and put it on a board supported on bricks (known as a 'spot' board) at a convenient distance from the wall. Wet the board first, to stop the mortar sticking to it.

TOOLS MATERIALS

- **builder's line and line pins**
- **short and long spirit levels**
- **trowel**
- **pencil**
- **gauge rod**
- **builder's square**
- **jointing tool or roller tool and blades**
- **medium-soft banister brush**

- straight length of timber
- mortar
- engineering and frost-proof bricks
- galvanised or stainless steel wall ties (twist or butterfly type)
- thin card

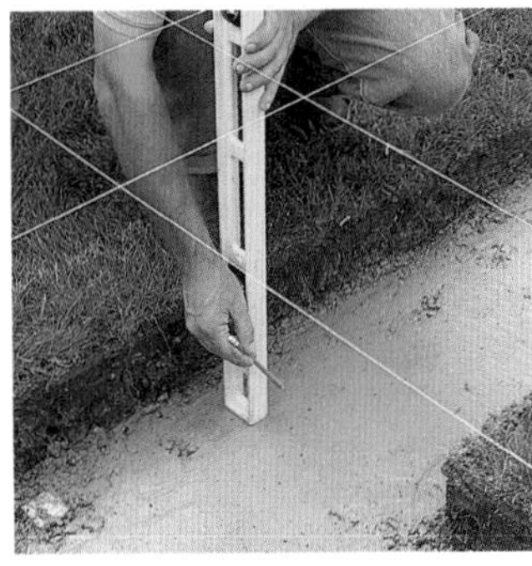

1 Attach lines to the inner nails on the profiles (those marking the edge of the wall). Hold a spirit level vertically against the lines and mark the outer edge of both skins of brickwork on the concrete. Join the marks using a length of timber as a straightedge.

2 Place a trowel full of mortar on the footing at the corner or end-of-line mark for the outer skin. Drag the point of the trowel towards you through the mortar, making a furrow in the centre. Lay the first brick, frog-side up if it has one. Level this brick along its length and across its width, using a spirit level.

3 Use a long spirit level to set another brick in position about a metre away from the first. This is a temporary brick and can be repositioned later. Continue along the line, checking that the bricks are level, until you can set the end-of-line brick in position.

4 Drive two line pins into the ground at each end of the wall, then stretch a builder's line between them as a levelling guide. (If you have a laser level – see IDEAL TOOL page 220 – you can use it to quickly level from one end of the wall to the other.) Then fill in the gaps in the first course, following the bricklaying techniques below. Move the temporary bricks as necessary.

5 Repeat the process to set out the first course of the inner skin. Use a builder's square to check corners are true right angles.

Basic bricklaying techniques

Use your gauge rod to ensure that the mortar in every joint between the bricks is 10mm thick – you'll get better at judging this with practice. From time to time, check the wall is vertical and level with a spirit level.

1 Scoop up a sausage shape of mortar and shape it to roughly the size of the trowel blade. Slide the trowel underneath the mortar and transfer it to the top course of bricks. Using the flat back of the trowel, stretch the mortar along five or six bricks then make a furrow in the centre with the point of the trowel. Remove any mortar overhanging the edge of the bricks.

2 Pick up a brick with one hand and apply mortar to the end of it with the trowel.

3 Push the brick into the mortar and give it a tap with the trowel handle. Aim for 10mm-wide horizontal and vertical joints. If a brick is too low, remove it and add more mortar. Lay the top front edge of the brick to the line but not quite touching it.

4 Scrape away any excess mortar from the front of the wall with a quick upwards movement with the edge of the trowel.

Building corners

Once the first course is in place, the corners and ends of the wall are laid next as a series of steps.

At each right-angled corner, ıy three bricks in each direction nd build up the corners with a eries of five or six steps. Check ıe height of each course with a auge rod.

2 Use the spirit level to make sure the wall is vertical and the builder's square to check that the corner is a true right-angle. To tie the two skins of the wall together, lay metal wall ties at intervals in the mortar. They should be no more than 900mm apart on the horizontal plane and 450mm apart on the vertical plane. (English and Flemish bonds do not require wall ties.)

3 Check that the steps are aligned by holding a straightedge or spirit level against the sides of the wall. Once the corners and ends are done, you can build the straight sections. Push two line pins into vertical joints at each end of the wall, then stretch a bricklayer's line between them as a guide to level the top of the second course. Raise the line as you complete each course. Fill the join between the two skins with mortar as you lay the courses.

YOU CAN DO IT

Builder's line

When using a builder's line, bend a small, thin piece of card in two, wrap it around the line and rest a brick on top. This will keep the line exactly on the edge of your bricks.

Pointing

he mortar between the bricks is smoothed to give it an attractive ppearance – this is called pointing. It also packs the mortar into he joints and makes them watertight. There are different pointing nishes, but the most common one is the concave or rubbed joint.

1 Leave the mortar until it is semi-dry; test by pressing your humb into a joint – it should eave an impression without the nortar sticking to it. Scrape a concave recess into the joint, ısing a jointing tool or even a bucket handle or piece of metal.

2 Let the shaped joints harden a little, then gently brush away any loose bits of mortar with a medium-soft banister brush. Take care not to dislodge the mortar in the joints.

IDEAL TOOL

Jointing tool

This roller tool makes it easy to achieve neat, regular pointed joints. You can also use it to rake out old mortar before repointing.

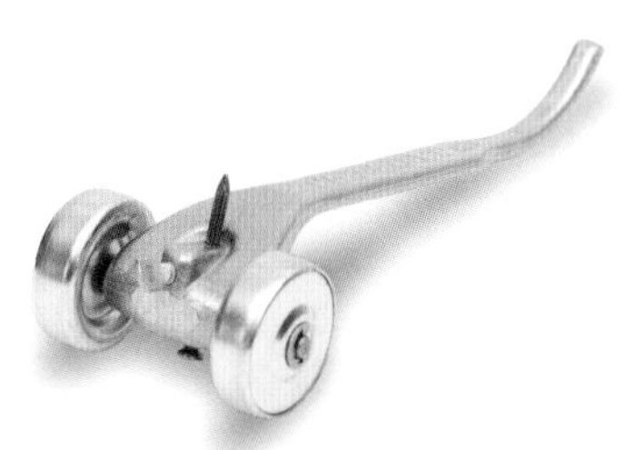

Coping and capping

Bricks, stones, slabs or special coping bricks and blocks can all be used to finish a wall. Coping is a top course that overhangs; capping is flush.

Slab coping

Slabs on a low garden wall can provide extra seating. When laying slabs, make sure they overhang the brickwork by 25mm–30mm and are firmly laid on a continuous bed of mortar. Always wet the back of the slabs, particularly on hot days, as this helps them adhere to the mortar. Use a line and spirit level in the same way as for the wall itself.

Brick capping

Bed one stretcher face of each brick into the mortar so that it spans the width of the wall and the header faces are flush with the faces of the wall. Use very strong mortar.

GARDEN WALLS BUILDING A BRICK WALL

Building a freestanding garden wall is quite straightforward, but sometimes a wall may need extra strengthening – if it is a retaining wall holding back heavy earth, for instance, or if it is a long wall. Or you may want to build a wall attached to the house. All these call for additional wall-building techniques.

Building a brick pier

Supporting piers, spaced no more than 3m apart, are necessary in single-skin walls over 450mm high. They can also be used in double-skin brick walls as a decorative 'full stop' on which to place a statue or potted plant, or as supports for gates or uprights for a pergola. (They are essential in double-skin walls of 1.35m and above.) The piers below are built in single-skin walls. Use stretcher bond and repeat the first two courses until the pier is the required height.

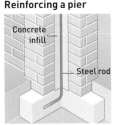

Support pier

To make a solid pier that projects on one side only, lay two header bricks in place of one of the stretchers on the first course, so they project from the wall. On the second course, cover the projecting part of the headers with a stretcher and cover the inner part with two ¾ brick stretchers, with a ½ brick between them.

Solid end pier

To build a solid pier at the end of the wall, projecting on one side only, lay a header brick against the end stretcher on the first course. Place a ½ brick parallel to the stretcher, butted against the header. On the second course, lay two stretcher bricks side by side.

Centred hollow end pier

End the first course with two ¾ brick headers. Butt a stretcher against each one, flush with the outer edge, and position a ½ brick stretcher to complete the final side of the square. On the second course, lay two ¾ brick headers on that final side and butt a stretcher brick against each one, flush with their outer edges.

Movement control joints

Weather conditions and ground settlement can cause movement in a brick wall, resulting in serious cracks. Control joints help to prevent this. A control joint is a continuous vertical gap of unmortared joints, completely separating one section of wall from the next.

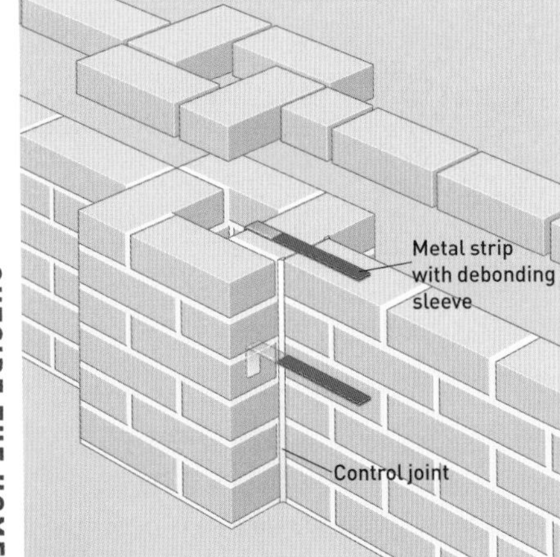

Control joints are not needed in a non-structural garden wall of less than 6m. In a wall longer than that, they should be incorporated at 6m intervals. The width of the control joint is normally 10mm, or a minimum of 1mm per metre of walling. Each joint should run right to the top of the wall, including the coping, but not into the footing.

A control joint is easier to disguise if you position it where the wall meets an intermediate pier. Build the wall and pier in the normal way, but instead of mortar insert a 10mm-thick polystyrene strip in the vertical joint between them. In the mortar of the horizontal joints embed galvanised metal strips with special debonding sleeves to allow for slight movement. When the wall is complete, run a bead of mastic masonry filler into the joint on both sides of the wall to hide the polystyrene strip.

YOU CAN DO IT

Reinforcing a pier

The hole in the centre of a hollow pier at the end of a wall is filled with concrete; if the pier is going to be attached to a gate or fencing or it is going to be more than 1m high, it will need extra reinforcement. If so, build the pier around a steel reinforcing rod or bar set in the concrete footing. The rod extends up to the top of the pier and the concrete is poured into the gap around it.

IDEAL TOOL

Laser level and tripod

A laser level with adjustable tripod will accurately extend a level line over long distances. This is extremely useful when building a fence or garden wall.

1 Build the first few courses of the garden wall up to the level of the damp-proof course in the house wall. Lay damp-proof polythene on the new wall at this level, sandwiched between layers of mortar, and lap it up the wall of the house by the depth of one brick.

Attaching a garden wall to a house

The simplest way to attach a wall at right angles to another is by using stainless steel connectors bolted to the existing wall. Special wall ties bedded in the new wall secure it to the connector. You will need a damp-proof course (DPC) in the garden wall or it could bridge the house's damp-proof course. Use a roll of polythene damp-proof course the same width as the wall.

TOOLS MATERIALS

- **power drill with masonry bits**
- **trowel**

- stainless steel connectors and wall ties
- expanding masonry bolts
- mortar
- bricks
- damp-proof course

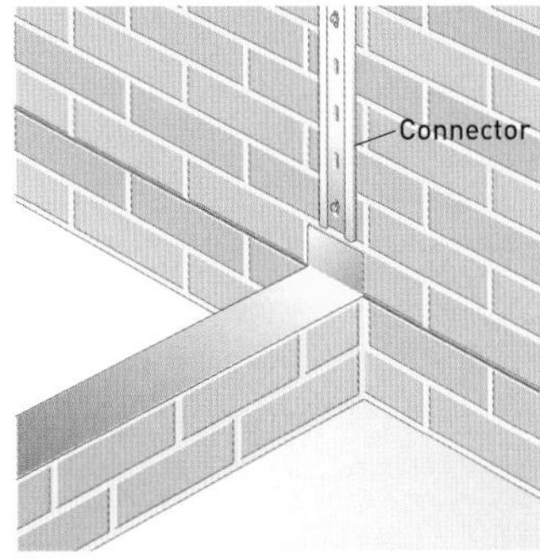

2 Attach the stainless steel connector to the wall of the house just above the damp-proof course, using expanding masonry bolts (see page 191).

3 Mortar and lay the end bricks against the connector so that a joint is formed with the existing wall.

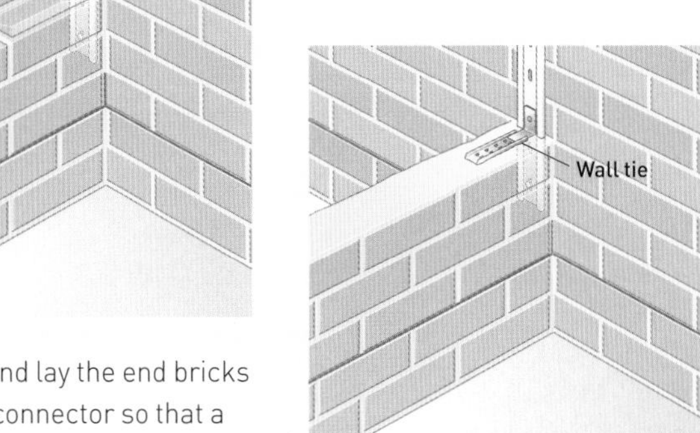

4 At every third course, hook one of the wall ties onto the steel connector and bed the other end in the mortar on the new wall.

Retaining walls

Retaining walls are used to hold back a bank of earth and, in turn, provide terracing on different levels in a garden. A steep bank can be held back by a series of small walls rather than one tall one. Retaining walls over 1m high should not be attempted without professional advice. Natural stone, bricks, concrete blocks and reconstituted stone are all suitable materials for a retaining wall. If you need a particularly strong wall, set reinforcing rods or bars in the footing concrete.

Excavate enough soil to give you room for the footing and the wall. If the soil in the bank is loose, hold it back with plywood or corrugated iron, secured with metal pegs, while you build the wall. Leave enough room to pack cleanstone – grit- and dust-free aggregate – between the back of the wall and the soil, and allow a 300mm depth of top soil.

Drainage is very important. Either leave some joints unmortared at ground level or just above to create weep holes, or fit a drainage pipe through the wall. Drainage will also be improved by a layer of geotextile permeable fabric on top of the cleanstone.

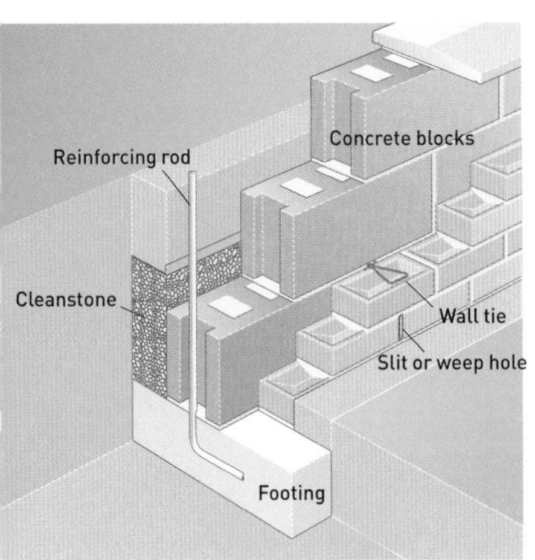

Hollow block and brick wall

This retaining wall is built with hollow concrete blocks and bricks and has reinforcing rods running through the holes in the blocks. Metal wall ties join the blocks and bricks.

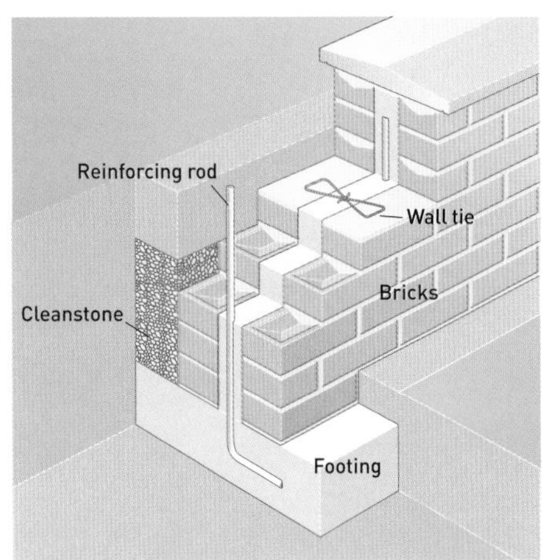

Brick retaining wall

Reinforcing rods are set between the two skins of this double-skinned brick retaining wall. Metal ties join the two skins of bricks.

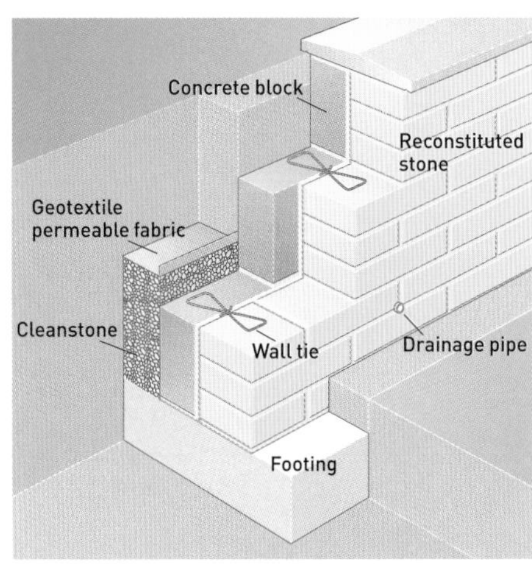

Concrete block and reconstituted stone

The inner skin of this wall is concrete blocks and the outer (facing) skin is reconstituted stone. The skins are joined by metal ties and drainage pipes are fitted about 1m apart.

GARDEN WALLS BUILDING A STONE WALL

TOOLS MATERIALS

- **bricklayer's hammer or stone axe**
- **heavy-duty gloves**
- **safety goggles**
- **trowel**
- **spirit level**
- **builder's line**
- **medium-soft banister brush**

- natural stone
- mortar
- metal wall ties

In buildings, natural stone is stuck together with mortar in much the same way as brickwork. For a garden wall, however, a 'dry-stone' effect – without mortar – looks very attractive. Proper dry-stone walling requires a great deal of skill and some wide bonding stones to span the width of the wall. An easier method, producing the same effect, is to build up the wall from both sides with a narrow layer of mortar in the centre, so that the joints look open, as if they have no mortar. Using a complete covering of mortar on each course and then raking some of it out once it has set won't achieve such a good effect.

Building a natural stone wall

Lay the footing as you would for a brick wall (see pages 216–17). The minimum width of a double-faced freestanding stone wall is 450mm and the footing should extend by 120mm on both sides of the wall. Mark the footing to indicate the line each face of the wall will follow.

1 Sort through your pile of stones and pick out some likely corner stones (quoins). If there are no obvious ones, shape a stone by chipping it with a bricklayer's hammer or a stone axe. Wear gloves and safety goggles to do this.

2 Apply mortar to the footing (see Step 2, page 218) and set a quoin at each end of the footing on the marked lines.

3 Continue filling in the line of stones between the two ends. You can use a mixture of stones; they don't all have to be the same height (see YOU CAN DO IT).

4 Build up the corners and ends first as you would when laying bricks (see page 219). Use a spirit level to make sure the quoins are vertical. Stretch a level line from one end of the wall to the other, 300mm–400mm above the footing. Move the line up the wall as you build, using it as a guide until you reach the finished wall height, which must be level.

5 Work on one side of the wall up to a height of no more than 500mm, then go to the other side of the wall and build that side up roughly level with the first side. Large stones, known as 'jumpers', can be introduced. These will change the height of the course.

6 Fit metal wall ties no more than 900mm apart on the horizontal plane and 450mm apart on the vertical plane. Fill the centre with mortar and small off-cuts of stone as you go.

IDEAL TOOL

Bricklayer's hammer
A bricklayer's hammer is made of particularly hard steel with a chisel end and a square head instead of a round one, which makes it easier to chip bits off natural stones.

YOU CAN DO IT

Fitting the stones
When filling in the line of stones between the quoins, there is no need to work from one end to the other. Good stone masons say they never put a stone down once they have picked it up – it will always fit somewhere!

1 Spread mortar on the top course of stones, then fit large and small stones alternately, standing them on end.

Capping a natural stone wall

There are various ways of capping a stone wall, including using slab or even brick. One of the most popular methods is 'cock and hen' capping, alternating upright large and small stones. The stones are usually held in place with mortar.

2 Before the mortar is completely dry, scrape away any surplus with a trowel and brush the stones with a medium-soft banister brush.

SAFETY FIRST

- Always wear safety goggles to cut bricks or blocks. Using an angle grinder creates a lot of dust, so you will need a gauze face mask too.
- An angle grinder continues to run for a few seconds after it has been switched off, so don't put it down until the blade has stopped turning.

1 Spread mortar on the footing and lay the first course. Build course by course, with mortar in all the joints. With these interlocking blocks there's no need to build up ends and corners first.

Reconstituted stone walls

Reconstituted stone comes in a wide range of colours, shapes and sizes (see page 213). The composite blocks used here are interlocking, making them very quick and easy to build.

2 When the wall is the required height, spread mortar on the top course and fit reconstituted stone slabs or special coping stones.

IDEAL TOOL

Angle grinder
An angle grinder is an electric or motorised stone cutter that makes easy work of cutting stone slabs or bricks.

Keybrick planter

Keybricks are quick and easy to lay on any level surface because they lock together without mortar. They are ideal for building a garden planter, which will last for years or can easily be taken down and rebuilt elsewhere. The bricks slot together along their smooth faces and their weathered faces are left exposed. Whole, half and corner bricks are available.

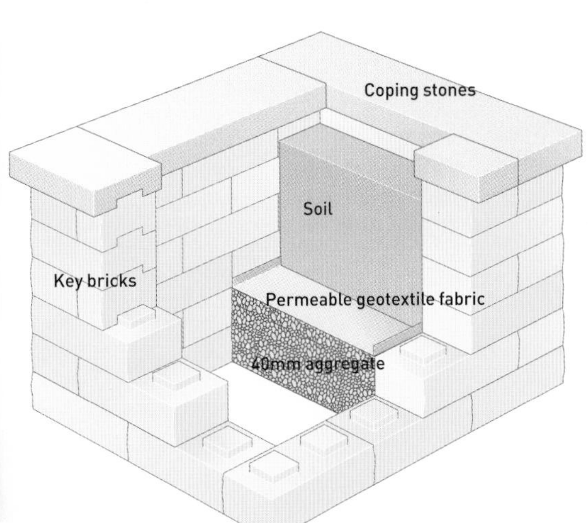

1 Arrange the first course of bricks on a flat level surface, hole side down, with the rough surface on the outside of the planter.

Drainage

To make sure water can drain away easily, fill the bottom third of the planter with 40mm aggregate and lay a sheet of permeable geotextile fabric on top. Fill the rest of the container with a mixture of top soil compost and horticultural grit.

2 Continue adding bricks, locking each course into the one below, until the planter is the required height. Fit locking coping stones on the top.

PAVING PATIOS AND PATHS

Patios and paths give character and definition to outdoor space. A patio designed as a sitting or dining area can be in any part of the garden, but will usually be sited next to the house for convenience. It can be paved with concrete slabs, paving blocks, reclaimed stone or even gravel, and is often connected to other parts of the garden by steps or a paved or gravel path.

Planning your garden

When you are designing major changes, it's a good idea to draw a simple plan of the house and garden to show where landscaped areas will be. It should also indicate any changes in level, because once out in the garden even slight gradients can present construction problems if they weren't thought about at the planning stage. Before you make any final decisions, use lengths of string to lay out your proposed plan on the ground.

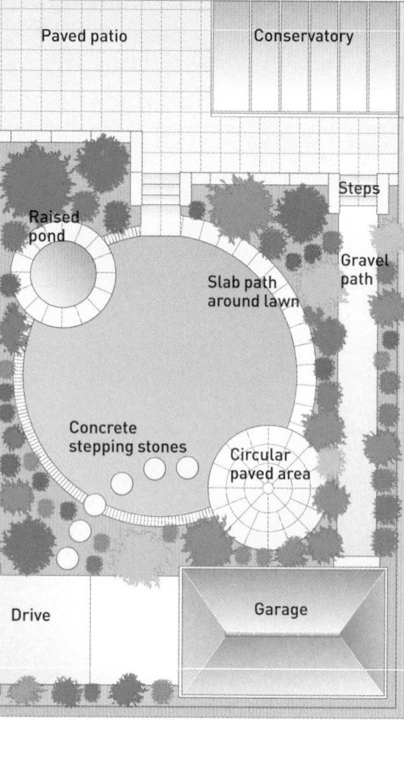

Paving slabs

Paving slabs are manufactured from hydraulically pressed concrete. Some have pigments added to give different colours, and you can buy them in a range of finishes: smooth, textured or moulded to resemble naturally weathered stone. They are straightforward to lay and come in a variety of shapes and sizes.

Smooth

These smooth-finished slabs look great in combination with slabs of different shades or texture.

Concrete deck tiles

These wood-effect deck tiles are actually made of concrete, and can be used anywhere in the garden.

Textured

Textured slabs, like smooth ones, are made in a range of natural-looking colours, including red, grey and buff.

Concrete stepping stones

Wood-effect stepping stones running through a gravel path or across a lawn will entice anyone to explore.

Weathered

Slabs with a natural weathered appearance provide a mature look and blend well in an established garden.

Reclaimed

Old reclaimed York stone slabs or flagstones are the most expensive paving options. They are heavy and the laying process involves a lot of cutting – but the 'been there forever' look can be worth it.

YOU CAN DO IT

It's a wash-out

If you don't want to pave a path or drive, you can use gravel – but don't use it on a steep slope, because gravel will wash downhill in wet weather; in this situation, it is better to use concrete or tarmac.

Paving slab designs

You can use one size and shape of slab to make regular grid or staggered patterns, or you can combine different sizes to create a random design. Hexagonal slabs can be used to create a honeycomb pattern, although if the edges of the paved area are straight, this will involve a lot of cutting.

Regular grid

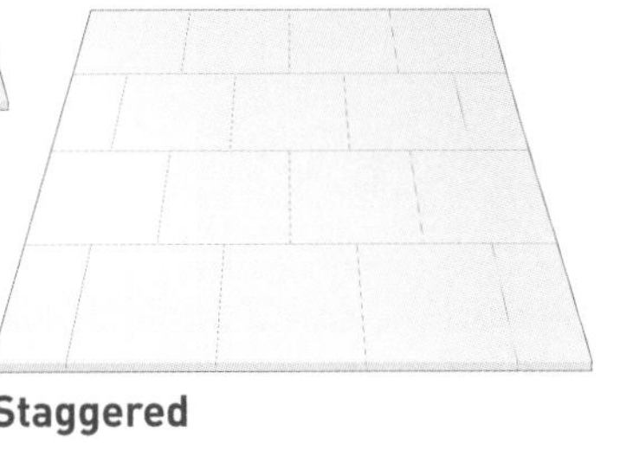

Staggered

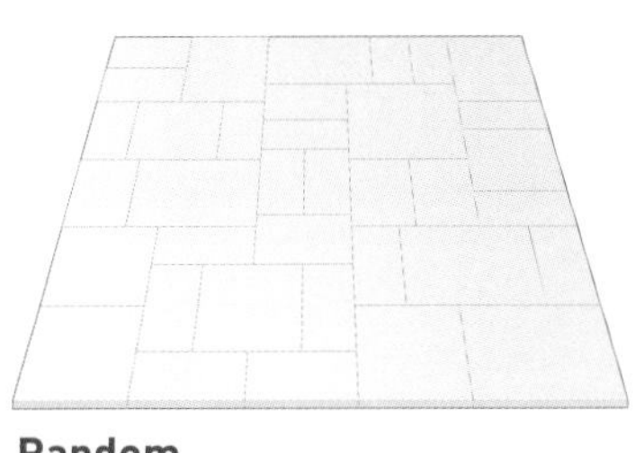

Random

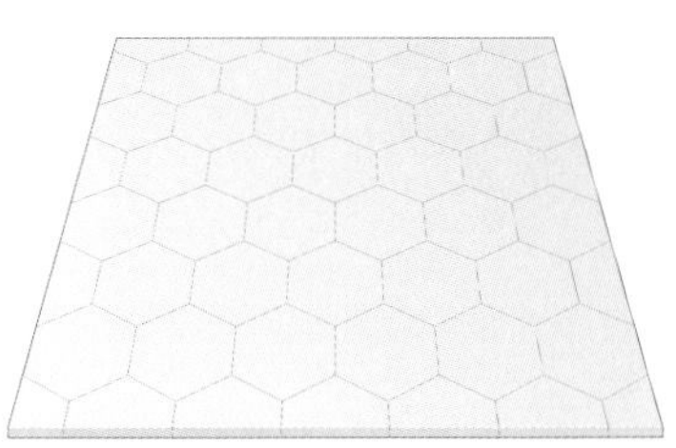

Honeycomb

Cobbles

As well as individual cobble stones, you can buy paving slabs made to resemble cobbles. Or you can even buy cobbling by the square metre. In this case, the stones are manufactured to look like real cobble stones, but they are joined together with nylon line, so fitting them is as simple as laying a rug. They can be laid on earth, hardcore or a concrete base. Sand, gravel or soil can be brushed into the joints, or if the cobbles are laid on a concrete base (either on mortar or straight on wet concrete) they can be pointed with sand and cement. If laid on a lawn, the grass can be left to grow through the gaps. They are not suitable for drives.

Linked cobbling

Slab cobbling

Paving blocks

Brick-shaped concrete paving blocks are another alternative to slabs. In addition to standard-sized blocks, you can buy specially designed edging and corner stones. Like slabs, they are available in a range of colours and textured finishes.

Paving blocks can be laid in various patterns. Herringbone is particularly good for a drive as it can withstand the movement of cars.

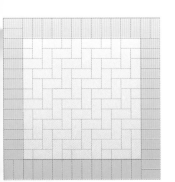

Herringbone

Angled herringbone

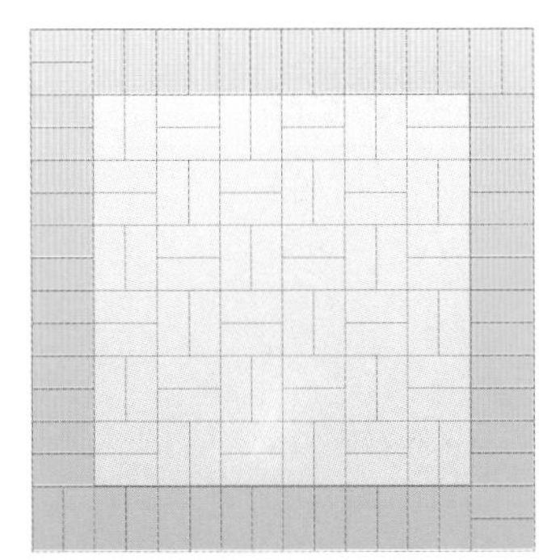

Basketweave

Stretcher bond

PAVING SIMPLE REPAIRS

Although concrete is very hardwearing, you may sometimes need to repair paving, paths or steps. A section of paving or even a single slab may sink due to minor ground movements or heavy use, and this allows rainwater to collect in puddles. Concrete steps can wear at the edges and other areas can develop holes or cracks.

Replacing a slab

If a slab has sunk or suffered damage, it is a fairly easy matter to lift it and either re-lay or replace it.

TOOLS MATERIALS

- **safety goggles**
- **heavy-duty gloves**
- **plugging chisel**
- **club hammer**
- **spade**
- **broom handle**
- **bolster chisel**

- timber off-cut
- sharp sand
- cement
- new slab, if required
- dry mortar of 3 parts sharp sand to 1 part cement

1 Wearing safety goggles and heavy-duty gloves, chip out the pointing around the slab with a plugging chisel and a club hammer.

2 Lift the slab with a spade, using a timber off-cut to protect the adjacent slab.

3 Insert a broom handle under the slab and roll it out of the way.

4 Use a bolster chisel and club hammer to break up and remove the old mortar. If the slab was laid on sand, use a piece of timber to level it and add more sand if necessary.

5 If the slab was laid on mortar, wet the back and lay it (or a new slab) in position on a fresh bed of mortar mixed with four parts sharp sand to one part cement. Make sure it is flush with the surrounding slabs. Use a timber off-cut and the club hammer to press the slab into position. Fill the joints with dry mortar (see Filling the joints, page 230).

IDEAL TOOL

Plugging chisel

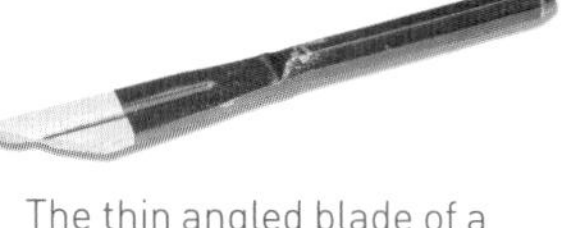

The thin angled blade of a plugging chisel is specially designed for removing mortar from joints in walls or paving.

YOU CAN DO IT

Slab sizes

There is a slight difference in size between older concrete slabs, produced in imperial sizes, and the new metric ones – the metric slabs are a fraction smaller. If you have to replace an old slab, see if it is possible to take one from somewhere else on the patio – from a position against a wall, for instance – and use that slab to replace the broken one. Fit the mismatched slab against the wall, where it will be less conspicuous – or you could fill the gap with earth and plants.

B&Q

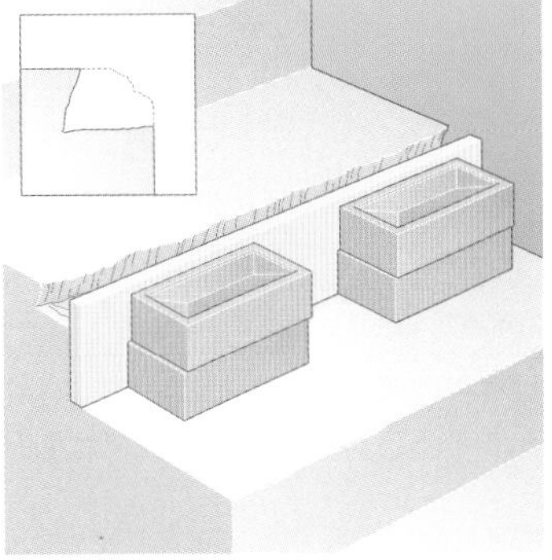

Repairing concrete steps

Years of use and exposure to the elements can cause concrete steps to deteriorate on the edges where the tread meets the riser. Repair the damage as soon as possible to prevent the steps becoming unsafe as well as unsightly.

TOOLS MATERIALS

- **safety goggles**
- **heavy-duty gloves**
- **cold chisel**
- **club hammer**
- **old paintbrush**
- **trowel or float**
- **arrissing tool**

- PVA adhesive
- piece of board
- bricks
- sharp sand
- cement
- polythene

1 Wearing safety goggles and protective gloves, chip out the loose and flaking concrete with a cold chisel and club hammer. Paint the damaged area with PVA adhesive diluted with water according to the manufacturer's instructions. Cut a piece of board to the same height as the riser and prop it against the riser with bricks.

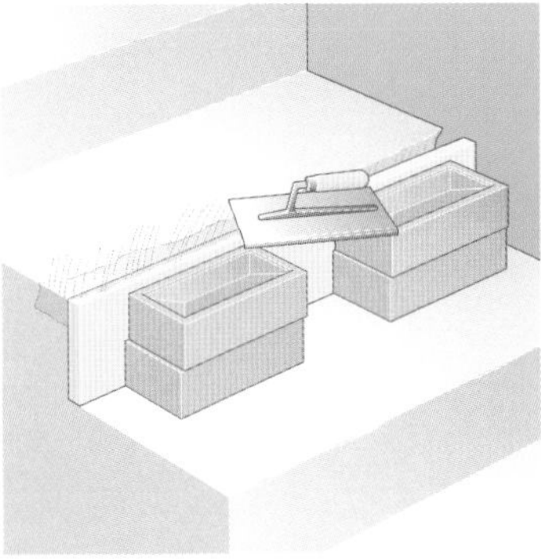

2 Let the adhesive dry to the point that it becomes tacky, then use a trowel or float to fill the damaged area with a concrete filler made by mixing three parts sharp sand, one part cement and a solution of equal parts of PVA adhesive and water mixed separately. Run an arrissing tool along the edge to create a neat, rounded front edge to the tread. Cover with polythene for three days while it hardens, then remove the bricks and board.

IDEAL TOOL

Arrissing tool

An arrissing tool is a metal float with a curved edge, which is used to round off and smooth concrete edges so they are less likely to be damaged. It also means there are no sharp edges to cause injury.

Repairing holes and cracks in concrete

Small hairline cracks in concrete are not a problem, but large cracks and holes should be repaired to prevent them filling with water, which could freeze and cause more damage. Chip away the damaged area to a depth of at least 15mm with a sharp cold chisel and a club hammer. Undercut the edge of the concrete with the chisel to hold the filler in place. Brush away any dust and debris from the hole and paint it with PVA adhesive diluted according to the manufacturer's instructions. When the PVA is tacky, fill the area with concrete repair filler mix (see above, Step 2). Use a float to level the surface with the surrounding concrete. Cover with polythene and leave to harden for three days.

TOOLS MATERIALS

- **safety goggles**
- **heavy-duty gloves**
- **cold chisel**
- **club hammer**
- **old paintbrush**
- **trowel**
- **float**

- PVA adhesive
- sharp sand
- cement
- polythene

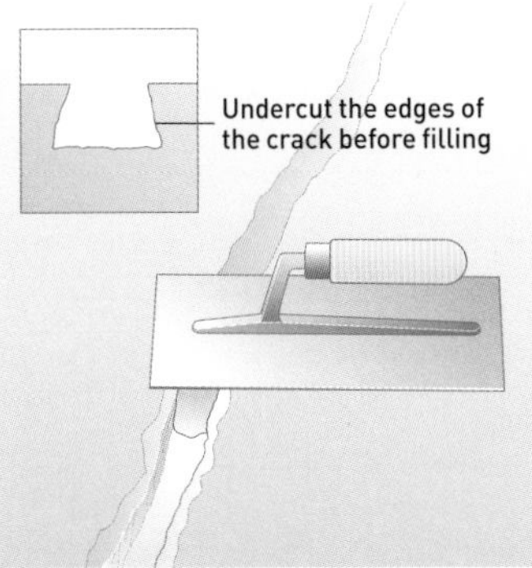
Undercut the edges of the crack before filling

YOU CAN DO IT

Clean paving

B&Q

Keeping paving stones clean will help to prevent a path or patio becoming slippery in wet weather. A pressure washer used with a chemical brick and patio cleaner will remove oil, grease and moss.

PAVING SUB-BASE AND FALL

TOOLS MATERIALS

- **builder's line**
- **hammer**
- **builder's square**
- **spade**
- **shovel**
- **wheel barrow**
- **club hammer**
- **spirit level**
- **straightedge**
- **earth rammer or vibrating plate compactor**
- **rake**
- **bucket**
- **soft brush**
- **heavy-duty gloves**
- **safety goggles**
- **dust mask**
- **bolster chisel or angle grinder**
- **watering can with rose attachment**
- **trowel**

- wooden marker pegs
- hardcore
- sharp sand or all-in ballast
- 5mm spacers
- recessed manhole cover, if required
- masking tape, if required
- polythene
- wooden shims
- large-headed nails
- mortar, made from sharp sand and cement
- 600 x 600 concrete slabs
- timber off-cut

A large area of paving cannot be laid straight on soft ground. Concrete slabs, gravel, paving blocks and asphalt all need the support of a sub-base. This consists of hardcore (crushed or broken bricks, block and stone) compacted with an earth rammer (see IDEAL TOOL, page 243) or a vibrating plate compactor (which can be hired) and then topped with a layer of sharp sand or ballast – called blinding – to fill any gaps. If you are laying slabs on a drive, which is likely to have to bear the weight of several cars, the sub-base is better compacted with a single-drum vibrating roller, and it needs a layer of concrete as well.

Preparing a patio sub-base

You will need to remove a depth of top soil equal to the depth of the sub-base plus the thickness of the paving and mortar (a minimum of 25mm). In firm well-drained soil, the sub-base should be 100mm deep; in soft ground it should be deeper. Clear an area slightly larger than the paved area will be. When a patio is built next to a house, the level of the finished surface must be at least 150mm below the damp-proof course.

1 Mark out the area for the sub-base using builder's lines attached to wooden pegs. Use a builder's square (see page 217) to make sure the corners are square before you start excavating. As a final check, measure the diagonals to make sure they are the same.

2 Cut the turf in strips with a spade and roll it up. Save some of the turf in case you need to make good between an existing lawn and the paved surface.

3 Dig the area to the correct depth and use marker pegs to mark the finished hardcore level, taking into account the required fall (see opposite).

4 Tip in enough hardcore to fill your sub-base to just above the top of the pegs.

5 Compact the hardcore with an earth rammer or a petrol-powered vibrating plate compactor, as used here.

6 Cover the surface with a thin blinding coat of sharp sand or all-in ballast and rake it level.

YOU CAN DO IT

How deep is your drive?
The depth of a drive sub-base depends on what you plan to pave it with. If you are laying concrete slabs, allow 150mm of compacted hardcore plus 125mm of concrete; if laying paving blocks, allow 150mm of compacted hardcore and 50mm of sand.

Setting the fall

Paved areas must have a slight slope or fall so that surface water drains away. Generally, it is only necessary to have a fall in one direction: the surface in the other direction can be level. In normal conditions, the ideal fall for a patio is 1 in 80 (that is, a 12.5mm drop in level per metre); for a path about 1 in 80 (across the width); and for a drive about 1 in 40. This is achieved in practice by using a spirit level, a 1m-long straightedge and a shim, a small strip of wood cut to the depth of the required drop in level per metre (see chart).

CALCULATING SHIM DEPTH

Fall	Drop in level per metre
1 in 80	12.5mm
1 in 60	16mm
1 in 40	25mm

Setting the fall in the sub-base

First decide which way the paving will slope. If you are building a patio against the house, it must slope away from the walls. Cut a number of softwood pegs. Measuring from the top of each peg, mark them with the depth of the sub-base. Hammer in a row of these pegs across the high side of the site. Cut a shim to the correct size and nail it to the underside of one end of a 1m-long straightedge. Then hammer in the next row of pegs in line with the first, exactly one metre away. Place the straightedge between two pegs with the shim on the lower peg and lay a spirit level on top. A level reading means that the lower peg is deeper by the exact depth of the shim: the correct amount to give the fall you need. Repeat this process at metre intervals across the entire area to be paved.

Setting the fall in the paving

Although the fall is already established in the sub-base, it's important to run builder's lines marking the top edges of the paving to ensure you maintain the correct slope as you lay the slabs.

1 Mark out the edges of the patio with builder's lines attached to pegs. Use a builder's square to make sure the corners are true right angles.

2 Hammer pegs at the four corners of the patio to mark the finished slab height. Allow a depth of at least 25mm for the mortar. To check the fall, rest a straightedge and spirit level between opposite pegs at the high and low ends of the site. The depth of the shim on the lower peg needs to be the drop per metre multiplied by the length of the paving. Check that the pegs are level in the other direction. Fix lines between the pegs, nailed into the top with large-headed nails.

Laying the first slab

Paving slabs are bedded in mortar mixed with four parts sharp sand to one part cement (see page 215). The first slab is the key one that is the guide for all the others and it should be positioned in a corner. You may need to fit slabs around drainage gullies or manhole covers (see page 231). Arrange them so that you have to do as little cutting as possible.

SAFETY FIRST

Look after your back! If you are laying slabs 600mm x 600mm or larger, you must have someone to help you lift and lay them.

1 Place five blobs of mortar on the ground for the slab, one at each corner and one in the middle. (If laying a drive, you need a continuous layer of mortar between the sub-base and the slab.) Wet the back of the slab with a brush – this will improve adhesion and make it easier to slide into position.

2 Carefully lift the first slab and lay it on top of the blobs of mortar.

3 Use a piece of timber and a club hammer to tap the slab into position.

4 Fill any gaps under the slab with mortar, cutting it flush with the edge as you go.

PAVING SLABS AND MANHOLE COVERS

SAFETY FIRST

Keep children and pets well away from an uncovered manhole. If necessary, build a temporary guard around it while new concrete dries.

Once you have positioned the first key slab, laying the rest of the slabs is quite straightforward. If there is a manhole (a drain inspection chamber) in the area you are paving, you can disguise it with a recessed manhole cover. If your finished paving is higher than the original ground level, you may have to raise an existing manhole cover.

Laying the remaining slabs

Whichever method you use to cut concrete slabs (see YOU CAN DO IT), it is difficult to achieve perfectly straight edges, so always place the cut edge against a mortar joint where it will be less noticeable.

1 Starting from your key slab, lay the first row of slabs in the direction of the slope. Fit 5mm spacers in all the joints to make sure they are the same size. Use a spirit level and shim to check and recheck that the surface is flat and the fall is correct. If you put a slab down and it rocks on the mortar, take it up and re-lay it; you are unlikely to be able to correct it by trying to push mortar underneath a slab once it's in position.

2 When the first row is complete, lay slabs along the two adjacent outer edges. If you are using a grid pattern, the first and last slabs on alternate rows will be half slabs.

3 Fill in the central area, working back row by row. Nail a line to pegs at either end of each row before you begin laying it. Keep checking that the fall is correct and that the surface is flat in both directions.

Filling the joints

Leave the mortar to set for 48 hours before walking on the slabs. Only then can the joints be filled. If the slabs are wet or it looks as if rain is imminent, wait for a drier day.

1 Mix a dry mortar of three parts sharp sand to one part cement. Remove the spacers and brush mortar into the joints. When all the joints have been filled, push the mix down firmly with a trowel or a piece of wood, then brush in more mortar. Repeat this process three or four times or holes will appear in the mortared joints. Finally, carefully brush away all the excess mortar – take time over this, as it's easy to end up with mortar on the slabs.

2 Using a watering can with a rose attachment or a spraying device, lightly wet the whole surface. This will make the mortar set.

YOU CAN DO IT

Cutting slabs

Cut a concrete slab on a bed of sand. Mark the cutting line in pencil on all its surfaces. Wearing safety goggles, cut a groove along the line using a sharp bolster chisel and a club hammer, cutting gradually deeper until the slab breaks.

For a quicker, cleaner cut, use an angle grinder with a stone-cutting disc. As well as safety goggles, you must wear heavy-duty gloves and a gauze dust mask while you work.

B&Q

YOU CAN DO IT

Skeleton manhole

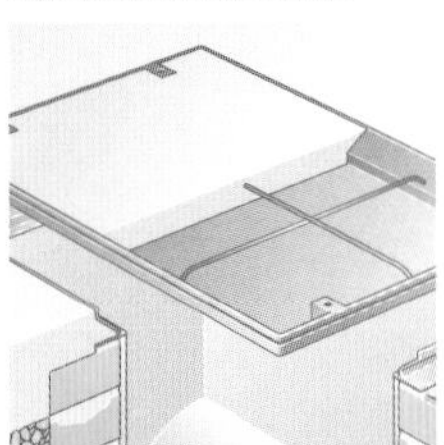

If you are making a concrete path or drive, use a skeleton type of manhole cover. This is installed in the same way as a recessed cover but the tray is filled with concrete which is reinforced by a metal grid.

1 Bed the manhole cover on concrete, making sure the lip is 2mm–3mm below the level of the finished paved surface. Haunch the concrete around the edges with a trowel, being careful to leave room for the depth of the paving and its mortar bed.

Recessed manhole cover

A recessed manhole cover is an open tray designed to disguise a manhole in a run of paving. The paving is laid right up to the rim of the cover, then more paving is laid in the tray on a bed of mortar, retaining the paving pattern. Cobbled paving is shown here, but the same principle applies with slab paving. The tray can be lifted out using special manhole keys if the drain needs to be inspected.

2 Lay the paving right up to the manhole cover, retaining the pattern.

3 Lift out the tray and cut the paving to fit inside it, still retaining the pattern. Remove the paving and spread a bed of mortar over the whole of the tray, then set the paving in the mortar. Cover the keyholes with masking tape while you fill the paving joints (see opposite).

Raising the height of a manhole cover

The surface of a new patio or drive will often be higher than the previous ground level, and the cover of any drain inspection chamber will need to be raised to the same level.

TOOLS MATERIALS

- **club hammer**
- **cold chisel**
- **trowel**
- **spirit level**

- polythene sheet or plastic bag
- engineering bricks
- soft sand
- cement
- timber off-cut
- board

1 Lift off the manhole cover and lay a polythene sheet or plastic bag in the bottom of the manhole to make sure the debris does not clog the drain. Chip away the old mortar from the edge of the manhole frame with a club hammer and a sharp chisel. Take care not to hit the frame – if it is an old one it may be made of cast-iron, which cracks easily. Lift off the frame and clean away any mortar covering the top surface of the brick walls of the manhole.

2 Build up the manhole with engineering bricks bedded in mortar made with three parts soft sand to one part cement. If you want to raise the height less than the depth of one brick, use brick slips, which are narrow sections of brick, cut to size.

3 Spread more mortar on the new bricks, place the frame on top and tap it into position using a timber off-cut and a club hammer. Use a spirit level to make sure it is level across its length and its width.

4 If you are gravelling the area, slope the mortar around the frame to direct rainwater away. If you are laying slabs or blocks, then cut the mortar flush with the bricks so that you can pave right up to the frame. Remove the polythene and any debris from the bottom of the manhole. Cover the frame with a board weighted down with bricks while the mortar dries.

PAVING AND GARDEN DRAINAGE

Patios, paths and drives are built with a slight slope or fall so that surface water can drain away. In some instances, particularly if you have a large paved surface or live in an area of heavy clay soil, simply allowing the water to drain on to a lawn or planted bed may not be enough. You may need to build a drainage channel to collect the surface water and direct it to a dispersal point which leads into an existing surface water drain or into a soakaway.

Concrete drainage channel

If your patio isn't draining efficiently, or if you are laying a new patio or drive, one of the easiest ways to create a drainage channel along its edge is by moulding a concrete strip using a length of plastic guttering.

1 Place a length of timber the required distance from the paved surface (in this case slightly wider than the guttering used to mould the channel). Hammer in wooden pegs at intervals and nail them to the timber. The channel should run at right angles to the fall of the paving. Use a 1m-long straightedge and a 12.5mm shim to set a fall of 1 in 80 along the drainage channel (see page 229).

2 Mix concrete using four parts mixed aggregate to one part cement. Fill the channel with the concrete to a level slightly lower than the edge of the timber, and smooth it with a float.

3 Press the guttering into the wet concrete to leave a clear imprint. Remove the guttering and smooth any ridges in the concrete. Use a spirit level to make sure the fall is set at the correct angle.

TOOLS MATERIALS

- **cement mixer**
- **shovel**
- **float**
- **spirit level**
- **1m-long straightedge**
- **hammer**

- 25mm-thick softwood plank
- wooden pegs
- 75mm nails
- 12.5mm shim
- mixed aggregate
- cement
- length of plastic guttering

YOU CAN DO IT

Drainage in the middle of a patio

You can fit a drainage channel in the middle of a paved area. The paving either side should slope towards the channel edges. The channel should have a fall of 1 in 80.

Plastic drainage channel

Instead of moulding a channel in concrete, you can buy ready-made drainage channel. This may be plastic, resin-bonded or vitrified clay.

1 The channel should run at right angles to the fall of the paving and have a fall of 1 in 80. Use a 1m-long straightedge and shim of 12.5mm to achieve this (see page 229). Excavate a depth of 100mm along the edge of the patio and fill it with concrete. Place the first section of channel on the concrete.

2 Use waterproof sealant to fill the specially designed recess in the end of each section of channel. Fit the next section. Keep checking the fall and repeat all the way along the required run, cutting the channel with a panel saw, if necessary.

3 Build up or haunch the concrete on the outside of the channel, sloping away from it. Point the joint between channel and paving with dry mortar (see page 230). Finally, fit metal grating over the top.

TOOLS MATERIALS

- **cement mixer**
- **tape measure**
- **shovel**
- **trowel**
- **spirit level**
- **1m-long straightedge**
- **panel saw**

- mixed aggregate
- cement
- drainage channel
- 12.5mm shim
- silicone sealant
- metal grating

AFETY FIRST

Check with your local authority how far a soakaway should be from a building and which is their preferred method of construction.
When constructing underground drainage systems – with the exception of perforated land drains – make sure that you can rod the pipes in case of a blockage (see page 167).
When working in an excavation, you must make sure that the soil does not collapse into the hole. If there is any danger of this, shore up the sides with plywood boarding and stout timbers.

Land drainage

If water builds up at the edge of a patio and takes a long time to drain away, you can install an underground drainage pipe system to cure the problem. Other wet areas of the garden can be drained the same way. However, there must be somewhere for the water to go. Rainwater should never exit into the main sewerage system. It must be diverted to a surface-water drain or, failing that, a soakaway in another part of the garden or even a river or lake (though in this case you will need permission from the local authority).

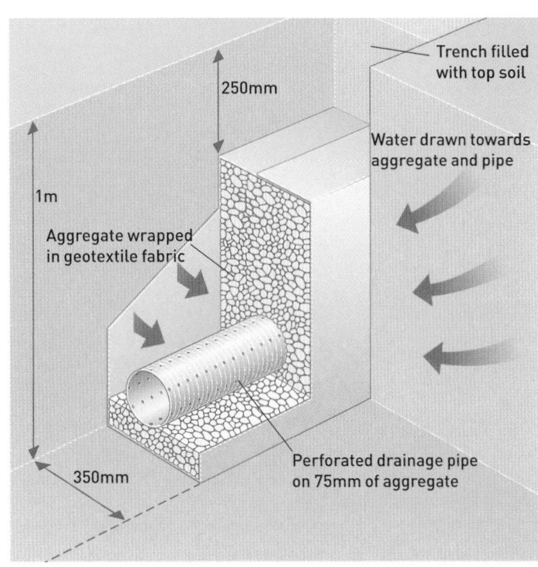

Constructing a land drain

Dig a trench about 1m deep and 350mm wide with a fall towards the outlet (to a soakaway or surface-water drain). The trench should run with the contour of the land, if possible. Line the trench with permeable geotextile fabric and lay clean aggregate (20mm–40mm) to a depth of 75mm in the bottom of the trench; the aggregate must be of a consistent depth and follow the fall. Lay a 100mm perforated plastic drainage pipe in the centre of the trench on top of the gravel bed. Work down the trench filling it with aggregate to within 200mm–300mm of ground level, being careful to keep the pipe central and running flat along the bed. Lay geotextile fabric over the aggregate and cover that with top soil.

Soakaways

Soakaways are used to disperse rainwater from drainage pipes and channels and land drains. They must not be used for household drainage or sewage and they should never exit into the sewerage system. You can buy a ready-made soakaway (right), which consists of open concrete blocks built up in rings. It has a concrete base and a manhole cover on top. It is buried underground with permeable geotextile membrane wrapped around the structure to keep soil out. Water entering the soakaway seeps out through the open blocks and membrane into the soil.

Ready-made concrete soakaway

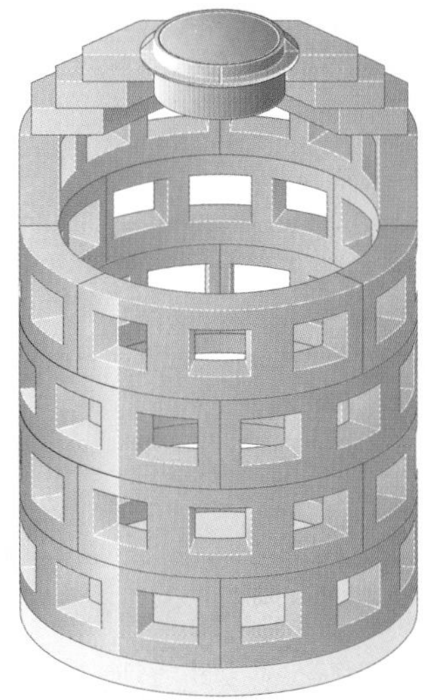

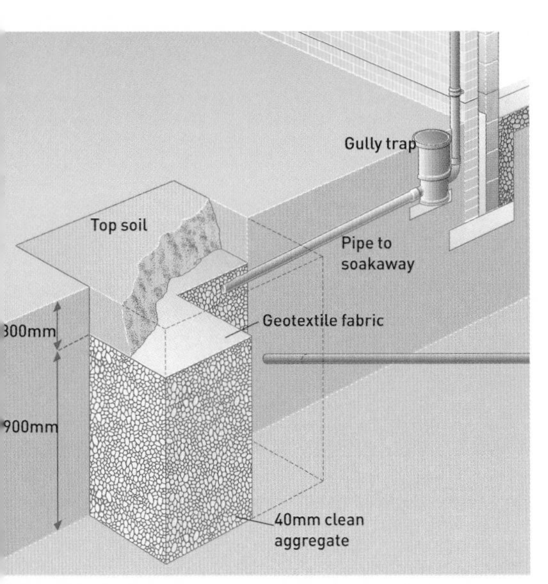

Digging a simple soakaway

A less expensive way of installing a soakaway is to dig a hole in the ground approximately 1.2m square and 1.2m deep. Break up the clay or rock at the bottom of the hole with a fork or crowbar. Cover the sides and bottom of the excavation with permeable geotextile fabric, overlapping it by 300mm where necessary. Fit a plastic underground drainage pipe from the drainage channel or rainwater pipe into the soakaway, fitting a gully trap at the top end of the pipe. Make sure that the pipe slopes towards the soakaway. Refill the hole with clean aggregate (40mm or larger), allowing for at least 300mm of top soil. Cover the aggregate with more geotextile fabric and top up with soil.

YOU CAN DO IT

Test your hole
Before excavating for a soakaway, dig a test hole at the required depth and check that it does not fill up with water from the ground. If it doesn't, half-fill it with water and check that this drains away. If the water takes a long time to drain, the soakaway may have to be bigger.

PAVING BLOCKS, GRAVEL AND ASPHALT

An edging kerb can give a decorative finish to all types of surfacing on paths, patios and drives. It is particularly useful for retaining paths of gravel or asphalt, and essential if you are laying paving blocks since these are simply bedded into a sub-base of sand over compacted hardcore. Without a securely laid kerb edging on concrete footings all around the edge, the unmortared blocks will soon fall away.

Laying paving blocks

Paving blocks are bedded into a layer of sharp sand with a light plate compactor (see page 228). You can use a club hammer and a piece of timber instead, particularly if paving a small area, but the blocks will not be so stable. Calculate the dimensions of your paving or patio in numbers of whole blocks to avoid waste and minimise cutting. Set out a sub-base at least 75mm deep in the same way as for slab paving (see pages 228–29). Allow the correct fall to ensure efficient drainage (see page 229).

TOOLS MATERIALS

- **tape measure**
- **builder's line**
- **spirit level**
- **spade**
- **builder's square**
- **trowel**
- **kneepads**
- **plate compactor or club hammer and piece of timber**

- mortar, made of sharp sand and cement
- timber levelling strips
- sharp sand
- edging blocks
- paving blocks

1 Excavate a strip around the edge of the sub-base and lay concrete footings for the kerb. The footing should project 75mm on the outside of the edging blocks and no more than 25mm on the inside. When the concrete is dry, lay the edging blocks on a bed of mortar consisting of three parts sharp sand to one part cement. Use a line and spirit level to position them and allow for the fall across their surface. Leave the mortar to harden for three days.

2 Place two timber levelling strips about 1m apart to form a bay. The strips need to be as deep as the sand, which in turn depends on the size of block and method of compaction: a plate compactor will reduce the sand by 15mm; bedding in the blocks by hand will reduce it by about 10mm. Pile sand in the bay, then spread it perfectly flat and level with the tops of the strips. Check the fall as you go.

3 Prepare two or three bays, then remove the timber strips and carefully fill the depressions they have left with sand, using a trowel. Make sure the surface stays completely flat. Do not walk on the sand.

4 Lay the blocks in the pattern of your choice, starting from one corner. Wearing knee pads, kneel on a length of timber to spread your weight over several paving blocks. Butt the blocks tightly against each other leaving no joints (they have small spacing nibs included in their design). Complete about 2sq m.

5 Press the blocks into the sand using a plate compactor, or a club hammer and piece of timber. If they drop too low, or they won't compact enough, take them up and adjust the sand bed. Continue paving in 2sq m sections.

YOU CAN DO IT

Levelling a path

When paving a path you can use the edging kerb on each side as a guide for levelling the sand. Find a length of timber longer than the width of the path and cut a notch out of either end so it will sit over the edging. The depth of board below the notches should be the depth of the paving block less 10mm or 15mm (depending on the method of compaction, see Step 2). Pull the board towards you, levelling the sand as you go.

B&Q

Laying a gravel path

A loose gravel path needs a retaining edging if it is not to become dispersed through use. Set out a sub-base 100mm deep, in the same way as for slab paving (see page 228).

TOOLS MATERIALS

- **tape measure**
- **builder's line**
- **spirit level**
- **spade**
- **trowel**
- **builder's square**
- **rake**
- **garden roller**

- mortar
- coarse gravel and sand mix
- fine pea gravel
- hardcore
- edging kerb

1 Excavate the hardcore sub-base to lay concrete footings for the kerb (see pages 216–17). The footings should be a minimum of 75mm deep and project about 75mm either side of the edging kerb line.

2 Use a builder's line to align the edging kerb as you set it on a bed of mortar (see page 218, Setting out the first course, Step 4).

3 Build up the mortar against the edging kerb on both sides with a trowel, keeping it lower than the path and ground level so that it will be out of sight.

4 Make sure the hardcore sub-base is firmly compacted. Cover the base with coarse gravel mixed with sand to a depth of 50mm. Rake it level.

5 Use a garden roller to roll in the coarse gravel and sand.

6 Cover the surface with fine pea gravel to a depth of 18mm–25mm and roll it with the garden roller.

Laying an asphalt path

Cold asphalt can be used to repair or resurface an existing asphalt surface, or to build a new path on a hardcore sub-base. It is not suitable for the construction of new drives. If you are resurfacing an old path, spray the path with weed killer about two weeks before applying the new layer. If you are building a new path, prepare a sub-base as you would for a patio (see pages 228–29) and lay edging kerb. Pick a fine day to lay the asphalt – water does not mix with bitumen emulsion.

TOOLS MATERIALS

- **old watering can without rose**
- **stiff broom**
- **shovel**
- **garden rake**
- **garden roller**

- hardboard sheet or timber for masking
- bitumen emulsion (5kg will cover about 3sq m of hardcore or 7sq m of an existing asphalt surface)
- cold asphalt (a 25kg bag will cover about 0.9sq m)
- paraffin or white spirit

1 To avoid staining the edging kerb, cover it with some hardboard or old timber (if you do get any splashes, remove them with some white spirit on a cloth). Spread a coat of bitumen emulsion on the sub-base using an old watering can without a rose. Brush it across the surface with a stiff broom, if necessary. Let the emulsion dry for about twenty minutes, in which time it will turn from brown to black.

2 Tip or shovel the asphalt on top of the emulsion and rake it over the surface to an even thickness of about 20mm.

3 Wet the garden roller to stop the asphalt sticking, then roll in several directions to level and compact the asphalt to a depth of about 13mm. Clean your tools with paraffin or white spirit.

CONCRETE PATHS, PADS AND DRIVES

SAFETY FIRST

- Wear safety goggles, gloves and a mask when mixing concrete.
- When mixing by hand work on a level surface, such as a sheet of plywood. When using a concrete mixer, position it on flat ground.
- Do not put your hands or a shovel into a mixer while it is running.
- Don't allow concrete to dry on your tools. Clean it off with a stiff brush.

Concrete is made up of cement, aggregate (particles of stone) and sharp sand. When the ingredients are mixed with water, they bind into a solid, hard material. In different proportions, they produce concrete of different strengths for different uses. It's important to get the proportions accurate: if there is too much aggregate, you will have difficulty producing a satisfactory finish; too much sand will mean that the mix will be weak and the finished surface could be damaged by the elements. Hardening begins after about two hours and the concrete is then unworkable, but it does not become really strong for several days and continues to harden as long as there is moisture in it.

Designing with concrete

Various factors must be taken into account when designing concrete paths, pads or drives if the concrete is to be strong enough for the job.

- The thickness of the concrete must be determined by the weight it will be supporting. A pad for a lightweight wooden shed would only need to be 100mm deep. For a stone, brick or block garage, you would need a 150mm sub-base of compacted hardcore and a 125mm concrete pad. The edges of the pad would need to be deeper (a minimum of 200mm) to support the walls.
- The mix must be determined by what the concrete is to be used for (see table below).
- The surface of the concrete must form a slight slope, so that water drains off. It should slope away from buildings or, in the case of a slab used to site a shed, away from the door (see Setting the fall, page 229).
- When laid against a house wall, the surface must be at least 150mm below the damp-proof course.
- In an area that will have to withstand considerable weight, such as a drive, concrete should be reinforced with a steel grid at half its depth.

CONCRETE MIXES

Ingredients	Amounts required for approx. 1 cubic metre of concrete
Paving mix **(strong mix suitable for exposure to all weathers, including frost), using separate aggregate**	
1 part cement	16 x 25kg bags
1.5 parts sharp sand	½cu m
2.5 parts 20mm coarse aggregate	¾cu m
Paving mix **(strong mix suitable for exposure to all weathers, including frost), using all-in aggregate**	
1 part cement	16 x 25kg bags
3.5 parts all-in aggregate	1cu m
Foundation or footing mix **(and for concreting in fence posts), using separate aggregate**	
1 part cement	11.2 x 25kg bags
2.5 parts sharp sand	½cu m
3.5 parts 20mm coarse aggregate	¾cu m
Foundation or footing mix **(and for concreting in fence posts), using all-in aggregate**	
1 part cement	11.2 x 25kg bags
5 parts all-in aggregate	1cu m
For garage or garden shed bases **(not exposed to weather), using separate aggregate**	
1 part cement	12.8 x 25kg bags
2 parts sharp sand	½cu m
3 parts 20mm coarse aggregate	¾cu m
For garage or garden shed bases **(not exposed to weather), using all-in aggregate**	
1 part cement	12.8 x 25kg bags
4 parts all-in aggregate	1cu m

Mixing by hand

Mixing concrete by hand is only really an option for small amounts. Prepare it in the same way as mortar (see page 215), mixing thoroughly and methodically – a longer job than you might think – until it is an even consistency, neither too dry nor too sloppy. When you pick up a shovelful, it should stay on the shovel and when you drop it onto the sub-base it should spread slightly but retain some shape.

Using a mixer

Start by pouring about a quarter of a bucket of water into the mixer. Add half the aggregate and half the sand (or half the all-in aggregate), and all the cement, then check the mix to see if you need to add more water. Add the rest of the aggregate (and sand, if using it), and more water if necessary. If you find it difficult to assess a shovelful, gauge the mix using buckets (see page 215).

If the final mix is too sloppy, add more aggregate and cement in proportion. An average-sized mixer will accept 12 to 14 shovelfuls of aggregate and two to three shovelfuls of cement.

Ready-mixed concrete

If you are planning to lay a large area of concrete or have little time, ready-mixed concrete is worth considering. Depending on the access to your site, the concrete is delivered in lorries and either poured directly on to the area or wheelbarrowed from the lorry to the site. It is a much more expensive way of buying concrete, but it cuts down on labour enormously and companies will deliver any quantity. If you decide to use ready-mixed, you will need to ensure that everything is organised before the lorry arrives and that help is on hand. Ready-mixed is ordered by the cubic metre: add 10% to allow for wastage and specify the job you are doing so the right mix can be prepared.

Estimating the amount

To estimate the amount of concrete required for a job, you need to apply a bit of basic geometry. Measure the surface area of the site by multiplying the length by the width (in metres). Multiply that figure by the depth or thickness required (as a fraction of a metre) and you will have the volume in cubic metres. In practice, figures are rounded up and about 10% added for wastage.

For example: (width) 2m x (length) 6m x (depth) 0.15m = 1.8 cubic metres. You would round that up to 2 cubic metres of concrete.

If the site is circular, use the formula πr^2 (π = 3.14 and r^2 = the radius of the circle squared). Multiply them together to get the surface area, then multiply that number by the depth of the concrete required to get the volume.

For example: (π) 3.14 x (radius) 2m x (radius) 2m x depth 0.15m = 1.884 cubic metres of concrete. Rounded up, you would require 2 cubic metres of concrete.

Irregular shapes

To work out the volume of concrete needed for an irregularly-shaped site, draw it accurately and to scale on graph paper. Each square should represent 1sq m of the site. Count the whole squares covered and roughly add up the part squares. Multiply that total by the depth of the concrete and round the figure up by 10%.

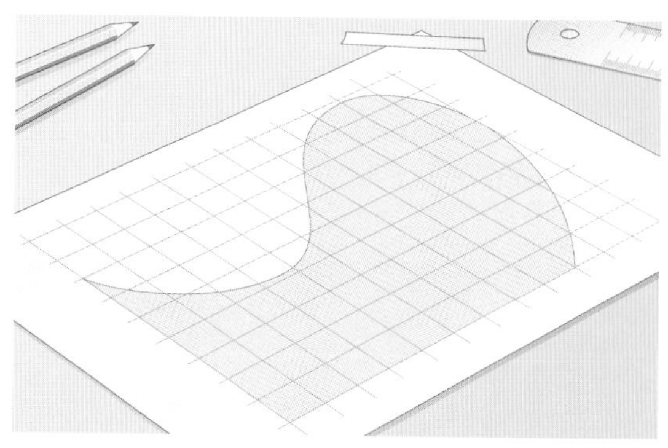

Constructing basic formwork

Concrete has to be supported by a frame or edging, known as formwork, until it has set. Timber formwork is sufficient for most domestic jobs but on larger projects, such as long drives, you can hire metal roadforms. The formwork is constructed directly on a prepared sub-base (see pages 228–29). Use rough-sawn timber planks about 25mm thick and as deep as the concrete. They are held in place by wooden pegs spaced at about 1m intervals.

TOOLS MATERIALS

- **builder's line**
- **builder's square**
- **panel saw**
- **club hammer**
- **spirit level**
- **straightedge**
- **hammer**

- 50mm x 50mm wooden pegs
- rough-sawn timber planks, 25mm thick and as wide as the depth of concrete
- 50mm nails

1 Set out the site using builder's lines and wooden pegs, cut to a point at one end: the lines should mark the edges of the concrete, which will be the inside of the formwork. Use a builder's square (see page 217) to check the corners are exactly 90º.

2 Cut a plank to length and place it in position along the high side of the site. Use a club hammer to drive a peg into the sub-base at each end, outside the area to be concreted. Hammer them in until they are flush with the top of the plank.

3 Use a spirit level to make sure the plank is level, then secure each end of the plank to the wooden pegs with 50mm nails.

4 Use a spirit level, straightedge and shim to set the fall on the two adjacent sides of the formwork. It should be about 1 in 80 for a single concrete pad (see page 229).

5 Attach the last plank to complete the square or rectangle. Make sure that there are pegs at the corners and that the corners are tight-fitting by nailing the planks together. It doesn't matter if the planks run past the edge of the square, as they do here.

6 Hammer in pegs at roughly 1m intervals along the outside of the formwork. The structure must be solid; it is very difficult to alter it once you begin concreting.

IDEAL TOOL

Club hammer

A heavy club hammer is needed for driving the wooden pegs into the hardcore sub-base.

CONCRETE FORMWORK

Curved formwork

If you want to make a curved path or drive, you will need to bend the timber formwork to follow the curve. Do this by making a series of closely spaced parallel saw cuts across the width of the plank along the length of the curve.

TOOLS MATERIALS

- **builder's line**
- **hammer**
- **workbench**
- **circular saw**
- **hosepipe or rope, if required**

- 50mm x 50mm wooden pegs
- 50mm nails
- bamboo cane
- rough-sawn timber planks, 25mm thick

YOU CAN DO IT

Check it's firm
As a final check to make sure the formwork is solid before you start concreting, try to flex the planking by pushing it backwards and forwards with your hand. If it moves, add more pegs.

1 To mark a curve, nail one end of a line to a peg, attach a bamboo cane to the other end and use this to draw an arc in the sub-base surface. If the curve is not circular, use a hosepipe or rope to define the shape and mark it with a cane. Drive in pegs at roughly 1m intervals along the curve.

2 Hold the plank in a workbench and use a circular saw to make a series of cuts, about 50mm apart and 20mm deep, along the entire length of the proposed curve. If it is a tight curve, the saw cuts should be slightly closer together.

3 Starting in the middle of the curve, nail the plank to the pegs with the saw cuts on the inside of the curve (if it is a very gentle curve, they can be on the outside).

Driveways

Even if you intend to surface a driveway with concrete slabs, you need a sub-base that includes a layer of concrete. This is because a drive has to bear a much greater weight than a path or other lightweight structure. It should have a sub-base of 150mm compacted hardcore covered with a thin blinding coat of sharp sand, then a 125mm depth of concrete, or 150mm of concrete if the drive is going to be used by heavy vehicles. The slabs should be at least 50mm thick.

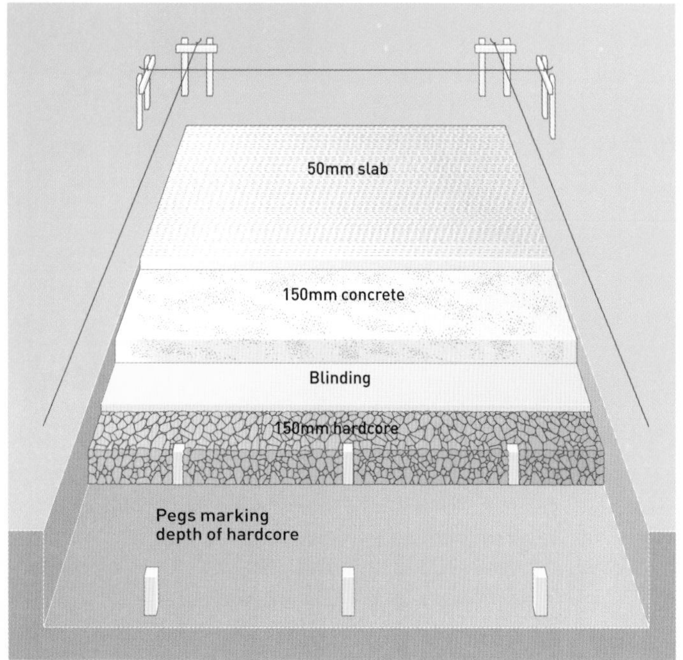

Extending a run of formwork

You may have a run of timber formwork that is longer than the length of the planks you are using. In this case, you need to butt-join two lengths very securely. Cut a section of plank about 200mm long.

Line up the two planks to be joined, end to end. Place the short length of timber across the join, outside the area to be concreted. Nail from the inside to join the short length to the long planks. Keep your feet well out of the way, and hit the spiked end of each nail when you have knocked it through to turn it safely over.

Control joints

In larger areas and along paths and drives, special control joints should be installed to allow the concrete to expand and contract without cracking as the temperature changes. Control joints usually consist of 12mm-thick bitumen-impregnated fibreboard (specially designed for the job), which is compressible and allows the concrete to expand and contract. The fibreboards are inserted as the concrete is being laid.

Control joints should be installed between concrete and a wall, between bays (see page 241), and around inspection chambers. The maximum size a concrete slab can be without danger of it cracking depends on its width and thickness: the more narrow and shallow the concrete, the more likely it is to crack (see table below). You don't need control joints in a concrete sub-base.

CONTROL JOINT INTERVALS

Width of concrete	Depth of concrete 75mm	100mm	150mm
Under 1m	2m interval		
1m–2 m	2.4m interval	2m–3m interval	3m–4m interval
3m	3m interval	4m interval	5m interval

Installing a control joint for a path

Cut the bitumen-impregnated fibreboard to size – each joint must be the width of the slab and the depth of the concrete.

IDEAL TOOL

Shovel
Unlike a garden spade, a shovel has raised edges designed for transporting loose materials like sand, gravel or cement.

1 Place the first board on the sub-base between the formwork. Hammer nails through the formwork into the board but do not drive the nails home. This will allow you to take them out easily with a claw hammer before the formwork is removed.

2 Shovel concrete against the board on both sides to hold it in position.

TOOLS MATERIALS

- **panel saw**
- **tape measure**
- **hammer**
- **shovel**

- bitumen-impregnated fibreboard
- 50mm nails
- concrete

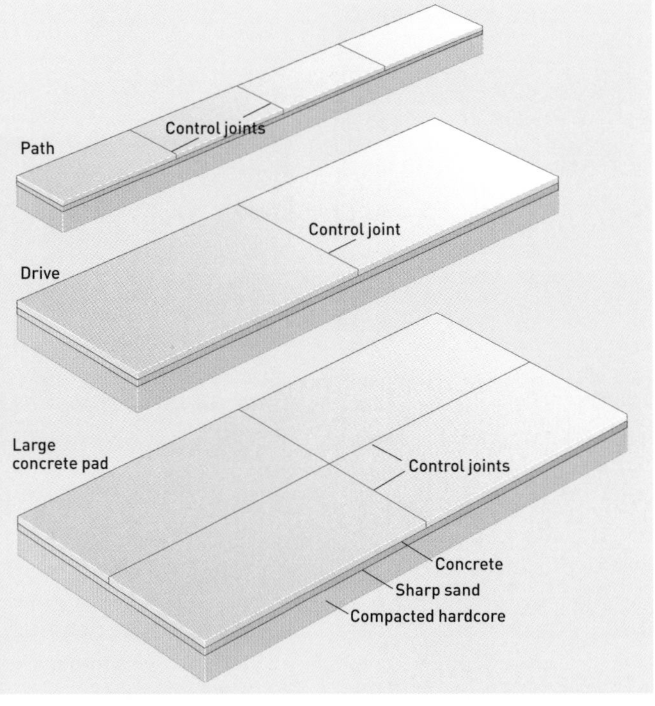

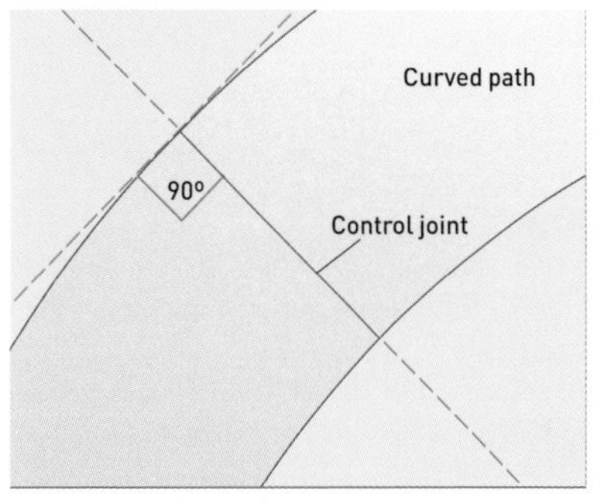

Regular and irregular shapes

Paths need a control joint every 2m in 75mm-deep concrete. Drives and parking areas need them every 4m in 100mm-deep concrete. In large concrete pads they should be installed no more than 4m apart in 100mm-deep concrete. On an irregular-shaped winding path, control joints are inserted at 90° to the path edges.

CONCRETE LAYING AND FINISHING

Concrete starts to harden and set about two hours after it has been mixed, so it must be laid, tamped (packed down) and given its finish within that time. Divide large areas into bays or sections which can be completed one at a time before they begin to set. You can walk on the concrete after three days, remove the formwork after five days and drive on it after ten days.

Laying concrete

Concreting is a two-person job. Using ready-mixed concrete, two people can lay an area of approximately 8.5sq m before it sets. Concrete will crack if it is allowed to dry too quickly during the first few days, so keep it moist by covering it with a polythene sheet.

TOOLS MATERIALS

- **watering can with rose attachment**
- **wheelbarrow**
- **shovel**
- **rake (optional)**
- **arrissing tool**

- concrete
- 50mm x 100mm timber longer than the width of your site
- polythene sheet
- timbers and bricks to support polythene sheet

1 Wet the sub-base and the formwork with a watering can fitted with a rose.

2 Starting in one corner, pour concrete into the formwork.

3 Push the blade of the shovel up and down in the wet concrete (particularly near the edges) to get rid of any air pockets.

4 Use a rake or shovel to spread the concrete, leaving it about 18mm higher than the top of the formwork. Fill about 1m–1.5m from the end where you started.

5 With a helper, compact the concrete using a straight piece of 50mm x 100mm timber that is longer than the width of your site (this is known as a tamping board). Start at one end and use steady blows of the plank, moving it along the site at a rate of about half its thickness at a time, until you have an even ridged surface.

6 To remove excess concrete and level the surface, go back to the end where you started and slide the tamping board backwards and forwards in a sawing motion across the site, moving it all the time away from the starting edge. Fill any depressions in the surface and repeat the procedure, if necessary, until you have an even surface flush with the top of your formwork. Continue to pour the concrete, tamp and level until you reach the end of the bay.

7 At this stage you have a rough tamped surface which can be given any of the finishes opposite. When you are happy with the finish, you can run an arrissing tool (see IDEAL TOOL, page 227) along the formwork to round off the exposed edges of the concrete.

8 Cover the concrete with a polythene sheet to slow drying and prevent cracking. Raise the sheet on wooden supports so that it does not touch the surface and weight it down with bricks around the edges.

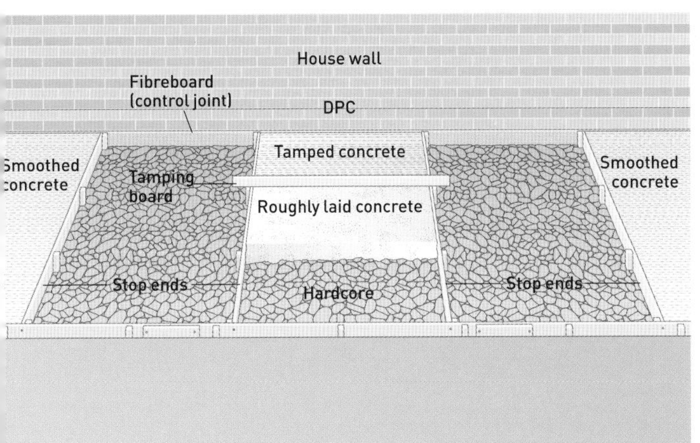

Concrete bays

Try to keep bays the same size and as square as possible. Their size will vary according to the shape of the site but it is impractical to make one more than 4m wide in the direction in which you will be tamping or packing down the concrete. Position pegged boards (known as stop ends) at right angles to the main run of formwork. Remember to install a control joint against a wall and to keep the surface of the concrete at least 150mm below the damp-proof course in a house wall. The pegs must be outside the area to be concreted. Lay the concrete in alternate bays so you can stand in the empty bays to tamp it. When the concrete is dry, take out the boards and pegs and fit lengths of fibreboard in their place. Then fill the gaps, using the edges of the dry concrete pads to level the concrete in the adjacent bays.

Concrete finishes

A rough tamped finish will often be perfectly adequate, or you can use brushes or floats if you want a smoother finish. Allow the concrete to dry a little before finishing with a float or you will bring moisture to the surface, which will weaken the concrete.

Tamped finish

For a roughish finish with plenty of grip, leave the tamped surface without any extra finish.

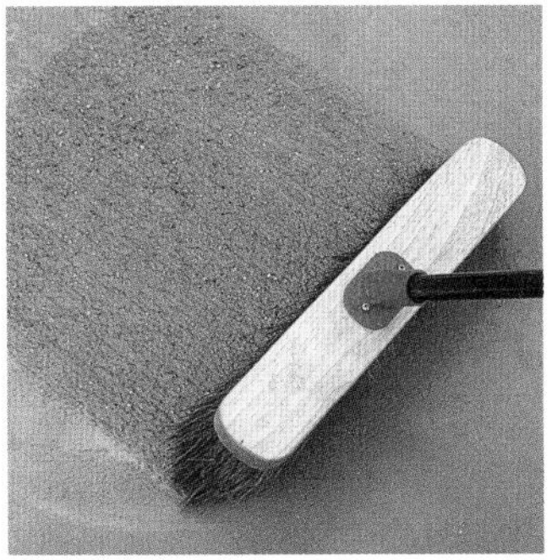

Brush finish

Pull a stiff brush at an angle across the surface. For a softer finish, use a soft brush.

Metal float finish

Use a metal float to create a polished, glass-like finish. This is time-consuming and requires some skill to get it perfectly smooth. It is usually impractical outdoors: on a path or drive algae growth will build up as it weathers and the surface will become very slippery in no time.

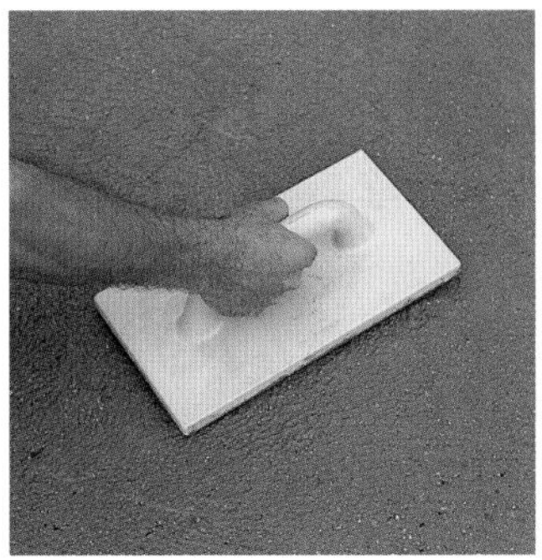

Wooden or plastic float finish

Create a pattern of overlapping circles on the concrete surface, using a plastic or wooden float.

Gravel finish

Smoothed concrete can be covered with a layer of gravel. Use small, same-size gravel such as 10mm pea gravel.

1 Finish the surface with a float then spread the gravel while the concrete is still wet.

2 Lightly tamp the gravel into the surface, using a block of wood. Let the concrete harden for a day or two then lightly spray the surface, using a watering can with a fine rose attachment. Brush away any loose material with a soft brush. Let the surface dry for a day, then hose it down and brush with a stiff broom.

IDEAL TOOL

Float

A wooden or plastic builder's float is very effective for smoothing the surface or for creating circular patterns on a concrete surface. For a really fine texture use a steel float.

GARDEN STEPS ON A SLOPE

Garden steps built into an earth slope can be constructed from a variety of materials: bricks and concrete slabs, timber and gravel, concrete or large flat stones. The design will depend on the type of material you use, the gradient and the length of the slope. But the treads – the horizontal part of the step – should never be less than 300mm from front to back, and the risers – the vertical face between the treads – no lower than 100mm and no higher than 180mm. Use longer treads on a gentle slope and shorter on a steep one.

Setting out and excavating the steps

The steps shown here are built from brick and concrete slabs. The first riser is laid on a concrete footing, while the rest of the risers are bedded directly on to the tread below. The tread lengths are all the same but the excavation for the first step is longer than the others.

TOOLS MATERIALS

- **builder's line**
- **builder's square**
- **hammer**
- **tape measure**
- **spirit level**
- **straightedge, if required**
- **spade**
- **wheelbarrow**
- **trowel**
- **earth rammer**

- 50mm x 50mm wooden pegs
- foundation-mix concrete
- bricks
- sharp sand
- cement
- hardcore
- 10mm shim
- slabs

1 Begin by marking out the site using builder's line and pegs. Fix two parallel lines down the length of the slope, marking the outer edge of the steps, and two more to mark the top and bottom of the steps. Use a builder's square to check that the corners form a right angle (see page 217).

2 To calculate how many treads and risers are required, you need to measure the vertical height and horizontal distance of the flight of steps. Knock in a peg to mark the back of the highest tread. Then hold one end of a long spirit level (or a level and straightedge) at the top of the peg. With a helper, measure the horizontal distance to the first riser, and the vertical distance to the ground at that point.

3 Divide the vertical height by your riser height and use the tread-riser combinations chart (opposite) to find an appropriate tread length. Strip away any turf in the marked-out area with a spade.

4 Use lines to mark the back of the treads, set back an extra 50mm or so to give you enough room to work. Roughly shape the steps with a spade. Allow enough depth beneath the concrete slab treads for 100mm of hardcore.

5 Dig a trench about 125mm deep for the footing for the first riser. Drive in pegs levelled with a spirit level to mark the surface of the footing before you pour in concrete. If there is to be a paved surface leading to the steps, then dig a deeper footing and lay one or two courses of engineering bricks on top of it, below ground level. You will then be able to lay paving right up to the first riser.

6 Concrete the footing, making sure the surface is level with your pegs, and leave it to dry for 24 hours before building on it.

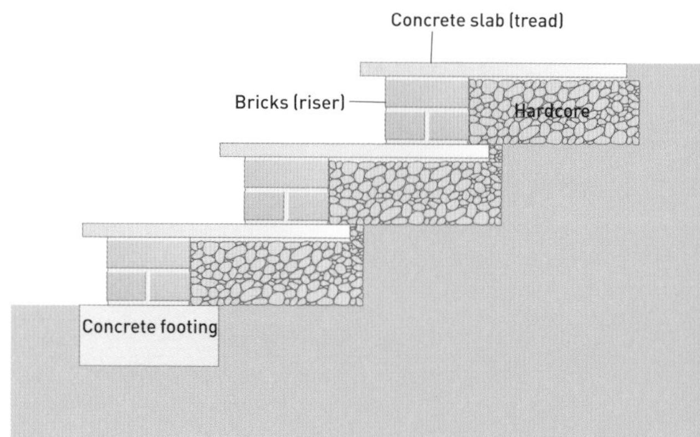

Tread-riser combinations

o work out how many risers you need, divide the vertical height of the light by the height of your riser. Then divide the horizontal length of the light into a suitable number of treads. The combinations of tread and iser measurements given here will make attractive, safe steps. It is ot always possible to follow them exactly: you may need to shorten or engthen treads, cut bricks or build up the ground to make your flight vork. But you should aim to approximate these measurements when naking your calculations, and don't forget that a tread should never e less than 300mm front to back.

TREAD-RISER COMBINATIONS

Tread length	Riser depth
460mm	100mm
430mm	113mm
400mm	125mm
380mm	140mm
360mm	150mm
330mm	165mm
300mm	180mm

Building the steps

It is a good idea to make a drawing showing the step dimensions once you have decided on the best tread and riser combination: you will find this a useful reference while you are building the steps. If you are using slabs that are 600mm square or larger, make sure you have a helper – they should be lifted and laid by two people.

IDEAL TOOL

Earth rammer
An earth rammer – a heavy steel club on a long handle – is ideal for compacting small areas of earth.

1 Mix a mortar using four parts sharp sand to one part cement see page 215). Build the first iser on the concrete footing ısing two skins of stretcher bond ›ricks (see page 214). Keep :hecking they are horizontal with a spirit level. Leave the mortar to dry for two hours.

2 Fill behind the riser with hardcore – it should extend beyond the back of the slab when laid. Compact the hardcore with an earth rammer (see IDEAL TOOL).

3 The hardcore should rise slightly towards the back of the step. Use a spirit level and 10mm shim laid across the front of the step to achieve this (see Setting the fall, page 229).

4 Lay a continuous bed of mortar on the riser and hardcore and position the slab for the first tread on top of it. The slab should overhang the riser at both the front and sides by approximately 40mm. Place the spirit level along the front edge to check the step is in line. If you are laying two slabs side by side, apply a pointing mortar (made with three parts sharp sand to one part cement) to the edge of the first slab before you lay the second. This will make it easier to fill the joints.

5 Confirm that the treads are showing a slight fall towards heir front edge with a spirit level and 10mm shim. Fill all the joints with mortar.

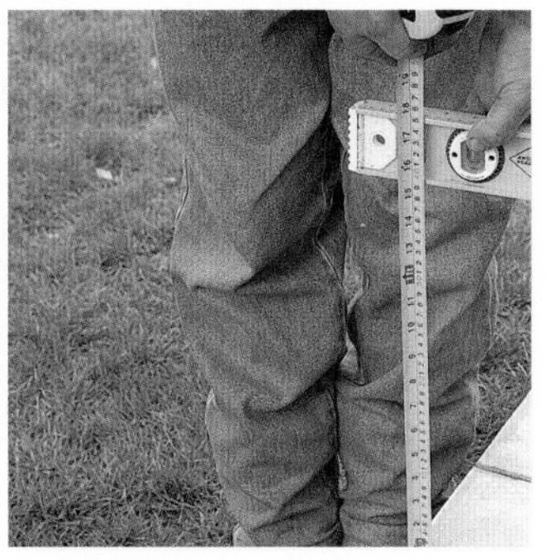

6 Build the next riser on the first tread. Check that its depth is the same as the first and make slight adjustments to the horizontal joints as necessary. It's very easy for slight errors to accumulate, so you should also check each riser against the overall height of the flight, measured from the top guide peg with a spirit level and tape measure. Lay the slabs of the next tread.

7 Continue building the steps, checking that the tread lengths are correct. Place a long spirit level or straightedge on the front edge of the treads to check they are in line. The slope on either side of the steps can be banked up with earth for planting or it can be grassed.

GARDEN STEPS FREESTANDING AND LOG

Freestanding steps constructed beside a brick wall should be built from brick and concrete, and need to be anchored to the wall to make them secure. In an informal part of the garden logs can be used to support a single step on a gentle slope, or they can be placed at intervals on a long incline.

Freestanding steps

Not all steps are built into a slope: freestanding steps can be built on a flat base alongside an existing garden wall (not a house wall, for they would breach the damp-proof course). They are supported by low walls built of bricks, which also form the risers. The walls are like a series of boxes and are filled with hardcore. For a flight of up to five steps, the supporting walls can be centred on concrete footing strips. For a longer flight, you need a concrete pad under the whole structure.

The brick risers can either be built up from ground level or you can lay a 100mm concrete footing at the back of each tread on built-up compacted hardcore before you lay the slab, and build the next riser on it. With brick steps parallel to a brick wall, the bricks in the risers should correspond to the bricks in the existing wall. The risers must be anchored, or toothed in, to the existing wall to make them more secure.

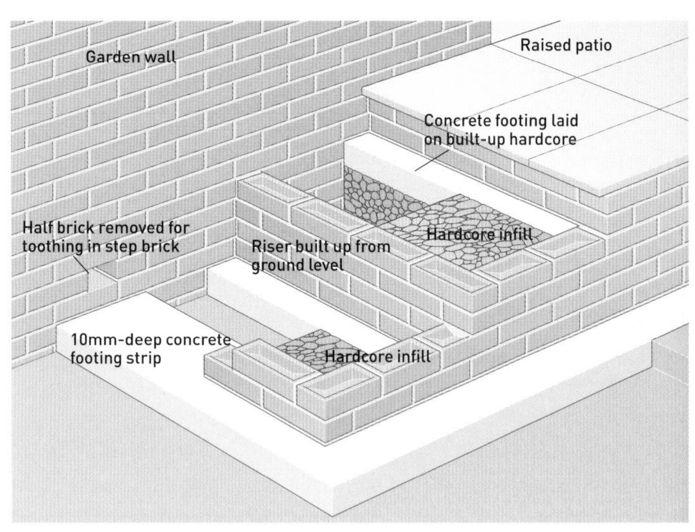

TOOLS MATERIALS

- **hammer action drill with 10mm masonry bit**
- **cold chisel**
- **club hammer**
- **builder's line**
- **tape measure**
- **trowel**
- **spirit level**
- **builder's square**
- **shovel**

- hardcore
- foundation mix concrete (see page 236)
- paving slabs
- bricks
- mortar

Anchoring steps to an existing wall

To anchor freestanding steps safely to the wall, the adjoining brick in every third course of their low supporting walls must be 'toothed in' to the brickwork of the existing wall. To do this half a brick is cut out of the existing wall and half of the adjoining brick is inserted and securely mortared in its place. All the appropriate half-bricks must be removed from the existing wall before you start building the steps.

1 Drill 10mm holes into the joints around the half of the brick that you are removing. Then drill down the centre of the brick.

2 Use a cold chisel and club hammer to remove the half-brick.

3 Build the steps and support walls up to the level of the cavity. Spread mortar on the top of the wall and into the cavity, then fit half of the adjoining brick into the cavity. Tap it into place with the trowel handle. Continue building the rest of that course of bricks and lay the tread.

IDEAL TOOL

Cold chisel

A cold chisel, which is made from solid steel, is ideal for chopping out a brick from a wall. The plastic handle has a built-in guard to protect your hand.

1 Excavate the ground either side of the step, roughly levelling it. Tread down the soil to compact it, if necessary. Cut your log or logs to the required length using a handsaw and paint the cut ends with wood preservative. Then lay one log in position to mark the first riser. Cut two lengths of log about 450mm long and sharpen one end of each to a point; these will be used as stakes to retain the riser. Use a sledgehammer to knock in the stakes in front of the riser at either side of the step, leaving them higher than the proposed depth of the riser.

Simple log step

This log step will blend well in an informal part of the garden. Instead of logs you can use railway sleepers or even sawn lengths of timber. Select one large log or two slimmer ones for each step (the logs shown here are 75mm in diameter). If you buy untreated softwood logs, be sure to give them a coat of wood preservative before you start.

TOOLS MATERIALS

- **spade**
- **tape measure**
- **spirit level**
- **handsaw**
- **sledgehammer**
- **power drill with twist bit**
- **earth rammer**
- **hammer**
- **rake**

- 75mm-diameter logs
- wood preservative
- 125mm galvanised nails
- hardcore
- gravel

2 Position the next log directly on top of the first and use a spirit level to ensure it is horizontal. Roll the logs away and adjust the earth below if necessary.

3 Use the sledgehammer to knock down the stakes to the level of the riser.

IDEAL TOOL

Sledgehammer

You will need a heavy-weight tool like a sledgehammer to hammer log stakes into the ground.

4 Take off the top log. Using a drill with a twist bit, drill pilot holes all the way through the lower log in line with the two stakes. Get a helper to hold the post steady from the other side with the sledgehammer and hammer in 125mm galvanised nails from the inside of the step to secure the bottom log to the stakes. Repeat with the top log.

5 Pack hardcore behind the riser to form the step tread and compact it with an earth rammer.

6 Cover the hardcore with a layer of gravel and rake it level.

Design your own steps

Reclaimed railway sleepers (left) have a rugged, weathered finish that works perfectly with the informality of simple garden steps. Fill the excavated part of the step with stones, chippings or wood bark. You could relay the turf, but it is likely to wear away with regular use. For a more hardwearing surface, let the grass grow between loose-laid log cobbles

SHEDS AND GREENHOUSES PLANNING

Shed or summerhouse, playhouse or gazebo, greenhouse or simple glass lean-to: garden buildings come in all shapes and sizes, and have more potential than you might at first think. What's to stop you adding a power supply and heating to a shed and turning it into a workshop or even a home office? Do the same in a summerhouse and you can relax or entertain in it day or night, winter or summer. These structures are very affordable, demand minimum planning, and are quick and easy to put together. Visit www.diy.com for inspiration and ideas.

Sheds, summerhouses and playhouses

Classed as temporary structures, sheds and wooden outbuildings rarely require planning permission, unless you live in a conservation area (see page 370). They can be built almost anywhere, so long as they are positioned on a level, firm surface. Thinking through the following issues before you buy should help you make the right choice:

Planning

- What size of outbuilding do you want? How big can it be without it overwhelming your garden?
- How will you gain access to the building? Would a path protect the lawn and make it more accessible in the wet?
- Where will you put it? Don't place a building where it will create dead space, where light is blocked and access limited. It is often sensible to back a shed onto an outside wall or fence.
- Will there be enough natural light in winter? Is there a danger of overheating in summer?
- Do you want an electricity supply? If so, how far away is the power source?
- Do you want a water supply? Is there an outside water tap from which a pipe can be run?
- Will your choice of building be useful if your needs change in the future? For example, an outbuilding designed as a playhouse could become a summerhouse or workshop when small children grow up.
- What can you do to make it look good and complement your garden? You could paint it with coloured wood stain, for example, and surround it with imaginative planting.

Greenhouses

Greenhouses come in many shapes and sizes, with frames in timber or, more often, aluminium, which has the advantage of being maintenance-free. Choose the biggest greenhouse you can afford or have room for, as you will find that plants fill the space very quickly.

Glazing

There are three main choices: horticultural glass is most common and is inexpensive; toughened glass is a stronger alternative and safer if there will be children in the garden; even tougher still are polycarbonate panels, which diffuse sunlight and so reduce scorching.

Ventilation

The correct amount of ventilation is very important for temperature control and air circulation. Poor ventilation will increase humidity and encourage plant disease. Most greenhouse frames include adjustable air vents. Thermostatically controlled automatic vents can be installed inexpensively, and they don't need a power supply. Louvre windows are another option, allowing adjustable, draught-free ventilation.

Shading

Greenhouse shading is necessary in the summer months to avoid overheating and scorching plants. There are three main options:

- Special greenhouse shading paint can be applied to the exterior surface of the glass. It is weatherproof but can be removed with a duster in late autumn.
- Shading panels or woven plastic netting can be clipped to the inside of the frame.
- Internal shelving can provide shade for the most delicate plants.

Heating

For cold seasons and for growing certain plants, you may need to heat your greenhouse. Again, there are several options available:

- Paraffin heaters are cheap to buy but they consume a lot of fuel, are difficult to regulate and they encourage condensation, which can increase humidity and lead to plant diseases.
- Bottled gas heaters are thermostatically controlled but again encourage condensation.
- Electric heating is the best option, but you will need connection to a power supply. Choose between heating pipes, a fan heater or even a warming cable laid under the soil in a bed of coarse grit.

Irrigation

Capillary matting, which retains water and releases it according to a plant's requirements, is enough for most greenhouses. Alternatively you could run a pipe along the soil from an outside water tap. You could even add a timer switch for automatic watering – particularly useful if you go away regularly.

GREENHOUSE CONSTRUCTION

A greenhouse will bring new life to your garden, providing a controlled environment in which to propagate plants, bring on hardy ones early, protect semi-hardy specimens from frost, and grow exotic species in year-round warmth. Choose an open sunny situation, with the longest side of the greenhouse facing south for maximum light penetration.

Securing the base to the ground

You can buy a separate purpose-designed galvanised steel base, also available as a flatpack, on which the greenhouse frame sits, secured by frame fixings. A base will usefully raise the height of the greenhouse, and make construction easier, though it is not essential. However, the frame or base must be firmly secured onto a level surface. There are different methods of doing this:

- Push specially designed metal hooks into isolated pockets of wet concrete. These are then attached to the base, securing it to the ground.
- Or you could install a concrete strip footing 200mm wide and 100mm deep. The base can then be anchored by drilling and bolting it into the concrete. Drill holes through the base, or directly through the bottom sill of the greenhouse frame in the centre of each bay (being careful to leave room for the glazing).
- Better still is to lay a single course of bricks on top of the concrete footing and fix the base – or the greenhouse frame without a base – to the bricks. This is the most attractive and sturdiest method, and it raises the height of the greenhouse by around 125mm.

If you are not using a base, the manufacturer may recommend wooden battens as a buffer between the brick/cement and the bottom of the greenhouse frame.

Installing the base

This is the procedure to follow if you want to attach your base and frame to a course of bricks on a cement footing. Check the kit before you begin to make sure all the base and frame fixings are included.

TOOLS MATERIALS

- **tape measure**
- **builder's line**
- **spade**
- **builder's square**
- **spirit level**
- **trowel**
- **flat-head screwdriver**
- **cross-head screwdriver**
- **10mm open-ended spanner**
- **hammer action drill with masonry bit**
- **protective gloves**
- **safety goggles**

- plywood or hardboard sheets, if required
- greenhouse base kit
- footing mix concrete (see page 236)
- bricks
- mortar
- 25mm frame fixings
- greenhouse kit

YOU CAN DO IT

Building paths

To make the job easier, construct paths around and inside your greenhouse before you erect it. Watering and trampling will make soil paths in a greenhouse turn to mud, so build a path from concrete slabs or paving stones, or simply lay down gravel or coarse wood chip between narrow retaining boards nailed to pegs hammered into the ground.

1 Construct the galvanised steel base, following the instructions supplied. It is best to work on a flat, level surface such as plywood or hardboard sheets. Make sure the site is firm and level, and lay down the base to mark out the position of the footing. The footing needs to be 200mm wide. Mark its edges by running two builder's lines parallel to each side of the base, one 50mm from the outside face, the other 150mm from its inside face.

2 Dig out the footing trench to a depth of 100mm and fill it with concrete (see pages 216–17). The surface must be absolutely level. When dry, rest the base on the concrete and pencil a line around its outside edge. Lay one course of bricks (see page 218) in the centre of the footing. The outer faces of the bricks should be flush with the outside of the frame. Leave the mortar to dry for 24 hours.

3 Lift the base onto the prepared brick foundation.

Building the greenhouse

Make sure you have the manufacturer's instructions and all the pieces to hand before you start. You need to assemble the whole frame and make sure it is straight and square before fully tightening the bolts and screws.

SAFETY FIRST

If you have children, or young children play in your garden, choose the safer option of polycarbonate glazing panels in your greenhouse. Ordinary horticultural glass is a potential hazard.

1 Lay the pieces for one gable end of your greenhouse on a flat surface. Arrange them carefully into position, with metal sections and bolts the right way round and angled pieces leaning in the correct direction.

2 Bolt the pieces loosely together to assemble the first side. Follow the same procedure for the other end and then for the sides.

3 Now bolt the sides and gable ends of the frame together and screw them to the base. Leave all bolts and screws loose at this stage.

4 Attach the roof ridge bar, screwing it loosely between the the two gable ends. Slide on the fittings for the roof vent then screw in the roof glazing bars.

5 Now use a builder's square and spirit level to check that the whole frame is straight and the corners are square.

6 When you are confident that everything is level and true, tighten all screws and bolts, including those attaching the frame to the base.

7 Secure the metal base to the brick plinth, using 25mm frame fixings. These must be drilled through the base and into the brickwork. Take care to drill only into brick, not cement.

8 Assemble the frame of the roof vent. Once it is tightly screwed together, slide it into place along the roof ridge.

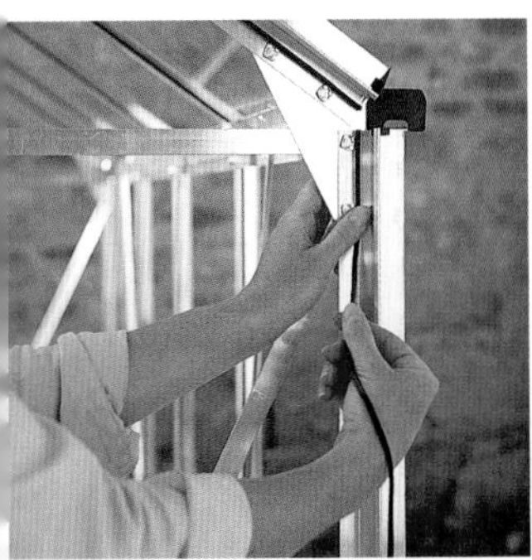

9 Push and slide the thin flexible rubber line into the tiny slots all around the frame.

10 Starting with the roof, place each pane of glass into the frame and secure it with clips. Be sure to wear gloves and safety goggles. Once you have the knack this process is quick and easy. Take care, be patient, and make sure you are working with the right-sized glass for the section of the frame you are glazing.

11 Position the glazing clips according to the manufacturer's instructions. Keep them evenly spaced.

12 Assemble the door, fit the glass and slide it into place.

SHED CONSTRUCTION

A basic garden shed is straightforward to assemble. Or you can choose something more elaborate: extra windows and double doors for additional light, easy access and good ventilation. A more substantial shed or summerhouse can be fully wired up, insulated or even heated; extra-secure locks can be fitted if you intend to store valuable items inside.

Building the shed

Lay a concrete pad (see pages 236–41) that is 25mm smaller on all sides than the base of the shed, to create an overhang and prevent water accumulating around the timber floor and runners. To ensure good drainage this should slope slightly (see Setting the fall, page 229).

TOOLS MATERIALS

- **tape measure**
- **pencil**
- **screwdriver**
- **power drill with twist and countersink bits**
- **hammer**
- **spirit level**
- **builder's square**
- **craft knife**

- shed kit
- timber prop

1 Centre the shed floor on top of your concrete pad so that there is an overhang of 25mm on all sides. Measure and mark in pencil the centre point of each edge, and do the same on the bottom batten of each of the side panels.

2 Lift the gable end without the door into place, and use a prop to hold it upright. Lift one side panel onto the base.

3 Screw the gable end and side panel together along the framing battens where they meet. Drill pilot holes then fit three 50mm countersunk screws at the top, middle and bottom.

4 Fit the other side panel in the same way. Then fit the gable end housing the door. But don't try to fix your shed frame to the floor yet.

5 Fit the roof support beam across the top of the shed, slotting it into the pre-cut grooves at the top of the gable ends. Check that the shed is sitting firmly on its base and that the door opens easily. Then use 30mm screws through an L-shaped metal bracket to fix the beam to each gable end.

6 Lay the roof panels on the ground, one at a time, with the eave sections (wooden strips) positioned underneath flush with the bottom edge of the panel. Measure and mark six evenly spaced fixing positions. Drill pilot holes and then hammer in the nails to attach the eave sections to the roof panels.

7 Lift the roof panels into place, one at a time. Line up the shed frame on the base using the centre markings then secure the roof panels with 30mm screws along the roof support beam. Fix them to the sides and gable ends of the shed using 40mm nails, or 30mm nails across the window heads. Check again that the shed is square on the base before finally nailing the sides and gable ends to the floor with 50mm nails.

YOU CAN DO IT

Square it up

You may find that the assembled shed is not quite square when you come to nail it to the base. If so, you will need to shift it slightly. Tap one corner with a club hammer, holding a timber off-cut against the shed timbers to avoid bruising them.

Felting the roof

Even if your shed kit comes with a roll of roof felt, you will probably still need to cut it to size with a sharp craft knife and a straightedge.

1 Unroll the roofing felt then measure and cut three pieces: one for each roof panel, and a third strip to be laid along the apex, to prevent water seeping in. The pieces covering the roof panels should run the full length of the shed with a 50mm overhang at either end. The third piece covering the apex should be the same length and extend at least 75mm over each roof panel.

2 Lay the first piece of felt over one side panel, with a 50mm overhang at the eave. Tack it along the top edge with felt nails about 300mm apart. Then fix it down along the gable ends and eave with felt nails at 100mm intervals. Repeat the other side. Place the third strip of felt over the top of the roof and nail it along each edge at 100mm intervals.

3 Tidy up the felt at the corners: cut it to the edge, fold it neatly and tack it down (see Steps 4 and 5, page 252). Hammer the roof fascia in place using 40mm nails over the felt on the front and back gable ends. Use four nails per strip.

4 Secure each corner trim with three evenly spaced 30mm nails.

Finishing touches

Shed windows are usually made of perspex, which slides easily into the window frames. Add a bolt, and then all that remains is to decorate the shed in the style of your choosing. You could treat it with coloured wood stain, and grow plants around it to help it blend in with the garden.

1 Standing outside the shed, slot the metal window sill into position along the bottom of the window frame.

2 Still outside, nail in the window cloaks (short strips of wood), using four 40mm nails in each. This secures the sills.

3 From inside the shed, slide the perspex into place, resting it on the sill. The beading is secured with 25mm nails. Start the nails first, then position the beading over the perspex sheet at the top and sides of the frame and hammer them fully home. Finally remove the protective film from the perspex.

4 Drill pilot holes and screw in the sliding bolt. This can be padlocked for additional security.

CHILDREN'S GARDEN

Kids will play safely for hours in their own playhouse. You could stain it a cheerful colour and add features such as a sand pit, a special planting area, a shallow wildlife pond (for older children) or a climbing frame.

Building a playhouse

You can buy playhouses in a kit containing all the materials you need. Look for non-toxic wood treatments and perspex-glazed windows for added peace of mind. As for a garden shed, you need to start with a firm and level base. This could be a concrete pad (see pages 236–41) or some purpose-built decking (see pages 200–1). Fit the glazing and window beading before you assemble the playhouse (see Finishing touches, Step 3, page 251).

TOOLS MATERIALS

- **screwdriver**
- **power drill with twist and countersink bits**
- **tape measure**
- **pencil**
- **builder's square**
- **hammer**
- **craft knife**
- **paintbrush**

- playhouse kit
- paint or wood stain

1 Position the floor and erect the gable ends and sides as you would if erecting a shed (see page 250). Use a builder's square to check the corners are all 90°, then fit the roof ridge bar. Nail in the roof support block and corner trims, using 40mm nails. Lift the roof panels into position, following the same procedure as for a shed (see page 250).

2 Align the building and hammer in evenly spaced 40mm nails through the side frames to secure the floor. This playhouse has a small verandah: position the verandah floor at the front of the playhouse.

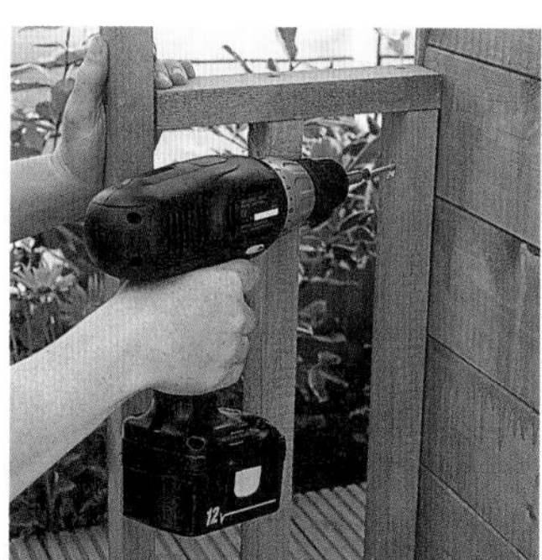

3 Secure the verandah rails onto the front of the playhouse. Screw the bottom of the rails down into the floor, and the tops into the eaves of the playhouse. Countersink all screws.

YOU CAN DO IT

Keep it straight

Use a builder's square (see page 217) to make sure all the corners form true right angles.

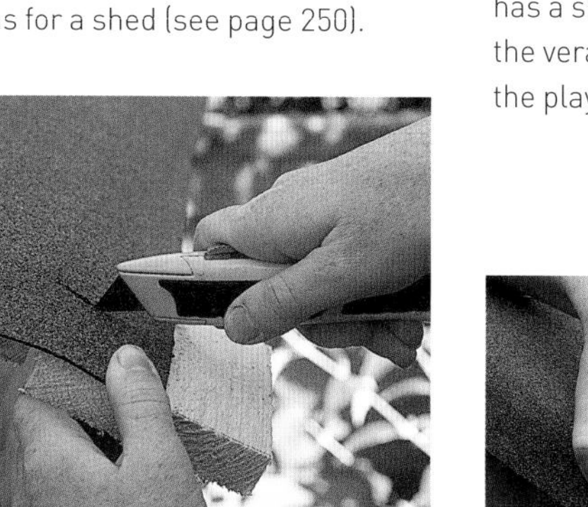

4 Felt the roof (see page 251). Where the gable end felt meets and overhangs the front eave, hold a piece of timber beneath the felt and use a sharp craft knife to make a straight cut from the corner of the roof to the edge of the felt.

5 Fold the cut flap under and nail the felt down at the corner.

6 Nail the fascia to the gable ends using two nails per section. If your playhouse is on a deck, you should screw it down to stop it slipping on the smooth surface. Drill 100mm countersunk screws through the runners inside the playhouse. (There's no need to fix it to a concrete surface.)

7 The playhouse can then be treated with wood preservative or stain. You could also paint it inside.

Building a sand pit

You can make a sand pit in any shape or size, but a simple 1m x 1m square gives ample space for play.

TOOLS MATERIALS

- **tape measure**
- **handsaw**
- **4 canes**
- **builder's line or string**
- **spade**
- **2 quick-release clamps**
- **hammer**
- **workbench**
- **try square**
- **power drill with countersink bits**
- **garden fork**
- **craft knife**

- 8 treated deck joists, 47mm x 150mm each
- 2 treated deck boards, 28mm x 144mm each
- 75mm deck screws
- 100mm and 25mm galvanised nails
- 10mm felt nails
- perforated metal fixing plates
- plastic pond liner or heavy-duty plastic sheet
- wood filler
- exterior wood adhesive
- paint
- play sand

1 Saw eight sections of deck joist to form two square frames or 'boxes' that will sit one on top of the other. Each box requires two lengths of exactly 1m and two of 1.056m to allow for the overlap at the corner joins. Drill pilot holes and fix the joists together at each corner using two 100mm galvanised nails.

2 Lay one box frame in position on the ground and mark the outer corners with canes; join the canes with builder's line or string to outline the hole. Dig the hole to the depth of the two stacked boxes. Put one box frame on top of the other and clamp them together, making sure they are flush and square. Then join them with a perforated metal plate in the middle of each side, secured with 25mm galvanised nails.

3 The exterior frame, made from deck boards, will rest on the ground, forming a seat around the top of the sand pit. To make it, take four pieces of 28mm x 144mm deck board. Secure each one in a workbench and cut one end to a 45° angle.

4 To cut the other ends accurately, line the deck boards up around the box, one at a time. Align the angled end with one corner and mark the point where it touches the next corner. Use this as the starting point for cutting the other end. If the box is exact, the inside, shorter edges of the frame sections will be exactly 1m long.

5 Working on a flat surface, glue the joints with a strong waterproof wood adhesive and then nail a perforated metal plate across the underside of each joint with 25mm nails. Wipe away surplus glue with a damp cloth, and leave to dry.

6 Once securely bonded, drill pilot holes and fix the seating to the top of the box with 75mm countersunk deck screws. Fill the holes with wood filler and sand smooth.

7 Now you can paint the frame. When it is dry, attach a sheet of pond liner or heavy-duty plastic to the bottom of the box with evenly spaced 10mm felt nails.

8 Scatter a thin layer of sand into the bottom of the hole and lower your finished box into it.

9 Use a garden fork to perforate the plastic liner. Make plenty of holes to allow for drainage and prevent your sand pit becoming soggy. Then fill it with play sand. It is best to cover a sand pit when it's not in use to stop it getting water-logged.

PONDS AND ORNAMENTAL FEATURES

SAFETY FIRST

Never forget that small children can drown in a few inches of water. Don't leave them unsupervised for a moment near a pond. For peace of mind, install a fence and gate around it until they are older.

Water has been used in landscape gardening for centuries, adding a precious extra dimension to the garden and providing an environment in which fish, frogs, newts and all sorts of wildlife can thrive. Ponds and water features can range in size from small lakes to tiny self-contained pebble water fountains.

Designing a pond

Make a rough sketch of the garden and draw in the proposed outline of the pond and its surroundings, including any plants. A symmetrical shape will produce a more formal effect, or you could create an irregular, informal pond that looks natural and fits in with the surrounding landscape.

Rigid pre-formed plastic ponds complete with a built-in planting shelf come in a wide choice of shapes and sizes. Installation is simple: dig a hole that is large enough to accommodate the mould, make sure the pond is perfectly level and back-fill around it. Flexible plastic liners, on the other hand, enable you to form the shape and size you want (see pages 256–58).

Fish will survive happily in as little as 400mm–600mm of water, but the heat and light from the sun will penetrate a shallow pond more easily and produce more algae growth. However, there is no need for a pond to be deeper than 1m.

The pond will need an edging. Avoid using small pieces of stone right on the edge as they may slip in. Paving slabs make one of the simplest and most effective edgings; or you can use large rounded pebbles. Alternatively, turf right up to the pond edge; if you do this, planting a narrow band of waterside grasses will create a more natural effect.

Where to site a pond

- Most pond plants need sun when they are growing, so you should position a pond where it will receive full sun in summer.
- Avoid windswept sites as pond plants can be dislodged in gales, and there will be increased evaporation from the surface.
- Don't site a pond on boggy or water-logged ground, unless you are prepared to install a drainage system. Water building up beneath a flexible liner can cause it to billow and come to the surface; it can also dislodge a pre-formed liner.
- A pond should be at least 5m–6m from a tree, to avoid being cast in the shade and the liner being damaged by roots, as well as the water being clogged with autumn leaves.
- Some species of tree can be harmful to ponds or pondlife: willow has a vigorous root system and its decaying leaves produce chemicals harmful to fish; water lily aphids over-winter in plum and cherry trees; laburnum and rhododendron are poisonous; horse chestnut and poplar have spreading thirsty root systems; and yew is both poisonous and has a spreading thirsty root system.
- Ponds need topping up from time to time, so a nearby water supply will be useful.
- Pumps and fountains need a power supply; take this into account before you decide where to position the pond. Or choose from the range of solar-powered lights, pumps and fountains now available.

Pumps

Domestic pond pumps can power waterfalls and fountains and run filters. To work out the flow rate of the pump required, you need to calculate the pond volume by multiplying average length (m) x average depth (m) x average width (m). This will give you the volume in cubic metres; to convert that to litres, multiply by 1000.

As well as the capacity of your pond, you need to know what filters you intend to use, the size of any waterfall you want to attach and the height the water will need to be pumped to reach the waterfall. As a rule of thumb, in order to run a 150mm-wide waterfall, you would need a pump with a capacity of 2750 litres per hour.

Pond filtration

It's possible to keep ponds clear and healthy without filters – by correct planting, keeping fish to a minimum and encouraging beneficial wildlife – but it is difficult and takes time. Filtration combined with planting is a better solution. There are various filters to choose from.

- **In-pond filters** consist of a plastic sponge that connects directly to the pump via a pipe. They are only suitable for small ponds up to 900 litres.
- **Tank filters** provide mechanical and biological filtration, using bacteria to remove pollutants. They come in various sizes and are sited outside the pond, either in a hole in the ground or hidden behind rocks or plants. And you can now buy them with integral ultraviolet clarifiers.
- **Ultraviolet clarifiers** (UVCs) bombard free-floating algae with ultraviolet light, killing it and causing it to clump together so that it can be filtered out by a tank filter.
- **Bioforce/Ecoforce pressurised filters** provide mechanical and biological filtration in combination with an ultraviolet clarifier (UVC). They can be buried in the ground.

Planting

Plants are essential to the health of a pond. Deep-water aquatics and lilies are submerged plants that sit on the bottom while their leaves and flowers float on the surface. Marginal aquatics are plants that line the edges of ponds, lakes and streams. Their roots need to be just below the surface so they should sit on a shelf no more than 250mm beneath the water level. In straight-sided ponds a plinth made of bricks and slabs can be built up to the required height to support them.

The most important of the submerged plants are the oxygenating ones, which absorb the mineral salts on which algae would otherwise thrive. They are usually sold as cuttings clamped together with a small piece of lead, and can be planted in baskets in the bottom of the pond. Or if there is a layer of soil on the liner, you can simply drop them into the water and they will grow until checked. In a healthy pond oxygenating plants multiply quickly and need to be thinned in summer.

PONDS WITH FLEXIBLE LINERS

Flexible liners made from PVC or polyethylene sheeting are ideal for small and medium-sized ponds, allowing you to choose whatever shape and size you want. The sheeting is inexpensive and reasonably durable, and is easily repaired.

Marking out the pond

If you have made a rough sketch of the proposed outline of the pond, use it as your guide when you mark out the shape of the pond on the ground.

TOOLS MATERIALS

- **hosepipe or rope**
- **tape measure**
- **spade**
- **pickaxe, if required**
- **wheelbarrow**
- **wooden mallet**
- **spirit level and straightedge, or laser level**
- **trowel**
- **plastering trowel**
- 50mm x 50mm timber pegs
- soft sand
- cement
- pond underlay or old carpet, if required

1 Mark out the pond area with a hosepipe or length of rope, trying different shapes and sizes until you come up with something you like.

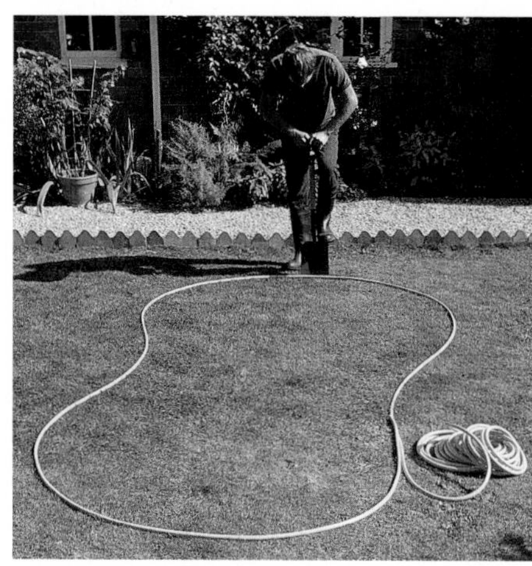

2 Use a spade to mark the edge of the pond clearly, following the hosepipe or rope.

3 Remove the hosepipe and cut a second line beyond the pond outline to mark the outer rim of the edging. The distance from your original line should be the width of a slab less 50mm, so that the slabs overlap the pond edge by 50mm – this not only hides the liner but also protects it from direct sunlight.

Excavating the pond

The best way to ensure the stability of a paved edging is to dig a trench round the pond before you excavate it. A concrete pad can then be laid in the trench once the liner is in place. This secures the liner and provides a base on which to rest the paving slabs.

1 Dig a trench between the two guidelines using a spade and a pickaxe if necessary. The depth should be 75mm for the concrete pad, plus the thickness of the edging slabs, plus a mortar joint of 15mm. Roughly level the trench as you go.

2 Cut a series of 50mm x 50mm pegs, about 300mm long, and sharpen them to a point at one end. Drive one into the centre of the trench with its top at the finished water level. This will be lower than ground level by the depth of the edging (with a 25mm-thick slab and 15mm mortar joint, the tops of the pegs should be 40mm below ground level). Mark the first peg so you can recognise it to level all the other pegs from. Drive in pegs not more than a metre apart around the trench and set them with a long spirit level or laser level (see IDEAL TOOL, page 220). The ground surface need not be wholly level but the pegs must be.

3 Start to dig out the pond to the level of the marginal planting shelf, using the inside line as your guide. The shelf should be about 230mm below water level and 250mm wide. For stability, the sides of the pond should not be vertical but should slope slightly inwards at an angle of 20° (or more in soft crumbly ground).

4 Dig out the central part of the pond to the required depth, sloping the pond sides between the marginal shelf and the pond bottom at 20°. Make sure there are no stones sticking out of the ground. Hammer a stake into the centre of your pond and use a spirit level and a straightedge to set it level with your first peg (or use a laser level). Use the stake to double check that all the other pegs are level, and make slight alterations if necessary.

5 When all the pegs are at the right level, mix a fairly stiff mortar using three parts sand to one part cement, and lay a line of mortar around the rim of the pond. The top of the mortar line should be level with the pegs. Make sure its edges are rounded off and the surface is smooth. Use the central stake to check the level again all the way around the rim of the pond. Leave the mortar to dry for 24 hours.

6 Using a plastering trowel, cover the excavated pond with a 25mm layer of damp sand. If the ground is particularly stony or there are sharp corners, use pond underlay or lengths of old carpet on top of the sand to protect the liner.

YOU CAN DO IT

Think big

Remember with ponds that bigger is better. The planting both in the pond and at the edges will make the water surface appear smaller as the plants increase in size.

IDEAL TOOL

Spirit level

Spirit levels come in a range of lengths. Choose one that is a metre long for checking horizontals and verticals outdoors. You can balance it on top of a straightedge for distances of more than a metre. If you get any mortar on your level, clean it straight away before it sets.

Calculating the liner size

When calculating the liner size, always allow for an overlap on the edge of the pond so that it can be secured either underneath a paved edge or buried in the ground if the grass runs up to the edge of the pond. Allow an overlap of 150mm all around, more if you plan to bury it.

- To calculate the length of the liner you need to buy, measure the maximum length (including overlaps) and add twice the maximum depth
- To calculate the width of the liner, measure the maximum width (including overlaps) and add twice the maximum depth

PONDS FITTING THE LINER AND PUMP

TOOLS MATERIALS

- **hosepipe**
- **scissors or sharp knife**
- **tape measure**
- **cement mixer (optional)**
- **shovel**
- **trowel**
- **angle grinder, or club hammer and bolster chisel**
- **protective gloves**
- **goggles and dust mask**
- **jointing tool**

- flexible plastic pond liner
- stones or bricks
- footing mix concrete (see page 236)
- edging paving slabs
- sharp sand
- cement

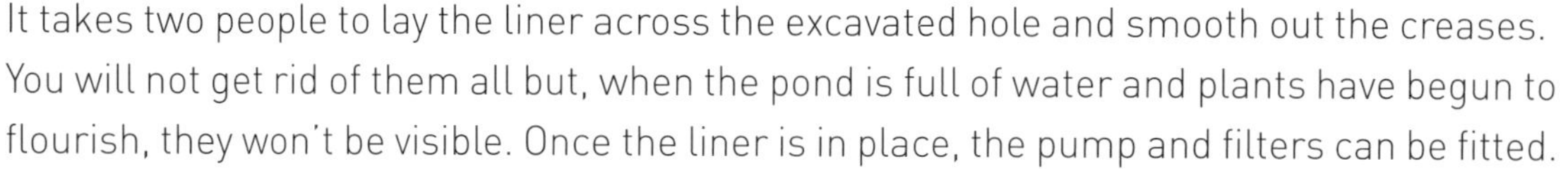

It takes two people to lay the liner across the excavated hole and smooth out the creases. You will not get rid of them all but, when the pond is full of water and plants have begun to flourish, they won't be visible. Once the liner is in place, the pump and filters can be fitted.

Fitting the liner and edging

The liner must be laid across the entire excavated area. Gently stretch and fold the sheeting so that it lies in the correct position with plenty of spare on all sides. Take great care not to puncture it on sharp stones; if you do, patch the hole on both sides with off-cuts of liner and an adhesive recommended by the manufacturer.

1 Lay the liner in the hole, smoothing out as many creases as you can. Place some stones or bricks round the edges to weight the liner and stop it slipping down.

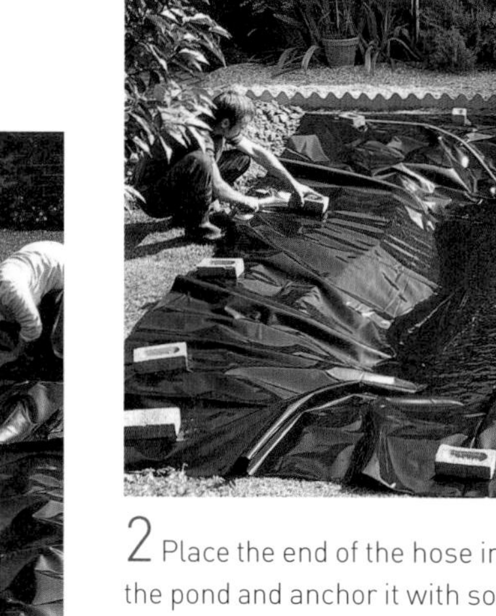

2 Place the end of the hose in the bottom of the pond and anchor it with something heavy but not sharp. Fill the pond with water, taking care to move the stones or bricks as it fills to release the liner and allow it to fit into the shape.

3 Smooth the liner over the mortar edge into the trench – it should cover almost half the trench. Trim off the excess with a pair of scissors or a sharp knife.

4 Fill the trench with concrete, bringing it level with the top of the mortar rim. This will anchor the liner in place and provide a firm base on which to place the edging slabs. Leave the concrete to dry for about 24 hours.

YOU CAN DO IT

Draining the pond

You will need to fill the pond to secure the liner, then empty it again to finish the edging. Either siphon out the water with a length of hosepipe, or use the pump to empty the pond – simply fit a hosepipe to its outlet. The pump must be covered with water at all times when it is operating, so you will need to scoop out the last of the water.

5 Lay the slabs on a continuous mortar bed on the concrete, overlapping the liner by 50mm. On a curved pond you will need to mark and cut each one to fit. Use a club hammer and bolster chisel, or an angle grinder (see YOU CAN DO IT, page 230) to cut slabs, and wear heavy-duty gloves, safety goggles and a dust mask. Mix the mortar using four parts sharp sand to one part cement. Allow for a 10mm mortar joint between the slabs. Finally empty the pond (see YOU CAN DO IT) and point the joint between the slabs and liner. Clean the liner thoroughly afterwards: mortar is poisonous to plants and fish.

Installing the pump and filters

Installing a pump is easier when the pond is empty. The pump must be raised off the bottom to prevent debris clogging the filter and so that you can reach it for cleaning. The pump shown here is a low-voltage pump with a fountain head. It is connected to an ultraviolet clarifier and a biological tank filter. You can connect it to the mains power as you would low-voltage garden lighting (see page 293).

TOOLS MATERIALS

- **spirit level**
- **hacksaw**

- piece of pond underlay
- 2 bricks
- slab or flat stone
- pump with fountain head
- plastic pipe to fit the pump (in this case 25mm)
- plastic conduit
- jubilee clip
- ultraviolet clarifier
- biological tank filter

SAFETY FIRST

A low-voltage pump is very straightforward to install and connect, but remember that water and electricity are a lethal mix. If you are in any doubt about your ability to do the installation yourself, do call in an electrician.

1 Lay a piece of pond underlay on the liner to protect it and place two bricks on top to act as supports. Rest a slab or a flat stone on the bricks and stand the pump on it.

2 Use a spirit level placed on the pond edging to determine the position of the fountain head. It should be set about 3mm–5mm above the water level. Fountain heads are usually adjustable and interchangeable to give different effects.

3 The pump's underground cables must be protected. The low-voltage cable shown here is run through a plastic conduit as it goes through a rockery beside the pond.

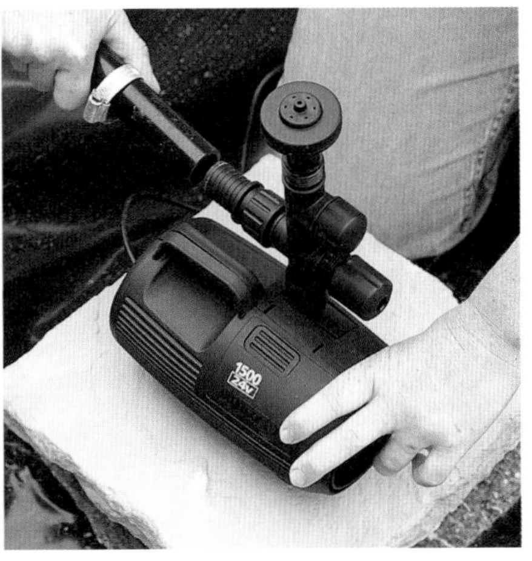

4 Attach the 25mm pipe to the pump outlet using a jubilee clip. This pipe will lead in turn to the ultraviolet clarifier and the biological filter.

5 Use a hacksaw to saw the end off the pipe attachment on the ultraviolet clarifier to fit the size of your pipe and allow you to connect it. An ultraviolet clarifier needs its own electricity supply, and it should be connected following the manufacturer's instructions.

6 Place the tank filter in a position that is higher than the pond – in this case, its outlet will feed a waterfall (see page 260). Connect a pipe from the ultraviolet unit outlet to the tank inlet.

PONDS WATER FEATURES AND PLANTS

Incorporating a waterfall will introduce a soothing, harmonious sound to your garden, and the movement of the running water will help to aerate the pond. Once the pond is finished you can add plants to create a rich, varied wildlife habitat.

Installing a simple waterfall

Attach another pipe to your pump (it will most likely have more than one outlet) and you can easily feed a waterfall. You can mould your own from an off-cut of plastic pond liner on compacted earth or concrete, or install a pre-formed plastic waterfall like the one used here.

TOOLS MATERIALS

- **trowel**

- pre-formed plastic waterfall
- sand or mortar
- pebbles or rocks (optional)

1 Place the pre-formed waterfall on a bed of sand or wet mortar at the edge of the pond. The sand or mortar makes it easier to position as you want it.

2 Test the waterfall by filling the pond and using the pump to circulate the water. Create a more natural effect by placing pebbles or rocks in the flowing water.

Plants for a pond

Even when a pond has filters, plants are essential for maintaining healthy water. About one-third of the pond surface should be covered with foliage during the growing season to deprive algae of the light they need to flourish. Lilies, which have large leaves, are ideal for this purpose. Deep-water aquatics and floating plants (see page 254) will starve the algae of mineral salts. Aquatic plants do not need rich soil. Use aquatic compost or a heavy garden soil; avoid sandy soils or soil containing farmyard manure.

TOOLS MATERIALS

- **protective gloves**

- pond plants
- planting baskets
- hessian, if required
- aquatic compost or heavy garden soil
- clean gravel

1 For most ornamental ponds, plants should be anchored in special planting baskets with latticework sides, which retain the soil while allowing water to permeate. Modern baskets have micro-mesh sides that prevent the soil making the water dirty. If the basket has large holes, line it with a square of hessian before filling it with compost. If you are planting tall plants like bulrushes, try to plant them in a basket that is large enough for you to place a brick in the bottom before filling it with compost, as this will keep the plant stable.

2 If you think the pond plant you have purchased will soon outgrow its basket, repot it into a larger one. Add clean gravel as a topping around the stem to prevent loss of soil from the surface of the pot. Gently lower the plant in the pond.

Turfing

If you site your pond on an existing lawn, you will probably need to make good the lawn around the edge. You can do this with turf or grass seed. Turf can be laid at any time of year, except in freezing conditions, but should be laid immediately since the grass will yellow if left more than a day.

TOOLS MATERIALS

- **spade**
- **wheelbarrow**
- **fork**
- **rake**
- **craft knife or garden edging tool**
- **garden roller**

- top soil
- new turf

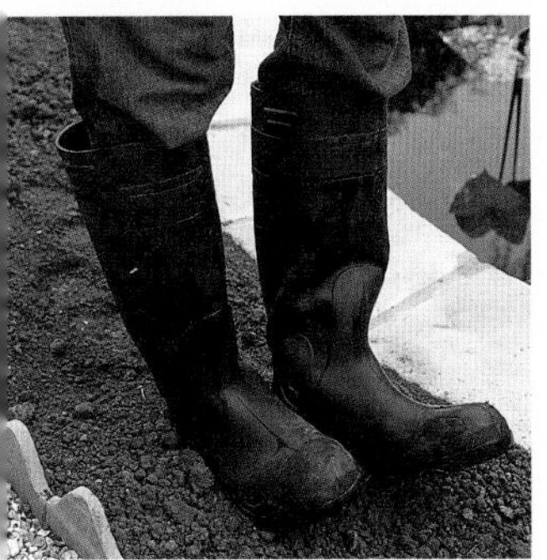

1 Cut out the existing turf round the pond and fork over the ground if it is compacted. Spread top soil over the area and rake it roughly level with the pond edging slabs. 'Heel' the soil by walking backwards and forwards over the area, using short steps and putting all your weight on the heels of your boots until the soil is firmly compacted. Rake the ground flat and if necessary add more top soil and compact it again until it is at the right level. Roll the ground with the roller.

2 Lay the turf on the surface. If you have to join strips, stagger the joints. Trim the turf with a craft knife or a garden edging tool.

3 Roll the turf flat with a garden roller. Keep it watered and apply fertiliser during the growing season.

Simple stand-alone water feature

In most stand-alone water features the water is pumped from a small underground reservoir to the feature and then flows back again. The pump may be solar-powered or, as here, it may run on low-voltage power and need to be connected to the mains electricity with cable run in plastic conduit and buried underground to a depth of at least 450mm, as for low-voltage garden lighting (see page 293).

TOOLS MATERIALS

- **spade**
- **wheelbarrow**
- **spirit level**
- **screwdriver**
- **hosepipe**

- water feature kit
- 4 nails
- string
- plastic conduit
- pebbles or stones

1 Turn the plastic reservoir upside down and mark out its position precisely on the ground by pushing a nail in at each corner and joining the nails with a length of string. Dig a hole the depth of the reservoir.

2 Place the plastic reservoir in the hole and use a spirit level to make sure it is level across its length and its width.

3 Screw the fountain to the lid of the reservoir, following the manufacturer's instructions. Make sure that the plastic pipe goes through the lid.

4 Use a hosepipe to fill the tank with water. Secure the plastic pipe from the reservoir lid to the pump. Sit the pump on the bottom of the reservoir, trailing the electrical cable out of the reservoir. Connect the pump to the mains electricity, following the manufacturer's instructions.

5 Arrange pebbles or large stones over the plastic lid of the reservoir to disguise it.

SAFETY FIRST

If in any doubt about your ability to make the electrical connections yourself, do call in a professional.

MARLEY
HOT

Home systems and services

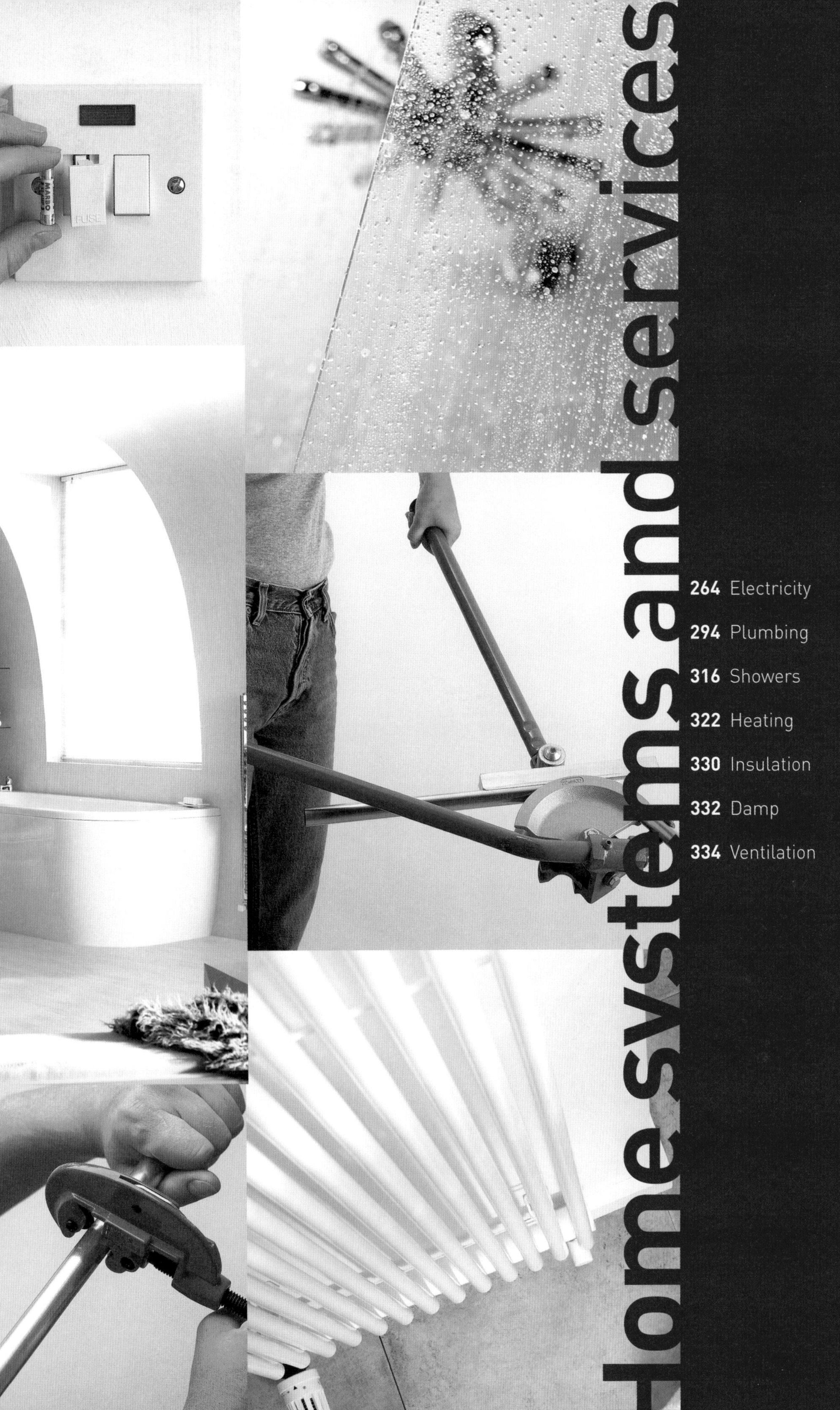

ELECTRICITY BE SAFE

SAFE ELECTRICS

Before beginning any kind of electrical work, you must always take the following safety precautions:

- Switch off the main power at the consumer unit (fuse box).
- Isolate the circuit you plan to work on by removing the circuit fuse and putting it in your pocket. Or switch off and lock the relevant circuit breaker (see page 271). If you can't lock it, tape the switch in the off position, and attach a very clear note to the unit stating that you are working on the circuit.
- Refit the cover and turn the main power back on.
- Check the circuit is dead with a plug-in socket tester or, in the case of a lighting circuit, a voltage tester (see page 270).

When you have completely finished, turn the main power switch off again before replacing the fuse. Never restore power until the faceplates and covers of all accessories have been installed.

YOU CAN DO IT

Preparation

A lot of electrical home improvements involve simple cable routing and socket fixing. These tasks require basic skills like chopping out and repairing plaster, drilling into walls and timber, or lifting and replacing floorboards. Even if you decide to play safe and employ an electrician, you will save money by doing the basic preparation and making good yourself.

B&Q

Electricity flows around a system of cables in your home. These are divided into several circuits, each supplying specific parts of the system – sockets, lights, cooker, immersion heater and so on. Making changes to electrical circuits is not as difficult as you may think but you must always maintain a healthy respect for electricity and observe the safety guidelines rigorously.

Follow the rules

You don't need to be a qualified electrician to make changes to your home's electrical system, but the work must be done in a professional manner and must conform to the IEE Wiring Regulations (or Scottish Building Regulations in Scotland). If in any doubt, always seek expert advice. The electricity supplier has the right to cut off the power if your system is judged to be unsafe.

All the advice given in these pages applies to systems that conform to the IEE Wiring Regulations for the UK and Northern Ireland only (other countries have their own regulatory organisations).

You shouldn't have any problems if you follow the instructions meticulously but if at any time you are uncertain of your ability, or you suspect that your system has been adapted or extended in an unorthodox way, always seek the advice of an electrical contractor registered with the NICEIC (the National Inspection Council for Electrical Installation Contracting), the ECA (Electrical Contractors Association) or the Electrical Contractors' Association of Scotland (trading as SELECT). It is a requirement of the Wiring Regulations that domestic electrical systems be checked periodically by a competent person. If your house is more than ten years old, get your system checked first before you start working on it – otherwise you have no way of knowing what dangers may be lurking.

Dos and don'ts of electrical safety

The potential danger of working on your home's electrical system should never be underestimated. Electricity can cause fire, burns and in extreme cases kill. What's more, poor workmanship in an electrical job may only become apparent when a fault or overload occurs. So follow these safety tips to prevent disaster:

- Be patient and methodical, and only embark on a job that you understand from start to finish.
- If in the slightest doubt about your ability to complete a particular electrical task, call in a professional.
- Always isolate the circuit you plan to work on at the consumer unit (see SAFE ELECTRICS, above).
- Wear rubber-soled shoes when you are working on an electrical installation.
- Use insulating tools and screwdrivers specifically designed for electrical work.
- When making connections, ensure that no cable or flex cores are damaged (see page 268); sheath the bare earth core of cable with green/yellow insulation; check that cores are connected to the correct terminals; and tighten all terminal screws fully. Always connect the earth core to the earth terminal at fittings and appliances, unless your appliances carry the double insulated symbol ⧈ or, as with some light fittings, have no metal parts.
- Make sure circuit and appliance fuses are of the correct rating (see page 269). Never be tempted to replace a fuse that keeps blowing with one of a higher rating; investigate the reason for the problem.
- Replace damaged electrical fittings or appliances immediately. Don't try to use anything you suspect may have a fault.
- Never patch a length of worn flex – always replace it.
- Don't overload sockets with adaptors and extra plugs. Fit additional sockets instead.
- Always unplug electrical appliances before working on them. Unplug power tools before changing blades or accessories.
- Turn off the light switch before replacing a bulb.
- Never use electrical appliances in a damp environment and don't touch anything electrical with wet hands.
- When using electrical appliances or tools in the garden, ensure they are protected by an RCD (residual current device), either plugged in at the power socket or permanently wired into the system at the consumer unit (see page 290).

Is your system safe to work on?

There are certain sure signs that your system is out of date and unsafe to work on – old-style rubber-sheathed cable, for example. But even in a modern property whose electrical system has been professionally checked and approved in the past ten years, things can go wrong. Make sure it's safe *before* you begin work, and if in doubt, get it checked by a qualified electrician.

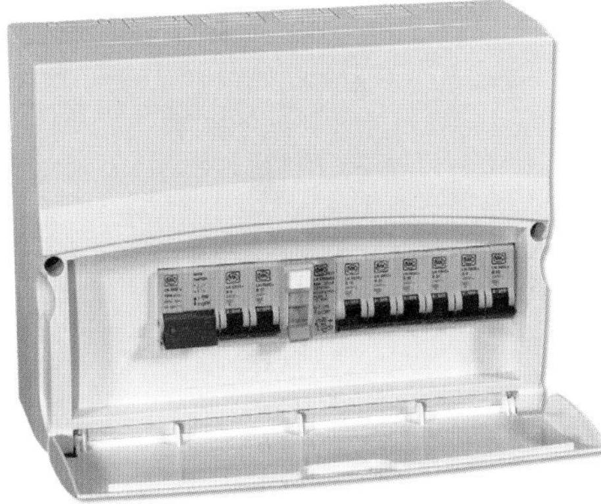

1 Is your consumer unit old-style or modern?

If your consumer unit cover gets cracked or broken, replace it straight away. In older houses, you sometimes find a mixture of old fuse boxes attached to the fuse board beside the electricity meter. These can be dangerous, and you are strongly advised to get a qualified electrician to change them for a modern all-in-one consumer unit (above).

2 Are the circuits labelled and fitted with fuses or circuit breakers of the correct rating?

If you are going to do electrical work in your home, you will need to isolate the circuit you are working on by removing the correct fuse or switching off the circuit breaker (see page 271). If the circuits are not already labelled, you can do this yourself. Identify each one by switching off the main power, disabling one circuit, restoring power and then investigating which sockets, appliances or lights are dead.

3 Are the cables in good condition?

Cables used to be sheathed in rubber, which perishes over time, potentially exposing bare wires. If you have rubber cabling, or if any cables are worn, get them checked by a qualified electrician and replaced if necessary. Any discolouring of modern cabling may be a sign of overheating, and should also be checked by an electrician.

4 Is the earth connection secure?

Running from the consumer unit there will be a thick cable with green-and-yellow-sheathing (or green in an older installation) which provides the vital earth connection. If this cable looks at all loose or damaged, you must get it checked straight away. See page 267 for more information on earthing.

5 Does your consumer unit have an RCD?

A residual current device, or RCD, will detect an earth leakage and isolate a circuit in milliseconds, before an accident can occur. You can test an RCD by pressing its test button.

6 How safe is your fixed wiring?

Fixed wiring runs in the walls, between floors and in the loft space. If you can get access to any part of it, check the condition. Is it rubber-insulated? Are any bare wires showing? Is it fixed securely? Does it run neatly into any junction boxes or accessories? If you have surface-mounted wiring, it should be clipped tidily to the walls, or preferably concealed behind them (see page 272).

7 Are any of your sockets damaged?

Watch out for warning signs that a connection may be loose inside. Does the socket or plug feel warm? Do you ever notice sparks when you pull out a plug or operate a switch? If so, you should check the connections inside the socket and plug, or contact an electrician for advice. If it is difficult to insert a plug into a socket, it could be a sign that the socket is worn and needs to be replaced. Cracked or broken faceplates on sockets should be replaced as soon as possible. Scorching on a socket may be caused by overloading, for example by plugging in an adaptor to supply several large loads; or by loose connections in a plug. Replace the faceplate (see page 274) and investigate the cause of the problem: reduce the load and if necessary replace the plug (see page 269).

8 Are your electrical appliances connected securely?

Even if an appliance appears to be working normally, it is worth checking the wiring from time to time. Is the insulation around the flex deteriorating? Is the flex securely attached? Are there any bare wires visible? Make sure that the earth cores have green-and-yellow sleeving. If the external casing of an appliance becomes cracked or worn, it should be replaced. If the switches are not working properly, get professional help or replace the appliance. Plugs should contain a fuse of the correct rating for the appliance (see page 269).

9 Are your light fittings wired correctly?

If there isn't an earth wire inside a ceiling rose, get an electrician to check it. All wiring inside the ceiling rose should be PVC-insulated. Old-style braided flex should be replaced with the correct PVC-insulated and sheathed flex (see page 268).

10 Do you use electrical appliances outdoors?

Any electrical appliance used outdoors must have the protection of an RCD rated at 30mA. An outdoor socket must have a permanently wired-in RCD; indoor sockets used to power appliances outdoors can have a plug-in RCD (pictured above).

ELECTRICITY THE BASICS

SAFE ELECTRICS

Before you start any kind of electrical work isolate the circuit by removing the circuit fuse or switching and locking the circuit breaker. Double-check it is dead with a socket tester or voltage tester. Never take risks with electrical safety! See page 264.

The consumer unit is the distribution point for the electricity supply in your home, where the flow is split to feed the various circuits. Socket outlets and fused connection units can be supplied with electricity via two types of wiring layout, known as radial and ring circuits. Your home may well have both types, since the power supply is usually split into at least two circuits.

Domestic circuits

The electrical circuits in your home all begin at the consumer unit, or fuse box, where the incoming supply is split as required. The cables leading from it contain three copper wires, known as conductors or cores. The electrical current flows to the appliance or fitting along the 'live' conductor (coloured red, or in lighting circuits sometimes flagged with red tape or sleeving). Then it flows back along the 'neutral' conductor (coloured black) to the source. The third conductor is the 'earth' core, which provides a safe escape route for the current should it leak from the circuit because of a fault or poor connection; without earth protection, the metal components of appliances and fittings could give you a fatal electric shock if they were to become live through a wiring fault. Thus, any metal appliance or fitting in your home that could come into contact with electricity must be earthed, and that includes the plumbing system.

The consumer unit

Also commonly known as the fuse box, the consumer unit is usually mounted close to your electricity meter and will contain the main isolating switch, which allows you to turn on and off the power to the entire house. Inside the consumer unit, the incoming current is split to feed a number of circuits – lighting, power, cooker and so on – each protected by a fuse or circuit breaker.

In addition, more modern consumer units incorporate an RCD (residual current device). RCDs shut off the power rapidly if an earth leakage develops, to prevent electrocution. Depending on the design of the unit, the RCD may operate on all the circuits or only some. Older consumer units may have a separate RCD mounted alongside. Any circuit that provides power to appliances used outdoors must have RCD protection (see page 290).

Each fuse or circuit breaker should be labelled with the name of the circuit it protects, so that you can isolate each one easily when you want to work on it.

Radial circuits

In the early days of domestic electrical systems, socket outlets were few and far between in homes, and each was supplied by an individual cable run from the fuse box. Modern circuits, whether radial or ring, can have multiple socket outlets. In a radial circuit, a single cable runs from the consumer unit and feeds a number of sockets. There is no restriction on the number of sockets fed by one circuit, but there is a limit on the floor area it can supply; a 20 amp radial circuit can supply up to 20 sq m, and a 30/32 amp circuit can supply up to 50 sq m. The cable simply runs into one socket or fused connection unit, then on to the next, until it terminates at the last socket on the line. Each radial circuit is protected by a fuse or circuit breaker at the consumer unit. This is designed to blow or trip if the circuit is overloaded.

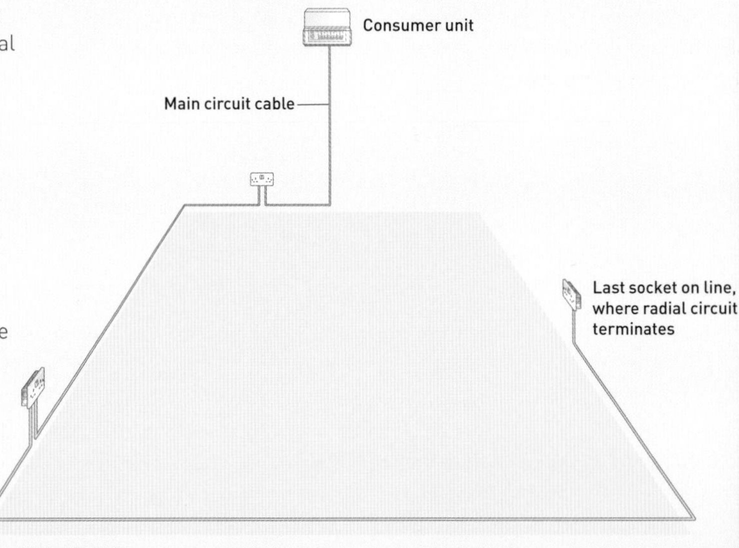

Radial circuit

Ring circuits

a ring circuit, the cable runs from the consumer unit, in and out f the sockets and fused connection units, and then returns to the onsumer unit (rather than terminating at the last socket on the line). he electrical current can flow from either end of the ring. This has ie effect of raising the current-carrying capacity of the circuit without icreasing the size of cable needed, which would be the case with a adial circuit.

As with a radial circuit, there is no restriction on the number of ockets that can be wired into a ring circuit, but there is a limit of 00 sq m on the floor area served. At the consumer unit, the circuit is rotected by a 30 or 32 amp fuse or circuit breaker.

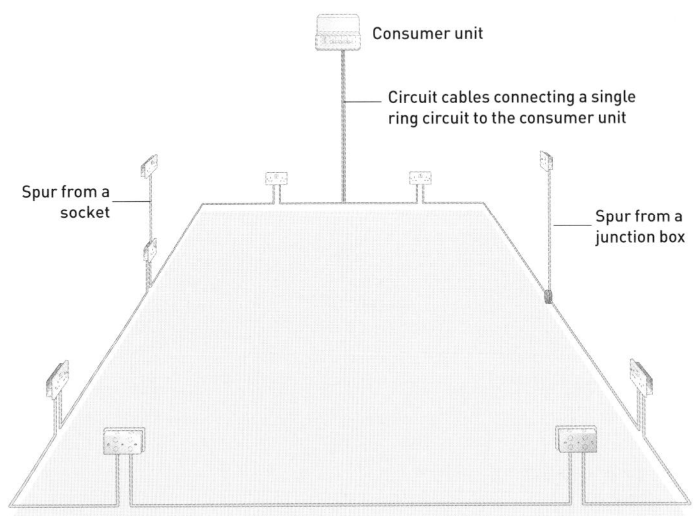

Ring circuit

Spurs

spur is a short branch cable from an existing socket outlet on the nain circuit or from a connection box, known as a junction box, vired into the main circuit cable. Each spur should only supply one ocket outlet (single or double) or fused connection unit (used for xed appliances), although the IEE Wiring Regulations used to allow wo. You can have as many spurs as there are sockets, or fused onnection units, on a main ring circuit. See pages 276–77 for advice n adding spurs.

Appliance circuits

Individual radial circuits are provided for appliances that require large amounts of current – cookers, immersion heaters, electric showers, storage heaters, and so on. Depending on the appliance, these may be wired in much heavier cable than normal power circuits and may be protected by a variety of fuse/circuit breaker sizes.

In most cases, the cable runs through a special double-pole switch, which interrupts the flow of current through both live and neutral cores of the cable – normal single-pole socket and light switches only interrupt the live supply – ensuring that the power to the appliance can be shut off completely if repairs are necessary, without the need to disconnect the wiring.

Earthing

The earth is a particularly good conductor of electricity. This means hat if you were to touch a live conductor, the electricity would take he shortest route into the ground via your body – with potentially atal consequences. If a live wire in an appliance accidentally comes into contact with a metal casing, the electricity will flow o the ground – this time harmlessly – along the earth wire. This s known as an earth fault, and the sudden change of route will cause a circuit breaker to operate or a fuse to blow.

Earth wires are either insulated with green and yellow sheathing or they are bare copper wires sandwiched between the live and neutral cores in cable.

Bonding

For safety, the main gas and water pipework in your home should be connected by bonding conductors to the main earthing terminal near the consumer unit. Main bonding wires – lengths of single-core cable, usually 10mm^2, with green-and-yellow sheathing – should be clamped within 600mm of the meter or main stopcock (on the household side). In addition, there must be supplementary bonding linking all the metallic elements within a bath or shower room, since these are particularly hazardous areas. This is done with 4mm^2 green-and-yellow-sheathed single-core cable. If you use plastic connectors on copper plumbing pipes, you must restore the earth connection across them, or your system will not be safely earthed (see page 302).

Supplementary bonding connection

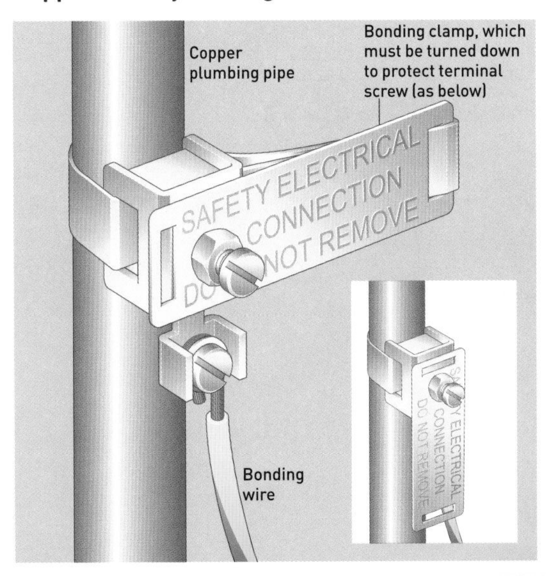

ELECTRICITY CABLE, FLEX AND FUSES

SAFE ELECTRICS

Before you start any kind of electrical work isolate the circuit by removing the circuit fuse or switching and locking the circuit breaker. Double-check it is dead with a socket tester or voltage tester. Never take risks with electrical safety! See page 264.

Electrical current flows in the home along different types of cable and flex. You have to strip these to bare the cores before you can connect them to new terminals. Fitting new plugs is one of the most straightforward electrical jobs, but it is important to make sure you insert the correct fuse for the appliance that will be supplied.

Flex

Flex is used to connect appliances and pendant lights to the fixed wiring. It is usually round in cross-section and normally contains three cores within a white or coloured PVC outer sheath, although non-kinking rubber-sheathed flex with a braided outer covering is also available for irons. All three cores have coloured insulation: brown for live, blue for neutral and green/yellow for earth. Two-core flex (with no earth core) is used for double-insulated appliances and some light fittings that don't have metal components. Special heat-resistant flex is available for immersion heaters. Different flex sizes are available. Check the box opposite to see the size required for different appliance ratings.

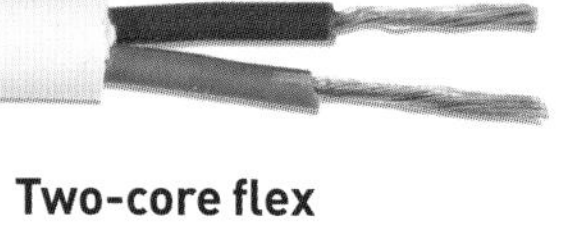

Two-core flex

Three-core flex

Cable

Cable is used for all fixed wiring, which is usually hidde behind walls, ceiling and floor. It has an oval cross-section and contains cores set side by side within a thick white or grey PVC outer sheath. The live core is separately insulated in red sheath, the neutral core in black sheath. The earth core is bare and runs between them. This is known as two-core-and-earth cable; special three-core-and-earth cable (with red, blue and yellow cores, plus a bare earth) is used for the two-way switching of lights. When connecting cable, the expose earth core must be protected by a length of green/yellow electrical sleeving. Bigger cable is needed for circuits with a higher current demand. Common sizes c cable are 1, 1.5, 2.5, 4, 6 and 10mm^2; the measurement represents the cross-sectional area of the individual cores. Normal cable sheathing is not frost-resistant, sc outdoors it must be protected by conduit or you must use steel-wire-armoured cable (SWA).

Two-core-and-earth cable

Three-core-and-earth cable

Steel-wire-armoured cable (SW

Safe stripping

To prepare flex or cable for connection, you have to strip back the plastic sheath to expose the copper cores. It is important not to damage the cores, which in flex are made up of a large number of fine copper strands. If any of these are cut through, the core's current capacity is reduced, which could lead to overheating.

IDEAL TOOLS

Side cutters

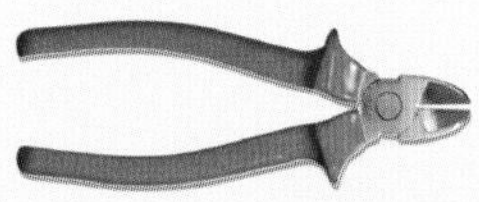

Side cutters are specially designed to give a clean, accurate cut through cable or flex.

Wire strippers

Use wire strippers to strip flex and cable safely, without risking damaging the cores. Some are adjustable to suit a range of core sizes; others have jaws with cut-outs for different sizes of core.

Stripping flex

Mark the amount of flex outer sheath you need to remove, then bend the flex double and make a shallow cut at the mark. This will open up automatically. Repeat around the flex until you can pull the piece of outer sheath free. Cut the flex cores to length with side cutters. Remove about 10mm of the insulation from the end of each core, using wire strippers. Twist the exposed fine copper wires of each core together so that they can be inserted easily in their terminals.

Stripping cable

Mark the amount of outer sheathing to be removed and lay the cable on a flat surface. Use a sharp knife to carefully slit the sheathing down the centre (above the earth core). Peel back the sheathing and cut it off using side cutters. Cut the cores to the required length. Use wire stripper to remove just enough of the coloured cores' insulation so that the cores extend to the full depth o the terminal, with no wire exposed Add green/yellow sheathing to the bare copper core.

Fitting a new plug

Jnscrew and remove the cover of the old plug. Turn the plug over and oosen the terminal screws so the flex cores can be pulled from the pins. Slacken the screws securing the flex clamp and pull the flex free. f the appliance was working fine, prise out and keep the fuse – but don't re-use it without checking it is the right rating for the appliance.

Make sure when you buy a new plug that the live and neutral pins are partly covered with plastic insulation. Depending on the plug's design, you may need to slide the cover over the flex before making the connections.

- Feed the end of the flex under the flex clamp or between the flex grips of the new plug.
- Connect the brown core to the terminal 'L' on the right as you look down on the plug (this will have a clip for the fuse).
- Connect the blue core to the terminal 'N' on the left.
- Connect the green/yellow earth core to the terminal 'E' or ⏚ at the top (the longest of the three pins). Make sure that the earth wire is longest and the live wire shortest – this way if the plug is ripped off the flex, the live wire will break away first and the earth last. If there is no earth core (the appliance is double-insulated) simply make sure that the terminal screw is tight.
- Check that the cores are pushed fully home with the insulation right up to the terminals and tighten all the screws.
- Confirm the rating of the fuse and replace it with one of the correct amperage if necessary.
- Tighten the flex clamp screws to grip the flex firmly.
- Finally, screw on the cover, ensuring that it fits properly all round.

TOOLS MATERIALS

- **screwdriver**
- fuse, if required
- new plug

Correct

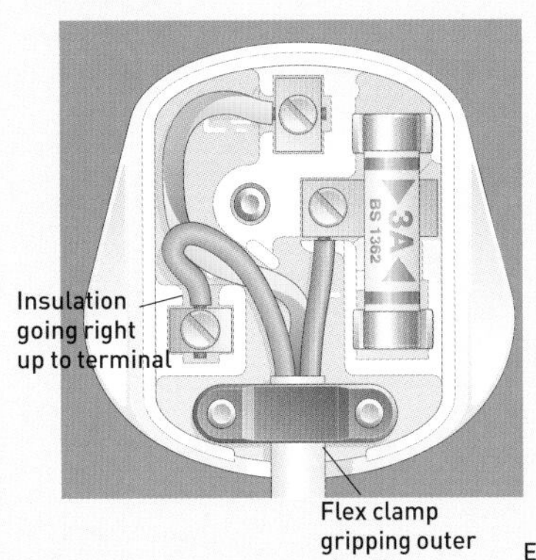

Incorrect

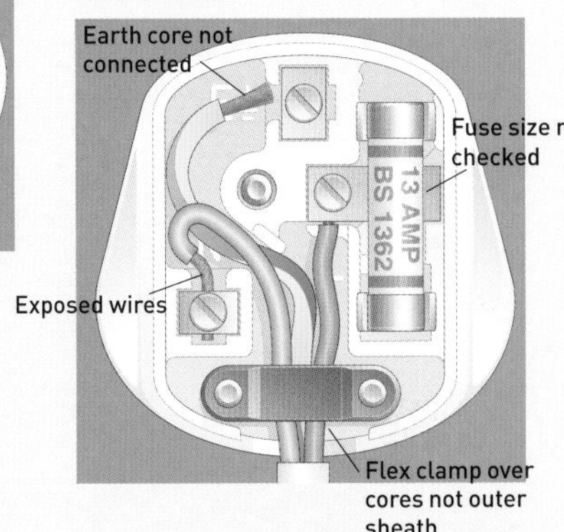

SAFETY FIRST

Not all plugs are manufactured to the same quality. A standard 3-pin plug should carry the British Standard kitemark and code BS1363 or BS1363A.

FLEX SIZES

Appliance rating	Flex size
700W	0.5mm²
1.4kW	0.75mm²
2.3kW	1mm²
3kW	1.25/1.5mm²

Changing a fuse in a plug

These days, all appliance plugs contain cartridge fuses, normally rated at 3, 5 or 13 amps depending on the wattage of the appliance. Appliances rated up to 700 watts should be protected by a 3 amp fuse while those rated above 700 watts should have a 13 amp fuse. Some appliances, such as videos and televisions, may require a 5 amp fuse. Always check the appliance manufacturer's instructions. A new plug will usually contain a 13 amp fuse; this may be too high for your appliance. Never fit a fuse with the wrong rating.

TOOLS MATERIALS

- **screwdriver**
- fuse

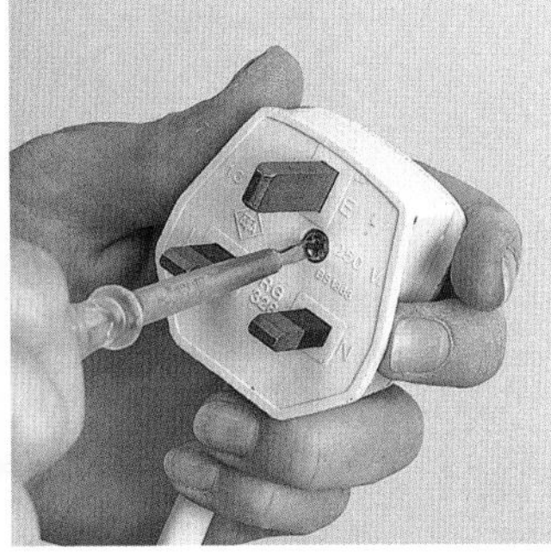

1 To replace a fuse, unplug the appliance, unscrew the cover of the plug and lift it off.

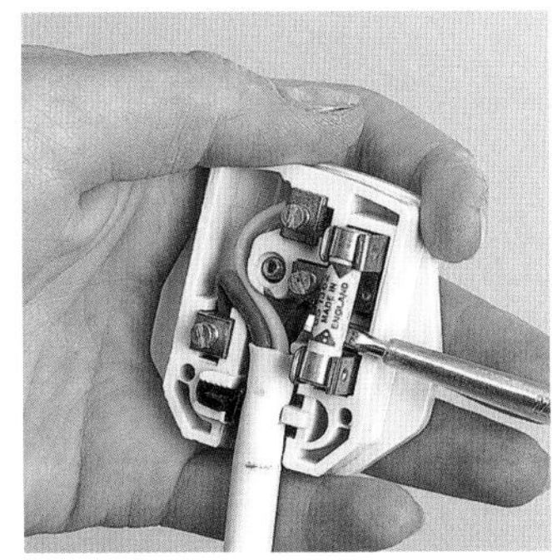

2 Prise the fuse from its clips and insert a new one of the correct amperage. Refit the cover. (Note that some plugs are moulded in one piece with the fuse in a lever-out holder in the base. After changing the fuse, make sure this holder is pushed back fully into the plug.)

Connection unit fuses

Fixed appliances – for example an extractor fan, or a central heating boiler – are permanently wired to a connection unit with an on/off wall switch. These must also be fitted with a fuse of the correct rating.

TOOLS MATERIALS

- **screwdriver**
- **voltage tester**
- fuse

1 Isolate the circuit and use a voltage tester to confirm the power is off. Then unscrew or prise out the fuse holder.

2 Remove the fuse and insert a new one of the correct rating. Push or screw the holder back fully before restoring the power.

ELECTRICITY IDENTIFYING FAULTS

SAFE ELECTRICS

Before you start any kind of electrical work isolate the circuit by removing the circuit fuse or switching and locking the circuit breaker. Double-check it is dead with a socket tester or voltage tester. Never take risks with electrical safety! See page 264.

It can be very irritating when an electrical socket or appliance doesn't work, but with a bit of logical detective work, you should be able to discover the cause of the problem and, in many cases, correct the fault yourself. But before you do any kind of electrical work, you need to know not only how to isolate a circuit, but also how to double-check that it is dead

Checking a circuit is dead

The safest option when working on an electrical fitting is turn off the entire household electricity supply at the mains. But if this would mean working in the dark, or prevent you from using power tools, you may need to isolate just the circuit you are working on. Do this by removing the fuse – put it in your pocket so it can't be replaced by accident – or switch off the relevant circuit breaker and lock it if you can, or failing that, leave a very clear note on the consumer unit stating that you are working on the circuit.

However it is also extremely important to check that you have turned off the *right* circuit. On a main power circuit, use a socket tester (see IDEAL TOOL) to confirm the power is off. On a lighting circuit you need a voltage tester, of which there are different types on the market. One option is a voltage meter, which has probes that are touched to the exposed cable. This is the most reliable method of checking whether a cable is live or not, but you do have to be extremely careful while opening up the fitting, just in case it is. The alternative is a voltage tester (or volt stick), which detects the presence of live wires without contact with a cable, and will even work through a fitting or faceplate. But it is vital to use it properly: always check first that it is working by testing it on a known live cable, otherwise you could get a false negative reading, with potentially fatal consequences. And be aware that a positive reading can sometimes be caused by static electricity in the environment. As always, read and follow the manufacturer's instructions.

Identifying a problem

Follow these step-by-step procedures to identify the cause of an electrical problem.

A plug-in appliance doesn't work

- If it is a plug-in light, try changing the bulb. For any other kind of appliance, first try plugging it into another socket. If it works, the original socket may be faulty and need replacing (see page 274). If it doesn't work, try again on a different power circuit (probably a different floor). If it works there, then you may have a dead circuit (see below).
- If the appliance doesn't work in a socket you know to be functioning, then check the flex connections in the plug and replace the fuse in the plug, ensuring that it is of the correct rating.
- Still not working? The appliance may have an internal fault, which will require professional attention.

A circuit is dead

- Turn off all lights or unplug all appliances on the affected circuit. Turn off the main isolating switch at the consumer unit and repair the circuit fuse/reset the circuit breaker. Then turn the main switch back on.
- Switch on each light or plug in each appliance in turn to find out which item on the circuit is causing the fuse to blow or the circuit breaker to trip. When you find it, isolate the circuit again and check the fuse, the connections and the flex (see above).
- If the fuse blows/circuit breaker trips again, then the fault may lie in the fixed wiring. Call in a qualified electrician.

A wall or ceiling light doesn't work

- Are the other lights on the circuit working? If not, then follow the steps for a dead circuit, below.
- If the other lights on the circuit are working, then turn off the light at the switch and replace the bulb.
- If that doesn't help, then turn off the power and check the cable/flex connections at the light. If necessary, strip back cores and remake the connections; make sure the terminal screws are tight. Still with the power off, check the condition of the flex with a continuity tester (see IDEAL TOOL, page 276), and replace if necessary.
- If that doesn't work, then turn off the power again, remove the switch cover and check the cable connections. If they are loose, remake them. If they are fine, then try replacing the switch (see page 282).
- Still not working? Call in a qualified electrician.

All circuits are dead

- If the circuits of your home are protected by an RCD (residual current device), check to see if it has tripped. If so, reset it. If it trips again, carry out the checks for faulty lights, appliances and a dead circuit. If the problem persists, call in a qualified electrician.
- Check with neighbours or your electricity supplier to determine whether the power to the neighbourhood has been cut. If not, and the problem cannot be traced within the domestic circuits, notify the electricity supplier who will check the main supply cable and service fuse.

IDEAL TOOL

Socket tester

A quick means of checking whether there is a wiring fault or incorrect connection at a socket is to use a plug-in tester. This has three pins, just like a normal plug, but on its face there are three neons. With the power to the circuit switched on, plug in the tester; the combination of neons illuminated indicates whether or not there is a fault, and if so where it lies.

SAFETY FIRST

Nuisance RCD tripping

To avoid nuisance tripping on RCD-protected systems you should work with the whole power supply switched off. Switching off a circuit breaker or removing a circuit fuse only isolates the L (live) side of the circuit. The N (neutral) remains connected to the mains. This is quite safe for working on the circuit, but it means that contact with the N wire will cause the RCD to trip and switch off the entire house supply. This can be irritating, even dangerous, when you are in the middle of a repair.

Fuses and circuit breakers

Each of the electrical circuits in your home is provided with a fuse or circuit breaker (also known as a miniature circuit breaker or MCB). These devices protect it against overloading, which could generate heat within the wiring, melting the insulation and causing a fire. They also react to short circuits caused when the current-carrying cores of cables come into contact with each other; this can happen if they become loose inside an electrical accessory or when the cable is pierced accidentally by a drill or nail.

Fuses contain a special wire that will melt and separate, cutting off the flow of electricity, if the circuit draws too much current or a short circuit occurs. The wire may be exposed within the carrier or it can be contained within a special cartridge. Circuit breakers are trip switches that turn themselves off under the same circumstances and can be reset by pushing a button or operating the switch.

The demand placed on circuits varies – light fittings consume less electricity than most plug-in appliances, for example – so as well as having different sized cable, the circuits are protected by fuses or circuit breakers with different ratings. Lighting circuits will be protected by 5 or 6 amp fuses; socket circuits by 30 or 32 amp fuses; an immersion heater by a 15 or 16 amp fuse, and so on. It is essential that fuses of the correct rating are used. One with too low a rating will keep blowing; one with too high a rating might not protect the circuit against overloading, with potentially fatal consequences.

Cartridge fuses

Circuit breaker

Changing a cartridge fuse

Cartridge fuses are easy to replace, but make sure you have the correct fuse rating for the circuit: fuses vary in size and colour coding according to their rating.

Switch off the power and remove the cartridge fuse. Some are simply held in spring clips and can be prised out; others require the fuse carrier to be opened by releasing a screw. Press a new fuse of the correct rating into the spring clips or insert it into the open ends of the carrier's pins. Then, if necessary, reassemble the fuse carrier. Check the main power switch is off and replace the fuse; usually the pins are offset to one side so that it will only fit one way round. Restore the power.

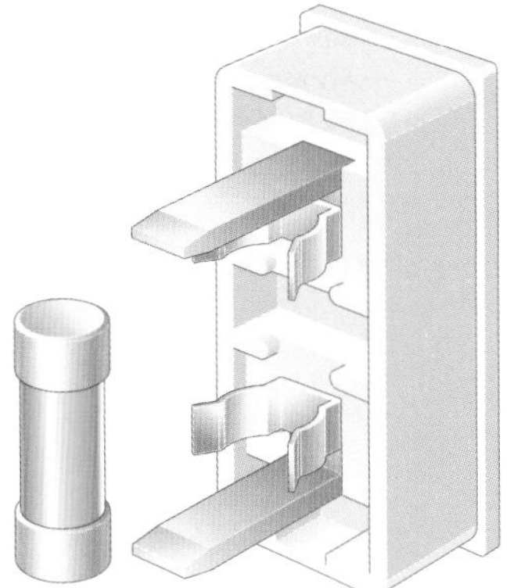

Spring-clip cartridge fuse holder

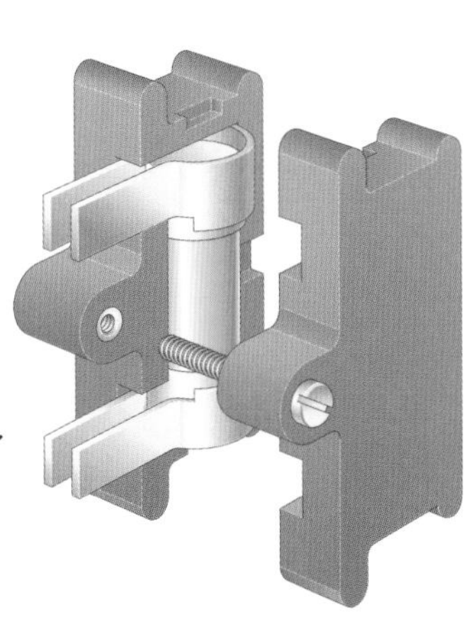

Enclosed cartridge fuse holder

Changing a fuse wire

If a rewirable fuse has blown, you should be able to see that the fuse wire has melted. Replace it with new fuse wire of the correct amperage. Turn off the power and lift the fuse cover on the consumer unit. Release the terminal screws and remove the fuse wire. Take a length of fuse wire of the correct rating and insert it in the carrier. Wind the ends of the wire around the terminals, but don't pull it taut. Cut off the excess then tighten the screws. Check the main power switch is off, and then refit the fuse. Replace the cover and turn the power back on.

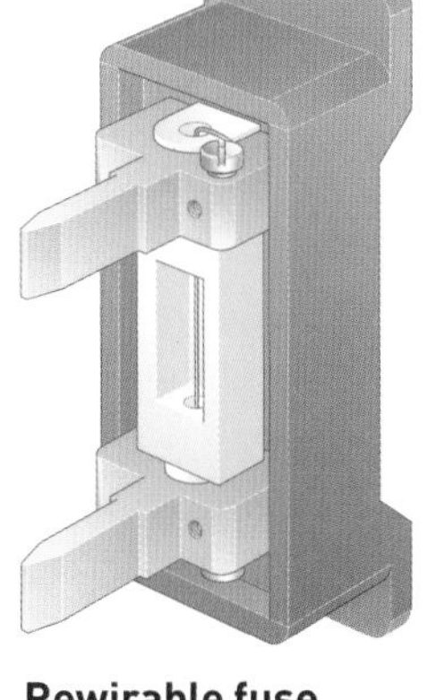

Rewirable fuse

ELECTRICITY RUNNING NEW CABLE

SAFE ELECTRICS

Before you start any kind of electrical work isolate the circuit by removing the circuit fuse or switching and locking the circuit breaker. Double-check it is dead with a socket tester or voltage tester. Never take risks with electrical safety!

Adding any new electrical outlet or light fitting will almost certainly involve running cable from a power source to the item concerned. You can simply clip cables to the surface of a wall, but it is safer and neater to conceal them. They can be run above the ceiling, below the floor, or behind walls. Where practical, mark where you run new cables for future reference.

Running cable between floors

- **Lofts** You can lay cables across the top of joists around the edges of a loft, well away from where anyone is likely to walk. Or clip them to the sides of joists, but keep them well above any thermal insulation, which can cause cables to overheat. Polystyrene insulation can also react with cable sheathing.
- **Intermediate floors/ceiling voids** Clip cables to the sides of joists, lay them on the ceiling or route them through holes drilled through the joists.
- **Ground floors** If you can gain access to the underside of the floor, clip cables beneath the joists.
- **Concrete floors** If a concrete floor has a timber sub-floor on top, you can lay cables on the surface of the concrete. But cables should only run through a concrete floor if they are passed through conduit inserted when the floor is laid, not through channels subsequently cut into the concrete.

Clipping cable to a joist

Run the cable along the centre of one side of the joist and space the clips at roughly 300mm intervals. Buy clips that match the size of cable.

Drilling through a joist

Always be cautious of drilling or cutting joists – it's very important not to weaken the structure. Drill a hole that will allow a 25% air gap around the cable – but no bigger than that. Keep to the central two-thirds of a joist's length and drill at the centre of its depth (or at least 50mm from either top or bottom) to minimise weakening and ensure you are clear of nails or fixings.

Running cable in a solid wall

You can simply mount cables on the surface of a wall with clips, or run them through plastic trunking nailed or screwed to the wall – some types are even self-adhesive. Route them along skirting boards and around door and window frames so they won't be conspicuous. But for a really neat finish you should conceal cables. In a solid wall you need to cut a channel (or chase) in the plaster and run the cable through an oval plastic conduit or, for longer lengths, 'top-hat' capping.

1 Always run cable vertically to a fitting in a solid wall so that you will know its approximate position when the work is finished. Plan the route of the channel using a spirit level or plumb line and mark it in pencil. Check it with a cable detector to ensure you won't accidentally damage an existing cable or pipe. Wearing thick gloves and safety goggles, cut the channel with a bolster and club hammer, making it 6mm wider than the conduit or capping. Cut away to the depth of the conduit, plus about 3mm.

2 Cut the plastic capping or conduit to length with a hacksaw and feed in the cable. Capping is fixed to the wall with masonry nails; conduit snaps into clips nailed to the wall, or can be simply held with masonry nails driven in each side. Either way, the cable will be held firm by the plaster when you fill the channel.

3 Fill the channel with skim-coat plaster or filler to within about 3mm of the wall's surface. When it has set, add another layer flush with the wall surface. When the filler has set, lightly sand it for a perfect finish.

TOOLS MATERIALS

- **spirit level or plumb line**
- **cable detector**
- **pencil**
- **thick gloves**
- **safety goggles**
- **bolster**
- **club hammer**
- **hacksaw**
- **screwdriver**
- **hammer**
- **filling knife**
- **sanding block**

- oval conduit or cable capping
- conduit clips or galvanised masonry nails
- cable
- filler or skim-coat plaster
- abrasive paper

Top-hat cable capping

Cable in stud walls: drilling a passage

A stud partition wall is ideal for concealing cables, but it is much easier to install them while the wall is being built, when holes can be drilled easily through the various parts of the framework (see page 66). In existing walls, it may be possible simply to drill the head or sole plate and feed the cable in, then fish it out at the appropriate spot with stiff wire. However, there may be a horizontal nogging blocking the way. One solution is to drill a passage for the cable through the plasterboard and nogging.

TOOLS MATERIALS

- **hammer**
- **bradawl**
- **pipe and cable detector**
- **stud finder, if required**
- **power drill with 20mm wood bit**
- **filling knife**
- **sanding block**

- stiff wire
- cable
- filler
- abrasive paper

SAFETY FIRST

Over-bending cable will damage its cores, so be sure to cut off the bent section before making the connections.

1 Bend the end of the cable before you drop it into the wall through the head plate, as this will help you retrieve it. If you encounter a nogging, determine its precise position with a stud finder, or by tapping the face of the wall with a hammer handle – the sound will be more solid over timber. Find the edges of the nogging by pushing a bradawl through the plasterboard. Check there are no hidden pipes or cables then use a 20mm wood bit to bore at a shallow angle through the plasterboard into the nogging from above and below. The holes should meet, allowing the cable to be passed through them.

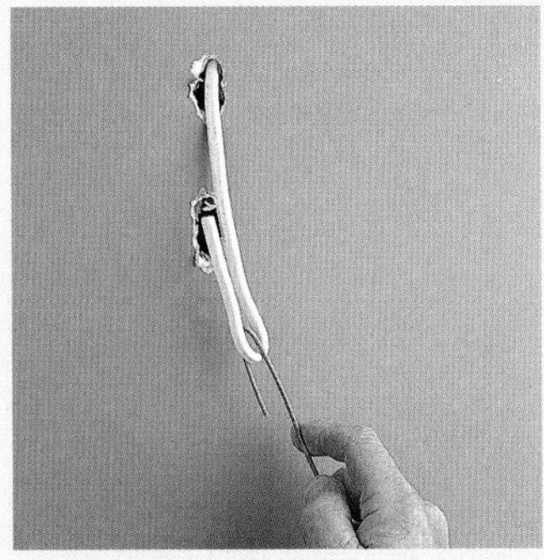

2 Bend the end of a piece of stiff wire, such as a coat hanger, into a hook shape and fish for the cable through the hole above the nogging. This is not as difficult as it sounds. Pull the end of the cable out through the hole.

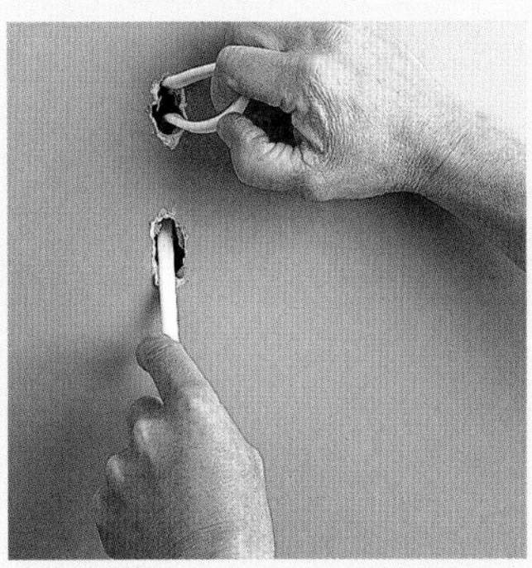

3 Feed the end of the cable back into the upper hole and through the holes bored in the nogging until it emerges from the lower hole.

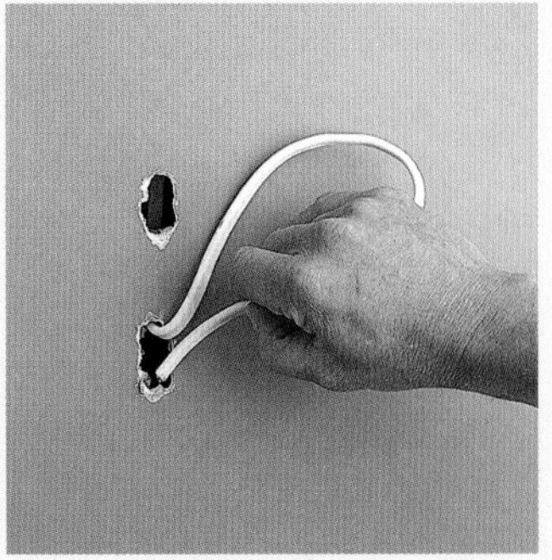

4 Pull enough cable through the lower hole to reach the fitting you want to supply. Take great care not to damage the outer sheathing – if you do, cut off and throw away the damaged length. Feed the cable back into the lower hole and down into the wall. Fish it out of the fitting's mounting box hole. Finally, fill the holes and sand smooth when dry.

Cable in stud walls: removing plasterboard

Another method of running a cable past a nogging is to remove a square of plasterboard then cut a shallow notch in the face of the nogging to accommodate the cable. You must shield the cable from accidental penetration with a nail or screw by screwing a flat steel plate over it, or hammer on a purpose-designed cable safeplate.

1 Before dropping the cable into the wall from above, mark its route in pencil using a spirit level or plumb line. Look for noggings with a stud detector or by tapping with a hammer handle and listening for a more solid tone. If you encounter a nogging, mark out a 125mm square at that position. Check for hidden pipes or cables and then drill holes in diagonally opposite corners. Insert the blade of a padsaw or plasterboard saw and cut out the square of plasterboard.

2 Using a chisel and mallet, cut a notch across the face of the exposed nogging, about 13mm deep and 20mm wide. Feed the cable into the wall. Protect it as it passes through the notch by screwing on a square steel plate or hammering on a cable safeplate.

3 Cut a square of plasterboard to fit the hole – or use the old piece if it wasn't damaged – and nail it to the nogging at each side. Fill the gaps around the edges and sand the filler when dry.

TOOLS MATERIALS

- **spirit level or plumb line**
- **cable detector**
- **stud finder, if required**
- **rule**
- **pencil**
- **padsaw or plasterboard saw**
- **20mm chisel**
- **mallet**
- **hammer**
- **filling knife**
- **sanding block**

- cable
- steel plate or cable safeplate
- plasterboard
- plasterboard nails
- filler
- abrasive paper

SAFE ELECTRICS

Before you start any kind of electrical work isolate the circuit by removing the circuit fuse or switching and locking the circuit breaker. Double-check it is dead with a socket tester or voltage tester. Never take risks with electrical safety! See page 264.

TOOLS MATERIALS

- **screwdriver**
- **socket tester**
- **wire strippers**

- socket faceplate, same size as original
- screws
- green/yellow sleeving, if required

Replacing a socket or converting a single socket into a double are simple jobs. Sockets can be surface or flush mounted. Surface mounting electrical fittings is easier – basically, a mounting box is screwed to the wall, the cable run in and the faceplate attached – but flush-mounted fittings look better and are less prone to accidental damage. Before adding a socket, you must work out whether the IEE Wiring Regulations permit it (see page 276).

Replacing a damaged socket

A socket can become damaged for a variety of reasons: a blow can break the faceplate or overheating may cause scorching. If the problem is scorching, it will usually have been caused by overloading the socket or by loose connections in a plug. Don't plug it back in without dealing with the problem or the same thing will happen again.

1 Isolate the circuit. Use a socket tester to double-check that it is dead. Unscrew the socket faceplate and pull it away from the wall. Keep the screws in case the new ones don't fit.

2 Loosen the terminal screws and free the cable cores. If the insulation is heat damaged, cut back the cores and strip the ends. Run green/yellow sleeving over the earth core if you find it bare.

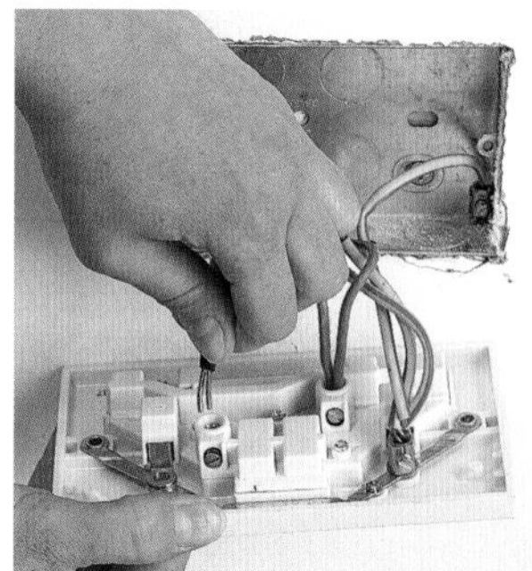

3 Connect the red core or cores to the live terminal (L) of the new faceplate, the black to the neutral terminal (N) and the earth to the earth terminal (E or ⏚). Tighten the terminal screws fully. Refit the new faceplate. If the new screws don't fit the lugs of the old box, use the original screws. Use the socket tester to check it is correctly wired.

Single flush socket to a double

If the socket is flush mounted, it is very easy to replace it with a surface-mounted double socket. There are special socket conversion boxes available for doing this, or you can use a standard double socket and drill and plug the wall, as shown here. If you want the socket to be flush mounted, however, you will have to remove the old box and make a larger recess for a new one (see opposite).

TOOLS MATERIALS

- **screwdriver**
- **socket tester**
- **pipe and cable detector**
- **hammer action drill with masonry bits**
- **wire strippers**

- new double socket
- wall plugs and screws
- green/yellow sleeving, if required

1 Isolate the circuit. Use a socket tester to double-check that it is dead. Unscrew the faceplate and disconnect the cables from the terminals of the single socket mounting box. Run green/yellow sleeving over the earth core if you find it bare.

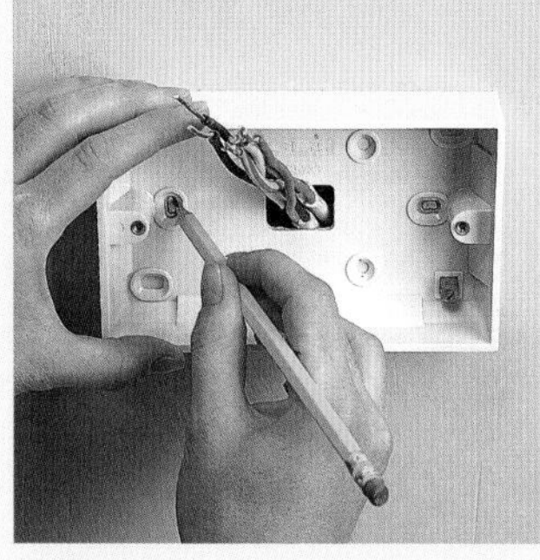

2 Remove the knockout in the new surface mounting box and pass the cables through. Then mark the fixing holes on the wall in pencil. Take the box away, check for hidden pipes or cables, and then drill and plug the wall behind.

3 Screw the new box in place and then connect the cables to the terminals (as above, Step 3). Fit the new faceplate. Use the socket tester to check it is correctly wired.

SAFETY FIRST

If the cable isn't long enough to reach the terminals of the new socket without straining, don't be tempted to pull it! Use a specially designed crimp or terminal block to attach a new short length of cable. But only do this if there is room for it inside the mounting box; all wiring connections must be accessible, not buried in the wall behind.

Flush fixing to solid walls

When flush mounting a box in a solid wall, you need to cut a neat recess through the plaster and into the masonry behind. It's dusty work, so wear gloves and protective goggles.

1 Test for hidden pipes and cables and if all is clear hold the mounting box in position. Use a spirit level to check that it is horizontal then draw its outline on the wall. Using a masonry bit and hammer action drill, make a series of holes within the outline to a slightly greater depth than that of the mounting box (use a socket template, if you have one – see IDEAL TOOL). Set the drill's depth stop, or wrap masking tape around the bit as a depth guide.

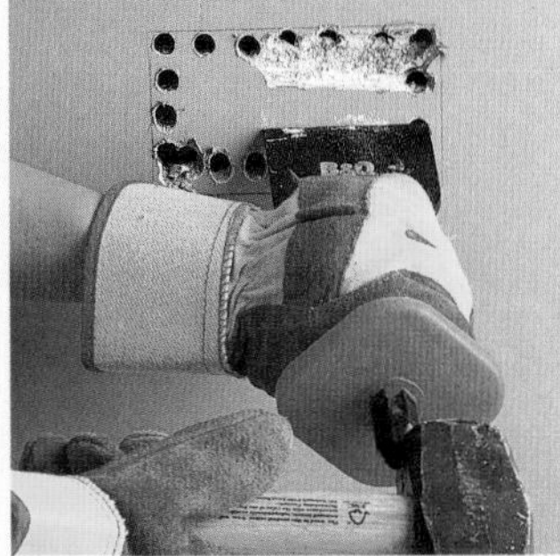

2 Chop out the plaster and masonry with a bolster and club hammer, cutting down to the bottom of the drilled holes. Brush out all the debris and check the fit of the box.

3 Hold the box in place, mark the fixing positions, and drill and plug the holes. Cut a channel for the cable (see page 272) before attaching the box. Then isolate the circuit and make the final connections (see Replacing a damaged socket, opposite). Fit the faceplate and check the wiring is correct using a socket tester.

TOOLS MATERIALS

- **spirit level**
- **pencil**
- **protective gloves**
- **safety goggles**
- **pipe and cable detector**
- **hammer action drill with masonry bit**
- **bolster**
- **club hammer**
- **screwdriver**
- **wire strippers**
- **socket tester**

- mounting box
- adhesive tape
- plastic wall plugs
- round-head screws

IDEAL TOOL

Socket template

When cutting out a recess for a flush mounting box, a socket template will allow you to drill a series of closely spaced holes for a single or double box without the need to draw around the box first. It will also prevent the bit from wandering.

Flush fixing to a stud wall

When flush mounting a socket in a stud wall, it is simplest to use a cavity fixing box. This has a flange that sits against the face of the wall and spring-loaded or rotating lugs that press against the back of the plasterboard, giving more flexibility when you are positioning the fitting.

TOOLS MATERIALS

- **stud finder**
- **spirit level**
- **pencil**
- **pipe and cable detector**
- **screwdriver**
- **padsaw or plasterboard saw**
- **wire strippers**
- **socket tester**

- cavity fixing box

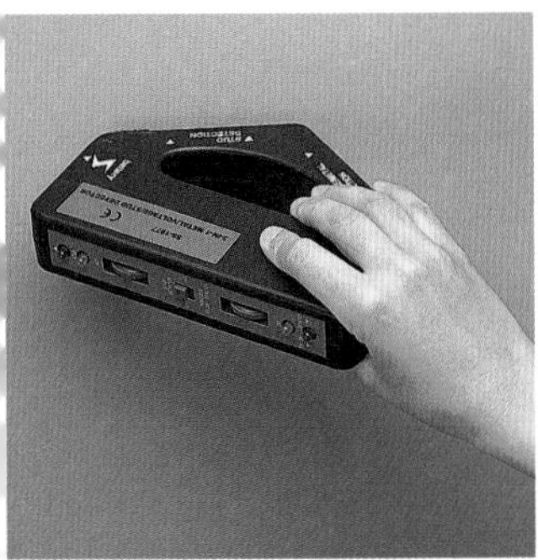

1 Decide where you want to put the new switch or socket. If you have a stud finder, use it to check that none of the wall's framework will be in the way. If you don't have a stud finder, tap the wall gently with a hammer handle, listening for the hollow note to change when you tap over the framework. Hold the box in place, use a spirit level to ensure it is horizontal, and then draw around it in pencil.

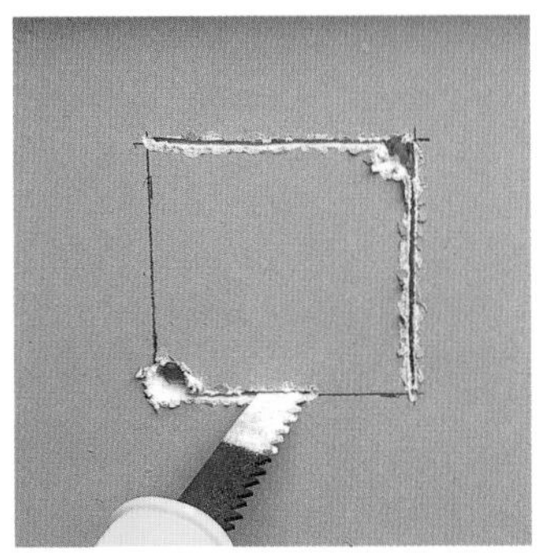

2 Check the area is free of hidden pipes or cables, then push and twist a screwdriver through at diagonally opposite corners of the outline so that you can insert the blade of a padsaw or plasterboard saw. Cut outwards from the holes, following the box outline, and remove the waste piece of plasterboard.

3 Check that the box fits snugly in the hole. Remove the knock-out from the box. Push the box back into the hole, feeding the cable through the opening.

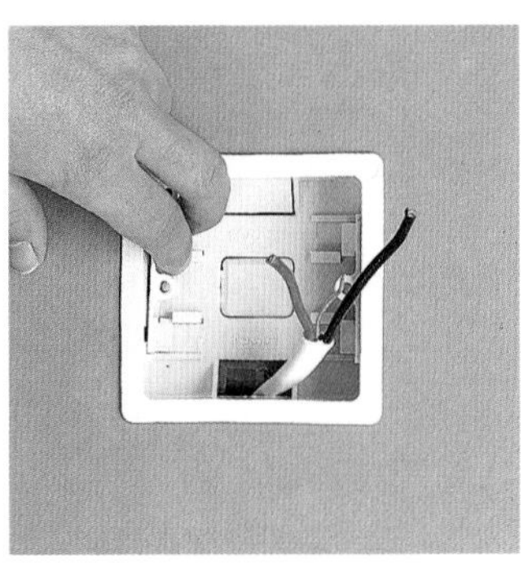

4 Push in or turn the securing lugs so that they grip the rear face of the plasterboard firmly. Connect the wires (see opposite) and fit the faceplate. Check the socket is correctly wired using a socket tester.

ELECTRICITY ADDING SOCKETS

SAFE ELECTRICS

Before you start any kind of electrical work isolate the circuit by removing the circuit fuse or switching and locking the circuit breaker. Double-check it is dead with a socket tester or voltage tester. Never take risks with electrical safety! See page 264.

Although you can increase the number of sockets in a room by converting single sockets to doubles (see page 274), there may be occasions when you need an extra socket where none exists to convert. In this case, you need to add a spur from a ring circuit. You can either run it from an existing socket or from a junction box connected into the cable run of a suitable ring circuit.

Adding a spur on a ring circuit

The easiest way of connecting into a ring circuit is to run a spur cable from the terminals of an existing socket – but you can't connect it to just any socket you please. The IEE Wiring Regulations are very specific about this. You must not run a spur from a socket that is already on a spur, or that already supplies a spur. And the new socket must not extend the floor area served by the circuit beyond the prescribed limit.

Finding the right socket

Isolate the circuit at the consumer unit and use a socket tester to double-check that the power is off. Then remove the faceplate from the socket you want to run a spur from. Count the cables entering the mounting box: one cable means it is already on a spur; three cables mean it already supplies a spur. You can't add a spur in either instance – try another socket.

What you need to find is a socket with two cables entering it. But before you add a spur, you must first confirm that this is a ring circuit. Disconnect the black cores and – with the power still off – test them with a continuity tester (see IDEAL TOOL). If the tester shows continuity, this is a ring circuit and you can add a spur – provided it won't extend the floor area of the circuit beyond 100 sq m (see below).

An alternative to running a spur from an existing socket is to run it from a 3-terminal, 30-amp junction box wired into the main circuit cable. The same regulations apply, however, so trace the cable to the nearest socket and run the above tests.

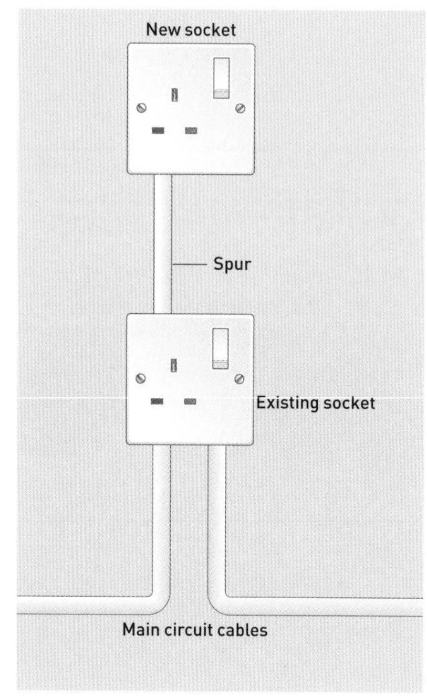

IDEAL TOOL

Continuity tester

This is a simple battery-powered tool for testing whether a cable is part of a continuous circuit. Isolate the circuit and double-check the power is off with a socket tester – never ever use a continuity tester with the power switched on. Then remove the faceplate of the socket, disconnect the two black cable cores from their terminal and touch the individual probes of the tester to each core simultaneously. If the cable is part of a ring circuit, the tester will give a continuity reading. If it doesn't, the cable is either part of a radial circuit or a spur.

Consider the floor area

Although the IEE Wiring Regulations permit you to have an unlimited number of socket outlets on each main circuit running from the consumer unit, there are restrictions on the floor area that each circuit can supply. A 30/32 amp ring circuit can supply a maximum area of 100 sq m. However, because ring circuits serving kitchens and utility rooms are usually the most heavily loaded, it is advisable to avoid extending them into other rooms wherever possible.

You should find that the rooms of the house covered by each circuit are written inside the fuse cover of the consumer unit, but you can check this by isolating the circuit and using a socket tester on each socket to see if it works. Once you have determined the extent of the circuit, you can measure the rooms it supplies and calculate the floor area. If you have a large house and were planning to run a spur through a wall to feed a socket in a different room, you may find it will exceed the limit. If so, you must run the spur from a different circuit.

Running a spur from a socket

Install the new socket and and run a length of 2.5mm² two-core-and-earth cable from the new outlet to the existing socket (see pages 272–75).

1 Isolate the circuit and use a socket tester to double-check that the existing socket is dead.

2 Unscrew the faceplate of the new socket, feed the cable into the mounting box through a rubber grommet and connect its cores to the faceplate terminals. Don't forget to add green/yellow sleeving to the bare earth core of the new cable, and make sure the terminal screws are tight.

3 Cut the cable and do the same at the existing socket.

4 If you have metal faceplates, cut a short length of earth core from 1.5mm² cable and run it between the earth terminals of the faceplate and mounting box.

5 Replace the faceplates and turn the power back on. Check that the new socket is correctly wired using a socket tester.

TOOLS MATERIALS

- **continuity tester**
- **side cutters**
- **wire strippers**
- **screwdriver**
- **socket tester**

- 2 rubber grommets
- green/yellow sleeving

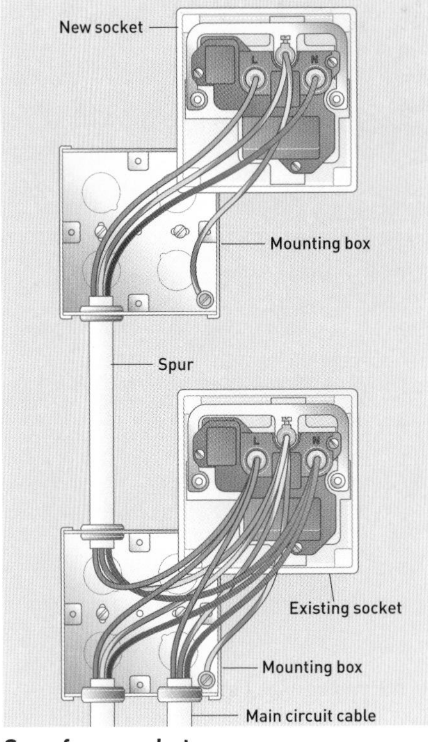

Spur from socket

Running a spur from a junction box

TOOLS MATERIALS

- **continuity tester**
- **power drill with twist bits**
- **panel saw, if required**
- **hammer, if required**
- **screwdriver**
- **side cutters**
- **wire strippers**
- **socket tester**

- rubber grommet
- 3-terminal 30-amp junction box
- timber battens, if required
- 50mm nails, if required
- green/yellow sheathing

Install the spur socket and run a length of 2.5mm² two-core-and-earth cable back to the point where it is to be connected to the main circuit cable (see pages 272–75). The junction box should have the same amperage as the circuit.

1 Isolate the circuit and use a socket tester to double-check that it is dead.

2 Unscrew the faceplate of the new socket, feed the cable into the mounting box through a rubber grommet and connect its cores to the faceplate terminals. Don't forget to add green/yellow sleeving to the bare earth core of the new cable, and make sure the terminal screws are tight.

3 If the faceplate is metal, cut a short length of earth core from 1.5mm² cable and run it between the earth terminals of the faceplate and mounting box. Replace the faceplate.

4 Screw the base of the junction box to the side of an adjacent joist or to a batten nailed between joists so that it will be within reach of the cut ends of the main cable.

5 Cut the cable, strip back the outer sheathing (but make sure it extends a few mm into the junction box), bare the ends of the cores and connect them to the terminals of the junction box. Connect the matching-coloured cores of the spur cable to the same terminals. Remember to add green/yellow sleeving to the bare earth cores.

6 Make sure the terminal screws are tight, then replace the cover of the box and turn on the power. Test the socket is wired correctly using a socket tester.

YOU CAN DO IT

Know your terminals
Make sure you are connecting to the correct socket terminals – their position varies between brands. Read any instructions that come with the new socket.

SAFETY FIRST

Grommets
When using metal mounting boxes, it is essential to fit rubber grommets to protect the incoming cable from being damaged by the sharp edges around the metal cut-outs.

Spur from junction box

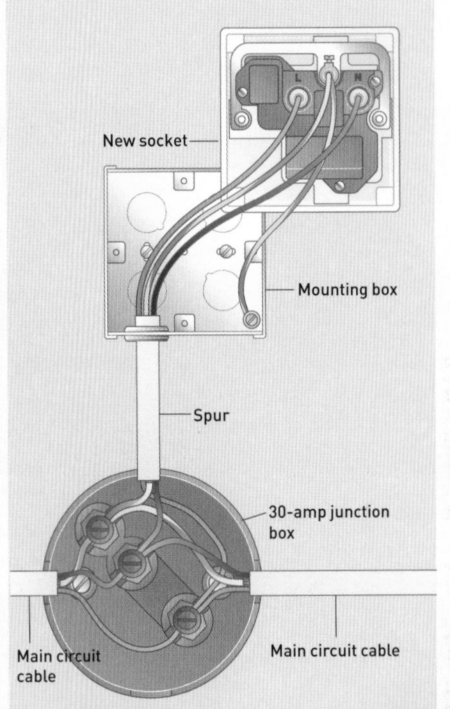

SAFE ELECTRICS

Before you start any kind of electrical work isolate the circuit by removing the circuit fuse or switching and locking the circuit breaker. Double-check it is dead with a socket tester or voltage tester. Never take risks with electrical safety! See page 264.

Lighting circuits are wired in two different ways, using either junction-boxes or loop-in ceiling roses. These days the loop-in system predominates, though individual circuits often combine the two for the most economical use of cable. But unlike power circuits, lighting circuits are always of the radial type: the cable leaves the consumer unit and runs to each outlet position before terminating at the last fitting on the line. Most houses have at least two lighting circuits – usually one upstairs and one down.

Junction-box circuits

The reason why the wiring of a lighting circuit is more complex than a power circuit is that each outlet or light fitting needs to be controlled by a separate switch. One way of providing for this is to install a four-terminal junction box in which the cable from a light and the cable from its switch can be connected to the circuit cable.

In practice, instead of a junction box for each lighting outlet, you may find that the cables run to a single, bigger junction-box in the attic or ceiling void, where all the connections for the circuit are made. Or there may be a combination of junction-box and loop-in wiring (see opposite) on one circuit.

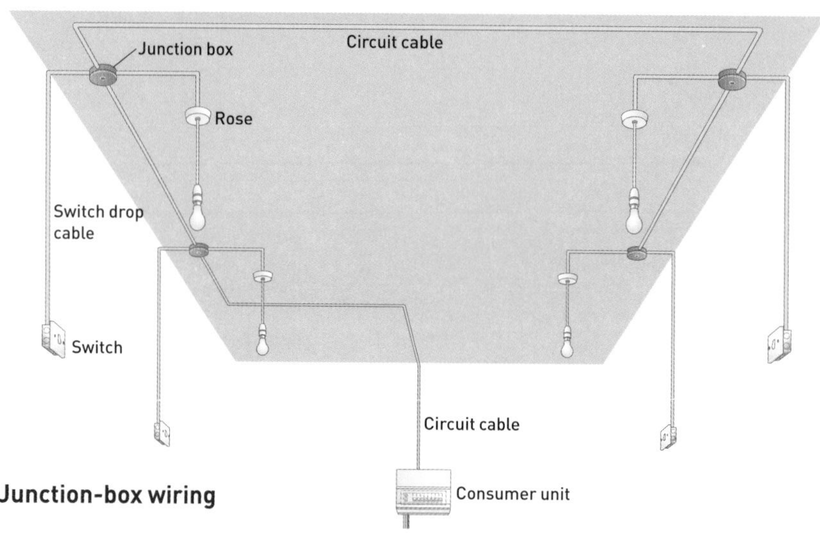

Junction-box wiring

The wiring of a four-terminal junction box

Two of the cables entering the junction box are the main circuit cables. Their red (live), black (neutral) and earth (green/yellow sleeved) cores are each connected to a different terminal. One of the other cables entering the box runs to the light, the last to the switch. The red core of the light cable is connected to the fourth terminal, while its black core is connected to the main circuit black cores; the earth runs to the earth terminal. The red core of the switch cable is connected to the main circuit red cores, while its black core is connected to the light cable red core.

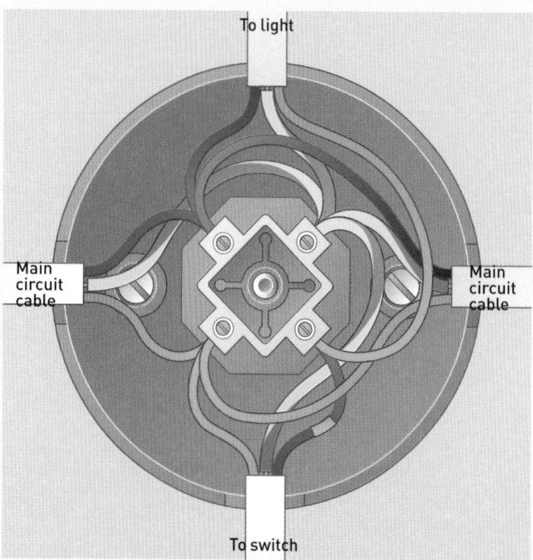

Current flows from the main circuit down the red core to the switch then (if the switch is on and the circuit therefore unbroken) back up the black core and along the red core to the light before finally returning through the light cable black core to the neutral terminal in the box. Because the switch cable's black core becomes the feed to the light when the switch is turned on, it must carry a warning 'flag' of red PVC electrical sleeving.

At the light unit itself, the current flows from the red core of the cable into the brown (live) core of the flex, then back up the blue (neutral) core of the flex to the cable's black core. In a pendant light fitting and some wall lights, the connections are made in the rose or base of the unit, but flush-mounted fittings require the connections to be made in a heat-proof conduit box set in the ceiling or wall.

Loop-in circuits

With loop-in wiring, the main circuit cable from the consumer unit loops in and out of multi-terminal ceiling roses, from which individual cables run to the light switches. The system does away with the need for junction boxes and separate cables to the lights. All the necessary connections are made within the rose. A separate terminal is provided in the rose for the switch cable neutral core, which passes current directly to the live core of the pendant flex.

Loop-in wiring

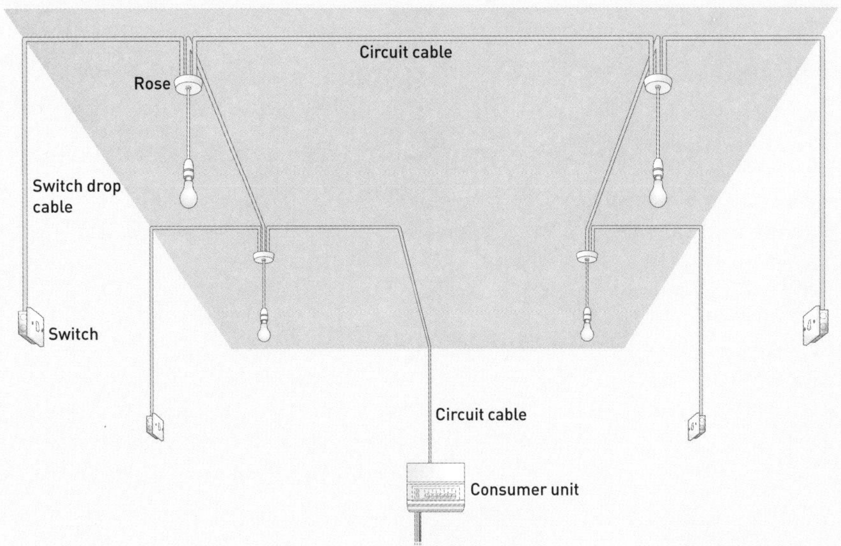

Circuit capacity

A lighting circuit is protected by a 5 or 6 amp fuse or circuit breaker. This fuse size allows bulbs with a maximum combined wattage of 1150 watts (5 amps x 230 volts) or 1380 watts (6 amps x 230 volts) to be run off the circuit. In practice it is best always to restrict the number of outlets per circuit to about eight; that means that even with a 100 watt bulb at every outlet, the total wattage is comfortably within the maximum. But if you are running high-wattage floodlights, or a big multi-bulb chandelier, you will need even fewer outlets if you are to avoid overloading the circuit.

Lighting circuits are generally run in $1mm^2$ two-core-and-earth cable, but particularly long circuits may use $1.5mm^2$ cable to compensate for the drop in voltage experienced on long cable runs.

Two-way switching

It is common for the light in a hall or on a landing to be controlled by two-way switching, whereby the light can be switched on and off both from upstairs and downstairs. In this situation, the switch connected directly to the light (either through a junction box or loop-in rose) is linked to a second switch using special three-core-and-earth cable.

Bathroom lighting

The steamy, damp environment of a bathroom greatly increases the potential dangers of any electrical fitting. Steam can easily cause a bulb to shatter, so it is advisable always to fit moisture-proof, enclosed light fittings wherever you position them in a bathroom. Switches must be ceiling-mounted pull-cords; any wall-mounted switches should be sited outside the room.

The IEE Wiring Regulations divide a bathroom into four Hazard Zones. You must check that any light fitting you install is suitable for the zone you are positioning it in; always read the manufacturer's instructions and measure the room carefully. A light fitting in Zone 2 must be approved as splashproof (with a minimum rating of IPX4, see page 290); in Zone 1, it must also be protected by a 30mA RCD. A ceiling-mounted switch must be in Zone 3 or beyond, although it is permissible for the pull-cord to dangle down into other zones. If in doubt, seek the advice of a qualified electrician.

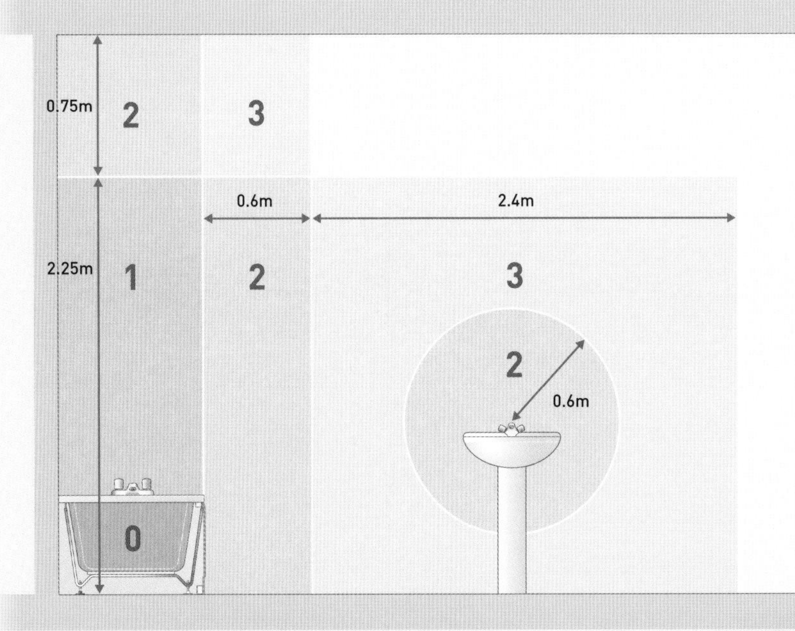

SAFE ELECTRICS

Before you start any kind of electrical work isolate the circuit by removing the circuit fuse or switching and locking the circuit breaker. Double-check it is dead with a socket tester or voltage tester. Never take risks with electrical safety! See page 264.

Lighting plays a functional role in the home, allowing you to see what you are doing when natural light is insufficient, but it can also make a major contribution to the decorative schemes of your rooms and can have a dramatic effect on the mood they produce. Lighting is the one aspect of your home's electrical system that really allows you to be creative, and you can personalise it for your own needs.

Lighting for effect

Many rooms in our homes have a single pendant light hanging from the centre of the ceiling; it's what builders invariably provide, and very easy just to take for granted. But that single pendant can leave much to be desired when it comes to getting the most from a room's lighting. Overhead lights of this type can make a room and its furnishings look flat and uninviting. Moreover, the diffused light they produce may not be strong enough for reading or similar close-up tasks.

By introducing a variety of light fittings, either in combination with a pendant or instead of it, you can change a room completely, adding atmosphere and making it feel cosy and welcoming. Different rooms in your home need different treatments, but always consider the purpose of the room first. Once you are sure that the lighting is sufficient for the required task, you can add the finishing touches that make the room come alive.

Living room

Here, you need to cater for a range of family requirements: reading, watching television, entertaining, children's play. So the general diffused lighting of overhead fittings is a start, but add directional lighting with spotlamps and reading lamps; use recessed or surface-mounted spotlamps to accent features or pictures, or 'wash' walls with light. Table and standard lamps can be used to provide soft pools of light to create a relaxing atmosphere, while dimmer switches will allow you to control the overall light levels.

Bedroom

Make the most of lighting to create a cosy atmosphere in a bedroom. Use recessed spotlights, wall lights and table lamps to generate a soft light, but provide task lighting for reading in bed and using a dressing table. Freestanding uplighters can also provide soft ambient lighting, but are not a good idea in children's bedrooms, where the temptation to throw paper or objects into them makes them a fire hazard.

Dining room

Dining should be a pleasurable experience, something to linger over, so you don't want a dining room to have a cold atmosphere. You need a light over the table, but control it with a dimmer switch so that you can adjust the light level; that way, you will be able to see what you are eating without being bathed in harsh glare. Again, picking out features in the room with accent lighting will provide added interest, and pastel-coloured bulbs will soften the atmosphere and enhance a colour scheme.

Hallway and stairs

In a hallway, choose lamps that will provide a warm welcoming glow for visitors – table and standard lamps or wall lights. Stairs, though, must be well lit to prevent anyone missing a step.

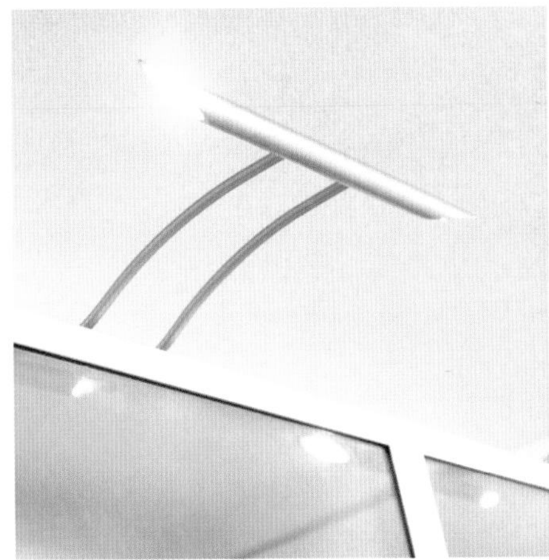

Kitchen

The kitchen is one room where you really need to see what you are doing, so good lighting is essential. Aim spotlights at the hob and sink; fit lights under wall cabinets to shine on to work surfaces. Don't use plug-in lamps, which may clutter work surfaces.

GLS (general lighting service)

These are the most commonly used lamps and are found in most light fittings. They may be clear, translucent (pearl) or opaque (in a choice of colours). They are available in a range of sizes and shapes, from the well-known pear and mushroom forms to candle types. Special large-diameter versions are available and are intended to be on view, without shades. All of these provide a general diffused light.

Halogen

Halogen lamps produce a crisp, clean, bright white light – brighter than a standard bulb of the same wattage. They bring out the detail of an interior, and are also particularly good for reading and close-work, helping avert eye strain. They do get extremely hot, so must only be used in a suitable fitting.

SAFETY FIRST

All lampshades have a wattage maximum. Don't exceed it or you could cause scorching or even a fire.

Types of lamp

Light bulbs and tubes are correctly known as lamps, and there is a vast range to choose from, meeting every conceivable practical and decorative purpose. Lamps usually have either a bayonet end cap or Edison screw cap. Tubes generally have two small pins projecting from each end that fit into spring-loaded holders.

Reflector

These lamps produce strong directional beams of light and are used in spotlamp and floodlight fittings. All have some form of silvering on the bulb that helps throw the light in a particular direction. Crown-silvered types direct light back on to a separate reflector that throws it forward; internally-silvered types have no need of a reflector, since their design aims the beam forward. A third type, the PAR (parabolic aluminised reflector), has a conical shape and comes in a variety of beam widths suitable for spotlamps and floodlights.

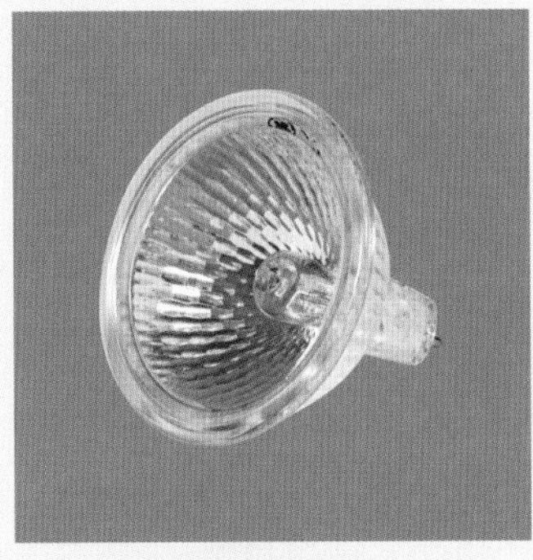

Low-voltage halogen

Low-voltage lighting, a relatively recent development, uses halogen bulbs that run at 12 volts rather than the usual 230. The current is supplied via a transformer which may be built into the light fitting, or in a separate location (see page 289). The bulbs provide a bright, directed light, ideal for highlighting particular features of a room.

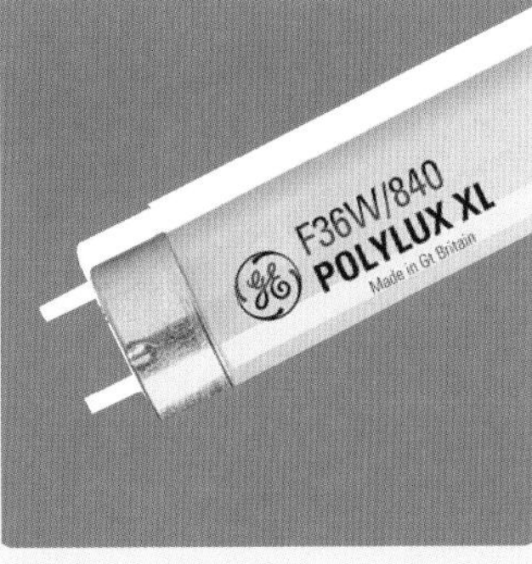

Tubes

These are long glass cylinders with metal end caps. Fluorescent tubes produce light ranging from a harsh bluish white to a much warmer pinkish shade. Various lengths, and even circular versions, are available for a range of fittings. Their use has limitations in domestic situations, although they are ideal for garages and home workshops. Another type of tube is the tungsten-filament type, essentially a tubular version of the standard GLS lamp. This is quite small (up to 285mm long) and may be clear or pearl. In the main, this kind of tube is used for concealed lighting.

YOU CAN DO IT

Dimmers

A dimmer switch will dramatically increase the potential of your home's lighting, however basic your fittings. It is wired in the same way as an ordinary switch (see page 282). But remember that not all dimmers are compatible with low-voltage halogen bulbs or most fluorescent tubes or lamps; check the manufacturer's instructions.

Compact fluorescent lamps

These combine the construction of a fluorescent tube with the compact dimensions of normal GLS lamps, and they will fit standard light fittings, as they have bayonet and screw end caps. They produce a bright light and reduce energy consumption, since they use about 20% of the electricity of a comparable GLS lamp. Moreover, they can last eight times as long. They are most useful in fittings where they will be left on for several hours at a time, since they can take a few seconds to warm up and reach full brightness, especially after a period of use.

SAFE ELECTRICS

Before you start any kind of electrical work isolate the circuit by removing the circuit fuse or switching and locking the circuit breaker. Double-check it is dead with a socket tester or voltage tester. Never take risks with electrical safety! See page 264.

Light switches are functional items, and many of the cheaper varieties – made from white plastic – look strictly utilitarian, but you can choose from a range of decorative switches that will add a finishing touch to many rooms. If you are replacing a switch that has become damaged, you could take the opportunity to improve its appearance.

Another reason for changing a switch is to provide the convenience of multi-way control of a light in a hallway, landing or stairwell.

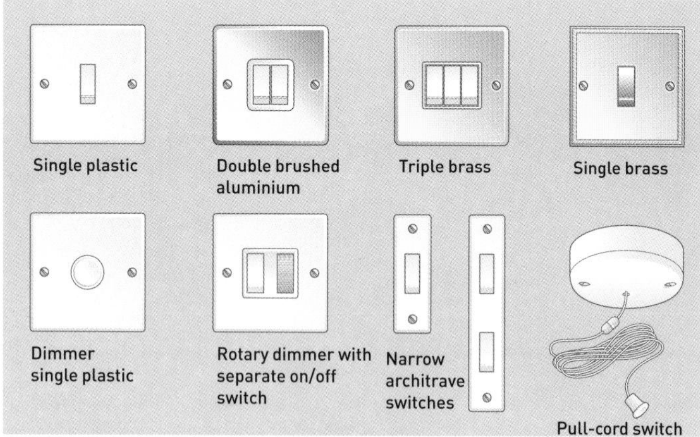

Types of switch

Wall-mounted light switch fittings (known as plateswitches) may contain one, two, three or even more individual switches (or gangs) to allow control of several separate light fittings from one position. In addition, versions are available to allow two- and multi-way switching. There's a huge range of fittings available, from functional plastic fittings to stylish metallic finishes.

Dimmers allow you to raise and lower the light level and may have a simple combined on/off and dimming control, or a separate on/off switch and dimmer control, so that you don't have to readjust the light level every time you turn on the light. They are wired in much the same way as a standard switch. Where space is limited, or for an unobtrusive installation, narrow architrave switches can be fitted into door frames. Switches generally require a 16mm-deep mounting box, although some dimmers may need deeper boxes. Ceiling-mounted pull-cord switches are required in bathrooms or shower rooms, where you are not allowed to have a wall-mounted switch within reach of anyone using the bath or shower.

Replacing a one-way switch

If a switch is damaged, or you simply want to update your fittings, replacing it is a fairly simple task. Just be sure to write down exactly how the old switch was wired before you disconnect it, and wire the new switch in the same way. Keep hold of the original screws – you may have to reuse them, since modern fittings will come with metric-sized screws and older fittings may have imperial threads.

TOOLS MATERIALS

- **voltage tester**
- **screwdrivers**
- **side cutters**

- one-way plateswitch
- green/yellow earth sleeving
- red PVC electrical sleeving
- screws

1 Isolate the circuit and confirm that the power is off with a voltage tester. Then unscrew the switch faceplate and pull it forward so that you can see the connections behind. Draw a clear diagram showing the colour and number of wires connected to each terminal, then release the terminal screws and pull the cores from the terminals. If the earth core is properly insulated in green/yellow sleeving and connected to the mounting box, leave this attached.

2 Connect the cores to the correct terminals of the new switch, tighten the screws and check that they are clamping the cable cores firmly by giving the wires a slight tug. If there isn't one already, fit a length of red PVC sleeving over the black core to indicate that it can be live.

3 Run a length of green/yellow PVC sleeving over the bare earth core of the switch drop cable and reconnect it to the earthing terminal of the mounting box.

4 Recheck that each connection is secure, then push the cable back into the mounting box and fit the faceplate.

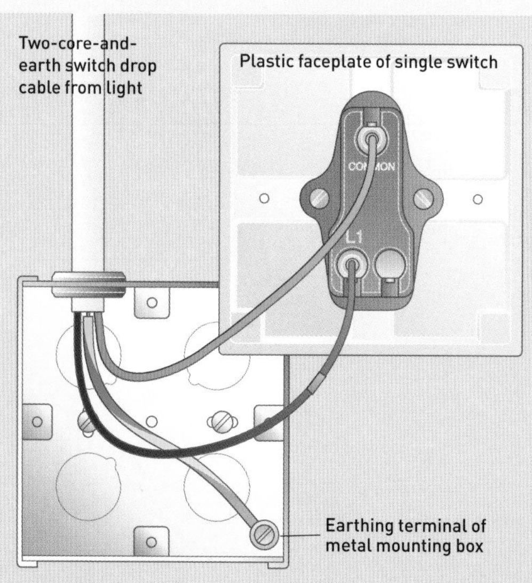

SAFETY FIRST

Earthing light switches

The commonest combination is a metal mounting box and plastic faceplate, as shown here, in which case the earth core or cores must be connected to the earthing terminal of the mounting box. If you have a metal faceplace you must *also* run a short length of earth core (cut from 1mm^2 two-core and earth cable and insulated with green/yellow sleeving) between the earthing terminals on the faceplate and the mounting box. If both mounting box and faceplate are plastic, there's no need to earth them, but it's a good idea to run green/yellow sleeving over the bare cores and clamp their exposed ends with a connector; that way if you decide to change to metal fittings in the future, you will be able to earth them safely and easily.

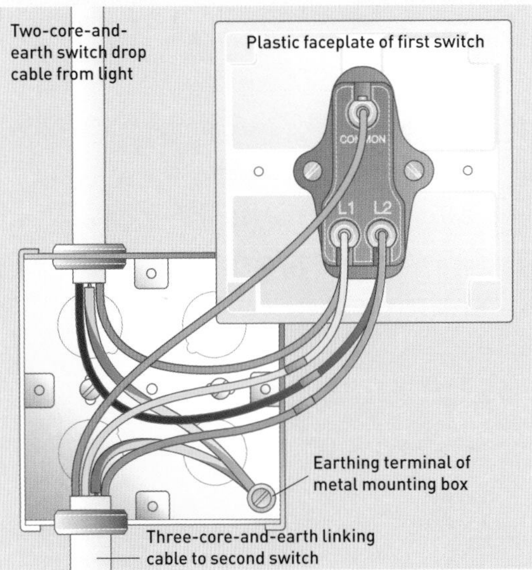

1 Isolate the circuit and double-check the power is off with a voltage tester; remove the faceplate from the existing switch and disconnect the cable cores. You may find that the switch has three terminals, indicating that it is actually a two-way fitting, in which case you can reuse it.

2 Each two-way switch will have three terminals, arranged as a single and a pair. They will either be labelled Common, L1 and L2, or L1, L2 and L3. At the original switch, fit a length of red PVC sleeving over the black core of the switch drop cable and the blue and yellow cores of the linking cable to indicate that they can be live. Then connect the red and black cores of the existing switch drop cable and the yellow and blue cores of the new linking cable to the pair of terminals. Take the red core of the linking cable to the single terminal. Fit green/yellow sleeving over the bare earth cores and connect them to the mounting box earth terminal.

Two-way switching

To change from the one-way control of a light to two-way switching you have to replace the original switch with a two-way fitting, install a new two-way switch at the second control point and link the two with 1mm^2 three-core-and-earth cable. Start by running the cable between the two switch positions and installing a mounting box at the new switch position (see pages 272–75).

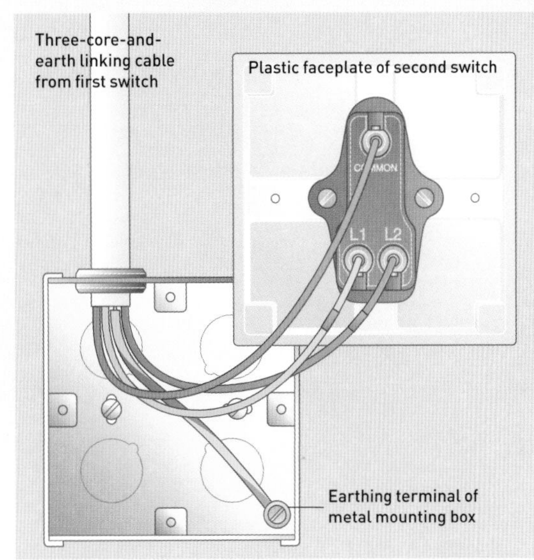

3 At the second switch, fit a length of red PVC sleeving over the blue and yellow cores of the linking cable to indicate that they can be live. Then connect the cores of the three-core-and-earth cable to the same terminals as the first switch. Fit green/yellow sleeving over the bare earth core and connect it to the mounting box earth terminal.

TOOLS MATERIALS

- **voltage tester**
- **screwdrivers**
- **side cutters**

- green/yellow earth sleeving
- red PVC electrical sleeving

SAFETY FIRST

Multi-way switching
Be extremely cautious when opening up multi-way switches. The lights they control *should* all take their power from the same circuit, but if yours are incorrectly wired and take power from different circuits, there will still be live cables at each switch position when one circuit is isolated. Be aware also that there is more than one method of wiring multi-way lights. If yours do not match the system shown here, that doesn't necessarily mean they are unsafe.

YOU CAN DO IT

Three-core-and-earth cable
The connections in two- and three-way light switches are such that the circuit can be made or broken at any of the switch points. For this to be possible you have to use cable with an extra core, so that the current can run in various directions, along various routes. Because the yellow, blue and black cores may all at times be live at a light switch, they must carry a warning flag of red PVC electrical sleeving or tape.

B&Q

Multi-way switching

You can control a light from more than two separate switch positions. The connections for wiring the first and final switches are the same as for two-way switching, but a special intermediate switch is wired into the three-core-and-earth linking cable between them. An intermediate switch has four terminals; fit a length of red PVC sleeving over the blue and yellow cores and connect the yellow cores to the top and bottom terminals on one side and the blue cores to the terminals on the other. The two red cores should be joined with an insulated strip connector. Fit the earth cores (protected by green/yellow sleeving) to the mounting box earthing terminal.

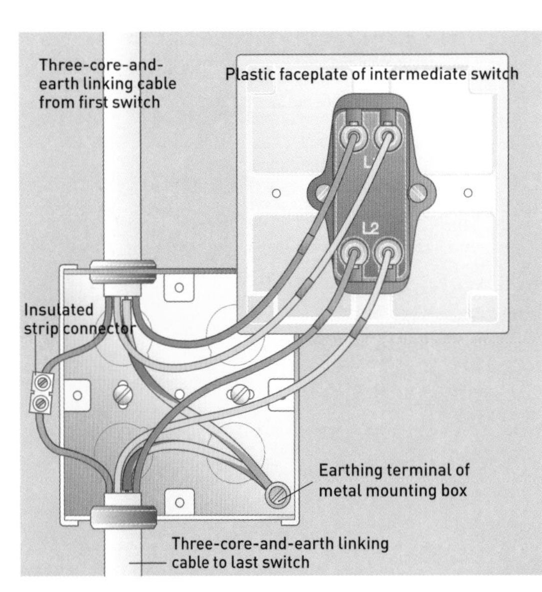

ELECTRICITY CEILING LIGHTS

SAFE ELECTRICS

Before you start any kind of electrical work isolate the circuit by removing the circuit fuse or switching and locking the circuit breaker. Double-check it is dead with a socket tester or voltage tester. Never take risks with electrical safety! See page 264.

A standard single pendant light fitting near the centre of the ceiling can sometimes leave a lot to be desired. Provided you can access the ceiling void from above without too much disruption, it's not complicated to move a light to give illumination where you really need it or to increase light levels by adding extra pendants, operated either by the existing switch or by a new one. Pre-wired lampholder-plus-flex combinations are widely available.

Identifying the circuit type

The first task is to identify the circuit type – junction box or loop-in. With the power turned off, remove the ceiling rose cover. You can't tell from the design of the rose; you need to count the cables entering it. If there is only one cable, you have junction-box wiring; if there are two or three, you have a loop-in system.

SAFETY FIRST

Pendants

Flex can only support a very light lamp and shade. Light fittings over 2kg must be chain-supported for safety. Fittings with metal parts must be earthed via three-core flex unless they are clearly labelled as double-insulated (⧈).

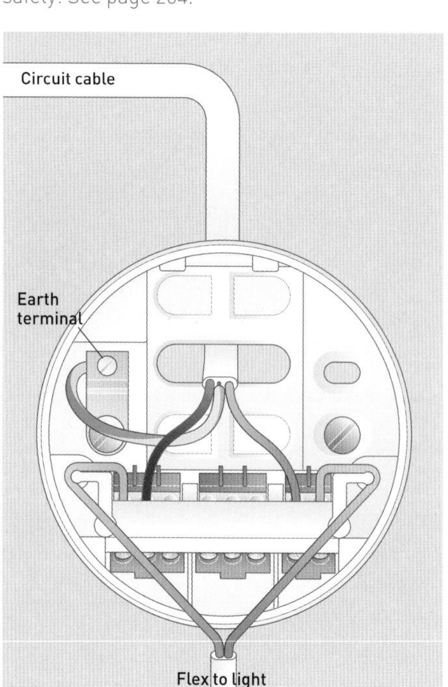

Single cable entering rose

A single cable at the rose indicates junction-box wiring.

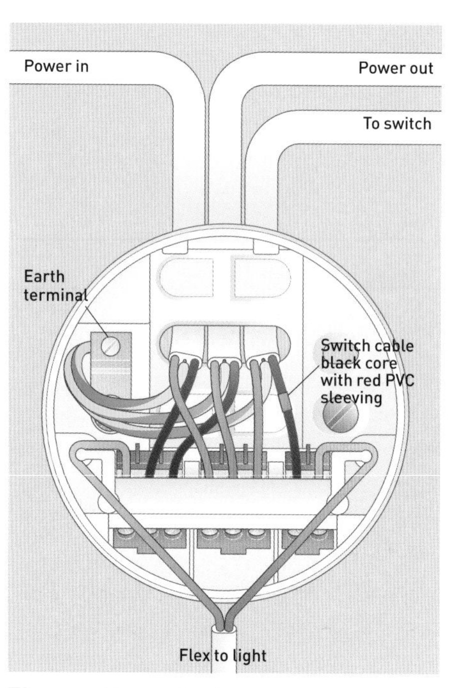

Three cables entering rose

Three cables at the rose indicate loop-in wiring; an intermediate rose on the circuit will have two circuit cables plus a switch cable.

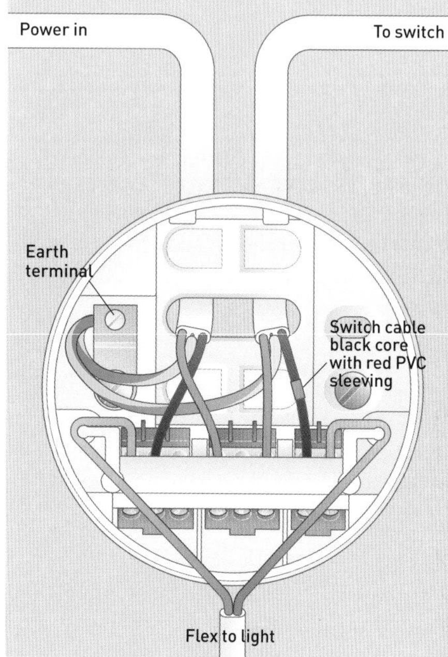

Two cables entering rose

Two cables also indicate a loop-in circuit. The last rose on the circuit will have one circuit cable plus a switch cable.

TOOLS MATERIALS

- **voltage tester**
- **screwdriver**
- **side cutters**
- **sharp knife**
- **wire strippers**
- **filling knife**
- **sanding block**
- **paintbrush**

- ceiling rose
- 1mm² two-core-and-earth cable
- green/yellow earth sleeving
- red PVC electrical sleeving
- cable clips
- 3- or 4-terminal junction box(es)
- new switch, if required
- filler
- abrasive paper
- paint

Moving a pendant light

Isolate the circuit, double-check it is dead and unscrew the rose cover. When you have identified the wiring type, disconnect the flex and feed cable.

With junction-box wiring

Unscrew the rose base from the ceiling and push the cable back through. Above the ceiling, connect the cable to a three-terminal junction box; run a length of 1mm² two-core-and-earth cable from the new light rose. Connect the red core to the live terminal, the black to the neutral terminal and the earth (insulated with green/yellow sleeving) to the earth terminal. Make good the ceiling at the old light position with filler.

With loop-in wiring

Unscrew the rose base from the ceiling and push the cables back through. Mount a four-terminal junction box (see page 278) above the original light position. Connect the red, black and earth cores of the main circuit cable(s) to three separate terminals. Then connect the red core of the switch cable to the circuit reds, the earth core to the circuit earths and the black core to the fourth (unused) terminal. Finally, add a fourth cable to feed the light, connecting its red core to the switch black, its black core to the circuit blacks and its earth to the circuit earths. Make good the ceiling at the old light position with filler.

Adding an extra pendant light to an existing switch

If a single pendant fitting doesn't provide enough light in a room, you can add another controlled by the same switch without too much trouble. The one limiting factor is the number of lighting outlets already powered by the circuit; don't risk overloading the circuit (see page 279).

With junction-box wiring

Double-check the circuit is dead and cut the feed cable to the original light at a suitable position to install a three-terminal junction box. Run a length of 1mm^2 two-core-and-earth cable from there to the new fitting.

With loop-in wiring

1 Double-check the power is off and run a spur cable from the original ceiling rose, connecting its red core to the same terminal as the switch drop black core (which should carry a length of red PVC sleeving to indicate that it can be live) and its black core to the black circuit cores, the earth core going to the earth terminal – as illustrated, right.

2 At the new rose, connect the red core to the terminal marked 'live' and the black core to the terminal marked 'neutral'. Take the earth core to the earth terminal, covering it in green/yellow sleeving. Connect the live (brown) core of the pendant flex to the live terminal and the neutral (blue) core to the neutral terminal.

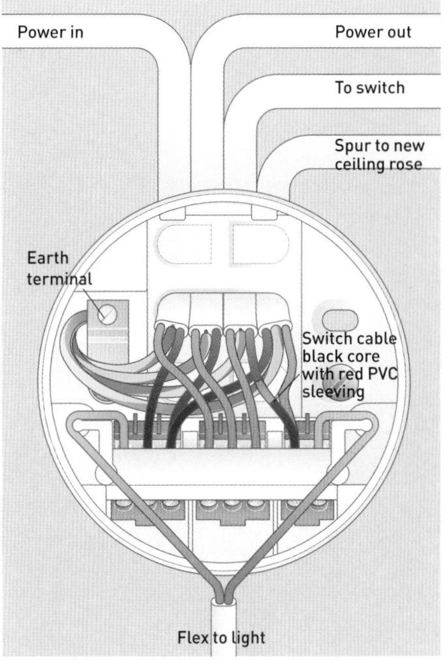

Running a spur from a loop-in rose

With a loop-in system, you can add a spur cable at the original ceiling rose to provide power to a second light controlled by the same switch.

Adding a pendant light and new switch

Whichever type of wiring you have, you may find it possible to run the switch cable back to the existing switch position, replacing the original one-gang switch with a two-gang unit. This will make for a neater installation.

With junction-box wiring

1 Double-check the circuit is dead then cut the main circuit cable and install a four-terminal junction box. Connect the red cores of the split circuit cable to one terminal, the black cores to another and the earth cores to a third, adding green/yellow sleeving.

2 Then run one length of 1mm^2 two-core-and-earth cable to the new light and another to the switch. Connect the red switch core to the circuit reds, its earth to the circuit earths and the black core to the fourth terminal; add a length of red PVC electrical sleeving to this core to show that it can be live.

3 Connect the red core of the light cable to the switch drop's black core, its black core to the circuit blacks and the earth to the earth terminal.

Alternatively

With either type of wiring, you have the alternative option of connecting a three-terminal junction box into the main circuit cable and running a spur from there to a loop-in rose with its own switch cable.

With loop-in wiring

1 Double-check the power is off and run a spur cable from an existing rose on the circuit, connecting its red core to the main circuit reds, its black core to the main circuit blacks and its earth to the earth terminal.

2 At the new light position, connect its red core to the central bank of terminals, which may be marked 'loop in' and its black core to the neutral terminal; connect the earth to the earth terminal, adding green/yellow sleeving.

3 Then run in the switch drop cable at the new rose, connecting its red core to the spur's red, its black core (flagged red) to the live terminal and its earth to the earth terminal.

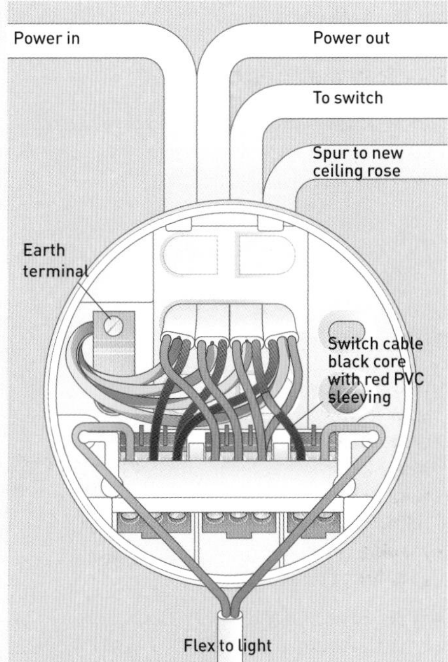

Running a spur from a loop-in rose to a new rose and switch

With a loop-in rose, you can add a spur cable to provide power to a second light position controlled by its own switch.

ELECTRICITY WALL LIGHTS

SAFE ELECTRICS

Before you start any kind of electrical work isolate the circuit by removing the circuit fuse or switching and locking the circuit breaker. Double-check it is dead with a socket tester or voltage tester. Never take risks with electrical safety! See page 264.

Even when controlled by a dimmer switch, a ceiling light can only produce very limited effects. For greater versatility, wall lights are hard to beat: they can be functional, providing directed light to accent particular features or to aid reading; and they can be decorative, creating pools of illumination that give a room an overall subtle glow.

Installing the lights

Fitting wall lights can be a messy, labour-intensive job, so start by planning the cable runs and connections, aiming to keep disruption to a minimum. If you have fitted carpeting on the floor above, for example, then accessing the lighting circuit cables in the ceiling void may be much more difficult than running a spur from a suitable socket within the room.

As a rule, wall lights are best placed about 1.8m above the floor. In some you can make the connections within the base of the light (using strip connectors), while for others you will need to fit a round conduit box in the wall at the end of the cable chase. In some cases, you may be able to screw the light fitting to the box; in others, it will have to be screwed to the wall.

Run all the cable first (see pages 272–73) and then fit the lights before finally isolating the supply circuit and making all the connections. If you are installing more than one wall light, you will need to cut the supply cable and install a three-terminal junction box for each additional fitting; simply connect the cores like to like and check they are secure.

Wiring options

You need to decide how you want the new lights to operate:

- Do you want wall lights that come on with the main ceiling light? If so, then you need to run a spur from the junction box or loop-in rose controlling the ceiling light.
- Do you want the wall lights to be separately switched from the main ceiling light? You need to wire a junction box into a lighting circuit and run new cable from there to both the switch and light fittings.
- Do you want the wall lights to replace the ceiling light? If so, you need to replace the rose with a junction box and run a cable from that to the new lights.

Don't risk overloading a lighting circuit (see page 279). If you want to install multiple wall lights, it may be better to power them from a spur run off a main power circuit.

Adding wall lights controlled by an existing switch

Your first task is to establish whether you have junction-box or loop-in wiring. Make certain that the circuit is dead, then unscrew the ceiling rose cover and count the cables entering it: one cable means junction-box wiring; more than one means loop-in wiring (see page 284).

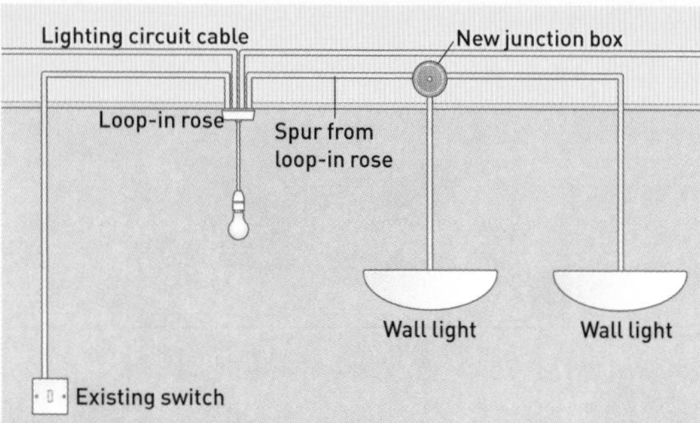

With loop-in wiring ▲

If you have loop-in wiring, you can run a spur from the rose to the new wall lights. Connect its black core to the same terminal as the blue (neutral) core of the ceiling light flex, and its red core to the same terminal as the brown (live) core of the flex. Add green/yellow sleeving to the bare earth core and connect this to the rose's earth terminal. Make sure the black core of the switch cable is 'flagged' with red PVC electrical sleeving and replace the rose cover.

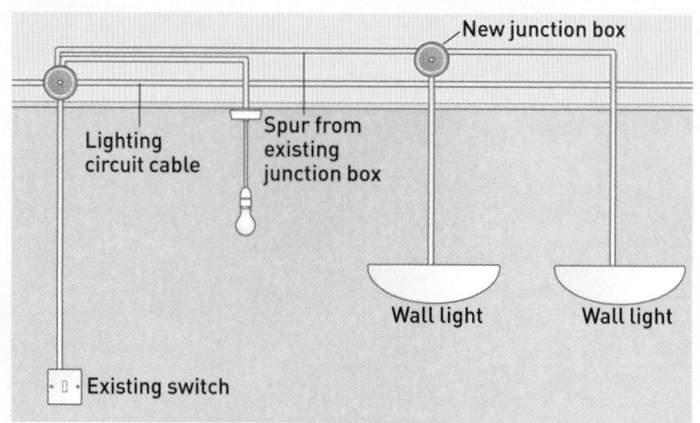

With junction-box wiring ▲

If you have junction-box wiring, use a cable detector to trace the cable from the ceiling rose back to the junction box where it connects with the circuit cable and switch drop. Entering the junction box, you may find three cables (one circuit, one switch and one light) or four (two circuit, one switch and one light). Remove the cover and connect the cores of the new wall light spur cable to the same terminals as the cores of the existing light cable, like colour to like terminal. Remember to add green/yellow sleeving to the bare earth core.

Check that the black core from the switch cable (which connects to the red cores of the light cables) has a length of red PVC electrical sleeving to indicate that it can be live. Replace the cover.

TOOLS MATERIALS

- **voltage tester**
- **screwdriver**
- **electronic pipe and cable detector, if required**
- **side cutters**
- **sharp knife**
- **wire strippers**
- **filling knife**
- **sanding block**
- **paintbrush**

- 1mm² two-core-and-earth cable
- green/yellow earth sleeving
- red PVC electrical sleeving
- cable clips
- 3- or 4-terminal junction box(es)
- new switch, if required
- 2.5mm² two-core-and-earth cable, if required
- switched fused connection unit, if required
- filler
- abrasive paper
- paint

Adding wall lights with a separate switch

If you want separately switched wall lights, you can take power from a nearby lighting circuit – provided you don't overload the circuit (see page 279). If possible, run the switch cable back to the existing switch position and replace the original one-gang switch with a two-gang unit; this will give you a much tidier finish.

1 First install the wall light or lights and the new switch. Run 1mm² two-core-and-earth cable from the switch back to a suitable position for cutting into the main circuit cable. Run another cable from here to the wall light, or to a three-terminal junction box from which you can run cables to two wall lights. You will need a three-terminal junction box for each additional light.

2 Isolate the circuit and check it is dead with a voltage tester. Then cut the main circuit cable, and connect it with the switch drop cable and new cable to the lights at a four-terminal junction box (see page 278).

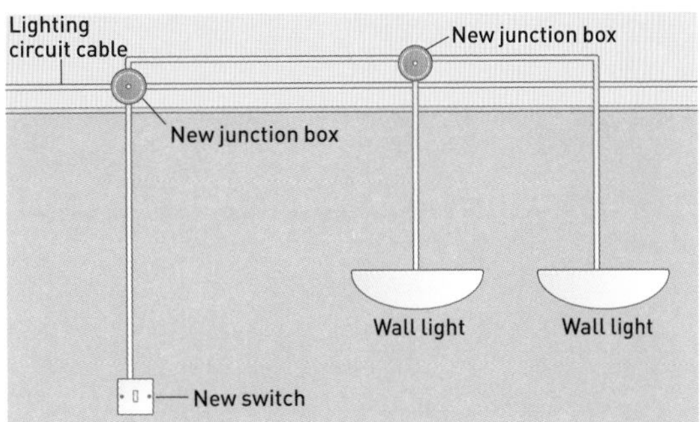

Replacing a ceiling light with wall lights

The advantage of replacing a ceiling light with wall lights is that you don't need to install a new switch. If you substitute a light there is also less risk of overloading the circuit (see page 279) – but check first, particularly if installing more than one wall light. Double-check the circuit is dead, unscrew the ceiling rose, and work out whether you have junction box or loop-in wiring: see page 284.

With junction-box wiring

Disconnect the cable entering the rose, push it back through the ceiling and connect it to a three-terminal junction box. Run new cable from that to the wall lights. If there is more than one wall light, split the feed cable with one or more three-terminal junction boxes. Make good the ceiling at the old rose position with filler.

With loop-in wiring

If you have loop-in wiring there will be two or three cables entering the rose. You need to identify them before disconnecting them. Look for the switch cable, the neutral (black) core of which should be connected to the live (brown) core of the pendant flex and 'flagged' with red sleeving. The other cable or cables will be the main circuit. Label the cables, disconnect them and remove the rose baseplate from the ceiling. Push the cables back through the ceiling and connect them to a four-terminal junction box (see page 278) from which you can run the new cable to the wall lights. Make good the ceiling at the old rose position with filler.

Connecting to a power circuit

If gaining access to a lighting circuit is difficult or adding the wall lights will overload a circuit, you can supply the new fittings from a nearby power circuit.

1 Make sure the circuit is dead and run a spur in 2.5mm² two-core-and-earth cable from a suitable socket or junction box on a main ring circuit (see pages 276–77) to a fused connection unit containing a 5 amp fuse and connect it to the 'feed' terminals. If you buy a switched fused connection unit, this can act as the on/off switch for the lights; otherwise, you will have to run a cable from the fused connection unit to a four-terminal junction box and run separate cables from this to the lights and switch.

2 The lights should be wired in 1mm² two-core-and-earth cable, which should run from the 'load' terminals of the fused connection unit. If more than one wall light is being installed, split the feed cable with one or more three-terminal junction boxes.

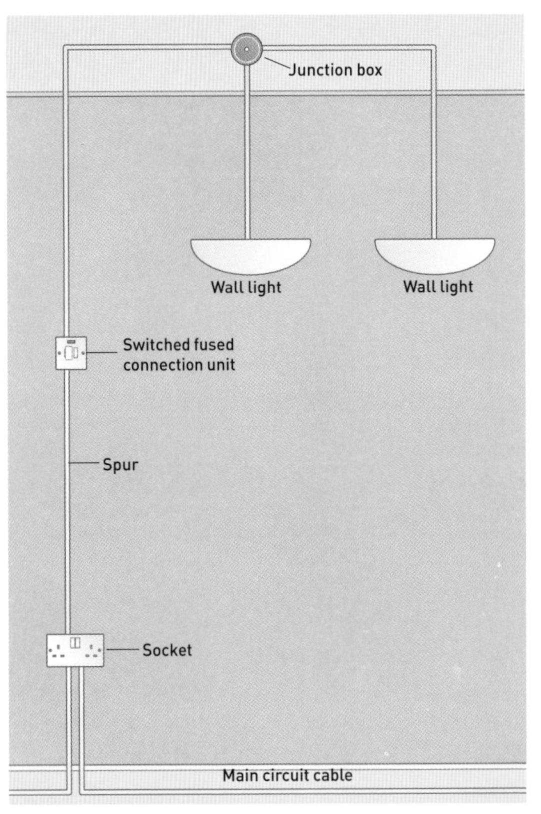

ELECTRICITY CEILING SPOTLIGHTS

SAFE ELECTRICS

Before you start any kind of electrical work isolate the circuit by removing the circuit fuse or switching and locking the circuit breaker. Double-check it is dead with a socket tester or voltage tester. Never take risks with electrical safety! See page 264.

TOOLS MATERIALS

- **pencil**
- **compasses, if required**
- **pipe and cable detector**
- **protective goggles**
- **face mask**
- **drill with twist bit**
- **padsaw or plasterboard saw**

- spotlights

For more interesting effects, replace standard pendant light fittings with streamlined recessed spotlights. If you want to save on running costs, consider low-voltage halogen fittings, which last longer than normal lights, produce much more brightness and require a third less power. If you have many ceiling fittings to install, think about assembling a work platform – it will make the job easier, quicker and safer (see page 349).

Fitting recessed spotlights

Installing recessed spotlights involves cutting holes in the ceiling, so you should always lift the floorboards in the room above to ensure that there are no joists or obstructions where you want to fit them. Most recessed spotlights are supplied with a template for marking the fixing hole; if not, use a pair of compasses to draw a circle in pencil on the ceiling. Use a detector to check for pipes or cables then drill a small hole through, just inside the circle. Go back up and double-check all is clear from above, then from below insert the blade of a padsaw or plasterboard saw and cut around the marked circle. Wear safety goggles and a mask when doing this. Remove the disc of plasterboard from the ceiling. The lights usually clip in place on spring clips that grip the surrounding plasterboard.

Mains voltage recessed spotlights

To replace a pendant ceiling light with recessed spotlights, start by installing the lights and running 1mm^2 two-core-and-earth cable back to the position of the ceiling rose. For each additional light you will need to split the supply cable at a three-terminal junction box, connecting matching cores at each terminal. Clip the new cables neatly to the sides of the joists (see page 272).

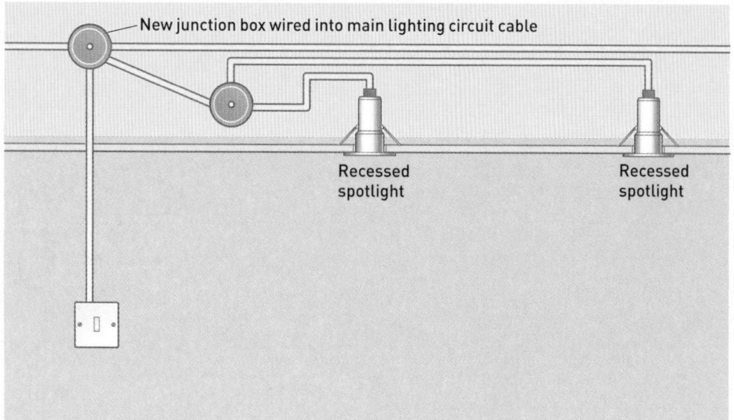

1 Isolate the lighting circuit and double-check the power is off with a voltage tester. Disconnect the cable or cables from the existing ceiling rose. If it is a loop-in system (see page 284), label the cables so that you can identify which are the circuit cables and the switch drop. There should be a length of red sleeving on the neutral (black) core of the switch drop cable; it will be connected to the live (brown) core of the flex to the light.

2 Unscrew the rose base plate and push the cables back through the ceiling.

3 If a single cable supplied the old rose, connect it to the new cable to the spotlights via a three-terminal junction box. If you find two or three cables, connect these to a four-terminal junction box as described on page 278.

4 At the spotlights, strip the outer sheathing of the supply cable, bare the ends of the cores and connect them to the light. Make sure the spring clips are positioned correctly and push the light into its hole. Check that the clips have engaged the plasterboard and are holding the light firmly in place.

5 Make good the hole where the ceiling rose was with filler, sand smooth when dry, then paint.

TOOLS MATERIALS

- **voltage tester**
- **side cutters**
- **sharp knife**
- **wire strippers**
- **hammer**
- **filling knife**
- **sanding block**
- **paintbrush**

- 1mm^2 two-core-and-earth cable
- green/yellow earth sleeving
- red PVC electrical sleeving
- cable clips
- 3- or 4-terminal junction box(es)
- filler
- abrasive paper
- paint

SAFETY FIRST

Spotlight and transformer heat

Spotlights and particularly transformers can get very hot, making them a potential fire risk if there is not adequate ventilation to prevent overheating. Always pull any insulation material well clear of the fitting. A transformer hidden in a ceiling void must be accessible from the floorboards above or a trapdoor below. Check the manufacturer's instructions before fitting a transformer; some are not designed to operate in an unventilated ceiling void. In a loft, it's a good idea to protect fittings from accidental damage by building a plywood box around them, but be sure to leave the top open for ventilation. The Building Regulations require recessed ceiling lights of all kinds to be enclosed in fire-proof compartments when installed in a multi-occupancy building.

Low-voltage (12 volt) recessed spotlights

A relatively recent innovation in domestic lighting, low-voltage lights cut running costs considerably. They are smaller than normal lights, with a neat, streamlined appearance. They offer a variety of lighting effects, making them useful for general lighting or picking out features in the room. They take their power from a 12 volt transformer, which can be linked to a spur taken from a nearby power circuit (see page 276) via a 5 amp fused connection unit. If the connection unit is switched, it can be used to turn the lights on and off. Or the lights and transformer can be powered from a lighting circuit. Install a four-terminal junction box (see page 278) at a suitable position and run cables to a new switch and transformer, and from there to the lights.

Transformers

The transformer output wattage must be matched to the combined wattage of the lamps that it will supply. Use 1.5mm² two-core-and-earth cable for the spur or circuit cable to the transformer. Low-voltage lights are usually supplied with cable for running between the transformer and the lights, and this should be used without modification. If a cable kit is not supplied, 1.5mm² two-core-and-earth cable can be used, provided the runs are short (up to 3m). The lights do not need to be earthed (always follow the manufacturer's instructions).

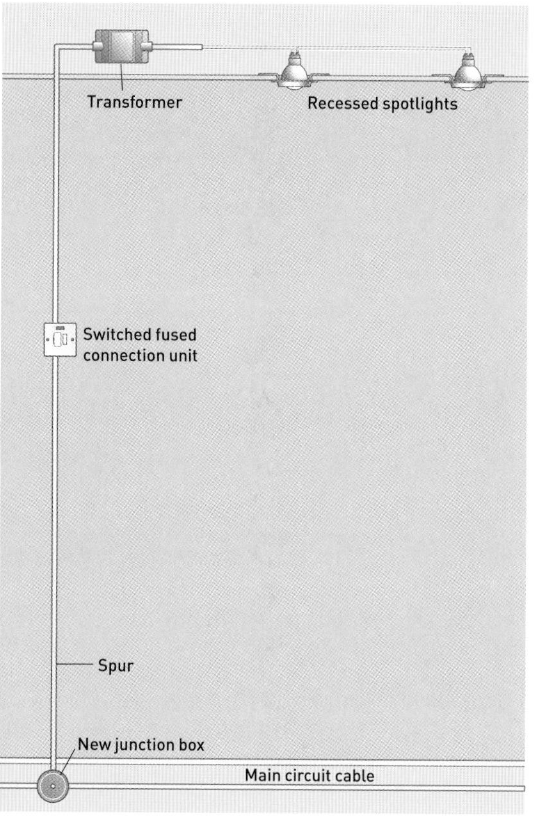

Low-voltage lighting from a power circuit

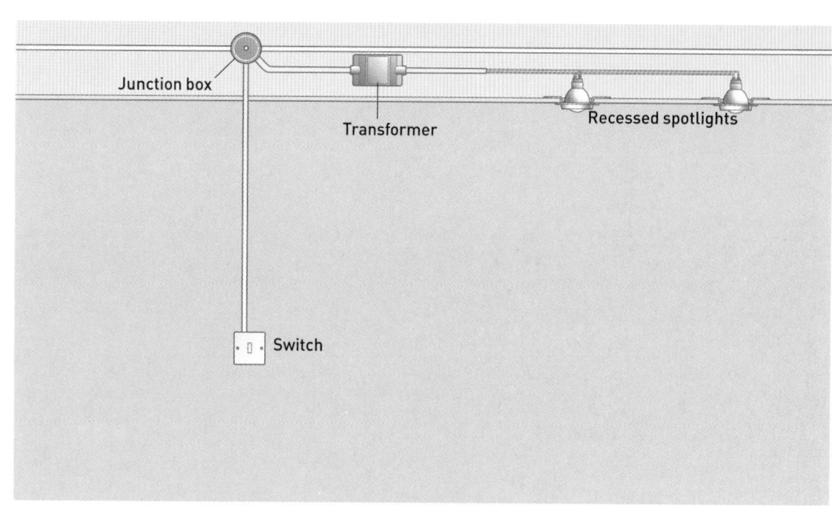

Low-voltage lighting from a lighting circuit

Practical and safe

Low-voltage halogen lamps consume around a third of the power needed by conventional lights. They last longer too, though when one blows you must replace it as soon as possible or the life of the other bulbs supplied from the transformer will be shortened. Low-voltage lighting is easy to install and a safe option, particularly in an environment like the kitchen, since it carries no risk of electrocution. You can simply clip low-voltage cables along the top or underside of your units. The light is very bright and directed – perfect over a kitchen work surface.

SAFE ELECTRICS

Before you start any kind of electrical work isolate the circuit by removing the circuit fuse or switching and locking the circuit breaker. Double-check it is dead with a socket tester or voltage tester. Never take risks with electrical safety! See page 264.

If you regularly use electrical equipment outdoors, such as a lawnmower or hedgetrimmer, an external power point will make life easier and safer by removing the need to drape a lead through a window or doorway from a socket indoors.

Basic requirements

You should wire an external socket in the same manner as a normal spur (see pages 276–77), running the cable from a socket or junction box on a main ring circuit and mounting the socket on an external wall. However, there are two important differences. One is that proper weatherproof outdoor fittings must be used, and the other is that the socket must be linked to or have an integral RCD – residual current device – which will provide protection against shock should you accidentally cut through the flex (see below). The socket will have a weatherproof cover for when it is not in use and a surface mounting box equipped with seals to prevent moisture from entering. Even so, it is wise to position it where it will not be exposed to the full force of the weather.

YOU CAN DO IT

IP ratings

Electrical fittings have an IP rating to tell you what environment they can be safely used in. IP stands for 'ingress protection' and is followed by two numbers: the first tells you how easily objects or dust can penetrate the fitting, the second how easily water can get in. The numbers run from 0 (or X), meaning wholly unprotected, to 6 (objects) or 8 (water). So a rating of IP68 would mean totally dust-proof and submersible.

B&Q

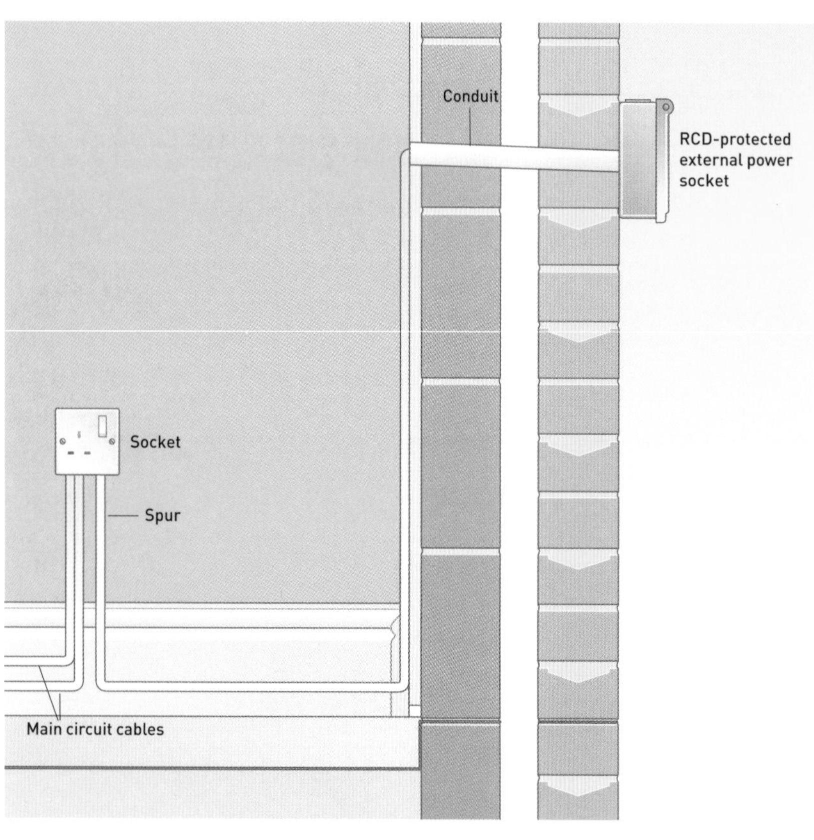

Modern timber-framed buildings

You cannot bore a hole for a cable through the external wall of a modern timber-framed building. This is because the interior cavity is filled with insulation material and contains a vapour barrier. It is essential that the vapour barrier is not broken. However, it may be possible to supply an outdoor power point from a socket in an attached garage, provided this is not already on a spur.

SAFETY FIRST

Electrocution protection

A simple plug-in residual current device could save your life. Even if you don't have an external socket with wired-in RCD, you must have RCD protection whenever you use an electrical appliance outdoors.

RCD – a life saver

An RCD – residual current device – is basically a fast-acting, safety trip switch that will cut off the power within a split second as soon as it detects an earth leakage fault, preventing injury from electric shock. Earth leakage can be caused by accidentally cutting through a flex with a hedgetrimmer or some other tool. All electrical equipment used outdoors must be protected by an RCD. While appliances connected to an indoor socket can have the protection of a plug-in RCD, an outdoor socket must have one wired into the system permanently. This must be in the spur cable from the main circuit to the outdoor socket; alternatively, you can buy an outdoor socket that contains an integral RCD. The RCD itself must be rated at 30mA (milliamps) to ensure the correct level of sensitivity.

Fitting an external power point

/hen fitting an outdoor socket, it is essential that the installation is weatherproof, and ɔu must always use purpose-designed fittings. Frost will damage cable insulation, so it ıust not be left exposed to the elements at any point. Fit the outdoor socket first then ɔmplete the installation by wiring the cable into a suitable socket or junction box on the ıain circuit – as for a spur (see page 276–77) – or into a separate RCD and then on to ıe main circuit if you are not using a combined outdoor socket/RCD unit.

TOOLS MATERIALS

- **electronic pipe and cable detector**
- **tape measure**
- **pencil**
- **heavy-duty hammer drill with 16mm-gauge long masonry bit**
- **small masonry bit**
- **spirit level**
- **screwdrivers**
- **sharp knife**
- **side cutters**
- **wire strippers**
- **filling knife**

- 16mm plastic conduit
- 2.5mm^2 two-core-and-earth cable
- external socket/RCD unit or separate socket and RCD
- socket mounting box
- weatherproof grommet
- plastic wallplugs
- round-head screws
- silicone sealant
- exterior-grade filler

1 Check the inside wall for hidden pipes or ables, then drill from the outside, about 0mm below the socket position, using a eavy-duty hammer-action drill and 16mm auge bit. Angle the drill slightly upwards.

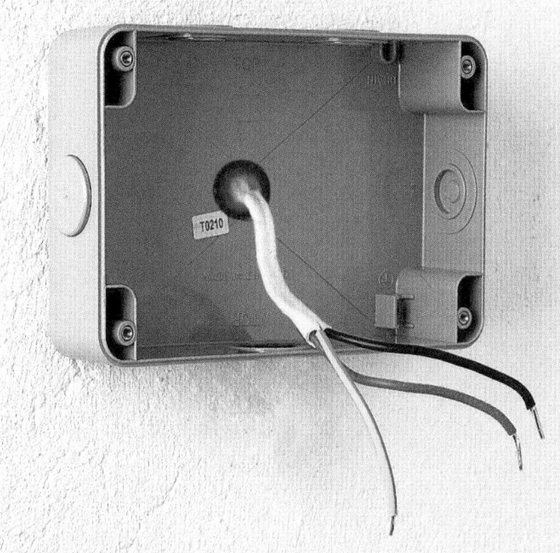

2 Feed the conduit and cable through the wall. Leave the conduit protruding out of the wall, and sufficient cable to connect to the new socket. Remove the central knock-out from the box and fit a weatherproof grommet. Hold the mounting box in place, use a spirit level to make sure it is horizontal, and mark the fixing holes. Drill the fixing holes with a masonry bit and fit plastic wallplugs. Feed the cable and the end of the conduit through the grommet into the box and fix the box to the wall with round-head screws. A dab of silicone sealant behind each screw head will provide a watertight seal. Run a bead of silicone sealant between the wall and outer edge of the box.

3 Strip off the outer sheathing of the cable and bare the ends of the cores. Slip a length of green/yellow sleeving over the bare earth core. Connect the cores to the appropriate terminals, making sure that the screws are tight. Then screw the faceplate to the mounting box.

YOU CAN DO IT

Running cable through an outside wall

Hold the drill at a slight upwards angle so that the hole will run uphill towards the inside. That will prevent rainwater running through and damaging the plaster inside. A normal cavity wall is about 275mm thick, excluding the interior plaster. Mark this depth on the drill bit with tape and as the hole approaches that depth, go slowly to reduce damage to the plasterwork as the drill bit breaks through. Sticking masking tape over the interior plaster before you drill will also help minimise damage. Line the hole with 16mm plastic conduit to protect the cable and ease installation.

B&Q

IDEAL TOOL

Power hammer drill

The average hammer-action drill is not powerful enough to drill through an exterior wall and will not take sufficiently long drill bits. But heavy-duty hammer drills are now widely available to buy or hire.

TOOLS MATERIALS

- **heavy-duty hammer-action drill with 16mm-gauge long masonry bit**
- **screwdrivers**
- **sharp knife**
- **side cutters**
- **wire strippers**
- **filling knife**
- **voltage tester**

- exterior light fitting
- plastic conduit
- 1mm² two-core-and-earth cable
- strip connectors and PVC electrical tape, if required
- 4-terminal junction box
- red PVC sleeving
- plastic wallplugs
- round-head screws
- silicone sealant

Providing some form of lighting outdoors offers a variety of benefits – it can illuminate your path to the front door and prevent you fumbling for your keys in the dark; it can help you to see who is calling at night and deter criminals from lurking; it can allow you to make the most of a patio during warm summer nights; and it can create dramatic visual effects of light and shadow among the plants.

Installing a light on the house wall

Lights attached to your house walls – at the front and back doors, or on corners to illuminate pathways – can be fed by spurs from existing lighting or power circuits. It is advisable to incorporate an RCD so that the power will shut off instantly if a fault develops. Some modern consumer units incorporate this, but you may need to wire in a separate RCD to older types; if in doubt, check with a qualified electrician. Only fit weatherproof lights specially designed for outdoor use.

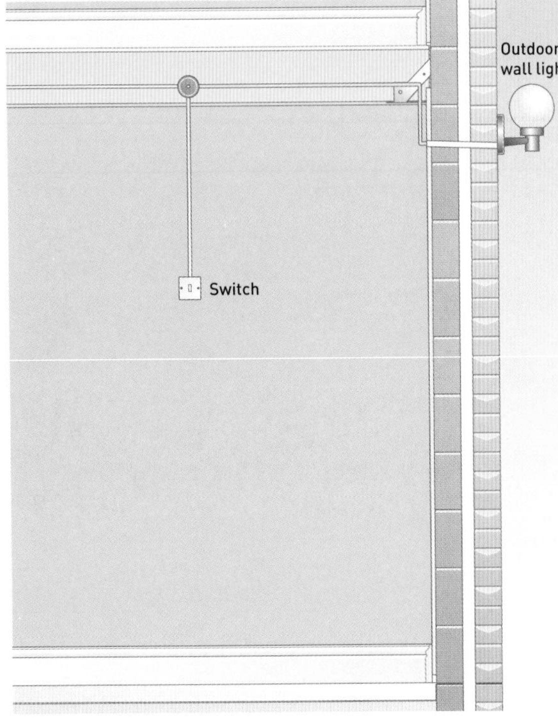

Connecting to a lighting circuit

A ground-floor lighting circuit will be the most convenient to supply outdoor wall lights, but make sure the additional fittings won't overload it (see page 279). If you want multiple outdoor lights or high-wattage floodlights, you may need to run a spur from a main power circuit (see below). Start by installing the light and switch, and run all the cables before isolating the circuit and making the final connections.

1 At the light position, drill a hole through the wall so that it runs downhill slightly towards the outside (see YOU CAN DO IT, page 291). Line the hole with plastic conduit and feed the cable through.

2 Connect the cable cores to the appropriate terminals within the unit or to its flex cores using strip connectors, which you should wrap tightly in PVC electrical tape to keep out damp.

3 Attach the light to the wall and seal out moisture with a bead of silicone sealant around its base.

4 Inside the house, run the light supply cable back to a suitable position for cutting into a main lighting circuit cable with a four-terminal junction box.

5 Install a switch and run a length of 1mm² two-core-and-earth cable back to the junction box position.

6 Isolate the circuit and double-check the power is off with a voltage tester. Then cut through the main circuit cable and make the connections in the junction box as described on page 278.

Running a spur from a power circuit

If you decide to run an outside wall light off a main power circuit, first identify a suitable socket from which to run a spur (see page 276). The spur must be run in 2.5mm² two-core-and-earth cable to the 'feed' terminals of a fused connection unit containing a 5 amp fuse. If this has a switch, it can be used to turn the light on and off; otherwise, you will need a separate switch. From the 'load' terminals of the fused connection unit, run 1mm² two-core-and-earth cable directly to the light (if the connection unit has a switch) or to a four-terminal junction box, from which you can run separate switch drop and light supply cables (see page 278).

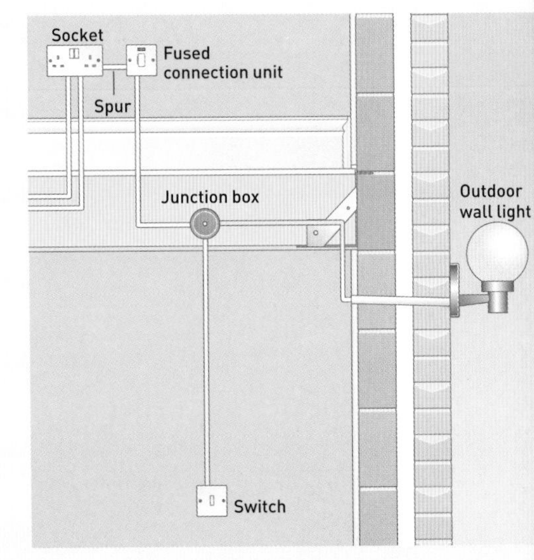

Installing mains-powered garden lighting

Garden lights can be powered from a spur off a ring circuit (see page 276), via a 5 amp fused connection unit. Once outdoors, the lights must be supplied by 1.5mm^2 three-core steel-wire-armoured cable (SWA). Only fit weatherproof lights recommended for outdoor use. The circuit must have RCD protection.

Working with steel-wire-armoured cable

- The cores of three-core SWA are coloured red, yellow and blue; it is essential to fit black sleeving over the blue core and green/yellow sleeving over the yellow core at every connection to indicate that these are being used as neutral and earth respectively.
- SWA must be buried: accidentally cutting through it could be fatal. Lay it in a trench at least 450mm deep under a path or driveway, or 750mm deep below unpaved areas that may be dug up at some point. Run electrical route marker tape above the cable at a depth of about 150mm as an extra precaution.
- SWA must be secured to the house wall with SWA cable clips, fixed to the masonry with suitable plugs and screws.
- Use a junior hacksaw to cut through SWA and pliers to strip back the armouring.
- Connect the SWA cores to those of 2.5mm^2 two-core-and-earth cable in a weatherproof adaptable box fixed to the house wall. The SWA must enter the box via a purpose-made gland covered in a plastic gland shroud – it is essential to use the correct fittings in order to minimise corrosion of the cable armouring. Also, if the adaptable box is painted, you should clean off the paint where the cable enters it, to ensure good metal-to-metal contact and so effectively earth the armouring.
- When connecting the cable to the lights, pay particular attention to the earth connections and any waterproof seals; it is vital that the units are weatherproof. You may also need glands to protect the SWA as it enters the lights – refer to the manufacturer's instructions.

SAFE ELECTRICS

Before you start any kind of electrical work isolate the circuit by removing the circuit fuse or switching and locking the circuit breaker. Double-check it is dead with a socket tester or voltage tester. Never take risks with electrical safety! See page 264.

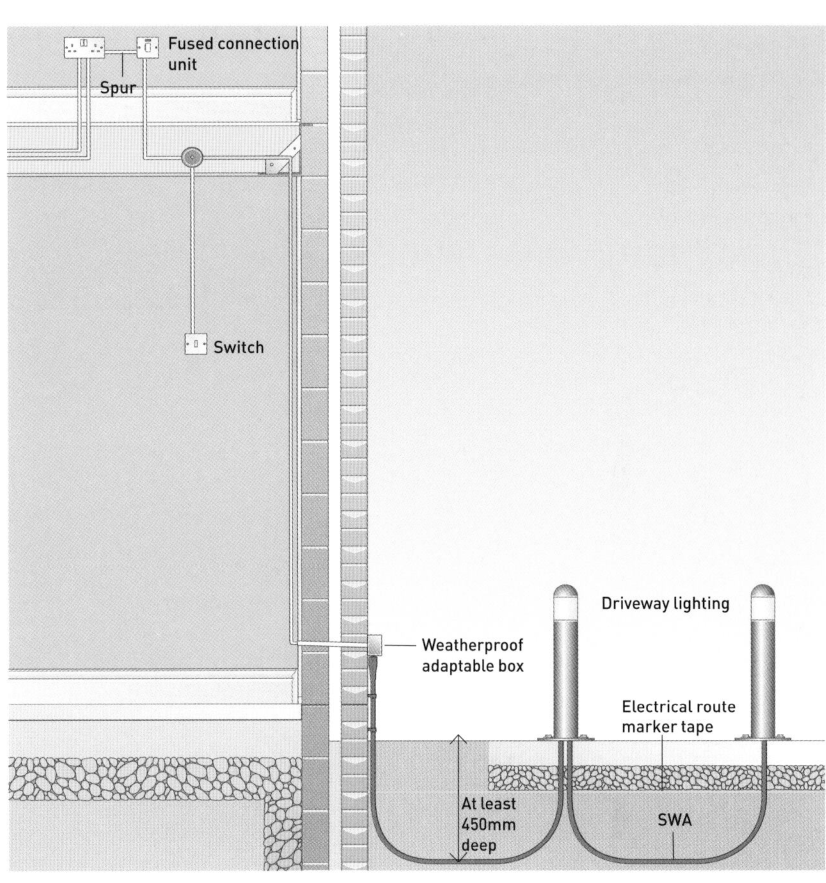

Installing low-voltage garden lighting

When it comes to garden lighting, a low-voltage set-up is the simplest to install and the safest. Often the light units are on spikes, which are simply pushed into the ground. The lights take their power from the transformer via ordinary two-core cable.

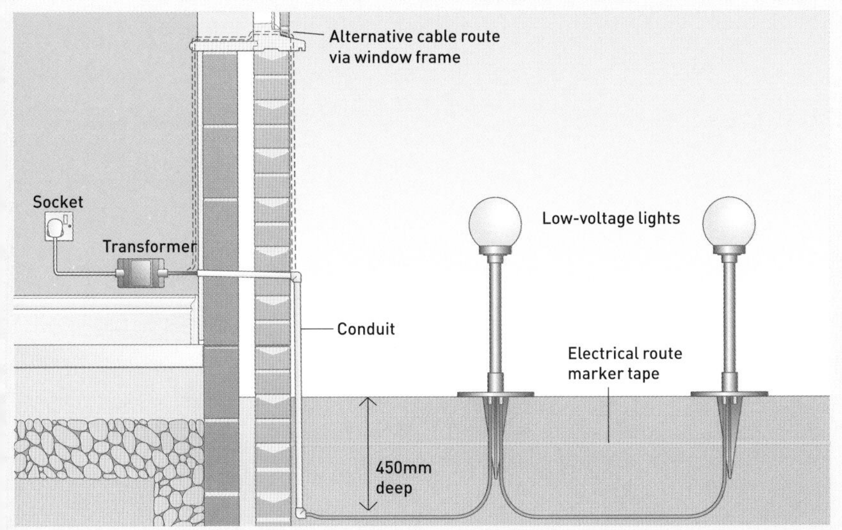

Running the cable

The lights are fed by a 12 volt transformer, which can be plugged into a convenient socket indoors or in a shed or garage – it must be protected from the weather. The cable size depends on the circuit length and load (see page 289). It can be passed through a hole drilled in the wall and lined with conduit, or through a hole in a door or window frame. Plug the hole with silicone sealant to keep moisture at bay. Because of the low voltage, the cable can be safely laid on or just below the surface. But to avoid the trip hazard of loose cable, not to mention the sheer inconvenience of putting a garden spade through it at some future date, it is better to bury it about 450mm deep. Lay electrical route marker tape above it at a depth of about 150mm to indicate its presence.

PLUMBING COLD AND HOT WATER

Your home's cold and hot water supply systems will be largely out of sight, with pipes concealed in walls and under floors. But knowing what type of system you have and the location of everything is essential for maintenance work, making improvements and, most of all, dealing with emergencies.

Your water supply

Your local water company is responsible for providing you with clean, drinkable water and for the removal of waste water and sewage. From the company's main supply pipe under the road outside your home, a branch pipe will run underground to a stop valve beneath a metal plate set in the pavement or somewhere in your front garden. This valve allows the company to control your water supply. From the valve, the water flows along what is known as the service pipe, passing through your home's foundations before rising up through the floor, usually in the kitchen, but sometimes under the stairs or even in a garage. The rising main, as it is known, is fitted with your main stop valve at this point. From the water company's underground stop valve onwards, the entire system is your responsibility, and you must make sure that it is properly maintained. Allowing water to be wasted through leaks is an offence.

Direct cold water systems ›

Some homes, particularly older properties, have a direct cold water system. Branch pipes lead directly from the rising main to feed all the cold taps and WC cisterns in the house. However, the rising main will usually also continue up to a storage cistern in the roof, which provides a supply of water at gravity pressure to a hot water cylinder.

One advantage of a direct system is that drinking water is available at all the cold taps (you should not drink water from a storage tank, which may be old and contaminated). There is also less pipework in the roof to worry about. However, many water companies will not permit direct systems because they expose the mains water supply to a greater risk of contamination through back-siphonage of dirty water from baths and wash basins.

Cold water storage cistern
Overflow pipe
Cold supply to hot water cylinder
Cold water supply to bathroom
Bathroom taps and WC supplied from cold water storage cistern
Rising main
Kitchen tap supplied from rising main
Draincock
Stop valve

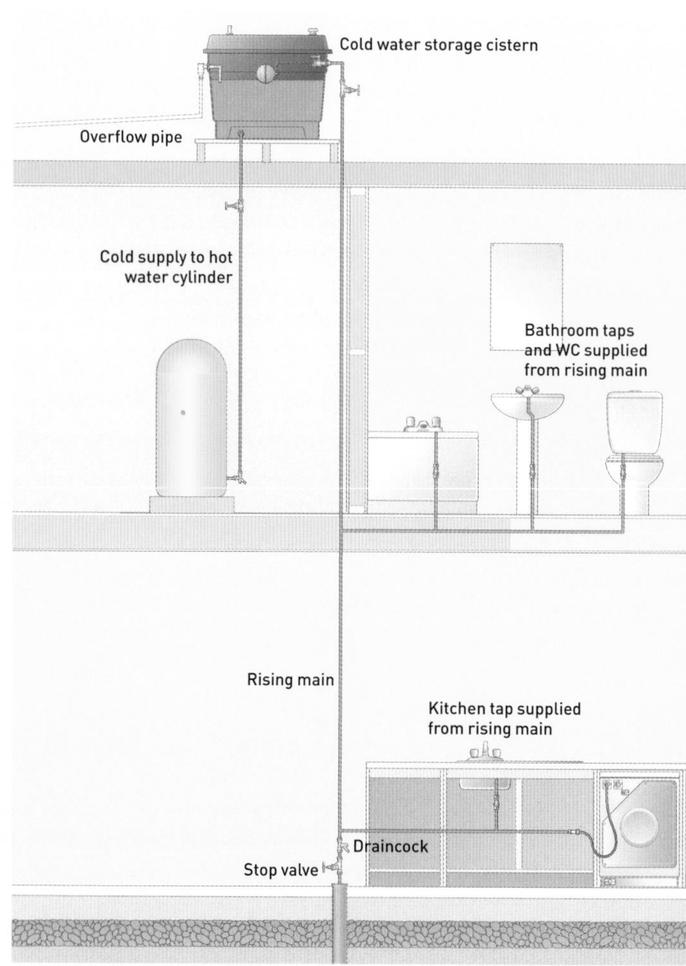

‹ Indirect cold water systems

Most homes have an indirect cold water supply system. A branch is run from the rising main after the householder's main stop valve to the cold tap at the kitchen sink to supply clean drinking water. Other branches may be taken off at this point to supply a washing machine, dishwasher or garden tap. The rising main runs up to the roof, where it terminates at a cold water storage cistern. This supplies all the remaining cold taps in the house, the WC cisterns and the hot water cylinder.

The advantages of an indirect system are that the storage cistern holds a reserve of water for washing and flushing WCs if the mains supply is interrupted, and the lower pressure of the gravity supply to most of the system causes less wear and tear and less noise as the water flows through the pipes.

Stored hot water systems

If your water is heated by a boiler and stored in a cylinder, the chances are that the water is heated indirectly. This means that you have two hot water systems – a primary circuit and a secondary circuit. In the primary circuit, a pipe runs from the boiler to a heat exchanger (usually a coil of copper pipe) inside the hot water cylinder and then back to the boiler. When the boiler is running, hot water flows continuously around the primary circuit. As the pipes of the heat exchanger warm up, so too does the water in the cylinder, which can then be drawn off from the top of the cylinder to supply the hot taps around the house (the secondary circuit).

The hot water cylinder, usually found in an airing cupboard, is kept topped up with water from the cold water storage cistern in the roof. The primary circuit has its own top-up supply of water from a small tank in the roof known as the feed-and-expansion cistern. The cylinder's hot water draw-off pipe continues to the roof and terminates over the cold water storage cistern; the boiler's hot feed pipe to the heat exchanger terminates over the feed-and-expansion cistern in the roof. This allows any air or steam in either circuit to escape safely.

A major advantage of the indirect system is that the water that passes through the boiler does not mix with the water in the cylinder and, effectively, is recycled time and again. Consequently, there is less build-up of scale in the boiler and corrosion inhibitor can be added to the water, leading to lower maintenance costs.

Some older properties still have a direct hot water system. In this there is no primary circuit; water is fed into the bottom of the hot water cylinder from the cold water cistern, piped from there to the boiler where it is heated, and returned to the top of the cylinder where it is drawn off to supply the taps. Although this arrangement is much simpler in terms of pipework and, therefore, cheaper, it does mean that a constant flow of fresh water passes through the boiler, leading to heavy scale build-up and higher maintenance costs. Furthermore, corrosion inhibitor cannot be added to the water and the boiler cannot be used to run a central heating system.

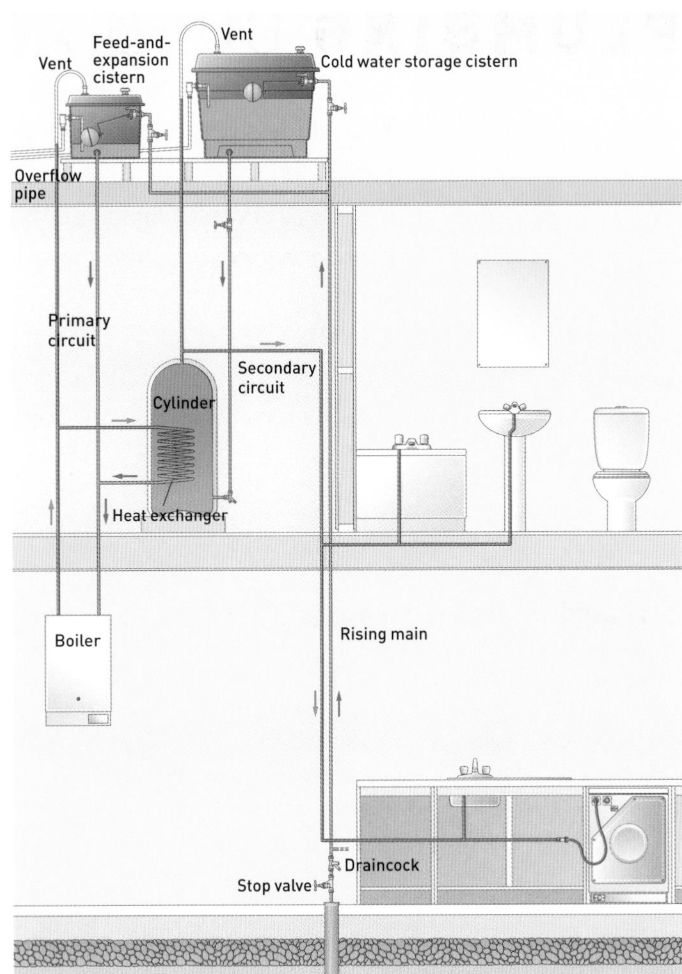

Indirect hot water system

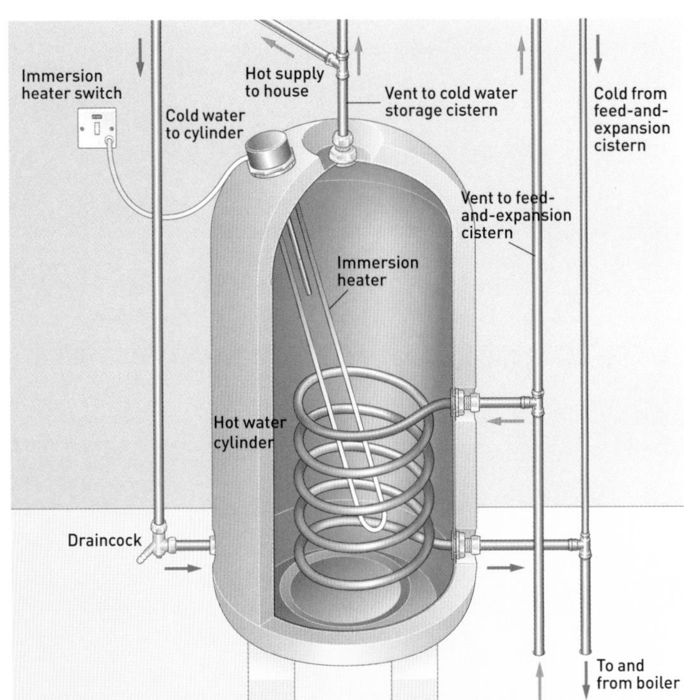

Hot water cylinder with immersion heater

Immersion heaters

An electric immersion heater fitted into the top of the hot water cylinder provides a means of heating water during the summer without having to run the boiler. It has a long, thermostatically controlled heating element that extends down inside the cylinder. Some have two elements, a short one and a long one, allowing just the top portion of the cylinder to be heated when only small amounts of hot water are required, or the entire cylinder for bigger demands, such as filling a bath. You can also have two immersion heaters with short elements fitted in the cylinder, one above the other. An immersion heater has a thermostat to control the maximum water temperature; this can be adjusted by turning an adjuster screw with a screwdriver. For most homes, 60°C is a comfortable level.

Instantaneous hot water systems

These days people are increasingly opting for combination (or combi) boilers, which do away with the need for a hot water cylinder by heating water on demand. In small properties, particularly flats where there is no room for a hot water storage cylinder, an instantaneous water heater, usually gas fired, can heat the water just before it is drawn from the tap. Single-point instantaneous heaters incorporate their own outlet and are designed to fit over a sink or hand basin, while multi-point units can supply several taps from a remote location. Electric single-point versions are also available for supplying showers.

PLUMBING CISTERNS AND CYLINDERS

The cold and hot water storage tanks are vital parts of a plumbing system. They rarely cause problems, but because of the quantities of water they hold, if anything does go wrong, they can create a lot of damage. Knowing where they are and how to look after them will help you avoid the worst.

Isolating pipe circuits

An indirect cold water system will have a storage cistern in the loft that is fed from the rising main through a ball valve. All the pipes that run from the cistern should be controlled by nearby stop valves, allowing individual pipe circuits to be turned off and drained for repair or maintenance work without having to empty the entire system. If there are no valves, the cistern itself has to be isolated – either by turning off a stop valve in the supply pipe or by tying up the arm of the ball valve – then drained. The cistern has an overflow pipe that runs to the outside if the water level is too high. It must have a lid to prevent anything from falling into the water and should be insulated to prevent freezing during winter.

A direct cold water system will not have a storage cistern, although there may be a similar, but smaller, cistern in the loft to provide top-up water for a hot water cylinder or a feed-and-expansion cistern to supply a wet central heating system. This is isolated in the same way as an indirect storage system.

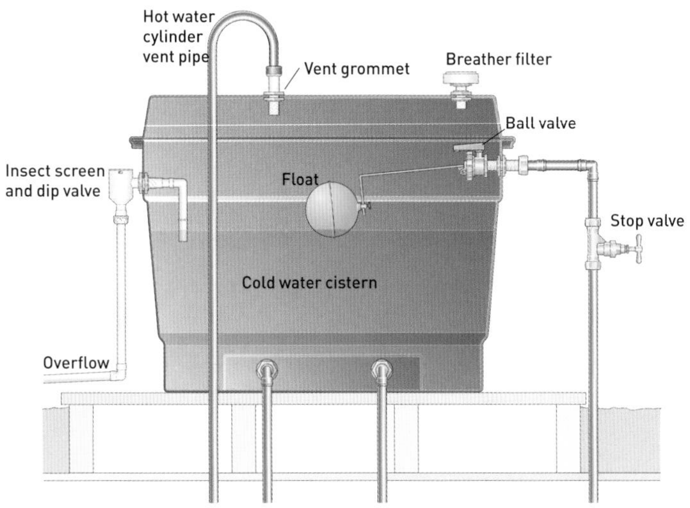

Ball valves

The water level in storage and WC cisterns is regulated by ball valves. These incorporate a long lever arm with a metal or plastic float (often ball shaped) at the end. When the cistern is full, the float holds the lever up, which keeps the valve closed; when the water level drops, float and lever fall, opening the valve. By altering the position of the float in relation to the valve, the point at which the valve opens and closes can be adjusted, thus varying the 'full' water level in the cistern.

The most important thing to remember about ball valves is that there are high- and low-pressure versions. High-pressure types must be used where the supply is at mains pressure (on a cold water storage cistern or WC cistern on a direct system), while low-pressure valves must be fitted to cisterns supplied under gravity pressure (WC cisterns on an indirect system).

Draining the system

The system should always be drained if you are going away for a long time in winter. You may also need to drain the system to repair or extend it. This is how to do it:

- Shut down the heating system or turn off the immersion heater.
- Close the main stop valve on the rising main, then open all taps. When the taps stop running, flush all WCs.
- Connect a hose to each draincock on the system in turn – probably above the main stop valve and at the foot of the hot water cylinder – and run it to an outside drain. Open the valve to empty any remaining water from the system. Close the draincock before removing the hose. Take care not to confuse draincocks on the heating system with those on the water supply system; there is no need to drain the former (see page 322).
- Pour a little salt down all plug-holes to prevent water in the waste traps from freezing.

Before refilling the system by opening the main stop valve, make sure that all taps and draincocks are closed. Inspect storage and WC cisterns to ensure that their ball valves have not become stuck open. Air may become trapped in the system during filling, causing taps to splutter and the water flow to be sluggish. If the problem persists, clear the air locks with mains pressure (see page 299).

Stop valve

Fitted to the rising main pipe close to where it comes into the house, the stop valve allows the entire water supply to be shut off.

Draincock

A draincock is a small tap fitted at a low point on the plumbing system to allow a pipe run to be emptied.

Adjusting a ball valve

Some ball valves are adjusted simply by bending the metal float arm; others have an adjuster screw and locknut. Some have floats that can be repositioned vertically. The float should be set so that the water level is about 25mm below the overflow outlet.

Replacing an immersion heater

After years of use, an immersion heater can become corroded and will eventually fail. Fortunately, replacing it is quite straightforward. Buy a heater with elements the same length as the old one, and make sure you include a new thermostat, which may not come with the heater itself.

1 Turn off any heating system and isolate the immersion heater power circuit (see SAFE ELECTRICS, right). Disconnect the flex from the old immersion heater. Shut off the cold water supply to the cylinder at the stop valve near the cold water cistern, and run the hot taps until the water stops. Attach a garden hose to the draincock at the bottom of the cylinder. Just slacken the nut of the immersion heater with the immersion heater spanner, then draw off about 400mm of water.

2 Pieces of the old sealing ring may be stuck to the cylinder's boss, particularly if a sealing compound was used. Scrape them off, taking care that they do not fall into the cylinder. Clean the boss with white spirit. This is essential to ensure a good seal with the new gasket.

3 Slide the new sealing gasket over the heater elements and the threaded portion of the heater's body.

4 Pass the heater's elements through the boss and carefully screw the heater into place by hand, making sure that the gasket is seated properly. Tighten the heater with the immersion heater spanner.

5 Then slide the thermostat through the opening in the centre of the immersion heater body. Make sure it is fully inserted.

6 Connect the wiring. The lead soldered to the heater's element runs to one terminal of the thermostat, while the flex brown (live) core goes to the other. The blue (neutral) core connects to the terminal at the other end of the element, and the earth core to the earth terminal.

7 Adjust the temperature setting with a screwdriver. Fit the cover, make sure the draincock is closed and restore the water supply to fill the cylinder. Turn on the power and test the heater.

SAFE ELECTRICS

Switch off at the mains. Isolate the immersion heater power circuit by removing the circuit fuse (put it in your pocket if you can). Or switch off the circuit breaker, tape it in the off position, and leave a clear note at the unit stating that you are working on the circuit. Never take risks with electrical safety! (See pages 264–65.)

TOOLS MATERIALS

- **garden hose**
- **adjustable spanner**
- **screwdrivers**
- **immersion heater spanner**

- cloth
- white spirit
- immersion heater
- thermostat

IDEAL TOOL

Immersion heater spanner
The large octagonal bosses on an immersion heater need a special spanner. Two kinds are available: you need the deep box type (right) if your cylinder has thick, moulded-on insulation.

YOU CAN DO IT

Soften the seal
If you can't shift the nut of an old immersion heater, try using a hot-air gun to just soften the sealant holding it in place.

PLUMBING EMERGENCIES

Water can cause serious damage to the fabric of your home, so prompt action is essential if a problem occurs in the plumbing system. Keeping a few basic repair materials in your tool kit and knowing what to do in an emergency will prevent most situations from getting out of hand.

Turn off the power and water

If you do suffer a burst pipe, a leaking cistern or flooding of any kind, the first thing to do is turn off the electricity supply at the consumer unit (fuse box) immediately. When the leak has been repaired and the water mopped up, examine all sockets, switches, ceiling roses and electrical equipment in the vicinity to make sure they are dry. If water has got into them, don't turn the power back on until they have dried out.

In such a situation, a knowledge of your plumbing system is vital: make sure you know the location of all the valves, particularly the main stop valve, which allows you to turn off the supply in an emergency or for essential work. Check valves every few months to ensure that they can be opened and closed easily. Applying a little penetrating oil to a valve shaft will help free it. Never leave a valve completely open, as this will make it more likely to seize up, preventing you from closing it when you really need to; close it by a quarter- to a half-turn.

Making a permanent repair

You can use any method of joining pipes to replace a damaged section (see page 301), but plastic push-fit joints are probably the easiest, especially for the plumbing novice.

TOOLS MATERIALS

- **mini pipe cutter**
- **measuring tape**
- **felt-tip pen**
- **narrow file**
- **deburring brush or wire wool**

- new length of copper pipe
- 2 straight push-fit connectors
- short length of $4mm^2$ single-core earth cable and 2 bonding clamps

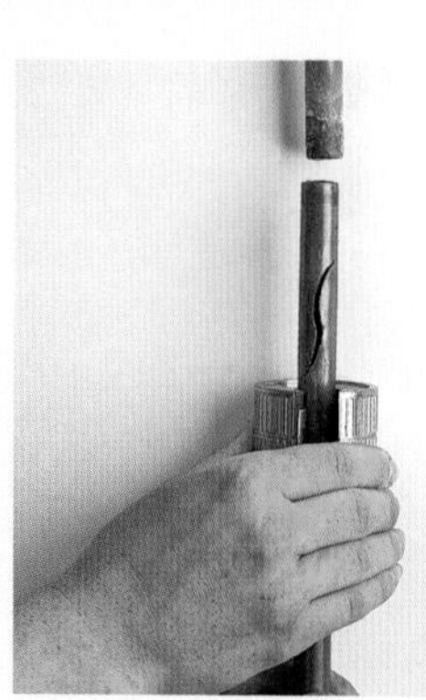

1 Turn off the water supply and drain the pipe (see page 296). Use a mini pipe cutter to make cuts on each side of the damaged area and remove that section of pipe. You may find that you have to free the pipe from any nearby clips so that you can rotate the cutter around it.

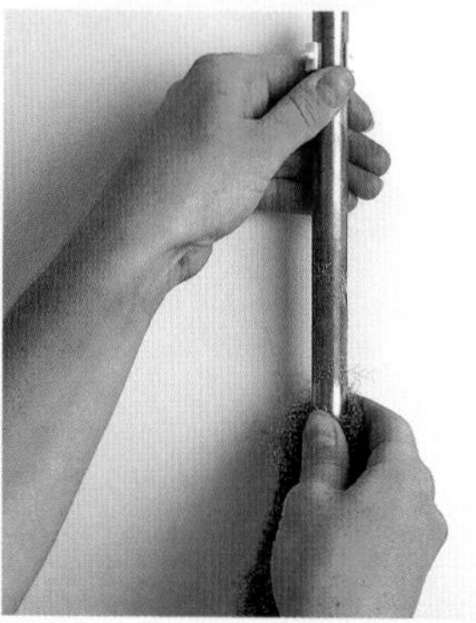

2 Use a narrow file to remove the burrs from inside the cut ends. Burnish the outside with wire wool or a deburring brush. Measure carefully for the new piece of pipe, making an allowance for the distance between the internal pipe stops of the push-fit joints – these will be marked on the outside of the joints. Cut the new section of pipe to length and file the ends.

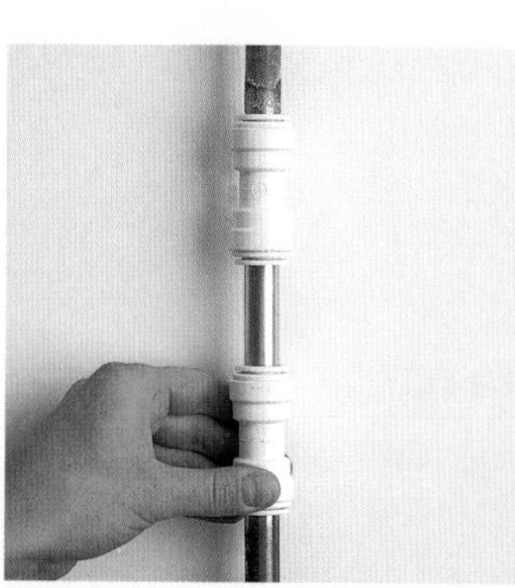

3 Insert each end of the new piece of pipe into a push-fit coupling. Fit this assembly onto one of the existing pipe ends, making sure it is pushed fully home. Unclip as much of the two lengths of original pipe as possible and push the remaining cut pipe end into its coupling. Restore the earth bonding across the plastic joints (see SAFETY FIRST).

SAFETY FIRST

Plastic push-fit joints on copper pipes destroy the continuity of a plumbing system's earth bonding (see page 267). This must be restored by joining the two copper pipes with a length of $4mm^2$ single-core earth cable, secured by earth clamps.

Fixing a burst pipe

A pipe repair clamp is the quickest means of stopping water leaking from a burst pipe, and it doesn't require the pipe to be drained before it can be fitted. However, it should only be regarded as a temporary repair.

TOOLS MATERIALS

- **screwdriver**

- pipe repair clamp with fixing screws

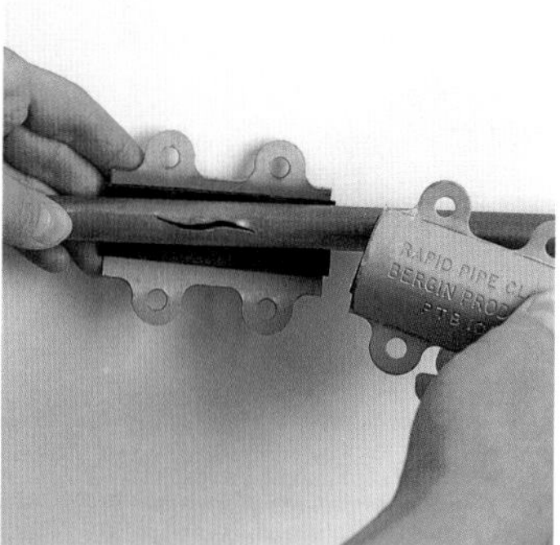

1 Assemble the two halves of the clamp over the damaged portion of pipe, double checking that the rubber sealing gasket is positioned correctly.

2 Fit the securing screws and tighten them fully to clamp the device firmly over the damaged section of pipe.

Repairing a leaking joint

Remaking a soldered pipe joint that is leaking requires some skill; much easier is to use a two-part epoxy repair compound, which will also stop the leak permanently. When hard, the material can be sanded smooth for painting.

TOOLS MATERIALS

- **wire brush**
- **rubber gloves**

- two-part epoxy repair compound

1 Shut off the water supply to the affected section of pipe and drain it down (see page 296). Dry the pipe, then key the area that needs to be repaired with a wire brush.

2 Wearing rubber gloves to protect your skin, twist or cut off enough two-part epoxy compound to carry out the repair.

3 Work the material between your fingers until it reaches a uniform colour. At this stage, you will have to work quickly, as you have only about five minutes before it begins to harden.

4 Press the material around the joint, forcing it into the gap between pipe and fitting. Smooth it as much as possible, then leave for 24 hours to harden fully.

Airlocks

If the plumbing system has been drained and refilled for any reason, air may have become trapped in the pipes, making taps splutter or possibly cutting off the flow completely. To cure this, connect a garden hose to the kitchen cold tap, which is on mains pressure (or any cold tap if you have a direct system: see page 294) and connect the other end to the affected tap. Open both taps and leave for a few minutes. The mains pressure should force the air out of the system, but you may have to repeat the process for a complete cure.

A frozen pipe

All pipes in lofts, under ground floors, in garages or any other areas where they will be exposed to very low temperatures should be lagged to protect them against freezing (see page 330). However, lagging will only delay the onset of freezing, and if temperatures are low enough for long enough, ice may still develop, stopping the flow of water to taps and other outlets; at worst, the ice may actually split the pipe or force apart a joint. For this reason, if you go away for a substantial amount of time in winter, you should take precautions. Set your heating thermostat at the lowest setting, or if there is one use the 'frost setting', which will cause it to come automatically on if temperatures drop near to freezing point. Or turn off the main stop valve and drain the system completely (see page 296).

To thaw a frozen pipe, warm it with a hair dryer, gradually working along its length from the tap or valve until the water starts to flow again. Alternatively, drape a hot water bottle over the pipe or soak hand towels in hot water, wring them out and wrap them around it. But whatever you do, don't use a blowtorch.

Water pouring from a ceiling

Water storage cisterns and tanks are usually situated in the loft or on the upper floor of a house. This means that if a leak occurs, the first you will know of it is water pouring through a ceiling. Given the amount of water stored, you must act quickly, as the ceiling may collapse, with disastrous results.

First turn off the electricity at the main power switch and the water supply at the main stop valve. Position containers to catch the leaking water and turn on all the taps and flush WCs. This will empty the pipes and cold water storage cistern, and they will not refill while the main stop valve is off. Investigate the cause of the leak, which may be a burst pipe, a loose joint, or the cistern itself leaking or overflowing due to problems with the ball valve and overflow (see page 296). If the leak is coming from a hot water cylinder, turn off the boiler and empty the cylinder by running a hose from the draincock near its base to an outside gully. Make repairs or replace items as necessary.

No water from a tap

- Turn on the kitchen cold tap – or any cold tap on a direct system (see page 294). If there is no flow, make sure the main stop valve is open; if the problem persists, call your water supplier.
- If the mains cold tap is working, inspect the cold water storage cistern in the loft; if it is empty, make sure the ball valve isn't jammed. Dismantle and clean the valve or replace it. If there is no flow when the valve is held open, your rising main is blocked – this can be caused by ice in winter.
- If the cold water storage cistern is full but there is no flow from the bathroom taps, there must be an air lock or blockage in the supply pipe from the cold cistern or hot water cylinder.

PLUMBING PIPES AND FITTINGS

In an ideal world, pipe runs would be made in one piece from one fitting or appliance to another, to minimise the number of potential leak sites. In reality, this simply isn't possible – pipes are not made in infinite lengths, and the complex shapes often required would make it impossible to feed a single pipe through the structure of a house. So shorter lengths must be cut, shaped and joined together.

Pipe materials and sizes

At one time, domestic plumbing systems used iron and lead pipes. These days, copper pipes are the usual means of carrying water around the home, with plastic pipes used for waste systems. The most common size of copper pipe has an outer diameter of 15mm, although you may find smaller sizes (10mm) feeding monobloc taps (see page 309) and radiators, and larger sizes (22mm and 28mm) feeding baths, storage cisterns, tanks and boilers.

If your plumbing system was installed before the mid-1970s, the pipework will almost certainly be of imperial dimensions (½, ¾ and 1 inch inner diameter). You can join modern 15mm pipe to ½ inch imperial and 28mm to 1 inch using standard metric compression fittings, but connecting 22mm pipe to ¾ inch requires a 22mm compression fitting with a special oversize olive. For soldered joints, there are metric/imperial connectors in the relevant sizes.

Copper

Copper is strong but lightweight, solders well and can be bent quite easily. Copper pipes can take capillary, compression or push-fit fittings (see opposite).

Plastic

Although plastic pipes are commonly used only for waste water, there are also types of plastic pipe that are suitable for hot and cold water supply pipes and central heating systems. They can be joined to copper pipework and are made to the same standard sizes, although the wall thickness of different makes can vary. They are easy to bend and install, are impact- and frost-resistant, and do not corrode.

Cutting copper pipe

Cutting copper pipe is not difficult. It is possible – but not ideal – to use a hacksaw: wrap masking tape around the pipe as a cutting guide, aligning its edges carefully. However, you will get a much cleaner and more square cut with a pipe cutter.

TOOLS MATERIALS

- pencil
- measuring tape
- pipe cutter
- wire wool or deburring brush

IDEAL TOOL

Pipe cutter

A pipe cutter (or pipe slice) has a hardened cutting wheel and adjustable rollers that allow it to be clamped tightly around a pipe. Rotating the tool causes the cutting wheel to bite into the pipe, leaving a narrow groove. By constantly tightening the rollers against the pipe, the groove can be made deeper until eventually the pipe is cut in two. Standard types have a reamer blade for removing the internal burr from the pipe. Special 'mini' versions are made for cutting through pipes that run close to a wall or other surface (see page 298).

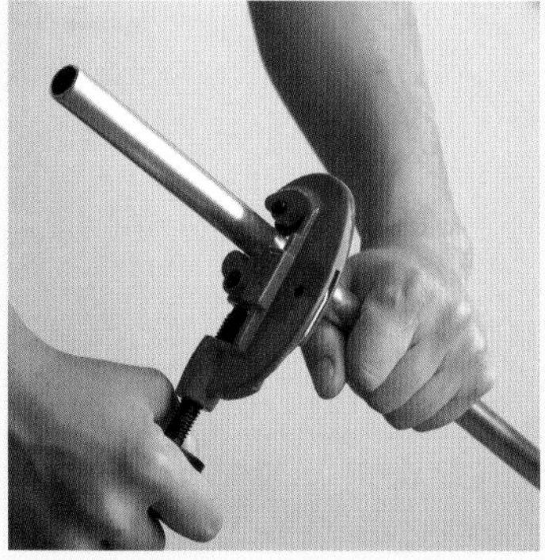

1 Measure the length of pipe required and mark with a pencil. Then place the cutter over the pipe so that the cutting wheel aligns with the mark and tighten the screw. Rotate the cutter around the pipe, steadily tightening the screw until you cut through the pipe.

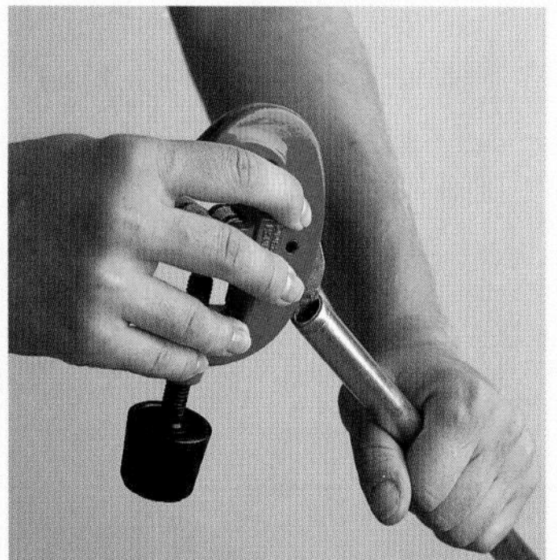

2 Remove the burr around the inside of the pipe's cut end by inserting the cutter's triangular reamer and rotating the tool. Make sure that no copper fragments remain in the pipe, as they could cause damage to valves or taps on the system.

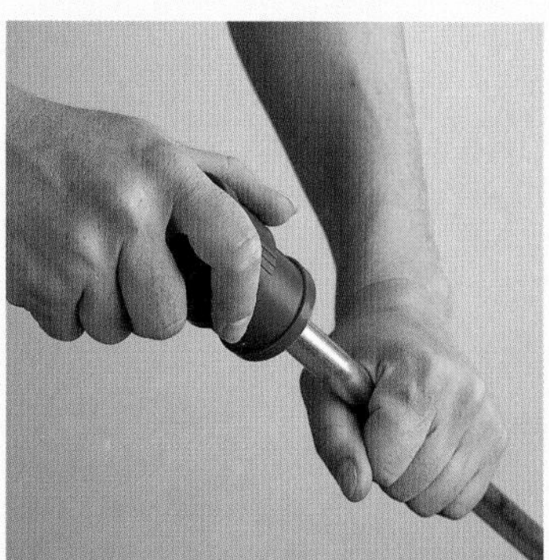

3 Clean the outside of the pipe by burnishing it with wire wool; this will provide a good surface for the joint, ensuring a watertight seal. Or use a deburring brush (shown), which will do the same job and prevent stray slivers of wire wool from sticking into your fingers or falling into the pipe.

Bending copper pipe

Small-bore (15mm) copper pipe can be bent by hand with the aid of a bending spring, which supports the pipe internally and prevents it kinking. Considerable strength is needed, however; bending machines make the job much easier and are essential for larger diameter pipes.

TOOLS MATERIALS

- **bending machine or bending spring**
- **length of cord, if required**
- **cloth**
- **screwdriver, if required**

- petroleum jelly

Using a bending machine

A machine applies considerably more leverage than bending by hand. Place the pipe on the correct size of curved former (several sizes will be supplied) under the pipe stop, then insert the straight former between the pipe and roller. Draw the handles together to bend the pipe; over-bend it slightly as it will tend to spring back a little.

Using a bending spring

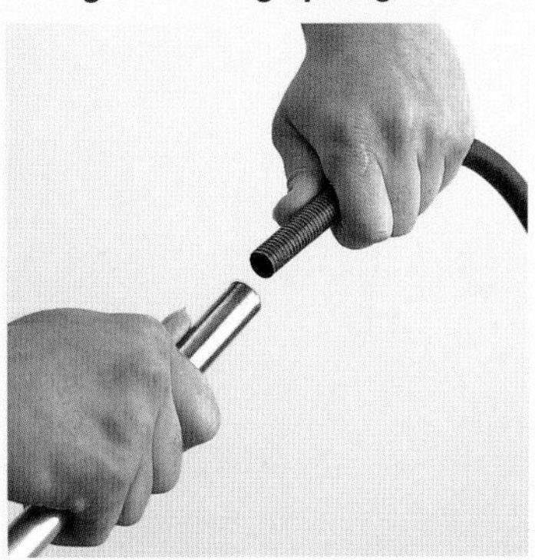

1 Coat the spring with petroleum jelly and slip it into the pipe. If the bend will be some distance from the end of the pipe, tie a length of cord to the spring.

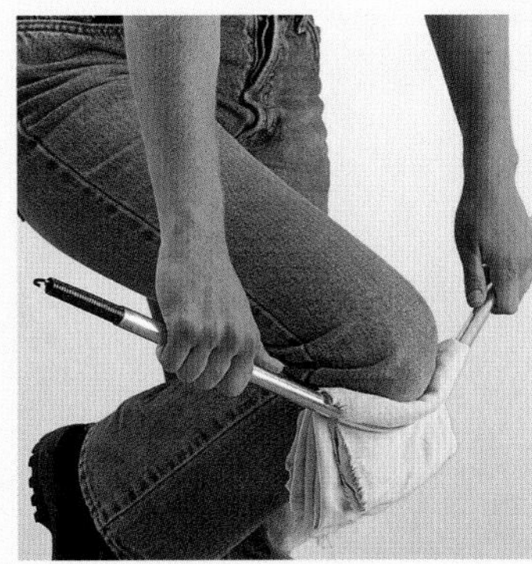

2 Bend the pipe around your knee, using a pad of cloth as a cushion. Over-bend it slightly. Check that the angle is correct, then pull the spring from the pipe. If you can reach the end of the spring, inserting a screwdriver in the spring eye and turning it to tighten up the spring coils should help in its removal.

YOU CAN DO IT

Flexible tap connectors

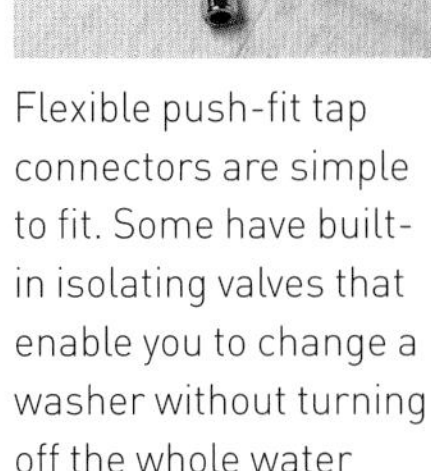

Flexible push-fit tap connectors are simple to fit. Some have built-in isolating valves that enable you to change a washer without turning off the whole water supply.

Joining pipes

The traditional methods of connecting copper pipes are brass compression joints that are tightened with wrenches, and capillary joints that must be soldered. Equally effective and much simpler are plastic push-fit joints, which incorporate rubber O-rings for sealing.

Push-fit joints

Developed originally for use with plastic pipe systems, push-fit joints are an easy and effective way of joining copper pipes too. Sharp metal edges can cut into the plastic, causing leaks, so you should protect the O-ring with a special insert. Then simply mark the depth of the joint on the cut ends of the pipes and push them fully home.

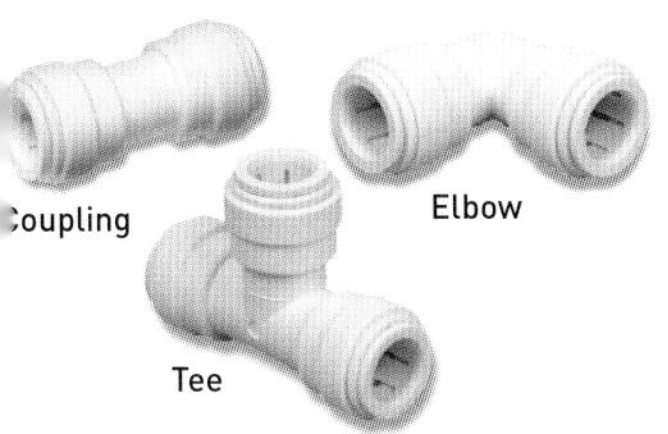

Compression joints

Usually made from brass, compression joints produce a watertight seal by squeezing a special metal ring, known as an olive, between the pipe and the body of the fitting. A capnut screws on to the end of the joint to provide the necessary pressure against the olive.

Capillary joints

Soldered fittings are known as capillary joints, because, when heated, solder is drawn between the fitting and pipe by capillary action. Two types are available: end-feed and solder-ring (or Yorkshire). With the former, lead-free solder must be added to the mouth of the joint as it is heated with a blowtorch; the latter are made with a ring of solder already inside the mouth of the joint, so only heating is required. In both cases, a chemical cleaner, known as flux, must be brushed on to the pipe end and inside the joint before heating. Pipes must be flushed thoroughly after joining to remove all traces of flux, which is corrosive.

End-feed joints

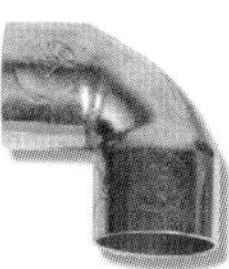

Solder-ring (Yorkshire) ioints

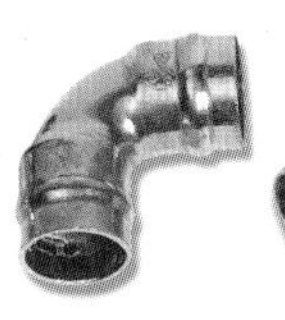

Push-fit joints

Plastic push-fit fittings are a very straightforward and reliable method of joining copper pipes. But don't forget to run earth wire across the fitting to restore the system's earth bonding (see SAFETY FIRST, page 298).

1 To ensure a good seal, burnish the end of the pipe with wire wool. Make sure none is left inside the pipe. Install the joint by simply pushing it firmly on to the end of the pipe until the pipe meets the joint's internal stop.

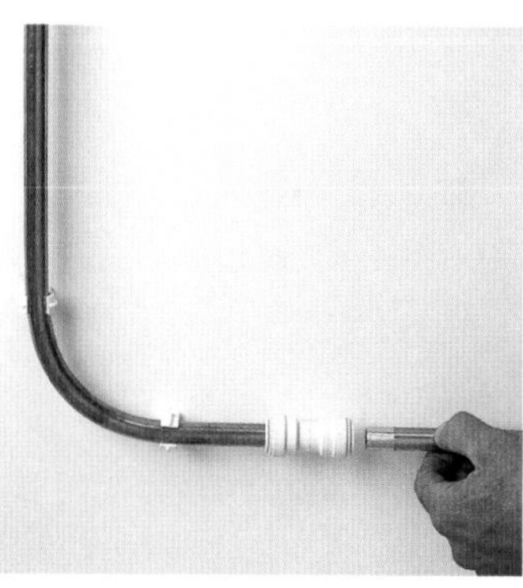

2 Connect the second pipe by pushing it into the joint.

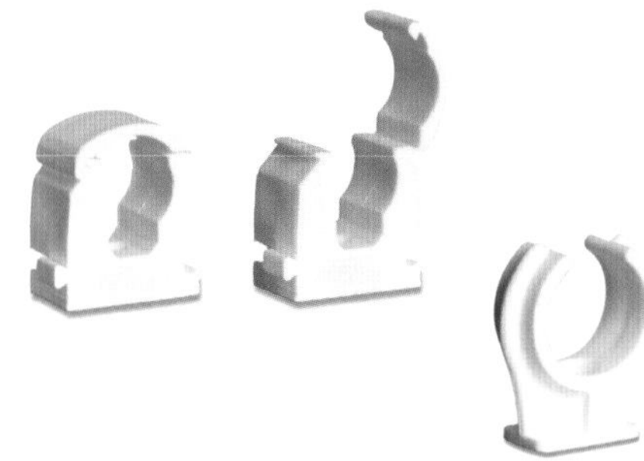

Pipe clips

Whether you are running pipes along a wall or concealed behind or beneath it, it is important that they are firmly clipped in place at regular intervals, otherwise they may creak or vibrate. Pipe clips come in all styles and sizes to suit all situations.

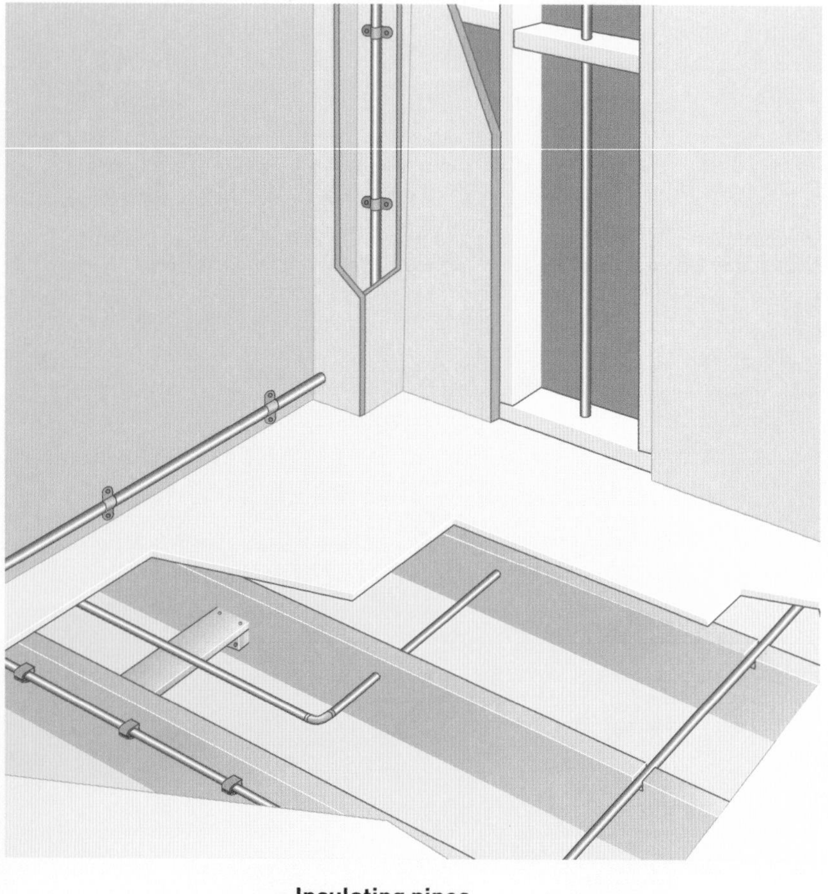

Insulating pipes

Use split foam tubes to lag any pipes that are at risk from freezing: pipes running under a ground floor, through a loft space, or against an outside wall. They could prevent a plumbing disaster.

Running supply pipes

Moving or modifying elements of your plumbing system will very often involve running new pipework. There are plenty of options for doing this. Plan the route first, and try to keep bends to a minimum so that the water flows freely.

Along walls

The easiest and quickest way of running new pipework is to simply clip the pipes to a wall. They will be less conspicuous if you keep them neat, straight and parallel, and if you run them up a corner, around a chimney breast, or along the skirting. You can buy plastic ducting to hide them, or box them in with plywood and timber battens. You can also remove the skirting and build a false skirting to contain them. If you are building a stud partition wall, run any new pipework through the studs and noggings before you close off the cavity with plasterboard (see page 66).

Under a suspended floor

Clip the pipe to the side of a joist; support it on battens attached between joists; run it in shallow notches cut into the top of joists; or – if there's space to insert it – pass the pipe through holes drilled in the joists. Run pipes at least 50mm below the top of the joists to avoid them being punctured by nails driven through the floorboards. Mark the pipe runs in pencil on the boards to remind you where they are. Always be wary of cutting into joists, however, since they are essential to a building's structure. Remove as little timber as possible.

Waste pipes

Waste pipes are bigger than supply pipes: sinks and hand basins have a 32mm waste outlet pipe, showers, washing machines and baths a 40mm pipe, and WCs a 110mm pipe, the same size as a modern soil stack. Another important difference is that waste pipes must slope downwards at the rate of at least 20mm in every metre to ensure that the water runs away freely.

In the past, waste pipes were made of lead, but modern systems are exclusively plastic. Depending on the type of plastic used, the pipes may be joined by simple push-fit connectors containing rubber ring seals, compression-type connectors with rubber 'olives' or by solvent welding, using specially formulated solvent cement that softens the plastic and dries to form a strong, watertight joint.

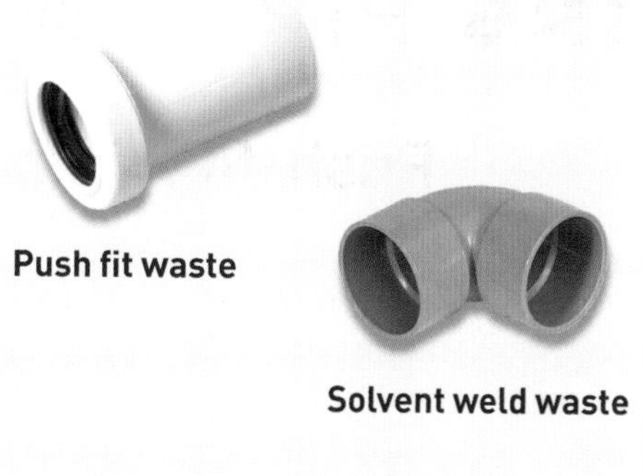

Push fit waste

Solvent weld waste

Compression fit waste

Cutting, gluing and fixing waste pipes

Cut plastic waste pipes with a hacksaw and then remove the burrs inside and out with a half-round file before fixing. Solvent-weld fittings are neat but permanent, so while they are ideal on visible pipework, it is better to use compression fittings under and behind sinks, so that you can take them apart again for cleaning and unblocking. When running pipes along an interior or exterior wall, hold them in place with waste pipe clips, which are available in different colours and sizes. Use wallplugs and screws to attach the clips to a masonry wall, or hollow-wall fixings on plasterboard (see pages 368–69). Don't forget to check for hidden pipes and cables before you drill!

Traps

A vital part of the drainage system is the trap, a water seal that prevents drain smells from entering your home through the waste outlets of the sinks, basins and WCs. Every plumbing installation that discharges waste water into the drainage system will be fitted with a trap, or incorporate one in its design. Essentially, a trap is a U-shaped loop of pipe directly below a waste outlet. Whenever you pull a plug or flush a lavatory, a small amount of water remains in the trap, providing a seal.

Traps are made from plastic and come in a variety of designs to suit different applications and situations. The most common is the P-trap, so-called because of its profile. It has a horizontal outlet. Special shallow versions of P-traps are made for fitting beneath baths and shower trays, although strictly speaking they should only be used in a two-pipe system (see page 305), as the water seal can be sucked out of them by the flow of water in a single soil stack. Then there is the S-trap, which has a vertical outlet, and the bottle trap, which is a compact device intended for use where the trap is exposed, such as under a hand basin. However, the bottle trap is more susceptible to blockage than P- and S-traps. Some bath traps provide a connection for an overflow pipe; there are traps with connectors or standpipes for washing machines; and WC pans and bidets have integral traps.

Early lead U-bend traps incorporated a threaded access plug at the bottom, which could be removed to clear blockages; modern plastic traps can be dismantled by unscrewing the capnuts that hold them together. This arrangement not only allows the trap to be cleaned completely, but also provides access to the waste pipe when a blockage occurs farther along the system.

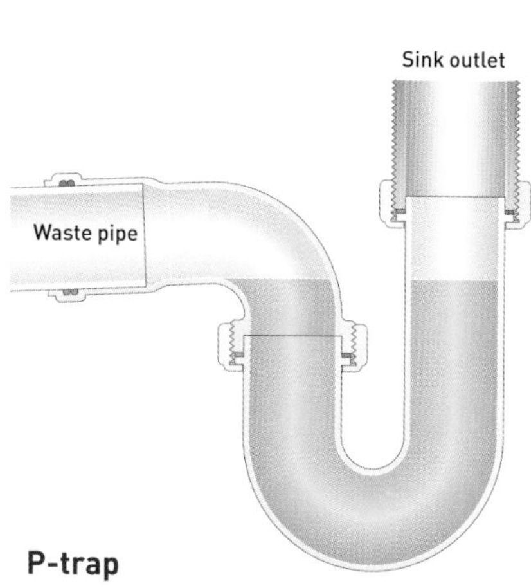

P-trap

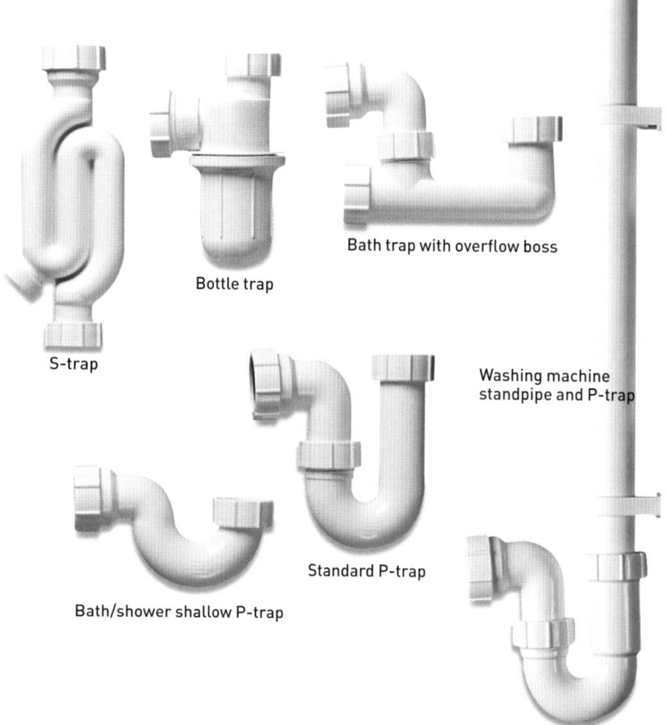

PLUMBING DRAINAGE SYSTEMS

Waste water is channelled from all the plumbing installations in your home into a large vertical pipe or pipes, and from there into the main underground drainage system. Newer homes have a single vertical pipe (single-stack system) whereas older ones may have two separate pipes (two-pipe system).

Where does the waste water go?

Waste water from your appliances either flows to the main soil stack and from there directly into the underground drain, or – in the case of a ground-floor sink, basin or appliance – may discharge into a special outdoor trap set into the ground known as a gully. This is linked to the underground drain and is fitted with a metal or plastic grid to prevent leaves and other debris from falling into the trap and blocking it. The drain itself may run to the main sewer or, in rural areas, to a cess pit or septic tank buried in your garden.

Rainwater drainage

Rainwater from gutters should be drained separately, as a heavy, prolonged downpour could risk overwhelming the system. Downpipes may discharge over the grid of an open gully or be connected directly to an underground drain pipe. From there, the water may run into a storm drain beneath the road or be piped to a soakaway, basically a rubble-filled pit somewhere in your garden, where it gradually percolates back into the soil.

Whose responsibility?

You are responsible for a substantial proportion of your home's drainage system, up to the point where it enters the main sewer; any blockages or damage must be put right at your expense. Because of the potential hazard to health presented by a drainage system, the rules concerning any changes are quite strict. Unlike the supply network, which is governed by the Water Regulations, the drainage system comes under the Building Regulations, and these are enforced by your local council, not the water company. If you are thinking about modifying any part of the drainage system, consult your council's Building Control Officer first (see page 370).

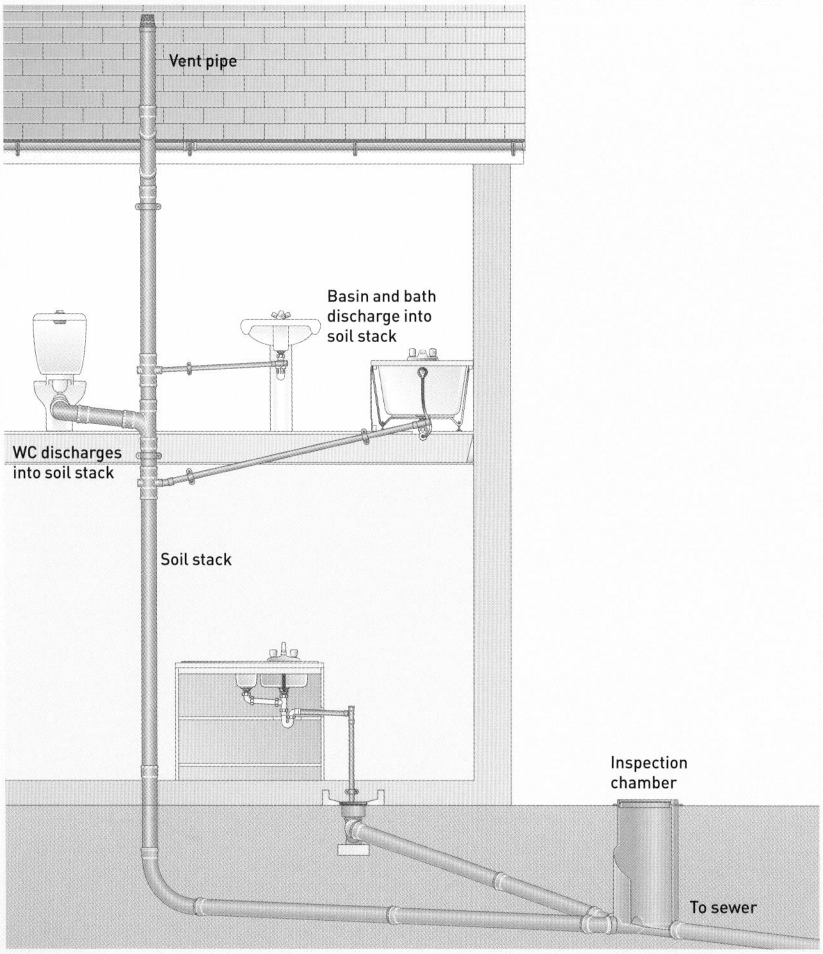

Single-stack system

Modern domestic drainage systems are based on the single-stack arrangement. In this, one large-diameter vertical pipe, known as the soil stack, provides the essential connection with the underground drain. The waste pipes of all upstairs basins, baths, showers and WCs will run to the soil stack. Downstairs waste pipes can also run into the soil stack but in some situations, it may be more convenient for a sink or basin to discharge directly into a gully. If this is the case, the waste pipe should terminate below the gully grid – unless the gully incorporates a special pipe connector behind the grid – and above the water level in the trap. A downstairs WC will almost certainly be connected directly to the underground drain.

In properties built nowadays, the soil stack usually runs up inside the house to provide a degree of frost protection. At the top, the stack emerges through the roof and extends above it; it is left open to vent any drain smells well clear of nearby windows and to prevent suction from occurring in the system that could empty traps of their water seals. Older single-stack systems, and conversions from two-pipe systems, will have the soil pipe on the outside of the house.

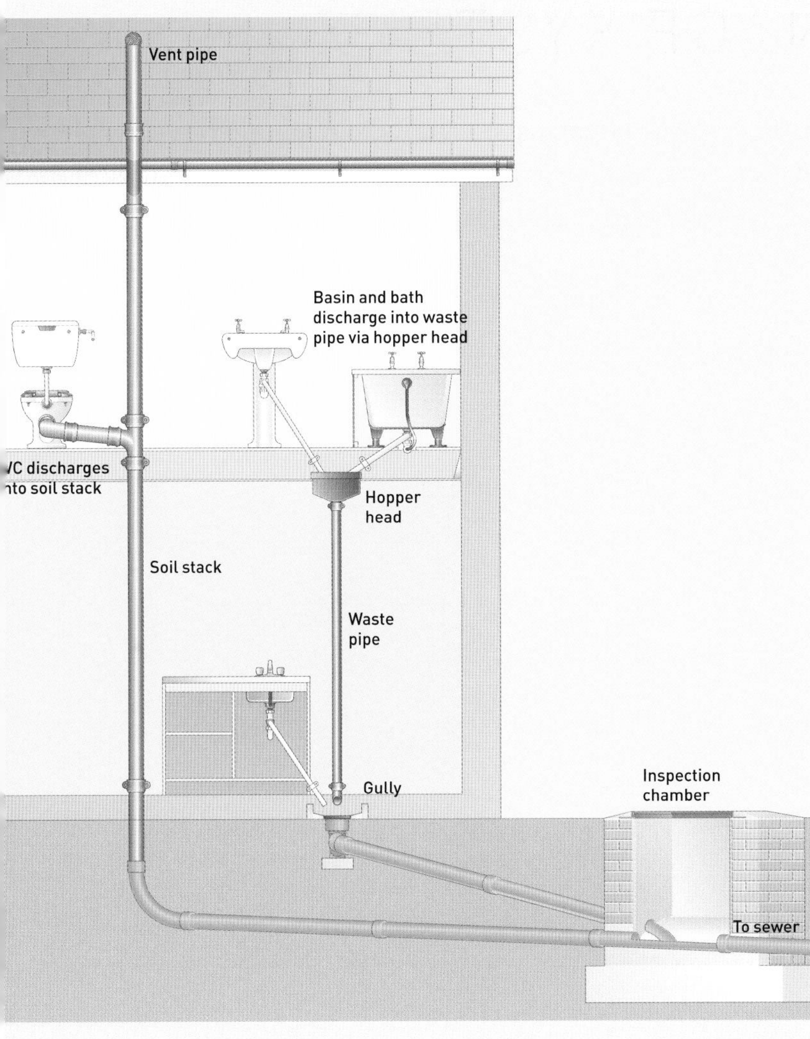

Two-pipe system

Traditionally, domestic drainage was provided by a two-pipe arrangement, whereby the waste and soil water were kept separate until they reached the underground drain. Although many older properties have been converted to single-stack drainage, two-pipe systems are still quite common.

WCs are connected to a large vertical soil pipe attached to an outside wall and extending above the roof. A second, smaller-diameter vertical pipe drains waste water. This terminates at about the level of the first floor in a funnel-like fitting called a hopper head, and all the waste pipes from the upstairs basins and baths discharge into this. At ground level, the waste pipe ends just above the grid of a gully. In most cases, downstairs fittings discharge into gullies, but their pipes terminate above the grids. This is one of the major disadvantages of the system, since grids may become blocked with sink waste, while the hopper is not self-cleansing and can suffer a build-up of soap. This can result in unpleasant odours and even overflows.

ECO WATER

Grey water describes water that has been used for showering, bathing, handwashing, low-intensity laundry and dishwashing. It can be treated and reused for flushing toilets and irrigating the garden. You will need a domestic grey water treatment unit installing: ask your water company for more information.

Joining up

If you need to run a waste pipe through an outside wall, you will need a power hammer drill, or better still a diamond-tipped core drill. Use an electronic pipe and cable detector to check there are no hidden pipes or cables behind the inside wall. Then drill from both inside and out to avoid a messy exit hole. With a core drill you will need to drill a few cm at a time, then stop to empty the drill core and clean out the hole in the masonry with a club hammer and cold chisel. Make sure the hole runs downhill slightly towards the outside.

There may be a spare boss on the soil stack suitable for connecting a new waste pipe; or you can bore a hole and use a strap-on boss and solvent-weld fitting. Alternatively new non-soil waste pipes can be fed into an existing network of hoppers and gullies. However, there are strict rules about where you can connect pipes into a soil stack, so you must contact your local Building Control Officer before making any modifications.

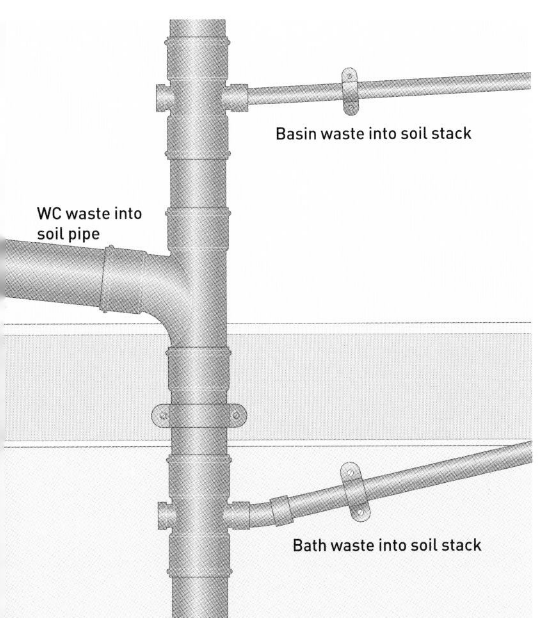

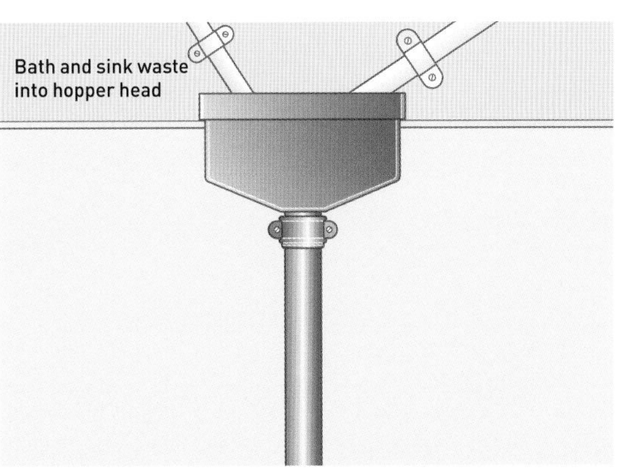

PLUMBING WASHING MACHINES

Washing machines and dishwashers need a power supply and a water supply. Connection will be easier if the machine is near existing pipes, but you can run branch pipes to it using the techniques on pages 300–2. Both kinds of machine must stand on a firm, level floor close to an outside wall or an internal soil stack to simplify running the waste pipe.

Water supply

Washing machines are normally connected to the cold and hot water systems, but many will work with a cold supply only – the machine's heater will simply spend more time bringing the water up to the right temperature, which may prove more expensive, depending on how you heat your hot water. Dishwashers usually only require a cold supply.

Pressure

If the machine is supplied from the pipe that feeds the kitchen tap, the water will be at mains pressure. If it also needs a hot water supply, this will be at gravity pressure from the cylinder upstairs. Usually, machines have a flow restrictor in the cold water inlet to even out the pressure differential. If the cold water supply is at gravity pressure you may need to remove the restrictor – check the machine's instructions. Pressure may be a problem if the machine is upstairs. The instructions will specify the water pressure required (usually 0.3–10 bar); to work out if there will be enough, measure the distance from the bottom of the cold water cistern in the loft to the machine inlet – every metre equals about 0.1 bar.

Waste connection

The machine's flexible waste has to discharge into a waste pipe or tra above the level of the top of the drum, otherwise water will drain from the machine by siphonic action. One option is to hook the hose into th top of an open standpipe with a P-trap at its base. From the trap, the waste pipe must run through the outside wall to a hopper head or gul or directly into a soil stack (see page 305). The air gap at the top of the standpipe stops back-siphonage of dirty water into the machine.

Some manufacturer's recommend a standpipe, and some water companies insist on it. But if possible, it is easier to position the machine next to a sink and change the sink trap to a washing machin trap. This has an inlet for the waste hose. When you attach the hose to the inlet, install a non-return valve to prevent back-siphonage of wast water; or fix a hook to the underside of the work surface and tie the hose to it, so that it runs higher than the level of the sink overflow.

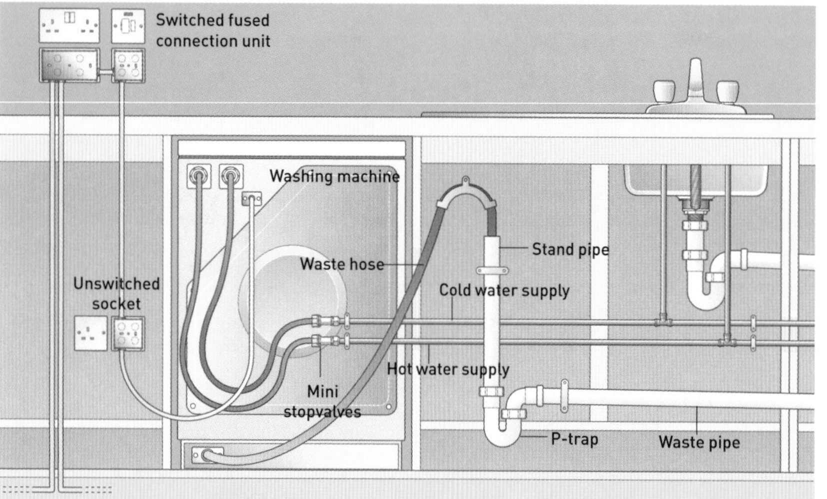

Pipe connections

There are various ways in which you can make the pipe connections. If the machine's hoses won't reach existing supply pipes, you will have to drain the pipes then cut them, add T-fittings and run branch pipes to the machine. These should terminate in mini stop valves (see YOU CAN DO IT, opposite), to which the machine's hoses can be connected. If the pipes run close to the machine, you can install T-piece stop valves and screw the hoses to them, or you may be able to use self-cutting connectors, which can be installed without draining the pipes.

Plumbing in a washing machine ▲

A typical washing machine installation: nearby hot and cold water pipes have been extended via T-fittings to reach the machine's supply hoses. Mini stop valves allow the machine to be isolated without having to cut off the water supply. The waste hose is hooked into a standpipe with P-trap.

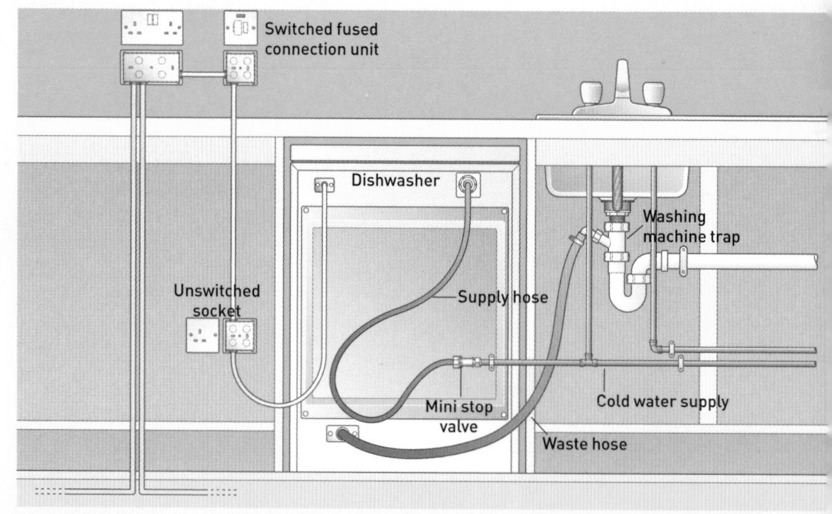

Plumbing in a dishwasher ▶

A typical dishwasher installation will have a cold water supply only. The mini stop valve connecting the supply pipe to the machine's hose allows the machine to be isolated without turning off the water. The waste hose is connected to a washing machine trap beneath the sink.

Power supply

Vashing machines and dishwashers need to be plugged into a standard socket. common problem in kitchens and utility rooms is that all the sockets are above ne work surfaces. The solution is to run a spur from a socket to a switched fused onnection unit above the work surface, then a cable from this to an unswitched ocket below the surface to serve the machine (see pages 272–77). The connection nit should have a neon so that you can see when the machine is switched on.

SAFETY FIRST

If you are installing a washing machine in the bathroom, remember that you cannot have a socket or a switched fused connection unit in there. Instead mount the fused connection unit outside the bathroom and connect the machine to a flex outlet plate in the bathroom.

OOLS MATERIALS

wire wool
screwdriver
spanner or wrench

self-cutting hose connectors

Self-cutting hose connectors

You will probably have to extend a water supply pipe (or pipes) to feed a washing machine or dishwasher, and if so, you should use mini stop valves to connect the hoses. But if your new machine is sited near existing water supply pipes, it is simpler to use self-cutting hose connectors, which contain isolating valves. The machine's blue hose should be connected to the cold supply, and the red hose (if it has one) to the hot. There's no need to drain the supply pipes before fitting the connectors. But check first that your machine is compatible with these fittings: some are not.

1 To ensure a good seal between he connector and pipe, the latter nust be perfectly clean; if the pipe s painted, the paint must be emoved. Use wire wool to clean the area of pipe where the connector vill be fitted, rubbing until you have achieved a bright copper finish.

2 Before fitting the saddle assembly to the pipe, make sure that the rubber seal is correctly positioned. Then place the backplate behind the pipe and fit the saddle over the top, aligning the screw holes. For added strength, the backplate can be screwed to the wall.

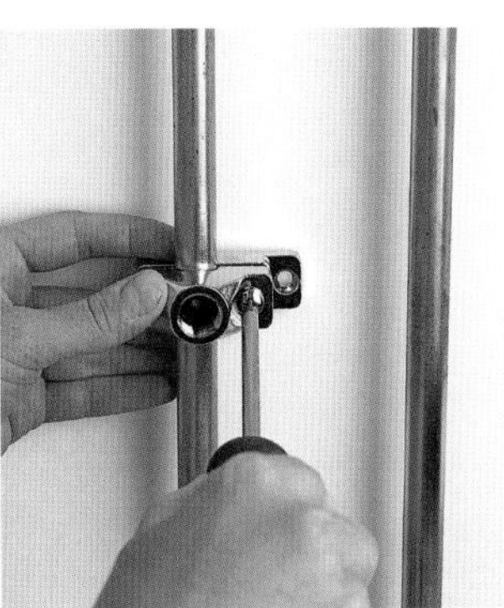

3 Clamp the saddle assembly in place around the pipe by inserting the screws and tightening them home fully. Make sure that the two halves of the saddle remain square to the pipe as you do this.

4 Make sure that the valve is in the 'off' position, then screw it into the saddle by hand; you will feel it cut into the pipe as you do so. Continue turning the valve until it is fully home and the body of the valve is at a right angle to the pipe – to allow you to turn it on and off easily.

5 Secure the valve by tightening its retaining locknut with a spanner or wrench, taking care that the valve does not move as you do so.

6 Attach the supply hose to the valve by screwing its capnut on to the threaded outlet, making sure it is tight.

YOU CAN DO IT

Mini stop valves

If you aren't using self-cutting hose connectors, you still need to install valves so that a dishwasher or washing machine can be easily removed for servicing or repair. Mini stop valves are ideal. They are fitted to the supply pipes with compression joints and are threaded to accept the machine's hoses. A small lever on the valve allows you to turn the water on and off. In-line, right-angled and T-piece versions are available.

PLUMBING BLOCKAGES AND DRIPS

If sinks, basins or baths become slow to drain, or stop draining completely, there must be a blockage somewhere in the waste pipe. Deal with the situation straight away to prevent the job becoming more complicated. Dripping taps should also be fixed immediately, or they will cause staining on your bath or sink and erosion inside the tap mechanism.

Clearing a blocked sink

An accumulation of grease in the trap, or fibres caught below the grid on the plug-hole, will result in water draining away slowly. If water doesn't drain away at all, then there is a complete blockage and there must be an obstruction in the waste pipe. There are different methods you can try to remedy the situation.

TOOLS MATERIALS

- **sink plunger**
- **cloth or rag**
- **safety goggles**
- **protective gloves**
- **bucket**
- **drain auger**

- chemical drain-cleaning product
- petroleum jelly

1 If a sink is completely blocked, partially fill it with water and place the cup of a sink plunger over the plug-hole. Stuff a damp cloth into the overflow to prevent loss of pressure. Then pump the plunger up and down vigorously. Take the plunger away and see if the water drains. You may need to do this a couple of times.

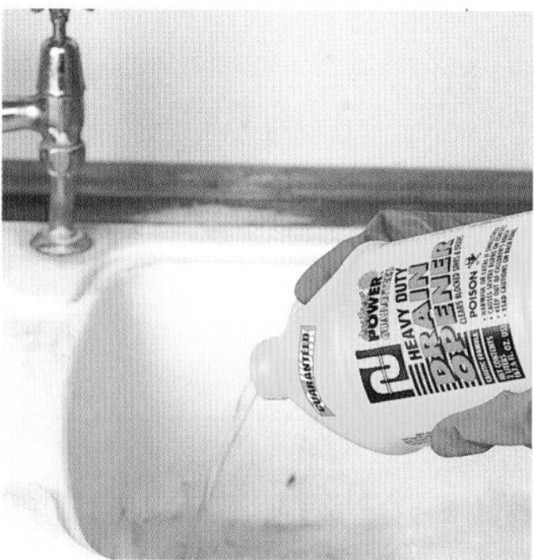

2 If that fails, try using a chemical drain-cleaning product. Wear protective gloves and goggles and follow the instructions carefully, as it will be highly toxic. Smear some petroleum jelly around the rim of the plug-hole to protect it from damage.

3 If you have not been able to clear the blockage, then you will have to remove the waste trap. Put a bucket underneath the trap to catch any spillage. Unscrew the trap, and empty the contents into the bucket. Replace the trap making sure you replace any washers or o-rings. Don't overtighten or it will be difficult to undo if it needs cleaning out in the future. If there was nothing blocking the waste trap, use a drain auger to probe into the waste pipe.

IDEAL TOOL

Drain auger

A drain auger has a flexible rod that extends into a waste pipe as you rotate the handle, dislodging any blockage as it probes. The rod then winds back into the handle for hygienic storage.

Clearing a blocked lavatory

A blocked lavatory pan causes the flush water to rise almost to the rim, and then drain away very slowly. It will probably be blocked in the pan outlet, but if not then it could be a problem in the main drainage system.

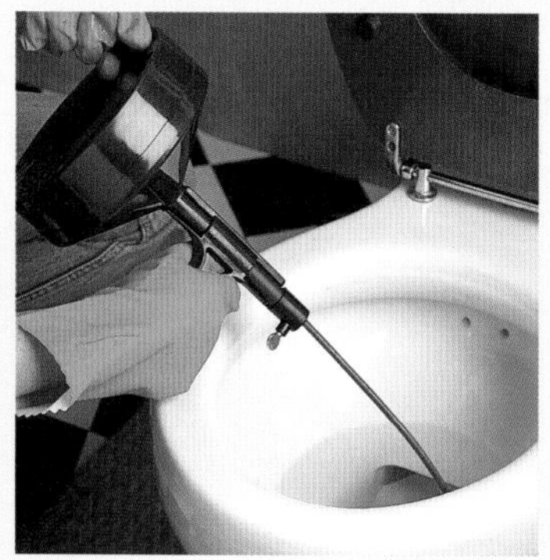

1 Try pouring a bucket of warm water into the pan from a height; this often clears a minor blockage.

2 Place a large WC plunger over the pan outlet and pump the handle up and down.

3 If that doesn't shift it, use an auger (left) designed for a lavatory. Its probe extends around the u-bend and rotates as you turn the handle, dislodging the blockage. Wear protective gloves and read the manufacturer's instructions.

TOOLS MATERIALS

- **protective gloves**
- **bucket**
- **WC plunger**
- **lavatory auger**

Repairing a dripping tap

Don't ignore a dripping tap! The sooner you tackle it, the easier it will be to fix, and the less damage will be done. Even if you don't have a spare washer, take a look inside the tap – if the washer is only slightly damaged on one face, you can reinsert it the other way up. But even if that stops the drip, do remember to replace it with a new washer as soon as possible. Standard mixer taps can be repaired as shown here, but monobloc taps – often controlled by levers, and needing only a quarter turn between fully off and fully on – have ceramic disks rather than traditional washers. The disks are very hardwearing, but if one does develop a problem you will need a replacement cartridge from the tap manufacturer.

TOOLS MATERIALS

- **adjustable spanner or pliers**
- **screwdriver**
- **pipe wrench**
- **cloth**

- tap washer
- silicone grease
- cardboard

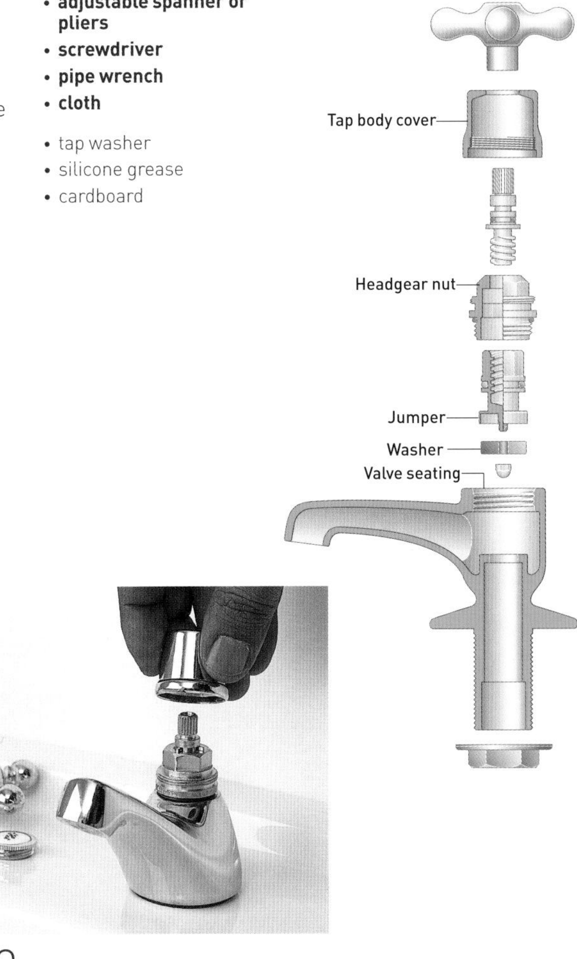

1 Turn off the water supply and open the tap to drain water from the system. Put the plug into the plug-hole, just in case you drop any small nuts or screws. Unscrew the top plate (this has the hot/cold emblem on it). You might be able to do this with your fingers, but if not use pliers or an adjustable spanner.

2 Not all taps are made the same way so you will have to work out how the handle comes off. In the type shown, you need to unscrew the retaining screw, and pull off the handle. This will expose the headgear nut.

3 Unscrew the tap body cover. If you can't do this by hand use an adjustable spanner or pipe grips, but protect the chrome with a cloth.

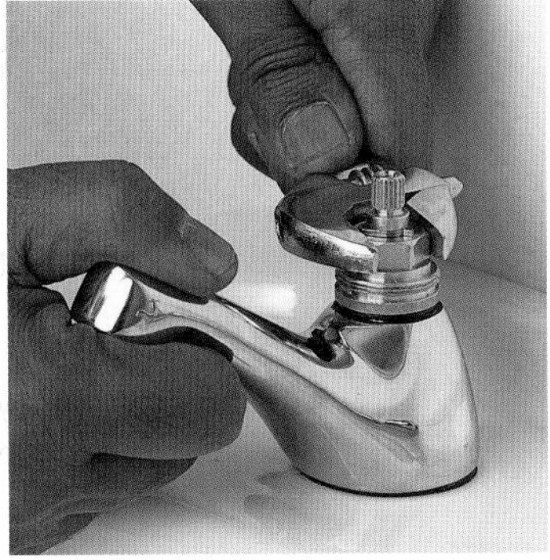

4 Undo the headgear nut using an adjustable spanner. If the nut is difficult to turn, don't force it or you risk twisting the base of the tap and putting a strain on the inlet pipe. Instead pad around the base of the tap with cardboard and use a pipe wrench to grip it firmly as you apply the necessary force to the nut.

5 Remove the headgear assembly by unscrewing the headgear nut. The washer sits in the jumper and is either pressed in place, often over a small button, or retained by a nut. If necessary, unscrew the nut holding the washer in place with an adjustable spanner. Prise out the old washer; you can use a screwdriver to dig it out if necessary.

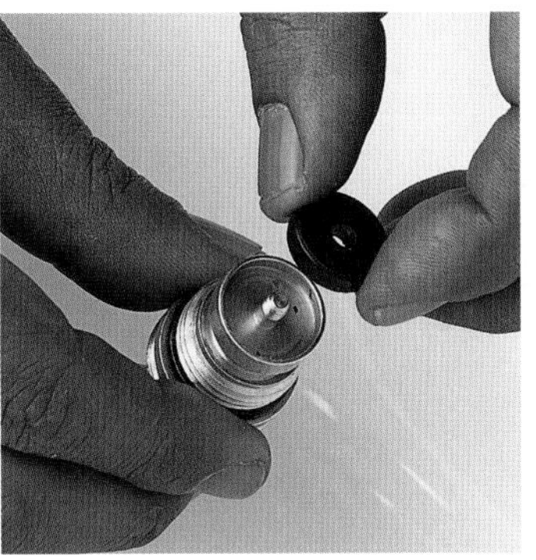

6 Insert a new washer and push it down into the jumper. Reassemble the tap in the same sequence. Apply a little silicone grease to the threads on the base of the headgear assembly before reinserting it in the tap body.

YOU CAN DO IT

Valve seating damage

If a tap carries on dripping even with a new washer, then the valve seating is probably eroded. This can be repaired with a special grinding tool or – much more easily – with a washer and seating set. The plastic seat fits into the existing metal seat, and a washer-and-jumper unit fits on the headgear. The sooner you replace a washer, the less likely the valve seating is to get damaged.

B&Q

You will usually be able to use the existing water supply pipes and waste outlet when replacing an old basin or sink. Try to choose a trap similar in size to the one you have removed as this will make fitting much easier. If you want to put a sink into a new location you will have to extend the pipework, which is more ambitious (see pages 300–5).

Fitting a new kitchen sink

If you are replacing an existing sink, measure the space carefully. To cut a hole in a new work surface to accommodate a sink see page 159. If necessary, extend nearby hot and cold water supply pipes so that you can connect them to the inlet pipes of the new taps. You may also need to extend the existing waste outlet pipes to meet the trap of the new sink (see page 303). Then you can install the sink.

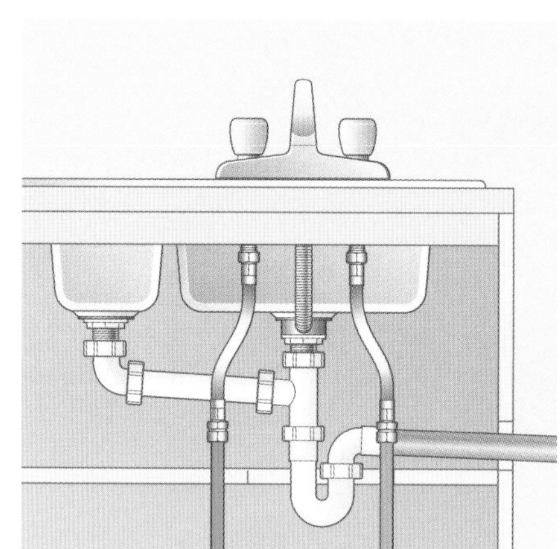

TOOLS MATERIALS

- **cross-head screwdriver**
- **hacksaw**
- **adjustable spanner or pipe grips**

- taps
- kitchen sink and waste fittings
- sanitary silicone sealant
- 15mm flexible tap connectors

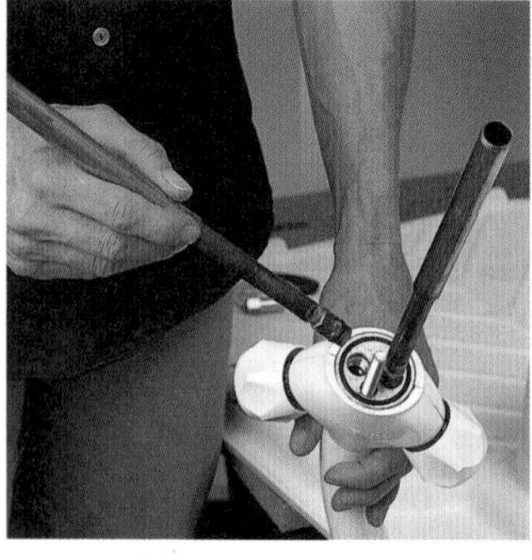

1 Assemble the tap according to the manufacturer's instructions, and attach the pipes to the correct inlets.

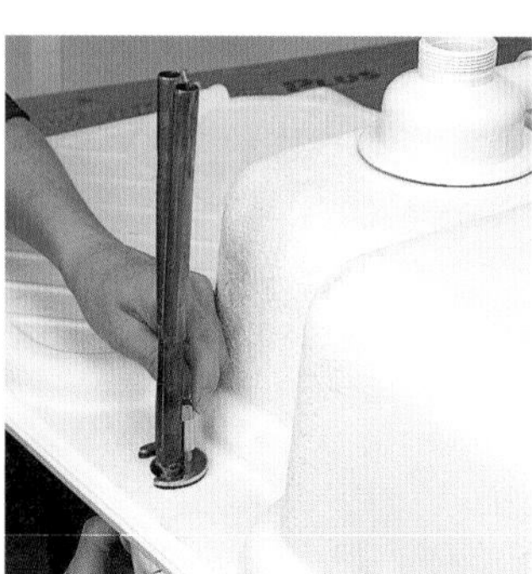

2 Insert the tap through the hole in the sink, including any washers or backing plates, according to the instructions supplied.

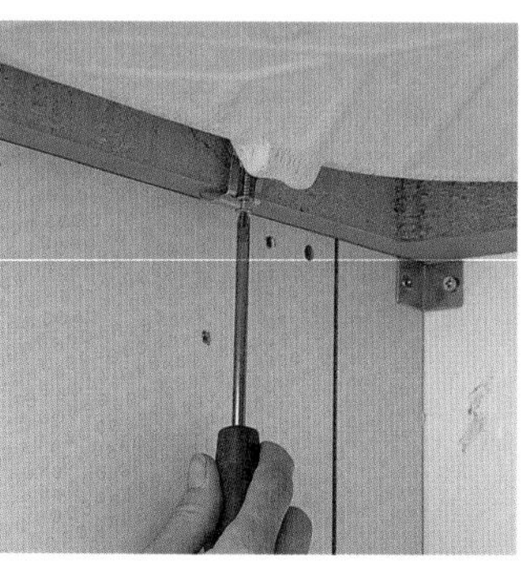

3 Fit the retaining clips to the underside lip of the sink, spacing them evenly. Run a continuous bead of sanitary silicone sealant around the outer edge of the sink. Then carefully turn the sink over and rest it into the cut-out in the worktop. Working from the underside, tighten the screws on each retaining clip. Take care not to overtighten.

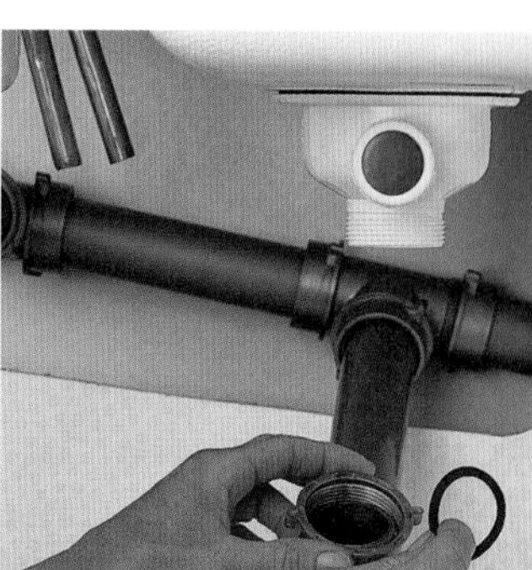

4 Assemble the waste pipes and trap. Place rubber o-rings onto the waste couplings.

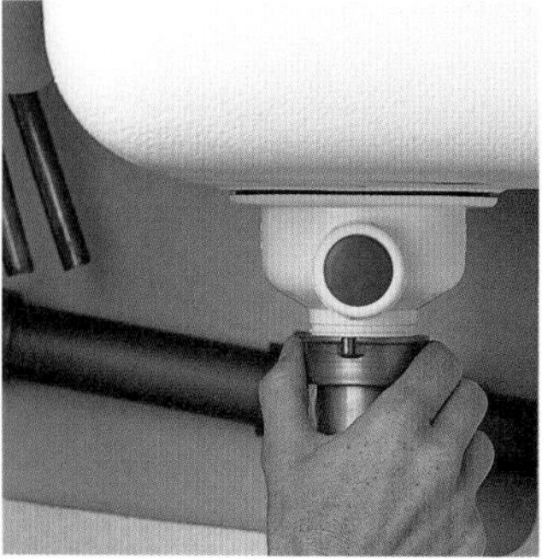

5 Fit the waste coupling to the outlet on the underside of each sink bowl.

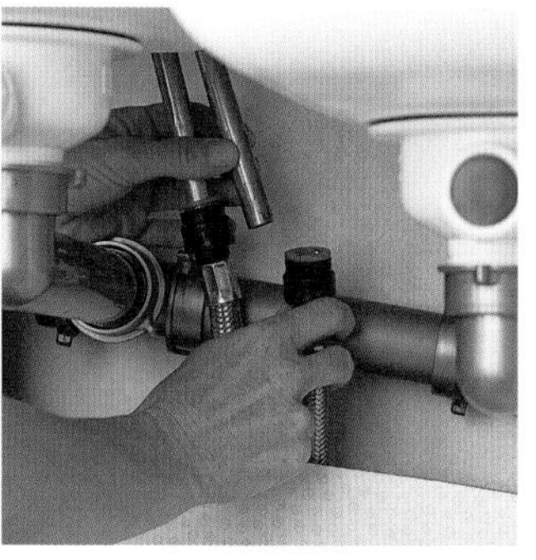

6 Join the hot and cold water supply pipes to the tap pipes with push-fit flexible tap connectors (see YOU CAN DO IT, page 301). Connect the overflow pipe between the sink's overflow outlet and the inlet below the bowl. Then turn on the water supply and check for any leaks, retightening the joints as necessary.

Fitting a new basin

There are several types of basin available. Wall-mounted basins can look extremely smart, but they need very strong fixings to support their weight, and hiding pipework can be difficult. Pedestal basins are the most popular choice. The hollow pedestal supports the weight and also hides pipework, making them fairly easy to install. Pedestal basins also come as a corner fitting; these are a good space-saving option for small bathrooms.

TOOLS MATERIALS

- **dust sheet**
- **cranked spanner**
- **spirit level**
- **pencil**
- **pipe and cable detector**
- **hammer-action drill with masonry bit**
- **pipe cutter**
- **narrow file**
- **screwdriver**
- **wire wool**

- pedestal and basin
- taps
- 15mm push-fit flexible tap connectors
- sanitary silicone sealant
- 50mm screws
- plasterboard fixings, if required
- wallplugs, if required
- waste trap
- waste pipe

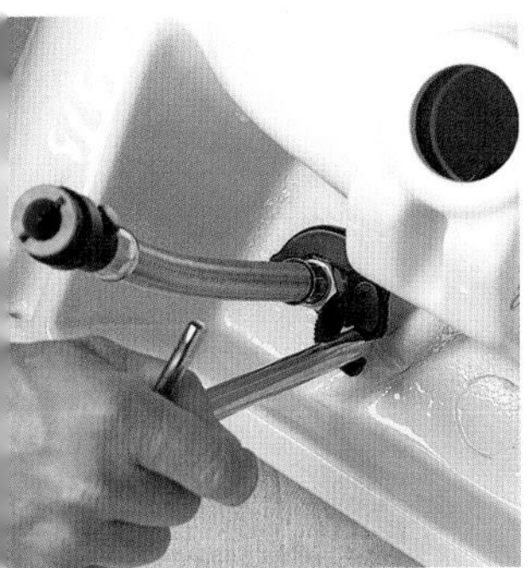

Lay a dust sheet on the floor nd rest the basin upside down. it the washers supplied over the ail of each tap and feed the tap rough the holes in the basin. crew the plastic nuts onto the ail end of the tap using a cranked panner. To prevent the whole ssembly from turning, hold the ap with your other hand while ghtening the nut. Connect 5mm push-fit flexible tap onnectors with built-in isolating alves to each tap; remember to nclude the fibre washers. Again, old the tap with your other hand hile tightening the nut with a ranked spanner.

2 Apply sanitary silicone sealant around the waste hole in the basin. Push the waste outlet through the hole and bed the rim of the grid into the sealant. Fit the rubber washer and plastic retaining nut. Run a bead of sanitary silicone sealant behind the washer to ensure a watertight fit. Stand the pedestal in position and put the basin on top. Adjust it until the whole unit is centrally placed over the pipework and touching the wall. Use a spirit level to get the basin level, then mark the position of the fixing holes on the wall and the floor.

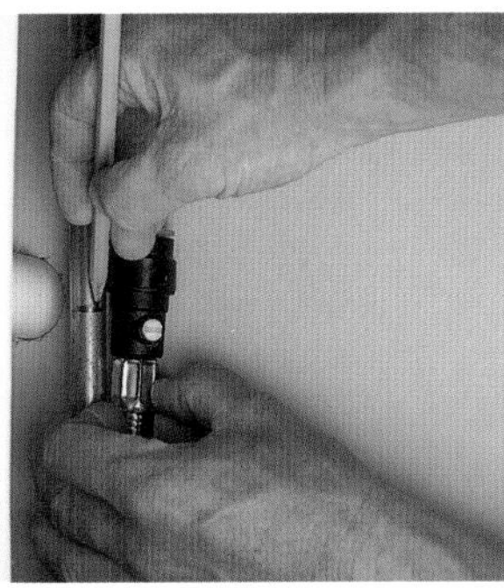

3 Arrange the flexible pipe connectors so that they fit behind the pedestal, and mark the inlet pipes where they will need to be cut. They must be long enough to fully engage with the fittings on the pipe connectors. Make sure the waste pipe is in the correct position to join to the sink trap.

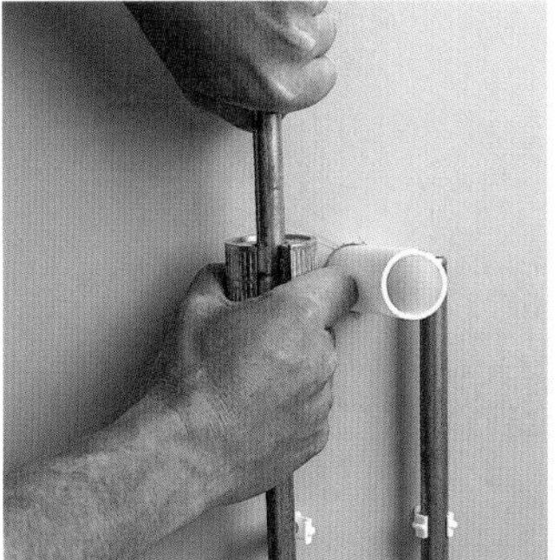

4 Remove the pedestal and basin. Check for hidden pipes and cables. If the area is clear, drill and plug the wall at the fixing positions. On a hollow wall, use plasterboard fixings (see pages 368–69). Check the floor-fixing positions for hidden pipes or cables, then drill the holes and, on a solid floor, plug them. Use a pipe cutter to cut the inlet pipes where you marked them, and file off any burrs. Fit the trap to the waste outlet pipe, remembering to include all rubber washers.

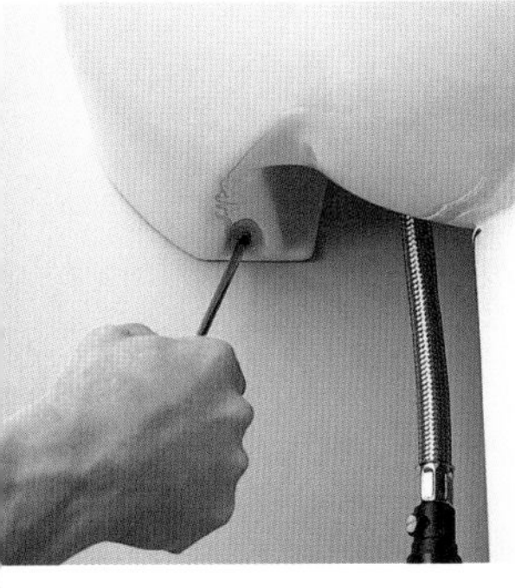

5 Put the unit back in position. crew the basin to the wall and he pedestal to the floor. Don't vertighten the screws.

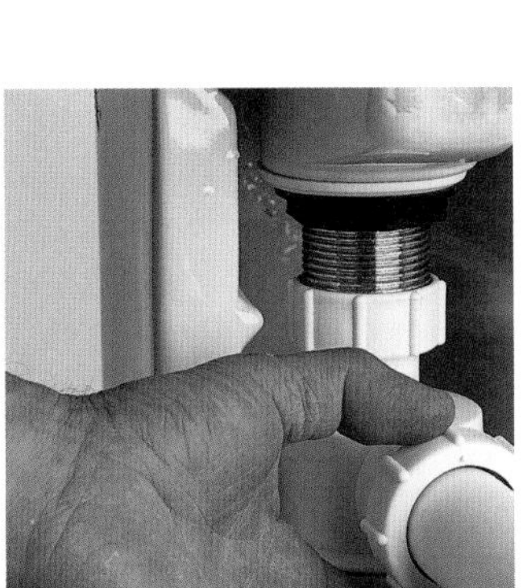

6 Push the flexible tap connectors onto the inlet pipes. If the inlet pipes are dirty, clean them with wire wool first. Insert the waste pipe into the trap and hand tighten the nut. Turn on the water, open the isolating valves and check for leaks. If you spot any drips, retighten the connectors as necessary.

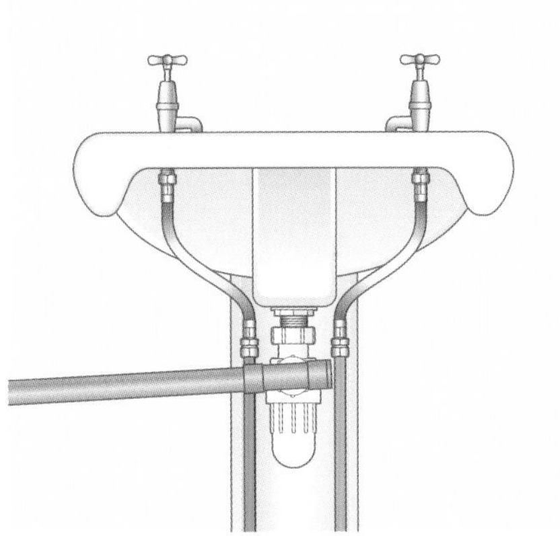

PLUMBING LAVATORY AND CISTERN

YOU CAN DO IT

Check first
Always unpack and carefully inspect a new WC or suite before you rip out your old fittings. You don't want to discover a fault, crack or missing part once your bathroom is already out of action.

There are many different lavatory designs to choose from, to suit every style of interior. Fitting a lavatory is not too difficult if you are replacing an old one and it can be connected to an existing branch of the soil pipe. If you want to add a new lavatory in another part of the house, however, you should get a professional plumber to connect into the main soil pipe. Apart from style, the main consideration will be your choice of cistern and flush mechanism.

Types of WC

Low-level cisterns are mounted on the wall just above the pan, and connect to the pan with a flush pipe. Close-coupled cisterns sit directly on top of the pan and are a particularly popular modern design. Other types include high-level cisterns, which are more old-fashioned, and concealed cisterns, which are designed to be hidden behind panelling.

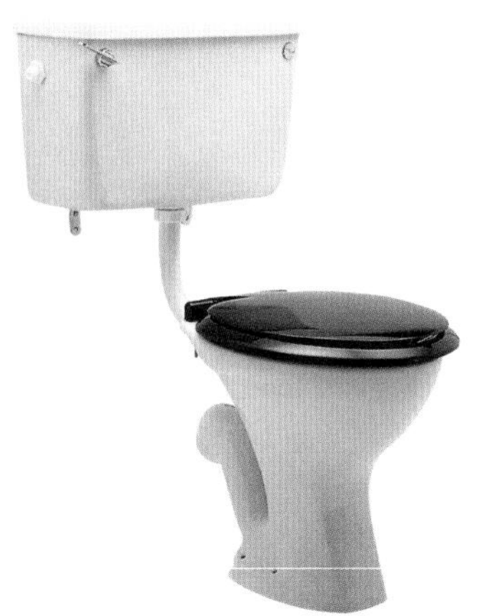

Low-level cistern

Close-coupled cistern

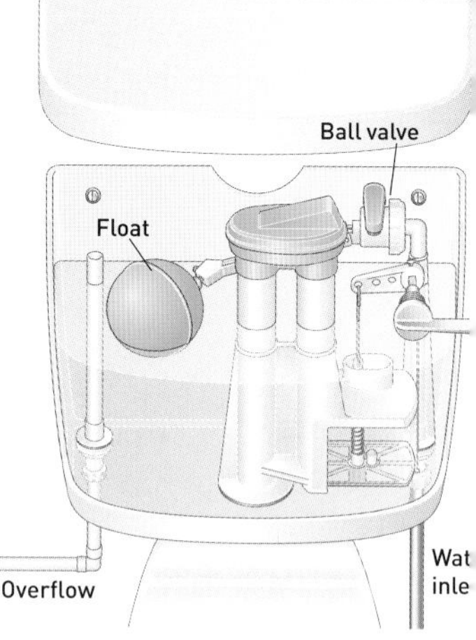

Standard lavatory cistern

A standard cistern has a siphon flush mechanism operated by a ball valve and float, with a lever handle on the front. However, flush mechanisms do vary between designs, so always read the manufacturer's assembly instructions.

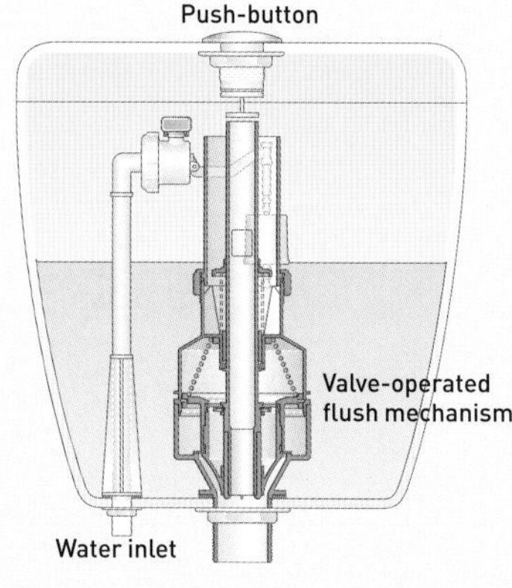

TOOLS MATERIALS

- **adjustable spanner**
- **screwdriver**
- **pipe and cable detector**
- **power drill with twist or masonry bit**

- WC and cistern
- silicone grease
- screws
- wallplugs, if required
- push-fit tap connector
- lavatory seat

Installing a close-coupled WC

Instructions are given here for fitting a freestanding cistern with a push-button flush. This type of cistern has a valve-operated flush.

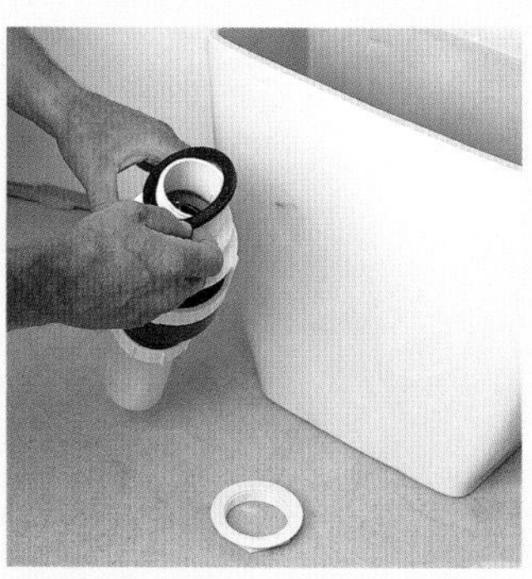

1 Follow the manufacturer's instructions to assemble the flush mechanism. Make sure you include the rubber sealing rings where necessary.

2 Place the flush valve mechanism into the cistern; slide the bottom threaded section through the hole in the base. Check that the rubber washer is on the mechanism, inside the cistern. Screw on the back nut securely, but don't overtighten.

3 Insert the push-button assembly through the hole in the cistern lid, and fit the nut.

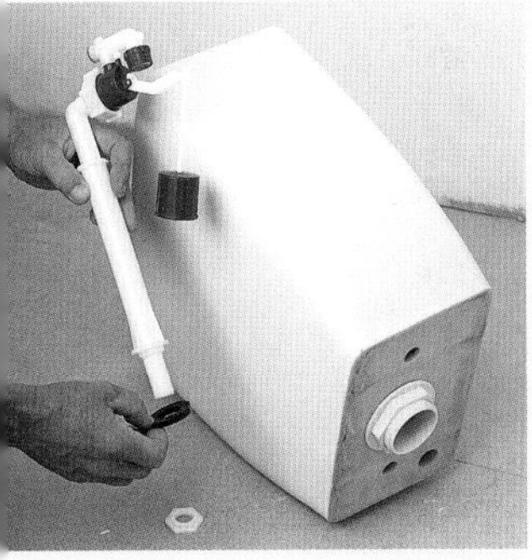

4 Insert the inlet valve assembly nto the cistern. Check that the ubber washer is in place on the ıssembly, inside the cistern, then ock it into position using the nut supplied. Tighten by hand and hen give a further half turn using an adjustable spanner or small vrench. Don't overtighten.

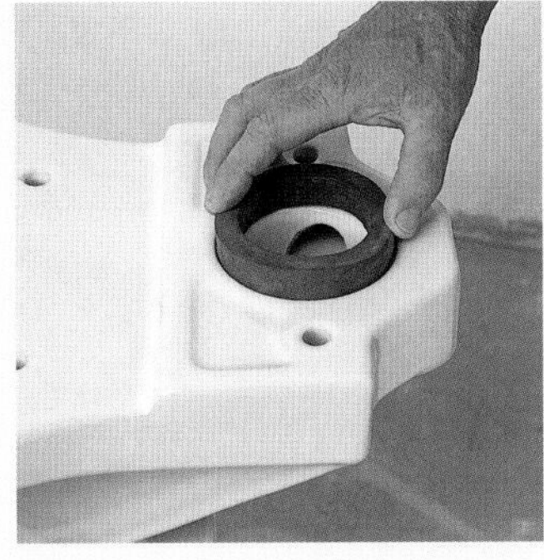

5 Place the large rubber gasket into the flush entrance of the pan.

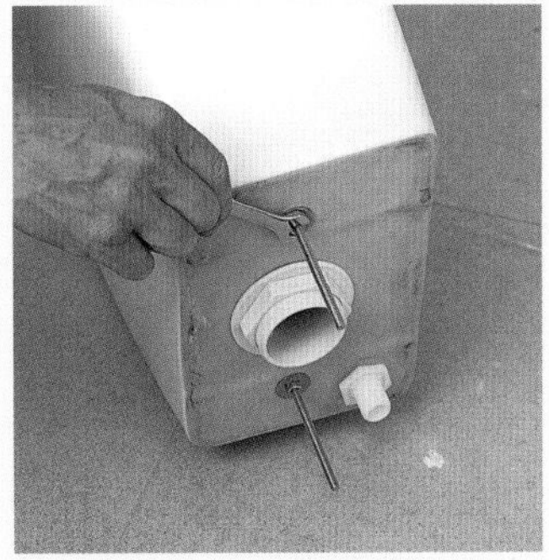

6 Insert the long fixing bolts through the holes in the cistern, using the rubber and large metal washers supplied.

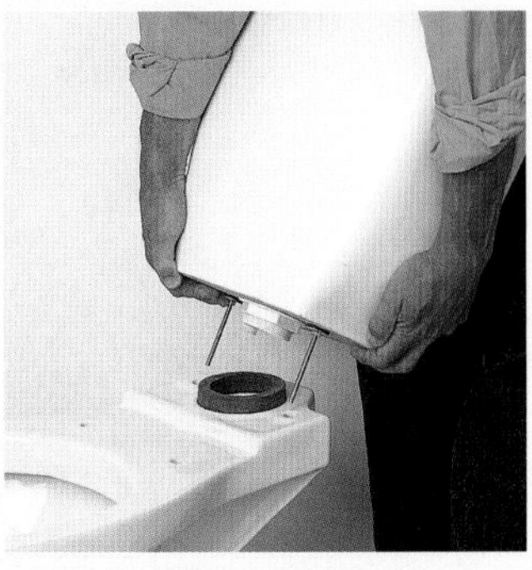

7 Lift the cistern onto the pan so that the connecting bolts locate through the holes. The threaded section of the flush mechanism should go through the rubber gasket on the flush entrance of the pan.

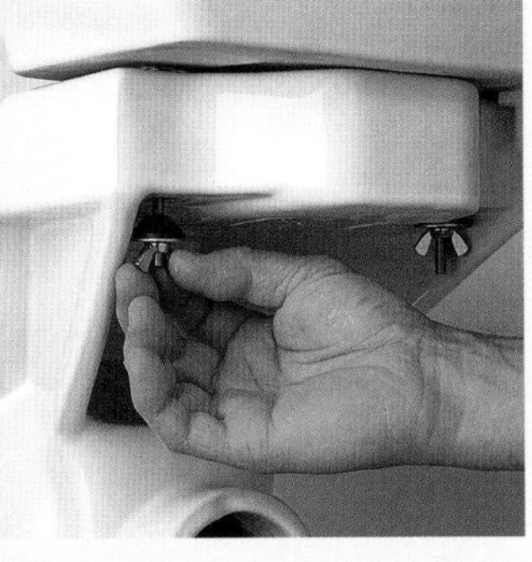

8 Fit washers to the connecting bolts, and tighten the wing nuts. Fit securely but don't overtighten.

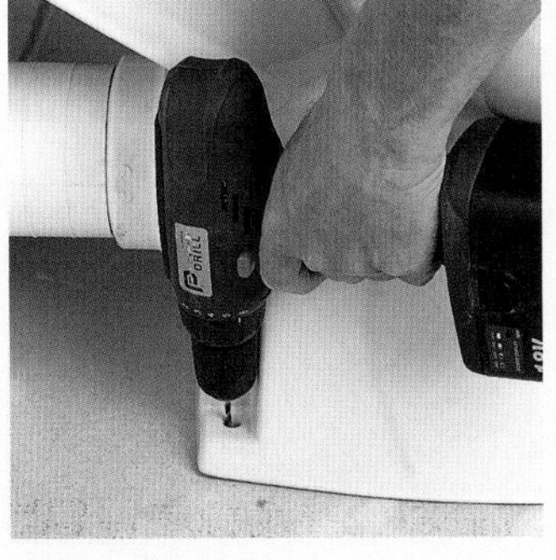

9 Check there are no pipes or cables beneath the fixing points, then position the WC and slide the pan outlet into the flexible connector attached to the soil pipe. A little silicone grease will ease it on. Drill pilot holes into the floor at the fixing points. If it's a solid floor you will need to drill the holes with a hammer-action drill and plug them.

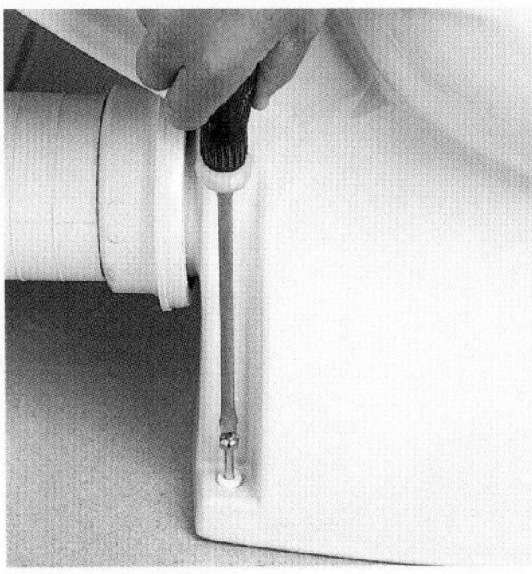

10 Push plastic protective inserts through the holes in the base of the pan and screw the retaining screws through and into the floor. If the cistern has fixing holes in the back, fix to the wall by drilling and plugging; remember to add rubber washers before tightening the nuts.

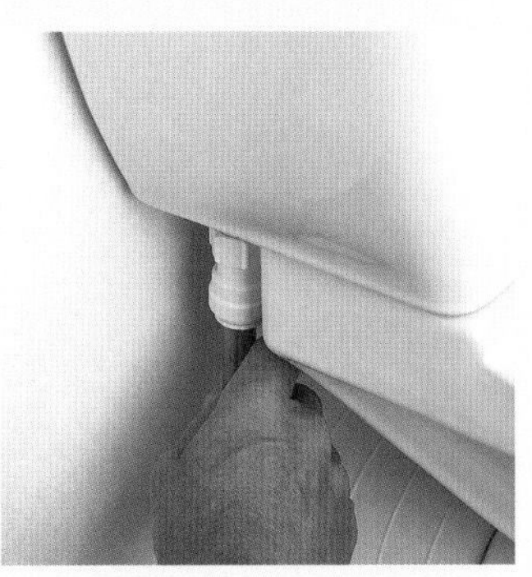

11 Connect the supply pipe for the cold water feed using a push-fit tap connector.

SAFETY FIRST

Use an electronic detector to check for hidden pipes and cables before you drill, both under the floor and behind the wall. Don't risk a flood or, worse, electrocution!

Fitting the seat

The lavatory seat and lid are fitted together, with a hinge to allow them to be raised and lowered.

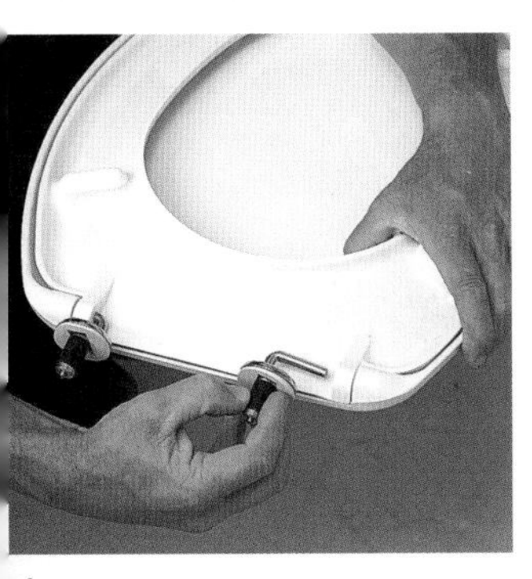

1 Fit the hinge assembly to the seat following the manufacturer's instructions.

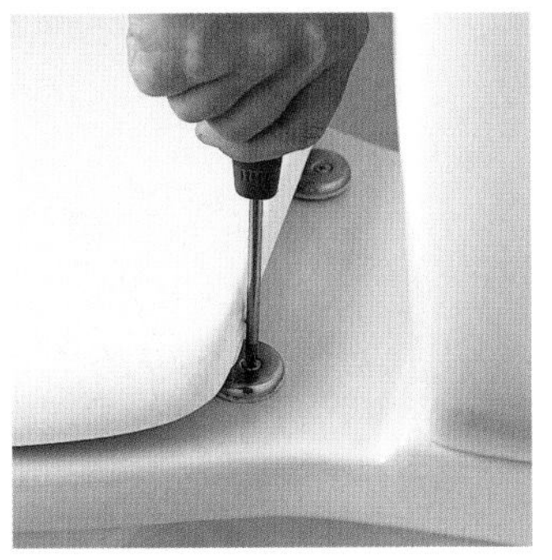

2 Connect the seat to the pan by securing through the holes at the back using the screws supplied. Adjust so that it sits in the correct position.

YOU CAN DO IT

Changing your seat
You can replace a cracked lavatory seat without changing the whole WC. Choose an exact match or go for a contrasting effect; for example, wood-effect seats look good on plain white pans.

PLUMBING INSTALLING A BATH

It is fairly simple to replace an old bath with a new one, though if you are installing a bath in a completely different position, you will have to re-route the waste pipe and extend the supply pipes (see pages 300–3).

Constructing the bath

If you are replacing an old bath, the simplest thing to do is to turn off the water supply and cut right through the existing supply pipes. Carefully file off any burrs ready for reconnection. Always read the manufacturer's assembly instructions, since different designs may be put together in slightly different ways.

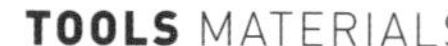

TOOLS MATERIALS

- **dust sheet**
- **cross-head screwdriver**
- **adjustable spanner or basin wrench**
- **pipe grips, if required**
- **spirit level**
- **pencil**
- **electronic pipe and cable detector**
- **hammer-action drill with masonry and twist bits**
- **fine-toothed saw or sharp knife, if required**

- bath and fittings
- bath trap
- bath taps
- flexible tap connectors
- wallplugs, if required
- 25mm, 40mm and 45mm screws
- 25mm x 50mm timber batten

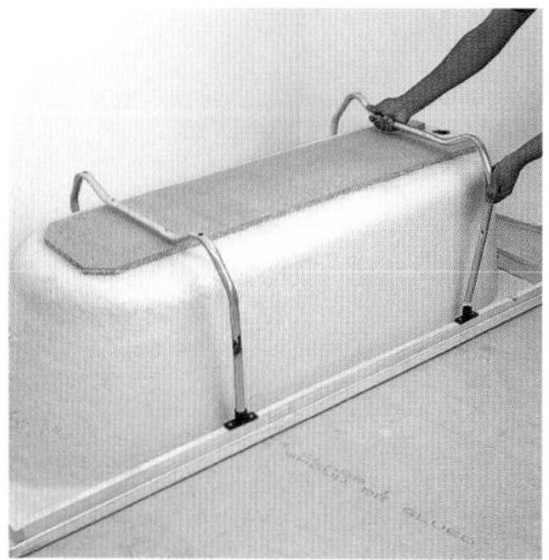

1 With a helper, lay the bath upside down on a dust sheet. Place the two leg cradles over the bath and fit them into their plastic mounting brackets.

2 Fix the leg cradles to the bath by inserting and tightening the locking screws into the plastic mounting brackets.

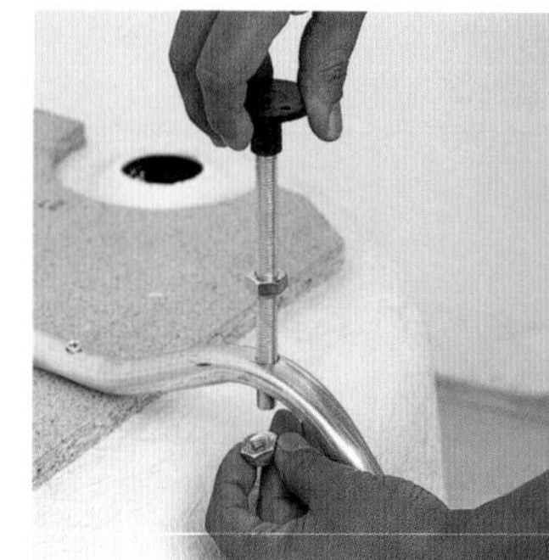

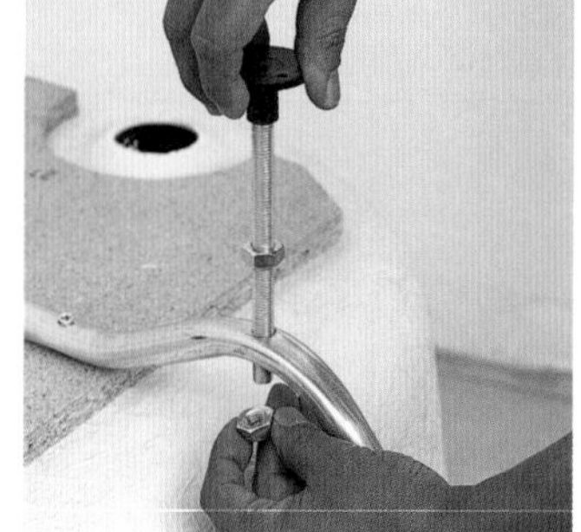

3 Screw each leg cradle to the baseboard through the pre-drilled holes. Place the adjustable bath feet into the holes in the cradles and loosely fit the locking nuts. Roughly set each leg to the same height.

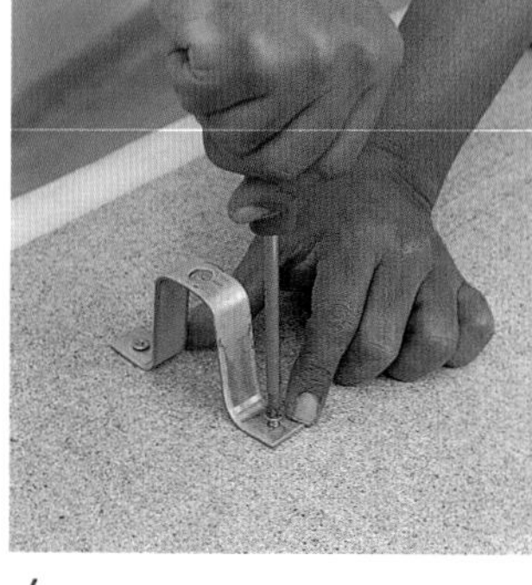

4 Screw the centre support foot bracket to the middle of the baseboard, and screw in the adjustable foot.

5 Screw the wall brackets to the timber frame on the sides of the bath. They should be about 150mm from each end. With a helper, turn the bath back over so it is standing on its feet.

6 Push the flexible overflow pipe into the back of the overflow hole, remembering to fit the rubber washer supplied. The other end attaches to the trap (see Step 8).

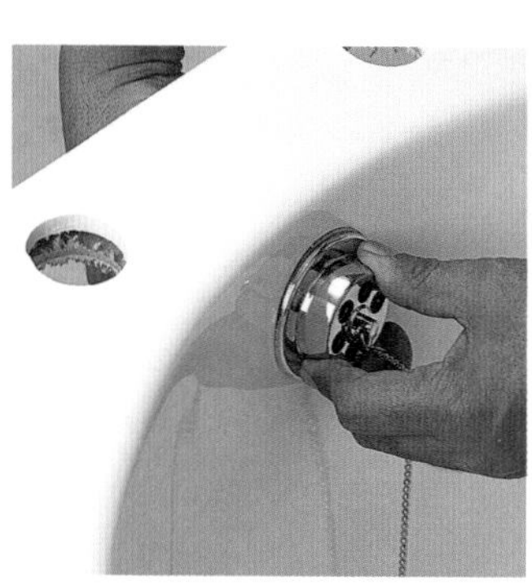

7 Insert the overflow outlet, check the washers are in place, and screw on the back nut.

8 Fit the waste trap to the bath's waste outlet.

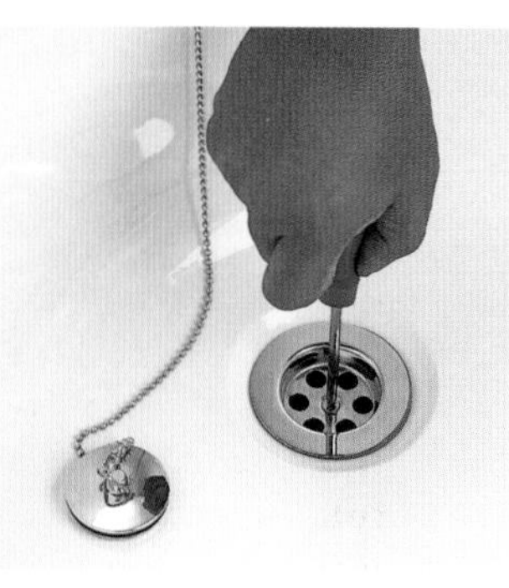

9 Run a bead of sanitary silicone sealant under the waste outlet fitting and screw it down, making sure any rubber washers are fitted according to the manufacturer's instructions.

IDEAL TOOL

Adjustable spanner

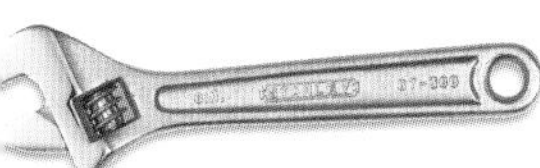

The movable jaws of an adjustable spanner can grip nuts of different sizes. The nut should fit right into the jaws of the spanner; don't try to grip it with the tips.

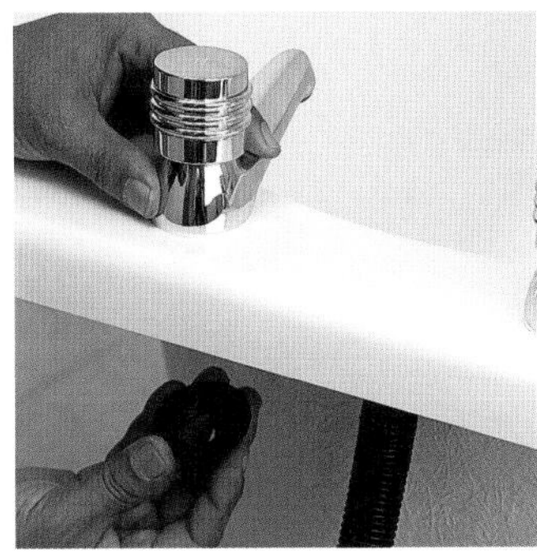

1 Insert the hot and cold taps through the holes. Put on the washers and plastic nuts using an adjustable spanner or basin wrench. Don't overtighten.

Fitting the taps

Check the diameter of the inlet pipes and join them to the taps with suitable flexible connectors. This will make adjustment easier if there is any misalignment.

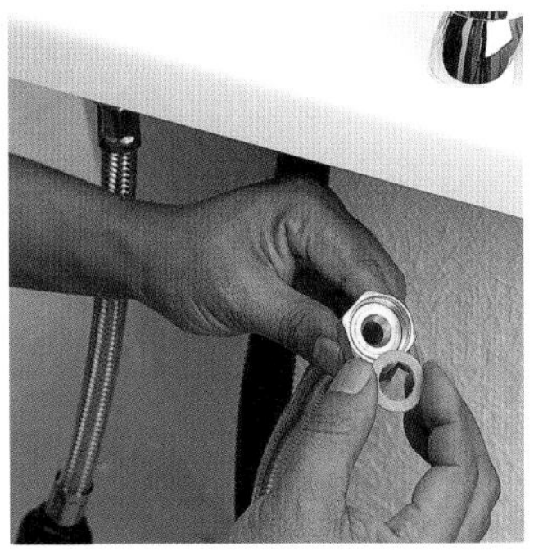

2 Fit a fibre washer to each tap connector, and screw on each tap.

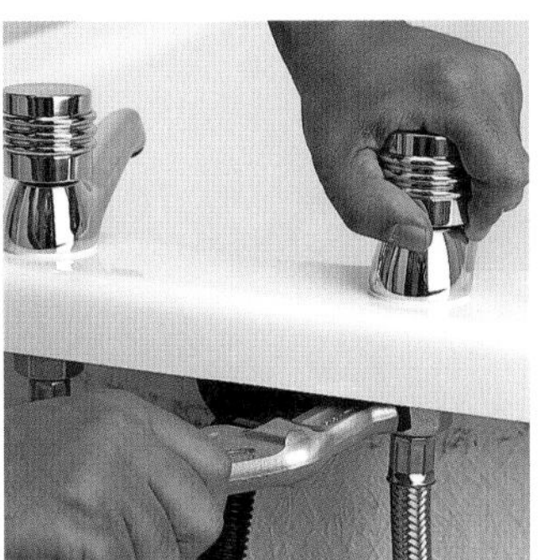

3 Grip each tap firmly and tighten the connector with an adjustable spanner or pipe grips.

Fixing the bath in place

Now you are ready to attach your bath to the wall and floor, and to fit bath panels to the sides and end. To cut the panels to fit around skirting or pipes, use a small fine-toothed saw or very sharp knife.

SAFETY FIRST

Use an electronic detector to check for hidden pipes and cables before you drill, both under the floor and behind the wall. Don't risk a flood or, worse, electrocution!

1 Put the bath in position and use a spirit level to make final adjustments to the feet. Allow for the height of the bath side and end panels. Mark the positions for the wall fixing brackets and the feet fixing screws.

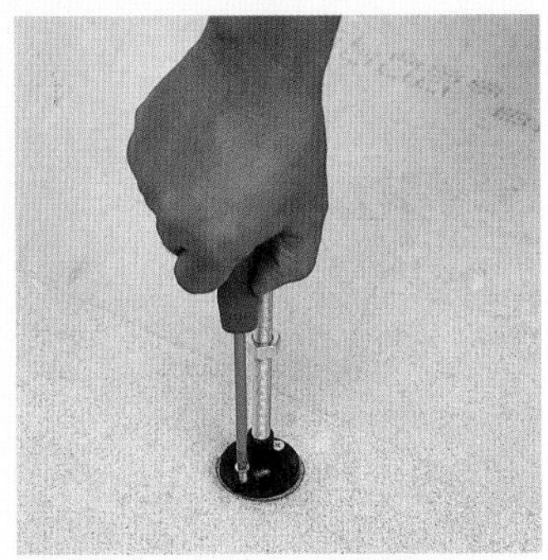

2 Lift the bath away. Remove the feet from the leg cradles. Check for hidden pipes or cables under the floor, then drill pilot holes and screw the feet down with 25mm screws. On a solid floor use a hammer drill and plug the holes.

3 Check for pipes or cables then drill the wall where you have marked the positions for the wall brackets. Get someone to help you lift the bath onto the feet. Double-check that the height is correct then tighten the locking nuts to secure the feet to the legs. Fix the wall brackets to a masonry wall with plugs and screws, or to plasterboard with hollow-wall fixings (see pages 368–69).

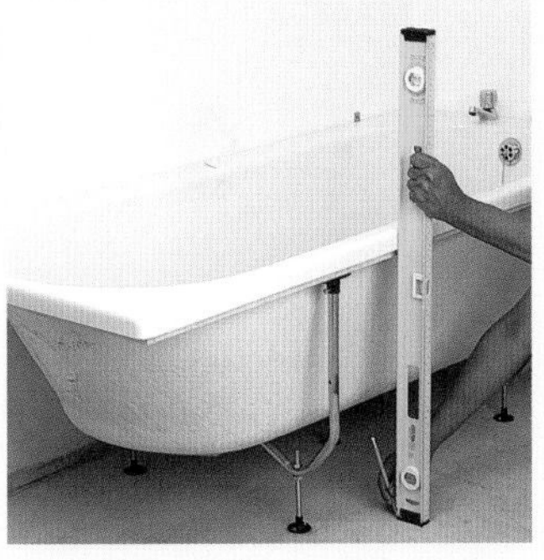

4 Stand a spirit level vertically against the side of the bath. Mark a pencil line against the inside of the spirit level on the floor. Do this in several positions along the side of the bath. Use a straightedge to join up the lines. The manufacturer's instructions will give you the thickness of the side panels (with profiled panels this can be tricky to measure). Use this to measure and mark the inside edge of the panel on the floor.

5 Cut four 150mm lengths of timber to make floor-fixing battens. Drill two pilot holes into each one and position them so that the outer edge of each is in line with the inner lines you have marked. Space them equally around the bath and fix them to the floor using 45mm screws.

6 Insert the top of the end panel behind the front flange of the bath and rest the bottom against the batten. Do the same with the side panel. Drill pilot holes through the panels and into the battens, and then screw them in place.

SHOWERS TYPES AND INSTALLATION

It's important to choose a shower that is compatible with your home's plumbing system (see pages 294–95 to identify the type you have). If you have a gravity-fed system – in other words you have a hot water cylinder and a cold water storage cistern in the loft – you have the most options: you can choose a mixer shower with or without a pump, a power shower or an electric shower. If you have a combination boiler or your cold water comes directly off the mains you can only install a mixer shower or an electric shower; you can't attach a pump to a combi boiler or a mains supply.

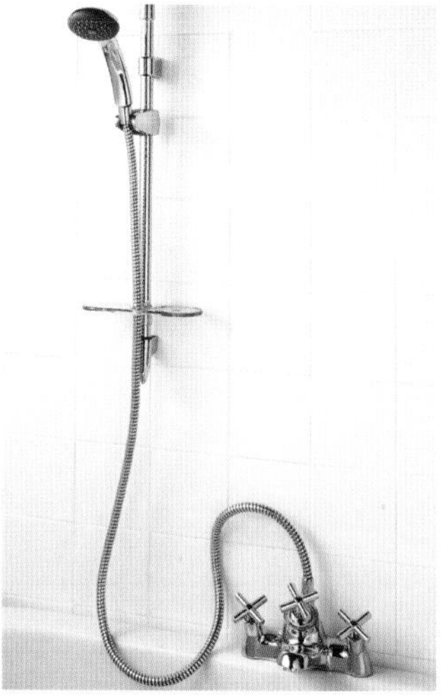

Basic mixer

A basic mixer shower is cheap and easy to install with no new plumbing or electrical connections. The supply of hot and cold water is controlled simply by turning the bath taps. The downside is that it can be fiddly to achieve the temperature you want, and the temperature can be affected if someone draws water elsewhere in the house.

Thermostatic mixer

With a thermostatic mixer, you set the temperature you want on a manual control and the thermostat maintains that temperature to within 2°C even if water is drawn off elsewhere in the house. You can install it over a bath or in a separate shower cubicle. And if you have a gravity-fed water system, you can add a booster pump (see below).

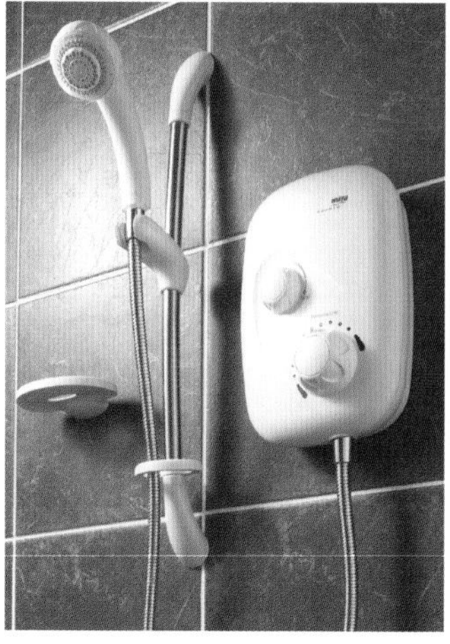

Power shower

A power shower works just like a thermostatic mixer, with one key difference: it has a built-in electric pump to boost the flow rate. It makes an excellent choice if you have low water pressure in your home – but like any pump, it's only compatible with a gravity-fed plumbing system.

Electric shower

This kind of shower works like a kettle: it requires only a cold water supply, which is warmed by heating elements inside the unit. The higher the kilowatt rating, the more powerful the shower, though the force of its spray may weaken in winter when the incoming mains water is colder and so takes longer to heat up.

Pump it up

Adding a booster pump to a thermostatic mixer shower can more than double the flow rate. The pump can be hidden under a bath or tucked away in an airing cupboard or loft, so you will not see it though you may hear it in action. But remember that you cannot connect a pump to a combi boiler or to a cold water supply coming straight off the mains. And to get the most out of your pump, it might be necessary to install a bigger hot water cylinder.

Fitting a thermostatic mixer shower

You can supply a thermostatic mixer shower, with or without a pump, via branch pipes from the hot and cold plumbing system. Try to join them as near as possible to the cold and hot water tanks, and run them to the shower position and through the wall using the techniques described on pages 300–2.

The hot and cold water pressure in a gravity-fed system is determined by the height of the cold water tank above the shower. Without a pump, you need a minimum of 1m between the bottom of the tank and the shower head to produce a reasonable flow rate and pressure. If you don't have enough difference in height then you must either raise the cold water tank or install a pump in the system.

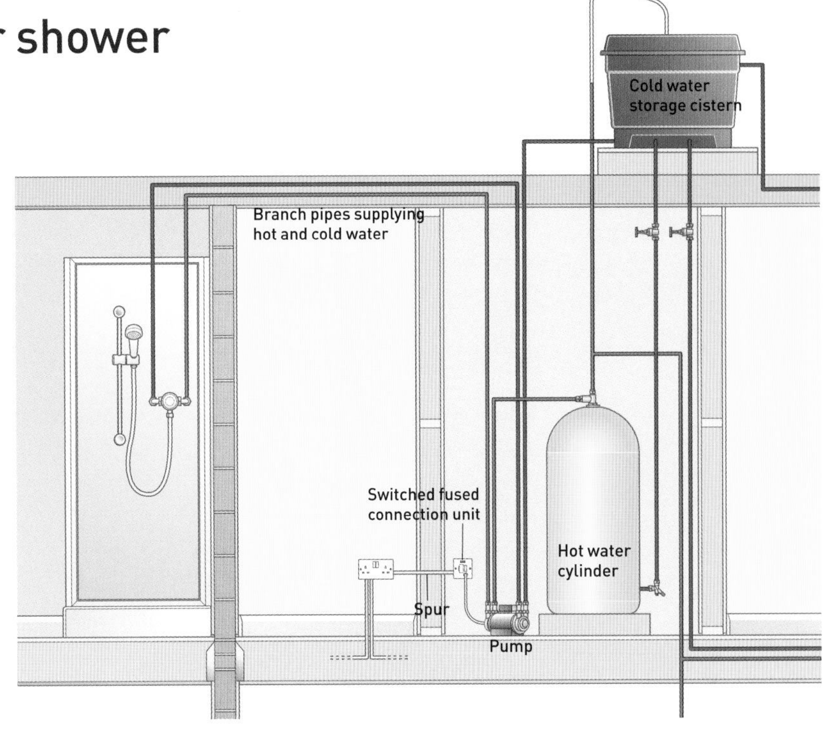

Fitting the mixer valve and rail

The rail should be set high enough to accommodate the tallest user – but not so low that the shower head will dangle any less than 25mm from the spillover level of the shower tray or bath, or a nearby basin. Otherwise you risk back-siphonage of used water into your household supply.

TOOLS MATERIALS

- **adjustable spanner**
- **chinagraph pencil**
- **pipe and cable detector**
- **hammer-action drill with masonry bit**
- **spirit level**

- sanitary silicone sealant
- thermostatic mixer shower and rail with fittings
- 2 couplers
- wallplugs

1 Seal the hole around each inlet pipe with sanitary silicone sealant. Flush out the pipework by briefly turning on the hot and cold water supply. Then – before attaching the pipe trims – fix a coupler onto each pipe and attach the thermostatic mixer valve using an adjustable spanner. Turn on the hot and cold water to check for leaks. If all is watertight, turn off the water again, remove the mixer, fit the chrome pipe trims, and refit the mixer valve.

2 Fit the lever and holder to the slider rail. Place the brackets on the ends of the rail and mark the position of the fixing hole for the lowest bracket.

3 Check there are no hidden pipes or cables with an electronic detector, then drill where you have marked the position of the lower bracket. Insert a wallplug and squeeze onto it a spot of sanitary silicone sealant.

4 Remove the slider rail from the brackets and fix the bottom bracket to the bottom hole using the screw supplied. To find the position of the top fixing hole place the rail back onto the bottom bracket. Put the other mounting bracket onto the top of the rail. Use a spirit level to check it is vertical and mark the top fixing hole on the wall.

5 Remove the rail and drill and plug the wall as before. Screw the top bracket in with the rail in place. Finally fit bracket covers onto the top and bottom brackets.

SHOWERS INSTALLING AN ENCLOSURE

Shower enclosures can be fitted into the corner of a room or against a flat wall. Buy one as part of a new bathroom or add one to your existing suite. The doors can be hinged, folded, sliding or pivoted. If space is tight, sliding or folding doors are the least intrusive option.

YOU CAN DO IT

Seal the joins

Sanitary silicone sealant gives a flexible waterproof seal around bathroom fittings. Run a bead of sealant around the top of the shower tray and the outside of the enclosure – but don't fill the drainage channels on the inside of a shower enclosure, or you will cause a flood.

The waste pipes and trap

Before choosing a shower enclosure, you need to work out how you are going to run the drainage pipes, and check how much height you need under the tray for the pipework. You may be able to cut a hole in the floor to install the waste pipe. If so, you will also need to make an access hatch: either extend the hole for the waste trap beyond where the outside edge of the shower tray will be; or make a separate hatch nearby, within reach of the trap. If your floor is solid, or you cannot achieve enough of a fall for drainage under a suspended floor, you could opt for an enclosure with a step up to the tray; or you could raise the tray above floor level by installing it on a plinth.

If you don't have enough space under the shower tray to fit a shallow P-trap (see page 303), you could fit a compact trap (right). This is specially designed to give the necessary water seal while being shallow enough to fit under most modern shower trays. It has a removable grid for easy cleaning.

TOOLS MATERIALS

- **adjustable spanner**
- **trowel**
- **spirit level**
- **junior hacksaw**
- **cross-head screwdriver**
- **chinagraph pencil**
- **pipe and cable detector**
- **hammer-action drill with masonry and twist bits**

- shower tray
- shower enclosure and fittings
- sanitary silicone sealant
- ready-mix mortar
- wallplugs

Fitting the shower tray

Once the waste pipework is prepared, you are ready to install the shower tray and connect its waste outlet to the trap. Read the manufacturer's installation instructions too, since different designs may be fitted in slightly different ways.

1 Hold the tray on its side and run a bead of sanitary silicone sealant around the waste hole.

2 Insert the waste outlet into the hole, so that it sits into the sealant. Make sure that you have fitted any washers supplied, and screw on the locking nut using an adjustable spanner. Fit the trap to the waste outlet.

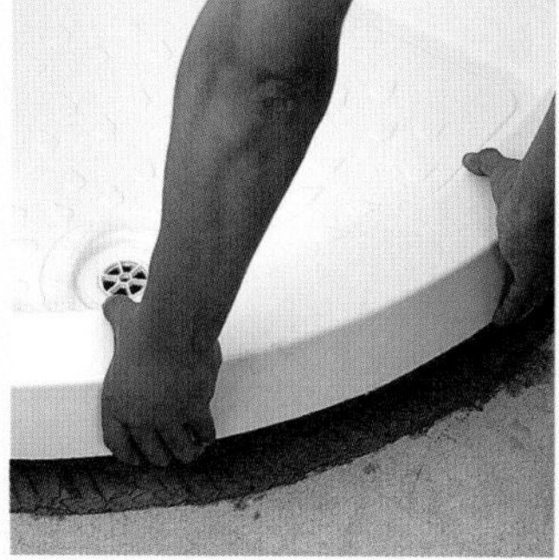

3 Mix the mortar and use a trowel to lay a thin bed on the floor where the tray will be positioned. Rest the tray in place.

4 Bed the tray down into the mortar and level it with a spirit level. If you can't get it exactly level you may need to take up the tray and adjust the mortar. Tidy the edges and remove any excess mortar with the trowel. Open the floor hatch and connect the trap to the waste pipe.

Fitting the shower enclosure

The shower tray, mixer valve and all pipework and tiling should already be in place before you fit the shower enclosure. Shown here is a corner enclosure with curved sliding doors; there are lots of designs available, each installed in a slightly different way, so do read the manufacturer's installation instructions. With any enclosure it is vital that the wall and tray are fully waterproof, and that the uprights of the frame are vertical.

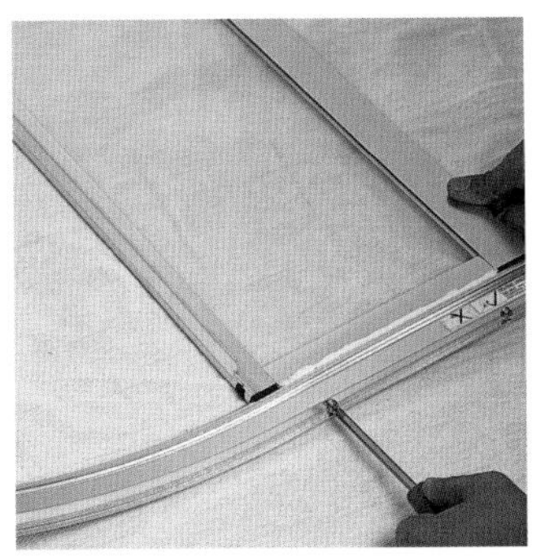

1 Lie the two fixed side panels flat and run a generous bead of sanitary silicone sealant into the curved channels at the top and bottom. Then attach the head and sill rails with the screws provided; don't overtighten them.

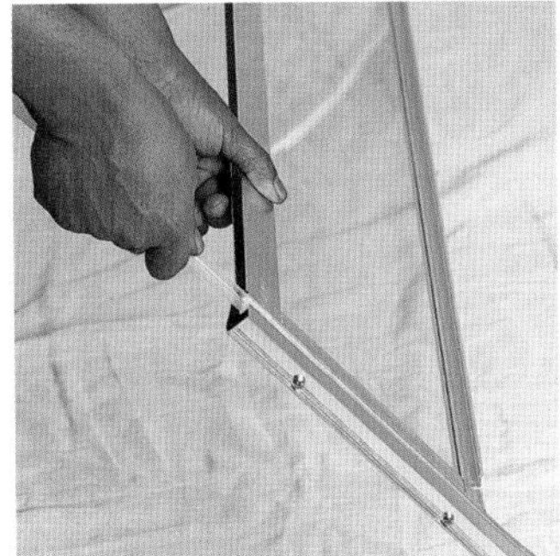

2 Slide the plastic guide tracks into the head and sill rails.

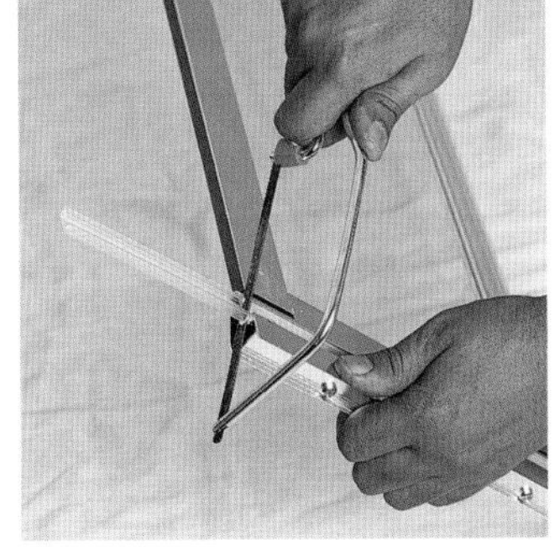

3 Use a junior hacksaw to shorten the plastic guide tracks if they are too long.

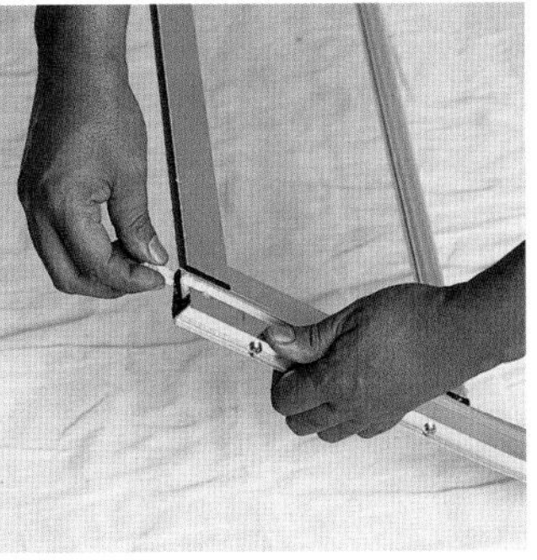

4 Push two door stops into the guide track in the head and sill rails. Move them into the middle but don't fix them yet.

5 Stand the shower enclosure upright and slide the curved sliding doors into the head and sill rails, making quite sure that the doors are the right way around. Then insert another doorstop into both the head and sill rails.

6 Attach the wall channels to each side of the enclosure and stand it on the tray. Check it is vertical using a spirit level. From the inside of the enclosure, use a chinagraph pencil to mark the position for the fixing holes through the pre-drilled holes in the wall channels.

7 Remove the enclosure and check for hidden pipes and cables behind the fixing positions with an electronic detector. If all is clear then drill fixing holes in the marked positions. Push wallplugs into the holes, making sure they go in beyond the depth of the tile.

8 Run a continuous bead of sanitary silicone sealant down both wall channels. Put the enclosure onto the base, and screw in the fixing screws. Remove any excess sealant. Refer to the instructions to make final adjustments to the sliding doors.

9 From the inside, drill through the holes in the wall channels and into the frame. Secure with the screws provided and cover the heads with screw caps. Drill through the plastic track and inner head channel then screw the doorstops in position.

10 Seal the join between the tray and the tiled wall with a continuous bead of sanitary silicone sealant. Do the same around the outside edges of the enclosure.

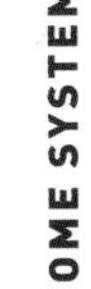

SHOWERS ELECTRIC SHOWERS

An electric shower has an element like a kettle that heats the water as it passes through. You control the temperature by modifying the rate that the water passes over the element. As most don't have a thermostat, if the temperature of the incoming water varies, then so too will the temperature of the shower. An electric shower can be mounted over the bath or set in a cubicle.

Preparing the pipework

Before you fit the shower you need to prepare the pipework and install an electricity supply. Run a single 15mm pipe from the cold water supply near the storage tank to the wall where you intend to fit the shower. Hold the shower unit in place and mark the position for the inlet pipe and power supply cable. Use a pipe and cable detector to check there are no hidden pipes or cables before drilling into the wall. Run the pipe through the wall at the marked position. Fit an isolating valve in the pipe and fit the correct connector for the unit.

Providing the power supply

Drill a hole in the wall for the electric cable, alongside the water inlet pipe. The size of cable required will depend on the length of the run and the kilowatt rating of the shower unit: check the manufacturer's instructions. Run cable from the shower unit position to a ceiling-mounted double-pole pull-cord switch. This should have an on/off indicator and must not be sited in Hazard Zones 1 or 2 as defined by the IEE Wiring Regulations (see page 279). An electric shower needs its own dedicated circuit from the consumer unit, and for safety you must get an electrician to make the final connection for you. To protect against electrocution, it is advisable that the circuit is protected by an RCD (residual current device, see page 290).

Fitting an electric shower

When you decide on the position of the shower unit make sure you leave enough room around the shower to remove the front cover, as it may need servicing some time in the future. Depending on the type of unit, the water supply pipe may enter from the top, bottom or rear. Make sure you have the recommended amount of cable emerging from the wall to connect to the terminal block. The instructions with the shower will tell you how to do this. Before you connect the unit, turn on the water to flush any debris from the water inlet pipe, as any small particles could damage the new shower. Then turn the water off and drain the pipe.

SAFE ELECTRICS

- Switch off at the mains then isolate the circuit by removing the circuit fuse (put it in your pocket) or locking it, or switching off the circuit breaker. Never take risks with electrical safety!
- Remember that different rules of electrical safety apply in a bathroom. If you prefer a wall-mounted switch, you must site it outside the room.
- Don't forget that all new pipework in a bath- or shower-room must be cross-bonded to earth (see page 267).
- If in doubt, always consult a qualified electrician.

TOOLS MATERIALS

- **chinagraph pencil**
- **pliers**
- **pipe and cable detector**
- **hammer-action drill with masonry bit**
- **screwdriver**
- **pipe wrench**

- sanitary silicone sealant
- 15mm compression fitting
- electric shower and fittings
- masking tape
- wallplugs

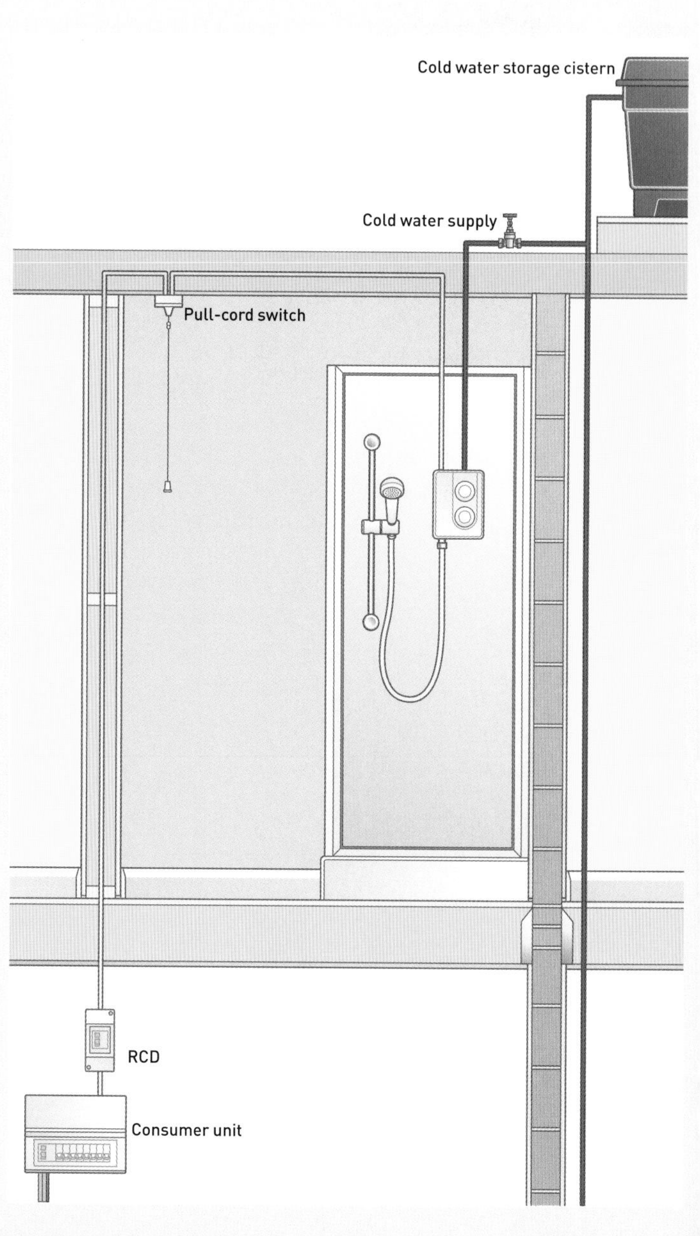

1 Hold the shower unit in position and mark the fixing holes with a chinagraph pencil. Drill holes at the marked positions with a masonry bit. On a tiled surface use a tile bit or stick masking tape on the tiles to stop the bit slipping. Fit wallplugs and squeeze a little sanitary silicone sealant onto each one.

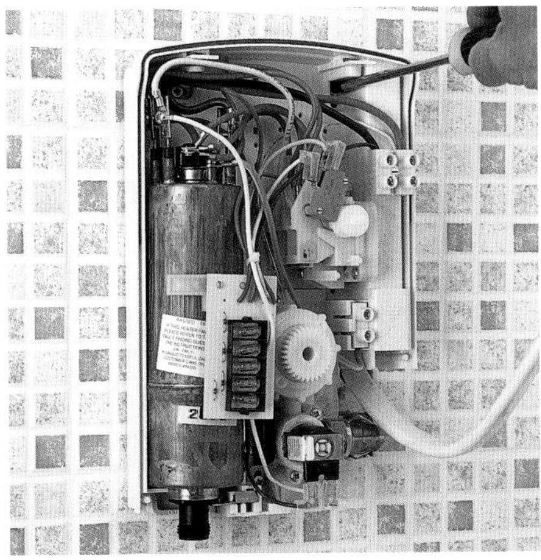

2 Feed the pipe and electric cable through the backplate of the unit. Screw it to the wall using the screws supplied.

ECO SHOWERS

Electric shower units are both economic and energy efficient. They use less water than any other system and because the water is heated as you need it there is no wasteful draw on the hot water. You only heat it as you use it.

3 Connect the inlet pipe to the shower unit using a pipe wrench to tighten the compression fitting.

4 Connect the cable to the unit by connecting its live and neutral cores to the terminals marked 'load' and its earth core to the earth terminal.

5 Fit the cover according to the manufacturer's instructions, ensuring that the rubber seal is in place.

6 To fit the rail, follow Steps 1–5 on page 317. Don't forget to position it high enough that the shower head cannot dangle less than 25mm from the spillover level of the bath, shower tray, wash basin or bidet, otherwise you might get back-siphonage of dirty water.

7 Screw one end of the hose to the handset and the other to the shower unit. Be sure to include any washers supplied. Follow the test procedure described in the instructions to ensure the shower is working correctly.

Most homes now have central heating systems and while you need a qualified professional to install them, there is a lot you can do to maintain them yourself if you understand the basic principles. The two main types of system are wet central heating, which works by circulating hot water through a system of pipes, and dry central heating, in which warm air is blown through a series of ducts.

What is central heating?

In a central heating system, heat is produced from a single source – usually a boiler – and distributed throughout the house, either in the form of hot water or hot air. Some systems allow the whole house or just a part of it to be heated according to your needs, usually much more economically than if you had individual heaters sited in each room. You can get central heating systems with automatic temperature control and, when teamed with efficient insulation, these can provide substantial savings on overall heating costs.

Wet central heating

In a wet central heating system, a boiler heats water, which is usually pumped around a circuit of pipes to radiators fitted throughout the house. Each radiator has valves that control the rate at which water flows through it, thus controlling the amount of time the water spends in the radiator and the amount of heat that is given off. When the water leaves the radiator, it is piped back to the boiler for reheating. The boiler may be gas- or oil-fired, or it may burn solid fuel, and it may also provide domestic hot water.

Although some heat is lost from the pipes as the water flows around the system, their narrow diameter and the speed of the flow keeps this to a minimum. A well-designed system may have several short circuits radiating from the pump, rather than one large one, ensuring that the last radiator on each circuit heats up just as efficiently as the first.

Modern systems are invariably forced-flow (pumped) but older systems may operate on gravity flow, with circulation around the system created simply by hot water rising and cold water sinking. Such systems use larger-diameter pipes, since the flow is much slower than in a pumped system. Modern solid-fuel boilers must be connected to a system designed at least in part to allow gravity circulation. This is because – unlike a gas- or oil-fired boiler – a solid-fuel boiler cannot be switched off instantly. If its pump were to fail, water in the boiler could overheat severely, with potentially explosive consequences.

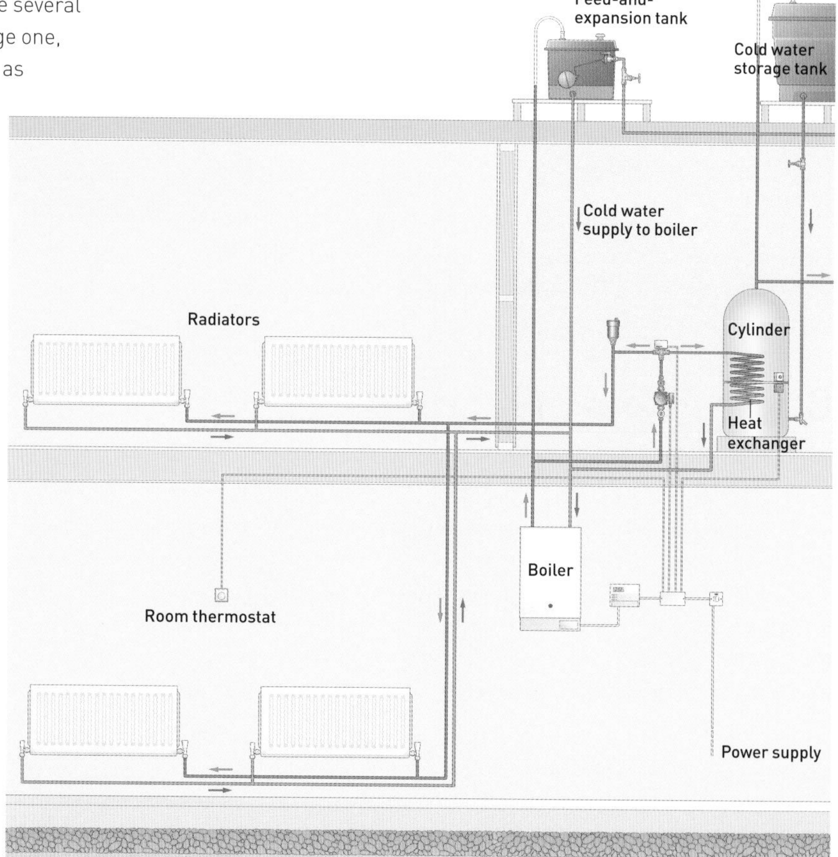

ECO HEATING

Although gas, oil and solid fuel all come from non-renewable resources, gas is the cleanest-burning of the three fuels, followed by oil and then solid fuel. Modern boilers, particularly condensing boilers (see page 324), are much more efficient than older appliances, extracting far more heat from a given quantity of fuel. So they are not only kinder on your pocket, by reducing fuel costs, but also better for the environment because they reduce emissions too.

Pipework

The radiator circuits in most modern wet central heating systems are run in standard 15mm copper pipe, while pipes linking the boiler and pump and the points where the circuits split off will be 22mm or 28mm diameter. Soldered capillary joints are best (apart from connections to boiler, pump and valves), as these are least likely to leak.

More modern systems have a two-pipe layout, where hot water is carried from the pump to the inlet valve of each radiator by a flow pipe, which terminates at the last radiator on the circuit. A second pipe, the return pipe, collects the cooled water from the radiators and carries it back to the boiler for reheating. In the older single-pipe layout, the hot water passes through one radiator, then is returned to the flow pipe to be carried on to the next and so on around the circuit, losing some of its heat each time. Consequently, radiators towards the end of the circuit have to be bigger in order to give off the same amount of heat.

A variation of the two-pipe layout uses small-diameter microbore pipe, which is available in 8mm and 10mm sizes. It is supplied in coils and is very easy to bend, so you can feed the pipe through cavities and around corners without the need for joints. However, these narrow pipes only carry enough water to heat one radiator at a time, so each radiator must have its own circuit. These radiate out from fittings known as manifolds – short sections of large-diameter pipe with a series of compression connectors down each side. The manifold is divided internally, allowing one end to be connected to the pipe from the pump and the other to the return pipe to the boiler. Thus, the flow pipes to several radiators are connected to one end of the manifold and the returns to the other. Plastic pipes have been developed for use in wet central heating systems, but they can't be connected directly to a boiler; a short length of copper pipe must be used instead.

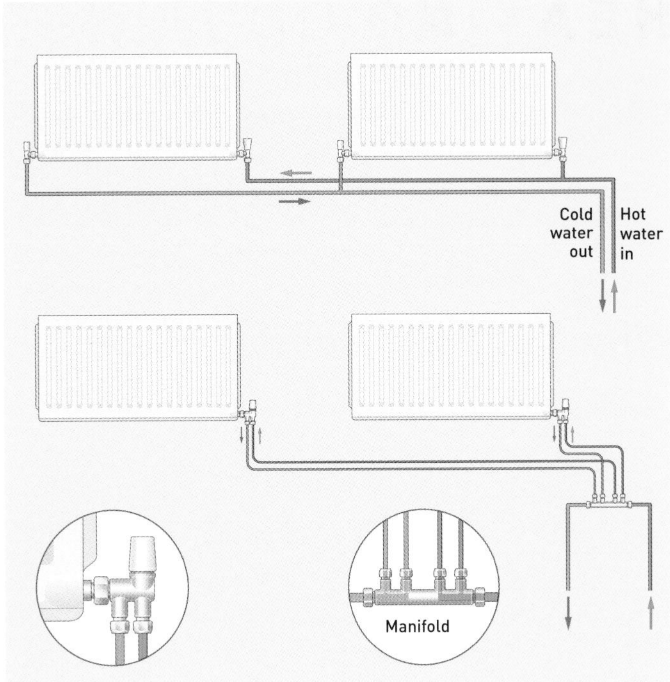

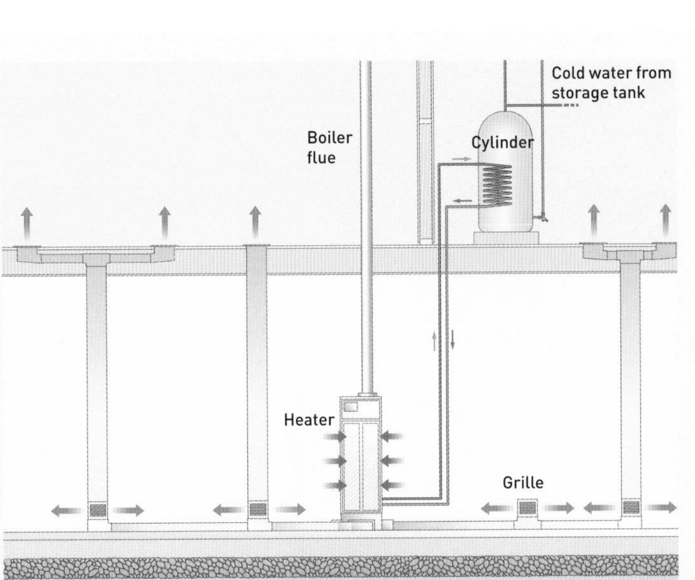

Dry central heating

In a dry central heating system, air is warmed by a single heat source and blown through a series of large ducts to heat the rooms of the house. Each duct terminates in a floor or wall grille, which can be opened and closed to control heat output. Some systems rely on an electric storage heater to warm the air; others use a fuel such as gas. You can use overnight off-peak electricity to heat firebricks in an electric storage heater, and then use their stored heat to warm the house during the day.

Depending on the type of heater, some systems are also able to provide hot water. This type of heating system is only really suitable for installation when the house is being built, since the ducts are very bulky and must be incorporated into the structure if they are to be unobtrusive.

Other forms of heating

Although strictly speaking not central heating, there are other dry systems that can be employed to heat a whole house. These include individual room storage heaters, which use off-peak electricity to heat firebricks that give off heat during the day.

Another option is underfloor heating, in which hot water pipes or electric elements are laid under the floors. These are designed to produce enough heat to warm the air of the room without making the floor uncomfortable underfoot.

HEATING BOILERS AND RADIATORS

ECO HEATING

Reduce your heating thermostat by 1°C – you won't notice the difference in temperature, but you will save energy and money.

Whether you already have a wet central heating system or are having one installed, understanding the various components will help you choose the most efficient use of the system for your home and keep running costs down.

What sort of boiler?

Condensing boilers

For maximum efficiency and economy, a condensing boiler is the best choice. It is designed so that the water passing through the boiler extracts heat from the flue gases – which normally would be lost to the atmosphere – before entering the heat exchanger. That means less fuel needs to be burned to bring the water up to the required temperature. As the flue gases are cooled, any water vapour present condenses out and is discharged through a small drainpipe. Gas and oil versions are available. If your boiler is powerful enough, it can also be used to heat a hot water cylinder by means of an indirect circuit. A professional heating engineer will advise on the heat output you need, which depends on the size of your property.

Combi boilers

If you are in a small property where it would be difficult to find space for a hot water cylinder, a combination (or combi) boiler is for you. This contains two heat exchangers – one for the central heating, the other to act as a multi-point instantaneous water heater. It is connected to the mains and is capable of supplying all the hot taps in the house. Gas and oil versions are available. The only disadvantage is that the hot water can run more slowly than the cold, because it is only heated when you turn on the tap.

Standard boilers

Standard, non-condensing boilers are run on a variety of fuels, including solid fuels. Modern fan-assisted boilers have good heat efficiency, but if your boiler is more than 15 years old, you may find that you make substantial savings on your heating bills by installing a modern version.

Back boilers

The final type of boiler is the back boiler, which is fitted behind a radiant fire, burning either gas or solid fuel. In gas-fired versions, the boiler may be operated independently of the fire, but in solid-fuel versions, the fire must be lit for water to be heated.

Where to install a boiler?

Standard, combination and condensing boilers may be freestanding or wall-mounted, although solid-fuel types are freestanding only. They are compact, too, which makes accommodating them in a kitchen, bathroom or utility room quite easy.

The other factor you must take into account when choosing the position for a boiler is the type of flue that will be required. Boilers must be connected to a flue so that the gases produced by burning the fuel can be discharged to the atmosphere. In many cases, this can be an existing chimney, although it must be lined to suit the fuel being burned because the gases can have a corrosive effect on the structure. When using a conventional flue of this type, it is essential that the room where the boiler is situated is well ventilated to ensure sufficient air for combustion and to prevent a build-up of poisonous fumes.

Fumes are not a problem if the boiler has a balanced, or room-sealed, flue. This is basically a divided horizontal duct that passes through an outside wall; air is drawn in along one passage and flue gases are discharged through the other. A balanced flue would be essential for a boiler in a garage, or there would be a danger of petrol fumes from a car being sucked into the combustion chamber and causing an explosion. There are special regulations regarding balanced flues – your heating engineer will advise on this.

What sort of fuel?

If you have access to mains gas, this is the cheapest fuel for your boiler to burn (see ECO HEATING, page 322). If not, the second cheapest option is oil, followed by solid fuel (such as anthracite), and then LPG (liquefied petroleum gas).

Oil and LPG can be stored in bulk tanks; LPG can also be supplied in large cylinders, but this is the least convenient and most expensive way of using the fuel. Solid fuel may be delivered loose or in pre-packed bags, but it is dirty, and you have to stoke the boiler regularly to keep it burning. That said, some solid-fuel boilers have hopper feeds that cut down on the amount of stoking required. You also need some means of disposing of the ash after burning.

In a standard boiler, the fuel is burned beneath a chamber, known as a heat exchanger, through which the water passes to be warmed. Then it is pumped around the heating circuit or circulates by gravity. This basic design can operate on gas, oil or solid fuel.

SAFETY FIRST

The quality of installation can affect the safe operation of a central heating system, so when having a new system installed or an existing one updated, it is essential to employ a qualified heating engineer. They will work to industry standards and will be able to advise on the correct and safe siting of the boiler and flue. The firm should be registered with the Council for Registered Gas Installers (CORGI) if you are using gas as a fuel, or the Heating and Ventilating Contractors Association (HVCA) for other types of fuel.

Types of radiators

A wet central heating system delivers its heat by radiation and convection. You can feel radiation as heat emitted from a hot surface, but convection warms the air and, in doing so, sets up a gentle circulation centred on the heat source – the warm air rises and cooler air flows in to take its place; in this way, the temperature of the whole room rises gradually.

The simplest form of heat emitter is the panel radiator. Although called a radiator, in fact over half of its heat output occurs through convection. It has a corrugated body to increase its surface area and ensure maximum heat output. Where space is limited, double-panel radiators are ideal. Another means of improving output is to use a convector radiator, which has a number of fins on the back to increase convection.

Convectors can also be installed in a wet central heating system. These emit heat purely by convection and comprise a large number of fins attached to the hot pipe and contained in a box-like housing. Warm air escapes from the top and cool air is drawn in at the bottom. Usually, an adjustable damper is provided to control heat output. Some convectors are designed for fitting inconspicuously at skirting level, while others have electric fans to boost output.

Radiator valves

Radiators normally have a threaded hole, or tapping, at each corner. The bottom two are for the valves – the lockshield valve, which regulates the flow of water through the radiator and thus heat output, and the wheel or manual valve, for turning the radiator off and on. One of the top tappings will be fitted with a bleed valve, a simple tapered screw that allows you to remove air from the system; the other has a blanking plug.

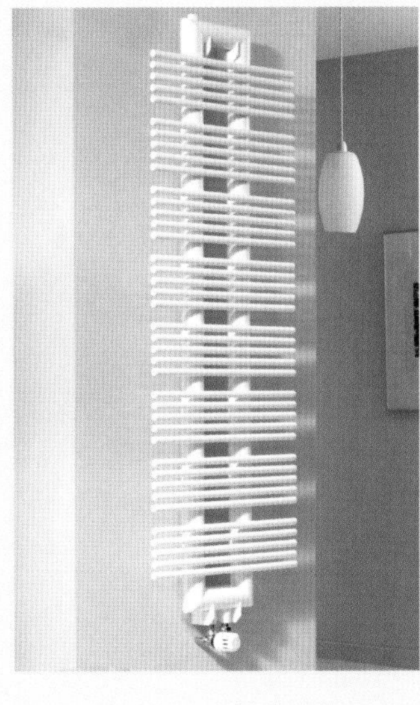

Radiator design

Radiators and towel warmers needn't just be functional heat providers. These days there are lots of stylish options to complement every interior – see www.diy.com for ideas.

Which controls do you want?

Gas- and oil-fired wet central heating systems can incorporate a number of controls that allow you to make the most efficient use of the system, directing heat where it is needed most and allowing you to shut them off when heat is not required. Solid-fuel systems are much less adjustable, simply because it is not possible to turn the heat off and on at will.

Gas and oil boilers have an internal thermostat that regulates the temperature of the heated water by turning the boiler off and on. Solid-fuel boilers have a thermostatically controlled damper that adjusts the amount of air being drawn in, varying the rate of burning and, therefore, heat output. Both types of control can be adjusted manually.

Roomstats

Many systems incorporate a room thermostat, or roomstat, which switches the heating on and off in accordance with the temperature you have selected. It is normally sited in the living room or hall, and it operates on the assumption that a rise or drop in temperature in its vicinity will be matched by a corresponding rise or drop throughout the house.

The problem with a roomstat is that it doesn't accommodate local temperature variations – caused perhaps by the sun shining through windows or an open fire in a living room. You can reduce the heat output of an individual radiator by closing a manual radiator valve, but much more efficient is to install thermostatic valves, which will do this automatically for you and then open again when the room temperature drops (see page 328).

Time switches and programmers

A simple time switch will turn the system on and off at pre-set times of the day, but a programmer allows independent operation of the heating and hot water circuits at different times of the day. Even greater flexibility is provided by a controller, which operates the system at set times and also responds to temperature fluctuations, while a boiler manager ensures that the boiler only runs when necessary by sensing a variety of conditions, including outdoor temperature.

Cylinder thermostats

The temperature of water required to heat radiators is much higher than that needed at the taps (82°C as opposed to 60°C), and a cylinder thermostat will prevent overheating of the hot water supply. When the temperature in the cylinder reaches the set limit, the thermostat operates a motorised valve, shutting off the flow to its heat exchanger. When the water temperature drops, the valve opens again.

Zone valves

Motorised valves, known as zone or mid-position valves, can also be used to shut off parts of the system at specific times of the day when heating is not required in certain rooms. This can be useful in a large house, where you may not want to heat all the bedrooms on upper floors during the day, and is now a requirement in systems heating more than 150m^2.

HEATING TACKLING FAULTS

Different makes and models of boiler have different controls, so keep your boiler operating instructions in a handy place in case of trouble. You can use this fault finder to diagnose some of the most common problems that occur. Many of them have simple solutions, which you should be able to do yourself – but if in doubt, call in an engineer.

Noisy system

Hissing/banging

- The water level in the system might be low. Turn off boiler and pump, and examine the feed-and-expansion cistern in the loft; if it's empty, check that the ball valve is not jammed closed and that the water supply has not been turned off or supply pipe frozen. If you can identify and fix the cause yourself, you can then top up the system water level again, following the boiler operating instructions.
- Substantial deposits of scale can build up in the system in hard-water areas – call an engineer to clean it out. They may decide to fit a hard water filter to stop it happening again.
- It could mean that your boiler thermostat is faulty – call an engineer.
- If you have a solid-fuel system, it could be that the chimney is blocked – try sweeping it (see page 139).
- In a solid-fuel system, noises could indicate that the pump is not working. You can check this yourself, using the boiler operating instructions. Shut down the boiler; check that the pump is turned on and the impeller running by feeling the casing for vibration; if the switch is set to on, but the pump is not running, turn off the power at the mains and check that none of the wiring connections has come loose. If the pump is running, but the outlet pipe is cool, open the bleed valve to release trapped air. If the problem persists, call an engineer.

Creaking from pipework

- This could be caused by hot pipes expanding and rubbing against floor/wall structure or other pipes. Locate the source of the sound; lift floorboards as necessary and open up the holes through which the pipes pass; widen pipe notches in joists (but don't make them deeper, as this will weaken the joists); clip long unsupported pipe runs; pack insulation around and between pipes; where pipes pass through walls, wrap them with fibreglass roof insulation.

Humming in pipes

- It could be that the pump speed is too high or that your pipes are too narrow for the system flow – call an engineer.

Rushing sound in pipes

- This probably means that you have air or gas bubbles in the system. Bleed the radiators (see page 328); if the problem persists, call an engineer.

Cold radiators

All radiators cold when boiler running

- This could mean that your pump is not working. You can test it by following the boiler operating instructions. Shut down the boiler then check that the pump is turned on and the impeller running by feeling the casing for vibration. If the switch is set to on but the pump is not running, turn off the power and check the wiring connections. If the pump is running, but the outlet pipe is cool, open the bleed valve to release trapped air. If the problem persists, call an engineer.
- It may be that your pump thermostat/timer is incorrectly set or faulty. Check and reset, if necessary. If the thermostat/timer is set correctly, turn off the power and check wiring connections, following the operating instructions. If the problem persists, call an engineer.

Some radiators cold

- First you should check if the zone valve thermostat/timer is incorrectly set or faulty; reset it, if necessary. If the thermostat/timer is set correctly, switch off the power and check the wiring connections, using your operating instructions. If the problem persists, call an engineer.
- The zone valve itself may be faulty, or the system may need 'balancing'. Call an engineer.

Single radiator cold

- It may simply be that the radiator's manual control valve is turned off – if so, open it.
- The thermostatic radiator valve could be incorrectly set or faulty. Check and reset, if necessary. If the valve is set correctly but the radiator still doesn't work, try replacing it (see page 328).
- You may have an incorrectly set lockshield valve (see page 325). Open the manual valve fully, then remove the plastic cap from the lockshield valve and use an adjustable spanner to open the valve until the radiator warms up. Next time you have the system serviced, ask the engineer to balance the radiator.
- Heavy corrosion deposits may be blocking the inlet and outlet. Remove the radiator and flush out or replace it, as necessary; add corrosion inhibitor to the system (see page 329).

Top of radiator cold

- This means there is air trapped. Open the bleed valve so that air can escape (see page 328); if the problem persists, call an engineer.

Centre and bottom of radiator cold

- Corrosion is probably restricting the water flow. Remove the radiator and flush out or replace it, as necessary; add corrosion inhibitor to the system (see page 329).

Boiler not working

- First of all, check if the pilot light is extinguished. If it is, re-light it in accordance with the boiler manufacturer's instructions.
- It may be that the temperature setting on the roomstat or boiler thermostat is too low. Check and reset as necessary.
- The system timer/programmer may be incorrectly set or faulty. Check and reset the timer/programmer, as necessary. If the problem persists, call an engineer.
- Overheating caused by the pump shutting down may have caused the thermostat to shut down the boiler too. Confirm that the pump is running and restart the boiler. If the problem persists, call an engineer.
- There may be a problem with the electricity supply. Check some other electrical circuits and if there is a power cut, wait for power to be restored. If a fuse has blown, repair it.
- With combination boilers, it's possible that the water pressure is at an incorrect level. Refer to the operating instructions for the correct figure and check the boiler pressure gauge; if it is too low, you may be able to top up the system at the mains water filling point; otherwise, call an engineer.

Overflow in the roof dripping

- The water level in the feed-and-expansion cistern may be too high, due to a leaking ball valve float or an incorrectly adjusted or faulty ball valve. Turn off the water supply and empty the cistern to below the level of the valve; examine the float and replace, if necessary. Bend the float arm or adjust the valve stop, if necessary. If the float arm/valve is adjusted correctly, fit a new washer to the valve; if the valve is in poor condition, fit a new valve (see page 296).

Leaks

- Leaks could be caused by loose pipe connections. Shut down the boiler and pump; tighten leaking compression fittings, but no more than a quarter-turn; if the problem persists, or soldered joints leak, drain the system (see below) and remake the joints completely (see page 301).
- A pipe may be damaged. Shut down the boiler and pump, drain the system (see below) and replace the damaged section of pipe (see page 300–2).
- If a corroded radiator is leaking, replace the radiator and add corrosion inhibitor to the system (see page 329).

Preventing the system from freezing up

If you go away during the winter and turn off the heating, a severe drop in temperature could cause the water in the system to freeze and burst the pipes, even if they have been lagged. To prevent this you can take one or more of the following steps:

- With gas- and oil-fired systems, turn the roomstat down to its minimum setting so that the heating will come on when the temperature falls.
- If you regularly go away in the winter, have a frost thermostat fitted; this will switch the system on when the temperature drops to freezing and off again when it rises.
- Pipes that are particularly susceptible to freezing may be wrapped with trace heat tape. This is used in conjunction with a frost thermostat; when the temperature drops low enough, the thermostat switches on the tape, which heats the pipe.

Draining and refilling the system

TOOLS MATERIALS

- **adjustable spanner**
- **batten, if required**
- **hosepipe**
- **radiator bleed key**

All wet central heating systems will be provided with at least one draincock to allow the system to be emptied for maintenance or repairs. Usually, this will be in the return pipe close to the boiler. However, where a solid ground floor prevents pipes from being run below it, the pipes will drop down from the ceiling void to supply ground-floor radiators. These sections of pipework will remain full of water when the system is drained from the boiler draincock and will have their own draincocks, allowing them to be emptied separately.

When refilling the system, make sure all draincocks and radiator bleed valves are closed before restoring the water supply to the feed-and-expansion cistern in the loft. As water flows into the system, air will become trapped in the radiators, so bleed each by opening the bleed valve about half a turn, starting at the bottom of the house and working upwards (see page 328). Before turning the pump back on, bleed this too.

1 Before draining the system, switch off the boiler, but allow the pump to run for ten minutes to cool the water. Then turn off the pump and close the stop valve in the pipe supplying the feed-and-expansion cistern. If there is no valve, place a batten across the top of the cistern and tie the ball valve arm to it to prevent the valve from opening. Push one end of a hose on to the outlet of the draincock. Run the hose to an outdoor drain.

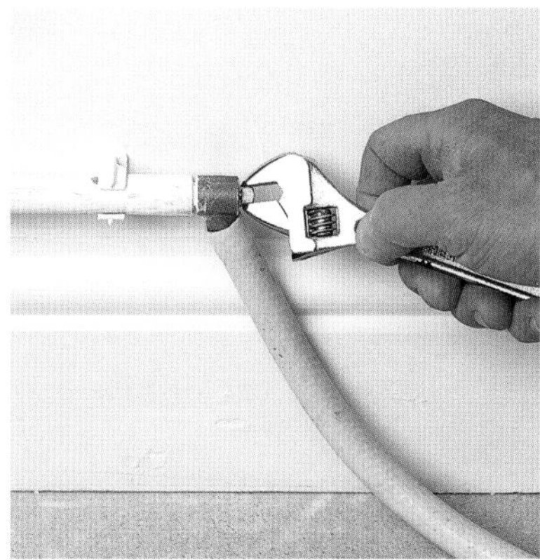

2 Use an adjustable spanner to open the draincock, but do not remove the square valve shank completely. When the feed-and-expansion cistern has emptied, work down through the house, opening radiator bleed valves to release any remaining water trapped in the radiators.

HEATING RADIATORS

Keeping your radiators well-maintained will save energy as they will function more efficiently. They should be bled from time to time to release trapped air, so that they heat up evenly. If a radiator has become corroded or damaged, replacing it with one of the same style and size is a simple job. Another easy improvement is to fit thermostatic radiator valves, which will provide automatic adjustment of each radiator's heat output, ensuring better temperature control throughout your home.

Bleeding radiators

All radiators are provided with a bleed valve in one top corner to allow trapped air to be released, ensuring that the radiator heats up evenly. The valve takes the form of a square shaft inside a threaded plug. Turn off the heating and use a radiator bleed key (or in some cases a flat-head screwdriver) to turn the shaft anti-clockwise by between a quarter- and a half-turn to open the valve – don't unscrew it by more than one complete turn. You will hear the trapped air hissing as it escapes. Hold a cloth beneath the valve to catch any water, and as soon as the first trickle appears close the valve. If you find you have to bleed your radiators frequently, have the system checked by a heating engineer, as there is likely to be a fault somewhere.

Fitting a thermostatic radiator valve

Many central heating systems are controlled by a single thermostat, usually sited in the hall. Unfortunately, this arrangement doesn't take into account local variations in temperature, and some rooms may become too hot or cold unless you keep adjusting the manual radiator valves. The answer is to fit thermostatic valves, which open and close automatically in response to room temperature. In many cases, a thermostatic valve will be a straight replacement for an existing manual valve, but do check first to ensure that it will fit.

TOOLS MATERIALS

- **adjustable spanner**

- thermostatic radiator valve
- new connector, if required
- wire wool
- PTFE tape

1 First drain the heating system (see page 327). Disconnect the valve from the radiator by unscrewing its capnut, but before releasing it completely, slacken the nut holding the valve to the pipe. Then unscrew both nuts fully and lift the valve together with its capnut and olive from the end of the pipe. The radiator here has been removed, but you can replace a valve without taking the radiator off the wall.

2 Clean the end of the pipe with wire wool and slip the capnut and olive of the new valve on to it. Hold the valve in place and screw the capnut on to the valve, making sure the olive is seated properly. Don't tighten the capnut fully at this stage.

3 Fit the radiator with a new connector if necessary, wrap a few turns of PTFE tape around its threads, align the valve and start turning the capnut onto it. Then tighten both capnuts fully. Refill the system, checking for leaks, and finally set the thermostatic valve in accordance with the manufacturer's instructions.

IDEAL TOOL

PTFE tape

This is used by plumbers to ensure a watertight joint on threaded fittings. Just wrap a few turns around the threads before you screw the fitting together.

With both valves turned off, se an adjustable spanner to lacken the capnut holding one f them to the radiator. You may eed to hold the valve body with second spanner to prevent it urning and buckling the pipe.

CO RADIATORS

osition the radiators in ach room with care. If ney are behind large eces of furniture, they ill heat the room much ss efficiently. If you want change the room layout, ou can reposition adiators by running extra engths of copper pipe. If our radiator is on an utside wall, up to 25% of he heat it emits can be bsorbed into the wall. To void this, fit reflective adiator foil behind the adiator to reflect heat ack into the room.

YOU CAN DO IT

Disguising a radiator

If you have ugly old radiators but don't want to replace them, you can install decorative cupboards around them. Wickerwork or lattice fronts allow the heat through into the room.

B&Q

Replacing a radiator

Fortunately you don't have to drain the entire heating system in order to replace a radiator, you just isolate it by closing off the valve at either end. Turn the manual valve clockwise until it won't turn any further. Pull off the plastic shield of the lockshield valve at the other end and turn the square shaft clockwise with an adjustable spanner. Count the number of turns so that you can reset it at the same flow rate; otherwise, you will alter the heat output of the new radiator.

TOOLS MATERIALS

- **2 adjustable spanners**
- **radiator bleed key**
- **drain tray**
- **bucket**
- **large allen key, if required**
- **pipe and cable detector**
- **hammer-action drill with masonry bit**

- cloths
- wire wool
- PTFE tape
- new radiator and brackets

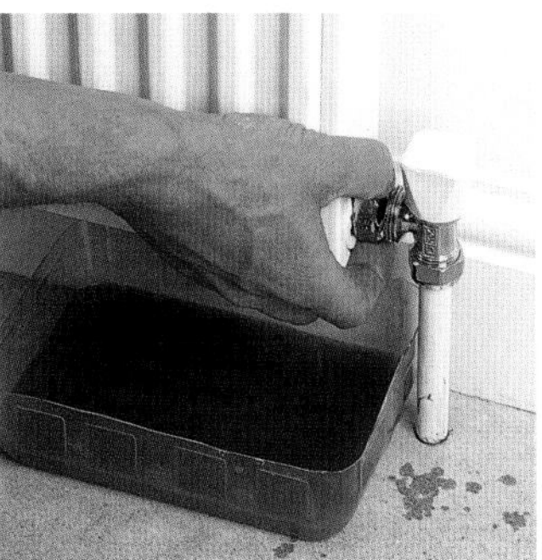

2 Place a shallow tray beneath the valve to catch the water as it drains out. Open the bleed valve at the top of the radiator and loosen the capnut. When the tray is nearly full, re-tighten the capnut and empty the water. Be ready with cloths to mop up any spillage – the water will be filthy. Repeat until all the water has drained out, then disconnect the other valve.

3 Lift the radiator from its wall brackets and tilt it to drain any remaining water into the tray. Get a helper to stuff tissue into the inlet the other end to stop it leaking dirty water. If the existing wall brackets don't suit the new radiator, unscrew them and fit those supplied with the new radiator. Don't forget to check for pipes and cables before drilling new fixing holes.

4 Remove the valve connectors from the old radiator, using an adjustable spanner or large allen key. Clean the threads with wire wool and wind PTFE tape around the threads about five times to ensure a good seal. Screw the connectors into the new radiator, making sure they are tightened fully. Hang the radiator. Connect the valves and reset them, allowing water to enter the radiator. You will need to open the bleed valve about half a turn so that air can escape; close it when water starts to appear.

Adding corrosion inhibitor

Corrosion inhibitor should be added to a system when it is installed, but it can also be added later if required. Make sure you buy a product compatible with the materials your boiler, pipes and radiators are made of; if in doubt, get expert advice. With an older installation, it is a good idea to flush the system first to remove any build-up of corrosion sludge, which can eventually cause the pump to fail. Turn off the heating and allow the water to cool, then drain the system completely (see page 327). Refill and drain again. Carry on in this way until the water runs clear. Partially fill the system, pour the correct quantity of corrosion inhibitor into the feed-and-expansion cistern (5 litres should be enough for most domestic systems, but check the manufacturer's instructions) and allow the system to fill completely. Turning the boiler and pump back on will cause the corrosion inhibitor to be mixed thoroughly with the water.

INSULATION HEAT AND SOUND

The average house loses about 35% of its heat through the walls, 25% through the roof, 25% through draughty doors and windows, and 15% through the floor. Insulating all these areas will save you money on your fuel bills in the long term. The initial cost can be fairly high, however, so the best way is to set your priorities – start with a few relatively inexpensive measures, such as insulating your hot-water cylinder and draught-proofing windows and doors, then do the more expensive things bit by bit. You can also use insulation to soundproof your home if you are troubled by noise from traffic or neighbours

Insulating the roof ▾

If you have access to the loft space, laying blanket or loose insulation between the joists will reduce heat loss by about a quarter. If the space has been converted into a living area, you can insulate the sloping underside of the roof (see page 102).

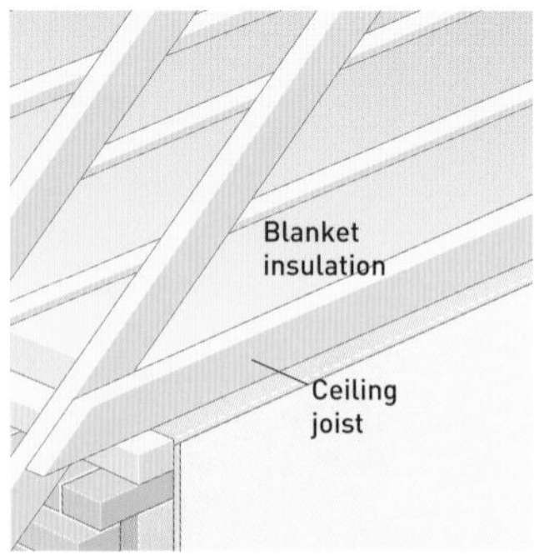

Insulating floors

In new houses the floors have to be insulated. With existing uninsulated floors, a good-quality carpet combined with underlay is often sufficient to minimise downward heat loss. Gaps below skirtings can be filled with flexible sealant or covered with wooden beading pinned to the skirting. Alternatively, the floorboards of a suspended floor can be lifted and blanket or sheet insulation laid between the joists. If you have a concrete floor, an insulated suspended floor can be built on top of it.

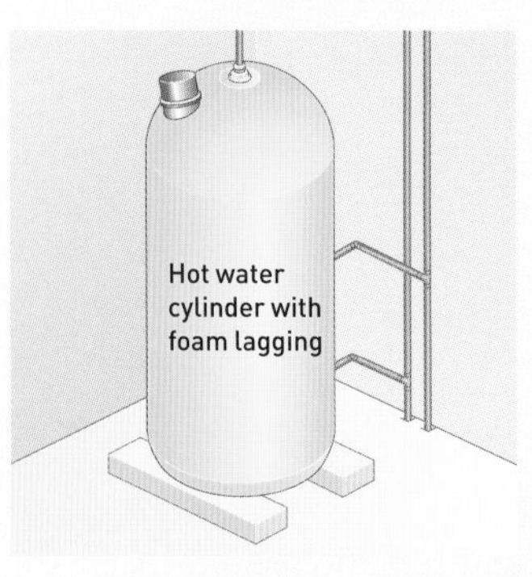

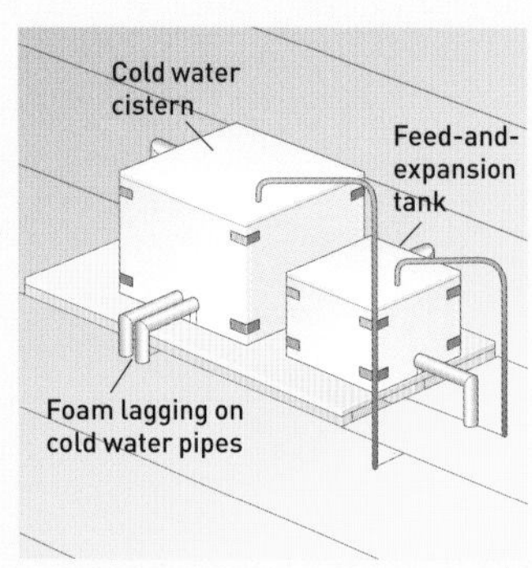

Lagging cylinders, tanks and pipes

It is well worth lagging your hot-water cylinder by fitting it with a jacket made from mineral-fibre insulation. If you are buying a new cylinder, choose one with foam insulation already fitted. Lag cold water pipes in the loft and any exposed hot-water pipes running through unheated areas of the house with split foam tubes. You should also insulate the cold-water cistern and the small feed-and-expansion tank (if you have one). The cistern can be wrapped in a purpose-made jacket or a glass-fibre blanket. But don't insulate the area underneath it – any heat rising from the room below will help to prevent the tank from freezing.

Insulating walls ▸

Insulating walls to reduce heat loss is a bigger, more expensive job than insulating the roof. Newer houses may have had insulating panel inserted between their cavity walls as they were built. This is less likely in older properties. Cavity walls can be insulated – the insulatin material is blown through holes drilled in the outside wall – but this is definitely a job for a professional.

You can insulate solid walls by dry-lining them, that is, by adding an extra layer of plasterboard to their inner faces. This is up to 50mm thick, so you will reduce your room space by this amount. The plasterboard is simply cut to size and glued or screwed to the existing wall but you may have to move electrical wiring, sockets and switches radiators, doors and windows.

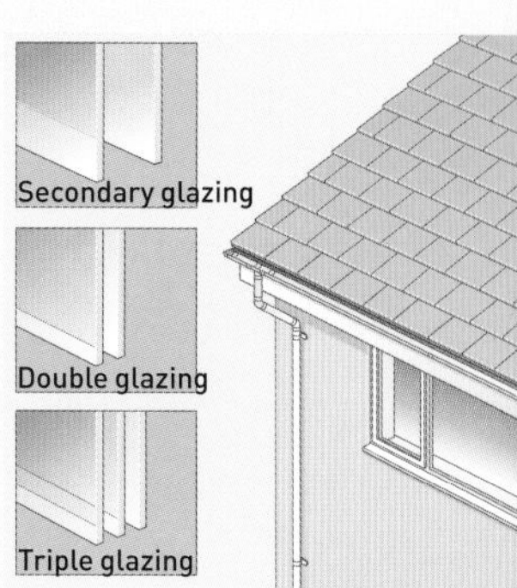

Secondary, double and triple glazing

Adding a second sheet of glass or plastic to a window traps a layer of air, which acts as an insulator and also reduces draughts, condensati and noise. It doesn't have a dramatic effect on overall heat loss – only about 5% – but does make rooms warmer and quieter near the windo

With secondary glazing, a frame containing a pane of glass (or plastic) is fixed over the existing window frame, leaving an air gap between. Simple secondary glazing kits, usually made from aluminiu and plastic, are available in a range of sizes.

Sealed double and triple glazing consists of two or three panes separated by spacing strips, bonded together and hermetically sealed at the factory before being fitted into the window frame. Inert gases that give extra sound and heat insulation may be sealed inside the gap

Draughtproofing windows

Fitting draught excluders to all gaps around doors and windows will keep your home warmer and reduce fuel bills. Self-adhesive foam strips of draught excluder are inexpensive, easy to fix in place and suitable for casement windows and interior doors. Make sure you don't stretch the strips when fitting them as this impairs their efficiency.

TOOLS MATERIALS

- **cloth**
- **scissors**

- self-adhesive foam draught excluder

1 Clean off all dirt and any loose paint from the window frame, using a damp cloth.

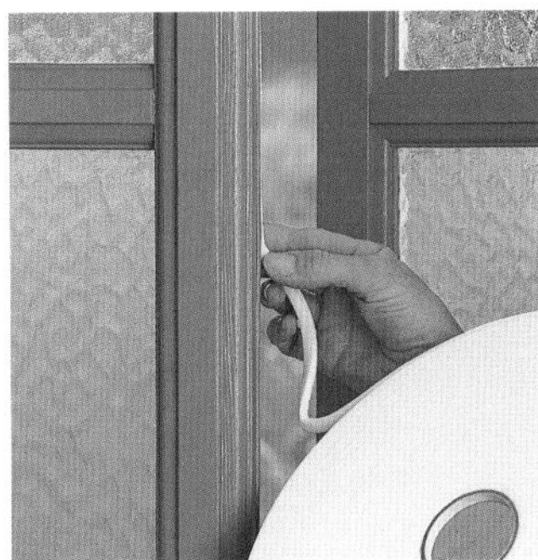

2 When the frame is dry, peel off the backing paper from the self-adhesive foam draught excluder a little at a time. Press it on to the outside of the window frame where the opening casement window will press against it when closed. Cut the ends of each length at a 45° angle to form a neat join at each corner. Close the window to press the strip firmly in place.

Draughtproofing doors

For doors, there is a variety of types of draught excluder to choose from, in different colours, and there are also complete sets for internal and external doors. The simplest is a self-adhesive foam strip – polyurethane foam for interior doors or vinyl-coated polyurethane, rubber or PVC foams for exterior doors. V-shaped strips are good for irregular gaps around doors. Sprung strip, in metal or plastic, is pinned to the rebates of the door frame. Self-adhesive foam is shown here.

1 Clean off all dirt and any loose paint on the door frame rebate using a damp cloth. When the frame is dry, apply self-adhesive foam draught excluder all the way around the edge in the same way as for a window and cut it to the correct length with scissors.

2 Make sure you attach the strip to the frame rather than the door stop, or it will be rubbed off when the door closes.

Sound insulation

Modern housing materials are not as soundproof as the traditional ones, and noise from neighbours can be a problem. However, there are various ways you can soundproof your home.

Soundproofing doors, windows and walls

A draught-proof exterior door and secondary or double glazing in entrance-hall windows will reduce noise levels. The joints between exterior and interior door frames and the masonry can be sealed with decorator's caulk. Lightweight interior doors can replaced with heavier ones. Fitting double glazing is the best way of soundproofing windows.

A party wall can be soundproofed by fitting a detached insulated lining, rather like a stud partition wall, in front of it. The gap between the lining and the party wall is filled with insulation – either glass fibre or mineral fibre blanket insulation – and then the lining is clad with plasterboard. This is effective, but does reduce the floor space a little.

Soundproofing floors and ceilings

A floor covering may not deaden the noise between the floors of a house, which can be a particular problem in properties converted into flats. Mineral-fibre insulating blanket can be laid under a suspended wooden floor to help deaden the sound.

A ceiling can be soundproofed either by adding a suspended grid-like ceiling of acoustic panels or by building a suspended ceiling from a timber frame of joists and battens with plasterboard fixed to it.

DAMP PREVENTION AND TREATMENT

IDEAL TOOL

Electronic moisture meter

If you're not sure whether a damp wall is caused by rising damp or condensation, check the moisture levels with an electronic moisture meter. Take readings up to about 1m above the floor all along the inside wall. Rising damp will give a high moisture reading up to that level and then drop sharply above it. Penetrating damp and condensation can give high moisture readings at any point on a wall.

Don't ignore damp: it can do serious damage to the structure of your house. Lots of different factors can cause it, however, and you need to find out what they are before you try to cure it, or you may treat the wrong thing and make the situation worse. Remedies that involve opening up external cavity walls or fitting a new damp-proof course should be left to the professionals. If your home is in an area prone to flooding, there are a number of precautionary measures you can take to protect it.

Diagnosing damp

There are three main kinds of damp: penetrating damp, rising damp and condensation. If you're not sure which kind you have, check the symptoms against the chart opposite and gauge moisture levels using an electronic moisture meter.

Rising damp ▸

Rising damp is confined to the lower part of walls – up to a height of about 1m – and to solid floors, and is caused by water soaking up from the ground. Modern houses are protected by a waterproof barrier built into the walls 150mm above the ground (the damp-proof course) and another laid under concrete floors (the damp-proof membrane).

Water from the ground will be drawn up into the structure of the house through any gap or breach in the damp-proof barrier. This can happen if the plastic membrane under the floor is torn by sharp stones, for instance. Very old houses built without damp-proof barriers frequently suffer from rising damp. The problem is aggravated by wet weather, but even in summer it never completely dries out, and you may require professional help to determine the cause and remedy it.

Penetrating damp ▸

Penetrating damp is caused by water seeping through the walls at any point (as opposed to rising damp, which is confined to the lower part of ground-floor walls). Damp patches may be visible when strong winds drive rain against the house wall and disappear when the weather improves. A semi-permanent damp patch may be caused by a leaking gutter or a crack in the render; if a whole wall is showing signs of damp, it may mean that old bricks have lost their weatherproof facings and become porous.

Penetrating damp is less likely to affect houses with cavity walls. If water does cross the cavity, it is usually because mortar has spread onto a wall tie.

Condensation

The warmth of a house causes moisture to evaporate into the air. If windows and doors are always kept shut, fresh air is unable to replace this water-laden air. When humid air comes into contact with a cold surface, it cools and condenses, depositing droplets of water. In cold weather the temperature of the external walls and windows is lower than the air indoors, so moisture condenses and runs down window panes and into the wallpaper and plaster.

Damp in a modern house in good condition is nearly always due to condensation. To reduce condensation, you can extract the moist air with an extractor fan (see page 335), reduce the moisture in the air by improving ventilation, and add double glazing and insulation so that the inner surfaces of walls and windows don't get so cold.

Flood prevention

More and more houses are prone to flooding as the frequency of severe wet weather appears to be increasing and because many homes have been built on flood plains. Apart from keeping your flood insurance up to date, there are several practical measures you can take.

- Check for and fix any leaks in walls, floors, windows or foundations.
- Keep gutters and downpipes free of leaves and debris. If surface-water doesn't drain freely, get a drainage specialist to check for blockages.
- Make sure that the outside ground surface slopes away from the house walls, and choose porous surfaces next to the house, that will allow rainwater to soak into the ground, rather than concrete.
- If you suffer from repeated flooding, your insurance company or drainage specialist will advise on installing a pump to redirect the water.

In the event of a flood, turn off gas and electricity supplies straight away. Keep sandbags or heavy boards to hand with which to block doorways and airbricks. Store the numbers for the emergency services and your insurance company in a safe, accessible place, along with a torch.

CAUSES OF DAMP

Symptom	Likely cause	Treatment
Penetrating damp		
Damp patches on the ceiling around the chimney breast.	The flashing sealing the joint between the chimney stack and roof (see page 181) may have cracked or become dislodged, allowing water through the joint.	Refit loose flashing; replace damaged flashing with the same type of flashing or with a self-adhesive flashing strip.
Damp patch or mould forming at the top of an upstairs wall.	Blocked or broken gutters will send water gushing down the wall and possibly saturate it.	Clear gutters or repair damaged ones (see pages 164–67).
Damp patch appears on upstairs ceiling when there is heavy rain.	A slipped, broken or missing roof tile or slate will allow water through the roof.	Replace the tile or slate (see pages 184–85).
The inner side of an external wall shows signs of widespread damp, which spreads even further in wet weather.	Old bricks can become porous and allow water though the wall.	Replace bricks or repoint and treat the area with exterior silicone water-repellent fluid (see page 164).
An isolated damp patch on an inner wall.	Cracks in brickwork or damaged pointing in the joints will allow water through the wall.	Replace damaged bricks and fill any gaps in the mortar (see page 171).
Damp patch appears on the inner wall of a cavity wall after heavy rain.	If the brickwork is not causing the problem, mortar on a wall tie in the cavity could be bridging the gap and allowing water to cross to the inner wall.	The only way to solve this is to remove some bricks, inspect the cavity and rake out or chip off any mortar on the wall ties.
Damp patches around windows.	Mortar may have fallen out of the gap between the wall and the window frame.	Seal any gaps with flexible frame sealant.
Damp patch along the underside of the window frame.	The exterior window sill should have a drip groove on the underside to stop rainwater running under the sill and into the wall. If the groove is filled with layers of paint, water can run on to the wall.	Clear the groove; if there is no groove, glue and nail a hardwood strip (about 6mm square) to the underside of a wooden sill about 35mm from the front edge to stop water reaching the wall. Paint it to match the sill.
Signs of rot at the base of an external door, or damp patches on the floor just inside the door.	A door in an exposed position is more weatherproof if it is fitted with a weatherboard (see page 173).	Repair any rotten parts of the wood and if necessary fit a weatherboard.
Rising damp		
Damp rising to about 1m up the wall.	If it is an old house, there may not be a damp-proof course or it may be damaged.	Repair or install a damp-proof course: call in a professional.
Damp concrete floor.	If there is no damp-proof course, a house is unlikely to have a damp-proof membrane under the floor. If there is a membrane, it may be damaged.	Paint the floor with two coats of bitumen latex waterproofing emulsion. For added protection, lay reflective foil building paper, foil side up, on the second coat before it has completely dried.
Widespread damp at skirting level.	The problem could be caused by render on the outside wall extending below the level of the damp-proof course.	Hack off render to a level just above the damp-proof course.
Damp at skirting level where there is a raised path beside the outside wall.	The damp-proof course should be 150mm above ground level. If it is closer than this – where a raised path has been built, for instance – water can splash above the damp-proof course and soak into the wall.	The ground outside needs to be lowered; re-lay the path; or dig a channel about 150mm wide between the wall and the path then fill it with gravel to aid drainage.
Damp spreading from the skirting level where earth has been heaped up against an outside wall.	Earth against a wall will breach the damp-proof course, allowing water to seep through.	Remove the earth and let the wall dry out.
Condensation		
Pools of water at the bottom of the windows or condensation on the glass.	The windows get colder than other parts of the room because they are thinner than the walls, so condensation will form on the glass first.	If better ventilation (see pages 334–35) doesn't help, double-glaze the windows (see page 330).
General condensation in a room in winter.	This can happen if a room gets too cold and the air cannot absorb the moisture.	Turn up the heating so the air can absorb more moisture, and increase ventilation so the damp air can escape.
Widespread damp or mould on upstairs walls and ceilings.	Lack of loft insulation.	Install loft insulation (see page 102) and apply fungicidal paint, which will prevent mildew.
Damp on the chimney breast of a sealed fireplace.	A sealed-off fireplace should always be ventilated or air will not be able to circulate inside the flue (see page 138); instead moisture in it will condense and saturate the brickwork.	Remove any wall covering on the chimney breast, make sure the wall is clean and sound, and fit an airbrick just above the skirting level. Then apply two coats of a damp-proofing liquid suitable for inside walls. Redecorate when the area has completely dried out.
Water dripping from cold-water pipes that are not leaking or damp patch on a wall or ceiling along the line of pipes.	Unlagged cold-water pipes in cold areas such as the loft can suffer from condensation.	Insulate the pipes with split-foam lagging tubes.
Mould on the timbers in the roof space.	If there is no ventilation to let air circulate around the roof space, condensation will form and, in time, lead to damp and mould problems.	Clear any blocked air vents. If there is no ventilation, fit soffit vents or tile or slate vents (see page 334).

VENTILATION FITTING VENTS AND FANS

In order to have a constant supply of fresh air in parts of the house where there are no windows, you must provide some means of ventilation. When there is no ventilation in the roof space, for example, there is a risk of condensation. The timbers become damp and can develop wet rot, and the insulating material will become wet and useless. This in turn can cause electrical wiring to short-circuit. Installing ventilation is a simple, inexpensive task that can prevent serious problems developing in the future.

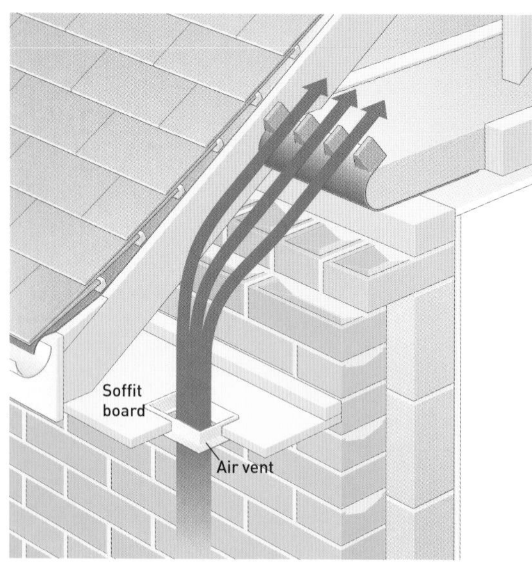

Ventilation in the roof space

The simplest method of ventilating a standard pitched roof is to fit plastic vents in the soffit board. If the roof insulation is likely to block the passage of air from soffit vents, eaves vents can be fitted between the rafters and joists to make a passageway for the air.

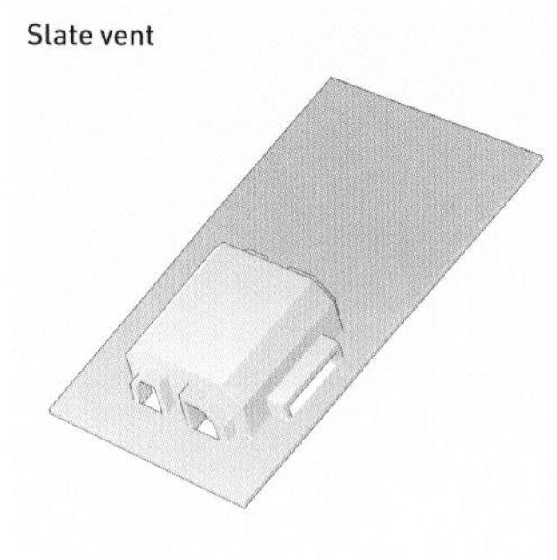

Slate vent

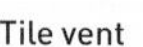

Tile vent

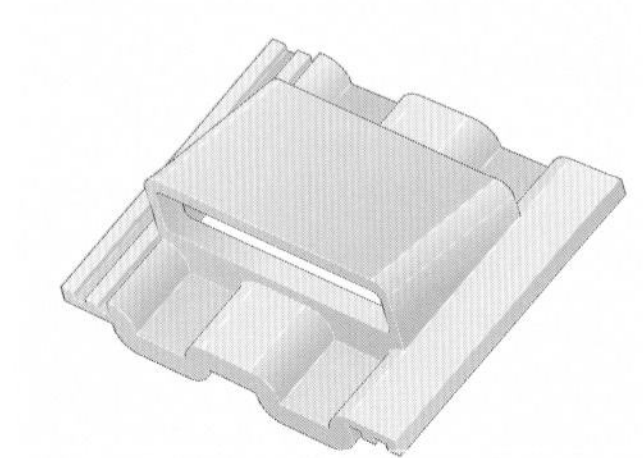

When there is an attic room with a sloping ceiling, tile or slate vents may be fitted near the ridge, and ridge vents can be fitted on the ridge itself, so they draw air over the ceiling in the roof space. Tile or slate vents may also be fitted where a solid wall, such as a party wall, is built across the loft space, stopping air flowing from the eaves on one side of the house to the eaves on the other side.

If a flat roof – on an extension, for example – is insulated, vents called over-fascia ventilators can be fitted at the eaves and where the roof meets the house's external wall (see page 183).

Ventilation under the ground floor

The external walls of a house contain airbricks to ventilate the space below suspended wooden floors. With a cavity wall, an airbrick is built into each side of the wall and a telescopic sleeve bridges the cavity between them.

Airbricks should never be blocked; check them regularly for leaves and other debris. Replace a broken airbrick immediately to prevent mice gaining access to the area under the floor.

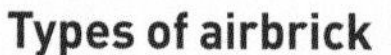

Types of airbrick

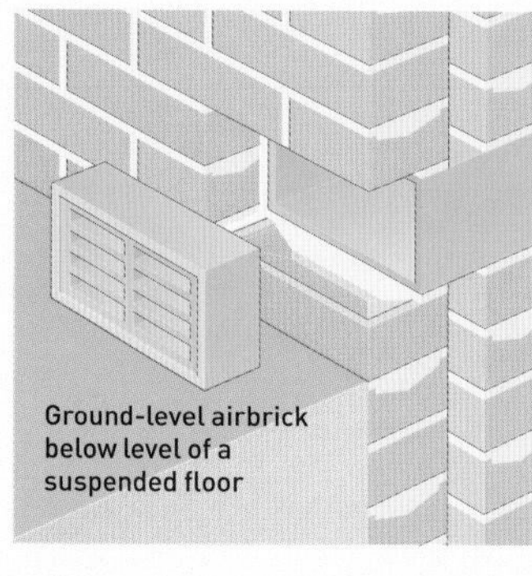

Ground-level airbrick below level of a suspended floor

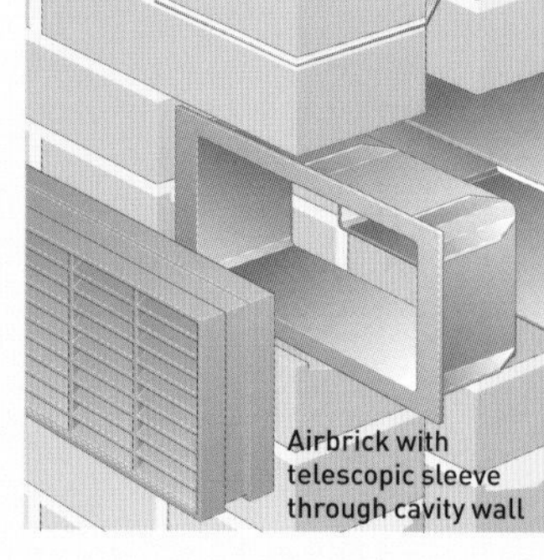

Airbrick with telescopic sleeve through cavity wall

Fitting a window vent

A simple way of ventilating a room is to fit a fixed window vent, which allows a free flow of air without causing draughts. Get a glazier to cut the required hole in the glass – it's not an easy job. It will be cheaper if you remove the pane and take it to the glaziers, though most will come and cut it in situ. If the window doesn't open, you will need someone outside to help you fit the vent.

TOOLS MATERIALS

- window vent
- silicone sealant

1 Remove the retaining ring from the vent. Apply clear silicone sealant to the retaining ring; this will help make it more weatherproof and secure.

2 Fit the vent on the inside and the retaining ring on the outside. Screw on the ring, taking care not to overtighten it.

3 Use the pull-cord to adjust the airflow into the room.

Fitting a window extractor fan

An electrically powered extractor fan in a fixed window will freshen a room very quickly. The unit needs to be powered from a switched fused connection unit connected to a spur cable that you should run from either a junction box or a socket on a ring circuit (see pages 274–77).

SAFETY FIRST

- Isolate the circuit and double-check the power is dead before beginning any kind of electrical work (see page 264)
- You cannot run a spur from a socket that is already on spur, or that already supplies a spur (see pages 274–77).
- If the fan has a choice of speeds, the wiring will be more complicated. Follow the manufacturer's instructions or call in an electrician.
- In a bathroom the fan must be operated by a pull-cord switch, or you should situate the switch outside the room. Both fan and pull-cord must be out of reach of a person using the shower or bath.
- Any fuel-burning appliance in the room, such as a boiler or gas heater, must have its own ventilation; otherwise the extractor fan could draw gases from it into the room, especially if the windows and doors are shut.

TOOLS MATERIALS

- **screwdriver**
- **claw hammer**

- extractor fan
- cable clips

1 Unscrew the fan cover and fit the rubber sealing ring.

2 Fit the extractor fan through the hole in the glass. Join the inner and outer sections with the screws provided.

3 Wire the flex to the connector block, following the manufacturer's instructions.

4 Push the flex into the cable grip to hold it securely.

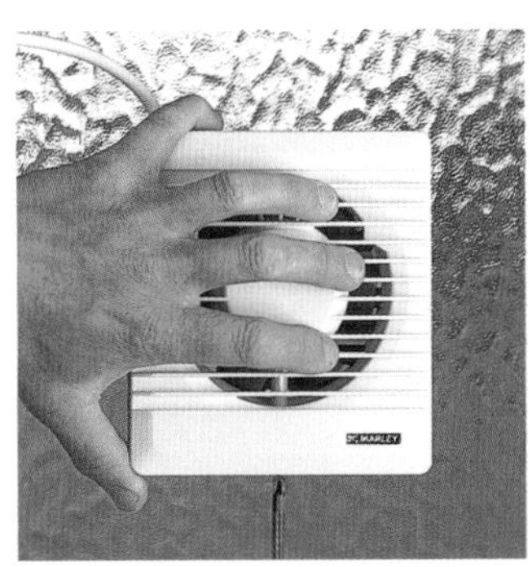

5 Screw the fan's cover back on.

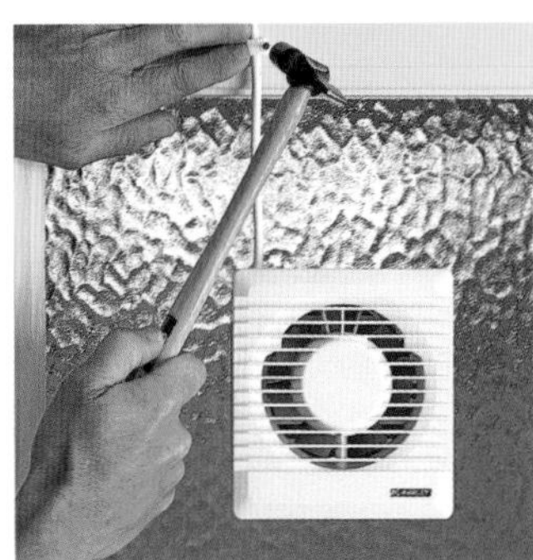

6 Secure the flex along the top of the window frame with cable clips and connect it into a switched fused connection unit. Fit a 3 or 5 amp fuse in the unit as recommended by the manufacturer.

OURS
silk
1700W
A PERFORMANCE POWER PRO PRODUCT

The basics

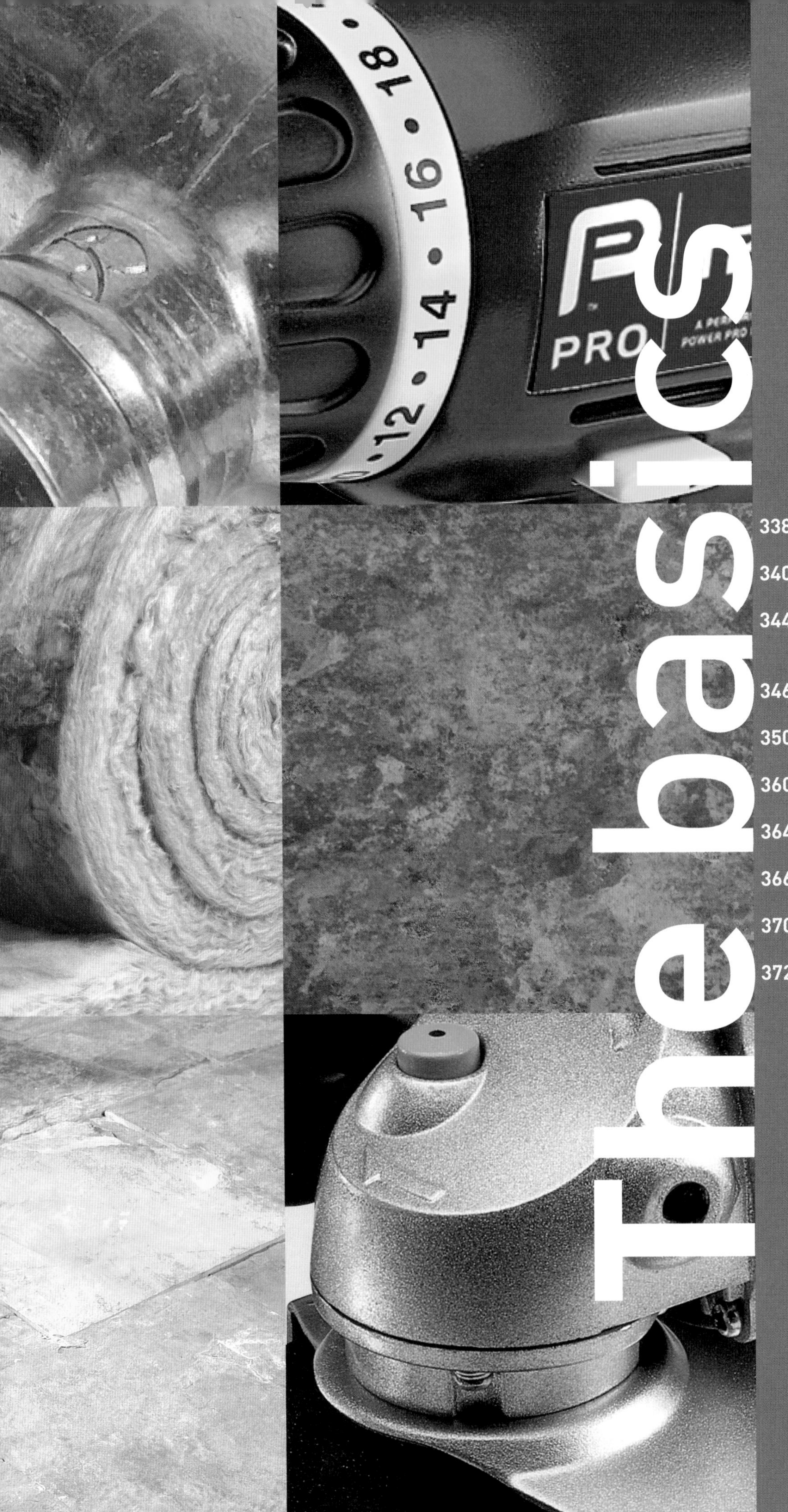

FIRE SAFETY BE PREPARED

Every home contains potential sources of fire – such as cookers, electrical equipment or candles – so it makes sense to be fire aware, to fit smoke alarms and to keep fire-fighting equipment to hand. Check your equipment regularly to make sure it is working; test the battery of a smoke alarm weekly, and be sure that your extinguisher is charged and hasn't passed its use-by date.

Smoke alarms

Fumes produced by a smouldering fire can kill you without you even waking up. This is where smoke alarms offer vital protection, giving early warning of trouble. They are very reasonably priced, but remember to check that your device carries the British Standard kitemark.

The more alarms you have around your home, the safer you will be. If you live on one level, fit a smoke alarm in the hallway between the living and sleeping areas. This will allow you to hear it throughout your home, particularly when you're asleep. The ideal site for a smoke alarm is on the ceiling, at least 300mm away from a wall or light fitting. On a wall the alarm must be 150mm–300mm below the ceiling. It is pointless installing an alarm in a kitchen or bathroom, as steam will set it off. If your house has more than one storey, fit one alarm at the bottom of the staircase and further alarms on each stair landing.

There are two types of smoke alarm. An ionisation alarm is very sensitive to particles of smoke from a fast raging fire. Photoelectric alarms are good for detecting the large quantities of smoke given off by smouldering or slow-burning fires.

Most of the less expensive alarms are battery powered, so it's important to check the batteries regularly. Better still, choose an alarm with a 10-year lithium battery. You can also buy mains-powered smoke alarms that are wired permanently to the household electricity supply.

Ionisation alarm

Photoelectric alarm

The 10 commandments of fire safety

- Teach your family all the dangers of fire, and practise your fire-escape plan thoroughly.
- Fit a smoke alarm on each level of your home. Test the batteries regularly, and always replace a dead battery immediately.
- Be prepared: install an all-purpose fire extinguisher in a prominent position, and a fire blanket close to (but not over) the hob.
- Unless a fire is very small and can be put out with a domestic fire extinguisher, do not tackle it yourself.
- Unplug all electrical appliances before going to bed, and keep them correctly maintained: no electrical flexes under carpets!
- Never leave a chip pan unattended. If a chip-pan fire starts, contain it by turning off the heat source then covering the pan with a damp cloth or fire blanket. Leave it there for at least 30 minutes while the heat subsides.
- Keep matches, lighters and candles out of sight and out of the reach of children.
- Do not plug electric blankets into multi-adaptors, or you risk switching them on accidentally.
- Never dry clothes or materials by the fire.
- In the event of a fire, get everyone out, shutting all doors behind you, and call the Fire Brigade.

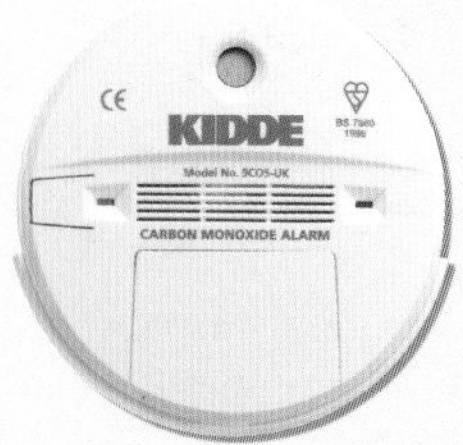

No fire, no smell – but beware!

Carbon monoxide is a colourless, tasteless, odourless gas produced whenever a fossil fuel is not burned efficiently. It can be emitted from inadequately maintained or badly fitted domestic heating appliances, such as wall heaters, fires and boilers. Carbon monoxide cannot escape from your home if the flue or chimney has a blockage, and it is well known that it can be fatal in high concentrations. Official figures indicate that in the UK over 50 people a year die from exposure to this dangerous poison within their own home. The symptoms of exposure often mimic many other common ailments, and so are easily misdiagnosed as flu, headache, fatigue or food poisoning.

Your best protection is to install a domestic carbon monoxide or combined smoke and carbon monoxide alarm that carries the British Standard kitemark, and test it regularly. Coal-burning and natural gas appliances should have their flues and chimneys swept regularly to ensure that blockages are identified and cleared. You should also have all your fuel-burning appliances serviced by a qualified installer every 12 months. Ensure there is adequate ventilation in each room. Air vents should be kept clear and never wallpapered over.

Fire extinguishers

Fire extinguishers over 1kg should comply with either the new European Standard BS EN3 or the old BS 5423. To meet the new standard, extinguishers have all-red bodies with a band of colour to indicate the extinguisher contents. You should make yourself aware of the different colours used for the different types of fire – see below.

SAFETY FIRST

Domestic fire extinguishers are not all used in the same way. Read and remember the instructions when you buy one – you may not have chance in the event of a fire.

Jsing an extinguisher safely

3efore tackling even the smallest fire, ensure that everyone has been evacuated and the alarm has been raised. Take up a position where access to the fire is unrestricted, but where a quick and safe retreat is possible. Crouching will help you keep clear of smoke, avoid heat and allow a closer approach to the fire. Always ensure that a fire is completely extinguished and not liable to re-ignite or continue smouldering.

Do not continue to fight a fire if:

- It's dangerous to do so
- Your escape route may be cut off by fire or smoke
- The fire continues to grow despite your effort
- There are gas cylinders threatened by fire

As you withdraw from the scene, close windows and doors behind you whenever possible.

Do not use an extinguisher to put out burning gas. Turn off the gas supply, if it is safe to do so, and call the Fire Brigade.

Water (red body)
Ideal for freely burning materials, such as paper, cloth and wood. Some contain water plus a special fire-inhibitor that prevents materials burning. These extinguishers are not suitable for flammable liquids or fires involving electrical appliances.

Foam (red body with yellow band)
Multi-purpose foam extinguishers are suitable for fires involving freely burning materials such as paper, cloth and wood, plus most flammable liquids.

Powder (red body with blue band)
Suitable for flammable liquids and electrical apparatus and most freely burning materials. But remember that powder smothers rather than cools the flames, so a fire may re-ignite.

Carbon dioxide (red body with black band)
For fires involving flammable liquids or electrical equipment like computers, photocopiers or generators. Not to be used in confined spaces where the fumes could be inhaled.

YOU CAN DO IT

Fire ladder

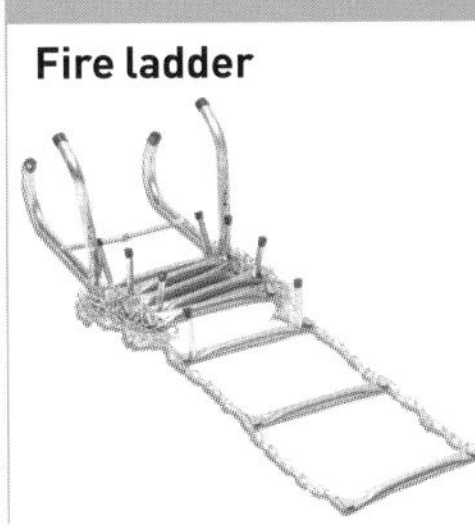

For peace of mind, consider keeping compact escape ladders in your upstairs bedrooms. These can be stored in a roll that fits under the average bed. Escape ladders are lightweight but strong, flame-resistant, and easy to use, and are available in different lengths.

Fire blankets

A fire blanket is the simplest and safest way to extinguish a cooking-oil fire. Turn off the heat source, hold the blanket so that your hands are protected behind it, then drape it over the pan. Flames will be smothered immediately, but you mustn't remove the blanket for at least 30 minutes to allow the heat to decrease. Never pick up a blazing pan and run outside with it; flames blowing back could make you drop the pan and you could get burned.

Most modern fire blankets are made of woven glass; some are coated to ensure oils and fats can't penetrate. If someone's clothes are on fire, wrap a fire blanket around them to smother the flames.

We all want to keep our homes, our valuables and our families safe from loss and harm, yet few would want to live in a fortress. Happily there are low-cost and easy-to-fit security devices that will significantly reduce the risk of burglary. These, combined with sensible precautions, will make your home more difficult to break into. Consult your local Crime Prevention Officer via your local police station for further advice and information.

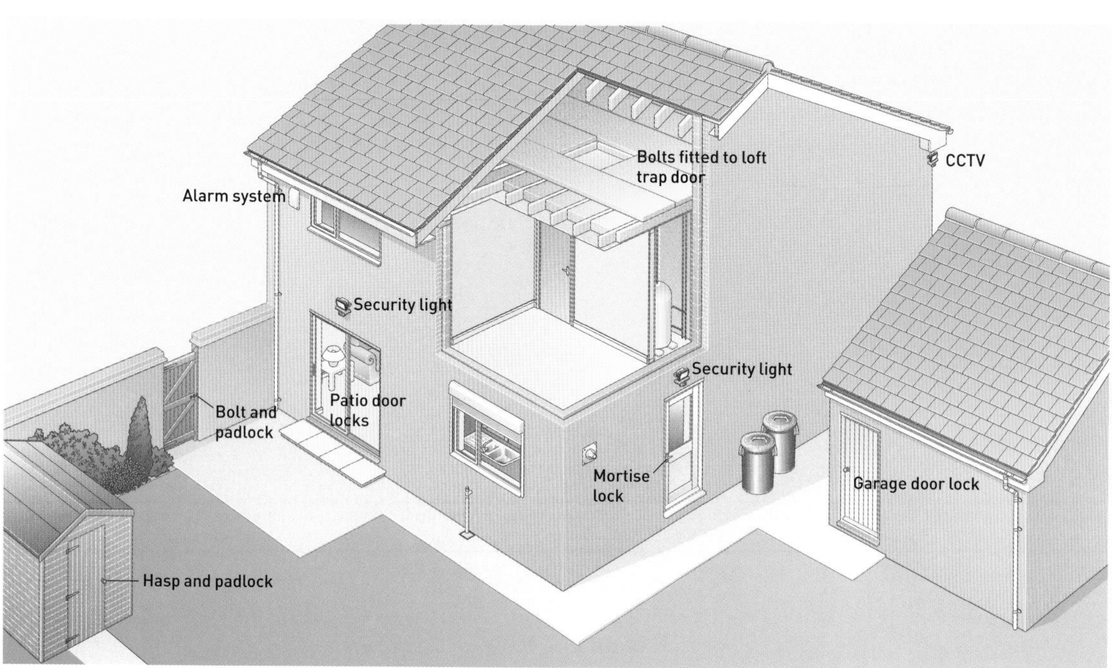

How secure is your home?

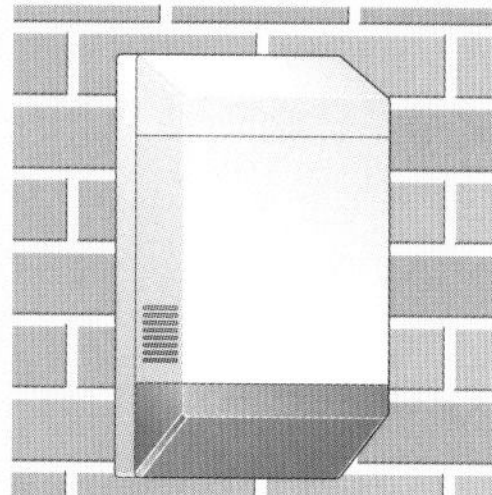

Alarms

One of the most effective burglar deterrents is an intruder alarm system with a bell box and strobe light at the front of the house. See page 343 for advice on the types of systems available.

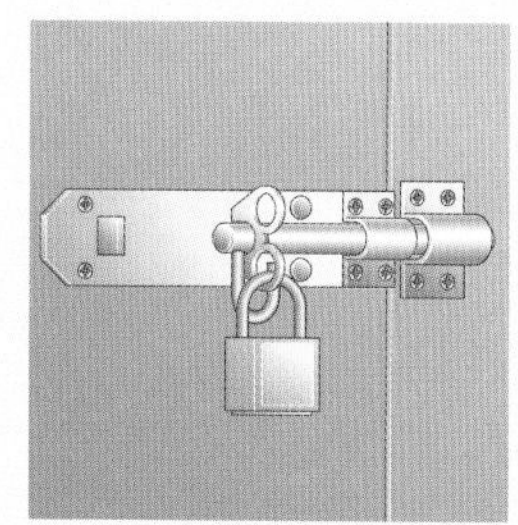

Side gates

Secure a side gate with strong bolts and locks and make sure it is difficult to vault over.

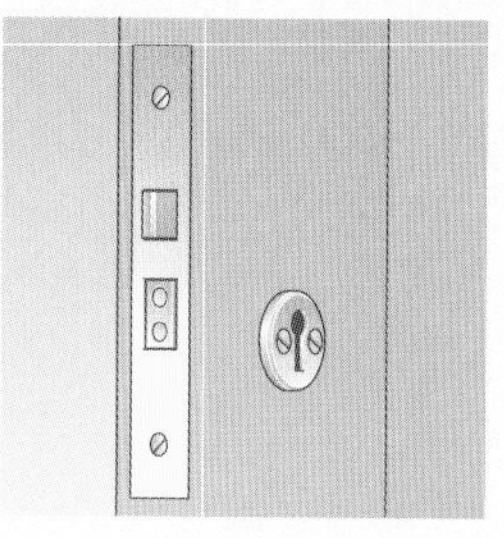

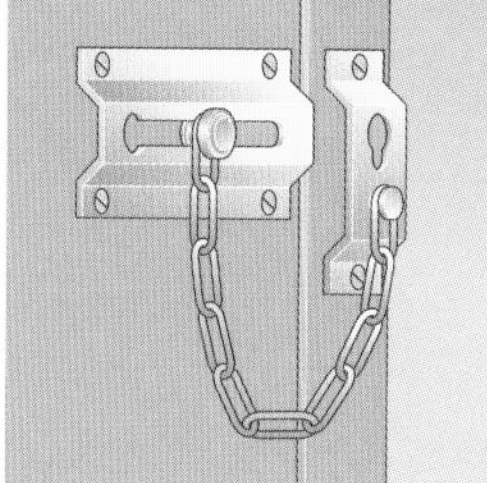

Doors

A front door should be fitted with a mortise lock that carries the British Standard kitemark, rack bolts top and bottom, a viewer and door chain (see pages 342–43). Fit a light in the porch or by the front door. If you live in an apartment, consider fitting an internal entrance door with a bolting system that secures the door to the frame on all four sides.

In fact burglars generally prefer to break and enter through side or back doors, where they are less likely to be seen. Security lighting will deter them – whether operated manually, automatically or on a time switch – but make sure it does not irritate your neighbours. Back doors should be secured with mortise locks and bolts.

Check with your insurance company – they may stipulate that particular kinds of locks must be fitted on exterior doors. Don't leave keys in the lock or on view, especially not lying around in the hall where they could be reached with a long implement inserted through the letterbox.

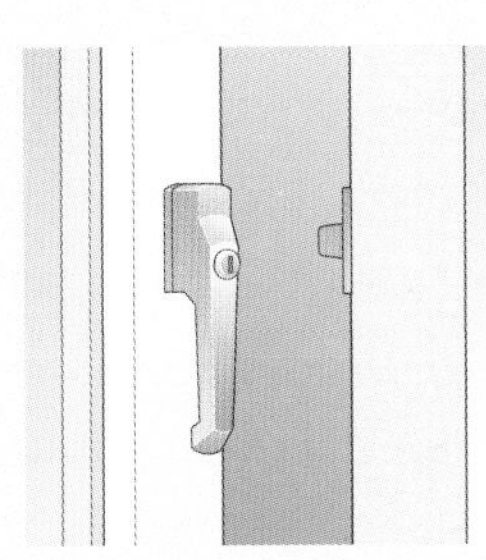

Windows and glass

Fit window locks to all frames – particularly if they are easy to access. Laminated glass or double glazing are more difficult to break through quietly. Make sure your putty or glazing beads are in good order so that a pane of glass cannot be easily removed. Metal grilles and rolldown shutters are good, if conspicuous, deterrents.

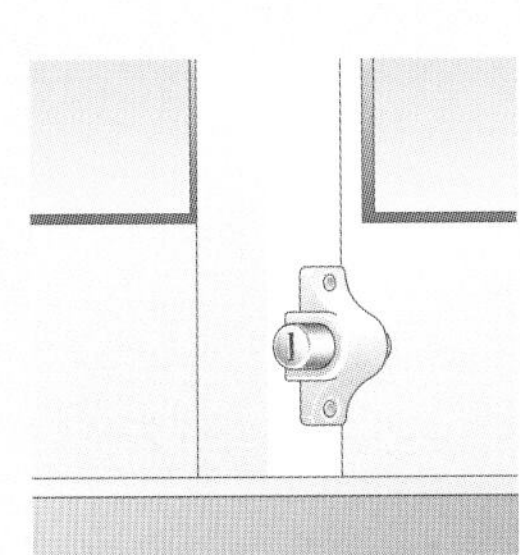

French windows

Each closing door should be fitted with locking bolts top and bottom. Make certain that sliding doors cannot be sprung or lifted off their runners.

Attics and skylights

If you live in a terrace or semi-detached house with a common loft, you are at risk from burglars breaking in from between houses and down through loft hatches or skylight windows. Fit bolts to your loft trap door and suitable skylight locks.

Understanding burglars

The last thing any common burglar wants is to find the house occupied. Most burglars will make themselves familiar with your routine before attempting to break in. Early to mid-afternoon is the favourite time for break-ins; night-time burglaries are comparatively rare. Burglars like to get in and out as quickly as possible, so anything that delays them, such as locks and bolts, will be a deterrent. They will also be put off by alarm systems and tend to avoid houses with barking dogs.

Once inside the house, they will head for the master bedroom first to look for personal possessions, such as jewellery. Your living rooms will be next, where they will seek out electronic and camera equipment.

If you surprise a burglar in your house, never confront him – just let him go. Don't risk your personal safety for the sake of a few possessions.

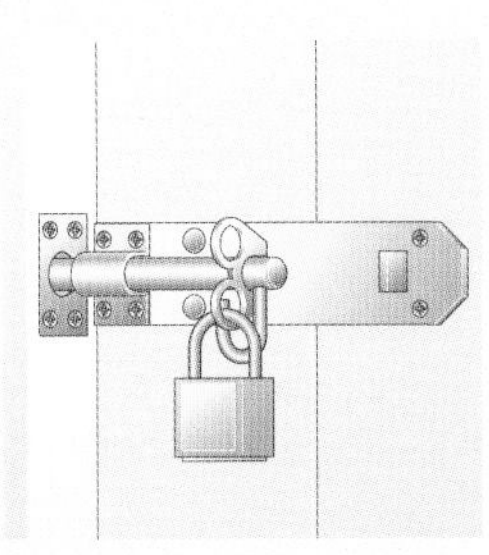

Garages and outbuildings

Garden machinery is attractive to thieves. Lock sheds securely with a robust hasp and padlock – but even so, remember that a shed is a lightweight construction and can be broken into with ease.

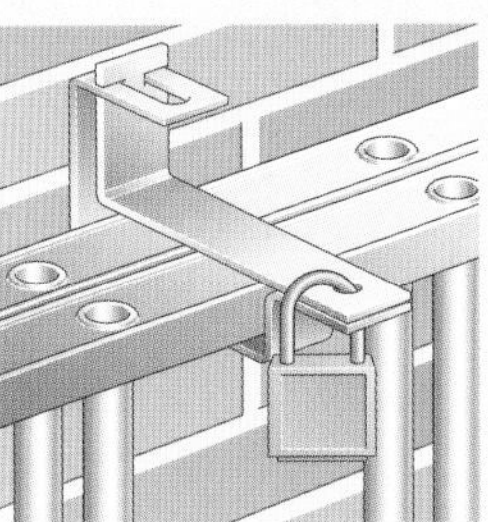

Tools

Any tools and equipment left lying around may be useful for breaking and entering, particularly a ladder. Lock away all tools and chain a ladder to a wall fixing.

Hedges and fences

Don't forget that if you create privacy with a solid wall, tall hedge or fence, you also provide cover for a burglar to work in peace.

Neighbourhood Watch

Active community awareness and cooperation does reduce local crime. Consider joining or setting up a Neighbourhood Watch scheme.

Taking sensible precautions

When you are going on holiday:

- Cancel milk and newspaper deliveries and ask the post office to hold mail for you.
- Buy timed light fittings that switch on and off automatically, making it look as though someone is at home.
- Driveway empty? It would be better to park a friend's or neighbour's car there.
- Portable valuables may be best transferred to your bank or safety deposit centre, or install your own safe.
- Tell a neighbour that you are away.
- Ask a friend or neighbour to visit from time to time to change the appearance of the home, for instance by opening or closing curtains or fitting time-switches to different lamps.

Marking and cataloguing

Write your postcode on your possessions with a UV pen, make a note of the serial and model numbers of electrical and camera equipment and keep a photographic record of jewellery and other valuables.

HOME SECURITY LOCKS AND ALARMS

Doors are a burglar's favourite entry and exit point, so it's important to make sure that yours are fitted with good-quality locks and security devices. Windows are also vulnerable – match the lock or locking system to the style or type of window. The new generation of alarm systems are effective and easy to fit, and can be adapted to suit your home, while intercoms and CCTV cameras are additional means of keeping intruders out.

Door locks

Mortise locks ▸

These are the most secure type of lock you can fit to any door. As the name implies, they fit in a slot called a mortise formed in the edge of the door, and shoot a hardened steel bolt into a keeper recessed in the frame when the key is turned. Make sure that any lock you buy is made to British Standard BS3621 and carries the British Standard kitemark. Versions with three, five and seven levers are available; pick one with at least five for greater security.

Mortise sashlocks ▸

A side or back door is often used during the day to allow access to the back garden from the house. The best security lock for these doors is a mortise sashlock, which combines a mortise lock and a handle-operated latch mechanism so the door can be opened and shut without the need to operate the key. The door can then be securely locked at night or whenever you leave the house.

Mortise sashlocks are left- or right-handed to suit the way the door opens, or may have a reversible latch bolt to enable the lock to fit either edge of a door.

◂ Cylinder locks

The locking mechanism of a cylinder lock is contained in a brass barrel that fits in a hole drilled through the door. On the inside there is a surface-mounted lock body fitted with a knob or lever so the door can be opened from inside without having to use a key. There is also a knob called a night latch that you can operate to prevent the latch being forced, but do remember that a night latch does not provide adequate security on its own.

Deadlock cylinder lock ▸

The most secure cylinder locks have a deadlocking facility that locks the latch securely with a key, used from inside at night and from outside when you leave the house. Again, make sure you buy a lock made to BS3621.

Patio door locks ▸

Sliding patio doors are relatively easy to force unless they have been designed with integral multi-point locking and anti-lift devices. Many older doors do not have these features, so it's wise to add a pair of key-operated surface-mounted locks to each sliding door, installed either at each side of the door or at the top and bottom. The lock body is screwed to the door frame or sill, and the bolt engages in a hole drilled in the door itself.

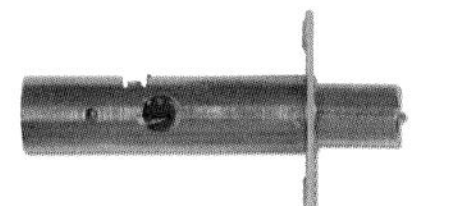

Bolts ▴

You can improve the security of any door by adding bolts, either surface-mounted bolts or concealed mortise rack bolts (above), which fit in a hole drilled in the door edge and are operated by a special key.

◂ Door chains

To restrict the door opening to a few inches, fit a door chain; this will prevent a caller from forcing entry as you open the door.

Hinge bolts ▸

These are fixed steel pegs that fit into holes drilled in the hinge edge of the door and engage in holes drilled in the door frame as the door closes. They prevent the hinged edge of the door from being forced.

Door viewers ▸

You can fit this small lens in a hole drilled through a solid front door, to allow you to see who the caller is before you open the door.

Window locks

The type and positioning of suitable locks depends on the type of window.

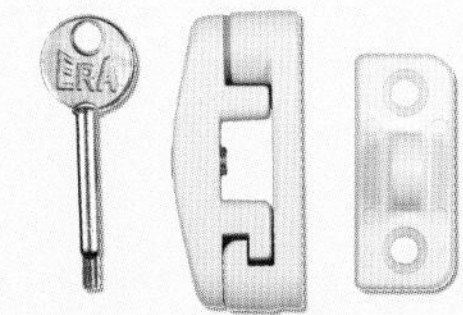

Casement windows ▸

Casement windows may have locking catches or stays, or you can fit special locks or rack bolts to secure the casement to the frame.

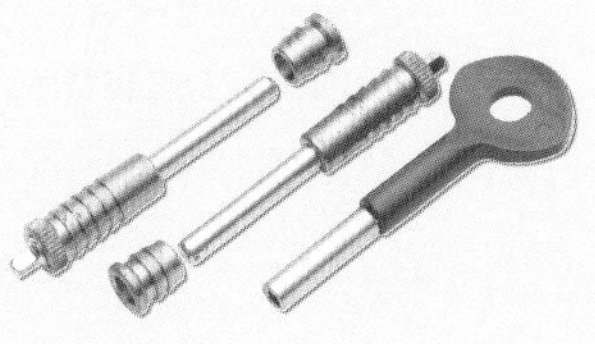

Sash windows ▸

Secure the sashes to each other with dual screws that clamp the rails together, or surface-mounted rail locks. Sash stops permit ventilation but prevent the window from being opened wide.

Alarm systems

There are several choices when it comes to installing security alarms in your home. Infrared movement detectors known as PIRs fitted high up in the corner of each room will activate the alarm if they sense a door opening or an intruder walking across the room. Magnetic contact detectors installed on doors or windows trigger the alarm if the magnetic plates are disturbed. Most alarm systems use a combination of these elements with an interior control panel and an exterior casing containing the bell or siren.

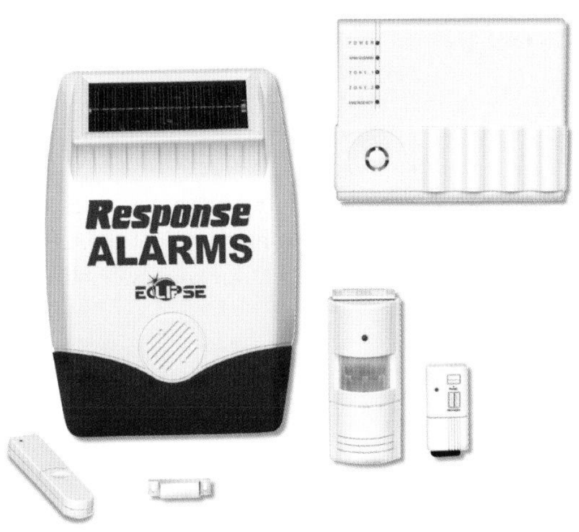

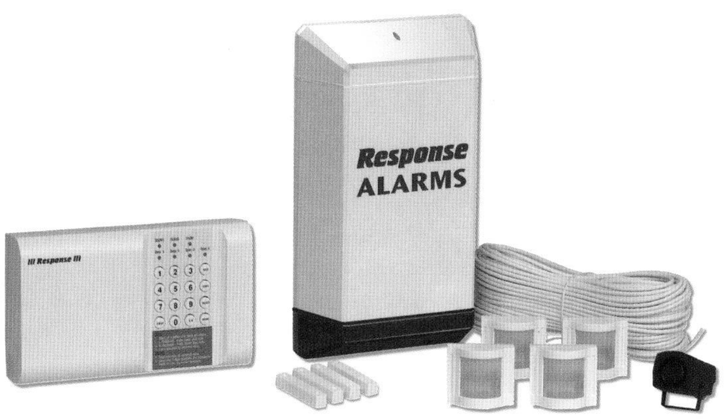

Wirefree or wired?

Wirefree alarms are much easier to install than wired alarms, but you will have to change the batteries from time to time. You can add as many PIR sensors or magnetic contact detectors as you wish to wirefree systems, while there are limits to the number of accessories that can be added to a wired system. All the components of wired alarms need to be linked and the control panel needs an electricity supply. It is possible to have wired alarms monitored by a security company, who will alert the police if they go off.

Zones

Some alarm systems allow you to isolate different zones in the house. For example, at night you can turn on the alarm downstairs but leave it off upstairs so you don't set it off on trips to the bathroom. If you have a cat or dog, you might choose to leave one room free of movement detectors, where your pet can be left when the alarm system is switched on.

CCTV and intercoms

CCTV cameras

No criminal wants to be captured on camera, so cameras are an extremely effective deterrent to intruders. An automatic video-starting system can be connected to your home VCR and when the PIR sensors positioned around the perimeter of your property detect a visitor or intruder, the CCTV cameras will be activated.

2-way intercom

Built-in speakers and microphones allow you to check who is at the gate or front door before you let them in. Some systems incorporate security cameras so that you can see as well as hear your caller.

SAFE HOME IMPROVEMENTS

SAFETY FIRST

Plan ahead

Before you tackle any home improvement job, think it through from start to finish. Read all the instructions and make sure you understand them fully. Check you have all the necessary tools and materials to hand. Consider any heights or weights you will have to deal with; will you need someone else to help? How long will it take, and will a room in the house be uninhabitable while you are working there? What are the possible consequences of the work you are planning? If you are in any doubt whatsoever about your capabilities, call in a professional to do the whole job, or just the parts of it that you are unsure about (see pages 372–73).

When embarking on a home improvement project, we take precautions to reduce the mess and disturbance that will inevitably result. We move furniture or possessions from the work area or lay dust sheeting in the room, even though this can be a painstaking and laborious process. But how much time do we spend protecting our own well-being, or that of our families and pets? One glance at the home accident statistics makes the answer all too clear: not enough!

Be aware that home improvement projects are almost always messy, often noisy, and sometimes dangerous. Take time to assess the risks. Protect yourself and, if necessary, those around you, and consider whether your activities may be disturbing others too.

Personal safety

What to wear for the job? The uniform of most builders is a pair of worn jeans, tough boots and either a T-shirt in summer or a sweatshirt in winter. Cheap, easy to replace and comfortable, this is sensible clothing for home improvement activities too. You may be in a hurry to get started, but do pause, change into old clothes or cover up with a set of overalls, many of which come with useful pockets for small tools and sundries.

Do not wear:

- Loose clothing, especially big sleeves or accessories such as a tie or jewellery. These may become entangled with a power tool, or snag on ladders or workbenches.
- Anything that restricts your movement.
- Very woolly sweaters when decorating – not only is it all too easy to brush against wet paint, but you will be amazed how many fibres are left stuck to the surface when you do.

Do consider buying and wearing:

- Overalls. These are inexpensive and worth every penny. Pick a material that is easy to wash and dry – cotton or cotton mix. They should be reasonably close-fitting to reduce the risk of interfering with machinery.
- Sturdy 'safety' boots or shoes with toe-cap reinforcement. These will protect your feet when you are handling heavy materials, such as bricks or stone slabs, as well as plasterboard, wooden sheets or large sections of timber. Wear rubber-soled shoes when working on electrical installations.
- A tool belt may look over-the-top, but it is very handy for holding your most useful and easily mislaid tools, such as a tape measure and claw hammer. And it can speed up repetitive tasks such as fixing with nails or screws, since you can have all that you need right there at hand.

Absolutely essential:

- Good lighting. Make sure you can see your work clearly; poor lighting is hazardous and tiring.
- A mobile phone is advisable whenever you are working alone, just in case of an accident.
- First-aid kit. Every household should have one, either bought or compiled according to your own needs. Include plasters and antiseptic salve as an absolute minimum, and consider reading an approved first-aid manual too. There is a Health and Safety executive standard for workplace use: if planning heavy work, check out their recommendations first.
- Beware of fatigue. You will need to concentrate and not rush, especially when working with electricity, using power tools, or beginning any new and costly home improvement. Take frequent breaks.

Essential gear for specific tasks:

- An industrial safety helmet may seem unnecessary for home improvements, but a hard hat is absolutely essential when there is any danger of either bumping your head or from falling objects. If you find a hard hat cumbersome, get a bump cap (this looks like an oversize baseball cap), which will give some protection from a knock.
- Will you be spending a lot of time on your knees? If you are going to put down any quantity of flooring, buy a pair of good-quality knee pads. Without them, laying a floor of any kind is a painful affair.
- Always protect your hearing. Even if the noise is not loud enough to damage your ears, you will find yourself becoming tired more quickly. Ear defenders will reduce the impact, but remember to be extra vigilant while wearing them.
- Wear the right gloves for the task – if exposed to liquids, protect your skin with throwaway thin rubber gloves. When doing work or handling materials that might damage your hands, wear cotton and leather reinforced gloves.
- Impact-resistant clear goggles will protect your eyes from dust and flying debris: another cheap but significant piece of safety gear.
- Take a breath. Protect your lungs from dust as well as from invisible fumes. There are breathing masks designed to provide different degrees and types of protection, from a simple gauze to screen out fine particles to a full facial respirator to isolate the wearer from poisonous fumes. Match the mask to the task!

Be tidy

It is important to clean your tools and keep your work area tidy as you go along. Paint, adhesive and mortar will be much harder – and in some cases impossible – to clean off when they have dried. Sharp tools, such as saws and chisels, must be hung up after use or the edges can become blunt. Safety guards should be replaced on power tools. Anything left lying around is a potential hazard.

Be especially careful when working with toxic substances. Follow the manufacturer's instructions to the letter and never decant substances into containers that are not clearly labelled.

Safety of family and pets

If you are going to make a lot of noise and a mess, do take into account your family and your pets. Keep them well clear of wet paint or cement until you are sure that it has dried. Seal off the work area if you can and make absolutely certain that all tools and materials are out of reach of children. You may be protected from dust and noise, but are all those around you?

Be a good neighbour

If you live in a community, think carefully about the impact your home improvement projects may have on your neighbours. Late-night drilling and hammering may get the job done more quickly, but could ruin your relationship with those around you. Be aware of the regulations concerning nuisance, and if in doubt about your rights, contact your local Environmental Health Department.

YOU CAN DO IT

Seek advice

If you hit a snag in the middle of a project and can't decide how to proceed, call your local store and ask a B&Q specialist for advice. They can explain the best tools and materials to use to achieve the effects you want. There's also a wealth of good advice at B&Q's website **www.diy.com**

LADDERS FOR DIFFERENT TASKS

Trying to reach up and work is tiring and uncomfortable. It makes sense to stand on a raised platform. But don't be tempted to improvise: always select the right equipment for the height and nature of the work at hand. Stepladders and multi-purpose ladders are ideal for indoor and light outdoor jobs, reaching up to 3m. Beyond that height, it's best to use ladders and scaffold towers. For specialist or one-off tasks, you will find it more economical to hire access equipment, and if your project is on a grand scale, you should commission an approved scaffolding company to erect a professional access platform.

◂ Small stepladders

A small collapsible stepladder may well be adequate for light tasks around the home and is compact enough to be stored inside the house, rather than the garage or shed.

Step-ups ▾

If you need a steady platform to work just above head height, a simple step-up is a good solution; easy to handle and sturdy, some are available with a handle – ideal if you feel unsteady when raised off the floor.

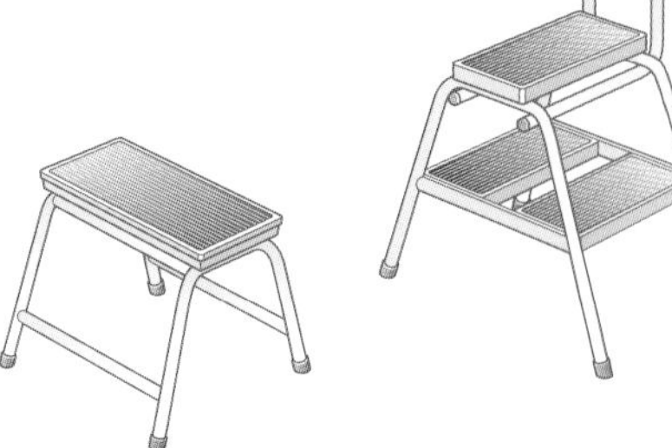

Double-sided steps ▸

Sturdier than a small stepladder, double-sided steps are good for more demanding home improvement tasks, both indoors and out.

◂ Stepladders

Choose a stepladder that will allow you to reach the ceiling and to the top of the ground-floor windows outside. Most are made of aluminium and have a top platform for resting tools or paint tins, and a projecting hand grip or guard rail for extra safety. All will have a locking mechanism to stop the two halves sliding apart – use it!

- Not sideways! Set the stepladder facing the work area, otherwise it will be unstable.
- Firm ground? If you are working outside make sure you are standing on firm, level ground. If the surface is soft, lay down a large wooden board to spread the load.
- No over-reaching! If you have to reach out or stretch, you need to move the ladder.
- Keep one hand on the guard rail and both feet on the treads while you work.
- One person at a time. Never let someone else climb on a stepladder while you are on it.
- Never, ever stand on the top platform. If you need to go higher, use a ladder or a platform.

SAFETY FIRST

Choosing a ladder

Only buy stepladders or ladders that conform to the relevant British or European Standard. All should be clearly marked with the load they can safely support. When you hire or borrow access equipment, inspect it very carefully before use – make sure there are no dents or splits, and that the feet are non-slip and in good condition; if appropriate check the locking action of a stepladder or multi-purpose ladder.

Multi-purpose stepladders and ladders ▸

Many aluminium stepladders also convert to a small extending ladder. An aluminium combination ladder can be arranged in different configurations for use as steps, a short ladder, a stairwell work platform or low-level staging, making it an ideal choice if you need access in a variety of different situations.

If you are using a combination ladder on a staircase, set the ladder in place and then, if possible, nail strips of scrap wood across the stair treads to prevent the ladder feet from slipping off the treads.

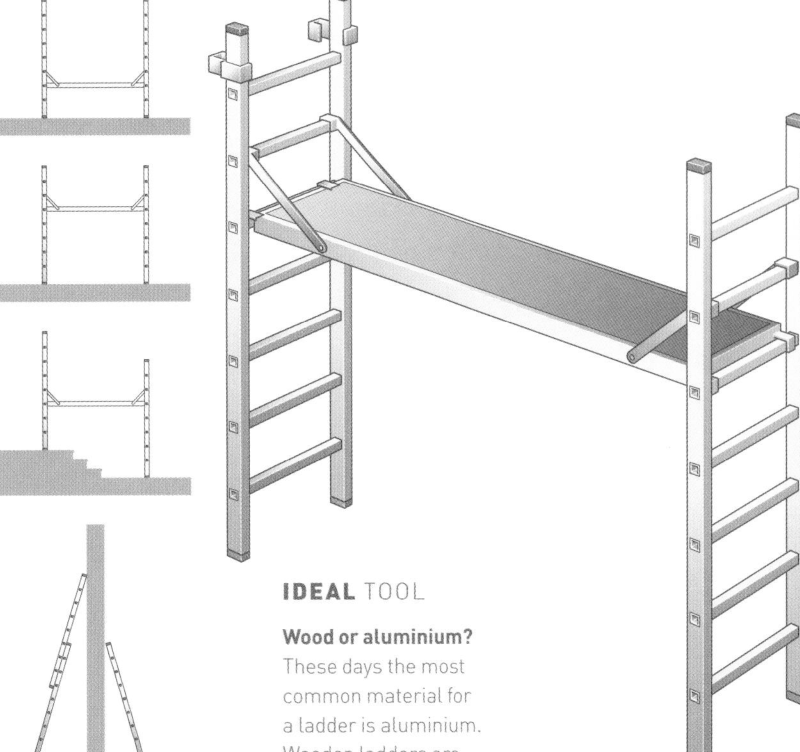

IDEAL TOOL

Wood or aluminium?

These days the most common material for a ladder is aluminium. Wooden ladders are heavier and less durable. If you must have a wooden ladder choose one with reinforcing metal rods beneath each rung. Be wary of buying or even borrowing a painted wooden ladder: the paint may be covering up potentially dangerous defects.

◂ Ladders

Once you need to go beyond the reach of your trusty stepladder it is time to buy, hire or borrow a ladder. The most popular buy is an extension ladder, and in particular a pair of ladders that can be used separately, or joined together for reaching up high.

Choose a ladder to match the dimensions of your home. Allow for at least 1m over and above the highest point at which you expect to work. A ladder that will extend to 7m–8m will probably be ideal. A double-extending ladder will measure up to 4.5m long when closed; if storage space is limited, look for a triple-extending ladder.

Roof ladders ▸

A proper roof ladder is essential for even minor repair work on a roof. It has wheels on one side and hooks on the other. Standing on an ordinary ladder, you push the wheeled side of the roof ladder up the roof then turn it over and slide the hooks down onto the ridge tiles to hold it in place. Don't be tempted to walk across the tiles or slates: this will damage them, and you may slip off. For more extensive work on a roof, you must by law install proper scaffolding.

Firm footing?

Always inspect the surface on which you intend to erect a ladder. If it is not level or firm, lay down a sturdy piece of board with a length of batten nailed in place to act as a stop, or find a ready-made ladder safety foot. If you can, use ladder stabilisers too; if not, drive stakes into the ground on either side of the feet and lash the ladder to these. On hard ground, lay a heavy sandbag over the bottom rung to prevent slipping. Finally – as ever – if in doubt, find a helper to stand on the bottom rung and hold on to the sides.

LADDERS WORKING WITH LADDERS

Ladders are one of the biggest common factors in accidents during home improvement activities. Be safe: don't add to the statistics.

Transporting a ladder

Carry the ladder upright to your place of work; hold the rungs and let the stile – the side of the ladder – rest in a balanced way against your shoulder. If the ladder is heavy or too long, find an assistant to help you. Look out for electricity and telephone cables as well as branches and other obstructions overhead. If it is windy, find a helper – or better still, leave the job for another day.

Raising a ladder into position

Lay the unextended ladder flat on the ground with its feet pushed against the base of the wall. Go to the other end of the ladder, pick up the top rung and raise the 'head' of the ladder above your head. Now walk forward under the ladder raising it to the vertical by moving your hands down from rung to rung. Once the ladder is vertical allow the head to rest gently against the building and move the feet out so that it is leaning at the correct angle according to the one-in-four rule (see YOU CAN DO IT).

Ladder stand-off

Stabiliser

Extending a ladder – in position

Once an extension ladder is upright, the top section can be raised by up to 2m by a person of average height. Unhook the lower end, carefully pull the ladder into a vertical position, and then slide the upper section skywards until the lowest rung is at approximately head height. Engage the hooks on the upper section to the ladder rung at that height. Rest the top of the ladder back on the wall and adjust the position of the feet according to the one-in-four rule.

Extending a ladder – before it's in position

You will have to do this if you need to extend the ladder by more than 2m. Lay it on the ground 'face up' and extend as necessary – use a tape measure to check you have the length you need. Then turn the ladder over and raise as described above. For a ladder with up to 18 rungs, always allow a minimum overlap of two rungs; for longer ladders, increase the overlap to three rungs.

YOU CAN DO IT

The one-in-four rule

For safety reasons always set a ladder up at the correct angle of lean. The foot should be one measure out from the wall for every four measures of wall height. So, for a ladder to reach the 5.2m eaves of a typical two-storey home, the foot of the ladder should be 1.3m away from the wall. One way of quickly assessing the correct angle is to stand with your toes touching the feet of the ladder, keep your back straight and upright, and extend your arms – you should be able to grasp the rungs at shoulder height.

IDEAL TOOL

Tool belt

The tool belt comes into its own when you are doing repetitive tasks up a ladder. It's an ideal and safe way of carrying nails and screws as well as the tools you need to have to hand.

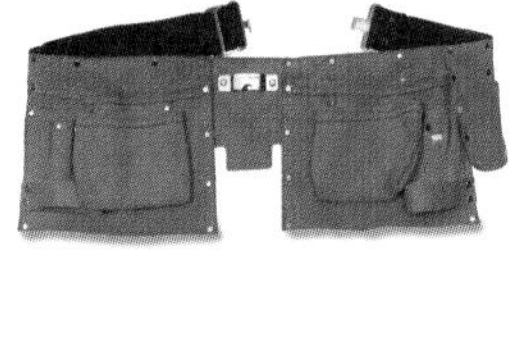

Be safe

- Wear thick-soled flat footwear, particularly if you'll be standing on one rung for long periods, and make sure that your shoelaces are securely tied. You can fit a hook-on foot platform to save your feet. Ensure that your shoes are free of mud or grease, to prevent slipping.
- Wear a helmet and do not wear loose clothing that might be snagged on the way up or down.
- Go slow – never rush when working at height.
- Do not climb the ladder with your hands full – use a tool belt, apron or shoulder bag. Haul up materials in a bucket or on a rope.
- Don't lean sideways or backwards from the ladder. Keep your centre of gravity inside the stiles. Keep both feet on the rungs – not one foot on the wall!
- When working on gutters and underneath eaves fit a ladder stand-off or stay (see IDEAL TOOL, opposite) before you erect the ladder – this is clipped to the top two or three rungs. Never, ever rest a ladder against guttering.
- Don't use a ladder in high winds or when it is raining.
- Always hold on to a rung with one hand when working.
- Fit a tool tray to keep the items you need to hand.
- Use cordless power tools wherever possible.
- Never leave a ladder unattended.

YOU CAN DO IT

Ladder stabilisers

If you need to put your ladder on an uneven patch of ground, you should bolt stabilisers to the bottom on both sides to stop the ladder rocking.

Get a grip and don't go too far

Climb the ladder by holding the rungs, not the ladder sides. Don't press against the ladder; climb with your arms straight and your body upright. Use the top four rungs of any ladder as handholds only.

Be secure

- Always store ladders and stepladders under cover, particularly if they are made of wood.
- Store stepladders standing against the wall, not suspended by a rung.
- Hang ladders horizontally on strong brackets.
- If you have to store a ladder outdoors or in view, make sure it is securely chained and padlocked to a well-fixed bracket. Don't give a leg-up to a thief!
- Never paint a wooden ladder – you may hide dangerous defects. Always use clear varnish or clear wood preservative.

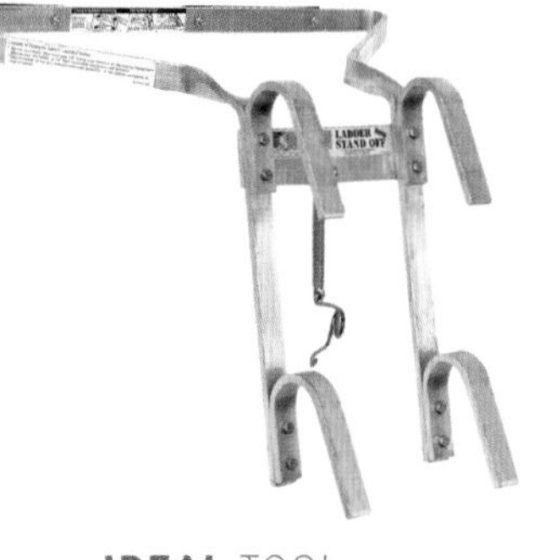

IDEAL TOOL

Ladder stand-off

It is very dangerous to rest a ladder against guttering. Instead, hook a metal stand-off to the top of the ladder to hold it away from the wall, so its full weight is not resting on the gutter.

Work platforms and scaffold towers

When you need access to a large area of wall or roof up to about 9m high, consider buying or hiring a tower made of lightweight alloy sections that clip together, framing a set of boards and guard rail that form a safe working area. The components, complete with lockable wheels, can be used to make a variety of mobile work platforms for inside and outside the home. Once a tower is erected, use the stabilisers to keep the structure solidly in place.

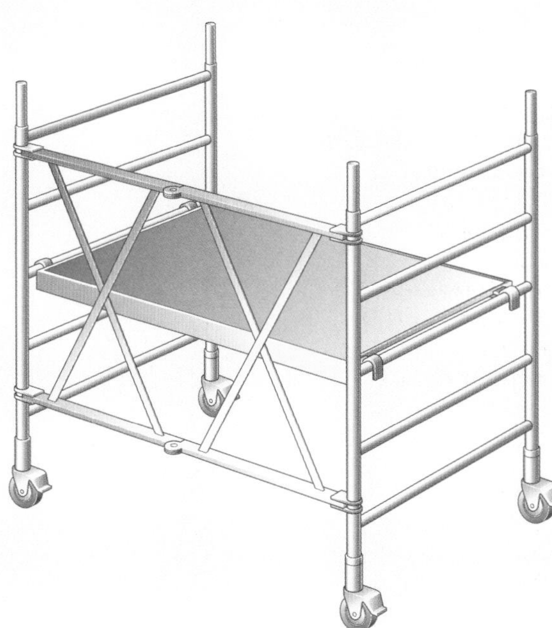

- Follow the instructions supplied carefully.
- Never build a tower beyond the specified dimensions.
- Never leave tools and materials on the platform.
- Only move a tower, once erected, when you are on completely level, solid ground. Once you remove the stabilisers the structure can become top-heavy.
- If in doubt, seek professional advice and have the scaffolding erected by a reputable firm.

Modern tools and equipment allow you to complete home improvement projects more easily than ever before. Yet despite all the new technology and design, the basic principles and techniques have not changed. With these essential tools you will be able to measure, cut, fix, assemble and finish most jobs.

Maintain order

◂ Tool box

Most of us buy tools haphazardly, as and when we need them. It doesn't take long to find that you need a storage box to keep them all safely in one place. Tool boxes, bags, belts or trays make it easier to carry and protect your tools. Be particularly careful how you store cutting edges in a tool box – keep and use the plastic guards that are usually fitted to new saw and chisel blades.

Storage box ▸

Every fixing requires a specific nail, clip, screw or bolt, often in combination with matching plugs, washers and nuts. If you keep them sorted in storage drawers, they will be easy to find when you need them. Many tool boxes have combination tool trays, compartments and drawers.

Hold firm

◂ Workbench

A secure working surface is essential for many tasks, and a portable workbench allows you to establish a solid platform in the house or garden. Workbenches are popular with professionals and home improvers alike.

Sawhorses ▴

A pair of lightweight plastic sawhorses will support materials while you cut them. Inexpensive and easy to store, these are a simple evolution of the carpenter's wooden sawhorse.

Clamps ▸

Hold materials securely in place while you work with modern spring-loaded or ratchet clamps, whose clever design makes them incredibly easy to use. They can also be a good substitute for an extra pair of hands.

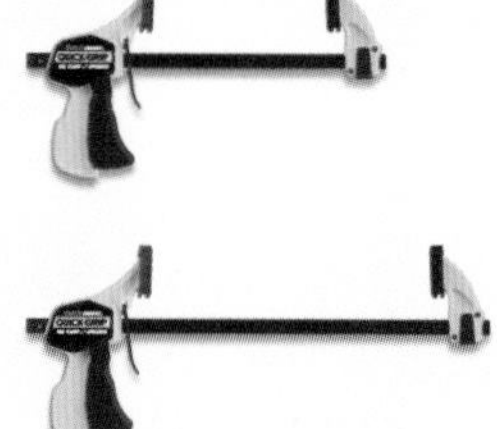

Measure and mark up

Accurate measuring is essential when working on home improvement tasks. And don't forget: always measure twice and cut once.

Retractable tape measure ▴

Buy a robust retractable tape measure – you will need it more than you might think.

Combination square ▸

The combination square can be used for measuring; for marking angles of 90° or 45°; and also has a small spirit bubble for levelling and a scribe for marking.

Steel rule ▸

Use a 300mm steel rule for accurate line drawing and measuring. When marking out over greater dimensions, use a wooden batten as a straightedge.

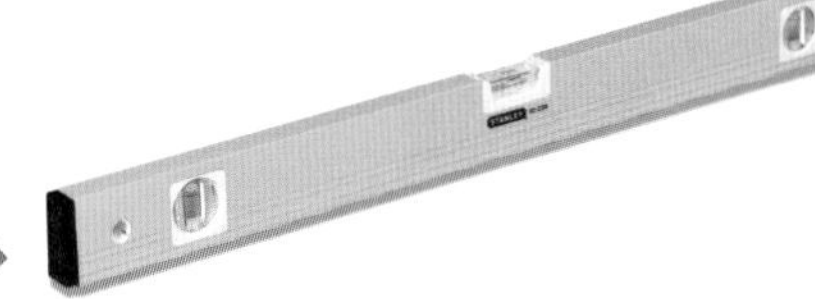

Spirit level ▸

Another must-have tool is a good-quality spirit level, designed to show you a true horizontal or vertical. This is essential when lining up shelving or cabinets on a wall, for instance. Spirit levels come in all lengths and prices.

Pencils ▸

Soft black pencils for marking cutting and drilling positions are one of the most useful tools of all.

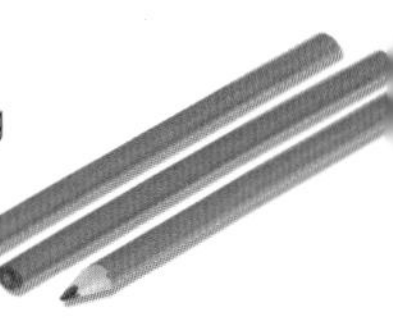

Bradawl ▸

The bradawl is a perfect tool for marking drilling positions on plaster, as well as for boring pilot holes in wood.

Cutting tools

Handsaw ▸

A handsaw will come in useful for many jobs. The panel saw is the most versatile, cutting sheet materials and timber well. As with all saws, the fewer teeth per inch (TPI) the more aggressive the cut, the more teeth the smoother the cut.

Hacksaw ▴

A good hacksaw will cut anything metal. It takes different blades, with different numbers of teeth per inch (TPI); for example, you might use 24 TPI to cut a thin metal sheet, 16 or 18 TPI for coarse metal.

Junior hacksaw ▴

For small-scale metal-cutting tasks, a junior hacksaw is an inexpensive and useful tool.

Grip and wrench

Combination pliers ▸

For everyday tasks such as gripping, twisting and cutting, a pair of combination pliers is invaluable.

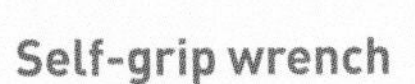

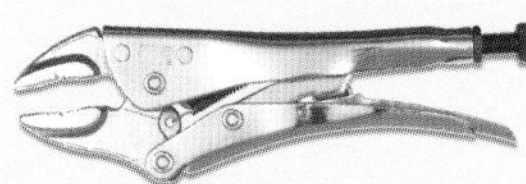

Self-grip wrench ▸

The best general-purpose wrench, useful for basic plumbing tasks too, is the mole or self-grip wrench, which is available in different sizes.

Adjustable spanner ▸

Always keep an adjustable spanner handy, to grip nuts of all different sizes.

◂ Socket set

When securing and releasing nuts and bolts you will find a simple socket set very helpful. It includes a range of different socket sizes which can be attached to a fixed rod or ratchet. Modern sets are not expensive.

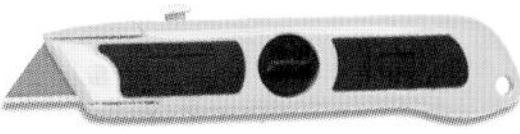

Craft knife ▸

Every tool box should include a craft knife; it can be used to cut many different materials. The simplest versions store spare blades in the handle. For safety in your tool box, buy a craft knife with a retractable blade.

Chisels ▸

A sturdy chisel with a synthetic handle that you can hit with a wooden mallet is essential for most woodworking jobs, such as fitting new door locks. Chisels need constant sharpening with a sharpening stone. Never use one to open a tin of paint!

Hit it home

There are different hammers for different jobs, but if you buy only one hammer in your life, make it a claw hammer.

Claw hammer ▸

This will drive in all but the smallest nails, hammer in wall plugs and generally knock things together and apart. Thanks to the curved claw opposite the hammer head, it will also pull out nails and can, at a pinch, be used as a small crowbar.

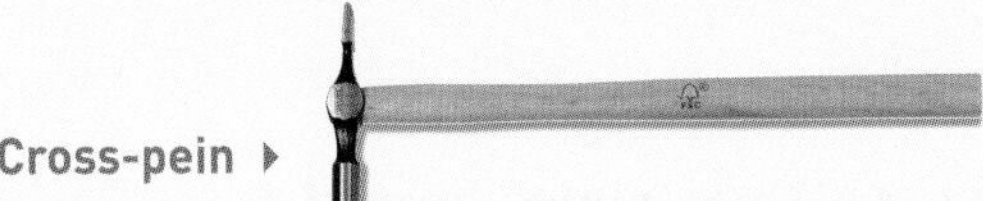

Cross-pein ▸

When you need to drive home lots of small nails – for instance, when securing hardboard to the floor – use a cross-pein or Warrington hammer.

Driving

Match your driver to your screw! Obvious but true – you will quickly strip the head from a screw if you use the wrong screwdriver.

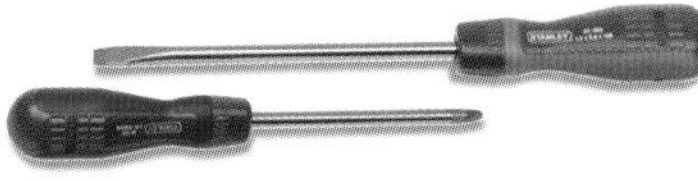

Screwdrivers ▸

Manual screwdrivers have moved on from simple wooden-handled tools; the new plastic and hard rubber handles are much easier to grip. But when you have a lot of screwdriving to do, a power screwdriver or drill-driver will save you time and effort (see page 352).

TOOLS POWER DRILLS AND SANDERS

Power tools are constantly being developed to be more effective and versatile than ever before – and at the same time cheaper and more reliable. This section will help you make the right purchasing decisions; visit www.diy.com for further information and advice.

Power drills

The most useful of all power tools is undoubtedly the drill. No other single tool can make so many tasks – particularly the repetitive ones – less of a chore. When you drill, or drive screws, you will want speed and control as well as accuracy. To help your selection, take a moment to consider your future drilling priorities:

Where will you drill?

If you buy a mains powered tool, you will also need to use an extension lead. A cordless drill will give greater mobility, although the most powerful cordless tools are more expensive than their corded equivalents. For maximum versatility, combination cordless and corded power tools are available, complete with easy-change adaptors for drilling, screwdriving, sawing and sanding.

What are you going to drill into?

Sooner or later you will almost certainly need to drill into masonry. To do this you will need a power drill with hammer action. If you wish to drill large-diameter holes in masonry, select a corded drill with a low speed gear. If you envisage drilling into a variety of materials – such as wood, plastic or metal – you should choose a drill with a multiple speed feature.

How much power do you need?

The motors of power drills are rated in watts, typically ranging from 400 watts for basic models to around 1080 watts for the biggest hammer drills. The more powerful the motor, the faster it will drill. However, for most basic jobs, a 450–500 watt drill is adequate.

Do you want a screwdriving function?

If so, look for a drill that has variable speed or torque control and is also reversible, so that it will not only drive in but also remove screws.

Electronic pipe and wire detector ▼

Never drill blind into a wall or floor – you might hit gas or water pipes or electrical wires. A pipe and wire detector is inexpensive and essential for making sure it is safe to drill. A triple detector will also find wood, so is extremely useful for locating studs in a partition wall.

Basic mains drill ▶

If all you ever want to do is to drill small holes in wood and occasionally masonry, the best choice is an inexpensive single-speed drill with hammer action. Pick one with an input power of at least 400 watts and a chuck size of 13mm – this means it will take drill bits of up to 13mm in diameter. Some of them have an old-fashioned chuck that needs to be tightened with a key, so always buy a spare key in case you lose the original.

Advanced mains drill ▲

More power means bigger drilling capacities – up to 40mm in wood, 20mm in concrete and 13mm in steel. Additional features include reverse gear and torque control, so the drill can do double duty as a power screwdriver. The most expensive models offer rotary hammer or percussion action – very useful if you do a lot of drilling into masonry.

Basic cordless drill ▶

The obvious advantage of a cordless drill is that you can take it anywhere without having to tow an extension cable behind you. The slow chuck speed, compared with mains drills, also makes it ideal for driving screws, and with a reverse gear it's easy to undo them as well. You can change drill bits by hand, but most have a maximum chuck capacity of just 10mm. Get a drill with variable speed and hammer action, allowing you to tackle masonry as well as wood and metal. A drill with a 12 volt battery is suitable for most jobs.

Advanced cordless drill ▶

As with mains drills, paying more for a cordless drill buys you a bigger chuck and more drilling capacity, as well as a longer battery life. Models with batteries of 12, 14.4 and a massive 18 volts are now available, offering drilling capacities of up to 30mm in wood, 13mm in metal and also 13mm in masonry if the drill has hammer action. Many have two speed ranges and torque control that allows them to be used as power screwdrivers.

Drill bits

A range of different sizes and types of drill bit is available, and they are often designed to make specific jobs easier and safer. For best accuracy when you start to drill a hole, select a bullet-point drill bit if there is one for your task. The sharp point will allow you to position the drill exactly on the right spot.

High speed twist ▲

For wood, metal and plastics, in sizes of 1mm–13mm.

Countersink ▶

These bits are for creating a shallow circular recess in wood to ensure that the head of a flat screw is set just below the wood surface to avoid snagging.

Screwsink ▶

These are designed to allow you to drill pilot and countersink holes in one operation, without needing to change bits.

Screwdriver ▲

For drills that also drive screws, these bits come in a range of sizes, often double-ended, like these.

Tile and glass ▶

The sharp tip and curved spade of these bits allow you to position and cut through glass and tiles with ease.

Masonry ▲

Hardened with a shaped tip of tungsten carbide, these are made specifically for boring into masonry when using a hammer-action drill. Sizes range from 6mm upwards.

Flat wood or spade ▲

For boring holes larger than 13mm in wood. Available in sizes 8mm–40mm.

Hole saw ▶

For making holes larger than 40mm in wood, plastic and light metal. Hole saws are available in 35mm–125mm sizes.

Sanders and planers

When you need to remove layers of varnish, stains, paint or rust, or you want to create a fine finish over a large area, a power sander is invaluable. There are many different types available. And a power planer will make easy work of reducing and smoothing timber.

◀ Orbital and sheet sanders

Ideal for light sanding work, such as finishing. Here the abrasive paper is stretched across a foam pad. Smaller versions are known as orbital palm sanders.

Belt sanders ▶

Perfect for heavy-duty shaping, preparing and finishing on large areas of timber. The continuous abrasive paper sheet is held in position by two rollers.

Delta sanders ▶

Use a delta sander, which is shaped with a triangular base plate, to finish tight corners.

Rotary sanders ▶

A simple, inexpensive fitting for a power drill, this is suitable for small-scale tasks.

Electric hand sander ▶

A small hand sander can help you work in less accessible areas where orbital and belt sanders can't reach. It can be fitted with various grades of abrasive paper to ensure a fine finish.

Electric planer ▲

A superb tool for shaving and smoothing sawn timber, this is quick and easy to use. You adjust the depth of cut by turning a knob.

Abrasive papers

Select the appropriate type of abrasive paper for the power sander you are using and use the grade of paper recommended for the work in hand. The golden rule is to work through the grit sizes, from coarse to fine. Note that the grit specification is common to all abrasive papers: 400 grit is finer than 200 grit.

SAFETY FIRST

Power tools reduce your labour but they also demand respect and careful operation:

- Read and observe the safety instructions for each type of tool you use
- Always work in good light and wear clear goggles when using powered cutting tools. Wear protective gloves when using a power saw to protect you from hot blades and sharp edges.
- When using power tools outdoors, you must have RCD protection against electrocution (see page 290). This is also a very good idea when using a power saw, or any tool that could cut into an electrical cable.

There are many other power tools apart from drills and sanders that will make your home improvement work easier, quicker and more accurate. The new generation of power saws is designed and built to be more sophisticated and easier to use, and you'll find that they are very affordable as well.

Jigsaws

These are highly portable, and there are now cordless versions available too. Select the right cutting blade and a jigsaw will cut through metal, timber, plastics, laminates and ceramic tiles. They are ideal for cutting curves and awkward shapes.

Advanced jigsaw ▲

More money buys you a range of additional features, including more power and a faster, deeper cutting performance. You can also expect variable speed control, pendulum action and an anti-splinter device for smoother, chip-free cutting – essential if you're cutting faced boards and laminated worktops. Dust extraction is a standard feature.

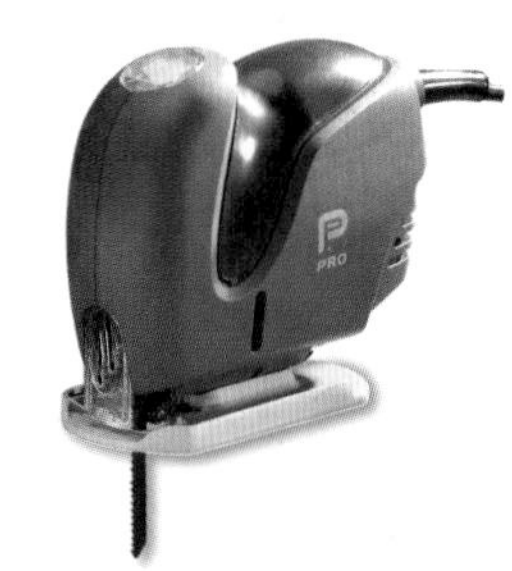

▲ Handheld palm jigsaw

Ideal for small jobs, this handheld jigsaw has an adjustable soleplate for 45° cutting. It has a palm grip handle for easy use and takes standard jigsaw blades.

Standard jigsaw ▲

A jigsaw has a slim reciprocating blade that cuts on the upstroke as you feed it into the edge of the wood or board (except for a laminate cutting blade, which cuts on the downstroke). If you do little more than the occasional sawing job, a single-speed jigsaw with an input power of 350–400 watts is ideal. Depending on the size of blade fitted, it will cut wood up to 50mm–55mm thick, and a model with an adjustable soleplate will allow you to make bevelled cuts at angles of up to 45°.

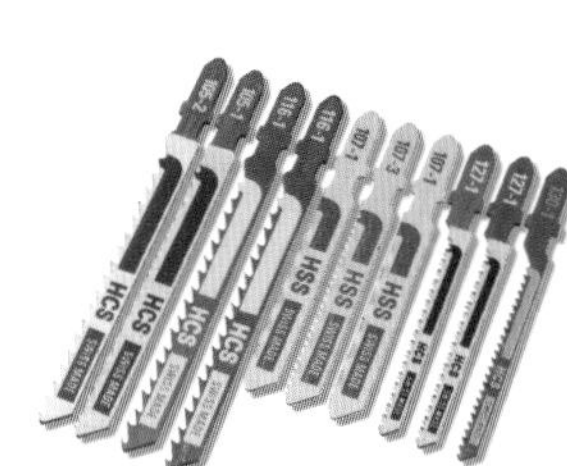

Jigsaw blades ▸

There are wood-cutting jigsaw blades for coarse, medium and fine cutting – the closer the teeth, the finer the cut – and the same blades will also cut plastic. Blades for metal have much finer teeth and should also be used for cutting wood that contains nails or screws. There are special blades for cutting ceramics and glass-reinforced plastics (GRP). The toothed section of the blade typically ranges from 50mm–105mm in length.

▲ Reciprocating and multi-saws

These saws are good for general and rough cutting. The pointed blade comes in different lengths up to 300mm, and is ideal for cutting through solid timbers like stud partitions during demolition work. With the correct blade it can also cut through metal pipework.

◂ Rotary cutter

This is a more precise cutting tool that will cut perfect circles or curves in a variety of materials, from ceramic tiles to wood and MDF. The cutting depth is adjustable.

Circular saws

The disc-shaped blade of a circular saw makes professional-quality straight cuts in man-made boards and timber. It can be used freehand, guided by a parallel guide fence, or it can be mounted in a saw table with the blade projecting upwards through a guarded slot.

Advanced circular saw ▲

More powerful saws take larger 180mm blades and will cut deeper and faster. Other features include adjustable cutting depth, a mitre and bevel facility for angled cutting, sight liner, adjustable fence guide and a vacuum cleaner attachment or dustbag.

Standard circular saw ▲

The cheapest models take blades around 150mm in diameter and have a maximum cutting depth of about 45mm. When selecting a blade for a circular saw you need to take three things into account:

- Pick the correct blade diameter for your saw.
- Select the right bore size (the diameter of the hole in the centre); this may be 12.7, 16, 20 or 30mm.
- Choose the tooth size and number to suit the job. A blade with a few large flat teeth will give a fast, coarse cut, while a blade with a larger number of alternately-offset teeth gives a medium or fine cut. Lots of small, flat, trapezoid-shaped teeth will give you the cleanest cut. All these blades have tungsten-carbide-tipped teeth for long life.

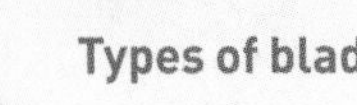

◄ Compound mitre saw

With the right blade, a power mitre saw will make clean and precise cross, mitre and bevel cuts in hard- and softwoods, plastic, alloys and non-ferrous metals. Additional features may include a laser guide for cutting accuracy, extension wings for larger materials, and dust extraction for cleaner operation.

Types of blade

Pointed tooth blade – suitable for cross-cutting solid timber, giving a reasonable finish.

Fine tooth blade – for fine cuts in chipboard and laminated board.

Ripsaw blade – rips through softwood, hardwood and man-made boards, leaving a rough-edged finish.

Chisel tooth blade – universal blade for soft- and hardwoods.

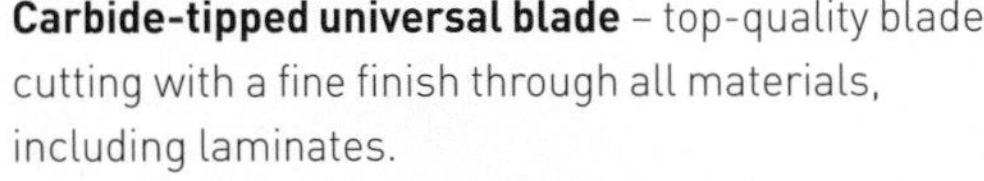

Carbide-tipped universal blade – top-quality blade, cutting with a fine finish through all materials, including laminates.

Router ▲

A router is used for accurate cutting in wood, such as shaping, edging, rebating, making grooves and decorative mouldings. This is a specialist tool, which is only essential for advanced home improvers, woodworkers, joiners and cabinet makers. But if you do a lot of wood machining, a router is for you. It will pay to take advice from an experienced user before you start, and practise first on some scrap wood. Wear a breathing mask, ear defenders and goggles or safety glasses.

Angle grinder ▲

Designed to cut and grind metal, as well as to cut stone, slabs, blocks, brickwork and concrete, an angle grinder is a powerful addition to a tool kit. Choose the right disc for the size of the grinder and for the job in hand: buy a metal cutting disc for metal, and a masonry cutting disk for masonry. Particle diamond discs are effective at cutting through blocks and brickwork. Do not cut or grind with excessive pressure, and wear heavy-duty gloves, ear defenders, a breathing mask and goggles.

TOOLS BUILDING, ELECTRICS, PLUMBING

SAFETY FIRST

Tool care

To keep tools safe and effective, they must be well looked after. All tools must be kept clean and stored in a secure place, out of reach of children. Paintbrushes and rollers should be cleaned straight after use. Cutting tools, such as saws, planes and chisels, must be sharpened regularly and stored hanging up so the blade is not blunted. Badly maintained tools can cause accidents, so don't take shortcuts with tool care.

Your general tool kit will provide most of what you need on a day to day basis, but for specific home improvement tasks you will need to purchase, hire or borrow other tools and equipment. Some tools, like a creosote paintbrush, are cheap enough to use once and throw away; others will last for a lifetime if they are properly looked after.

Building and landscape gardening

For building and outdoor projects you will need a mixture of specialist builders' tools and general-purpose gardening implements.

Cement mixer

If you are concreting or mixing mortar on a large scale, consider buying or hiring a cement mixer. Be sure to wash the drum thoroughly after use.

Wheelbarrow

For heavyweight tasks, such as moving rubble or sand, you will need a robust builder's barrow. An ordinary lightweight garden wheelbarrow is not strong enough.

Extension reel

Essential when using power tools without a nearby power point. Make sure you keep your extension reel away from water, and if the electrical load is heavy, unwind the reel so that the wires do not overheat. You must have RCD protection when using electrical devices outdoors (see page 290).

Bucket

Choose a sturdy one, preferably with measurements marked inside.

Soft short-handled brush

A handbrush with soft bristles is perfect for finishing off mortared joints in bricks and stone.

Long bar

The long bar is good for prising, levering and also breaking up surfaces.

Tape measure: 30m

An extra-long tape measure is essential for jobs like fencing or building a garden wall.

Straightedge

Any straight piece of rigid and easy to handle timber will make a good straightedge.

Builder's line and pins

This nylon line is an essential guide for lining up and maintaining a level when building a structure of blocks or bricks.

Cold chisel

This is used for cutting through masonry. Strike it with a club hammer, and get one with a plastic safety sleeve to protect your hand from misplaced hammer blows.

Bolster chisel: 100mm

Use this to cut bricks and concrete blocks as well as for general levering.

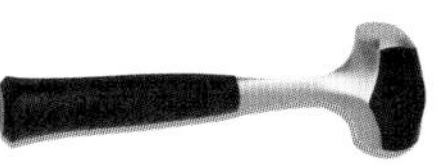

Club hammer

Use a club hammer for small-scale demolition work, or for jobs like driving lightweight posts into the ground.

Bricklayer's trowel

Builders use 300mm-long trowels but you will find it easier to use a shorter trowel until you are more experienced.

Pointing trowel

This small-bladed trowel (between 75mm and 100mm long) is handy for repairing and shaping mortar joints in bricks.

Builder's float

For finishing concrete or applying render and plaster to walls.

Pointing hawk

This lightweight handheld platform is ideal for carrying small quantities of mortar to the wall when pointing.

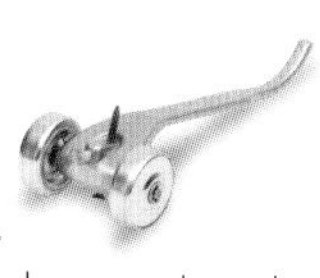

Jointing tool

This is used to shape neat mortar joints in brickwork, and also to rake out old mortar ready for repointing.

Pickaxe

Break up ground with a pickaxe or long bar rather than a spade or shovel, especially if there is buried rubble and rocks.

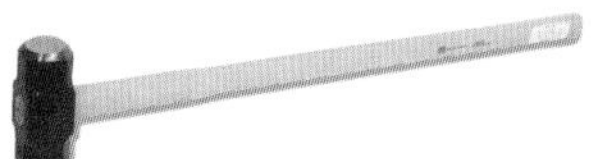

Sledgehammer

This is the tool for smashing up hardcore or slabs, and is also good for driving in fenceposts and stakes.

Shovel

The curved edges of a shovel make it ideal for moving aggregates as well as mixing and shifting mortar or concrete.

Spade

Dig holes and trenches with a spade. Steel alloy is good, and stainless steel best.

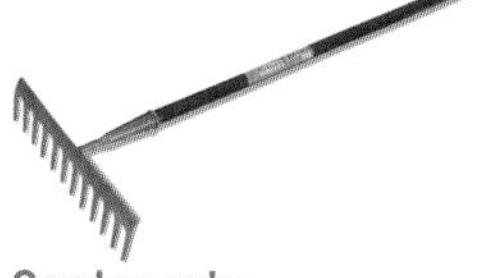

Garden rake

A common garden tool, useful for smoothing and spreading sand and gravel into place.

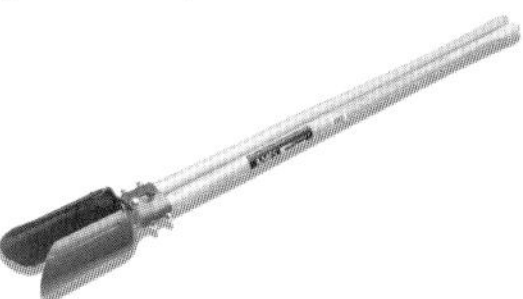

Post-hole borer

Use this to make neat holes in the ground for fence and gate posts.

Electrics and wiring

Besides general building tools, electrical and lighting improvements require a few specialist electrician's tools. It is also a sensible idea to keep a group of essential electrical tools together for emergencies, and store it in an easily accessible place.

EMERGENCY KIT

- Small terminal screwdriver
- Medium-sized flat-head screwdriver
- Pliers
- Retractable-blade knife
- Torch (with fresh batteries)
- PVC insulating tape

- Replacement 3–13 amp fuses

- Replacement cartridge fuses or fuse wire

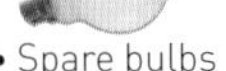

- Spare bulbs

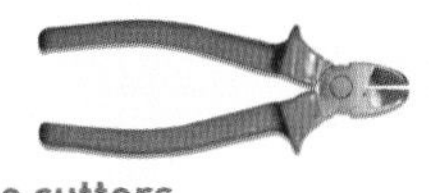

Side cutters

The best tool for cutting cables to an exact length.

Wire strippers

Remove the insulation from cables and flex cores with a wire stripper. The jaws will accommodate most core diameters.

Long-nosed pliers

For bending, twisting and positioning cable cores. Available with insulating handles for extra safety.

Terminal screwdriver

For tightening small terminal screws only – the driver blade is too delicate for anything else.

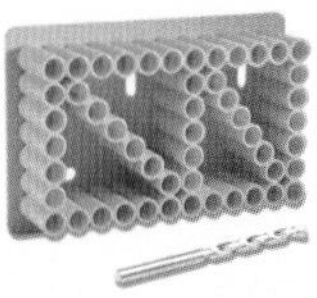

Socket template

Useful for installing flush-mounted socket boxes. The hard plastic guide provides an easy-to-use drilling template.

Immersion heater spanner

This inexpensive tool is specially designed for removing and fitting the electrical element in an immersion heater.

Socket tester

A plug-in tester that confirms that a circuit is dead – and so safe to work on – and also whether a socket is wired correctly.

Voltage tester

Test that a lighting circuit is dead with a voltage meter or a volt stick (pictured). Either way, be sure to use it properly and safely (see page 270).

Hand lamp or torch

Whenever you have to work without light or power, you will need a good battery-powered torch or lamp.

Plumbing

Plumbing repairs and improvements require a few specialist items and a variety of general-purpose tools as well.

Pipe cutter

It's possible to cut copper pipe with a hacksaw, but you will do a more accurate and neat job with a pipe cutter. Some come with a built-in reamer to remove burrs and rough edges from the inside of the pipe.

Mini pipe cutter

Works like a pipe cutter, but is circular-shaped and ideal for working in confined spaces.

Bending springs

You can bend copper pipes up to 28mm in diameter by hand. To stop the pipe kinking, insert a bending spring; they are available in 15mm and 22mm sizes.

Pipe bending machine

If you are running a lot of new copper pipes, this tool is invaluable. Its levers make easy work of bending pipes to the profiles you require.

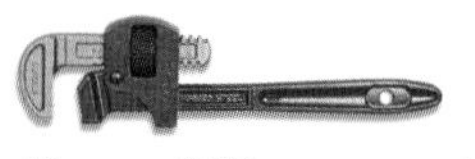

Pipe or Stillson wrench

Designed for gripping pipework, the jaws of the wrench self-tighten as you apply force.

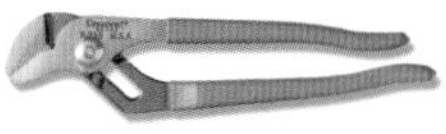

Slip-joint or waterpump pliers

With long handles and an easy-to-adjust slip jaw, these pliers are a useful tool for undoing fittings. But if you want to avoid damaging the finish, use a precision spanner instead.

Pipe cleaning rods

Flexible 1m-long polypropylene rods that screw together so you can reach blockages in drains and inspection chambers. There are a range of cleaning heads, including scrapers, plungers and corkscrews.

Radiator bleed key

For releasing trapped air from a radiator.

Basin wrench or crowsfoot spanner

This has a pivoting jaw that can be set for tightening or loosening tap connectors.

Cranked spanner

Double-ended wrench, also for use on tap connectors.

Half-round metal file

For removing burrs inside the ends of cut copper pipe.

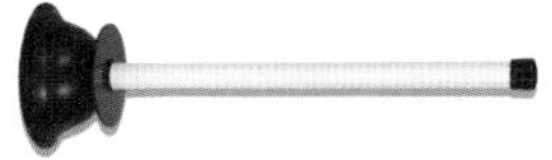

Plunger

The traditional device for clearing a blocked sink, basin or bath; pump up and down to create pulses of air and water.

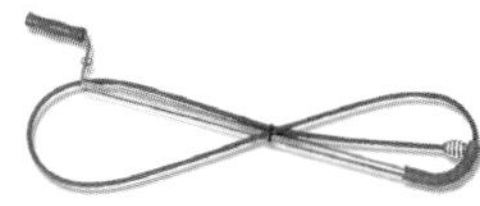

Lavatory auger

Insert the wire and rotate the handle to clear the blockage.

EMERGENCY KIT

Pipe repair clamp

For instant but temporary repairs to pipes, clamp this rubber-lined collar over the leak and tighten the screws to seal it.

Freezing kit

When you want or need to do plumbing work without draining the system, use a freezing kit to create temporary ice plugs in the pipework.

Epoxy putty

For patch repairs to all types of leaking pipework

- Short lengths of copper pipe

- Push fit couplings for joining pipes

- Tap washers
- Plunger
- Adjustable spanner
- Self-grip wrench
- Pliers
- Junior hacksaw
- Screwdrivers

TOOLS WOODWORKING, DECORATING

Woodworking

Lots of home improvements involve simple carpentry tasks, and these tools will help you work accurately and effectively.

Try square

To mark up and cut timber square, or to check the accuracy of right angles, use a try square (or a combination square, see page 350).

Sanding block

To smooth flat surfaces or square edges, wrap abrasive paper around a flat-based sanding block, often made of cork, and grip the paper with your fingers as you work.

Jack plane

The jack plane is a good all-purpose plane, used for shaving fine layers off the surface of wood to smooth and reduce it.

Smoothing plane

Larger than the jack plane, a smoothing plane gives a finer finish.

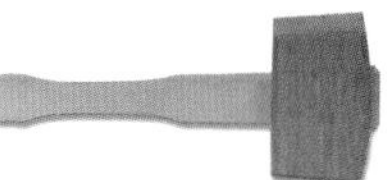

Carpenter's mallet

Often made from solid beech, a carpenter's mallet is specially designed for use with a chisel.

Pincers

The broad jaws of pincers are perfect for removing nails; grip and roll the nail out of the surface. Some pincers are also equipped with a tack lifter in the handle.

Padsaw

A padsaw or keyhole saw is used for cutting curves and enlarging holes in timber. Some have interchangeable blades for cutting plasterboard too.

Tenon saw

One of the backsaw family, all of which have a stiffened metal top edge the tenon saw has fine teeth, making it ideal for precision workworking and joinery.

Floorboard saw

Designed to cut accurately into or across floorboards, a floorboard saw is invaluable when renovating a home with old wooden floors.

Mitre box

The perfect device for cutting 45° and 90° mitres in all types of wood and plaster mouldings. Available in plastic or wood, and different sizes too. Use a tenon saw in a mitre box.

Painting

Manufacturers are constantly introducing new tools and equipment (as well as materials) that can reduce the labour of painting and speed the process.

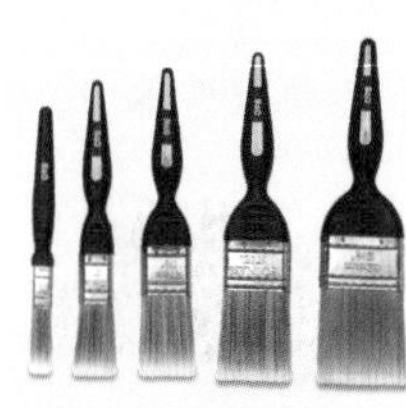

Paintbrushes

A good-quality bristle brush that is well looked after will give the best results over the years, but the new generation of synthetic bristle or mix-bristle brushes are great value and also give an excellent finish, particularly with water-based paints. Smaller brushes (12mm or 25mm) are for fiddly work; 50mm for doors and skirtings; 100mm and 150mm are ideal for walls and ceilings.

Cutting in (sash) brush

The angled cut of these bristles helps you get a neat result in the corners and inside edges of window frames.

Paint kettle

Life is easier if you carry around small quantities of paint at a time – so decant into a plastic or metal paint kettle.

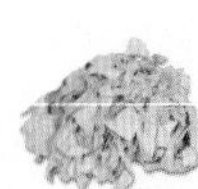

Special effects brushes, sea sponge, rags

Some paint effects can be created using everyday objects like a clean cotton rag or a plastic bag, but others – such as sponging and dragging – require specific tools.

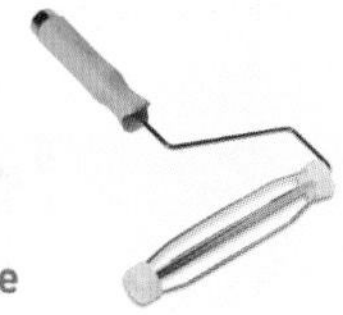

Roller handle

When you want to paint walls and ceilings quickly, a roller is the answer. Buy a durable roller handle with wire cage, which makes it easy to change the sleeve, but also makes the sleeve less likely to slip off than cheaper push-fit roller handles.

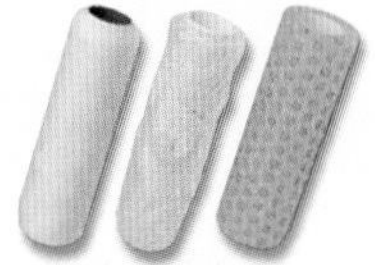

Roller sleeves

Suit your roller sleeve to your type of paint or the desired effect. The most common sleeves are finished with cropped wool or synthetic pile – ideal for painting smooth surfaces with a water-based paint.

Tack cloth

This will remove all traces of dust before you apply a final coat of paint or varnish.

Roller tray

A metal or plastic roller tray is essential when painting with a roller. Pour paint into the deep end of the tray and roll the roller across the ribbed surface so that the paint is applied evenly across its sleeve.

Corner roller

A normal roller will not reach into corners. You will need a corner roller to finish the job, or use a brush.

Radiator roller

A special long-handled roller designed for painting behind radiators.

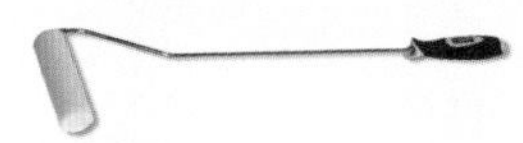

Telescopic pole

You can extend your reach to the ceiling with a telescopic pole that slips onto the handle of a roller or paint pad. Or look out for rollers with a shorter but still useful built-in extension handle.

Paint shield

A paint shield or 'george' can be used to create a clean edge at skirting boards and cornices, or for keeping paint off windows when you are painting the frames.

Paint pads and trays

Often sold in kits complete with trays or a roller applicator tray, paint pads are quick, light and easy to use, particularly on large areas with a smooth, flat surface.

Paintbrush cleaning kettle

Looking after good, and expensive, paintbrushes is well worth it – and now you can buy cheap and easy-to-clean pots to store and clean all types of paint and brushes.

Wallpapering

Having the correct tools will make the job simpler and the finished result much neater.

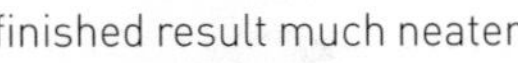

Paste brush
You can use any 100mm or 125mm paintbrush to apply paste, but a paste brush has a thicker wedge of soft bristles and is easier to use.

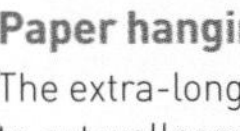

Paper hanging scissors
The extra-long blades make it easier to cut wallpaper in straight lines.

Wallpaper table (pasting table)
Higher than a kitchen table and just wider than a roll of wallpaper, this lightweight folding platform is perfect for measuring, cutting and pasting paper. W-leg tables are more stable than cheaper versions, and plastic ones are sturdiest of all, as well as being the easiest to clean and store.

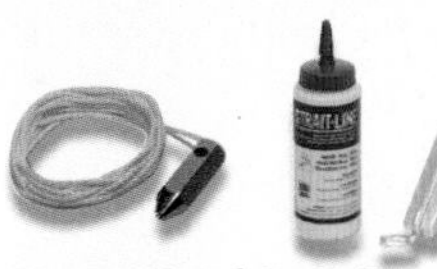

Plumb line/chalk line
Use a plumb line – a weight on the end of a string – to establish a vertical. For drawing a straight line on most surfaces, snap a chalk line.

Paper hanging brush
The soft bristles on this brush are designed to smooth wallpaper by squeezing out bubbles and excess paste. Wash the bristles in warm water when you've finished.

Seam roller
Smooth the seams between lengths of wallpaper with this tiny roller – but don't use it on embossed or fragile papers.

Wallpaper scorer
When soaking wallpaper ready for stripping, score the surface first with a rotary scorer to enable the water to penetrate. Then use a scraper to lift the paper off the wall.

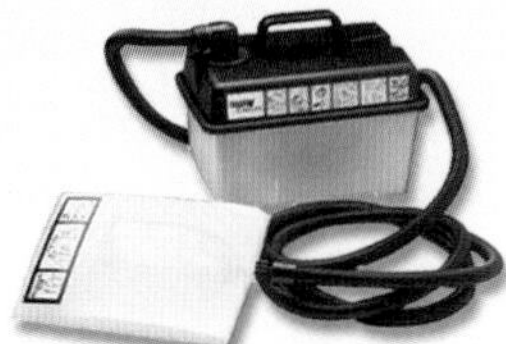

Wallpaper steamer
Steaming is the fastest way to strip wallpaper. It makes good sense to buy a steamer when you have a lot of paper to strip.

Combination smoother/cutter
Smooth the wallpaper into place then cut around obstructions with the retractable snap-off blade. Don't press too hard on fragile papers.

Tiling

When using tile-cutting and snapping tools, don't forget that you will need safety goggles and gloves to protect you from flying fragments and sharp edges.

Tile scorer
Get a clean break in a tile by scoring first through the glaze using a tile scorer with either a tungsten carbide tip or steel wheel.

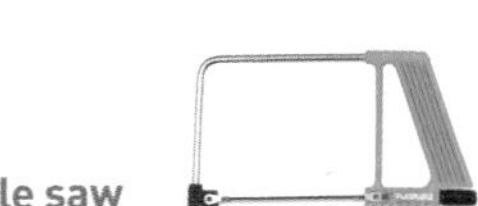

Tile saw
Used for cutting curved lines through a tile. You can also use a jigsaw or rotozip with a ceramic blade for this task.

Tile file
Removes rough edges from a cut tile.

Tile snippers or nibblers
For very narrow cuts, score first and then nibble to the line with these tungsten carbide-edged pincers. Also ideal for cutting mosaic tiles.

Tile snapper
Snap a tile in two by scoring and then squeezing the marked line between the jaws of a tile snapper. Some have an integral scoring blade too.

Electric tile cutter
The rotary blade on this machine will cut through all types of tiles; if you are tiling a large area, it's worth buying this relatively inexpensive power tool.

Heavy-duty tile cutter
Lever-actioned tile cutters, which score and snap, are available for both wall tiles and thicker floor tiles.

Notched spreader
A notched spreader will give you the correct depth of adhesive, evenly spread. Buy one for either wall or floor tiles, or choose a multi-toothed tool for both surfaces.

Grout spreader
Designed to spread grout across tiles and into the joints; you can buy different sizes of spreader for wall and floor use.

Stripping and filling

Choose your stripping method with care so as not to damage the surface (see pages 128–29).

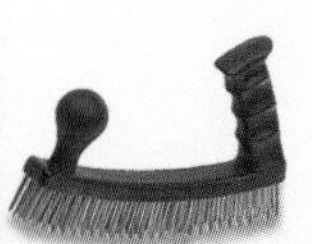

Wire brush
A good stiff wire brush will loosen flaking paint and surface rust from metalwork.

Hot-air gun
A safer alternative to the old-fashioned blowtorch, a hot-air gun lets you control the heat easily when softening paint before stripping.

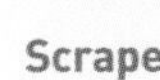

Scraper
A must-have for preparing any surfaces – particularly removing old paint or wallpaper. Scrapers have stiff blades, and though they can be used to apply filler, you will get a neater result with a filling knife.

Combination shavehook
For use with chemical paint stripper or a hot-air gun. The blade is designed for scraping paint from flat, concave and convex surfaces.

Profile gauge
Mould the profile of an obstruction onto this tool and then transfer the pattern to your tile, or any floor covering.

Glass scraper
If you accidentally spatter mirrors and glass with paint, scrape it off when dry with this scraper.

Putty knife
Shaped to allow you to smooth and finish putty in window frames.

Sponge
Synthetic and tough, a decorator's sponge is useful for wiping and mopping up after decorating tasks.

Filling knife
This has a similar appearance to a scraper, but the flexible blade makes it ideal for forcing filler into cracks and crevices in walls.

Cartridge gun
Tubes of various types of sealant or grab adhesive will fit this easy-to-use spring-loaded applicator.

MATERIALS TIMBER, MOULDINGS

Timber falls into two categories – softwood and hardwood. It is generally more expensive than man-made boards, of which there are many different kinds with different uses. Mouldings have a whole range of uses, including holding glass in place in doors and windows, hiding expansion gaps and joins, or just adding a decorative touch to an interior.

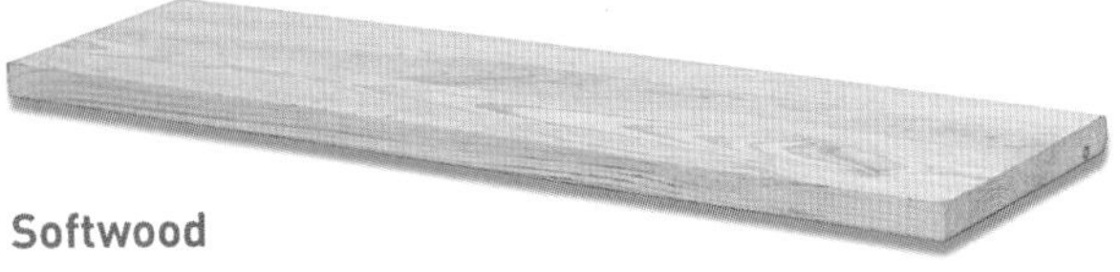

Softwood

Softwood is sold as rough (sawn) or smooth (planed) timber. Use planed timber when the appearance of the wood matters; it is often sold as the size before planing, and if so you need to take this into account when planning a job as planing can remove 4mm–6mm. When buying softwood, avoid timber with black knots (unlike brown ones, they will shrink and may drop out), warping, splits and wide cracks.

Wood is sold in standard thicknesses and widths, ranging from 12mm x 25mm to 75mm x 225mm. It can also be bought as tongue-and-groove boards for flooring and panelling. Wall panelling may be flush tongue-and-groove or V-jointed (known as TGV) to emphasise the junction between the boards. Buy all the TGV boards you will need at the same time as batches can differ slightly.

ECO TIMBER FSC

Always buy timber bearing the stamp of the Forest Stewardship Council. That way you can be certain it has come from a well-managed source that isn't adding to global deforestation and climate change.

Hardwoods

Hardwood can be bought machined or as whole planks cut from the log and seasoned. The colour can vary even between trees of the same species. Tools need to be sharp for cutting hardwood and screw fixings require pilot holes to be drilled first. Brass or plated screws should be used in oak – the acid in the wood will turn steel screws black.

Hardwood veneers are thin sheets of wood used to cover softwood or man-made boards such as plywood and chipboard. Nowadays there is a wide range of veneers, and you can buy several sheets or single pieces.

Man-made boards

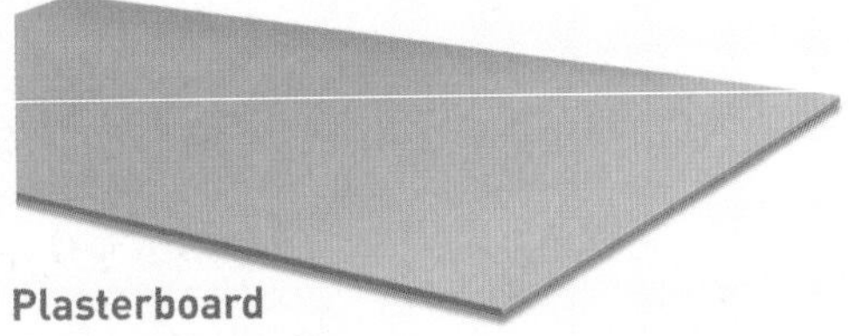

Plasterboard

Plasterboard is ideal for covering walls and ceilings to give them a clean flat surface for painting or papering. It is made by covering gypsum plaster with heavy-duty paper on both sides, and it comes in a variety of thicknesses and sizes. Standard plasterboard is usually grey on one side and ivory-coloured on the other side. You can decorate straight on to the ivory side or give it a coat of finishing plaster before decorating.

Thermal plasterboard and urethane laminate board have a polystyrene layer which makes them suitable for use as insulating linings. Vapour-check thermal board also has a water-resistant membrane between the plasterboard and the polystyrene.

Plasterboard can be fixed to timber studs using plasterboard nails, or metal studs using special self-tapping dry-wall screws.

Chipboard

Chipboard is manufactured by bonding small chips of softwood together under pressure. Standard chipboard and moisture-resistant chipboard are available. Melamine- and wood-veneer-coated chipboard are popular for shelves and kitchen worktops. Chipboard is sold in thicknesses of 9, 12, 15 or 18mm and a standard sheet is 2440mm x 1220mm.

MDF

MDF, short for medium-density fibreboard, is the best known type of fibreboard, which is a type of board made from wood fibres that are compressed and stuck together under pressure. MDF comes in a range of thicknesses in a sheet size of 2440mm x 1220mm. Cut edges can be painted; they don't need to be covered with veneer or wooden lipping.

Plywood

Plywood consists of thin wooden sheets bonded on top of each other, with the direction of the grain alternating at right angles in each layer. Edges are smooth enough to leave plain or they can be covered with a thin strip of veneer or wooden lipping. Thicknesses range from 3mm–18mm and the standard sheet sizes are 2440mm x 1220mm, 1220mm x 1220mm and 1220mm x 610mm.

Hardboard

Hardboard is made from compressed softwood pulp. The thin sheets are easy to cut, but they are not as rigid or strong as other man-made boards. However, hardboard is a cheap alternative, ideal for drawer bottoms or as underlay for some floor coverings. Standard hardboard is 3.2mm thick and shiny one side, textured the other.

Mouldings

There is a vast selection of mouldings available. They are usually made from softwoods, but hardwood and MDF (medium-density fibreboard) are also sometimes used, while ceiling mouldings are made from plaster or polystyrene.

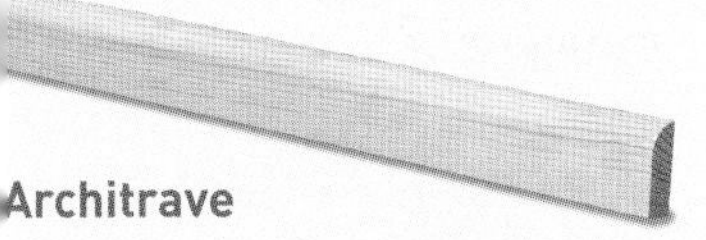

Architrave

Used to hide the join between a door frame and the wall.

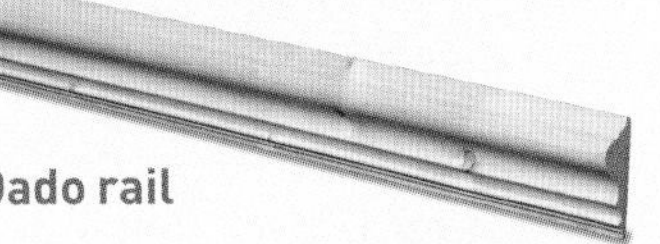

Dado rail

Divides the lower (dado) and upper area of wall.

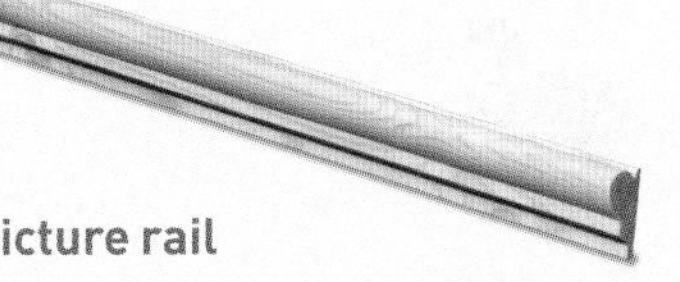

Picture rail

Positioned on the upper part of a wall, it may be used to hang pictures from or serve simply as a decorative feature.

Dowelling

Ranges in size from tiny dowels for plugging screw holes to diameters suitable for use as curtain poles.

Staff and parting beads

Used in sash windows to keep the sashes in place.

Glass beads

Used to hold glass in place on doors and window frames.

Quadrant

Covers the gap between skirting and floor, and between wooden windows and the window sill.

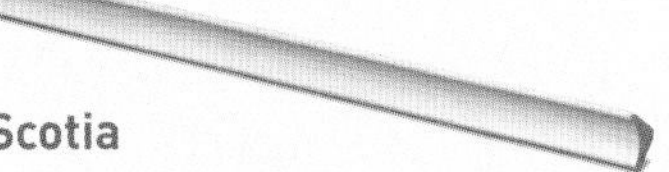

Scotia

A more decorative moulding that is used like quadrant.

Square or rectangular moulding

Can be used as retaining beads for glass panels in doors or for finishing the edges of chipboard and plywood shelves.

Half-round moulding

Gives a curved finish to man-made boards like chipboard.

Triangle moulding

Used as a finishing for internal corners.

Skirting

Used to hide the join between a floor and a wall, skirting is sold in a variety of heights and profiles. In older houses skirtings can be as tall as 300mm; in more modern homes they are generally about 175mm high. Newer houses often have either torus, ovolo or a bevelled/rounded skirting. Most standard skirting boards are made of softwood, ready for painting. Moulded reverse skirtings have a different profile on each side of the board, so always check you are using the correct profile as you cut and fit them.

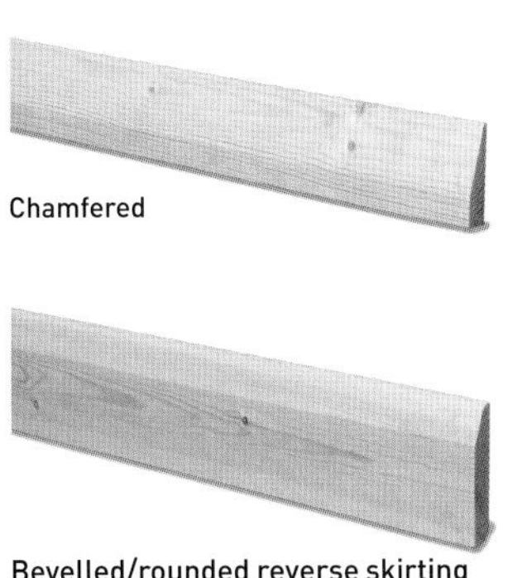

Chamfered

Bevelled/rounded reverse skirting

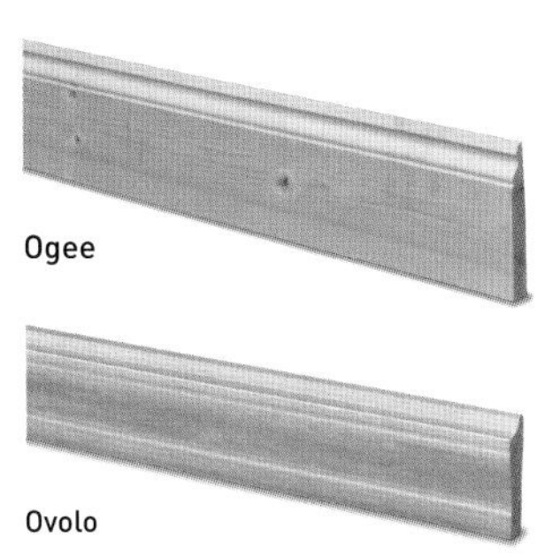

Ogee

Ovolo

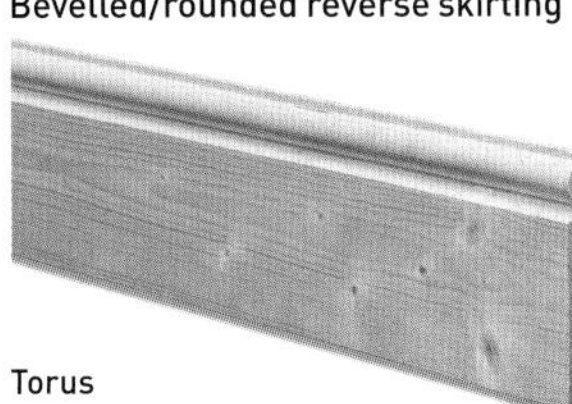

Torus

Coving

A prefabricated decorative plaster or polystyrene moulding fitted at the wall/ceiling junction in a room.

Cornice

A highly ornate form of coving found in some period houses.

Masonry

The term masonry refers to the stone, brickwork or concrete from which the walls of a house are built.

Stone

Few houses are built of natural stone these days, though there are plenty of old stone houses around, many coated with render on the outside to make them more weather-resistant. Stone may be used for building garden walls but it is far more expensive than other building materials.

Brick

Bricks are made from baked clay and their colour varies according to the type of clay used. They come in a standard size of 215mm x 112.5mm x 65mm and various special shapes are available for decorative brickwork.

There are three varieties: facings, commons and engineering bricks. Facings are used for exposed brickwork because of their attractive appearance as well as their structural qualities. Commons are general-purpose bricks that are not as finely finished as facings, so they are used for building walls that will be plastered or rendered or for the inner leaf of cavity walls. Engineering bricks are extremely strong bricks which are impervious to water. They are usually used underground for constructions like manholes. Bricks are made with differing levels of frost-resistance (see page 213).

Concrete blocks

Cast-concrete blocks are widely used in house-building. Lightweight concrete blocks are made from aerated concrete so they are easy to cut and drill. They are used for both internal and external walls, and are good for acoustic and thermal insulation. Dense concrete blocks, also known as medium-density or dense-aggregate blocks, are heavier and less common. Frost-resistant, moisture-proof blocks are used for foundations and walling below ground level. Blocks measure approximately 450mm x 225mm (length and height) while the thickness can vary from 75mm to 230mm.

Glass

Glass is sold by its thickness in mm. Most glass in domestic doors or windows is 4mm thick.

Float glass

The modern method of making glass involves floating a layer of molten glass on a bath of liquid tin to produce a flat sheet with no distortion. Known as float glass, this has now replaced plate glass, which was made by casting glass on a flat surface and then grinding and polishing both surfaces. Float glass is made in thicknesses of 3mm–25mm and is very strong, so is used for picture windows and glass items such as tabletops.

Safety glass

The term safety glass refers to any kind of strengthened glass, including toughened, laminated and fire-resistant wired glass. It is used for glazed doors, low-level windows and shower screens.

Toughened or tempered glass

To make toughened glass, ordinary glass is cut to shape, heated and then cooled rapidly. This makes it more shock-resistant and much stronger. The glass breaks into granules rather than sharp shards, making it suitable for doors or other areas that could be subject to sudden impact.

Fire-resistant glass

A steel mesh is sandwiched between two layers of glass during manufacture so that if the glass cracks, the mesh holds it in place for a time, helping to prevent the spread of fire and smoke.

Laminated glass

Two or more layers of glass are bonded together with clear plastic film between them. The film helps to hold the glass in place if it is broken.

Patterned or obscured glass

One side of the molten glass is given a textured surface or a decorative pattern with a special roller. Patterned glass is available in plain or tinted versions and in thicknesses of 3mm and 5mm. It is used for decorative effect and for privacy, such as in bathrooms.

Low emissivity glass

This is ordinary glass with a special chemical coating on one side that helps prevent heat loss. It may be used in double glazing or in greenhouses.

Non-reflective glass

Mainly used in picture frames, this glass looks clear but has a slightly textured surface that reduces reflections.

Solar-control glass

Laminated or patterned glass can be tinted or coated to reduce heat penetration in summer and heat loss in winter.

Insulation

There are various insulating materials you can use to reduce heat loss through floors and ceilings.

Blanket insulation

Blanket insulation is made from mineral fibre or glass fibre. It is sold in rolls usually 100mm, 150mm or 200mm thick and comes in two widths – 370mm, which matches the joist spacing in older houses, and 600mm for more modern houses. Measure the gap between your joists and buy rolls the same width so you can simply unroll and lay the insulation between them. Some types of blanket insulation have a paper backing to prevent tearing; others have a foil or polythene backing which acts as a vapour barrier, stopping moist air passing into the material. If using blanket insulation with no backing, lay a vapour barrier underneath it, either reflective foil building paper (sold in rolls) or sheets of polythene.

Slab insulation

Mineral-fibre insulation is also available in slabs 50mm thick, measuring about 1140mm x 465mm. These are easier to handle, but are more expensive than blanket insulation.

Loose insulation

Loose-lay or loose-fill insulation is made from mineral fibre, vermiculite granules or polystyrene granules and comes in bags ready to be tipped between the joists. It needs no cutting or fitting and is easier to use in lofts where the joist spacing is not of a standard size. Granules can blow about in a draughty loft; to prevent this, lay granules level with the top of the joists and then cover them with sheets of building paper.

Rigid insulation

Semi-rigid sheets of glass fibre or mineral fibre are also available, or you can get rigid blocks of foamed polystyrene or polyurethane, some with foil on each side.

Draught excluders

Draught excluders reduce heat loss through gaps around doors and windows, and are available in a variety of shapes and sizes.

Self-adhesive foam strip

Use on casement windows and interior doors; simply peel the backing strip off and cut to length. Cheap strips harden and need replacing after a year or two; better-quality ones will last up to five years.

Self-adhesive rubber strip

This is used in the same way as foam strip but is tougher and longer lasting.

Flexible tube

This is fixed to interior doors and wooden casement window frames. The rubber tube is compressed to form a seal when the door or window shuts onto it.

Brush strip

This consists of nylon pile on self-adhesive strips or in a metal or plastic holder. It can be used on doors or windows, tacked to the frame.

Sprung strip

Made from thin metal or nylon, this is stronger than foam or rubber strips. It is good for sealing around doors and windows where the gap is uneven because the strip springs to form a flexible seal between the surfaces. It has pre-drilled holes and is supplied with pins. It can be used on interior and exterior doors, and wooden casement and sash windows. Self-adhesive sprung strip is also available but is not so hardwearing – fit it to windows that are not often opened.

YOU CAN DO IT

Sealing gaps

You can use silicone rubber sealant to draught-proof doors or casement windows with irregular gaps around the frame that might be difficult to seal with other forms of draught excluder.

TREATMENTS AND FINISHES

Interior walls are usually finished with paint, wallpaper or tiles, and there are endless colours and styles to choose from. Before you start, you may need to prime or seal the surfaces.

SAFETY FIRST

Paint with a high lead content can cause poisoning. Most paints are now lead-free but before stripping old paint, always check it first with a lead-testing kit (see page 128). If the result is positive, you must use a special chemical stripper and take all the precautions advised by the manufacturer.

Primers and sealers

On bare wood, plaster or metal surfaces you will get a better result if you use a primer first. The primer provides a surface to which the paint can bond, and will stop paint being absorbed. There are primers to suit different surfaces, inside and outside the house.

PRIMERS AND SEALERS

Type of surface	Primer/sealer	Use
Bare plaster plaster or wood	All-purpose primer, or wood or plaster primer	Seals porous surfaces and gives the paint a surface to grip.
New or exposed plaster	Plaster sealer	Prevents paint being absorbed by the plaster.
Bare wood	Primer-undercoat	Saves time and effort because you can go straight to the top coat afterwards.
Stained walls or plaster, or areas treated with preservative	Stain block primer	Has aluminium scales which form a barrier, sealing in the stain. Two coats may be needed.
Knots in wood	Knotting solution	This is a shellac (resin) solution which prevents the resin in the wood from bleeding through and discolouring the paint. Coat with primer when dry.
Interior or exterior surface with mould, algae or lichen	Fungicidal wash	Kills the spores. Brush them away and apply a second coat.
Flaking external walls (usually render but can be used on exposed brick and stone)	Stabilising solution/primer	Binds chalky/flaky surfaces to make a sound base for paint. If there is any sign of mould, apply fungicidal wash first.
Metal	Metal primer	Contains zinc to help prevent rust. Different types available for different metals. Rusted metal should be cleaned and primed with a rust-inhibiting primer.

How to decide on the right type of paint

Paint comes in two main types: oil-based and water-based. Oil-based paints need an undercoat; with emulsion paint the first coat acts as an undercoat. When painting large areas like walls and ceilings, you should only use water-based paint. Oil- and solvent-based paints give off fumes that are harmful to your health and to the environment, so use them only on small areas like woodwork and trims, and make certain there is very good ventilation both while you apply them and while they dry. Even better, use water-based alternatives. The chart below covers general-purpose paints and where to use them. You can also buy specialised paints, such as floor and radiator paint.

CHOOSING THE RIGHT PAINT

Paint	Surface	Use
Undercoat	Interior and exterior surfaces. Apply over primer, where necessary, and before the top coat.	Apply a second coat if colour underneath shows through.
Vinyl or acrylic emulsion (interior)	Walls and ceilings.	Water-based paint that does not need separate undercoat. Available as matt, silk or soft sheen finishes.
New-plaster emulsion	Newly plastered walls and ceilings.	New plaster takes months to dry out fully; this type of emulsion is more permeable than ordinary emulsion, allowing moisture to pass through and evaporate.
One-coat emulsion	Walls and ceilings.	Better coverage than ordinary emulsion.
Anti-condensation emulsion paint	Bathrooms and kitchens.	Semi-porous emulsion that reduces condensation by preventing water droplets forming on the surface of the wall.
Emulsion (exterior)	Exterior walls.	Hardwearing water-based paint.
Multi-surface acrylic emulsion	Walls, ceilings, wood, metal and radiators.	Water-based paint similar to emulsion. Available as matt and satin finishes.
Gloss paint (water-based)	Interior wood and metal.	Fast-drying, high-sheen paint.
Gloss paint (oil-based)	Any undercoated surface.	Oil-based paint that is slow to dry but very hardwearing.
Non-drip one-coat gloss paint	Woodwork.	Combines undercoat and top coat.
Masonry paint	Exterior render.	A stronger exterior emulsion paint. Paint walls first with stabilising solution and a fungicide, if necessary.
Textured paint	Uneven plaster surfaces.	Much thicker than ordinary paint so can hide cracks. Can be over-painted with emulsion.

How much paint do you need?

Manufacturers specify on the paint container the area that the paint will cover; this varies according to the surface you are painting. To calculate your surface area, measure the height and width in metres, then multiply the figures together to get the area in square metres.

To calculate the total wall area of a large room, or more than one room, break it down into smaller areas, multiply the height by the width of each area, then add all the numbers together.

Choosing the right type of wallpaper

Wallpapers come in numerous finishes and range from everyday, hardwearing, economical papers to very expensive hand-painted ones that need to be treated with care. Porous surfaces should be coated first with size, a special sealer that prevents them soaking up the paste.

CHOOSING THE RIGHT WALLPAPER

Paper	Description	Uses
Lining paper	Plain undecorated paper.	Hung on bare wall surfaces under wallpaper. Can be papered or painted over.
Standard wallpaper	Flat wallpaper with a design machine-printed on its surface.	Price and quality vary. Cheap papers tear easily, making them harder to hang.
Woodchip	Small chips of wood glued between two layers of paper.	Hides rough wall surfaces. Should be painted with emulsion.
Vinyl	A printed PVC surface laminated to a paper backing.	Water-resistant, so wipes clean. Heavy-duty vinyls are good for kitchens and bathrooms.
Blown or textured vinyl	Screen-printed and then heated to create a textured effect that can also be painted.	Covers uneven surfaces and cracked walls. Flat underside means it is easy to paste and easily peeled off. Relief doesn't crush, as embossed paper can.
Embossed	Raised pattern is imprinted in the paper during manufacture.	Must be hung with care to avoid flattening the relief pattern.
Flock	Fibres such as velvet pile are bonded in patterns to the surface of the paper.	Expensive paper; hung the same way as standard paper.
Hand-printed/ screen-printed	Screen-printed or block-printed paper that is printed one roll at a time.	Attractive but expensive paper. Hand prints are very delicate and need expert hanging.
Paste the wall	Wide variety of printed and textured papers.	Special backing that doesn't expand when wet, so paste can be applied straight to the wall. Quick and clean to hang. Can be trimmed with a knife.

Choosing the right wall tiles

Wall tiles can vary in size from 25mm-square mosaic tiles up to 400mm x 250mm tiles, but the most commonly used sizes are 108mm and 150mm squares. Tiles can resist fairly high temperatures without cracking, but if you are tiling around a cooker or fireplace, check that the tiles you plan to use are suitably heat-resistant.

Standard field tiles

There is a huge choice available of ceramic wall tiles, in different colours, patterns and sizes, including hand-painted ones. Standard tiles have square edges, but you can buy tiles with two rounded glazed edges for using at the corner of a panel, and tiles with one rounded edge for panel borders or for turning external corners.

Mosaic tiles

These tiny tiles are usually sold in sheets on a mesh backing or with a paper facing that holds them together while laying.

Marble tiles

Genuine marble tiles are very expensive but marble-effect tiles are also available and these are much more affordable.

Insert tiles

Some tiles are specially shaped with one corner cut off so that they can be laid in a continuous pattern that includes smaller decorative insert tiles. Larger insert tiles can contain bathroom accessories such as soap dishes or lavatory paper holders.

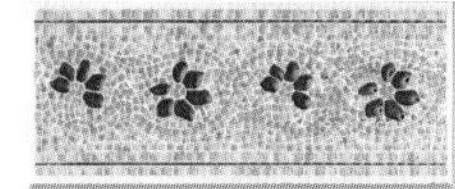

Borders

Borders can be used to create a decorative edge around the room. Special angled tiles and square corner mouldings are available for fitting to the edge of a worktop.

Tile adhesives, grout and sealants

Tile adhesives, available as a powder or ready-mixed, are used to stick tiles to the wall. Grout, also available as powder or ready-mixed, fills the gaps between tiles, and sealant is used to give a waterproof seal. Grout reviver will clean up dirty old grout to look like new.

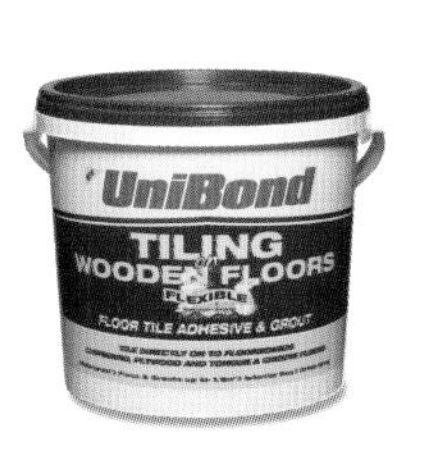

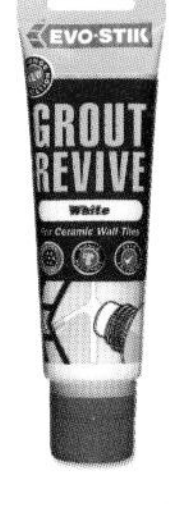

FIXINGS NAILS, SCREWS, GLUES

Whether you want to put up shelves or ceiling coving, fit a new kitchen or lay floor tiles, you will need some kind of fixing. There is a vast array of nails, screws and glues to choose from: those shown here are some of the most useful for general domestic jobs.

Nails

Steel nails come in all shapes and sizes. Outdoors, use zinc-plated galvanised nails to delay rusting.

Lost-head nail
Round nail that can be punched below the surface with a pin punch.

Masonry nail
Grips well in bricks and breeze blocks and is used for fixing wood to masonry.

Plain-head wire nail
General-purpose round nail. Can sometimes cause wood to split.

Oval wire nail
Oval shape helps to prevent wood splitting as it is hammered in.

Plasterboard nail
Jagged shank helps it to grip plasterboard.

Panel pin
Small, slim nail, easily punched in. Used for mouldings, joinery and general carpentry.

Cut floor brad
Nail with a rectangular cross-section used to fix floorboards to joists.

Ring-shanked nail
Round nail with rings around shank that make the fixing more secure.

Clout nail
Used for fixing slates and window sash cords.

Felt nail/large-head clout nail
Shorter than the clout nail; used for attaching roofing felt.

Screws

Screws provide a stronger fixing than nails and most of them can be unscrewed again. They are usually made of mild steel, but hardened steel, stainless steel, solid brass and steel plated with chromium or brass are also available, as are galvanised rust-proof screws for outdoor use.

A screw consists of the head, the shank and the thread. Its length is measured from the pointed tip of the thread to the part of the head that lies flush with the surface it is screwed into. The gauge is the shank diameter. Screws can be raised-head, which means the head sits above the surface, or countersunk, when the head is flush with or sinks below the surface. They can have either a slotted-head or a cross-head, which requires a cross-head screwdriver. Cross-head screws are easier to drive in than slotted-head ones, especially with a power screwdriver.

Countersunk woodscrew
The traditional unhardened woodscrew has a single thread. A pilot hole and a shank-clearance hole need to be drilled before it is fitted.

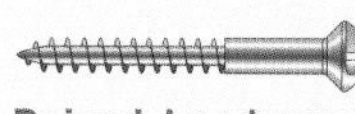

Raised-head woodscrew
Used for decorative hardware fittings, this screw is countersunk to the rim of the head.

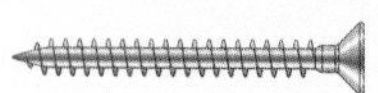

Hardened-steel woodscrew
Double threads enable fast insertion with no need for a pilot hole if screwing into softwood.

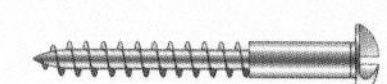

Round-head woodscrew
Used for fitting decorative door furniture.

Chipboard screw
Deep threads extend right up to the head of this screw. It can be used in wood as well as chipboard.

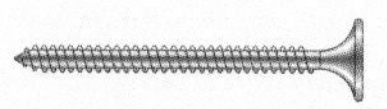

Dry-wall screw
A twin-threaded screw used for fixing plasterboard or fibreboard to timber studs.

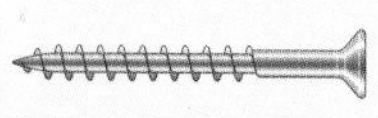

Carcass screw
With a thick shank and coarse thread, this can be useful for securing chipboard.

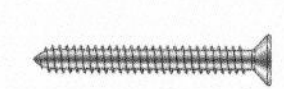

Self-tapping screw
Cuts its own thread in thin sheet metal and plastic.

Pilot and clearance holes

Screws go in more easily and accurately if you drill a narrow pilot hole to guide them. When you are screwing one thing to another you will need to drill a clearance hole through the top layer so that the screw thread cuts only into the lower one.

Countersunk screws

To countersink a screw, use a countersink drill bit to drill a shallow crater at the top of the pilot hole so that when you screw it in the head lies flush with the surface of the wood. For a completely smooth finish, fill the recess with wood filler and sand it when dry.

Screw gauges

The imperial system of screw gauges ranked the shank diameter as a number from 1 to 20 – the higher the gauge, the bigger the screw. Their metric equivalents are not nearly so user-friendly, but they are the way screws are now increasingly sold. The table below will help.

SCREW GAUGES

Gauge		Clearance hole	Pilot hole
Metric	Imperial		
2mm	2	2.5mm	1.6mm
2.5mm	3	3mm	1.6mm
3mm	4	3.5mm	2mm
3.5mm	6	4mm	2mm
4mm	8	5mm	2.5mm
5mm	10	5.75mm	3.5mm
5.5mm	12	6.5mm	3.5mm
6.5mm	14	6.5mm	4mm

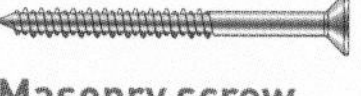

Masonry screw
A strong screw that can be driven into masonry without using a wallplug.

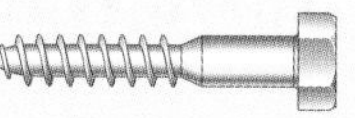

Coach screw
This has a square or hexagonal head that is driven with a spanner. It gives a very strong, heavy-duty fixing.

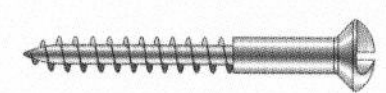

Security screw
The shape of the countersunk head prevents the screw being removed once it is in place.

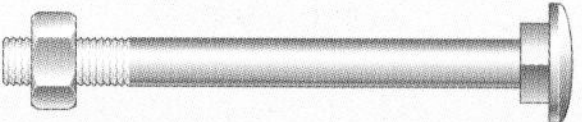

Coach bolt (cup square bolt)
Coach bolts have a square neck under a domed head that locks into the wood as the nut is tightened.

Fitting wallplugs to solid walls

A normal screw won't stay in masonry without a wallplug. The wallplug expands to grip the sides of the hole when the screw is driven in, so holding the screw securely in place. To drill into masonry, you need a power drill with hammer action and masonry bits. Make sure your wallplugs, screws and bit are of matching size.

SAFETY FIRST

Check for pipes and cables

Never drill into a wall blind – always check first for hidden pipes and cables using an electronic detector. Don't risk a flood, or worse, electrocution!

YOU CAN DO IT

Hold the power

If you don't have much experience using a drill, you may find it easier to achieve a neat, accurate result if you start the hole without the hammer action turned on.

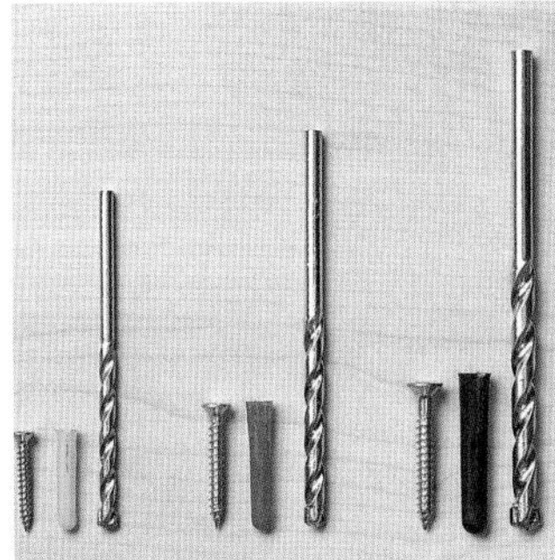

1 Select the correct size of plugs and drill bits for your screws. The yellow plugs here take 4mm gauge screws, the red take 5mm and the brown take 5.5mm (but note that wallplug colours can vary).

2 Hold the plug up to the drill and mark its length on the bit with tape. You should drill into the wall slightly deeper than the length of the plug.

3 Check for hidden pipes and cables (see SAFETY FIRST) then use a hammer setting to drill the hole. Keep the drill square to the wall and hold it steady or you will end up with a tapered hole.

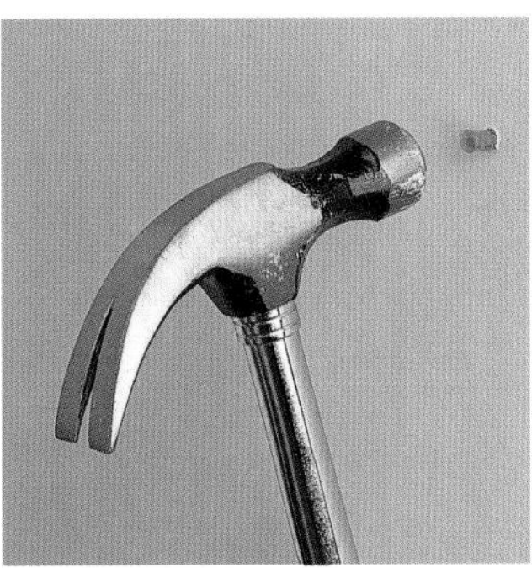

4 The wallplug should only require finger pressure to insert, but it should be a firm fit. Lightly tap the plug with a hammer to level it with the wall, if necessary.

Wallplugs

Moulded plastic wallplugs are produced on plastic 'trees' and the size of drill bit will be printed on the tree. Some manufacturers make different-sized wallplugs in different colours, but colours are not standard across all brands.

Straight plastic plugs

These are tubes with ribs running lengthways. They take the screw thread only, so they have to be cut shorter than the depth of the hole.

Moulded plastic wallplugs

These have a split end and take a range of screws.

Hammer-in plugs

Hammer-in plugs are the alternative to wallplugs and screws, good for fixing timber battens to masonry. One type has a wallplug with a ready-fitted screw. It is inserted into a drilled hole with a hammer and the screw then driven home. There is also a version of this designed for plasterboard. The other type has a flanged expansion sleeve fitted with a masonry nail.

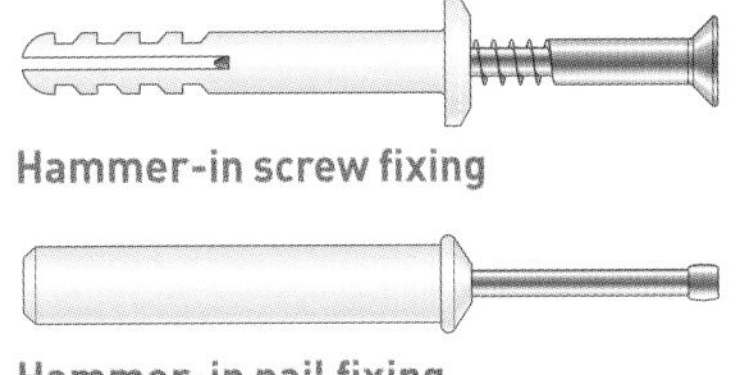

Hammer-in screw fixing

Hammer-in nail fixing

Heavy-duty fixings

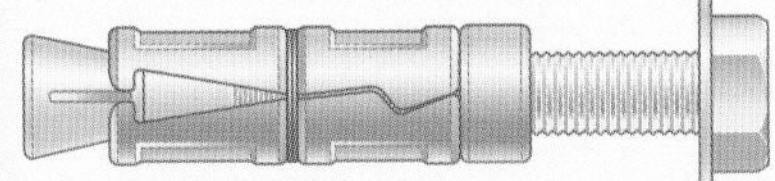

Expanding masonry bolt

This is an extremely strong fixing for attaching heavy items like fence posts to masonry walls. A bolt is screwed into a metal or plastic segmented shield which fits into a drilled hole. As the bolt is tightened, the segments are forced apart to expand and grip the sides of the hole.

Frame fixings

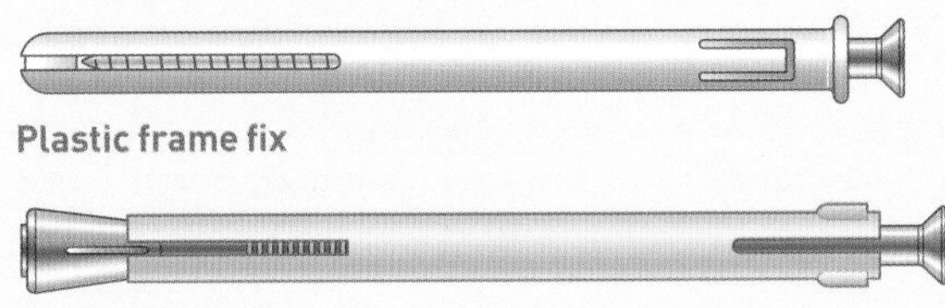

Plastic frame fix

Metal frame fix

These are long plastic or metal fittings which can be used for fixing wood, metal or plastic window and door frames to the wall. They fit into a hole drilled through the frame into the wall.

Knock-down fixings

You can't screw into the sides or ends of laminated board with an ordinary screw or it will split. Knock-down fixings are used for secure fixings in laminate that give strength and avoid splitting.

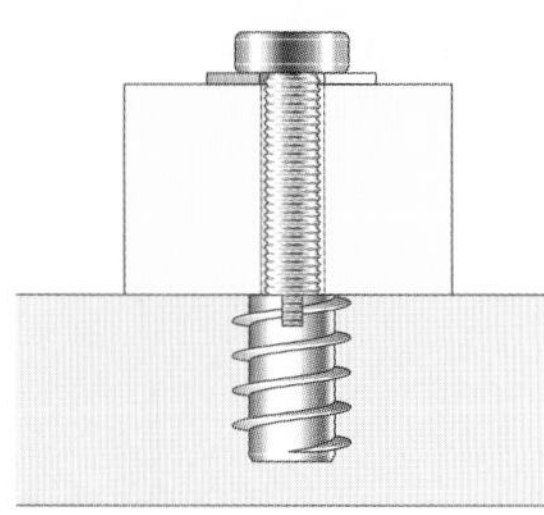

Chipboard fastener

This nylon plug has a thread on the outside which grips the board to make a secure fixing for woodscrews.

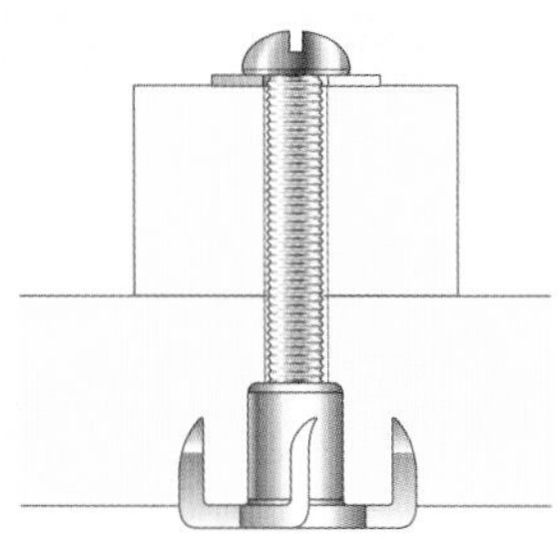

Tee nut

The projecting prongs of this metal nut grip into the wood. It is stronger than a chipboard fastener, but shows both sides.

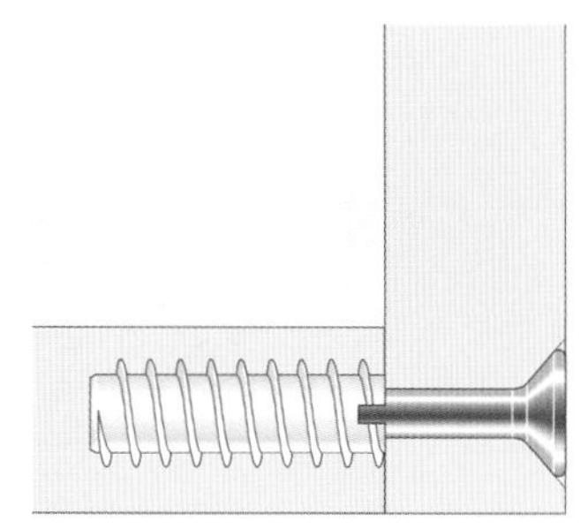

Screw socket

This is a threaded metal plug into which a screw is fitted. It is slightly less strong than a block joint, but much neater.

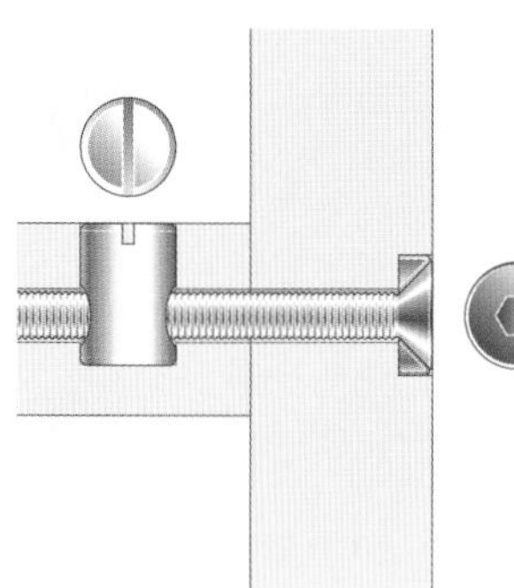

Cross dowel

A cross dowel consists of a steel dowel with a hole drilled through it and a screw. The screw fits through the dowel, which has a slot so it can be turned with a screwdriver to align it correctly. This makes a strong fitting for joining the ends of rails to side panels.

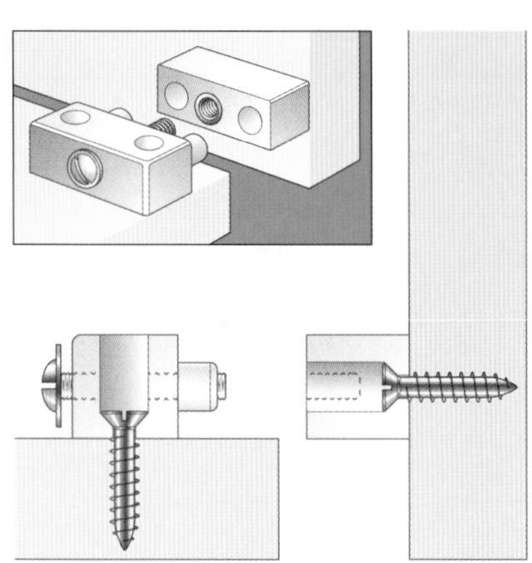

Block joints

These fittings are plastic blocks in two sections, which are used to join panels of man-made boards, such as chipboard, at right angles to one another. One block is screwed to each of the sheets being joined, then a longer screw joins the two plastic blocks together.

Hollow-wall fixings

When fixing screws into hollow walls of plasterboard, you must use specially designed fixings. The strongest kind open up once they are inside the cavity. None, however, are strong enough to take a heavy load; for this, you need to locate the timber wall studs with a detector and fix the load with wood screws.

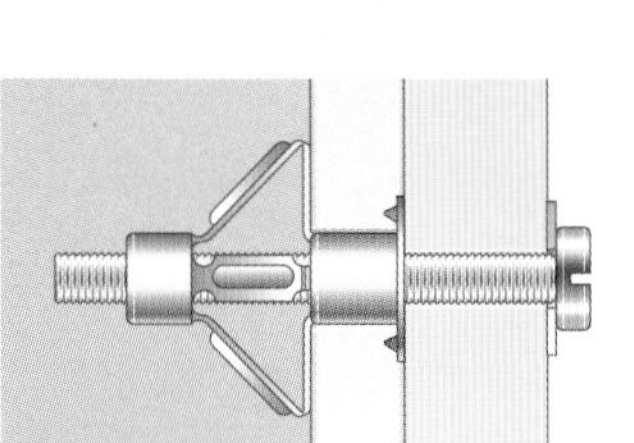

Metal anchor

This has metal segments that open out in the hollow wall.

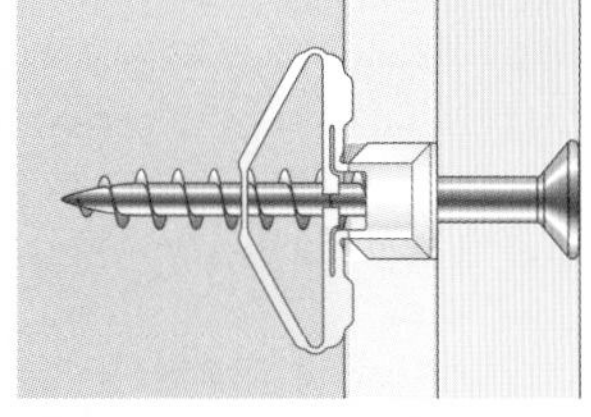

Plastic anchor

This has a plastic anchor with segments that open out once it is in the hollow wall.

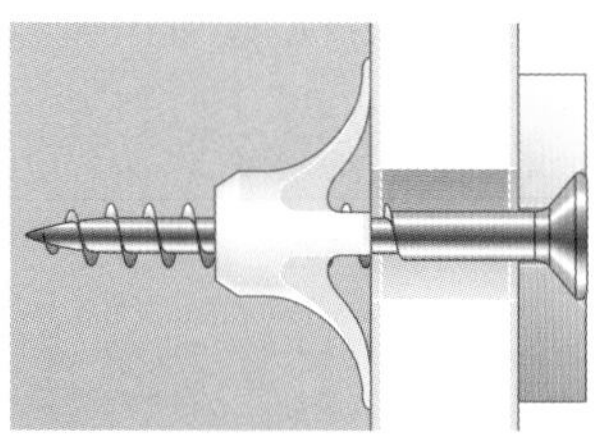

Nylon petal plug anchor

This has nylon wings that open out like petals to grip the back of the plasterboard.

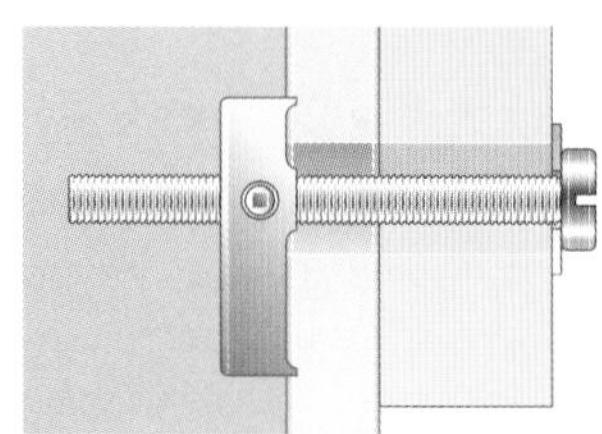

Gravity toggle

This is a screw with a swinging metal bar (toggle) attached. When inserted, the toggle swings down and grips the back of the wall. The toggle is lost in the cavity if the screw is removed. A gravity toggle is a strong fixing for plasterboard or lath-and-plaster walls.

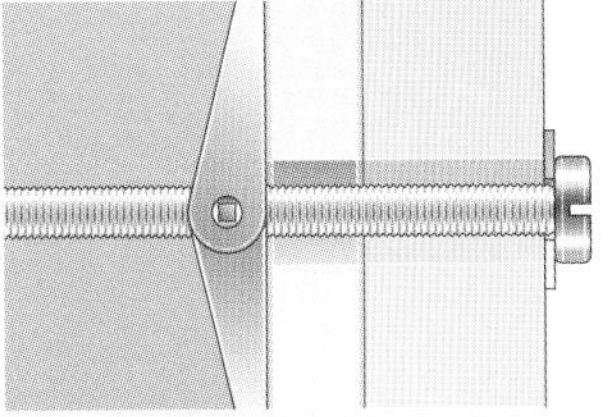

Spring toggle

This screw has a spring-operated toggle bar that folds flat for insertion and springs open inside the cavity. As the screw is tightened the bar is pulled tight against wall. The toggle is lost in the cavity if the screw is removed. This is a strong fixing for plasterboard or lath-and-plaster walls.

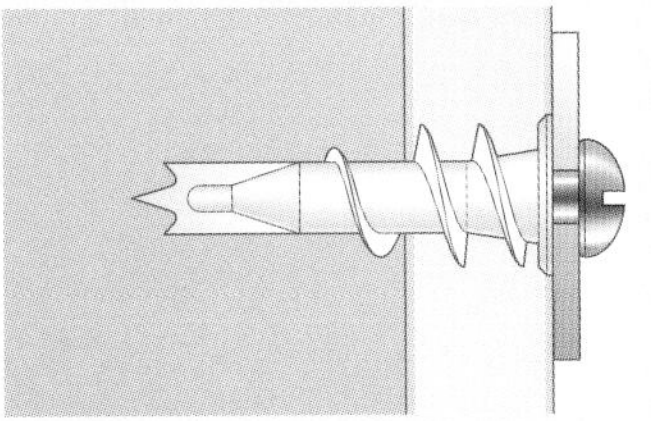

Plastic screw-in plug

This has a coarse thread designed to cut through plasterboard.

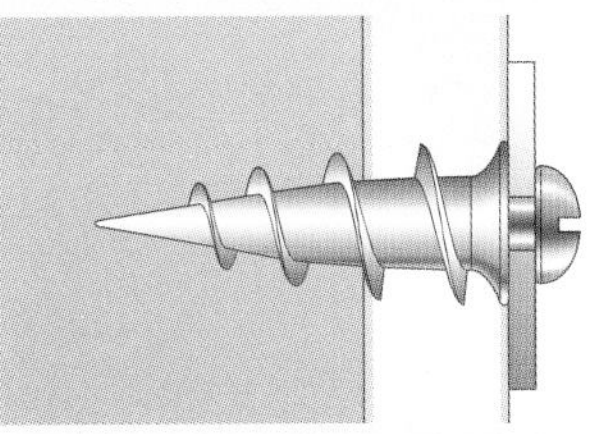

Metal screw-in plug

This has a coarse thread on the outside and a sharp point that cuts its own hole in plasterboard.

SAFETY FIRST

Using adhesives

Always read and follow the manufacturer's instructions. Work in a well-ventilated area because some glues contain solvents that give off fumes. Check which solvent is needed for the glue you are using, in case of accidents. Take particular care with super-glues, which can bond human skin. Note also that many adhesives are flammable.

Adhesives and sealants

There are many good general-purpose adhesives on the market, but for some materials you need a specific product. Whatever surfaces you are sticking, make sure they are clean and free of dust, and not damp or wet. If necessary, hold them together with tape, clamps or even temporary nails until the adhesive has dried. Check the recommended setting times and note that they may vary in summer and winter, due to differences in temperature and humidity.

PVA (Polyvinyl adhesive)

Polyvinyl adhesives, commonly known as PVAs, are available in a range of general-purpose formulas, as well as wood adhesives and building adhesives. Some PVAs are waterproof. They are milky white when squeezed from the tube, but dry transparent.

Rubber-based contact adhesives

These are used for gluing synthetic laminates to wood, man-made boards and plaster. Adhesive is normally applied to both surfaces before they are pressed together.

Epoxy resin adhesives (two-part adhesives)

Metal, ceramic, stone, glass and rigid plastic can be glued to materials such as wood and glass with these adhesives. Always check the product label as some adhesives will not join all the materials. Two-part epoxy resins can be used outdoors or for joints that need to be waterproof; take care because in powder form these can be toxic.

Flooring adhesives (rubber resin adhesives)

These, and synthetic latex adhesives (see below), are used to stick floor coverings to floors. They are able to withstand a certain amount of water and they are slightly flexible, so they will not crack when you walk or put furniture on the floor.

Tile/coving adhesives (synthetic latex adhesives)

These adhesives will fill gaps, which makes them good for fixing expanded polystyrene ceiling tiles and coving to plaster or plasterboard. They are also used for floor tiles. Like rubber resin adhesives, they allow a certain amount of movement without cracking.

Grab adhesives (acrylic polymer adhesives)

These adhesives can be used instead of nails and screws to fix wooden mouldings and skirting-boards.

Filler adhesives (polyurethane-foam adhesives)

Sold in pressurised cans, these adhesives make good gap-fillers in wood, masonry, plaster and stone because the foam expands when dispensed. To remove them you need a specially formulated solvent.

Super-glues (cyanoacrylates)

These fast-working glues will stick all kinds of small household objects, including metal, glass, ceramic and plastic. Special super-glue remover is needed to prise apart any items that are accidentally bonded. Use with great care as super-glues will also glue skin.

Mastics

Mastic sealants are available in different colours, for sealing around window and door frames to prevent water leaking into cracks and rotting the wood. They are usually sold in a cartridge that fits in a mastic gun. Use flexible acrylic mastic to fill joints subject to cracking, such as along skirting boards.

Roof and gutter sealants

Repair small cracks in asphalt roofs and plastic gutters quickly and easily with the appropriate type of sealant.

Silicone sealants

These form a waterproof seal around wash basins, baths and shower cubicles.

What are planning and building controls, and why do they exist? Can you sort it out yourself or is it best to consult a specialist (see page 372)? As with any task, you can decide that for yourself once you know what's involved. First of all, it's important to understand what planning and building regulations do, as it's easy to think of them as restrictive and bureaucratic tools put in place purely to thwart your ambitions. In fact, they are essential safety mechanisms devised to protect you, your neighbours and the local environment. The regulatory bodies will grant permission for you to carry out your plans unless there are very sound reasons for refusal, in which case they must explain their decision and you have a right to appeal to the Secretary of State for the Environment.

What's the difference between planning permission and building regulations?

Planning permission regulates the use, siting and appearance of buildings and other structures. It is required for any extension, outbuilding or conservatory that will:

1. Increase the size of the original house by more than 15% or 70 cubic metres.
2. Rise higher than the original roof.
3. Cover more than half the land around the original house.
4. Encroach nearer to a public highway.
5. Stand more than 3 metres high.
6. Abut a party wall or come within 3 metres of a neighbour's property.

What might seem to you a minor alteration could have far-reaching implications. A structure that could obscure a driver's vision near a junction, for instance, might constitute a traffic hazard. Equally, a local authority may refuse planning permission on the grounds that the proposed scheme would not blend in with its surroundings. If you live in a listed building, you will need listed building consent for any significant exterior or interior works. Conservation areas are also subject to stricter rules than normal.

Building regulations are concerned with structural integrity and the suitability of the materials used. Most building works, including alterations or extensions, have to meet certain standards to safeguard public health and safety. It's important to note that even when planning permission is not required, building regulations might need to be taken into account (see chart opposite).

Liability

It is crucial, and your responsibility, to be aware of the regulations, because if you proceed without permission you might later be forced to restore the property to its original state – probably at considerable expense – or face prosecution. It can also be difficult to sell a property if you have made alterations without the necessary authorisation. Look into the relevant regulations when you are planning your job.

Working together

Don't be afraid to consult a representative of the planning department and the Building Control Officer before you submit your application. They will be happy to discuss your proposal with you and offer advice about the best way to comply with the rules. They will also know from experience whether it is necessary to approach other authorities about related aspects of your project, such as sanitation and fire escapes. Such consultations can save you time and money.

Hiring a specialist

If you prefer, you can employ a builder or preferably an architect to handle your application. Even so, it is still your responsibility and in your interest as the owner of the property to keep an eye on developments. For example, do not ignore a request from the Building Control Office's surveyor to inspect the site, or you could incur the cost and inconvenience of having to expose covered work at a later stage.

How can I learn more?

Information on planning permission and building regulations is available from local councils and the Department of the Environment. Planning requirements can be complex and may require detailed drawings, but there is nothing to prevent you doing them yourself if you feel you are capable.

PLANNING PERMISSION AND BUILDING REGULATIONS

Project	Planning permission necessary?		Building regulation approval necessary?	
Installing central heating	No		Yes	Seek advice
Installing an oil-storage tank	No	As long as you leave at least 20m between the tank and a highway. Maximum capacity of 3,500l. Maximum height 3m	No	
Improving bathroom or kitchen	No		Yes	Seek advice
Erecting a small building	Likely	If it is within 5m of the house and more than10cu m in volume	Yes	Seek advice
Building an extension	Likely	Seek advice	Yes	Seek advice
Adding a garage	Likely	Treat as erecting a small building or, if it is within 5m of the house and more than 10cu m in volume, as an extension	Yes	Some exempt, but seek advice
Laying a drive	No		Yes	Seek advice
Painting and decorating	No	Seek advice if the building is listed	No	
Replacing windows	No	Unless they extend beyond the foremost wall of the house facing a public road, or if it is a listed building	Likely	Seek advice
Installing solar tiles or panels	No	Provided that the installation does not cover a space greater than the roof	Yes	Seek advice
Improving the garden	No		No	
Electrical work	No		No	
Converting the loft	Yes	Seek advice	Yes	Seek advice
Building a conservatory	Yes	Seek advice	Yes	Seek advice
Building a porch	Yes		Yes	Seek advice
Converting a house to flats	Yes		Yes	Seek advice
Converting a house into business premises	Yes		Yes	Seek advice
Knocking down internal walls	No	Unless the building is listed or if you change its use	Yes	Seek advice
Wall cladding	No	Unless the building is listed or if you live in a conservation area	No	
Demolition	Likely	Seek advice	Likely	Seek advice
Building a garden wall	No	Unless the building is listed building or if the wall is higher than 1m by the boundary or higher than 2m elsewhere	No	

Independent advice and further information

Architects Accredited in Building Conservation (AABC)
01625 523 784 **www.aabc-register.co.uk**

Association of Building Engineers (ABE)
List of members 01604 404 121
www.abe.org.uk

Bat Conservation Trust
If you have bats in your attic, you must call the Bat Conservation Trust before working in there.
Help line 0845 1300 228 **www.bats.org.uk**

British Standards Institute (BSI)
Tests materials and practices and defines product and industry standards
020 8996 9000 **www.bsi-global.com**

Builders Merchants Federation (BMF)
List of builder's merchants
0870 901 3380 **www.bmf.org.uk**

Building Conservation Group of Royal Institution of Chartered Surveyors
Advice on good practice in conservation
020 7222 7000 **www.rics.org**

Building Research Establishment (BRE)
Helpful research on building techniques and problems
01923 664 000 **www.bre.co.uk**

Centre for Accessible Environments (CAE)
Advice on accessibility for the disabled
020 7357 8182 **www.cae.org.uk**

Chartered Institute of Building
List of members
01344 630 700 **www.ciob.org.uk**

Construction Confederation
List of members and guarantee information
020 7608 5000
www.constructionconfederation.co.uk

Council for Registered Gas Installers (CORGI)
List of registered members and gas safety advice
01256 372 200 **www.corgi-gas.com**

Double Glazing Glass and Glazing Federation (GGF)
List of members
020 7403 7177 **www.ggf.org.uk**

Electrical Contractors' Association (ECA)
List of members
020 7313 4800 **www.eca.co.uk**

Electrical Contractors' Association of Scotland (SELECT)
List of members
0131 445 5577 **www.select.org.uk**

Energy Saving Trust (EST)
Gives advice and administers grants on energy conservation
0845 727 7200 **www.est.org.uk**

Environment Agency
Government body responsible for controlling air, land and water pollution in England and Wales
0845 933 3111 **www.environment-agency.gov.uk**

Federation of Master Builders (FMB)
List of members and guarantee information
020 7242 7583 **www.fmb.org.uk**

Health & Safety Executive (HSE)
Advice on safety at work in construction
08701 545 500 **www.hse.gov.uk**

Heating and Ventilating Contractors' Association (HVCA)
List of members
020 7313 4900 **www.hvca.org.uk**

Institution of Electrical Engineers (IEE)
List of members and electrical safety advice
020 7240 1871 **www.iee.org**

Institution of Gas Engineers
List of members
020 7487 0650 **www.igem.org.uk**

Institution of Structural Engineers
List of members
020 7235 4535 **www.istructe.org.uk**

National Association of Scaffolding Contractors (NASC)
List of members
020 7608 5090 **www.nasc.org.uk**

National Federation of Roofing Contractors Ltd
List of members
020 7436 0387 **www.nfrc.co.uk**

The National Inspection Council for Electrical Installation Contracting (NICEIC)
Independent electrical safety regulatory body
020 7564 2323 **www.niceic.org.uk**

Office of Fair Trading
Protects consumers and ensures that businesses operate fairly
020 7211 8000 **www.oft.gov.uk**

Ricability
Information on products and services for older or disabled people
020 7427 2460 **www.ricability.org.uk**

Royal Institute of British Architects (RIBA)
List of members
0207 580 5533 **www.architecture.com**

Royal Institute of Chartered Surveyors (RICS)
List of members
0870 333 1600 **www.rics.org**

Scottish Office
Advice on environmental and building regulations in Scotland
0131 556 8400 **www.scotland.gov.uk**

WORKING WITH SPECIALISTS

SAFETY FIRST

Don't try these yourself:
- Gas installations
- Demolishing or knocking through loadbearing walls
- Any job that may compromise the structural stability of your home, such as sawing through ceiling joists.

The golden rule of home improvements is be realistic. Most of us love to feel a sense of achievement but even the most gifted amateur cannot hope to complete every task alone. Beware: if you allow your enthusiasm to run away with itself, you are likely to take on too much! There are some circumstances – such as buying a home – in which you may have no choice but to call in a professional. And remember too that some home improvement work can be physically demanding. Don't let determination override common sense. Be kind to yourself!

Getting help from the professionals

If a potentially dangerous task requires more skill than you can realistically offer, then do play safe and call in an expert. But it's not only health and safety concerns that may lead you to call in a professional: timing, budget or even the law may require it.

Buying a home

When buying a property you will need to complete a survey, and you will have no choice but to call in an expert. If you need a mortgage, a survey will be a condition of the loan. If you are a cash buyer, it is highly recommended, whether in the form of a valuation, a 'home-buyer's report' or a full structural survey. If you opt for the full survey, every accessible nook and cranny of the property will be checked. However, those parts too difficult to reach during the inspection can be overlooked, and although surveyors point out major and minor pitfalls, you should not assume a report is a legally binding guarantee.

Spend wisely

With larger jobs you will probably be making a considerable investment in materials; it would be foolish to waste this because of inexperience. If you run into difficulties during a job, specialists at your local B&Q store will be able to advise you about the best way to proceed.

Know your limitations

Be honest with yourself. If you don't feel confident, or you will need to invest huge amounts of time acquiring skills that you might never use again, then surrender, and take the well-trodden path to the door of the tradesmen.

Share the task

If time is a constraint then consider calling in a contractor to do the major work in order to let you get on with smaller tasks that you know you can complete on schedule.

Know the law

Any maintenance or installation work on a gas appliance must by law be carried out by a qualified fitter registered with CORGI (Council for Registered Gas Installers). Do not attempt it yourself.

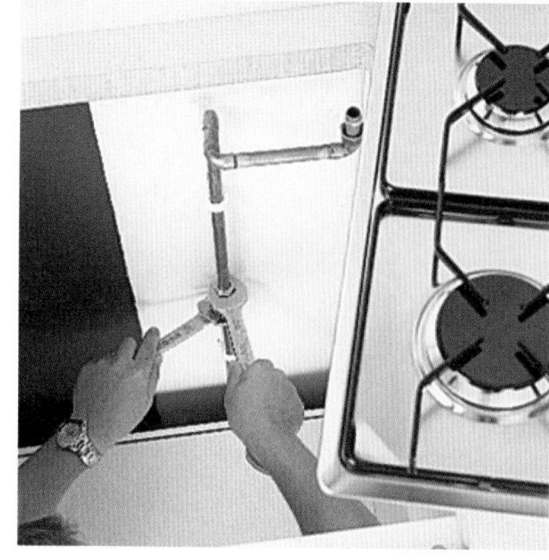

Using architects

Complicated projects such as extensions benefit from the overview, draughtsmanship and management of an architect. An architect, particularly a local one, will be able to prepare and adapt the plans in order to maximise your chances of success in securing the permission of local authorities, with whom they will have had previous contact. They will also make up a budget for you and oversee the work of any other professional tradesmen you are using.

Which professional?

Some jobs require a combination of professionals – a kitchen or bathroom makeover, for example.

Plasterer: Bear in mind that it takes a minimum of six months (and a maximum of a lifetime) to acquire the skill needed to create a smooth, even surface ready for painting.

Plumber: Always be cautious where there's any risk of flooding.

Electrician: Put safety first at all times. Never forget that electricity is potentially lethal. To find an approved contractor, get in touch with the NICEIC or ECA, or in Scotland SELECT (see page 371 for contact details).

Builder: Essential if major structural alterations are required. The Federation of Master Builders has a strict code of conduct for members.

Surveyor: A qualified professional – always go for a 'chartered' or listed surveyor when you need a report.

Carpenter: Joinery can be a highly skilled craft. Use a professional if a neat and accurate job is essential.

Finding a reliable professional

Having made your decision to call someone in, how do you go about finding them?

Word of mouth

Personal recommendations offer the very best form of endorsement. If a friend or acquaintance has engaged a builder, this is a perfect opportunity to see a completed job, get a valuable opinion of their experience and make an informed decision that you've found the right person.

A reputable tradesman will be proud to show you a portfolio and might even suggest you visit one or two of the jobs to see for yourself. Local tradesmen will have an advantage here, particularly if you have seen a project take shape quickly and efficiently in your neighbourhood.

Trade organisations

Failing a personal introduction, contact the relevant trade associations (see page 371) or look in the telephone directory for professionals displaying the relevant association's emblem. Although membership is no guarantee of competence, it is a good indication of professional intent.

If the work you are having done is the result of accidental damage and will be paid for by your insurance company, always check with them first. Insurance companies often have a list of local tradesmen they prefer to use, with whom they have worked before.

Estimates and quotations

Always get at least two estimates for the job, and remember the cheapest is not always the best – low prices may indicate cutting corners, poor-quality materials or shoddy workmanship; decide how much you value a good finish.

Peace of mind

Make sure that as many separate tasks are itemised as possible. An 'estimate' is not legally binding, since it is just an approximate cost, so you will need a 'quotation' to get a fixed price. Some builders' estimates will include 'provisional sums' to cover work they intend to subcontract and do not have a firm quote for. Insist that you are consulted before any final sums are agreed.

Schedules and contract management

Having determined the principal tasks and the individual prices, then it's a very good idea to agree a 'schedule of work'. This is an important document allowing both you and the expert to see clearly what is involved and when it is to be completed. A schedule should be a statement of agreement for both parties, and it is a good idea on larger jobs to tie payments to agreed completion dates (see also right).

When to give the go-ahead

Once both parties are happy, a contract should be drawn up that includes all of these elements. This should help ensure that nothing is left unplanned or uncovered. It should set out clearly exactly what is expected of you and of the professional you are hiring.

When to pay

With small jobs, most professionals will accept payment on completion, so long as they don't have to buy any special materials. With larger jobs it is normal for a builder to ask for an initial payment on receipt of materials and further interim payments to cover outlays until completion of the job. Never pay for the entire job in advance. If the job requires 'making good' or involves decoration, it is sensible to hold back some of the funds until after completion. You should also allow for 'snagging', when the builder returns after a six-month settling period; hold back a significant sum (5–10% is the accepted norm) to ensure a happy return. Make sure this final sum is mentioned in the contract, to insure you against any defects that may arise.

GLOSSARY

Aggregate
Mixture of small stones and particles of stone used in making concrete or in decorative finishes.

Architrave
Wooden moulding fixed around a window or door frame to hide the join between frame and wall. There is a variety of architrave mouldings available to suit the style of your home.

Arris rail
Timber beam, triangular in cross-section. The vertical timbers of a closeboard fence are attached to horizontal arris rails.

Balustrade
Protective railing along a stairway, landing or deck. It consists of a handrail and a set of vertical posts or balusters.

Batten
Any narrow strip of sawn timber. A length of straight batten used as a straightedge is surprisingly useful for measuring and marking out.

Beading
- A painting technique for achieving a clean, sharp edge where two colours meet.
- A type of moulding, often semi-circular in cross-section. Wooden beading is used to hold panes of glass or door panels in place. Metal or plastic corner beading is used to reinforce repairs to crumbling plaster at an external corner.

Blown
- A surface layer such as plaster or cement render that has begun to separate from the wall behind.
- A fuse wire that has melted and broken an electrical circuit due to overloading.

Building membrane
Water-permeable sheeting used in outdoor construction projects, usually to keep materials – for example earth and gravel – separate from one another.

Burr
Rough edge left behind after cutting a piece of wood or a copper pipe, for example.

Butt joint
Joint in which the two elements are cut square and fastened end to end without overlapping or interlocking.

Chalk line
Length of string or cord saturated with brightly coloured chalk, used to mark out a straight line on walls, floor or ceiling.

Circuit breaker or miniature circuit breaker (MCB)
Trip switch in a consumer unit that operates automatically to cut off the power to a particular electrical circuit in the event of a short-circuit or fault. Once the problem has been remedied, power can be restored by simply resetting the switch – much easier than old-fashioned fuses which, once blown, had to be replaced or rewired.

Cleanstone
Grit- and dust-free aggregate, used for example in the construction of garden retaining walls or when laying land drains.

Clearance hole
When screwing one thing to another, drill a clearance hole right through whatever you are fixing. This must be big enough to take the unthreaded part of the screw (the shank). *See also* pilot hole.

Consumer unit
The point from which mains electricity is distributed to the various circuits around the home. It contains a set of circuit breakers or fuses that protect the circuits against overloading.

Control joint
Helps prevent cracking caused by slight movement, expansion or contraction in a garden wall or concrete pad. In a wall a control joint consists of a continuous vertical row of unmortared joints; in a concrete path or pad it is a strip of compressible fibreboard inserted at intervals within the concrete.

Coping
The top course of a garden wall. Often sloping or overhanging, it helps direct water away from the body of the wall, as well as providing a decorative finish.

Cornice
Decorative moulding running along the joint between a wall and ceiling.

Countersink
A countersink screw has a head designed to lie flush with the surface it is fixed to. As well as a pilot hole, you have to drill a slight recess in the surface to take the screw head using a countersink bit. Or use a screwsink bit to drill a countersunk pilot hole in a single operation.

Coving
Moulding running along the joint between a wall and ceiling. Modern coving may be made of plaster or polystyrene.

Cross-head
A type of screw with a cross-shaped recess on the head rather than a single slot. Cross-head screws include Phillips and Pozidriv, and need a compatible screwdriver. They are the best type of screw to use with a power screwdriver since they are easy to locate and the screwdriver is less likely to slip.

Dado
The lower portion of an internal wall. Because it is the part most subject to wear and tear, the dado was traditionally protected with wallpaper or panelling. A wooden moulding dividing a wall horizontally at about waist height is known as a dado rail.

Damp-proof course
Layer of waterproof material that stops moisture rising up and into a wall.

Damp-proof membrane
Layer of waterproof material that stops moisture rising through a solid floor.

Distemper
Traditional water-based paint that is powdery to the touch and wipes off with a damp cloth. To redecorate, you must first scrape or wash off distemper completely, or seal it with a special stabilising solution; otherwise the new paint will not stick.

Dowel
Cylindrical wooden peg used to secure butt joints in wood.

Flashing
Thin metal strip used to seal the junction between a chimney and a roof, or along the valley between two sloping roofs.

Flatpack
Self-assembly (or knock-down) furniture is supplied by the manufacturer as a flatpack.

Flue
Passage in a chimney that allows the escape of smoke, hot air and gases.

Flush
Two surfaces that are perfectly level with each other are flush.

Formwork
Temporary timber frame that shapes and supports concrete as it sets.

Gauge rod
Purpose-made measuring rod used in tiling and bricklaying for setting out and for maintaining regular joints.

Geotextile permeable fabric
Hardwearing, long-lasting sheeting available in various thicknesses. Used in outdoor construction projects, for example to keep earth out of land drains and soakaways, or to stabilise soft ground before building a sub-base.

Grommet
A protective ring of rubber or plastic used to line the knockout hole through which an electrical cable enters a fitting.

Grout
Fills and seals the joints between tiles. Used to finish the tiled surface once the adhesive is dry. Available in different colours and formulas suitable for wall and floor tiles.

Hardcore
Crushed or broken bricks, block and stone, used in the construction of foundations and sub-bases.

Housing
Slot or hole made in one timber to receive another.

Insulation
- Non-conductive protective covering of electrical flex or cable.
- Material that inhibits the passage of heat or sound.

Joist
Horizontal beam supporting a roof or floor. Joists are usually timber, but may also be made of reinforced concrete or steel.

Junction box
Electrical fitting used for making connections between cables on a power or lighting circuit. Usually plastic with a screw-on lid, junction boxes are normally hidden from view behind the ceiling, walls or floor. They contain varying numbers of terminals.

Key
To key a surface is to roughen it either by scoring or by rubbing it over with abrasive paper so that plaster, adhesive or paint bonds more effectively.

Lagging
Insulating material that reduces heat loss. It is fitted over a hot water cylinder, or over pipes and tanks in unheated spaces to protect them from frost.

Laths
Narrow strips of wood that the plaster is stuck to in a traditional lath-and-plaster wall.

Melamine
Tough synthetic resin used to coat man-made composite boards such as chipboard.

Mitre
Corner joint made by cutting two pieces of material at an equal angle.

Mortise
Slot or recess cut to receive a matching projection or tenon in a mortise-and-tenon joint.

Moulding
Shaped strip usually made from timber or man-made board that is used for interior trims such as dado rails and skirting, as well as in the construction of glazed and panel doors and many types of window.

Nogging
Short horizontal reinforcing timber fixed between the vertical studs in a wood-framed partition wall.

Olive
Sealing ring in a compression plumbing fitting.

Pilot hole
Drilling a pilot hole helps to prevent wood splitting when you drive in a screw. It must be of a smaller gauge than the screw so that the thread bites into the wood. When fixing one thing to another, drill a clearance hole for the screw shank through whatever you are fixing and a pilot hole into whatever you are fixing to.

Plinth
Detachable panel that covers the feet and base of self-assembly units such as kitchen cabinets.

Primer
Substance applied to a surface to seal it in preparation for subsequent decoration. Metal primer prevents rust; plaster and wood primers make a surface less absorbent.

Render or rendering
Thin layer of cement-based mortar coating the surface of an exterior wall.

RCD or residual current device
Fast-acting trip-switch that cuts off the power in the event of an earth leakage.

Riser
The upright part of a step or stair that rises from the back of a tread.

Scribe
Score a line with a pointed instrument.

Sheathing
Insulating outer covering of electrical cable and flex.

Shim
Thin wooden strip used as a measure to establish a fall across a surface. Cut a shim of the right size from any scrap of timber.

Size
Sealer used to coat plastered or papered surfaces in preparation for wallpapering. It prevents the surface from absorbing the paste, which means the paper sticks better and is easier to hang.

Slot-head
Traditional screw with a single slot into which the flat blade of a screwdriver is fitted.

Soakaway
Rubble-filled pit or underground receptacle into which water is drained, and from which it soaks away into the surrounding earth.

Spur
Branch cable that extends an existing electrical circuit.

Straightedge
Long metal ruler, or any long straight piece of timber. Use it to check that something is flat or straight, or as a guide when drawing a line.

Striker plate
Plate set in a door frame containing a cutout into which the latch fits when the door is shut.

Stud
Vertical timber support in a wood-framed partition wall.

Sub-base
Layer of compacted hardcore that provides a stable base for a patio or path.

Tamp
Pack down by repeated blows to the surface.

Tenon
Projecting peg that fits into a matching mortise in a mortise-and-tenon joint.

Terminal
The connection to which the bared cores or conductors of flex or cable are attached inside an electrical fitting.

Trap
U- or S-shaped waste pipe fitting attached to the outlet of a sink, bath, washing machine or lavatory. The shape means that it always retains water, which acts as a seal, preventing insects, bacteria and smells re-entering your home from the drains.

Tread
The horizontal part of a step or stair – the part you tread on.

Tongue-and-groove
Type of joint between boards in which a projecting tongue along the edge of one board fits into a corresponding recess or groove along the edge of the next.

Wall tie
Metal connector used to bind different sections of a masonry wall together.

INDEX

D

M

N

O

P

T

U

V

W

Y

Z

ACKNOWLEDGMENTS

Project director and writer Nicholas Barnard

Consulting editor Ken Schept

Project manager Keith Brooks

Photographer Lucy Pope

Illustrations Peter Bull Art Studios

Planning and technical advice
James Hayward
Alan Emery
Grant Fay
Andrew Cray
Geoff Harris

Contributing writers
Felicity Jackson
Christina Heath
Ian Penberthy
Jessica Wheeler
Patrick Renouf
Elizabeth Lewis

Demonstration and set construction
James Hayward
Christina Heath
Colette Duthie
Camilla Blench
Mehari Mengisteab
Jessica Wheeler
Victoria Brooks
Julia Barnard
Alan Emery
Stuart Young
Dominic Emery
Grant Fay
Andrew Cray

Research David Spenser

Home and garden owners
James Hayward and Christina Heath
Vanessa Dowding
Victoria and Keith Brooks
Alan Emery and Lisa Williams

Indexer Hilary Bird

B&Q Marketing
Project manager Geoff Long
Maria Sealey
Keith Bibby
Sarah O'Brien
Violet Leahy
Lorian Coutts
Ross Marshall
Jin Kaur

inspire gloss style
B&Q
prepare
practical make good
sheen
greenhouse
loft
you light colour
sensual ceramic
green can
shade
calm soft
drill secure
brush
renew functional
achieve wallpaper
low-voltage skil
natural design
base coat welcom
belief my home
timber plasterboar
fresh outdoors laminate floorin